THE RI[S]
THE SPANIS[H]

IN THE

OLD WORLD AND IN THE NEW

BY

ROGER BIGELOW MERRIMAN

PROFESSOR OF HISTORY IN HARVARD UNIVERSITY

VOLUME I
THE MIDDLE AGES

1918

British Library Cataloguing-in-Publication Data
A catalogue record for this book is available from the
British Library

Roger Bigelow Merriman

Roger Bigelow Merriman was born on 24th May 1876, in Boston, America. He spent his early education at Dalzell's School in Worcester, and Noble's School in Boston, after which he progressed to study at Harvard University. Merriman graduated in 1896 with a degree in history. He then went on to study at Balliol College Oxford, where he studied for a B.Litt degree (in 1897), before returning to Harvard for one year – then back to Europe where he spent two years studying in Berlin, and travelling in France and Spain.

Regarding his future ambitions, Merriman reportedly stated that 'the road to become a *good* professor nowadays is long, and I won't be a third-class one or in a third-class college for anything, so I am taking my time.' This patient attitude paid off, and on completing his PhD (from Harvard) in 1902, he was immediately employed as an instructor in history at the university. Six years later, Merriman was promoted to assistant professor, and in 1918, to a full professorship.

Merriman, as well as being responsible for the General Examinations in History, also served on the Committee of Athletics (he had been a keen football player in his youth). He championed the Harvard rule requiring all freshmen to be subjected to compulsory exercise. As well as this substantial administrative work, Merriman also published many academic texts, including the *Life and Letters of Thomas Cromwell* (1902), *The Rise of the Spanish Empire* (4 vols., 1918-34) and a well-received study of *Suleiman the Magnificent* (1944).

During the First World War, he travelled to France in order to lecture and aid the Allies. In May 1918, he was appointed as a captain of Ordinance, and worked on the staff of General W. S. Graves. This took Merriman to Vladivostok, Russia, where he discovered an intense dislike of both communists, and communist principles. He had a great reputation in Europe though, and received many honorary degrees, and was a member of several European honorary societies.

Merriman enjoyed life to the full, and was never one to be deterred. For example, even after the loss of an eye in a shooting accident – he continued improving his game of tennis. Despite this attitude, in his last days a prolonged and painful illness brought down his spirits, leaving Merriman to quote Cromwell that his 'chief desire here is to make what haste I may to be gone.' He died at his summer house at St. Andrews-by-the-Sea, New Brunswick, on 7th September 1945, and was buried at Clinton, Massachusetts (America). He was survived by his widow, Dorothea Foote, and by his four children; Roger, Daniel, Dorothea and Helen.

TO

THE HONORED MEMORY

OF

WILLIAM HICKLING PRESCOTT

PREFACE

THE history of Spain is one of the most attractive fields that lie open to the historical student. Its variety is infinite, and the possibilities of new and important discoveries are unexhausted. To most Americans the principal interest of the subject will inevitably centre around Spain's activities as a great conquering and colonizing power; for the increased importance of the countries of Iberian origin has been perhaps the most remarkable political and economic fact in the recent development of the Western Hemisphere. Popular attention has been focussed as never before on their language, government, and commerce during the past twenty years; and much progress has also been made in the line of historical investigation. The labors of writers and students, however, have thus far been directed chiefly to the more recent periods of the Revolutions and of national independence. The long centuries of colonial administration have been less thoroughly explored, and the history of Spain herself, which forms the background for the entire picture, has not hitherto been considered from the standpoint of the great Empire which sprang from her.

The following pages are an attempt to supply this deficiency. It is my purpose to carry the story, in four volumes, down to the death of Philip II, under whose rule the Spanish Empire attained its greatest territorial extent, through the annexation of Portugal and of her dominions. The long period of 'decline and fall' I am content to leave to others, the more so because the tendency to regard Spain and the Spanish administration as synonymous with inefficiency and decadence is so common that it is a pleasure to emphasize the other side. The reader must not be surprised to find that practically the whole of the first volume is devoted to the mediaeval period. If he is willing to accept the first and most fundamental of my theories in regard to the development of the Spanish Empire, he will readily agree that a knowledge of the early stages of its development is indispensable to any real comprehension of what follows.

The original plan of the chief divisions and the principal chapters of the book was drawn up nine years ago, in general accordance with the scheme of a course of lectures at Harvard University which I had been giving intermittently since 1903. Although there have been some changes of detail, the main features of that plan have never been altered. The first two volumes, published herewith, are almost exclusively based on printed sources and standard secondary works. Manuscript material has been utilized in Chapters IV, V, XV, and XVI; but most of the unpublished documents that I have collected deal with the period of Charles V and Philip II, and therefore concern only my last two volumes. It would have been by no means difficult to find more manuscripts in the archives on the mediaeval period and on the reign of the Catholic Kings, but the field to be covered was so vast and so little known outside of Spain, that I felt that I could employ my time to better advantage in a thorough exploration of the material already in print. The fact that an unusually large number of documents, edited by Spanish scholars, have remained almost unutilized by historians, confirmed this decision.

Great pains have been taken to indicate fully the authorities for all important facts. Whoever has consulted the Spanish historians, except perhaps the very most recent, must remember long and weary hours spent in attempts to verify statements for which no specific reference was given; it is in the hope of sparing my readers such labor that so many footnotes have been inserted. On the other hand, it has not seemed worth while to include a complete bibliography, in the ordinary sense of that term. A mere list of titles is of little value, unless it be accompanied by some indication of their merits, defects, and relative importance; it occupies much space, and has been deservedly characterized as "a rather specious credential of erudition." Instead, the plan has been adopted of describing, in a bibliographical note at the end of each chapter, the most important authorities on which it is based; and of giving, in a "Note on the General Authorities" at the end of the Introduction, a brief account of the principal collections and histories which cover the entire field. These notes do not generally contain the titles of books or pamphlets which have been cited only once or twice; the latter may be found by examining the references in the text. For the names of important works constantly employed, abbreviations have been used; a list of these will be found on page xxvi.

My thanks are due to the editor of the American Historical Review for permission to reprint several paragraphs of an article on "The Cortes of the Spanish Kingdoms in the later Middle Ages" which I published in the issue of April, 1911 (Vol. XVI, No. 3). The genealogical tables which I have inserted are largely based on those of H. B. George (Oxford, 1916); but I have corrected some minor errors, and have made various additions and excisions.

The signs and abbreviations used to indicate the different relationships are taken from his book: any doubts as to their meaning may be cleared up by consulting his preface. The maps have been constructed, with much care, from a number of different atlases. Those of Spruner and Lane-Poole have laid me under the deepest obligations, but there are several sites, routes and boundaries, which I have had to work out, unaided, from the texts.

The list of friends and scholars both here and in Europe who have aided me in my work is very long: for the ramifications of my subject have been so divergent that I have been obliged to depend, to an unusual degree, on the knowledge and counsel of others. The names of Professor Edward Channing of Harvard and of Professor Henry Morse Stephens of the University of California come at the head of the list; for without their advice and encouragement I should hardly have ventured even to undertake the task. Their methods of exhortation have been characteristically different; but they have always pointed in the same general direction, and the measure of my gratitude to them both is difficult to express. I have had the great privilege of discussing some hard problems with Professor Rafael Altamira of the Universidad Central at Madrid, and with Professor Alfred Morel-Fatio of the Collège de France; and the help which they have freely given me, both in letters, and by word of mouth, has shown the way to the solution of many difficulties. My Harvard colleagues have been unfailingly generous in placing at my disposal the results of their learning and experience, and I would gratefully acknowledge my deep obligations to them; particularly to Professor C. H. Haskins for invaluable assistance on the chapters on mediaeval constitutional history; to Professor A. C. Coolidge for helpful sugges-

tions in regard to North African affairs and matters of
foreign policy; to Professor J. D. M. Ford for answering
perpetual questions in regard to Spanish literature, language
and accentuation, and to Professor J. R. Jewett for guidance
in the spelling of Moorish names; to Mr. G. P. Winship
for his criticisms of the chapter on the Indies; and to Professor C. N. Greenough for advice in regard to style. Mr.
G. W. Robinson of the Graduate School of Arts and Sciences
has not only made the index and helped me to prepare the
manuscript for the press; he has saved me from numerous
errors of fact and faults of expression, and he has offered a
number of positive suggestions of the highest value, particularly concerning the field covered by the Introduction
and the earlier chapters of Volume I. Finally I cannot
forbear to pay tribute to the constant and devoted assistance of my wife; she has gone over my work again and
again at the various stages of its progress, and has never
failed to improve it.

When one's knowledge of a subject is largely derived
from the teaching of it, one must not forget to render thanks
to one's pupils. Certainly my indebtedness to four friends
who have studied Spanish history with me at Harvard in
the course of the past twelve years is fully as great as any
services that I may have rendered them. The researches
of Professor C. H. Haring of Yale have furnished a large
part of the material for my account of the early administration of the Indies; and those of Dr. Julius Klein of
Harvard form the basis for my paragraphs on Castilian
economic history, and more especially on the Castilian
Mesta. The investigations of Professor J. G. McDonald
of the University of Indiana have been of material assistance to me in studying the office of the *corregidor*; and Dr.
C. E. McGuire of the International High Commission at

Washington has indicated the solution of several puzzling problems, by giving me the benefit of his wide knowledge of mediaeval ecclesiastical history and institutions. All these gentlemen, moreover, have helped me with suggestions concerning passages not directly connected with their special fields. Their criticisms, always unrestricted, and often severe, have afforded me the highest satisfaction that a teacher can enjoy, namely the knowledge that his pupils have gone beyond him.

Eighty-one years have now elapsed since William Hickling Prescott published the first edition of his "History of the Reign of Ferdinand and Isabella." Much new material has been discovered since that day, and the fashions of historical writing have greatly changed; but Prescott's work still remains the standard authority on the reign of the Catholic Kings. For fifteen years I have had the rare privilege of using his books and manuscripts in the Harvard College Library; I have scrutinized the passages he underscored, and read his pencilled notes in the margins. I have thus had the opportunity to follow, step by step, the process of the composition of his masterpiece, and can testify to the profound learning, deep insight, and above all to the unfailing honesty with which his work was done. Such errors as he made were due to lack of material, and to a really noble inability to comprehend a policy of treachery or deceit. My debt of gratitude to him is the deepest of all; and his granddaughter has kindly permitted me to give expression to it, by dedicating these volumes to his memory.

R. B. M.

CAMBRIDGE, March 10, 1918.

CONTENTS

xiii

BOOK I
CASTILE

CHAPTER I

CHAPTER II

CHAPTER III

CHAPTER IV

CHAPTER V

BOOK II

THE REALMS OF THE CROWN OF ARAGON

CHAPTER VI

CHAPTER VII

CHAPTER VIII

CHAPTER X

CHAPTER XI

MAPS AND GENEALOGICAL TABLES

MAPS

TABLES

LIST OF ABBREVIATIONS

Altamira . . . Rafael Altamira y Crevea. *Historia de España y de la Civilización Española.* Barcelona, 1909–11. 4 vols.

B. A. E. . . . *Biblioteca de Autores Españoles.* Madrid, 1846–80. 71 vols.

B. H. . . . . *Bulletin Hispanique.*

Bofarull . . . . Antonio de Bofarull y Brocá. *Historia crítica de Cataluña.* Barcelona, 1876–78. 9 vols.

Colmeiro, *Curso* . Manuel Colmeiro. *Curso de Derecho Político.* Madrid, 1873.

Colmeiro, *E. P.* . —— —— *Historia de la Economía Política en España.* Madrid, 1863. 2 vols.

Colmeiro, *Introd.* —— —— *Cortes de los antiguos Reinos de León y de Castilla: Introducción.* Madrid, 1883–84. 2 vols.

Colmeiro, *Reyes* . —— —— *Reyes Cristianos desde Alonso VI hasta Alfonso XI.* Madrid, 1891.

Cortes . . . . *Cortes de los antiguos Reinos de León y de Castilla, publicadas por la Real Academia de la Historia.* Madrid, 1861–1903. 5 vols.

D. I. A. . . . *Colección de Documentos inéditos del Archivo General de la Corona de Aragón.* Barcelona, 1849–1910. 41 vols.

D. I. E. . . . *Colección de Documentos inéditos para la Historia de España.* Madrid, 1842–95. 112 vols.

D. I. I. . . . *Colección de Documentos inéditos relativos al descubrimiento, conquista, y colonización de las posesiones Españolas en América y Oceania.* Madrid, 1864–84. 42 vols.

D. I. I., 2d ser. . *Colección de Documentos inéditos relativos al descubrimiento, conquista, y organización de las antiguas posesiones Españolas de Ultramar.* Madrid, 1885–1900. 13 vols.

Diercks . . . Gustav Diercks. *Geschichte Spaniens.* Berlin, 1895–96. 2 vols.

Lafuente . . . Modesto Lafuente. *Historia General de España.* Madrid, 1850–67. 30 vols.

Lecoy . . . . Albert Lecoy de la Marche. *Les relations politiques de la France avec le royaume de Majorque.* Paris, 1892. 2 vols.

M. and M. . . Amalio Marichalar and Cayetano Manrique. *Historia de la Legislacion y Recitaciones del Derecho Civil de España.* Madrid, 1861–72. 9 vols.

Mariéjol . . . J. H. Mariéjol. *L'Espagne sous Ferdinand et Isabelle.* Paris, 1892.

Mas Latrie . . Louis, Comte de Mas Latrie. *Relations et commerce de l'Afrique septentrionale ou Magreb avec les nations chrétiennes au moyen âge.* Paris, 1886.

Mercier . . . Ernest Mercier. *Histoire de l'Afrique septentrionale.* Paris, 1888–91. 3 vols.

N.B. A. E. . . *Nueva Biblioteca de Autores Españoles.* Madrid, 1905–12. 20 vols.

Prescott . . . W. H. Prescott. *History of the Reign of Ferdinand and Isabella, the Catholic.* 4th ed. London, 1846. 3 vols.

R. A. . . . . *Revista de Archivos, Bibliotecas, y Museos.*

R. A. H. . . . Real Academia de la Historia.

R. H. . . . . *Revue Hispanique.*

R. St.-H. . . . Eugène Rosseeuw Saint-Hilaire. *Histoire d'Espagne.* Nouvelle éd. Paris, 1844–79. 14 vols.

Schott . . . . Andreas Schott, Johann Pistorius, and Franciscus Schott. *Hispaniae Illustratae, seu Rerum Urbiumque Hispaniae, Lusitaniae, Aethiopiae, et Indiae scriptores varii.* Frankfort, 1603–08. 4 vols.

Zurita . . . . Jerónimo Zurita. *Anales de la Corona de Aragon.* Saragossa, 1610. 6 vols.

INTRODUCTION

INTRODUCTION

THE Spanish Empire of Ferdinand and Isabella and their successors has its origins in the earliest periods of antiquity. Far more than the British Empire, to which it has often been compared, it is linked with the history and traditions of the past. England's insular position, which ultimately forced her into a maritime career, is of course the fundamental explanation of her modern imperial domain; but this insular position did not actually bear fruit in voyages of distant exploration and conquest until after she had practically relinquished her mediaeval ambitions to win land on the European continent from France. The Tudor period, which witnessed the beginning of the one and the abandonment of the other, forms a sharp dividing line in English history; and it is possible to make an intelligent study of the British Empire without going back of the sixteenth century. But the story of the empire of Spain is at once more complicated and more continuous. The geographical position of the Iberian Peninsula tempted its inhabitants to expand both by land and sea. From the very dawn of history its fate has been closely associated with that of North Africa, southern France, and the islands of the western Mediterranean. At times it has formed a portion of empires which controlled all these territories, either wholly or in part; and at times its own rulers have, in turn, dominated large portions of them. The European lands outside the limits of the peninsula which acknowledged the rule of Spanish sovereigns in the year of the dis-

3

covery of America were already extensive, and they were to be substantially increased during the first century of the conquest and exploration of the New World. At the greatest crises of her imperial career Spain has been confronted by a bewildering array of irreconcilable opportunities. In her refusal to choose between them, in her heroic but misguided attempts to utilize them all, lies the explanation of some of her most disastrous defeats. The present chapter will endeavor to trace some of the earlier geographical and historical antecedents of this intricate imperial development.

Whoever glances at the map of the Iberian Peninsula with a view to investigating the history and civilization of the different peoples who have occupied it will first be impressed by the apparent definiteness of its external limits. On three sides and more than one half of the fourth it is bounded by the waters of the Mediterranean and of the Atlantic. Across the greater part of the remaining portion of its perimeter is built the mountain barrier of the Pyrenees, whose loftiest summits reach a height of over ten thousand feet. For the casual observer Iberia seems to be almost as completely shut off from contact with the outside world as if it were an outlying island.

More careful scrutiny, however, reveals a number of facts which considerably modify this original impression. First let us glance to the southward. One of the most important things for every student of Spanish history to bear in mind is the narrowness of the Straits of Gibraltar, the ease with which they may be crossed, and the essential similarity of the coasts of Spanish Andalusia and Morocco. The well known phrase "Africa begins with the Pyrenees" should always be interpreted to mean rather that Spain and North Africa are one, than that Spain and France are divided. The fact that Spain and Morocco are today regarded as belonging to two different 'continents' has blinded many people to the intimate connection that exists between them. In times comparatively recent, geologically speaking, they were probably joined.[1] The flora and fauna of Spain resemble those of Africa rather than those of France. The hilly coasts of both sides of the Straits are very much like one another; a glance over the intervening waves suggests, rather than discourages, the idea of crossing. The Pillars of Hercules were indeed the western barrier of the ancient world, but the water that flows between them has never offered serious hindrance to peoples who have been desirous of travelling north and south.[2]

From the very earliest times we encounter many evidences of this. Controversy still rages so hotly over the primitive inhabitants of Spain that it would be the height of folly for a layman to step in where specialists fear to tread; but from all the welter and confusion of polemic a few fundamental facts emerge unscathed. The ancient inhabitants of Spain and North Africa are unquestionably branches of the same Mediterranean race, far more closely allied to one another than were the Iberians with the primitive inhabitants of the greater part of France. On both sides of the Strait we find the same generally dolichocephalic type — predominantly brunette, but with an appreciable element of blondness, which gradually diminishes on the African

[1] There is reason to think that there was a water-way from the Mediterranean to the Atlantic, to the north of the Sierra Nevada, through the valley of the Guadalquivir, and another south of the Riff, by the valley of the Sebu, before the Straits of Gibraltar were opened up.

[2] A. Bernard, Le Maroc, pp. 3, 12;

S. Gsell, Histoire ancienne de l'Afrique du Nord, i, pp. 31 f., 38, 183, 189, 192. Cf. also Lucan's Pharsalia, ix, 411 ff.:

"Tertia pars rerum Libye, si credere famae
Cuncta velis; at si ventos caelumque sequaris,
Pars erit Europae."

side as one moves east. Some of the Riff Berbers today
can only be distinguished from Europeans by their slightly
curlier hair, which is doubtless to be ascribed to inter-
mixture with the negro tribes south of the Sahara.[1] Many
recent scholars incline to favor the theory that the Berbers
were not indigenous, but migrated to their present territory from Europe (probably about 1500 B.C.); or, at least,
that the indigenous Libyans were powerfully affected by
such a European immigration. Others maintain, on the
contrary, that the current flowed chiefly in the opposite
direction, and that the Iberians, who are generally regarded
as the primitive inhabitants of Spain, originated in North
Africa and crossed over thence into Europe.[2] For our
purposes it. is immaterial whether the trend was north to
south, or south to north; but it is difficult to exaggerate
the importance of the fact that Abyla and Calpe were in
constant and intimate relations with one another throughout this early period.

The primitive inhabitants of Spain were also closely in
touch with those of the eastern Mediterranean lands at a
very early date, and these relations led, indirectly, to the
first incorporation of the Iberian Peninsula in an empire
whose seat was in North Africa. It is not necessary to take
seriously the opening sentence of Stevens's translation of
Mariana's famous history, to the effect that "Tubal, the
son of Japheth, was the first man that peopled Spain
after the Flood"; yet its incessant repetition for several
centuries past has unquestionably invested it with a very
real importance. The Tarshish of the Old Testament is

---

[1] W. Z. Ripley, *The Races of Eu-*
rope, pp. 272–280; Bernard, *Le Maroc*,
pp. 63 f.

[2] Full references for these conflicting
theories may be found in the footnotes

to Gsell, *op. cit.*, i, pp. 306 ff. Cf.
also E. Philipon, *Les Ibères*, pp. 37–
60, and E. Meyer, *Geschichte des Alter-*
tums, ii, p. 687.

generally understood to signify Spain; though the "navy
of Tarshish" which brought to King Solomon "gold and
silver, ivory and apes and peacocks" [1] was a general term
used to designate any large vessels built for distant voyages,
rather than those specifically limited to Spanish ports.[2]
The date of the Biblical reference to Tarshish is usually
given as approximately 990 B.C.; but it was probably more
than a century earlier than that when the Phoenicians first
visited Spain, set up trading posts, and pushed through to
the shores of the Atlantic,[3] and certainly less than three
centuries later that the Greeks made their first appearance
there.[4] Archaeological discoveries, and the persistence
in Spain of certain eastern mythological legends, have done
something to illuminate the history of this obscure period,
and it is abundantly clear that the new visitors were intent
rather on commerce and the search for metals than on
colonization or conquest; certainly they made no effort to
subjugate the original inhabitants, or to penetrate into the
interior.

For us the main importance of the occupation by the
Phoenicians lies in the fact that their presence in Spain
ultimately paved the way for a new union of Iberia and
North Africa. In 585 B.C. Tyre, the centre of the Phoenician empire in the east, was overpowered by Nebuchad-
nezzar, king of Babylon, after a siege of thirteen years;[5]
and the heiress of Tyre was Carthage in North Africa,
originally a Phoenician colony, but now fast rising towards
the zenith of her fame, and destined to control the entire
western Mediterranean. The Carthaginians had already

[1] I Kings, x, 22; Jeremiah, x, 9;
Esekiel, xxvii, 12; Jonah, i, 3.
[2] Just as the modern word 'India-
man' does not necessarily signify a ship
trading with India.

[3] Gsell, i, pp. 359 ff.; Meyer, ii, pp.
689 ff.
[4] Gsell, i, pp. 412 ff.
[5] Esekiel, xxvi, 7–12; G. Rawlinson,
History of Phoenicia, pp. 472 f.

established a small colony in the island of Iviza in the year
654;[1] less than a century later they had ousted the Greeks
from the western portion of the island of Sicily; about the
same time they occupied Sardinia, Majorca, and Minorca,
and seized Malta and Gozzo.[2] To complete their great
political and economic system, to make the western Mediterranean a Carthaginian lake, the control of Spain alone
was lacking. Here they would have to deal with their
kinsmen, the Phoenicians, as well as with Greeks and natives,
but that did not deter them. Indeed, the historian Justin
tells us that it was an appeal by the Phoenician colonists of
Cadiz, for aid in repelling an assault by the primitive inhabitants, that gave the new conquerors the needed excuse
for interference.[3] At any rate, the Carthaginians entered
the peninsula, attacked and defeated both the natives and
the Phoenicians there, and finally established themselves
as lords of Cadiz, the key to southern Spain and to the
commerce of the far West. They subsequently extended
their sway over most of the neighboring settlements, and
they also engaged in sundry rather unsuccessful conflicts
with the Phocaean Greeks, whose headquarters were at
Marseilles, and whose chief settlement in Spain was at
Ampurias, north of the Ebro. Like the Phoenicians before
them, they were apparently unable to advance into the
interior of the peninsula, at least down to the time of Hamil-
car Barca; but they controlled the entire coast from Cadiz
to Mastia (the modern Cartagena), and also the opposite
shore of North Africa. The position they had won for themselves gave them unchallenged predominance in the western

---

[1] Gsell, i, p. 423, and reference there
to Diodorus Siculus, v, 16.

[2] Gsell, i, pp. 424–433, 439. It is
curious to note that the Carthaginians,
like the Spaniards two thousand years
later, failed definitely to possess themselves of Corsica.

[3] Justin, *Historiae Philippicae*, xliv,
5, 2 f.; and Gsell, i, p. 443.

basin of the Mediterranean.[1] And it is interesting to note several curious parallels between the way in which the Carthaginians regarded and treated Spain, and that in which Spain subsequently regarded and treated her American colonies. In both cases the metropolis looked upon the colony primarily as a place from which to derive revenue: Carthage expected Spain to furnish funds for the prosecution of her wars, just as Spain, two thousand years later, strove to utilize the Indies for a similar purpose. Both powers also made strenuous efforts to maintain rigidly monopolistic control of the territories they had won, and to exclude all outsiders from participation in their profits. Eratosthenes tells us that the Carthaginians made it a practice to "drown any strangers who sail past on their voyage to Sardinia or to the Pillars; hence much of what is related of the parts towards the west is discredited."[2]

The transference of Spain from Carthaginian to Roman domination was simply part of a larger movement which embraced the entire western Mediterranean world, both north and south of the Straits of Gibraltar. There was a change of masters, indeed, and the capital to which men owed allegiance was shifted to southern Italy; but Spain, North Africa, and the other neighboring lands all ultimately shared the same fate; the combination was virtually unbroken. The ensuing period of the Roman occupation of the peninsula lasted roughly six centuries, of which the first two were marked by a series of desperate conflicts, and the last four by comparatively uninterrupted peace. It was a far more serious occupation than that of the Phoenicians or Carthaginians. The newcomers were not satisfied with

---

[1] Gsell, i, pp. 440–447.
[2] Eratosthenes, cited in Strabo's *Geography*, xvii, 1, 19 (vol. iii, p. 240. of Falconer and Hamilton's translation).

mere commercial control. They were determined to make themselves the real masters of the land, and thoroughly to Romanize its inhabitants. They left their stamp on the peninsula in a way that none of its previous or subsequent invaders were able to do. Not until the reign of Augustus was the process really complete, but in the course of the long struggle the native Spaniard and the invading Roman learned to respect one another;[1] the terrible war was succeeded by a lasting reconciliation, and the victors and the vanquished fraternized and intermarried. The Romanized native type that emerged furnished the empire with some of her most distinguished men; it gave her Trajan, Hadrian, and Theodosius, and almost all the great names of Roman literature from Ovid to Martial.[2] It subsequently imposed a large share of its civilization and culture on its Visigothic barbarian conquerors. Under Roman domination, then, the native Spaniard cannot be regarded, as under the Carthaginians, in the light of a mere passive spectator of the development of the empire of which he formed a part. He was conquered, indeed, but respected and finally taken up into the life of the great system to which he had given his allegiance. He bore his share in guiding and controlling it. He was given the elements of an imperial education.[3]

The development of the provincial divisions of Roman

[1] The Roman poet Manilius, writing shortly before the death of Augustus, speaks of "Hispania maxima belli." Bk. iv, v. 693.

[2] Cf. Drepanius Pacatus, *Panegyricus Theodosio dictus*, iv, 2–5. "Hispania . . . terris omnibus terra felicior. . . . Haec durissimos milites, haec experientissimos duces, haec facundissimos oratores, haec clarissimos vates parit; haec judicum mater, haec principum est; haec Trajanum illum, haec deinceps Hadrianum misit imperio, huic te debet

imperium."

[3] In addition to the standard authorities on Roman Spain cited in the bibliographical note at the end of this Introduction, may be mentioned E. S. Bouchier, *Spain under the Roman Empire* (Oxford, 1914), and J. J. Van Nostrand, *The Reorganisation of Spain by Augustus* (Berkeley, California, 1916). The latter contains a valuable bibliography. E. Pérez Pujol, *Historia de las Instituciones sociales de la España Goda*, is also very useful.

Spain presents certain interesting features. At first, Spain was treated as an entity by itself; its political boundaries were drawn to coincide with its natural ones; it was separated from North Africa and from Sardinia and Sicily. From 197 B.C. to 27 B.C., except for a short period before 167,[1] it was divided into two provinces, Citerior and Ulterior, the boundary between them being the Douro from its mouth to the modern city of Toro, and an irregular line drawn thence in a southerly and southeasterly direction, through Villanueva de la Serena and Jaen, to the mouth of the Almanzora in the Mediterranean.[2] In 27 B.C. Hispania Ulterior was divided into two parts, Baetica [3] to the south, with the capital Corduba (Cordova), 'the patrician colony,' and Lusitania to the west, with Augusta Emerita (Merida) as its capital. Hispania Citerior, or Tarraconensis, as it was sometimes called from its capital Tarraco (Tarragona), was partitioned also, but not until much later; in 216 or 217 A.D., the northwest portion of the peninsula was marked off from it as a fourth province, called Asturia and Gallaecia, or Hispania Nova Citerior.[4] Meantime, from at least as early as the second half of the second century, the rich lands of Baetica, on the south, had been constantly raided by pirates from Mauretania Tingitana, the westernmost of the two new provinces on the opposite North African shore, which the Romans had somewhat neglected since it had

---

[1] Livy, xliv, 17, 10; xlv, 16, 1. The date 27 has been questioned by certain recent German writers, and a controversy on the whole subject has arisen which is well summarised in Van Nostrand, op. cit., pp. 95–97, with full citations of authorities.

[2] Van Nostrand (cf. map at the end of his monograph) places the southern part of the boundary between Citerior and Ulterior somewhat farther west than the Almansora. I have followed Péres

Pujol, i, p. 148, here. Mommsen thinks that the northwest originally formed part of the Ulterior province, and was transferred under Augustus.

[3] Also still called Hispania Ulterior (cf. Tacitus, Annales, iv, 13) or Hispania Ulterior Baetica.

[4] This had been foreshadowed by the erection of Gallaecia into a 'diocese' in the reign of Augustus: Van Nostrand, pp. 107 f.

fallen into their hands.   No convenient land route connected
Mauretania Tingitana with its eastern neighbor, Mauretania
Caesariensis.   The journey was a voyage of over two hundred miles along the desolate and insubordinate coast of
the Riff, while Baetica was not only nearer, but also much
more important to keep in touch with, on account of the
hostile incursions that surged to and fro across the Strait.[1]
Of all these facts the Emperor Diocletian took full account
when he reorganized the empire in 293, and erected Hispania
into a diocese of the prefecture of Gaul.   To the four
provinces already existing, three more were added.   One,
Carthaginiensis, was carved out of the southeast of Tarraconensis, as Gallaecia had previously been carved out
of the northwest.[2]   A second, established between 369 and
386, comprised the Balearic Islands.[3]   The last was the
African province of Tingitana, whose union with the diocese
across the Strait was, in Mommsen's words, "only the outward carrying out of what in reality had long subsisted.   It
was for Baetica what Germany was for Gaul; and, far
from lucrative as it must have been, it was perhaps instituted and retained for the reason that its abandonment
would even then have brought about an invasion of Spain
similar to that which Islam accomplished after the collapse
of the Roman rule."[4]   Such was the organization of Spain

[1] Mommsen, *Roman Provinces*, tr.
Dickson, i, p. 67; ii, p. 324.
[2] If we accept the view of J. Marquardt (*Römische Staatsverwaltung*, 2d
edition, 1881, i, pp. 254 ff.) that Hispania Citerior was divided from the
time of Augustus into three great districts or 'dioceses,' Asturia and Gallaecia, Tarraconensis, and Carthaginiensis, each under a legate, we may infer
that the substitution of three provinces
for one represents a change in the form
of administration rather than in its substance, and that the new provinces inherited, in general, the boundaries and
functions of the old districts.   The more
recent writers who have discussed the
subject differ impartially from Marquardt and from one another.   Ernst
Kornemann, in Pauly-Wissowa's *Real-
Encyclopädie*, ix, col. 719, *s.v. Dioecesis*,
quite misunderstands Strabo's account
of the administration of Hispania Citerior.
[3] Marquardt, *op. cit.*, i, p. 255.
[4] Mommsen, *Roman Provinces*, tr.
Dickson, ii, pp. 321 f.   Cf. also Altamira,
§§ 49, 52; and Mercier, i, p. 90.   Accord-

in the last century before the barbarian invasions.[1] It
bore striking witness to the closeness of its natural association with North Africa and the adjacent islands of the
Mediterranean; and the memory of it endured, so that
its influence can be plainly traced at many subsequent
stages of the development of the Spanish Empire.

During the fifth, sixth, and seventh centuries Spain,
like the rest of Western Europe, was inundated by barbarian hordes. First the Suevi, Alans, and Vandals poured
over the peninsula; then came the Visigoths, whose rule attained some measure of permanence, but was at best little
more than that of a dominant minority, which gradually
lost its power and ended by adopting the religion, the
language, and a great measure of the law of the Romanized
natives already on the ground.[2] In such turbulent times
it was inevitable that many of the political bonds which
had previously united the peninsula with the rest of the
Mediterranean world should be snapped; but the tie with
North Africa was strong enough at least partially to survive the shock. Certainly the Visigoths had their eye on
Morocco from the moment of their first occupation of Spain.
King Wallia (415–419) attempted to supply the agricultural
deficiencies of the peninsula by an expedition to North Africa
in search of corn; King Theudis (531–548) made a strenuous
though not permanently successful effort to cross the Strait
and capture Ceuta, in which he recognized, like the
Romans before him, an indispensable bulwark for southern

ing to Galindo y de Vera (*Historia de
las Vicisitudes de España en África*, p.
22), Mauretania Tingitana was virtually
incorporated in Baetica as far back as
the reign of the Emperor Otho, and
commonly spoken of as Hispania Tingitana or Transfretana. See also Tacitus, *Historias*, i, 78; *España Sagrada*,
i, pp. 181, 183, 185, 210, 216. Even
earlier, the colony of Julia Constantia

(Zulil, Arzila), founded by Augustus
on the Atlantic coast twenty-five miles
south of the Straits, was "regum dicioni
exempta, et jura in Baeticam petere
jussa." Pliny, v, 1, 3.

[1] Péres Pujol, *op. cit.*, i, pp. 144–151.
[2] See bibliographical note at the end
of this Introduction for the standard
authorities on the Visigoths in Spain.

Spain.[1] In this enterprise he encountered the East Romans, who had already conquered the Vandals in North Africa (533–539), overrun southern Italy and the islands of the western Mediterranean, and were now, like others who had possessed the adjacent lands before them, beginning to cast longing eyes at the Iberian Peninsula. An internal war among the Visigoths, in which one of the parties called on their Byzantine neighbors for aid, furnished the needed pretext, and the Emperor Justinian seized upon it at once. In 554 Liberius, governor of Africa, was ordered to cross the Straits with a large force. After uniting with the party that had invited him into Spain, he defeated the rival army, whose chief was soon after murdered. But the Visigothic faction who had summoned the East Romans to the peninsula soon discovered that their guests were by no means anxious to depart. The orthodox natives welcomed them; and although they were sometimes defeated in the open field by their Visigothic rivals, they clung closely to the walled towns, and soon commanded a strip of the southern coast of Spain extending from Cape St. Vincent to the mouth of the Jucar in the Mediterranean.[2] Had it not been for internal trouble in Constantinople, and the invasion of Italy by the Lombards, it is probable that the entire peninsula would have been conquered and the days of the Roman occupation renewed. As it was, the East Romans were not expelled from Spain until the reign of the Visigothic king Swintila (621–626); and it is not impossible that certain Spanish ports were subsequently reconquered by them from the Visigoths in the end of the seventh century.[3]

[1] Stevens's Mariana, p. 69; Gibbon (ed. Bury), iv, pp. 298 f.; v, p. 472; Galindo y de Vera, op. cit., pp. 23–26; Diercks, i, pp. 95, 112.

[2] Gibbon, iv, p. 299; Diercks, i, pp. 112–114.

[3] Gibbon, iv, p. 299, note; v, p. 472, note; Diehl, L'Afrique byzantine, p. 587; but see also Galindo y de Vera, op. cit., pp. 15, 25, and A. Bernard, Le Maroc, p. 83.

The decisive event in mediaeval Spanish history is the great Moorish invasion of 711; it determined the lines of the development of the peninsula during the next five centuries, and explains, more than anything else, the special features which differentiate Spain and Portugal from the other European states. The Arabs, who had become masters of Egypt before the middle of the seventh century, began, soon afterwards, to send out conquering expeditions into the regions farther west. In 670, Okba, the son of Nafi, founded the city of Kairawan south of Tunis, and carried the standard of the Prophet to the eastern confines of modern Algeria. In 682 he penetrated to the Atlantic, and rode his horse into its waves; but this expedition was only a raid, and left no enduring traces.[1] The native Berbers remained unsubdued and unconverted; indeed, in the following year they slew Okba in battle, and even recaptured Kairawan. The next four decades were full of furious fighting. When the Arabs were victorious in the field, the Berbers had recourse to the weapons of famine and devastation. Under the leadership of the savage queen El Kahéna, 'the African Pythoness,' they turned what was once a prosperous country into a howling wilderness. Not until the arrival in 705 of the famous Musa Ibn Nusair, with the title of Governor of Ifrîkia, were the invaders able definitely to extend their conquests to the shores of the Atlantic.[2] Even after that date we cannot regard the Berbers as fully subjected to Oriental domination and civilization. In government they were still virtually independent, while in religion — if anything more important [3] — they were no sooner converted than they became fanatics, distrustful of the more sceptical Arabs, and even hostile to

[1] Mercier, i, p. 206.
[2] Mercier, i, pp. 206–218.
[3] Bernard, *Le Maroc*, p. 86: "L'his-

toire de l'Afrique du Nord . . . est essentiellement une histoire religieuse."

them. An excellent foundation had been already laid for
the various subsequent revolts which prevented the eastern
caliphate from exercising any effective domination over
northwestern Africa, and were ultimately to exert a decisive
influence on the future of both sides of the Straits of Gibraltar.

The history of the events that led to the crossing of the
Saracens into Spain will probably never be accurately known.
That the Gothic empire was tottering to its fall and furnished a tempting quarry is certain; that the representations
of oppressed Israelites hastened the inevitable is highly
probable. The famous story of Count Julian and Florinda
la Cava is scarcely more than a legend; some authors have
gone so far as to deny the existence of Count Julian; and
if there ever was such a person it seems more likely that he
was an East Roman or a Romanized Berber than a Goth.[1]
But it is somewhat curious that historians should have been
at such pains to search for the cause of an action which, to
any one who has been on the scene and has known its earlier
history, must inevitably seem perfectly natural — so natural, indeed, as not to require any explanation at all. The
barrier between Spain and Morocco, as we have already observed, is far more imaginary than real; one cannot possibly
stand on either side of the Strait without feeling an impulse
to cross it. Lastly, we must never forget that what is often
somewhat misleadingly designated as the 'Arab invasion
of Spain' was in reality to a far greater extent an incursion
by North African Berbers such as the Iberian Peninsula
had several times experienced before. The relative numbers of Arabs and Berbers under Tarik's command in 711
have been very variously estimated. Some authorities

---

[1] Gibbon, v, pp. 472 ff.; Altamira,
§ 124; F. Codera, *Estudios de Historia*
Árabe Española, first series, pp. 45–94; C.
Diehl, *L'Afrique byzantine*, pp. 587–589.

place them at 17 and 7000; but, in any case, it is clear that the latter were enormously preponderant, so that the conquering army may, in effect, be regarded as an essentially North African force.[1]

The story of the subsequent development of the political and administrative relations of Moorish Spain to North Africa and the East further emphasizes this point. In theory, during the years immediately following the conquest, the so-called dependency of Andalusia (including the Iberian Peninsula, Gascony, Languedoc, and part of Savoy) was an integral part of the caliphate, and its governor was appointed from Damascus. Practically, however, during this period Spain was regarded as a subordinate dependency of Ifrîkia,[2] and the viceroy of Kairawan usually nominated the governors of Andalusia, without sanction from the capital.[3] Sometimes, when there was not time even to apply to Kairawan, the ruler of Spain was elected on the spot by the army. Such was the case when Yusuf, a descendant of the conqueror Okba, was chosen in 745–747, as a sequel to a series of bitter factional struggles; and this event is taken by some historians to mark the beginning of Spain's virtual independence of all connection with the East.[4] Whatever the final verdict on this point may be, it is certain that the control of Spain by Damascus was definitely terminated a few years later, with the fall of the Omayyad caliphs in the East at the hands of their rivals, the Abbassides. One of the members of the deposed dynasty was fortunate enough to escape the vengeance of his triumphant foes; he was a

---

[1] Mercier, i, p. 220; Diercks, i, p. 185.

[2] In the sense here used, this name includes the whole of North Africa west of Egypt; in its more restricted meaning it denotes the territory between Egypt and modern Algeria.

[3] Ameer Ali, *A Short History of the Saracens*, pp. 123, 144; Mercier, i, pp. 222 ff.

[4] Ameer Ali, *op. cit.*, pp. 161 f.; G. Faure-Biguet, *Histoire de l'Afrique septentrionale*, p. 38.

son of the Caliph Hassan, and bore the fortunate name
Abd ar-Rahman. After a series of romantic adventures
and hairbreadth escapes he found refuge at last among the
hospitable Berbers of Morocco, crossed the Straits, and
possessed himself of Spain, where he founded a dynasty
that endured until the eleventh century. A formal declaration of independence of the caliphate followed; prayers
in the mosques were no longer offered for the Abbasside
ruler in the East, but for the new Omayyad upstart in Spain;
in 763 an attempt of the Abbassides to reassert their supremacy suffered disastrous defeat, and the heads of their
generals, preserved in camphor and salt and wrapped in
the black banner of the Abbassides, were sent scornfully
back to the Caliph at Bagdad. Finally, in 929, when the
Abbasside dynasty had reached the nadir of its fortunes,
the greatest of the Spanish Omayyads, Abd ar-Rahman
an-Nasir, dared openly to take to himself the title of Caliph;
thus incidentally asserting his Abbasside rival to be a pretender, and Cordova to be the centre of the Moslem world.[1]

We revert to the relations of Spain and the Moorish
powers in North Africa. As long as the Berber states
continued to acknowledge their dependence on the Abbasside Caliph, they were naturally committed to an attitude
of semi-hostility towards the Spanish Omayyads; and at
first they made some small show of aiding the efforts of the
Abbassides to reconquer the Iberian Peninsula.[2] They
soon found, however, that nothing was to be gained by
fighting the battles of a distant overlord against their immediate neighbors; before long they reversed their policy,
and, following the example of their coreligionists across the

[1] There can be but one Caliph in
the world, according to Moslem law;
hitherto the Omayyad sovereigns in
Spain had styled themselves Emirs or
Sultans. Dozy, *Histoire des Musulmans
d'Espagne*, i, p. 367; Ameer Ali, *op.
cit.*, pp. 224, 300–302, 502 f.

[2] Faure-Biguet, *op. cit.*, pp. 40 f.

Straits, declared their independence of the caliphate of the
East. First in Morocco, in the year 788, the founding of
the Idrisite kingdom ended the rule of the Abbassides there,
and gained for western Mauretania complete autonomy.[1]
Twelve years later, in 800, the Abbasside Caliph, Harun
al-Rashid, in return for an annual grant of forty thousand
dinars, ceded to Ibrahim, the founder of the Aghlabite
dynasty, hereditary possession of Ifrîkia, which thenceforth
also became an independent principality.[2] But the Aghla-
bites retained possession of Ifrîkia for little more than a
hundred years. In 909 they were themselves dethroned
by a new dynasty, the Fatimites, who shortly afterwards
made a determined effort to oust the Idrisites from Morocco.[3]
In 920 they besieged Fez, forced the Idrisite ruler there to
recognize their sovereignty, and would probably have ultimately annexed all his lands, had it not been for the interference of the Omayyad Caliph in Spain, Abd ar-Rahman
an-Nasir, then at the summit of his power. From private
information Abd ar-Rahman was convinced that the Fatimite conquerors entertained aggressive designs on Spain,
and he fully realized that the possession of the southern
shore of the Strait would afford an admirable vantage
ground, as it had so often done before, for a descent on the
Iberian Peninsula. It scarcely seemed worth while to bolster
up the tottering buffer state of the Idrisites, after the proofs
of incompetence which they had already given. Abd ar-
Rahman had been helping them since 917, but they had
proved far too feeble a barrier to arrest the Fatimite onslaught.[4] The corollary was obvious. If Spain was to be
safe, Abd ar-Rahman must possess himself of the strong

[1] Mercier, i, p. 259.
[2] Mercier, i, pp. 263 f.
[3] Ameer Ali, *op. cit.*, p. 591; Mercier, i, pp. 316 ff.
[4] Ibn Khaldûn, *Histoire des Berbères* (trad. Baron de Slane), ii, pp. 567
ff.

places on the North African coast. In 926, accordingly, he sent over a large force to attack and take Melilla. Shortly afterwards he made common cause with an independent Berber tribe, which had shown more ability than the Idrisites in resisting the Fatimites, and persuaded it to conquer for him the whole strip from Tenes to Oran. Five years later the Caliph himself intervened and seized Ceuta. His mind was cast in an imperial mould; and had it not been for internal revolts in Andalusia and the Christian advance in northern Castile, he would doubtless have devoted all his energies to this Barbary campaign and driven back his foes to the boundaries of Ifríkia. As it was, a long and desultory struggle was waged in Morocco between the Omayyad and Fatimite powers,[1] in which the dwindling faction of the Idrisites espoused first one side and then the other, according to the ebbs and flows of victory and defeat. Finally, in 973, the Fatimites renounced all efforts to maintain themselves in Morocco, and departed to the eastward. The Omayyads thereupon redoubled their efforts, defeated the last remnants of the Idrisites, repelled several invasions from Ifríkia, and gradually secured the submission of the independent Berber tribes. Thenceforth they were unquestionably the leading power in Morocco down to the dissolution of their empire in the eleventh century; though they probably never exercised effective political control there, in the modern sense of the term. The pressure of the Christians in northern Spain prevented the Omayyads from giving their exclusive attention to the African problem, and forced them, against their will, to follow the policy of utilizing the more powerful of the Berber chieftains as the repre-

---

[1] It is interesting to note, in view of the subsequent history of the Spanish Empire, that Ifríkia and also Sicily were brought into this conflict: cf. Dozy, *Histoire des Musulmans d'Espagne*, iii, pp. 76 ff.; Mercier, i, p. 359; Faure-Biguet, *op. cit.*, p. 82.

sentatives of their own overlordship. Very often these
Berber viceroys renounced their allegiance to their masters
across the Straits; sometimes they even took the leading
part in revolts against the sovereign power at Cordova.
It would be quite useless to attempt definitely to fix the
boundaries of the lands in North Africa which theoretically
acknowledged Omayyad suzerainty during this period;
but it is doubtful if Spain has ever claimed sway over an
equally large extent of territory in that region, though her
power may have often been more effective within the limits
of the places she has held. Abd ar-Rahman an-Nasir
deserves an honorable place in the long list of rulers who
have pointed the way to the foundation of the modern
Spanish Empire.[1]

The fall of the Omayyad caliphate in the first part of the
eleventh century put an end to the power of Spain in North
Africa for many years to come. None of the twenty-eight
states into which the Iberian Peninsula was divided after
the central authority had broken down could possibly hope
to control any territory in Morocco, where anarchy reigned
supreme.[2] But the eleventh century was not to close without seeing Spain and North Africa once more reunited under
another empire; this time, however, the centre of gravity
was to be in the south. The Berbers of the Sahara had
been converted to the Moslem faith in the ninth century,
and as usual had developed rapidly from converts into
fanatics. They were inspired and led by holy men, or
Morabitin; hence the name Almoravides, by which they
are known to history.[3] Their religious enthusiasm soon

---

[1] Mercier, i, pp. 327–333, 353–385;
Dozy, op. cit., iii, pp. 73 ff., 222 ff.;
Faure-Biguet, pp. 82–93.
[2] Mercier, ii, pp. 1 ff.; Faure-
Biguet, p. 107.

[3] Mercier, ii, pp. 23 ff.; Faure-
Biguet, pp. 115–137; J. A. Conde,
History of the Arabs in Spain, tr. Foster,
ii, pp. 205 ff.

B

made them a mighty conquering power; by the middle of
the eleventh century, they came into hostile contact with the
scattered Berber tribes in southern Morocco and Algeria.
Then arose the great leader who was to become the real
founder of their empire — the famous Yusuf Ibn Tashfin,
simple, austere, devout, warrior and mystic combined. In
1063 he seized Fez. Shortly afterwards a revolt against
his power gave him the pretext for an atrocious massacre,
by which he rid himself at one blow of all possible rivals to
his authority. In 1084 he pushed through to the shores of
the Mediterranean and took Tangiers and Melilla; meantime one of his lieutenants farther eastward conquered
Tenes and Oran, and besieged Algiers.[1] But the prospect
to the north, on the other side of the Strait, was far more
alluring to Yusuf than the extension of his dominions in
North Africa, and the distance between the headlands was
not sufficient to deter him from crossing. On June 30,
1086, he landed at Algeciras. With reënforcements furnished by the Emir of Seville, he pressed forward to meet
the army of Alfonso VI; and on October 23 he utterly
routed his Christian foes at Zallaka, near Badajoz.[2] Troubles
in Morocco soon recalled the conqueror to North Africa,
and enabled the Christians to maintain their southern boundary at the Tagus, but the petty Moorish states in the south
of the peninsula were forced to submit to the harsh domination of their arrogant guests. Yusuf's Puritan spirit had
been shocked by the luxury of his coreligionists in Spain;
at Zallaka, indeed, he apparently rejoiced in their slaughter,
on the ground that they were his enemies as well as the
Christians.[3] One by one they were dethroned and replaced
by the faithful adherents of the North African zealot.

---

[1] Bernard, *op. cit.*, pp. 95–97. [2] Mercier, ii, pp. 46–48.
[3] Mercier, ii, p. 47.

By the year 1095 the whole of Moorish Spain was in the hands of the new invaders, forming an integral part of a vast empire whose centre of gravity was in Morocco, and whose southern limit was in Senegal.[1]

Yusuf died in 1106, and the empire that he had founded rapidly crumbled away;[2] but it was almost immediately succeeded by another of a very similar sort. About the year 1120 a new movement, that of the Al-Muwwahhidin, Almohades, or Unitarians, arose in the mountains of Morocco, its aim, like that of the Almoravides which preceded it, being to bring back pure religion to the Moslem world.[3] Its founder, Ibn Tumart, was an Arab who had been adopted by one of the Berber tribes;[4] but the real source of the greatness of the new sect, and one of the most notable figures in the entire history of North Africa, was his chief lieutenant and successor, Abd al-Mumin.[5] For several years the struggle between the Almoravides and the Almohades for the domination of Morocco hung in the balance; in 1143, however, the death of the son of Yusuf the Almoravide turned the scale. The Almohades promptly overran the whole of Mauretania, making a clean sweep of the Almoravide rule there; in 1149 they crossed to Spain. The Christians of the north had meantime improved the opportunity afforded by the dissolution of the Almoravide empire and advanced again into Andalusia, but they were powerless to resist the onslaught of the new invaders. In various minor encounters the Almohades drove them back, and at the same time they reduced the remaining Almoravide governors to obedience. By 1157 nearly half of the

---

[1] Ibn Khaldûn (trad. de Slane), ii, pp. 67 ff.; Mercier, ii, pp. 49–53; Faure-Biguet, op. cit., pp. 115–129.
[2] Cf. F. Codera, Decadencia de los Almoravides en España.
[3] Mercier, ii, pp. 65 ff.

[4] Ameer Ali, p. 534; cf. also Abd al-Wahid al-Marrakusi, Histoire des Almohades, trad. E. Fagnan (Algiers, 1893).
[5] Faure-Biguet, op. cit., p. 132.

Iberian Peninsula recognised their rule.[1] Curiously enough,
their most notable military victory over their Christian
foes did not occur until July 19, 1195, at Alarcos, after their
empire had reached its zenith.[2] In fact, that great battle
may be justly regarded as the event that gave the signal
for their decline. It caused the Christians in the north
to forget their internal quarrels, and, uniting in an effective
advance against the common foe, to win the final and decisive victory of Las Navas de Tolosa in 1212. In the succeeding years "the whole of Andalusia became a prey to
civil war,"[3] and the Christians, pouring down from the
north, reaped a rich harvest out of the quarrels and selfish-
ness of the Moslem chiefs. One only of the Moorish rulers
showed sufficient ability to withstand them — Ibn al-
Ahmar, 'the Conqueror through God,'- who, by a mixture
of military skill and political astuteness, finally succeeded
in possessing himself of Granada and the adjacent lands,
and in welding them together into a little kingdom which
defied the efforts of the Christians to conquer it for two and
one half centuries to come. A little later the authority of
the Almohades across the Straits was challenged by that
of a new rival, the Merinites, who established themselves
at Fez in 1248, and completed the conquest of Morocco in
1269; the king of Granada, moreover, immediately sought
and obtained the alliance of the new dynasty, just as his
predecessors had gained that of the Almohades.[4] In a
subsequent chapter we shall see that throughout the fourteenth and fifteenth centuries the different powers to the
north and south of the Straits were constantly in relations

---

[1] Ibn Khaldûn (trad. de Slane), ii,
pp. 161 ff.
[2] Ameer Ali (p. 537) wrongly places
Alarcos near Badajos; it lies much
farther up the valley of the Guadiana,
not far from Ciudad Real. Cf. map at
the beginning of this volume. Mercier
(ii, p. 125) erroneously assigns the battle
to the year 1196.
[3] Ameer Ali, op. cit., p. 542.
[4] Faure-Biguet, op. cit., pp. 167 f.,
176 f.

with one another in a multitude of different ways. The destinies of Spain and Morocco had been too often and too closely linked in the past to be permanently separated, even though the Christian conquest of the peninsula was virtually complete. During at least three stages of her history — under Carthaginians, Almoravides, and Almohades, and, occasionally, during the half century which immediately followed the first Moorish invasion — the whole or part of Spain had been more or less completely controlled by powers whose seat was in North Africa. Under the Romans, possibly under the Visigoths, and certainly in the reign of Abd ar-Rahman an-Nasir, Spain had held considerable possessions in Morocco. North Africa was perhaps the most normal and natural field for her expansion, when the days of her internal union and imperial greatness should come.

The historical bonds that united Spain with North Africa are in some degree rivalled by those which connected her with the islands of the western Mediterranean, and particularly with Majorca and Minorca. The Carthaginians had controlled western Sicily, Sardinia, and the Balearics, as well as the Iberian Peninsula, and the Romans succeeded them in all; moreover, the Balearics, from the time of their conquest by Quintus Caecilius Metellus in 123 B.C., were regarded as part and parcel of Spain, and in the fourth century, as we have seen, they were definitely erected into a province of it.[1] The Vandals, who entered Spain in 409, mastered Majorca and Minorca before they left it, and subsequently united them with Corsica and Sardinia under a single government.[2] Whether or not the Visigoths

[1] Cf. ante, p. 12; Vaquette d'Hermilly, Histoire de Majorque, p. 10; Lecoy, i, p. 8.

[2] Ludwig Schmidt, in Cambridge Medieval History, i, pp. 305, 311, 320.

followed them in the Balearics is still a matter of dispute, but it is certain that the East Romans made their presence felt in those islands and all the others of the western Mediterranean, as well as on the southern coast of Spain.[1] The Arabs crossed over to Majorca and Minorca soon after their arrival in the peninsula, and established there a pirates' nest; in the course of the ninth century it appears that both islands were for a time definitely subjected to the authority of the Moorish king of Bona in North Africa, so that we find the bishoprics of Majorca and Minorca assigned to the ecclesiastical province of Mauretania in a clerical schedule of the period.[2] Meantime Corsica and Sardinia were constantly raided by Moslem corsairs who sailed from Iberian ports; the conquest of Sicily for the Crescent was also in some measure accomplished through the efforts of invaders who came from Spain.[3] Even Crete was seized about the year 823 by certain Moorish adventurers who had been expelled from Andalusia by the Omayyad Caliph of Cordova.[4] They were evicted by Nicephorus Phocas in 960, and their coreligionists in Sicily shared the same fate a century later at the hands of the Norman Roger; but during a long and important period it is not too much to say that the Spanish Moslems exercised a dominant influence over the destinies of all these islands. As to the Balearics, despite incessant Christian raids, and their temporary association with Africa, they soon fell back completely into the control of the Moors of the Iberian Peninsula. The Almoravides took them from the Saracen chieftain who was in possession soon after their advent in Spain, but were ousted in turn by the Almohades in

[1] D'Hermilly, op. cit., pp. 20 f.; Piferrer y Quadrado, Islas Baleares, p. 25, note.
[2] Lecoy, i, pp. 9 f.
[3] Amari, Storia dei Musulmani di Sicilia, i, pp. 286 ff.
[4] Gibbon (ed. Bury), vi, p. 37; J. H. Freese, History of Crete, pp. 49-51.

1187.[1] Clearly there were abundant precedents in the previous history of the Iberian Peninsula for the acquisition by Aragon of the islands of the western Mediterranean in the thirteenth, fourteenth, and fifteenth centuries.[2]

From the Straits of Gibraltar and the Mediterranean, on the south and east, we now turn to the mountain wall on the north, whose importance as a natural boundary, or rather as an historical barrier, in the development of the Iberian Peninsula has also been somewhat overestimated. It has been justly said that the idea contained in the phrase already cited, "Africa begins at the Pyrenees," may be equally well expressed by the formula, "Europe ends at the Sahara."[3] The famous words, "Il n'y a plus de Pyrénées," which Voltaire placed in the mouth of Louis XIV in 1700, when his grandson, Philip of Anjou, was recognized as heir to the Spanish realms, might have been spoken with even greater truth at various earlier stages of the history of Iberia.

We must observe at the outset that the mountain chain of the Pyrenees does not extend unbroken all the way across the neck of land that connects France and Spain. There are passes to the westward and in the centre, and the whole range gradually fades away as it approaches the Mediterranean, so that its eastern end is comparatively easy to cross. Of the first occasions on which men availed themselves of these breaks in the mountain chain we have no definite information. It seems reasonably certain, however, that the Celts, who arrived in Spain at a very early date and mingled with the primitive Iberians there, came into the

---

[1] Lecoy, i, pp. 10–17.

[2] Cf. also on this paragraph *Historia General del Reino de Mallorca*, by J. Dameto and others (second edition, by Miguel Moragues and J. M. Bover), i, pp. 131–240.

[3] A. Bernard, *Le Maroc*, p. 3.

peninsula from France, and traversed the mountain barrier, probably to the westward.[1] In the days of the conflict of the Carthaginians and the Romans the armies of both sides crossed and recrossed the Pyrenees at the other end, over the foothills near the Mediterranean Sea. During the subsequent struggles between the Romans and the native Spaniards, there are at least two occasions when parts of southern France were administratively joined to Spain. When Pompey was sent to invade the peninsula, in 76 B.C., he appointed one of his subordinates as governor of Narbonese Gaul. Again, from 43 B.C. until after the battle of Philippi, the province of Narbonese Gaul was united with Hispania Citerior and Ulterior under the direct command of the triumvir Lepidus.[2] Of course these were extraordinary and exceptional arrangements, justified by the unprecedented conditions of the time. But the fact that it should ever have been found convenient to unite the political destinies of Spain and France at this period is not without interest in its bearing on the future.

The Visigoths, at the time of their arrival in Spain, were already in possession of southern Gaul; and though they were seriously threatened there by the armies of the Emperor Honorius, they succeeded in retaining and increasing their lands north of the mountains, while they subdued or expelled the other barbarian tribes who had preceded them in the Iberian Peninsula. In the second half of the fifth century, under the mighty Euric, the Visigothic kingdom attained its greatest extent. It stretched from the Loire on the north, to Gibraltar on the south, from the Rhone and the Mediterranean on the east, to the Bay of Biscay and the Atlantic on the west; its capital and centre of

[1] Philipon, Les Ibères, p. 139.
[2] Dio Cassius, xlvi, 55; xlviii, 1, 2; Appian, De Bellis Civilibus, iv, 2; v, 3;
E. von Herzog, Galliae Narbonensis Historia, pp. 66 f., 103 ff.

gravity was on French soil, at Toulouse, Bordeaux, and Narbonne. But the bulk of the Gallic portion of it was soon to be lost. It is curious to think of Spain, whose loyalty to the faith in later times was so potent a cause of the increase of her imperial domain, as being ruled by sovereigns whose espousal of the heretical side of one of the first religious wars of Europe resulted in a serious limitation of her territories. Yet such was the undoubted fact. King Clovis of the Salian Franks, recently victorious over Romans and Alamanni, was the hero of the hour in northern Gaul. He burned with jealousy of his Visigothic neighbors to the south of him; he longed to extend his territories at their expense; a pretext for an aggressive campaign alone was lacking, and Clovis finally found it in the fact that the Visigoths clung to Arianism, while he was ardently, though recently, orthodox. In the year 507 he defeated the armies of his Visigothic rival Alaric II in a terrible battle on the Campus Vocladensis,[1] near Poitiers, slew the king, and drove his forces in headlong flight. Had it not been for the intervention of Theodoric the Ostrogoth, grandfather of Alaric's son and successor, Amalaric, the Frankish conquest would scarcely have stopped short of the Pyrenees. As it was, the Visigoths were finally able to preserve a strip extending along the Mediterranean coast of France eastward from the end of the mountain range to the Rhone, known as the province of Narbonne, or Septimania, and sometimes as Gothia. In the succeeding years the Franks appeared before Narbonne, besieged it, and strove at every favorable opportunity to drive the Visigoths south of the Pyrenees; in 532–533 they actually crossed the mountain barrier farther westward, and occupied Pamplona. The

---

[1] On the exact site of this battle, cf. A. F. Lièvre in *Revue Historique*, lxvi, pp. 90–104.

centre of the Visigothic realm was indeed transferred to
Spain, and Toledo became its capital before the middle of
the sixth century; but Septimania continued to form a part
of it down to the Moorish invasion of 711. The region
was doubtless difficult to administer, and was the theatre of
dangerous revolts, the most serious of which occurred in
the reign of the famous King Wamba, and required royal
intervention to put it down. It was not, however, till a
thousand years later that the last portions of it were finally
reunited to France.[1]

The Moorish invasion did not stop at the Pyrenees.
Recklessly ignoring the small band of Christians who had
intrenched themselves in the mountain fastnesses of the
northwest of Spain, the Saracens began within eight years
of their arrival in the peninsula to carry their raids into
southern Gaul. In 720–721 the conquest of France was
systematically taken up. Narbonne was besieged and
captured, and Toulouse only rescued at the last extremity
by Duke Eudes of Aquitaine. A subsequent expedition
under another leader saw the invaders follow up the valleys
of the Rhone and the Saône into Burgundy.[2] After another interval of five years a new viceroy, Abd ar-Rahman
al-Ghafeki, having set the peninsula in order, marshalled
all his available forces and once more crossed the mountains by way of Navarre. First he crushed the army of
the Duke of Aquitaine, which attempted to oppose his
passage of the Dordogne; then, turning westward, he
seized and plundered Bordeaux. He then advanced northward, ravaging and devastating as he went, finally to
encounter the hosts of Charles Martel in October, 732, in

[1] On this paragraph cf. Ortega y
Rubio, *Los Visigodos en España, passim*,
and the bibliographical note on pp. 48–
50 of this book.
[2] St. Boniface, *Letters*, 73 (40 in

Kylie's translation); *Marca Hispanica*,
bk. iii, cap. i; C. Bayet in Lavisse,
Histoire de France, ii, 1, pp. 259 ff., and
the monographs of Reinaud] and of
Dorr, there cited.

the famous battle of Tours. The Frankish victory there
was rendered more decisive by the death of the Arab leader;
a rapid retreat of the Moslem army, and the loss of the bulk
of their recently won possessions north of the mountains
were the inevitable consequences, though the army of the
conqueror was at first too exhausted to pursue.[1] The
region of Septimania, however, still remained for a time in
Moorish hands; nay more, its limits were temporarily somewhat extended by several subsequent invasions from the
south, one of which reached so far eastward as to threaten
the Lombard kingdom in northern Italy. It was not
until the year 759 that Pippin, the father of Charlemagne,
succeeded in taking Narbonne and permanently driving the
Moors to the south of the mountain range.[2]

The Frankish conquest did not stop at the Pyrenees.
Expeditions by Charlemagne and his son Louis the Pious
carried their armies southward as far as the Ebro. Saragossa they were unable to win; but along the Mediterranean
shore they had better fortune. Barcelona was permanently
taken in 801; Tarragona and Tortosa were besieged and
temporarily captured in the immediately succeeding years.[3]
The last two were soon retaken by the Moors, and the
limits of the Frankish territories were pushed back nearly
as far as Barcelona; but the northeastern corner of the
peninsula remained in Christian hands, and was connected,
politically and administratively, for three quarters of a
century to come, with a greater or lesser portion of the
south of France. At first the Spanish conquests formed an
integral part of the great duchy of Aquitaine, owing to the
fact that the bulk of them had been gained by Louis the

[1] Mercier, "La bataille de Poitiers," in *Revue Historique*, vii, pp. 1–13.
[2] *Marca Hispanica*, bk. iii, caps. iii and iv; Ameer Ali, pp. 129, 146 ff., 162–164.
[3] *Marca Hispanica*, bk. iii, caps. xvi, xviii; Bofarull, ii, caps. iv and vi; C. Bayet in Lavisse, *Histoire de France*, ii, 1, p. 295.

Pious, who was established during his earlier years in the Aquitanian capital, Toulouse. In 817 this connection was severed, but when the break occurred the nearer Septimanian territories followed the lead of the Spanish lands with which they had previously been so long united, and together with them were erected into the so-called county of Barcelona, or Catalonia.[1] For a time the county owed feudal allegiance to the crown of France, so that French rule continued, in theory at least, to prevail south of the Pyrenees; but before many years had elapsed the situation was exactly reversed. The weak Carolingians found it impossible to exert any real authority over territories so remote. The counts whom they appointed as their local representatives were for the most part able men, ambitious to attain complete autonomy; finally, towards the close of the ninth century, the inevitable occurred, and Catalonia declared and vindicated its independence.[2] Most of the territories north of the mountains had been meantime stripped away through the efforts of Charles the Bald; but now that independence had been won, the counts of Catalonia set themselves busily to work to regain them. In this task they had history and tradition on their side, and were extraordinarily successful. An excellent start was made by Ramon Berenguer I (1035–76) who was able to leave to his son Carcassonne, Redes, Lauraguais, and "all that he had in the county of Toulouse, in Minervois, in Narbonne, in Foix, and in Comminges."[3] The bulk of the work, however, was done by Ramon Berenguer III (1096–1131), partly through skilful diplomacy and superior military power, but still more by a policy of advantageous marriage. His most important acquisition was the county of Provence,

---

[1] Dieroks, i, p. 257; Bofarull, ii, pp. 120 ff.

[2] *Marca Hispanica*, bk. iv, coll. 370 ff., 539 f.; Bofarull, ii, caps. ix, x.

[3] Bofarull y Mascaro, *Los Condes de Barcelona*, ii, p. 42.

together with Millau and Gévaudan, through his union with its heiress Dulce in 1112;[1] other adjacent territories followed under his immediate successors, so that in the early years of the thirteenth century the influence of Catalonia (which had meantime been strengthened south of the Pyrenees by its union with Aragon in 1137) may be justly described as preponderant in the south of France.[2] The story of the loss of the greater part of these territories in the reigns of Pedro II and James the Conqueror will be told in another place. Yet in the present connection it is well to remember that, even after James the Conqueror had been forced, at the treaty of Corbeil in 1258, to give up the bulk of his French holdings and renounce forever his grandiose plan of founding a single Romance state which should extend from the Durance to the Segura, the boundaries of Catalonia were not driven quite back to the line of the Pyrenees. Montpellier was not wholly lost until 1349, and Cerdagne and Roussillon, save for one brief interval at the end of the fifteenth century, remained in Spanish hands until the days of Louis XIV. Though territorially insignificant, stirring memories were sure to be roused by the mention of their names, and later Spanish kings went to desperate lengths to retain them. They remained for many years to come a possible nucleus for further conquests in the north, a lure to induce the descendants of the ancient counts of Catalonia to emulate the deeds of their ancestors and to enlarge their holdings beyond the mountain range.

The early history of the little saddlebag kingdom of Navarre may also be adduced as evidence that the Pyrenees do not set so formidable a barrier between France and Spain

---

[1] Devic and Vaissete, *Histoire générale de Languedoc* (revised edition in 15 vols.), iii, pp. 610 ff.

[2] F. D. Swift, *Life and Times of James the First of Aragon*, pp. 6, 7, 14, 96 f.

as might at first sight appear. Navarre lay partly to the north though mostly to the south of the range; its passes were a frequent route of invasion in both directions; previous to its division in the reign of Ferdinand the Catholic, its sovereignty had been held for long periods on both sides of the mountains.[1] It was a link, as well as a bone of contention, between Spain and France, and furnished a medium of institutional exchanges between the two countries. The fact that Basque is spoken today on both slopes of the Pyrenees, and the close linguistic affinity between Valencia, Catalonia, and Provence are also significant in the same connection. Not only, then, to the south, on the Straits of Gibraltar, nor to the east, in the Mediterranean Sea, but also to the north, across the Pyrenees, did Spain inherit precedents for expansion beyond her natural boundaries. Small wonder if, at the time that the daring and faith of Christopher Columbus opened up a new and far greater field of development, the possibilities of which were at first but remotely conceived, she should tend in some respects to neglect it, in favor of other enterprises nearer at home, and sanctioned by some of the strongest precedents of Spanish history and tradition.

We have thus far considered some of the external geographical features of Spain, and also certain events of her ancient and mediaeval history, with reference to her capabilities for external expansion, and her fitness for the possession of an imperial domain. But before the background for the foundation of the Spanish empire can be regarded as complete, we must supplement what has gone before with a few words concerning some of the most salient internal peculiarities of the peninsula — peculiarities which, though

[1] Codera, *Estudios*, 1st series, pp. 134–234; J. de Jaurgain, *La Vasconie.*

at first sight they may seem of slight importance in moulding
Spain's imperial career, were destined ultimately to exert
an influence fully as great as the external ones.

Of these internal peculiarities the first, and by all odds
the most fundamental, is the tendency towards diversifi-
cation and separatism. It is almost impossible to exaggerate its importance; even more than is the case with
Germany down to the nineteenth century, the whole history
of Spain "may be summed up in the one word 'Particular-
ismus.'" Geographical and climatic conditions form the
basis of it. Racially, historically, socially, and economically the effect of the separatistic trend may be traced from
the beginning to the end of the story. Its influence has
been deep-seated and permanent. It is the key to many
of the most important problems with which the Spaniard
is confronted today.[1]

Let us take, in the first place, the geographical features
of the peninsula. The average altitude of Spain is very
great; in fact it ranks next to Switzerland among the
European countries in this respect. The whole of the
north central portion forms a high, arid plateau, which
slopes off somewhat abruptly toward the Mediterranean
on the east, and more gradually toward the Atlantic on the
west. On the eastern half of the northern side it rises
rapidly into the mountain chain of the Pyrenees, while on
the western it merges into the rainy pastures of Asturias
and Galicia. On the south it falls away quite suddenly,
but far inland, leaving the wide, rich Andalusian plain,
watered by the Guadiana and Guadalquivir, and cut off

[1] On the physiography of Spain, cf.
Strabo's *Geography* (tr. Falconer and
Hamilton), i, pp. 205–263; Robert
Gaguin (c. 1468) in Martène and Du-
rand, *Thesaurus Novus Anecdotorum*, i,
coll. 1833–1840; Jules Gounon-Loubens,
Essais sur l'administration de la Castille,
chap. i; A. Blásquez, *España y Portugal* (Barcelona, 1914). Other references
may be found in Altamira, iv, pp. 459 f.

in turn from the Mediterranean by the snowy summits of the Sierra Nevada, whose loftiest peak (Mul-Hacen) exceeds in altitude the highest of the Pyrenees. Then, in addition to these general physiographical differentiations, the peninsula is subdivided by a number of minor mountain chains, which run for the most part in an east and west direction, and form the valleys of the five principal Spanish rivers — the Ebro, on the east, and the Douro, Tagus, Guadiana, and Guadalquivir, on the west. A river may be either a highway for those who desire to travel along its course, or a barrier for those who wish to cross it; but the Spanish rivers, with the possible exception of the Guadalquivir, are emphatically the latter rather than the former. Since they all rise on the high north central plateau, their current is for the most part so swift as to render it impossible for those journeying east and west to navigate them, while the same fact renders them the more difficult to ford for travellers going north and south. By its rivers and mountain chains, as well as by its high north central plateau, low-lying coasts, and Andalusian plain, the Iberian Peninsula is parcelled out into a number of sharply separated districts, each of which naturally tends to lead a life of its own.

Peculiarly and widely divergent climatic conditions follow as an inevitable corollary of these physiographical facts. Moisture is never evenly distributed in a mountainous country, and Spain is no exception to the general rule. The long and parching droughts, followed by sudden inundations, which are a familiar feature of the great plateau, result from a concentration of the rains among the mountain peaks, and the sudden flooding of the swiftly rising streams, which either carry the water off to the sea before it has had any opportunity to benefit the surrounding lands, or else, if the rain has been unusually heavy, overflow their banks. Sudden alternations of heat and cold are another characteristic feature of the high north central plain or meseta. These unfavorable conditions, however, do not obtain on all the coasts, while in Andalusia moisture is abundant and the temperature warm and even. In the extreme northwest, in Galicia and Asturias, the action of the Gulf Stream brings equable weather, though it is also unusually wet. In Spanish climatic as well as physiographical conditions, variety is again the dominant note.

Let us turn for a moment to some of the effects of this internal geographical and climatic variety and separatism on the historical development of the peninsula. The earliest writers on Spain were struck by it. There are even faint traces of it in the Carthaginian *Periploi*, or accounts of the earliest voyages along the coast, and Strabo's famous treatise may be described without exaggeration as an extended commentary thereon.[1] It is evident that the number and variety of the tribes which inhabited the peninsula made a profound impression on all observers. The prolonged and heroic resistance of the native Spaniard to the Roman legions in the last two centuries B.C. would have been impossible in a less mountainous and divided land; the Lusitanian shepherd Viriathus and his followers won their greatest victories by skilfully taking advantage of the deep ravines and rocky summits of the west. "The Romans," says Strabo, "lost much time by reason of the number of different sovereignties, having to conquer first one, then another."[2] That the victors, after their conquest

[1] Strabo, *Geography* (tr. Falconer and Hamilton), i, pp. 205–263; W. von Christ, "Avien und die älteste Nachrichten über Iberien," in *Abhand. der k. bayer. Akad. der Wiss.*, philos.-philol. Classe, xi, 1, pp. 113–187; for other references see Meyer, ii, pp. 686–688.

[2] Strabo, *Geography* (tr. Falconer and Hamilton), i, p. 238.

was complete, found it convenient to exchange their original partition of the land into Hispania Citerior and Hispania Ulterior for a division into three, four, and finally seven provinces is certainly significant, as is the difficulty which the Visigoths subsequently experienced in subjecting the remoter part of the land to their control, and in blotting out the various distinctions which separated them from the mass of the Hispano-Roman inhabitants. The whole internal history of Moorish Spain may be said to centre around the efforts of the sovereign power to check its subjects' natural proneness to dissolve themselves into a number of petty states, and the tendency to division and subdivision among the Christian rulers in the north is the key to many of the most difficult questions in the mediaeval period. The common statement that the history of united Spain begins with the marriage of Ferdinand of Aragon to Isabella of Castile is in some respects very misleading. The particularistic trend was much too strong to be eradicated by mere personal union of the crowns. Through Hapsburg and Bourbon days it continued to mould the destinies of the Iberian Peninsula; and it presented one of the most serious problems which confronted the builders of the Spanish Empire.[1]

The results of the peculiar geographical features of the Iberian Peninsula are also plainly visible in its constitutional, social, and economic life. Variety and differentiation are the dominant features of the national assemblies, of the municipal *fueros*, of the ranks and classes of men, and of their multifarious interests and occupations. The difficulty of communication between the different parts of Spain has always discouraged internal commerce, and accounts in

[1] Cf. on this paragraph F. Romaní y Puigdengolas, *Antigüedad del Regionalismo Español* (Barcelona, 1890).

some measure for the average Spaniard's marked economic incapacity and his proverbial aversion to a business career. Generally excellent harbors, on the other hand, furnish admirable opportunities for maritime intercourse with other lands, of which the inhabitants of the Mediterranean coast took advantage at an early date. On the Atlantic seaboard, however, the rise of Portugal as an independent kingdom in the twelfth century deprived Castile of her best ports, crippled her foreign commerce, and probably postponed for at least a century her brilliant career of foreign discovery and exploration. The climatic and physiographical conditions within the peninsula are especially favorable to pasturage — perhaps the principal national occupation in the fifteenth and sixteenth centuries. The rainy slopes of the Asturian mountains afford the best of summer grazing grounds, and the sunny regions of Andalusia are correspondingly valuable in winter. On the other hand, the barrenness of the meseta is profoundly discouraging to the agriculturist; it goes far to explain, if not to palliate, the prevalence of the sentiment expressed in the phrase "deshonor del trabajo;" it is one of the principal reasons why the Spaniard has always tended to concentrate in cities. It is true that this agricultural poverty is in some measure compensated by a plentiful supply of running water and considerable mineral wealth. But the full significance of the first of these natural advantages was not perceived until very recent times, and foreigners fully as much as Spaniards have been the ones to profit by it; while the second, at least in the influence which it indirectly exerted on the Spanish fortunes in the New World, was certainly not an unmixed blessing. The mineral richness of the peninsula was not sufficient to make the search for it a national occupation, but it was so much more considerable

than its agricultural possibilities that it led the inhabitants
to neglect to till the soil, and to confuse real wealth with
its outward and visible symbol. It partly accounts for
the proverbial thirst for gold which was the bane of the
Spaniards in the New World, and for their inability to realize that agriculture is the most permanent and stable source
of a new country's material prosperity. Some of the most
disastrous blunders in the Spanish administration of the
Indies are in large measure to be attributed to the peculiar
conditions under which the conquerors had been reared in
the peninsula.

Everything considered, then, Spain is a country whose
natural advantages for the life of mankind have been fully
counterbalanced by its disadvantages. There have always
been a number of unfavorable and hostile facts to be wrestled
with and overcome, and the age-long struggle against these
hostile conditions has powerfully affected the character of
the inhabitants, and their fitness for the difficult and arduous task of building an empire. The internal divisions
of the peninsula, and the tendency of each portion of it to
live a life apart from the rest, reacted most unfavorably
upon the development of Spain's external possessions.
They have kept the inhabitants of the peninsula as a whole
from concentrating their efforts in any one direction. They
are the fundamental explanation of the extreme complexity
and diversity of interests, which prevented even the powerful monarchs of the sixteenth century from endowing their
immense and widely scattered territories with that unity
which is the best result of absolutism. They account in
large measure for the essentially decentralized character of
Spanish imperial administration. On the other hand, we
may be sure that the inhospitality of the meseta was an
important element in encouraging the Spaniards to seek

pleasanter lands abroad ; and it is hard to conceive how any explorer born and brought up in a more smiling country than the desolate plains of Old Castile could have persevered in his advance across the yellow wastes of Arizona and New Mexico, which bear such striking resemblance to them. Certainly the predominantly unattractive interior of the peninsula helped to make its earliest inhabitants perceive the advantages of a seaboard existence, the first step on the road to empire. From the days of the Phoenicians and Carthaginians the coasts have been the most rich, populous, and progressive portions of the land. Spain is, in fact, one of the classic examples of the truth of the famous dictum of Plato that "men tend to establish themselves on the shore of the sea, like frogs on the edge of a pond."

NOTE ON THE GENERAL AUTHORITIES ON SPANISH HISTORY

Bibliographies. — Though lagging far behind most of the other Western European nations today in scientific bibliographical work, Spain was the leader in this field two and a half centuries ago. The *Bibliotheca Hispana Vetus* and the *Bibliotheca Hispana Nova* of Nicolas Antonio (1617–84) have rightly been described as "incomparably superior to any previous bibliography," "still unsuperseded and indispensable." The *Bibliotheca Hispana Vetus* is a literary history of Spain from the time of Augustus to the year 1500 A.D. The *Bibliotheca Hispana Nova* deals with the works of Spanish authors from 1500 to 1684. The best (revised) edition of both was published at Madrid, the *Vetus* in two folio volumes, 1788, the *Nova* also in two folio volumes in the same year. Both are in Latin, and in the *Nova* the titles are arranged alphabetically according to the authors' Christian names; a little practice, however, and constant use of the different indices will enable the student to find his way about in it: cf. M. Menéndez y Pelayo, *La Ciencia Española* (Madrid, 1887–88), i, pp. 50 ff. The elaborate but unsystematic *Ensayo de una Biblioteca Española de Libros raros y curiosos* by Bartolomé José Gallardo (Madrid, 1863–89, 4 vols.) is on the whole more valuable than the *Diccionario bibliográfico-histórico de los antiguos reinos, provincias, ciudades, villas, iglesias, y santuarios de España*, by Tomás Muñoz y Romero (Madrid, 1858). The "Índice de Manuscritos de la Biblioteca Nacional" at the end of the second volume of Gallardo is especially useful, though far from complete. Finally, we have Rafael Altamira's "Guía bibliográfica," the only up-to-date general bibliography of its kind, which occupies the last 92 pages of vol. iv of his *Historia de España y de la Civilización Española*. Though necessarily very incomplete, and lacking in any critical estimate of the value of the works cited, it furnishes a starting point for the serious study of Spanish history down to 1808, particularly on the institutional and economic side, and it is especially useful in its indications of important articles in historical journals and reviews.

Bibliographies of special topics abound, though they are often by no means scientific or complete. Felix de Latassa y Ortin's *Biblioteca antigua y nueva de Escritores Aragoneses* (new ed., Saragossa, 1884–86, 3 vols.) may be cited as a good example of a bibliography of a definite region; Prosper Boissonnade's *Les études relatives à l'histoire économique de l'Espagne*, down to 1453 (Paris, 1913: first published in the *Revue de synthèse historique*), and José Almirante's *Bibliografía Militar de España*

(Madrid, 1876), as bibliographies of special subjects. Much miscellaneous bibliographical information may also be obtained from *Cultura Española*, from the *Revista de Archivos*, and from the *Bibliographie hispanique*, edited annually since 1905 by the Hispanic Society in New York. Each volume of this last gives a list of the books that have appeared in the preceding year. Excellent brief critical accounts of the mediaeval chroniclers may be found in Rafael Ballester y Castell's *Las Fuentes narrativas de la historia de España durante la Edad Media* (Palma de Mallorca, 1908), and in the " Historiografia de Catalunya " by José Massó y Torrents in *R. H.*, xv, pp. 486–613: there is crying need for more of this sort of work in the different fields of Spanish history.

General Collections of Sources.— *Hispaniae Illustratae, seu Rerum Urbiumque Hispaniae, Lusitaniae, Aethiopiae, et Indiae scriptores varii* (Frankfort, 1603–08, 4 vols., folio) is a miscellaneous collection of the works of famous Spanish historians, from the early Middle Ages to the end of the sixteenth century. It includes the Chronicles of Lucas de Tuy, the *Historia Hispanica* of Rodrigo Sanchez de Arevalo, the first twenty books of Mariana's History, the Commentaries of Blancas, and many other similar works. The first two volumes were edited by the learned Belgian Jesuit Andreas Schott, or Schottus (1552–1629), the fourth by his brother Franciscus, and the third by Johann Pistorius. *España Sagrada* (Madrid, 1747–1879, 51 vols.) is a vast mine of information for the history of the Spanish Church: it corresponds to the *Gallia Christiana* for France. All the minor monastic chroniclers will be found in it. It was begun by the Augustinian theologian Enrique Flórez, and continued by Manuel Risco, José de la Canal, Antolin Merino, Pedro Sainz de Baranda, and the Real Academia de la Historia. A key to it will be found in vol. xxii of the *D. I. E.*, and a table of contents of the first 47 volumes in *El Bibliógrafo Español*, año iii, pp. 106–112, 115–117.

The Real Academia de la Historia (founded in 1735) has printed an enormous mass of valuable material on Spanish history. The most important of the sources it has published are as follows. (1) The text of the proceedings of the *Cortes de los antiguos reinos de León y de Castilla* from the beginning to 1559 (Madrid, 1861–1903, 5 vols.). Manuel Colmeiro has written an excellent *Introducción* to this set (Madrid, 1883–84, 2 vols.). The work of the Academy has been continued by the Congreso de los Diputados for the period after 1559, thirty-five volumes (*Actas de las Córtes de Castilla*) having been already published for the years 1563–1620. This collection is of course indispensable for the internal history of Castile. (2) A similar set for the *Cortes del antiguo principado de Cataluña* is now in progress; it has already reached the year 1458 in twenty-two volumes, and when it is terminated, the publication of the proceedings of the Cortes of the other realms of the Crown of Aragon will doubtless be taken up. (3) A *Colección de Documentos inéditos, relativos al descubrimiento, conquista, y organización de las antiguas posesiones Españolas de Ultramar* (2d series, Madrid, 1885–1900, 13 vols.). Most of these deal with the first century after the discovery of America. (4) *Memorial Histórico Español* (Madrid, 1851– , 46 vols. so far published): a miscellaneous collection of letters, documents, and articles, covering the entire field of Spanish history. A *Catálogo de las obras publicadas por la Real Academia de la Historia* (Madrid, 1901) gives a very brief summary of the contents of these collections: it is particularly valuable for the *Memorial Histórico Español*.

The *Colección de Documentos inéditos para la Historia de España* is a collection of 112 volumes (Madrid, 1842–95), edited by various scholars, the most important being the Marquis de la Fuensanta del Valle, who has brought out the last 56 volumes of the set. Most of the documents contained in this collection deal with the sixteenth and seventeenth centuries, but there is also valuable material for the earlier periods. An inadequate table of contents of the first 102 volumes was published at Madrid in 1891; and a list of titles of documents relating to America in the first 110 was compiled by G. P. Winship in 1894. — An invaluable collection of documents on Spanish constitutional history was undertaken some years ago by Professor Hinojosa; and a large part of the material is already in type.

Various collections of the laws of Spain (especially of Castile) from the *Fuero Juzgo* to the *Novísima Recopilación* have been published at different times. The best is that entitled *Los Códigos Españoles concordados y anotados* (Madrid, 1847–51, 12 vols.), published by M. Rivadeneyra, and the most convenient the one-volume *Códigos antiguos de España*, edited by Marcelo Martínez Alcubilla (Madrid, 1885).

The *Biblioteca de Autores Españoles*, published by M. Rivadeneyra (Madrid, 1846–80, 71 vols.), provides much valuable historical material: the two volumes of *Historiadores de Sucesos Particulares* (1858–63), and the three which contain the *Crónicas de los Reyes de Castilla* from Alfonso X to Ferdinand and Isabella inclusive (1875–78), are particularly important; these five volumes are all edited by Cayetano Rosell. The *Nueva Biblioteca de Autores Españoles*, edited under the direction of M. Menéndez y Pelayo (Madrid, 1905–12, 20 vols.), is also most useful; in it, for example, may be found the Primera Crónica General, four chronicles of the Great Captain, and two volumes of historians of the Indies. The publications of the Sociedad de Bibliófilos Españoles, the Sociedad de Bibliófilos Andaluces, and of the Sociedad de Bibliófilos Madrilenos, the *Colección de Libros Españoles Raros ó Curiosos*, and the set known as the

Libros de Antaño contain various writings of the earlier chroniclers and historians.

General Histories of Spain.—At the head of this category comes the famous *Historia de Rebus Hispaniae*, by the Jesuit Juan de Mariana, first published in 1592 (first edition in Spanish in 1601). Since this work has been made the subject of a most exhaustive study by Georges Cirot, *Mariana Historien* (Bordeaux, 1905), it is unnecessary to add anything more concerning it here. As I have cited it rarely, and rather for legendary and descriptive matter than for historical fact, I have felt justified in utilizing the much abridged and somewhat inaccurate English translation of John Stevens (London, 1699), for the sake of its exceedingly picturesque language. The two long and elaborate eighteenth century Spanish histories of Juan de Ferreras (Madrid, 1700–27, 16 vols.) and of J. F. de Masdeu (Madrid, 1783–1805, 20 vols.) are now almost entirely obsolete; but with the middle of the nineteenth we have two others, which demand more careful consideration. The first, by the French Protestant Eugène Rosseeuw Saint-Hilaire, began to appear in Paris in 1837 and was completed in 1879 in 14 volumes, down to the end of the reign of Ferdinand VII: 2d edition, 1844–79, 14 vols. The second, by Modesto Lafuente ('Fray Gerundio'), covers the same field and was first published in 30 volumes in Madrid, 1850–1867: there have been many subsequent editions in various forms. Lafuente was apparently incited to undertake his task by the appearance of the first volumes of Rosseeuw Saint-Hilaire, and his Spanish biographer takes evident pleasure in pointing out that his diligence was such as to enable him to complete his work first, and in more than twice as many volumes as that of his French contemporary (Antonio Ferrer del Rio, "Vida y Escritos de Lafuente," published in vol. xxx of Lafuente's *Historia*, pp. xli, clviii–clix). It is but fair to add, however, that Lafuente sometimes followed the work of Rosseeuw Saint-Hilaire more closely than the canons of modern historical scholarship would approve. A comparison of Lafuente, vol. vii, p. 412 (first paragraph) with Rosseeuw Saint-Hilaire, vol. v, p. 167 (middle paragraph); of Lafuente, vol. vii, pp. 446 f. with Rosseeuw Saint-Hilaire, vol. v, p. 183 (bottom); and of Lafuente, vol. viii, pp. 164 f. with Rosseeuw Saint-Hilaire, vol. v, pp. 212 f. will illustrate this statement; there are also striking resemblances in the general arrangement of the paragraphs in the two works. Both books are good typical products of the period in which they were written. They make reasonably good use of chronicles and memoirs (Lafuente also cites an occasional document); they give a mass of interesting detail, and are in general fairly accurate as far as they go. The constitutional, social, and economic sides of the story, however, are largely neglected, and the subsequent discovery of manuscript material has necessarily modified a number of their verdicts. The *Geschichte von Spanien* in the Heeren and Ukert series was written by F. W. Lembke, Heinrich Schäfer, and F. W. Schirrmacher, and is being continued at present by Konrad Häbler; its composition has been strung out in eight volumes from 1831 to 1907, and it has only reached the end of the reign of Charles V. Necessarily very uneven, its best portions do not measure up to the highest standards of German scholarship; occasionally, however, it forms a useful supplement to Lafuente and Rosseeuw Saint-Hilaire.

Of the general histories of Spain of more recent date may be mentioned the *Historia General de España*, written for the Real Academia de la Historia under the direction of Antonio Cánovas del Castillo. Eighteen volumes of this work appeared during the last decade of the nineteenth century, but the assassination of Cánovas in 1897 seems, temporarily at least, to have put a stop to it. The work was done by different specialists, but it was written rather for the general reader than for the historical student; the published volumes cover various non-consecutive periods and fields, so that there are many gaps. The most valuable are Cesáreo Fernández Duro's *La Marina de Castilla* (1895), and Manuel Colmeiro's *Reyes Cristianos desde Alonso VI hasta Alfonso XI* (1891). Far more useful for serious workers is Rafael Altamira's *Historia de España y de la Civilización Española* (Barcelona, 1909-11, 4 vols.), which marks an epoch in the study of Spanish history. By reducing the narrative portions to the smallest possible compass, the author leaves himself a chance to devote the greater part of his book to social, constitutional, economic, and cultural history. The emphasis on these phases is doubtless disproportionate; but when one considers the almost complete neglect of the various non-political fields of history by previous Spanish historians, one will doubtless be grateful to the author for the use that he has made of his space. The work is really indispensable for the study of any period of Spanish history previous to 1808, when it stops. Of recent histories of Spain by non-Spanish writers, Gustav Diercks's *Geschichte Spaniens* (Berlin, 1895-96, 2 vols.) is by far the best. It is scholarly, well arranged, and clearly expressed. M. A. S. Hume's revised edition of Ulick R. Burke's *History of Spain from the Earliest Times to the Death of Ferdinand the Catholic* (London, 1900, 2 vols.) should be used with the utmost caution. There are numerous inaccuracies, and the proportions are manifestly absurd; the footnotes, however, often show considerable research, and contain useful references to other works.

The following, though not strictly speaking general histories of Spain, belong rather in this category than in any other, and are consequently inserted here. M. Colmeiro's *Curso de Derecho Político* (Madrid, 1873) is the best single account of the institutions of Castile and Leon, with excellent footnotes and references. The same author's *Historia de la Economía Política en España* (Madrid, 1863, 2 vols.) is still useful as a general guide, though superseded in a number of important respects: Jules Goury du Roslan's *Essai sur l'histoire économique de l'Espagne* (Paris, 1888) is nothing more than an abridged translation of it. Amalio Marichalar and Cayetano Manrique's *Historia de la Legislacion y Recitaciones del Derecho Civil de España* (Madrid, 1861-72, 9 vols.) is an exhaustive work which forms the basis for many later books. It is especially valuable for the realms of the Crown of Aragon, where the student has not Colmeiro to guide him. It seems on the whole trustworthy, though the complete absence of references renders it difficult, if not impossible, to verify its statements. Manuel Danvila y Collado's well known *Poder Civil en España* (Madrid, 1885-86, 6 vols.) is too hastily put together to be of much value: the first volume extends from the earliest times to the year 1516. The standard ecclesiastical history of Spain by P. B. Gams, *Die Kirchengeschichte von Spanien* (Ratisbon, 1862-79, 3 vols. in 5), leaves much to be desired.

Periodical Publications and Reviews. — The *Boletín de la Real Academia de la Historia*, begun in 1877 and at present in its seventy-second volume, is a vast mine of miscellaneous historical information, and contains articles, documents, and bibliographical notes. The longer monographs published by the Academy are issued under the title of *Memorias*; fourteen volumes have so far been put forth (Madrid, 1796-1909). By far the most valuable of the different Spanish reviews for the historical student is the *Revista de Archivos, Bibliotecas, y Museos*, edited by a committee of the most eminent scholars in Spain, headed by Juan Menéndez Pidal. It was started in 1871, but its recent numbers are far more valuable than the earlier ones. An elaborate index, covering the first forty years of this publication, was put forth by Róman Gómez Villafranca in 1911. *Cultura Española* (previous to 1906 the *Revista de Aragón*) gave promise of becoming a very notable periodical; unfortunately its publication ceased in the year 1909. The *Revista Crítica de Historia y Literatura Españolas, Portuguesas, é Hispano-Americanas* lasted from 1895 to 1902, and is primarily useful for bibliographical purposes. Two reviews exclusively devoted to Spanish topics are at present published in France. The *Revue Hispanique* began in 1894, and is edited by Raymond Foulché-Delbosc; since 1905 it has been the official organ of the Hispanic Society of America. The *Bulletin Hispanique* was started in 1899, and is edited by a group of well known French scholars, most of them from the South. Both periodicals are of the highest standards, and are indispensable for the study of Spanish history and literature.

BIBLIOGRAPHICAL NOTE TO THE INTRODUCTION

Contemporary Authorities. — On the earliest and classical periods see *Geographi Graeci Minores* (ed. K. Müller, Paris, 1855, 3 vols.), which contains the text of the early Periploi. The *Ora Maritima* of Ruf[i]us Festus Avienus (in *Avieni Carmina*, rec. A. Holder, Innsbruck, 1887, pp. 144–171), which was written about 360 A.D., is a poetical rehash of an ancient Greek periplus of about 400 B.C.; on its value cf. W. von Christ, *Avien und die ältesten Nachrichten über Iberien und die Westküste Europa's* (Munich, 1865: *Abhand. der k. bayer. Akad. der Wiss.*, philos.-philol. Classe, xi, 1, pp. 113–187), G. F. Unger in *Philologus*, Supplementband iv (1884), pp. 191–280, and A. Blásquez y Delgado Aguilera, *El periplo de Himilcon según el poema de Rufo Avieno titulado Ora Maritima* (Madrid, 1909). The *Inscriptiones Hispaniae Latinae*, ed. E. Hübner in the *Corpus Inscriptionum Latinarum*, vol. ii and two supplements (Berlin, 1869, 1892, 1896), and the same editor's *Inscriptiones Hispaniae Christianae* and its supplement (Berlin, 1871, 1900), are the principal sources for the history of Roman Spain. Invaluable material is also contained in the *Codex Theodosianus*, the *Corpus Juris Civilis*, and the *Notitia Dignitatum*. The most important classical authors are Strabo, Caesar, Livy, Lucan (*Pharsalia*), Pliny the Elder, Tacitus (*Annals* and *Histories*), Appian, and Dio Cassius. The most significant Spanish Christian writers of the fourth and early fifth centuries are the historian Orosius and the poet Prudentius. On the Visigoths we have the *Leges Visigothorum*, ed. K. Zeumer in the *Monumenta Germaniae Historica* (Hanover and Leipsic, 1902), the Chronicles of Prosper, Idatius, and John of Biclaro; Isidore of Seville's *Historia Gothorum*, Gregory of Tours's *Historia Francorum* (standard edition by W. Arndt and B. Krusch in *Monumenta Germaniae Historica, Scriptores Rerum Merovingicarum*, i, 1; latest by R. Poupardin, 1913); the Chronicle of Fredegar; Julian of Toledo's *Historia de Wambae Expeditione*; and the anonymous Cordovan *Epitoma Imperatorum* or " Chronicle of the last kings of Toledo and the conquest of Spain by the Arabs " (formerly attributed to Isidore of Beja). On the value and different editions of these chronicles see Auguste Molinier's *Les Sources de l'histoire de France*, i, pp. 55–63, 91–94, and Rafael Ballester y Castell's *Las Fuentes Narrativas de la Historia de España*, pp. 13–28.

Later Works. — On the geography of the Iberian Peninsula, the most recent book is Antonio Blásquez y Delgado Aguilera's *España y Portugal* (Barcelona, 1914), vol. iii of the *Curso de Geografía* edited by V. de La Blache and P. Camena d'Almeida. F. Romaní y Puigdengolas, *Antigüedad del Regionalismo Español* (Barcelona, 1890), is a suggestive monograph; and A. Bernard, *Le Maroc* (Paris, 1913), gives a good idea of the geological and ethnological resemblances of Spain and North Africa. On the primitive inhabitants of Spain and the Iberian question, there is a vast mass of controversial literature, to which Eduard Meyer, *Geschichte des Altertums*, ii, p. 687, and Stéphane Gsell, *Histoire ancienne de l'Afrique du Nord*, i, pp. 306 ff., notes, are good guides. W. Z. Ripley, *The Races of Europe* (New York, 1899), pp. 272–280, summarizes the generally accepted conclusions of the leading scholars. Édouard Philipon, *Les Ibères* (Paris, 1909), should be used with caution: cf. review by F. N. Robinson in *American Historical Review*, xv, pp. 170 f. On the Phoenician and Carthaginian periods, E. Meyer, *Geschichte des Altertums* (Berlin, 1884–1901, 4 vols. so far published), and S. Gsell, *Histoire ancienne de l'Afrique du Nord* (one volume so far published, Paris, 1913), are standard works. For the Roman occupation Theodor Mommsen's *Römische Geschichte*, vols. i–iii and v, with the authorized English translations by W. P. Dickson of i–iii as *The History of Rome* (new ed., New York, 1903, 5 vols.), and of vol. v as *The Provinces of the Roman Empire from Caesar to Diocletian* (new ed., London, 1909, 2 vols.), is fundamental. Valuable suggestions and references may be found in the chapter on Spain in Julius Jung's *Die romanischen Landschaften des römischen Reiches* (Innsbruck, 1881), pp. 1–89. References to special monographs on the provincial divisions of Spain and other points will be found in the notes to pp. 10–13 and 28, *ante*. For the Visigoths the most important works are Felix Dahn's *Die Könige der Germanen*, vols. v and vi (Würzburg, 1870–71), well summarized by Thomas Hodgkin in the *English Historical Review*, ii, pp. 209–234; Eduardo Pérez Pujol, *Historia de las Instituciones sociales de la España Goda* (Valencia, 1896, 4 vols.); Juan Ortega y Rubio, *Los Visigodos en España* (Madrid, 1903); and Rafael de Ureña y Smenjaud, *La Legislación Gótico-Hispana* (Madrid, 1905). The intimate relations between Spain and North Africa in this and the succeeding periods are well brought out in Ernest Mercier's admirable *Histoire de l'Afrique septentrionale* (Paris, 1888–91, 3 vols.) and in León Galindo y de Vera's *Historia de las Vicisitudes y Política tradicional de España en las Costas de África* (Madrid, 1884). Edward Gibbon's *History of the Decline and Fall of the Roman Empire* (ed. J. B. Bury, London, 1896–1900, 7 vols.) is still one of the best authorities on the East Romans in Spain, as well as on the later period; it may be supplemented by Charles Diehl's *L'Afrique byzantine: Histoire de la domination byzantine en Afrique* (Paris, 1896). Most of the books on Moorish Spain and the early days of the Spanish Mark will be found in the bibliographical notes at the end of Chapters I and VI, *infra*. Besides these, the following may be mentioned: *Marca Hispanica*, by Pierre de Marca

(1594–1662), archbishop of Paris (ed. E. Baluze, Paris, 1688); this volume also contains the important *Gesta Veterum Comitum Barcinonensium* written in the end of the thirteenth century by a monk or monks of Ripoll, and other early histories (cf. Ballester y Castell, *Fuentes Narrativas*, pp. 59 f.); Francisco Codera's *Estudios críticos de Historia Árabe Española* (two series: Saragossa, 1903; Madrid, 1917); and the same author's *Decadencia y desaparición de los Almoravides en España* (Saragossa, 1889); and, finally, Gabriel Faure-Biguet, *Histoire de l'Afrique septentrionale sous la domination musulmane* (Paris, 1905).

BOOK I

CASTILE

CHAPTER I

THE RECONQUEST

THE mediaeval history of Spain is first and foremost the history of a crusade. For nearly eight centuries the Christians of the North devoted themselves to the task of expelling the Moors from the peninsula. It was in the accomplishment of that task that the different Spanish kingdoms were gradually evolved, and the final victory at Granada in 1492 celebrated the union of the crowns of Aragon and Castile. Many of the distinctive features of modern Spain are to be directly traced to the influence of this age-long struggle, and it powerfully affected the destinies of the Spanish Empire. In fact the reconquest of the peninsula and the conquest of an imperial domain beyond the sea really form two intimately connected chapters of the same story. From the cave of Covadonga to the annexation of Portugal and her dominions in 1580, which carried the Spanish Empire to its greatest territorial extent, the process of expansion is continuous.

We have seen that the Iberian Peninsula had been ruled both in ancient times and in the early Middle Ages by sovereigns who had also dominated parts of northern Africa, southern France, and the Mediterranean islands. Spain's connection with all these territories was traditional, natural, and intimate. When, therefore, the mediaeval Spaniard looked back at the previous history of his native land, he did not see her boundaries as we see them today. After the Reconquest had reached the shores of the Mediterranean and of the Atlantic, he saw no reason why it should stop. Expansion overseas had in fact begun even before the peninsula was clear of infidels. James I of Aragon captured the Balearics before he took Valencia. Castile won the Canaries before Granada fell, and the year of the surrender of that stronghold was the year of the discovery of America. The foundations of the Spanish Empire were thus laid before the mother country was wholly in Christian hands. Moreover, the interlocking and continuity of the two movements are as easy to recognize in the spheres of constitutional and social development and of national ideals as they are in that of political affairs. The early divisions of the Christian kingdoms have their counterpart during the sixteenth century in the regulations limiting the participation of the Aragonese in the affairs of the Indies; they are vividly recalled by the difficulties which the Hapsburgs experienced in bringing the institutions of the Mediterranean states into alignment with those of Castile. The same religious fervor with which Archbishop Roderic of Toledo strove to inspire the Christians to do or die on the bloody plains of Las Navas de Tolosa was invoked by Hernando Cortez when he burned his ships on the shore of Vera Cruz, and planted the symbol of the Faith above the reeking altars of the Mexican war god; it was utilized by Francisco Pizarro in justification of his ruthless slaughter of the Incas. The Cross of Christ was alike the emblem of reconquest and of conquest; Santiago was the Spanish battle cry in the old world and in the new.

No apology, then, is needed for beginning the story of the foundation of the Spanish Empire in the earliest days of the Reconquest. During the entire period of the Middle Ages, however, it is important to observe that the allied tasks of expelling the Moors from the peninsula, and of winning new territories beyond it, were very unevenly distributed between the eastern and western parts of Spain. It was Castile on the westward that assumed the lion's share of the work of recapturing Spain from the infidel, while the realms of the Crown of Aragon to the eastward took the lead in the great work of expansion in the Mediterranean Sea. The relative geographical extent of the lands held by Castile and Aragon within the peninsula and without it at the accession of the Catholic Kings bears striking testimony to this. While Castile and Leon occupied more than three times as much territory as did the Aragonese realms in Spain, their sole external possession, the Canaries, was less than one seventeenth the size of the Mediterranean islands and Italian lands that had been won by the eastern kingdoms. The mediaeval Castilian background of the Spanish Empire is primarily, therefore, a history of internal expansion, while that of the realms of the Crown of Aragon deals for the most part with the conquest of realms abroad; and this fundamental difference in national occupation and object was to give rise to an enormous number of subsidiary ones in a multitude of other respects. Two very divergent currents united under Ferdinand and Isabella to form Spain and the Spanish Empire, and much study will have to be devoted to the growth and development of each, before any adequate appreciation can be gained of the nature and complexity of the problems with which the Catholic Kings and their successors were confronted. The present chapter will deal with the narrative history of Castile during the first five and a half centuries after the Moorish invasion.

Time-honored tradition, so often more significant and important than established historic fact, assigns the cradle

of the Christian reconquest of the Iberian Peninsula and
of the modern Spanish Empire to the cave of Covadonga
in the Asturian mountains.   To this cave a small band of
Christians, led by a certain Pelayo, who gave out that he
was a descendant of the ancient line of Visigothic kings,
retired before the advancing hosts of one of the Arab
chieftains; and, favored by the mountainous character of
the country, offered desperate resistance to the overwhelming forces of the invaders.[1]   The date usually assigned to
this episode is the year 718, and the ancient Spanish historians vie with one another in telling of the marvels that
were there performed.   "The Infidels," says Mariana,
"attack'd the mouth of the Cave, powring in a Shower of
Stones and Darts.   Here the Hand of God appeared in
defence of the Christians; for all the Weapons cast against
them, flew back upon the Moors, with great slaughter of
them.   At this Miracle the Infidels stood astonished, and
the Christians taking heart, rusht out upon them; the
Fight was Disorderly, but the Enemy amazed at what
they had seen, turned their Backs and fled.   20000 were
killed in the Battle and Pursuit."[2]   If we cannot accept
this astounding story word for word, we may well believe
that a desultory guerilla warfare was waged in the Asturian
highlands, and that the Moors, discouraged by the difficulty of the country, and thinking perhaps that the Christian forces were too insignificant ever to cause them serious
trouble, finally decided to withdraw without crushing the
last embers of resistance.   It was a terrible mistake, as
they were afterwards to learn to their cost.   "Would to
God," exclaims the Moorish historian Makkari, "that the
Moslems had then extinguished at once the sparks of a fire

---

[1] *Primera Crónica General*, written at the command of Alfonso X, ed. Menéndez Pidal, in the *N. B. A. E.*, v., pp. 304, 306, 318 ff.; E. Saavedra, *Invasión de los Árabes en España*, pp. 138 f.
[2] Stevens's Mariana, p. 103.

that was destined to consume the whole dominions of Islam in those parts." [1]

Slowly Pelayo and his little band increased their territories, and gradually other scattered groups of neighboring Christians joined with them. Before long their united holdings came to be known as the kingdom of Asturias; and the capital which Pelayo had established at Cángas de Onís was transferred before the end of the eighth century to Oviedo.[2] The boundaries of the little realm in this period are impossible definitely to determine. They varied from day to day, though in general the Christians gained more than they lost, particularly during those times when the Moorish part of Spain was in confusion, as in the years immediately preceding the arrival of the first Omayyad. Most of the fighting in the eighth century occurred in the Douro basin; but the limits of the Christian kingdom did not extend so far south as that river, nor those of the Moorish territories so far north. Whenever the infidels withdrew from a district they deliberately devastated it, so as to prevent their foes from following close upon their heels; they thereby created a wide neutral zone or 'No Man's Land,' which, coupled with the natural poverty of the great meseta, opposed the most effective barrier to the Christian advance. These intermediate devastated regions were constantly raided by both parties, but they could not permanently support large armies; hence the desultory haphazard character of the wars of the Reconquest, and the notable absence of important pitched battles.[3] The progress of the Christians was also considerably impeded, during this early period, by the unwillingness of

[1] Translated by Pascual de Gayangos, *Mohammedan Dynasties in Spain*, ii, p. 34.
[2] Lafuente, iii, pp. 70, 123 f.
[3] Altamira, § 152; Diercks, ii, pp. 241–243; and J. Caveda, *Restauracion de la Monarquia Visigoda*, in *Memorias de la R. A. H.*, ix (1879).

these sturdy warriors to permit their monarchs to enter into any alliance with the Emperor Charlemagne against the Moors, lest the terms demanded should imply a derogation of Spanish autonomy, and possibly connote some measure of inferiority to foreign imperial power. The famous legend of Bernardo del Carpio, voicing the national disapproval of such external entanglements, is no longer accepted, but its constant repetition for many generations is a striking proof of the haughty pride of independence and bitter hatred of every kind of restraint, which are traditionally associated with the ancient Spanish aristocracy.[1]

Before the middle of the ninth century, however, several causes had combined to endow what had begun as a mere struggle for existence with a new aim and purpose, and to strengthen the foundations of the Spanish Empire with the sanction and blessing of the church. In the first place the Christians who flocked to the standard of Pelayo and his successors brought with them all the later Visigothic traditions of ecclesiastical power in the government, so that there was fruitful ground ready prepared for the perpetuation of theocratic rule. Secondly, the kings of Asturias soon began to realize that under the peculiar circumstances in which they found themselves the clergy could readily be converted into priceless allies in the task of expanding the boundaries of their little state. The churchmen could easily be induced to represent the work of driving back the Moor as a sacred duty obligatory on all, in fact even to threaten with ecclesiastical censures those who held back, and thus to contribute directly to the enlargement of the territories of the Christian king. In return for this favor the Asturian sovereigns would hand over to the church a generous share of the lands they conquered — the more

[1] Menéndez y Pelayo, *Antología de Poetas Líricos Castellanos*, viii, pp. 15–27.

readily since the clergy was a far less dangerous foe to
the monarchy than the proverbially restive nobility; they
would further the building of churches, cathedrals, and
monasteries, and maintain as far as possible ecclesiastical
influence in the government of the realm. It was a remarkably harmonious case of mutual and reciprocal aid: king
and clergy played into one another's hands to a very unusual
degree. The credit for originating this practice of alliance
with the church in the cause of territorial expansion is usually
given to Alfonso I (739–757), of whom the Moorish chronicler tells us "that he slew tens of thousands of the Faithful, burned houses and fields, and that no treaty could be
made with him." [1] His services to his country and to
Christendom have earned him the appellation of 'the
Catholic'; and though the policy which he inaugurated
seems to have perished temporarily at his death, it was
subsequently revived and continued, and in the ninth century received additional impetus from the birth of the
national Spanish legend of Santiago.

The story of the miraculous discovery of the remains of
St. James the Greater in the rocky fastnesses of Galicia is
picturesquely related in the following words by the trans-
lator of Mariana's famous history. "Theodomerus, Bishop
of Iria Flavia, hearing great Lights were seen in a wild part
of a Mountain, went thither, and causing the Bushes and
Briars to be cut down, and digging up a heap of Earth,
found the holy Body in a Marble Sepulcher. Overjoy'd
at this, he went to Court to acquaint the King, who in Person repair'd thither, and caus'd a Church to be Erected in
that place, dedicated to St. James, but mean, as having
only mud Walls. He also instituted Benefices belonging
to it, and assign'd them Revenues. The Fame of it being

[1] El Laghi, cited in Lafuente, iii, p. 81.

spread abroad, brought People from all parts of Christendom;
and to this day it is one of the most frequented Pilgrimages
in the World. Some grave and Learned Persons have
made a doubt, whether St. James the Apostle ever was in
Spain, and consequently of the Invention of his Body. I
will not undertake to discuss the point, but must confess I
think the general consent of all Christendom in this behalf
appears to me more convincing than all the Arguments
they can bring to oppose it." [1] It is the last sentence in
this account that contains the gist of the whole matter.
The story spread and was universally believed. A noble
church was erected on the sacred spot and consecrated in
899. During the succeeding centuries it became the goal
of pilgrims so numerous that Spaniards use the phrase 'the
road to Santiago' to express the myriad of stars that com-
pose the Milky Way.[2] But the effect of the legend within
the peninsula and the empire subsequently to be controlled
from it was far more important than Santiago's distinction
as the Mecca of the pilgrims of the West. Arising as it
did just as the kingdom of Asturias was completing the
first century of its troublous existence, it furnished an inspiration, an ideal, a battle cry, which committed the Christians to a steady continuance of their advance up to and
beyond the borders of Spain. It gave the vigorous but
disconnected efforts of the Asturian warriors the added
inspiration of a crusade. It cemented the alliance of church
and state in the sacred duty of reclaiming the peninsula
for the faith and of carrying that faith beyond the seas.
It linked the Reconquest to the Empire and emphasized
the continuity of their development. Never was national
legend of deeper and more lasting significance.

[1] Stevens's Mariana, p. 110.   17 f.; Burke, *History of Spain*, i, pp.
[2] *España Sagrada*, xix, pp. 64 ff.;   156 ff.
xxx, pp. 53 ff.; , Dante, *Paradiso*, xxv,

Powerful as was its influence for the advance of the Christian arms, the legend of Santiago was unable to endow the Asturian realm with the internal unity which was essential for lasting success. The clergy, indeed, had been brought into line, though the grants which rewarded their loyalty played havoc with the royal patrimony; but the nobles, whose existence did not depend on the success of the crusade, grew steadily more restive and uncontrolled. The tradition of elective kingship, inherited from Visigothic days, had not been forgotten, and served to keep the central power weak. Often the haughty barons revenged themselves for fancied insults at the hand of their monarchs by deliberately taking sides with the infidel, who suffered them to enjoy complete religious liberty and a considerable measure of political autonomy as well. The fact that the Cid, the most faithless of them all, could so easily attain the position of national hero shows that such betrayals were not generally regarded as in the least reprehensible. The nobles moreover were continually fighting among themselves; and the deadly feuds, sometimes prolonged for centuries, between the different aristocratic houses of the West Spanish realms, were the most fruitful of all the sources of internal anarchy and unrest, and of impotence abroad.[1] From the earliest days of the Reconquest to the times of Ferdinand and Isabella, the management and control of the baronage was much the hardest problem with which the West Spanish sovereigns were confronted, harder by far than the crusade against the Moors.

It is a singular fact, in view of these tendencies toward decentralization, that the monarchs themselves, whom every

[1] One of the most characteristic and certainly the most celebrated of these baronial feuds — related in countless works of prose and poetry, fact and fiction — is that which centres around the murder of the seven infantes de Lara in the last years of the tenth century. Cf. Stevens's Mariana, p. 129; Lafuente, iv, p. 61, note; M. Menéndez y Pelayo, *Antología*, viii, pp. 37–54.

consideration would naturally urge to work for the unity of their kingdom and the increase of their own power, deliberately adopted the ruinous policy of parcelling out their realms among their children at their deaths. The first instance of this disastrous practice occurred in the end of the reign of Alfonso the Great, who died in 910, and whose long rule of forty-four years had witnessed a considerable extension of the Asturian state. Victorious against the infidel, the old king was not master in his own house; sick at heart over the revolts of his turbulent children, he finally determined to renounce the throne. Plainly foreseeing, however, that his sons, who had previously joined forces against him, would not, after his abdication, permit the elevation of any one of their number to a position of supremacy over the rest, he weakly attempted to satisfy them all by dividing his inheritance between them. To the eldest and most ambitious, named García, he left the southerly territories of Leon, relatively newly won, and probably carrying with them a certain measure of suzerainty over the rest. To the second, Ordoño, he gave the western lands of Galicia and northern Lusitania, and to the third, Fruela, the parent kingdom of Asturias; while he himself retired to the town of Zamora, stipulating that it should remain in his hands till his death, which occurred shortly afterwards.[1] During the next four years the energy of García, king of Leon, which was chiefly directed toward the repeopling of the devastated lands, carried all before it, and made his portion unquestionably the centre of gravity of the Christian state. The capital was definitely transferred from Oviedo to Leon, which had the advantage of Roman fortifications, and the name Leon began gradually to be adopted as the general designation of the Christian

[1] Lafuente, iii, pp. 318–361.

kingdoms of the northwest.[1] But in 914 García died,
leaving no children, so that his younger brother Ordoño,
to whom his father had assigned Galicia, succeeded him in
Leon as well; and ten years later Ordoño died also. In his
case there was no lack of surviving sons, but it seems that
the nobles, to whom considerable influence in the choice
of monarchs still belonged, determined that none of these
was so fit to rule as Ordoño's younger brother Fruela, the
heir of Asturias, whom they accordingly elevated to the
throne of Leon. The kingdoms of the northwest, deliberately separated into three parts by Alfonso the Great, were
thus after fourteen years reunited.[2] The episode is of no
special importance in itself, but the process of division was
constantly repeated, and had not a considerable number
of the early monarchs died leaving only a single son, there
is no telling where it would have ceased. Whenever such
partitions occurred, defeat by the Moors was the inevitable
consequence; but the fact that repeated disasters did not
lead to the abandonment of the practice shows how deeply
the trend toward separatism was ingrained in the character
of the mediaeval Spaniard. Certainly the sort of *divide*
which he practised was not calculated to produce *impera*.

The tenth century witnessed important events on the
eastern frontier of the kingdom of Leon, which were destined
to give wider scope to this same tendency toward division.
The Leonese kings had found it advisable to intrust the
government of the eastern portions of their domains to vassal
counts who resided there, and would consequently be interested for their own sakes both in repelling the raids of the
Moors and in winning new territories at their expense.
The plan worked well, at least in the ninth century: under
the leadership of their counts, the inhabitants of these east-

---

[1] Diercks, i, pp. 292 ff.   [2] Lafuente, iii, p. 415.

ern regions made steady advances to the southward. In 860 their capital was at Amaya; in 884 it had been moved forward to Burgos. During the succeeding years still further progress was made; even Leon to the westward was outstripped, and the Christians came in sight of the Guadarramas. But the Moorish resistance was fierce; every mile was stubbornly contested, and conquered territory was likely to be immediately retaken. The inhabitants were therefore constantly under arms, and, in order to protect themselves against sudden raids, they covered the land with castles, so that it soon became known as Castile. Consciousness of military power naturally begat aspirations for autonomy, and the counts of these eastern regions gradually became restive under the control of the Leonese kings. The nature of their relationship in this early period is impossible accurately to define. The principle of hereditary succession in the countship had not yet formally prevailed over that of royal appointment; but it is evident that at an early date son often followed father without interference from Leon. It seems probable, moreover, that the counts of Burgos soon established a certain right of suzerainty over the less ambitious lords of the territories adjacent to them. They occasionally refused to obey their sovereigns' summons to military service, and we are even told that they sometimes nominated judges on their own authority, thus arrogating to themselves what had been invariably regarded as a royal prerogative. Out of the different and variously authenticated statements that have come down to us one fact emerges clear. By the end of the first quarter of the tenth century the counts of Burgos were aiming to secure complete independence of the kingdom of Leon and absolute control over their own dominions. It was only a question of time when a man should come to the head of affairs at the Castilian capital with sufficient ability to realize these ambitions.[1]

Such a man was found at last in the valorous Fernán Gonzales, who was established at Burgos about 930, and was master of the destinies of the Castilian lands till his death in 970. Legend has been very busy with his name, and many of the main facts of his career are still in doubt. We do not even know how he succeeded in gaining his place; but it seems likely that his own efforts were quite as important in effecting this result as any appointment by the king of Leon; and he was apparently the first definitely to assume the title of 'count of Castile.' He was a bold, resourceful man, equally proficient at plotting and at war, and it was by skilful and unscrupulous utilization both of the internal broils of the Christians in the north and of the ebbs and flows of the war of the Reconquest that he finally achieved Castilian autonomy. A disastrous expedition of his Leonese overlord Ramiro II against the mighty Caliph Abd ar-Rahman III, in 939, gave Fernán Gonzales his first opportunity. Instead of aiding his liege lord against the infidel he began by remaining neutral; then later, when Moorish bands began to penetrate the Christian territories, he joined forces with the invader and broke out into open revolt. On the field of battle Fernán Gonzales was defeated and taken prisoner; but Ramiro was so hard pressed by the troops of the Caliph that he dared not reap the fruits of the victory he had won, and, yielding to the almost unanimous demands of the Castilians, soon sent back the rebel to his own dominions. Nay more, he even sought to cajole his turbulent vassal into friendship and alliance by arranging a marriage between the latter's daughter Urraca and his

[1] B. Montejo, "El principio de la independencia de Castilla," in *Memorias de la Academia de la Historia*, iii (1799), pp. 245-316; Diercks, i, pp. 306-310.

own son Ordoño. Small wonder that Fernán Gonzales was
not won over by methods like these. Rightly regarding
the match that had been made as a confession of Ramiro's
weakness and of his own strength, he promptly returned to
his plots with greater zest than ever. The history of the
period that follows is one long chronicle of anarchy and
intrigue.   Fernán Gonzalez permitted Abd ar-Rahman
to use Castile as a base for new attacks on Leon, and continually interfered in the internal affairs of that kingdom.
When, in 950, his son-in-law Ordoño III succeeded Ramiro
there, he supported against him his younger half-brother
Sancho the Fat: then, six years later, when Ordoño died
and Sancho ascended the Leonese throne, Fernán Gonzales
reversed his policy and made common cause against the
new monarch with his cousin, Ordoño IV. The situation
was also complicated at this critical moment by the entrance
upon the scene of the king of the little realm of Navarre.
The Navarrese monarch was uncle to King Sancho of Leon,
and warmly espoused his cause: but even his help was not
sufficient to enable his ally to recover his throne, still less
to bring the terrible Fernán Gonzalez to his knees. The
intrigues of the count of Castile were shaking all the realms
of Christian Spain to their foundations.[1]

There was only one method by which the wretched
Sancho could possibly hope permanently to extricate himself from his difficulties. No combination of Christians
had so far been successful in vanquishing Fernán Gonzalez:
the only chance of bringing him to book was to outbid him
for the friendship of the great Caliph in the South. A
strictly personal reason, moreover, confirmed the Leonese
king in his resolution to apply for aid to Abd ar-Rahman.

---

[1] *Primera Crónica General*, ed. Menéndez Pidal, pp. 389 ff.; Lafuente, iii,
pp. 424–439, 451–454.

His corpulence was so excessive that it amounted to a serious infirmity and made him a jest in the mouths of his
subjects; his sole hope of being cured rested in a Jewish
doctor, named Hasdai, residing in Cordova, whom Abd ar-
Rahman would not permit to go to Leon. The Caliph,
however, was only too glad to have Sancho come to the
Moorish capital for his treatment: he also was not averse
to a political alliance, and before long the two sovereigns
came to terms.[1] Sancho journeyed southward to Cordova,
where Hasdai's cure was highly successful; Abd ar-Rahman
gave him Moorish troops to aid him in the recovery of his
dominions, in return for the surrender of ten fortresses;
in 959 he was able to regain possession of his realm.
His triumph, however, was but short. It had by this time
become the fashion for dispossessed Christian kings to seek
reinstatement through alliance with the infidel: Sancho
had used that weapon against Fernán Gonzalez, and now
his cousin, Ordoño, the protégé of the count of Castile,
determined to use it against him. The death of Abd ar-
Rahman and the succession of Hakam II at Cordova
(961) made the reversal of policy all the easier, and the
remaining years of Sancho the Fat saw Leon constantly
raided by Moorish troops.[2] Ordoño did not live to reap the
reward of his treachery, but the indefatigable Fernán
Gonzalez utilized the result of it for his own purpose —
namely, the winning of Castilian independence. The details of the story are wellnigh impossible to follow. We
can only be sure that during the last years of the life of
Sancho the Fat, who died in 966, and still more during the
minority of his infant son, Ramiro, the count of Castile
was unceasingly active; and that at his death in 970, his

[1] Dozy, *Histoire des Musulmans
Espagne*, iii, pp. 80-89.

[2] Gayangos, *Mohammedan Dynasties
in Spain*, vol. ii, lib. vi, cap. vi.

title was recognized as hereditary in his house, and passed to his son García Fernández without interference from Leon.

Castilian autonomy had thus been attained, in practice at least, if not in theory; but greater things were soon to come. The countship was ultimately destined to dominate and virtually to absorb the land that gave it birth. During the half century after Fernán Gonzalez's death several marriage alliances were made between the ruling families of Leon, Castile, and Navarre—an incidental evidence that the middle countship was now recognized as of equivalent standing with the kingdoms to the west and east of it. In 1029 these alliances resulted in a close union of Castile and Navarre under a certain King Sancho the Great, who thereafter attempted to carry his power even farther into the west and to possess himself of the kingdom of Leon. This ambitious project he was unable completely to accomplish before his death in 1035; furthermore, he followed the evil example of many of his predecessors, and divided his realms between his different children at his death. But his ambitions to conquer Leon survived in his second son Ferdinand, who succeeded him in Castile,[1] defeated and slew the Leonese monarch on the field of battle in 1037, and finally celebrated his triumph by assuming the royal title in the eastern countship, so that he ruled over both states as king of Castile until his death in 1065. The two realms were again separated from 1065 to 1072, reunited from 1072 to 1157, and separated for the last time from 1157 to 1230, only to be finally reunited under St. Ferdinand. At the time of their last amalgamation in 1230 the younger kingdom had begun to prevail over and swallow up the

[1] In fact Ferdinand took the title of king of Castile in 1033, two years before his father's death, when he married Sancia, heiress of Leon; cf. Lafuente, iv, p. 148.

elder, and as time went on, it continued increasingly so
to do.[1]

The rise of Castile as an independent countship and kingdom thus ended, fortunately for the cause of Spanish progress, with its union on somewhat better than even terms
with the realm from which it sprang. In the early twelfth
century there arose on the western confines of the kingdom
of Leon another state, whose independence of the parent
realm, attained with considerably less difficulty than was
Castile's, has endured, save for one short interval of about
sixty years, until today. The creation of the kingdom of
Portugal was an event of the gravest import for the development of the Spanish Empire.

The eleventh century had been on the whole a period
of rapid Christian advance. The realms of Castile and
Leon were much less often at odds than in the stormy days
of Fernán Gonzalez. From 1037 to 1065 and from 1072
to 1157, as we have just seen, they were united under a
single king. Among the Moors, on the other hand, everything was in anarchy and confusion. The most glorious
days of the Caliphate were gone with the death of Abd ar-
Rahman III in 961; for a few years the versatile Almanzor
revived its splendors, but when in 1002 he died ("and was
buried in Hell," as the *Chronicon Burgense* tersely puts it),[2]
the central power began visibly to crumble away. For
a few years more the farce of maintaining a puppet Caliph
in the Golden Palace of Az Zahra was continued; but soon
that hollow mockery was abandoned, and in 1031 Moslem
Spain became in name what it had been in fact since the

[1] Lafuente, iv, pp. 123–155; Montejo
in *Memorias de la R. A. H.*, iii, pp. 303–
316.

[2] In *España Sagrada*, xxiii, p. 308:
"Mortuus est Almanzor et sepultus est
in inferno" is the sole entry under the
year 1002. Cf. also *Lucae Tudensis
Chronicon Mundi* in Schott, iv, p. 88.

death of Almanzor, a group of petty independent states.
The Christians of the north, temporarily united, were quick
to seize the advantage afforded by this favorable turn of
affairs. Their southward march was resumed, and the
ever shifting boundary, which had hitherto advanced and
receded along the general line of the valley of the Douro,
was now carried forward towards the banks of the Tagus.
The capture of Toledo by Alfonso VI in 1085 marked the
culmination of the Christian success. French, German,
Norman, and Italian warriors were enrolled in the Castilian
army which received the surrender of the ancient Visigothic
capital. For a moment it seemed as if a united Spain,
supported by allies from north of the Pyrenees, would drive
the infidel across the Straits of Gibraltar.[1]

Then suddenly came the inevitable reaction, and the horizon darkened in every quarter. The year after the fall of
Toledo saw the fanatic Berber Almoravides cross the
Strait and win a smashing victory over the Christian hosts
at Zallaka near Badajoz. Farther advance by the Castilian
armies to the southward was effectively checked. That
Toledo was not retaken by the infidel was solely due to the
failure of the Almoravide leader vigorously to follow up his
initial success. More ominous still, disunion, anarchy,
rebellion, and treason broke out in Castile; for the time
being the royal authority was virtually extinguished. But
so little did Alfonso VI comprehend the necessity of concentrating such resources as remained to him, that he actually
contributed to the increase of the confusion by deliberately
rewarding several of his military followers from France
and Germany with large territorial grants in the north of
his own dominions. Among these followers, the two most
prominent were Henry, a younger brother of Eudes, duke

[1] Lafuente, iv, pp. 185-242.

of Burgundy, and his cousin Raymond, count of Amaous, who was descended from the collateral line of Burgundian counts. Both had speedily attracted the favorable notice of the Castilian sovereign, who was himself connected with them by marriage, and their services in the siege of Tudela were recompensed with unusual lavishness. To Raymond Alfonso gave in marriage his only legitimate daughter Urraca, in the year 1093, together with the governorship of Galicia; their son Alfonso VII was subsequently to occupy the Castilian throne, and their granddaughter Constance became the wife of King Louis VII of France. Henry of Burgundy was meantime wedded to Alfonso's natural daughter, Teresa, and received at the same time certain lands on the west coast of the peninsula between the valleys of the Minho and the Tagus; these regions had anciently formed the southern part of the kingdom of Galicia, but were now erected into a separate county, with the name of Portucalia or Portugal. At the outset it appears that Count Henry was in some degree subject to his cousin the ruler of Galicia, and that, in consequence, the relations between them were considerably strained in the ensuing years. Each distrusted the other, and wished to absorb the other's dominions in his own. Both, however, were united in a common jealousy of their father-in-law and feudal suzerain Alfonso of Leon and Castile, whose lands they both coveted, and of whom they were resolved to render themselves independent. A long and bitter struggle ensued, and Portugal in the end was the only power to reap any permanent benefit from it.[1]

The conflict began in earnest with the death of Alfonso VI in 1109. Though five times married, he left no legitimate

[1] E. Petit de Vausse, "Croisades Bourguignonnes contre les Sarrasins d'Espagne au xi° siècle," in *Revue Historique*, xxx, pp. 259-272; Herculano, *Historia de Portugal*, i, pp. 185-208.

male children, and was succeeded in both Leon and Castile
by his daughter Urraca, whose Burgundian husband Raymond, the ruler of Galicia, had died two years before, leaving her with an infant son Alfonso. But Urraca was not
long to remain a widow. · Partly owing to the pressure of
the nobles, who did not wish to see an unmarried woman
occupy the throne, and partly because she dreaded the
consequehces of refusing him, she accepted, as her second
husband, her kinsman, Alfonso the Warrior, the restless
and ambitious sovereign of Aragon, who looked with covet-
ous eyes upon the Leonese-Castilian inheritance.[1] At first
it was hoped that the union of all the Christian kingdoms
of the north, effected by this marriage, would bring peace
and quiet to the land, and bear fruit in glorious Christian
victories against the Moors; but precisely the reverse was
the case. Urraca profoundly disliked her Aragonese husband, whom she had married rather from fear than from
inclination. She dreaded his ambition to make himself king
of Leon and Castile. Open quarrel soon broke out between
them. It was clear that the queen desired a divorce;
and in this she was supported by the mass of the clergy,
who had always protested against the Aragonese marriage
on the ground that the parties were within the forbidden
degrees of kinship. The Galicians also, who hated the
thought of the intrusion of the Aragonese sovereign in their
affairs, took sides at first with Urraca, and, under the lead
of the famous Diego Gelmirez, archbishop of Compostela, supported the claims of Alfonso her son against those of Alfonso
her husband.[2] In 1113 a solemn decree of a church council
at Palencia annulled the marriage of Urraca and Alfonso
of Aragon, but did not thereby eliminate the latter from

[1] Lafuente, iv, pp. 463–469.
[2] M. Murguía, D. Diego Gelmires, pp. 111 ff.

the affairs of western Spain.[1] A furious war broke out
between the divorced husband and wife; and the situation
was further complicated by the fact that Urraca also became
involved in a conflict with Alfonso her son, whose Galician
supporters had previously aided her in getting rid of Alfonso
her husband, but in whom she now recognized a dangerous
rival to her own power.

The prevailing confusion afforded the rulers of Portugal
a golden opportunity to win their independence, and they
did not neglect it. Vigorous campaigns were launched in
Leon and in Castile, invariably directed against whichever
of the parties in those unhappy realms threatened to become predominant : even when, for one brief interval, Urraca
and her son united their forces against the powerful rebel
to the west of them, they were forced to agree to a peace
which granted their foes a large addition to their territories.
At one moment it almost seemed as if Count Henry's ambition would not be satisfied with the mere winning of freedom, but would extend as far as the conquest of the thrones
of Leon and of Galicia; but after his death in 1114, the sepa-
ratist forces in Portugal once more gathered headway, and
independence rather than the annexation of adjacent realms
became the national watchword. For fourteen years
Teresa, the widow of Count Henry, ruled in the name of her
son Affonso Henriquez, and tided Portugal over one of the
most critical periods of her existence; in 1128, however,
she was forced to retire in favor of the Infante, who, though
but seventeen years of age, refused to be kept longer in
tutelage.[2] In 1130 he invaded Galicia; and after a struggle
of varying fortune, was obliged (1137) to sign a peace with
Alfonso, the son of Urraca, in which he specifically acknowledged the condition of feudal vassalage which it was his ob-

[1] Lafuente, iv, p. 479.   [2] Herculano, *op. cit.*, i, pp. 223–290.

ject to shake off. But this state of affairs was not destined
to endure. The restless Portuguese ruler could not stay
his hand from fighting. If he could gain nothing at the
expense of his Christian neighbors to the north and east,
he would enlarge his dominions by attacking the infidel.
In 1139 he won a creditable victory over the Moors at
Ourique, far to the southward, and then returned with
enhanced prestige to Galicia. After an indecisive battle,
in which the Portuguese king was slightly wounded, it
was apparently agreed, in accordance with the customs of
chivalry, to commit the question of Portuguese independence to the issue of a tourney, between picked knights of
the two opposing hosts, in the historic meadow of Valde-
vez.[1] From the encounter the Portuguese emerged victorious,
but long delays ensued before full acknowledgment of their
freedom could be extorted from the king of Castile; for
though the latter recognized his rival's right to the royal
title, he craftily arranged to cede him certain Castilian lands
to be held by him in feudal vassalage, and thus in some
measure to preserve the relation of dependence which had
previously existed. To elude this danger, the king of Portugal approached the papacy, and asked permission to hold
his kingdom as vassal of the Holy See. This plan of playing off the pontiff against the king of Castile was not immediately successful; there were further difficulties about
titles and tributes; but all the time the position of Affonso
Henriquez grew steadily stronger. He was greatly helped
by the conquest in 1147, with the aid of foreign crusaders,
of the town of Lisbon.[2] Finally, in 1179, Pope Alexander
III not only acknowledged the validity of his title as king,
but also the independence of his realm, and thenceforth the
result of the struggle was a foregone conclusion.[3] Whatever

[1] Herculano, i, pp. 290–329.   [2] *Ibid.*, i, pp. 339–403.   [3] *Ibid.*, i, pp. 449 f., 535.

the claims of his rival in Castile, the king of Portugal had won virtual autonomy for his kingdom, and in the immediately succeeding centuries, while the tendency of the other peninsular realms was on the whole to coalesce, its destinies continued to remain separate from them.[1]

A few comments on the significance of the attainment of Portuguese independence for Spain and for the Spanish Empire will not be out of place. The fact that it could be attained and maintained at all is, of course, the strongest evidence of the intensity of Spanish particularism, and of the weakness of the central power in Leon and Castile. There was almost no natural or geographical reason for it. The rivers and mountain chains run on the whole east and west, and consequently form no barrier between Portugal and Spain. Though the character of the country changes somewhat as one crosses the present frontier, "it is impossible to find an adequate explanation of the separate existence of the two nations in the land: history furnishes the only key to this phenomenon."[2] And the results of Portuguese independence are of even more immediate interest to us than its causes. That another nation held the greater part of the western coast of the Iberian Peninsula retarded the process of Spanish expansion in the Atlantic, and, when it finally came, probably altered its direction. The Portuguese sailed south and east before they sailed west, and thus forestalled Spain in Africa and India. Had Portugal not been there, Spain would probably have won extensive lands in these regions before she was tempted out into the western seas. On the other side of the peninsula also the effects of Portugal's presence are distinctly traceable. Had the western seacoast been free for the use of Castile,

[1] On these last two paragraphs, cf. also Lafuente, v, pp. 102–122; and Morse Stephens, *The Story of Portugal*, pp. 34–59.

[2] A. Blásquez, *España y Portugal*, p. 679.

it is difficult to believe that she would have been so completely outstripped by the realms of the Crown of Aragon in maritime expansion during the fourteenth and fifteenth centuries. Imperial experience would have been much more evenly divided between the two component parts of Spain before their union; and the Mediterranean possessions would not have been suffered to divert so large a share of her attention from the Indies. The course of Spain's imperial development was thus largely moulded by the fact that Portugal had won her independence; and when at last, in 1580, the destinies of the two nations were temporarily joined, the divergences of over four centuries proved ineradicable, and the union was really never more than a union in name.

The progress of the Reconquest was naturally much impeded by the constant recurrence of quarrels such as we have just described among the Christians of the north. That it progressed at all is indeed a wonderful tribute to the energy and valor of the mediaeval Spaniard, whenever he could spare time and attention from his particularistic strivings to aid in the completion of the national task. Obviously also, the rapidity of the Christian advance, besides being dependent on the state of internal affairs in Castile and Leon, was bound to vary in inverse proportion to the strength and unity of the Moslem foe to the southward. The Douro valley had been attained during the period of confusion in Moorish Spain which preceded the arrival of the first Omayyad. The boundary was pushed forward to the Tagus in the days when the infidels were divided into a number of petty states. The third great forward movement by the Christians, which was to limit the foe to the little kingdom of Granada, coincides with the gradual disintegration of the Almohade empire in the first part of the thirteenth century. In the long intervals that elapsed between these advances there was a constant series of raids and forays by both combatants, in which the offensive was naturally assumed by whichever side had temporarily attained preponderance. Under Abd ar-Rahman III and Almanzor, in the latter part of the tenth century, when the general line lay just south of the Douro basin, Moorish expeditions were constantly penetrating to the Galician and Asturian mountains and even to the Bay of Biscay. In 997 Almanzor removed the bells from the great church of Santiago de Compostela and carried them south to Cordova, to make lamps for the ceiling of the Mezquita there.[1] On the other hand, Alfonso VII of Castile and Leon, seizing the favorable moment which succeeded the decline of the Almoravides and immediately preceded the arrival of the Almohades (1144–47), carried fire and sword throughout Andalusia, and finally crowned his achievements by temporarily capturing the town of Almeria with the aid of the fleets of Catalonia and Genoa.[2] Whenever to the rare and happy circumstance of domestic peace and unity in Leon and Castile there was added the still rarer one of aid and succor from the realms of the Crown of Aragon, progress was invariably rapid and decisive. Aragon and Castile tended normally to diverge. The Aragonese with their more limited possibilities of territorial expansion in the peninsula naturally took far less interest in the task of the Reconquest than did their neighbors on the west. But in supreme crises they stood loyally by their Castilian coreligionists, and bore them precious aid in advancing the cause of Christendom.

Such a crisis was occasioned by the Almohade victory

[1] Dozy, *Histoire des Musulmans d'Espagne*, iii, pp. 227–235.

[2] "Chronica Adefonsi Imperatoris," in *España Sagrada*, xxi, pp. 398–409.

at Alarcos, on July 19, 1195, over the forces of Alfonso
VIII of Castile.[1] The Christians in the north had been
lulled into a false sense of security by the fact that the
Almohades had been in the peninsula since 1149 without
achieving any notable military success. They felt no fear
of the infidel, and in time-honored fashion were quarreling
among themselves. Portugal and Navarre were too much
occupied with their own affairs to think of bearing aid to
the king of Castile in his distress. The sovereign of Leon
was actively hostile, and permitted some of his most prominent warriors to serve in the armies of the infidel leader,
while others ravaged the Castilian lands. In 1197 an attempt was made to secure peace between the two realms by
the marriage of Berengaria, the daughter of Alfonso VIII
of Castile, to Alfonso IX of Leon; but the union was declared void on the ground of consanguinity by Pope Innocent III. The pair were commanded to separate, and, on
their refusal to yield, were promptly excommunicated, while
the kingdom of Leon endured for seven years all the horrors
that accompanied a thirteenth-century interdict. But the
haughty pontiff was concerned for the welfare of Christian
Spain, as well as for the observance of the laws of the church.
When Berengaria and Alfonso acknowledged their fault
and the invalidity of their marriage, he consented to legiti-
matize their offspring: so that the eldest of their children,
known to history as St. Ferdinand, was able in 1230 to ascend the united thrones of Leon and Castile.[2] Furthermore, Innocent promised to excommunicate any Iberian
potentate who should refuse to bear a part in the crusade
on which the salvation of the peninsula depended, and which
was preached with feverish energy by the clergy throughout

---

[1] Conde, *Dominacion de los Arabes en España*, English translation, pt. iii, caps.
lii–liii.
[2] Colmeiro, *Reyes*, pp. 82–87.

the length and breadth of the land. By threats and concessions the kings of Portugal and Navarre were brought into line. Pedro of Aragon was enthusiastic for the cause. Only the jealous king of Leon held aloof, but his opposition was enough to cause disastrous delays; in 1211 an expedition into Andalusia had to be given up because Alfonso did not dare to leave his realm. Finally, however, in the spring of 1212 all was ready. Toledo was the rendezvous, and thither the knights of all the Iberian realms as well as crusaders from southern France and other European lands flocked for the great adventure. On June 20 the united forces turned southward. Whether they were discouraged by the long hot march across the desolate plains and by the lack of plunder, or whether treachery again was rife in the ranks, it is hard to tell; but the fact remains that despite all that clerical exhortation could do to prevent it, there were numerous desertions, particularly among the foreigners from north of the Pyrenees, who ravaged the Castilian lands in the course of their retreat, and were justly rebuked for their disgraceful conduct by being refused admission at the gates of Toledo.[1] But the bulk of the Spanish levies remained loyal to the cause. The enemy, in superior numbers and confident of victory, permitted the Christians to occupy the chief passes of the Sierra Morena, and, guided by shepherds, to issue out into the great plain of Las Navas de Tolosa. The battle that ensued there on July 16 was the greatest of the Christian victories over the Moors recorded in the long annals of the Reconquest. Prodigies of valor were performed by King Alfonso of Castile, and also by Archbishop Roderic of Toledo, who animated the spirits of the Christian troops and has left us a personal

[1] *Primera Crónica General*, ed. Menéndez Pidal, pp. 695 f.; Lafuente, v, pp. 209 f.

description of the fight.[1] A sudden and desperate rush of
the Castilians against the silken tent of the Moorish leader
was the crucial event of the day. The Christian losses
were apparently small, while those of their foes are reported
in all the contemporary chronicles to have been enormous:
the figures given are obviously absurd, but there is every
reason to think that the infidels suffered very heavily in
the battle and still more in the flight that ensued.[2]

Las Navas was unquestionably a glorious triumph; but
it proved absolutely impossible for Alfonso to hold together
his heterogeneous forces long enough to reap all the fruits
of it. No sooner was the Moorish danger past than the
allies began quarrelling among themselves, and the Castilian
king spent the last years of his life in vain attempts to reconcile their differences. Then on his death (1214) all the elements of anarchy and discord broke forth afresh.[3] Henry,
the son and heir of Alfonso, was a boy of ten; a regency
was installed first under his mother and then, on her death
a month later, under his sister Berengaria, the divorced wife
of Alfonso, king of Leon. The Laras disputed the control
of the government and were supported by the Leonese monarch; nay more, when in 1217 Henry was killed by the fall
of a tile, and Berengaria, chosen queen in her own right,
abdicated in favor of her son Ferdinand, the king of Leon
forgot that Ferdinand was *his* son also, and prepared to
wage war on Castile. The rebel barons aided him, and the
wretched strife began anew. The father fought the son,
and the son was supported by his mother. But Ferdinand
had the better cause, and Berengaria proved the wisest of

[1] "Rerum in Hispania gestarum
Chronicon," in Schott, ii, pp. 183 ff. A
good translation into Spanish may be
found in vols. cv–cvi of *D.I.E.* The
most recent authority on the battle is
A. Huici, *Estudio sobre la Campaña de
las Navas de Tolosa* (Valencia, 1916).
[2] Colmeiro, *Reyes*, p. 71.
[3] Lafuente, v, pp. 235–249.

counsellors. All the hostile coalitions were put down. The Laras were forced to flee to the Moors, and Ferdinand strengthened himself by his marriage to Beatrice of Swabia, cousin of the Emperor Frederick II. In 1230 Alfonso died, and although he attempted in his will to oust Ferdinand from the succession in Leon, the energy and skill of Berengaria prevented this catastrophe, so that the two kingdoms were finally brought together under her son, never again to fall apart.[1] And even before this happy consummation of his hopes, the new sovereign had signalized his advent to power by an outburst of renewed activity against the Moors.

Peace had been made between Castile and the infidels in December, 1213, just before the death of Alfonso VIII; and eleven years later, the uprisings of a number of local Moorish rulers rang the death knell of the empire of the Almohades in Spain.[2] The opportunity was most favorable for Ferdinand of Castile; he made common cause with the principal one of the rebel chieftains, and carried fire and sword through the upper valley of the Guadalquivir. The ruler of the Almohades crossed over shortly afterwards to Morocco, where another insurrection had broken out against his power; nay more, he even applied to the Castilian king for aid in suppressing it. Ferdinand was fully alive to the importance of establishing the Christian faith on the North African coast, and though the conquest of Andalusia was far from complete, he hastened to take advantage of the embarrassments of the Moorish ruler across the Strait. He promised the latter the military aid which he desired, but demanded in return a money payment, the cession of ten Andalusian fortresses, and finally the right to construct a Christian church in Morocco, where Spanish soldiers

[1] Lafuente, v, pp. 313–337.   [2] Conde, op. cit., pt. iii, caps. lvi–lvii.

could worship undisturbed, and the bells announce the hours
of service. These conditions were fully carried out. The
Almohade power was reëstablished in Morocco for the time
being, by the soldiers of the king of Castile; the price of
his intervention was duly paid; the church was built, and
in 1233 a bishopric of Fez and Morocco was established
by Pope Gregory IX — its first incumbent being a certain
Agnellus. It continued to exist under the Merinite dynasty,
which soon replaced the Almohades in Morocco. Its flock
was composed of Christian soldiers serving in the Moorish
armies, of Christian captives, and of Christian merchants
established in the North African ports; but it finally perished after the fall of its Merinite protectors in the early
years of the sixteenth century.[1]

Meantime in Andalusia the Castilian conquests advanced
apace. The departure of the Almohades for Morocco
had left three principal centres of Moorish influence in
Spain, each of which acknowledged the sway of a different
ruling family. With the first of these, Valencia, we shall
deal when we come to take up the affairs of the kingdom of
Aragon. The other two, at Murcia and at Jaen, were reserved by King Ferdinand for Castile. Of these the former,
under the dynasty of the Beni Hud, was at this time the
more important. Though its capital lay to the eastward,
its domains stretched right across the peninsula and included Cordova and Seville; clearly the Castilian king
would have to attack and subdue it before any further advance to the southward could be made.[2] An intermittent
warfare, interrupted by a three years' truce during which

[1] On this Christian bishopric in
Morocco, see Mercier, ii, pp. 151 f.; L.
Godard, *Description de Maroc*, pp. 362
ff., and "Les Évêques de Maroc" by
the same in *Revue Africaine*, ii, pp. 124–
130, 242–249, 433–440; iii, pp. 1–8;
iv, pp. 259–273, 332–346; Mas Latrie,
pp. 134 f., 455–457; and *Traités de paix
et de commerce* by the same, p. 10.

[2] Ibn Khaldûn, *Histoire des Berbères*
(trad. de Slane), ii, pp. 319–322; Conde,
op. cit., pt. iv, caps. iii, iv.

Ferdinand and his foe made common cause against the Emir of Jaen, culminated in the capture of Cordova, which fell after a prolonged siege on June 29, 1236. It was a notable triumph for the Christian arms, not only for sentiment's sake, but because it opened up the entire valley of the Guadalquivir for future operations; and Moorish captives were obliged to carry back on their shoulders to Santiago de Compostela the bells which had been taken by Almanzor in his famous raid of 997.[1] The murder of the leader of the Beni Hud shortly afterwards caused Seville on the west to renounce its allegiance to that family, and place itself under the suzerainty of the Almohade ruler across the strait, while to the eastward it enabled the armies of Ferdinand to penetrate to Murcia, whose submission was received in 1241. The Moorish ruler there was permitted to remain for some time longer and to exercise most of his functions, but as he paid one half the state revenues to the king of Castile, and specifically acknowledged his overlordship, he can scarcely be regarded as more than a viceroy. Ferdinand had thus carried the confines of his realm to the Mediterranean, and cut off Aragon from the possibility of further expansion in the peninsula at the expense of the Moor.[2]

Finally, in 1246, Ferdinand turned on Ibn al-Ahmar, the Nasride Emir of Jaen. The siege was well under way when the Moorish leader deemed it prudent to surrender his capital to the Castilian king, in return for permission to retain the bulk of his lands to the south of it in feudal vassalage to his victorious foe, and under payment of an annual tribute; he thereupon removed the seat of his authority to Granada, where he and his successors were to maintain themselves for two centuries and a half.[3] One clause

[1] Lafuente, v, p. 343.

[2] Conde, pt. iv, cap. iv; Colmeiro, Reyes, p. 105.

[3] Conde, pt. iv, cap. v; Mercier, ii, p. 167; Lea, The Inquisition of Spain, i, p. 49, with the references there given.

in the treaty between the Christian sovereign and the Granadan Emir stipulated that the latter should bear aid to his liege lord in besieging Seville, which, with the support of its Almohade sovereign across the Strait, now prepared to make a last desperate resistance. Situated as it was near the mouth of the Guadalquivir, where it could easily be relieved by its Moroccan master, it was plainly essential that the besieging army be supported by a fleet; and this was furnished for Ferdinand by a certain Ramón Bonifacio, a native of Burgos, and a well known naval enthusiast and connoisseur, who managed to collect no less than eighteen vessels for the purpose in the Biscayan ports, hitherto the centre of the shipping interest of western Spain. With these vessels he contrived to defeat a Moorish squadron off the mouth of the Guadalquivir; and he followed up this achievement by launching two of his victorious ships, on a favoring wind and tide, against a bridge of boats, which had enabled Seville to recruit its forces and replenish its provisions from the town of Triana across the river. The destruction of the bridge settled the fate of the city, which finally capitulated after a heroic resistance on November 23, 1248.[1] With its fall the reconquest of southern Spain was practically complete, save for the Nasride realm of Granada, which stretched from Tarifa to the mouth of the Almanzora on the seacoast, and inland as far as Antequera and the upper waters of the Guadalquivir. Had Ferdinand turned at once on the Emir of Granada, he probably could have conquered that kingdom then and there, and anticipated by nearly two centuries and a half the work of Ferdinand and Isabella. But as Ibnar al-Ahm had loyally supported him against Seville, he saw no reason to break his

[1] Fernández Duro, *La Marina de Castilla*, pp. 25 f. and references there; Mercier, ii, p. 168; A. Navarrete, *Historia Marítima Militar*, i, pp. 142–149.

treaty with him, and turned his attention instead to making ready a great expedition against Morocco, where the Merinites had supplanted the Almohades soon after the fall of Seville, and had furnished him an excuse for intervention by their incomplete fulfilment of the stipulations concerning the Christian bishopric at Fez. In the midst of his preparations, however, the king was overtaken by an untimely death (May 30, 1252) — one of the noblest figures in the history of the Spanish Empire, and deservedly venerated by his successors and their subjects long before he was canonized by Pope Clement X in 1671. He had dedicated his life with singlehearted devotion to the work of the Reconquest: he was valiant in war, generous in victory, loyal in the observance of his plighted word.[1]

The first paragraph of the present chapter attempted to emphasize the continuity of the story of the reconquest of the peninsula from the infidel and that of the conquest of an imperial domain beyond the sea. But like every long and complicated development, it naturally divides itself into a number of different stages, and the end of the reign of St. Ferdinand is one of the obvious places for such a division. It marks the close of the most glorious and fortunate phase of the Reconquest, of the period when the national energies, save when dissipated by internal strife, were chiefly concentrated on the advance against the infidel. Before passing on to the more complicated period which follows the death of St. Ferdinand, a few general observations may be properly inserted in regard to the achievements of the preceding age.

Of course the constant pressure of the war against the Moors preserved and stimulated all the fighting qualities

[1] Cf. *Memorias para la vida del Santo Rey D. Fernando*, edd. Burriel and Rodrigues; A. Nuñes de Castro, *Vida de S. Fernando el III* (Madrid, 1787).

for which the Spaniard has always been justly famed. The profession of arms was the most highly esteemed of all; it was the typical gentleman's occupation; the only others that could compare with it were the church, the navy, or the service of the crown. The fact that the Reconquest was preëminently a war of raids is moreover reflected in the military methods and armament of the time. The mediaeval Castilian soldier, as we shall later see, was in general much more lightly armed and better equipped for guerilla warfare in difficult country than the contemporaneous warriors of other European states. Two other distinctively Spanish characteristics, which took their rise in the physiographical peculiarities of the peninsula, were greatly accentuated by the war against the Moors: namely, aversion to agriculture and concentration in cities. The devastation caused by the interminable incursions of hostile troops rendered the naturally infertile meseta more barren still, and discouraged men from any attempt to till the soil; moreover, when any region changed hands, the complete or partial displacement of the local population could not possibly be accomplished without immense economic loss. Fear of a Moorish raid also contributed to cause men to desert the open country; they simply dared not live scattered in the fields where they would be at the mercy of a sudden attack, and the same consideration fostered the development of the cities, whose moats and walls alone furnished adequate protection. The immense importance of the municipalities in the history of Castile, as well as the absence of that concomitant of a predominantly agricultural existence — a full-fledged feudal system — are primarily explained by the ceaseless struggle against the infidel. The fact that the western Spanish realms counted for so little in the affairs of mediaeval Europe is also largely traceable to the war of the Reconquest. They were too much occupied at home to care what was going on abroad; and though their isolation was somewhat diminished in the fourteenth and fifteenth centuries, the effects of it were sufficiently permanent to instil into their inhabitants a spirit of dislike and suspicion of foreigners, which powerfully affected the destinies of Spain and the Spanish Empire at a later day.

The nature of the relations of Christians and Moors during the wars of the Reconquest also calls for some explanation.[1] We have already characterized the history of mediaeval Castile as first and foremost the history of a crusade; we have emphasized the fact that the reconquest of the peninsula and also the conquest of an imperial domain beyond the sea were both undertaken in the name of the Christian faith. But in view of what we know of the relations of the Moors and Christians during most of the Middle Ages, it cannot be maintained that religious enthusiasm was as much of an actual motive force in the Reconquest as it was in the struggle for the dominion of the New World. It was constantly invoked as a means to an end; it was called upon to furnish symbols and war cries; but it was not until the reign of Ferdinand and Isabella that the Spanish soldier became a real religious zealot, and the resolve to propagate the Christian faith a dominant factor in his life. We have already met with numerous instances when Leonese and Castilian sovereigns sought the alliance of their infidel foes against their Christian rivals and rebel subjects at home. When cities and territories were captured by a Christian advance, it was the usual thing for the conquered Moors to remain there in the enjoyment of their own religion, laws, and property, and under the rule of their own local magistrates.

[1] For the various authorities on this topic, cf. Lea, *The Inquisition of Spain*, i, pp. 35–79, notes.

They were generally and rightly regarded as a most valuable portion of the population from a financial and industrial point of view; they bore priceless aid to the Christians in restoring some measure of prosperity to the devastated lands. Down to the middle of the thirteenth century it is scarcely too much to say that they were not only gladly tolerated but highly esteemed. Many of the early Castilian monarchs deliberately strove to render the lot of the Moors who resided on their domains more agreeable than that which would have been their fate had they remained in the territories of the infidel. Any attempt to persecute them was vigorously resisted; they were protected, and often actively favored. After the early years of the fourteenth century, when the Pope and the ecclesiastical authorities began deliberately to inculcate intolerance, there is, as we shall later see, a different tale to tell; but during the period with which we are at present concerned, the history of the relations of the two faiths remains as an eternal refutation of the still too common statement that the Spaniard has been a bigot and a fanatic at every stage of his development. He has always shown a tendency in that direction; his religious antipathies have always been easy to rouse; and he has unquestionably won his most notable victories when inspired by the conviction that he was fighting the battle of the Cross. But it would be mistaking the outward symbol for the actual substance to assert that the reconquest of the peninsula was primarily due to zeal for the faith, as many of the victories of Spain in the sixteenth century unquestionably were. "A Spanish knight of the Middle Ages fought neither for his country nor for his religion; he fought, like the Cid, to get something to eat, whether under a Christian or a Moslem prince."[1] What had been a

---

[1] Dozy, *Recherches sur les Musulmans d'Espagne*, ii, pp. 203, 233.

means to an end in the Middle Ages first became under Ferdinand and Isabella an end in itself. In their efforts to instil the largest possible measure of religious fervor into their subjects, the Catholic Kings and their successors had the inestimable advantage of being able to utilize ancient battle cries, and thus to make their programme of militant Catholicism seem the logical consequence of what had gone before. Yet the continuity between reconquest and conquest, so striking in a multitude of ways, is in this single respect perhaps more apparent than real.

One other phase of the period we are considering demands passing comment — namely, the occasional use of the title of Emperor in Spain and the gradual development of the imperial idea during the first five centuries of the war of the Reconquest. We have repeatedly pointed out that progress against the Moors was constantly being hindered by the rivalries of the different kingdoms in the north : if, therefore, any Christian sovereign should succeed in attaining sufficient preëminence over his fellow monarchs to justify him in proclaiming it to the world by the assumption of the imperial title, he would further the cause of Spanish unity and the advance of the Cross against the Crescent. The first of the Castilian kings to do this was Alfonso VI, the conqueror of Toledo, who took the title of Emperor as a means of asserting his superiority over the other Christian kings in the peninsula. It even appears that he went so far as to style himself 'Emperador de los dos cultos' in order to emphasize the fact that some of the Moorish kings in the south had declared themselves his vassals.[1] But the imperial title and idea were developed much further in the reign of Alfonso's grandson, usually reckoned as Alfonso VII, whom we have already

[1] *Discurso de Recepción* in the R. A. H. by Francisco Fernández Gonsales and *Contestación* by Amador de los Rios (Madrid, 1867), p. 46. Cf. also Lea, *op. cit.*, p. 59.

encountered as a protagonist in the terrible conflicts of his mother Urraca, his Aragonese step-father Alfonso the Warrior, and the early rulers of Portugal. By the year 1135 he had extended his power over all the West Spanish realms; many of the Moorish kings of the peninsula paid him tribute; in fact his authority reached so far that Aragon and Catalonia and even some of the counts and dukes of the south of France acknowledged his overlordship. In token of his greatness he elicited from a church council at Leon a solemn declaration that as King of Kings he should assume the imperial title. A coronation ceremony of unprecedented magnificence ensued: it was repeated at Toledo (which thenceforth took the name of the Imperial City) and also at Santiago de Compostela.[1] Over and above all this, Alfonso demanded and obtained from Pope Innocent II permission to style himself King of Kings; and it is by no means fanciful to suppose that this new dignity was intended to connote some measure of derogation of the vague overlordship claimed by the Holy Roman Emperors, with whom Innocent was not on the best of terms.

Certainly Alfonso VII had carried the whole imperial idea much further than his grandfather before him. His assumption of the imperial dignity had been so much more formal and conspicuous than that of the conqueror of Toledo that it made a far deeper impression on his subjects: he is, in fact, usually known as Alfonso the Emperor in the interminable list of Spanish kings. Furthermore, his negotiations with Innocent II had invested the title with a new significance. What had hitherto been employed merely as establishing a claim to preëminence over the other kings of Spain could henceforth also be interpreted as an assertion of independence of any sort of subordination to any out-

[1] Fernándes Gonzales, *op. cit.*, pp. 48 f.

side power, a matter on which the Spaniard had been proverbially sensitive since the days of Bernardo del Carpio.[1]
From the time of Alfonso VII, however, the imperial title
gradually drops out of sight. St. Ferdinand, who so greatly
enhanced the extent and prestige of Castile, was most anxious to revive it,[2] and was unusually well fitted to do so,
both by his character and by the circumstances of his reign;
but he did not live to realize his ambition, and the subsequent
attempt of his scholarly son to win for himself the crown of
the Hohenstaufen was destined to result in a most miserable
fiasco. Still the imperial tradition had been too firmly
planted in mediaeval Castile to be entirely forgotten.
Coupled with her greater geographical extent, it gave the
western kingdom a certain preëminence over the realms of
the Crown of Aragon, which is significantly revealed in the
fact that her monarchs were not seldom loosely spoken of
as 'Kings of Spain' long before the accession of Ferdinand and Isabella.[3] When the imperial dignity was finally
revived under Charles V, it was bound to arouse many
stirring memories, and the glories which the Spaniards had
never ceased to associate with it went far to reconcile
them to the government of a foreign dynasty.

[1] Altamira, § 439.

[2] "Anhelando que su sennorio fuesse
llamado Emperio et non regno et él
coronado por Emperador, segunt lo
fueron otros del su linaje." Cap. ix of
Setenario, cited in Fernández Gonzales,
op. cit., p. 51.

[3] Cf. Rymer's Foedera (second edi-
tion), v, p. 304 (under date of March 28,
1342); Calendar of Patent Rolls, Henry
III, vi, p. 704; Edward I, i, p. 147;
Edward II, iii, pp. 53, 55. See also
Clavijo's Embassy to the Court of Ti-
mour (ed. C. R. Markham for the
Hakluyt Society), p. 133.

BIBLIOGRAPHICAL NOTE

See the bibliographical note at the end of the Introduction, and add:
Contemporary Authorities.— *Primera Crónica General. Estoria de España que mandó componer Alfonso el Sabio*; first published at Zamora in 1541 by Florian de Ocampo; I have used the latest edition, by R. Menéndez Pidal (*N. B. A. E.*, vol. v, Madrid, 1906). It extends from the beginnings of Spanish history to the death of St. Ferdinand, with a continuation to 1289. For further information about it, see Ballester y Castell, *Fuentes Narrativas*, pp. 85–113. On its two principal sources, the *Chronicon Mundi* of Lucas de Tuy, and the *De Rebus Hispaniae* by Roderic of Toledo, as well as on the still earlier minor chronicles, which are for the most part published in *España Sagrada*, see also Ballester y Castell, *op. cit.*, pp. 29–55, 71–84. The *Memorias para la vida del Santo Rey D. Fernando*, edd. A. M. Burriel and M. Rodríguez (Madrid, 1800), contains an anonymous *Crónica del Santo Rey Don Fernando tercero de este nombre, el que ganó a Sevilla*, and a number of useful documents.

Later Works.— On the Moorish side: Ibn Khaldûn, *Histoire des Berbères, et des dynasties musulmanes de l'Afrique septentrionale*, trad. William MacGuckin, Baron de Slane (Algiers, 1852–56, 4 vols.). On this author, who lived from 1322 to 1406, and his work, see his autobiography, translated by de Slane, in *Journal Asiatique*, 4th ser., vol. iii, pp. 5–60, 187–210, 291–308, 325–353. Al Makkarí, *The History of the Mohammedan Dynasties in Spain*, tr. and ed. Pascual de Gayangos (London, 1840–43, 2 vols.), is very valuable. Al Makkarí was born in Tlemcen in the latter part of the sixteenth century. J. A. Conde, *Historia de la Dominacion de los Arabes en España* (new edition, Barcelona, 1844, 3 vols.); English translation by Mrs. J. Foster (London, 1854–55, 3 vols.); my references are to this. On the value of this important work, see Louis Barrau-Dihigo in *Homenaje á F. Codera*, ed. Eduardo Saavedra (Saragossa, 1904), pp. 551–569, which also contains a number of other brilliant monographs on Moorish topics. R. P. A. Dozy, *Histoire des Musulmans d'Espagne* (Leyden, 1861, 4 vols.) and *Recherches sur l'histoire et la littérature de l'Espagne pendant le moyen age* (Leyden, 1860, 2 vols.). Dozy was one of the greatest Arabic scholars of his day. The *Histoire des Musulmans* has been translated into English by Francis Griffin Stokes, under the title of *Spanish Islam* (London, 1913). Ameer Ali, *A Short History of the Saracens* (London, 1900), gives the point of view of an enlightened Moslem of today.

On the Christian side: M. Colmeiro, *Reyes Cristianos desde Alonso VI hasta Alfonso XI* (Madrid, 1901), in the *Historia General de España*, edited by the R. A. H., gives the best general account of the period with which it deals. Alexandre Herculano, *Historia de Portugal* (4th edition, Lisbon, 1875–88, 4 vols.), is a standard work, but goes only to 1279. The first volume of Edward McMurdo's pretentious *History of Portugal* (London, 1888–89, 3 vols.) is a bad translation of it, considerably abridged. Louis, Comte de Mas Latrie, *Relations et commerce de l'Afrique septentrionale avec les nations chrétiennes au moyen âge* (Paris, 1866), is an invaluable summary; it is a reprint of the author's preliminary discourse to his *Traités de Paix et de Commerce et documents divers concernant les relations des Chrétiens avec les Arabes de l'Afrique septentrionale au moyen âge* (Paris, 1865). José Caveda, *Examen Crítico de la Restauracion de la Monarquia Visigoda*, in vol. ix of the *Memorias de la R. A. H.* (Madrid, 1879); Benito Montejo, " Disertacion sobre el Principio de la Independencia de Castilla," in *Memorias de la R. A. H.*, vol. iii, pp. 245–316 (Madrid, 1799); Manuel Murguía, *D. Diego Gelmirez* (Corunna, 1898); Ernest Petit de Vausse, " Croisades Bourguignonnes contre les Sarrazins d'Espagne au XI° siècle," in *Revue Historique*, vol. xxx, pp. 259–272; and Francisco Fernández Gonzalez, *Discurso [sobre la Idea del Imperio en España] ante la R. A. H.* (Madrid, 1867), are all useful monographs.

CHAPTER II

FROM ALFONSO THE LEARNED TO THE CATHOLIC KINGS

THE two centuries of Castilian history which elapse between the death of St. Ferdinand and the middle of the fifteenth century form a period of transition, in which the national energies, hitherto principally occupied with the work of the Reconquest, begin to expand in other directions. Measured by the progress which it sees made against the infidel, it is very disappointing. Though often attacked, and somewhat diminished in extent,[1] Granada remained in Moorish hands till after the union of the crowns of Aragon and Castile. But there are brighter if less immediately obvious sides to the picture. The foreign relations of the kingdom, not only with the other states in the peninsula, but also with England, France, and the remoter European nations, developed rapidly and assumed an importance which they had never attained before. In the early fifteenth century Castilian ambassadors penetrated beyond the steppes of Bokhara, and Castilian conquistadores to the islands of the Atlantic. Rapid social and constitutional development is also a notable feature of this period. The growth of the territory and population of the kingdom rendered necessary the creation of new institutions to deal with the problems which arose in connection with it, and a very large portion of the story of this stage of the national development will be found in later chapters on constitu-

---

[1] Cf. map at the beginning of this volume.

tional affairs. The narrative history may, in the meantime, be conveniently treated in topical fashion. Only certain phases of it are essential to a comprehension of the development of the Spanish Empire, and we can therefore omit entirely many subjects which would unquestionably deserve space in a history of Spain. The present chapter will deal with the internal affairs of Castile and her relations with her European neighbors; while the next one will be devoted to an account of her earliest ventures overseas.

Anarchy and disruption at home — the inevitable result of the inability of the majority of the Castilian kings to control and dominate their rebel baronage — are the most prominent features of the history of the time. The struggle which raged between the Castilian crown and the nobles during the fourteenth and fifteenth centuries has its parallel in contemporary England and France and indeed over all Europe, but it is doubtful if the English monarchs in the darkest days of the Wars of the Roses, or the French during the evil years of the Armagnacs and Burgundians, ever reached such a depth of degradation as was the lot of some of the Castilian sovereigns in the epoch between St. Ferdinand and the Catholic Kings. It is happily unnecessary to describe in detail the ebbs and flows of this paralyzing internal strife: we need only bear in mind that it was almost uninterrupted, and touch briefly upon its course at those points where its history becomes relevant to the matters which more immediately concern us. Yet it may not be amiss to say a word or two about the reasons for it, and to try to explain why the anarchy should have been so unrestrained. Over and above the general tradition of separatism and disunion, always dominant in the Iberian Peninsula, over and above the immediate memories of the humiliation of previous Castilian monarchs at the hands of insubordinate vassals like the Cid, there were several special causes which go to explain the pitiable weakness of the Castilian crown during the period at present under review.

In the first place the fact that the Reconquest was virtually accomplished was inimical to the interests of the monarchy. The energies of the nobles, hitherto largely employed in crusades against the Moors, now found vent in internal rebellion. The fact that Granada remained so long unconquered was also probably more harmful than favorable in its effect. The Moorish realm was not powerful enough to evoke an immediate, united effort to destroy it: yet it constituted a perpetual annoyance, sufficient to prevent Castile from embarking wholeheartedly on any other great national enterprise, which might have served to divert the attention of the nobles from their internal grievances.

Secondly, the period we are considering saw an unusual number of minorities, no less in fact than four out of ten reigns. Ferdinand IV became king at nine, Alfonso XI at one, Henry III at eleven, and John II at two. "Woe to the land whose king is a child." Moreover, when there was not a minority, there was often a disputed succession. Despite the law of Las Siete Partidas, the grandchildren of Alfonso X were despoiled of their just inheritance by their uncle Sancho: though their rights were never recognized, their claims were not speedily forgotten, and constituted a rallying cry for malcontents until well into the fourteenth century. The whole reign of Pedro the Cruel (1350–69) is one long struggle of the king to maintain himself against his illegitimate but more attractive half-brother, Henry of Trastamara, who finally emerged victorious after the bloody drama of Montiel.[1] During the entire conflict, in

---

[1] The scene of Pedro's death, in hand-to-hand conflict with Henry. It lies on the northern slopes of the Sierra Morena, southeast of Ciudad Real.

which the Castilian nobles took opposite sides, and France
and England intervened, the nation was in confusion and
uproar, and the claims of the legitimate monarch were not
satisfied till the marriage of Henry the Invalid to the
daughter of John of Gaunt in 1388. Even Isabella the
Catholic had to fight for her throne against a rival candidate
— La Beltraneja — whose legal claims were stronger than
her own, and who was supported by King Affonso the
African of Portugal. Under such circumstances no monarchy could expect to thrive.

In the third place, the characters and policies of most of
the Castilian kings of the fourteenth and fifteenth centuries
were certainly not calculated to hold the aristocracy in
check. The average level of the ability as rulers of the ten
sovereigns between St. Ferdinand and Ferdinand and
Isabella was not high. Alfonso X's remarkable talents
were scientific and literary rather than political. Of his
nine successors only Alfonso XI, Henry III, and possibly
John I have any claim to greatness, while kings like John
II and Henry IV were merely the sport of factions, and
moved along the line of least resistance, incapable of following any policy of their own. Lavishness in gifts of land
and money was also a besetting sin. While the Reconquest was in full blast, there was ample reason why a successful monarch should reward his faithful followers with
grants out of the territories that he had conquered, more
especially as he would naturally be desirous to repeople
the areas devastated by the war; but now that the boundaries of the realm were approximately fixed, the continuation
of such gifts could only mean that the sovereign was obliged
to bid for the loyalty of his powerful subjects, which he
could not command. Alfonso X distributed his favors
without reserve in order to bribe his nobles to support his

versatile but ineffective foreign policy. Henry of Trastamara was so eager to reward the supporters of his newly
established dynasty that he has gone down to history as
El Dadivoso. In neither case did the misplaced generosity
of the monarch attain the desired end. The nobles who
had enjoyed the largest measure of the royal munificence
were almost invariably the leaders in the next revolt. In
addition, then, to being crippled by minorities and disputed successions, the Castilian sovereigns were on the whole
singularly unfortunate in their methods of handling the
principal problem with which they, like other mediaeval
monarchs, were perpetually confronted — that of controlling a rebel baronage.

Finally, there can be little doubt that all the disruptive
and anarchical tendencies of the time were enormously
accentuated by the lamentable inefficiency of the very
notable scholar who succeeded St. Ferdinand on the united
thrones of Leon and Castile. The reign of Alfonso X saw
the Castilian nobility gain a vantage point in its age-long
struggle with the Castilian monarchy which it was not
forced to relinquish until the time of Ferdinand and Isabella.
It also witnessed the beginnings of some of the most significant external developments of Castile during the fourteenth and fifteenth centuries. It came at a most critical
moment in the national development, when the Reconquest
had been virtually accomplished, when Leon and Castile
had been permanently united, when the nation was easily
amenable to new influences and unusually ready to follow
whithersoever it was led. To the character and career of
Alfonso the Learned many of the mightiest currents in the
subsequent history of Spain and the Spanish Empire are
directly traceable. It is therefore essential that we should
become familiar with the principal events of his reign.

It has been well said of Alfonso X that he would have had more success in any other rôle than that of a king. His intellectual gifts were of the highest order: he was famous for his *sabiduría* to the ends of the earth. As a lawgiver and codifier he was unsurpassed. His astronomical tables were a distinct improvement over those of Ptolemy; his historical and poetical contributions to the literature of his native land place him in the front rank of mediaeval Spanish authors.[1] "If I had been present at the Creation," he is reported to have said, "I could have arranged the world better."[2] The same extraordinary versatility which marked his activities as a scholar was at once the distinguishing feature and the ruin of his career as a monarch. He closely resembled the Emperor Maximilian I of Germany in his fondness for prosecuting a number of inconsistent projects at the same time, and in his complete inability to carry any one of them to its definite logical conclusion. In this respect he forms the sharpest possible contrast with most of his predecessors, who had usually been so completely absorbed in expelling the Moors from the peninsula, and in dominating their rebel subjects, that Castile had often been completely isolated from the rest of Europe. It was under Alfonso X that the nation began to have more irons in the fire than it could handle, to be launched on a career more ambitious than was warranted by its resources, a foretaste of the imperial days of the sixteenth century.

[1] On Alfonso as a poet, historian, and compiler, cf. Ballester y Castell, *Fuentes Narrativas*, pp. 85–98; Ticknor, *History of Spanish Literature* (3d ed., 1864), i, pp. 32–50, 143–151; and Fitzmaurice Kelly, *History of Spanish Literature* (New York, 1917), pp. 63–72; his astronomical works have been carefully edited and annotated by Rico y Sinobas, *Libros del Saber de Astronomía de*

Alfonso X (Madrid, 1863–67, 5 vols.).

[2] Pedro the Ceremonious of Aragon is apparently the authority for this statement: cf. R. Sanches de Arevalo, *Historia Hispanica*, bk. iv, cap. v (in Schott, i, p. 196), and Zurita, i, ff. 274–275. Further references and discussions may be found in Bayle, *Dictionnaire*, s.v. *Castille*, and in Mondéjar, *Alfonso el Sabio*, pp. 637–648.

From his father, the Scholar King had inherited the project of carrying the Christian arms across the Straits of
Gibraltar — certainly a logical path of development, though
it might have been wiser to finish with Granada first.
Armies and a fleet were prepared; the papacy promised
support; but before the expedition could get under way,
Alfonso's attention was distracted by other cares, and the
whole affair had to be abandoned.[1] The internal state of
the realm gave the gravest cause for alarm.   In addition
to impoverishing himself by lavish grants to the *ricos hombres*, Alfonso had debased the coinage under the delusion
that he could thus alleviate the pitiable poverty of the
third estate.   Naturally the remedy proved worse than the
disease; the evil was increased instead of diminished.[2]
Though the king of Granada was, for the time being, friendly,
chiefly owing to the fact that Alfonso at his accession had
voluntarily diminished by one sixth the tribute annually
paid him by his Moorish vassal in recognition of his overlordship,[3] the Scholar King's relations with all his Christian
neighbors were in a most parlous state.   With James the
Conqueror of Aragon he had already had his difficulties
before his accession, over the frontiers between their realms
in the region of Murcia and Valencia.   To this ground for
hostility, others were added by the two kings' treatment
of their respective wives,[4] and by the fact that both were
ambitious to control the destinies of the little realm of
Navarre, which had recently fallen to the family of the
counts of Champagne.   Though naturally anxious above

[1] Mondéjar, *Memorias del rei Alfonso
el Sabio*, pp. 72 f.
[2] *Ibid.*, pp. 373 f.
[3] Colmeiro, *Reyes*, p. 111.
[4] James divorced his first wife
Eleanor, the daughter of Alfonso IX of
Leon, in 1229 (Swift, *James the First of
Aragon*, pp. 37 f.); Alfonso X planned
to do likewise with his wife Violante,
daughter of James the Conqueror, but
characteristically drew back at the last
moment, after a Norwegian princess
whom he had brought to Castile to replace her had actually arrived within
the realm (Colmeiro, *Reyes*, p. 112).

all to safeguard their own independence, the Navarrese
were less averse to Aragon's domination than to that of
Castile; and shortly after Alfonso's accession, a marriage
had been arranged between the young Navarrese sovereign,
Teobaldo, and Constance, the daughter of James the Conqueror, with an implied agreement that the king of Aragon
should protect his son-in-law in case of a Castilian attack.
Alfonso was not the man to disappoint them, and desultory
hostilities along the Navarrese frontier ensued till 1257,
when peace was made without advantage to either party;
but the whole affair had served to distract Alfonso's attention from other far more important matters, and to draw
off troops which might much more profitably have been
elsewhere employed.[1]

Another madcap adventure of the Scholar King carried
him across the Pyrenees into France. His great-grandfather, Alfonso VIII of Castile, had been married in 1169
to Eleanor, the daughter of Henry II of England, and his
wife had brought him the duchy of Gascony as her dowry.[2]
In 1204 Alfonso VIII had failed in an endeavor to substantiate his claims to the territory in question; but they
had not been forgotten, and in 1253, taking advantage of
the fact that the Gascons were in revolt against their English suzerain, Alfonso X determined to revive them. He
prepared a large army, which apparently was in great
measure composed of Moorish troops. Not satisfied with
the mere prospect of taking Gascony, he laid plans for the
invasion of the British Isles.[3] But Henry III of England
was in no mood to fight, and at the last moment Alfonso

[1] Swift, *James the First of Aragon*,
pp. 37, 50 f., 59, 79, 91–94.
[2] R. St.-H., iv, pp. 9, 43.
[3] That this project was taken seriously in England is proved by a letter of
Henry III, bearing the date of Dec. 29,
1253, and addressed to the archbishop
and bishops of Ireland. It is printed in
full in Rymer, *Foedera*, 2d ed., i, p..497,
under the title "De Alfonso Rege Castel-
lae et Exercitu Saracenorum invadendo
Aquitaniam, Angliam, et Hyberniam."

listened to his overtures for peace. Prince Edward of
England was married to the 'good queen' Eleanor, Infanta
of Castile, in the cathedral of Burgos, on October 18, 1254;
and was knighted on the occasion by his erratic brother-in-
law, who also seized the opportunity to renounce all
Castilian claims to Gascony without any countervailing
advantage. Episodes of this kind were not calculated to
raise the Scholar King's prestige with his own subjects.[1]

With Portugal also, Alfonso had his difficulties; and their
history goes to show that in addition to embarking on remote and hazardous adventures in which he had no reasonable chance of success, the Castilian king not seldom made
the complementary error of failing vigorously to pursue
more valid claims in matters nearer at home. After being
driven back across the Tagus by the Almohades, the Portuguese had again advanced to the southward, hand in hand
with their Castilian brethren to the east of them, during
the first half of the thirteenth century.[2] Whether or not
any boundary between the conquests of the two Christian
kingdoms had been agreed on beforehand seems doubtful;
the current of the Guadiana was certainly the logical line
of demarcation, but it is clear that the Portuguese, as they
advanced, captured a number of towns on its eastern bank
without the slightest protest from Castile, and they finally
drove a wedge through to the sea at the Guadiana's mouth
which included places on both the Castilian and Portuguese sides.[3] In the course of their conquests, moreover,
they made extensive territorial grants on both banks of
the stream to the Hospitallers and other orders of military
knighthood who had borne the brunt of the campaign,

[1] C. Fernández Duro, *La Marina de
Castilla*, pp. 36 f.
[2] Herculano, *Historia de Portugal*,
vol. ii, libros iii, iv, v.

[3] Herculano, *op. cit.*, iii, pp. 11 ff.,
398; H. Schäfer, *Geschichte von Portugal*, i, pp. 206 ff.

thus further increasing complications already great.[1] Meantime, in 1248, St. Ferdinand had captured Seville. Since its sovereign had considered himself overlord of the whole Moorish province of Algarve, which stretched westward along the southern shore of Portugal to the Atlantic, the Castilian king not unnaturally maintained that he had inherited this distinction; and his claim derived additional strength from the fact that his vassal, the Moorish king of Niebla, who had been permitted to retain his kingdom on acknowledgment of the suzerainty of Castile, also strenuously asserted that western Algarve fell within the limits of his dominions.[2] In fact, it was on the pretext of safeguarding the rights of the king of Niebla that Alfonso, while still Infante, made the first move to prevent the Portuguese occupation of the territory in question. For some time the matter hung fire, owing to the reluctance of St. Ferdinand to quarrel with a coreligionist; though it seems probable that Castilian troops had several times penetrated into western Algarve before the accession of Alfonso X.[3] After he had become king, however, the campaign was prosecuted with greater vigor. The claims of the king of Niebla had by this time fallen into the background; the disputed territory was obviously destined to become either Portuguese or Castilian; and several towns had fallen before the assaults of the soldiers of the Scholar King, when the representatives of Pope Innocent IV, who wished to see the rival nations coöperate in a crusade against the Moor, induced their respective sovereigns to make peace. In June, 1253, it was arranged that Beatrice, the natural daughter of Alfonso X, should wed Affonso III, king of Portugal, in order to unite the warring dynasties; but there is the widest discrepancy among different his-

[1] Herculano, iii, pp. 6 f.   [2] Herculano, iii, pp. 12–16.   [3] Herculano, iii, pp. 6 ff.

torians as to the political conditions which accompanied the marriage. It seems probable, however, that the agreement was that Affonso of Portugal should cede to Alfonso of Castile the usufruct of Algarve, including all the lands conquered by Portugal east of the Guadiana, for a certain specified time, at the expiration of which the entire territory east and west of the stream, including Moura and Serpa, and even Aroche and Aracena, should revert to Portugal.[1]

But Affonso of Portugal was not willing even to allow Alfonso of Castile to enjoy in peace the rights in Algarve which the treaty of 1253 had vouchsafed to him. Taking advantage of the many outside affairs which constantly distracted the attention of the Castilian king, he set himself to work to elbow him gradually out of the disputed territory. For a time, Alfonso X tamely submitted to this invasion of his lawful rights; he even ceased to call himself king of Algarve; but finally in 1257 a revolt on the part of his quondam protégé, the king of Niebla, induced him to make a fresh effort to assert his claims. In alliance with the king of Granada, he attacked Niebla, and after a nine months' siege (in which it seems possible that explosives of some sort were used for the first time in the peninsula [2]) captured it.[3] Its surrender included that of the neighboring territories over which its ruler held sway, and also apparently such claims as he exercised over Algarve: certainly the hold of the Castilian king on the towns claimed by Portugal east of the Guadiana was immensely strengthened by the victory which he had won. It is possible that Alfonso might have pushed his victory further across the

[1] Mondéjar, *Memorias*, pp. 74–85; Herculano, iii, pp. 21–25, 399–407; H. Schäfer, *op. cit.*, i, pp. 209–212; Lafuente, vi, p. 12.

[2] On the Moorish side: cf. Altamira, § 370.

[3] Herculano, iii, pp. 37–51, 408–412.

river into western Algarve in the succeeding years, had
not his ally, the king of Granada, deserted him and broken
out into revolt. But in order to deal with this new foe, he
needed peace with his rival in the west; so on April 20,
1263, he appointed delegates to arrange with representatives of Affonso III for the drawing of a permanent boundary
between the two realms.[1] In September, 1264, a treaty
was made, in which the whole of western Algarve was
definitely ceded to the king of Portugal in return for the
latter's promise to aid his brother of Castile either in money
or in men in his war against the infidel.[2] Three years later,
in 1267, at a fresh treaty at Badajoz, this last condition,
which possibly carried with it some slight implication of
feudal inferiority, was voluntarily removed by Alfonso X
in a burst of family gratitude and affection occasioned by
the sending to the Castilian court of his little five-year-old
grandson, Diniz (the son of Beatrice and Affonso of Portugal and heir to the Portuguese throne), to receive at the
hand of his famous grandfather the honor of knighthood.
The Scholar King also apparently seized the occasion to
renounce the title of king of Algarve and "ceded to Affonso
III without any restriction all right which might belong
to him in that region in virtue of any former treaty or in
any way."[3] This cession, however, can only be construed
as applying to those parts of the ancient Algarve lying west
of the Guadiana, for the Castilian conquest of the territories of the king of Niebla and the Portuguese surrender
of the castles of Aroche and Aracena confirmed the title
of the Scholar King to the territories to the east of it.[4] The
natural river boundary between the two realms was thus

[1] Herculano, iii, pp. 64 f.
[2] Herculano, iii, p. 74.
[3] Mondéjar, *Memorias*, pp. 88–92;
Herculano, iii, pp. 78–80; H. Schäfer,
i, pp. 214–216.
[4] Burke's preface to map lx in
Poole's atlas is very inaccurate on this
point.

established from the confluence of the Caya and the
Guadiana to the sea, save for the small triangle in which
the towns of Moura and Serpa lay. These places were
in the hands of the Portuguese Knights Hospitallers, and
long negotiations were necessary before Alfonso finally
managed to get a temporary hold on them in 1281.[1] The
Castilian tenure of them, however, was but short: the
Portuguese held that they were included in the dowry of
Beatrice under the treaty of 1253, and were determined to
get them back. The opportunity came during the minority
of Ferdinand IV, when Castile was so weakened by internal
confusion that the Queen Regent Maria was glad to purchase immunity from a Portuguese invasion by the surrender
of the disputed lands.[2]

With this arrangement the Castilian-Portuguese boundary in this region was finally fixed on the line which it has
retained without substantial alteration until this day.[3]
It may seem as if Alfonso X lacked adequate justification
for a more strenuous assertion of his claims to western
Algarve. Geographical considerations were clearly against
him, for the channel of the Guadiana was certainly the
natural boundary between Portugal and Castile. On the
other hand, the history of the previous relations between
the two realms, the need of Castile, which Alfonso fully
appreciated, for a more extended seaboard on the Atlantic,
and finally the fact that, as conquerors of the kings of Seville
and of Niebla, the Castilian sovereigns had a right to con-

---

[1] Herculano, iii, p. 79, note.
[2] R. St.-H., iv, pp. 320–322; Memorias de Fernando IV (ed. Benavides),
ii, pp. 53, 140–143. On the political
vicissitudes of the eastern corner of this
piece of land — usually known as the
'Contienda de Moura' — cf. Revista de
Geografia Comercial, iv, pp. 150–153.
[3] The only important exception to

this statement is afforded by the town
and region of Olivensa, which were
ceded by Ferdinand IV to Portugal, as
dowry of his sister Beatrice, who was
betrothed to the Portuguese prince in
1297. It was not finally recovered by
Spain till 1801. Memorias de Fernando
IV (ed. Benavides), i, p. 47; Lafuente,
xxii, p. 319.

sider themselves the heirs of their claims, may all be urged in support of the view that in this matter he was unwarrantably slack in enforcing his just rights. Moreover, there is every reason to believe that if he had pursued a more vigorous policy in regard to the land in southern Portugal, the subsequent loss of Moura and Serpa and the territories east of the Guadiana, to which the western kingdom had far less valid title, might have been effectually prevented.[1] In any case, Alfonso's rights in this whole Portuguese affair were certainly far better worth insisting on than his pretensions to Navarre or Gascony; but the very fact that they were nearer and more obvious was probably what caused him to neglect them. That his successors continued after his death to bear the title of kings of Algarve showed plainly that they never wholeheartedly approved of his renunciation.

From Alfonso's dealings with Portugal, it is natural to turn to his relations with Ibn al-Ahmar, the king of Granada, who at first had supported him in his struggle for Algarve, but subsequently became a thorn in his side. The Granadan ruler had loyally, though somewhat reluctantly, obeyed the summons of his Christian suzerain to aid him in suppressing a revolt of the Moorish town of Jerez, which lay within the limits of Castile, during the early years of Alfonso's reign; but it seems highly probable that on that occasion, as well as in the subsequent operations against the king of Niebla, Ibn al-Ahmar had taken the measure of the inefficiency of the Castilian king, and began to plan to rebel against him when opportunity offered. Cautious by nature, however, he determined to put on others the responsibility for the initial step. He secretly encouraged a

---

[1] On this whole question cf. Herculano, iii, pp. 399–404, and the works there cited.

new revolt at Jerez, and secured money and troops to support it from Yusuf, the Merinite ruler of Morocco across
the Strait; he even waited until the rebellion spread eastward into Murcia (where it will be remembered that St.
Ferdinand had permitted the local Moorish ruler to remain
in the enjoyment of a considerable measure of autonomy)
before he was willing openly to join the insurgents.[1] Even
then his loyalty to his coreligionists was but evanescent.
The power of the king of Castile was still considerable, as
was proved by his surprise and capture, on September 14,
1262, of the important town of Cadiz, which the Moors
had neglected to defend.[2] James the Conqueror of Aragon,
moreover, effectively supported the Scholar King on the
eastward by invading the rebel kingdom of Murcia, and
finally taking the capital in January–February, 1266; according to previous agreement he loyally handed over his
conquest to Alfonso of Castile, who lost no time in definitely incorporating it into his dominions.[3] The significance of these events was not lost on Ibn al-Ahmar, who
was the last man in the world to be caught on the losing
side. He was jealous, moreover, of the extent of the authority of Yusuf of Morocco, which he feared might ultimately prove inimical to his own; while, on the other
hand, he seems to have been considerably impressed by the
news of an understanding which had been reached between
Alfonso X and the king of Tlemcen against the Merinite.
The net result was that in 1265, even before the final fall of
Murcia, the Granadan Emir deserted his allies, and made
peace with the king of Castile, declaring himself once more
the latter's loyal vassal, in return for Alfonso's promise not

[1] R. St.-H., iv, pp. 192–194.
[2] Fernández Duro, Marina de Castilla, p. 42.
[3] Swift, James the First, pp. 114–116.

to aid the walis of Guadix, Malaga, and Comares, who had
recently broken out in revolt against him.[1]

During the next few years the scene shifted again.   In the
latter part .of the reign of Ibn al-Ahmar, who died in 1273,
and in the earlier years of that of his son and successor,
Mohammed II, a number of important Castilian malcontents and rebels had found refuge at the Granadan court.
At first, they were utilized by the Emir to drive Yusuf the
Merinite out of Spain, but finally they persuaded their new
lord to reverse the process, and, taking advantage of a
temporary absence of Alfonso from the peninsula, to call
back the Moroccan sovereign to coöperate in a joint attack
upon Castile.   Tarifa and Algeciras were surrendered to
him to facilitate his landing; in 1275 Yusuf arrived with a
force of seventeen thousand men, and, in alliance with the
Emir of Granada, carried fire and sword into Christian
Spain.   The Castilian troops which opposed him were not
on the whole effectively led; the only pitched battle of
the campaign — at Écija — was a Moorish victory, and
in 1276 Yusuf returned, gorged with booty, to Morocco.[2]
In 1277 he came again, followed by his son with reënforcements, and from that time onward, till after the end of
Alfonso's reign, incessant fighting took place by land and
sea up and down the southern coasts of the peninsula.[3]
But it must not for one moment be assumed that in these
combats the sides remained the same: quite the contrary,
they changed from day to day.   A new element was introduced by the alliance of the Emir of Granada with Sancho,
the younger son of Alfonso X, who desired to oust his
nephews, the Infantes de la Cerda, from their just inheritance.   On the other hand, Mohammed's jealousy of the

[1] Colmeiro, *Reyes*, pp. 118–120; Mas
Latrie, p. 255.
[2] Colmeiro, *Reyes*, pp. 121, 123–125.
[3] R. St.-H., iv, pp. 202–206, 208–
212, 309–311; Fernández Duro, *Marina
de Castilla*, pp. 44–46.

power of Yusuf, whenever the latter's star was in the ascend-
ant, prevented any very effective coöperation between the
two Moorish sovereigns. Each was quite as often in
alliance with Castile against the other, as he was with the
other against Castile.[1]   Peace was finally made in the first
year of the following reign.   Yusuf the Merinite, by all
odds the ablest of the combatants, was the only one who
could boast that he was any better off than when he began.
Tarifa, Algeciras, Ronda, and Guadix remained for the
time being in his possession, and a number of precious
Arab books and works of art, which had fallen into Christian hands at the capture of Cordova and Seville, were
delivered over to him.[2]   The whole course and final issue
of the conflict affords a significant illustration of the fact
that Granada during this period owed a large share of its
power, and perhaps even its continued existence, to the
protection which was from time to time extended to it
from across the Strait.[3]

All the various plans and projects of the Scholar King
which we have thus far examined concern themselves
with the affairs of the peninsula, or at least with those of
the lands directly adjacent to it.   But Alfonso was also
much involved with the other states of Western Europe.
Rightly or wrongly, he was convinced that the name of
Castile was not sufficiently often heard beyond the Pyrenees.
He was exceedingly anxious to gain for his nation a more
considerable place in the eyes of the other sovereigns of
the time.   He married his half-sister to one of the greatest
of English kings, and his eldest son to the daughter of
Louis IX of France.[4]   His cousin was the wife of the Latin
Emperor of Constantinople, and when she came to beg

[1] Mas Latrie, pp. 256 f.; Mercier, ii,
pp. 211–214, 224–226.
[2] Diercks, ii, p. 11; Mercier, ii, p. 212.

[3] A. Giménez Soler, *La Corona de
Aragón y Granada*, p. 8.
[4] Diercks, ii, pp. 30, 37.

his aid in ransoming her son Philip from the hands of the
Venetians, Alfonso granted her thrice the sum she asked
for — a proceeding which evoked the bitterest complaint
from his people, and foreshadowed the way in which Spain
was to be drained of its wealth for totally non-Spanish
objects in the sixteenth and seventeenth centuries.[1] But
there was another opportunity to advance the dignity and
preëminence of the Castilian name beyond the borders of
the realm which appealed more intensely to the Scholar
King than all the rest. Through his mother, Beatrice of
Swabia, he was near of kin to the Hohenstaufen emperors,
whose dynasty in Germany had come to such an unhappy
end only two years after he ascended the throne. The
imperial title, as we have already seen, had a certain tradition behind it in Spain, and had been actually assumed,
though with a somewhat limited and special significance,
by two of Alfonso's predecessors and namesakes on the
Castilian throne. It is not difficult to understand why a
man of Alfonso's peculiar makeup should have hit upon
the idea, in the prevailing uncertainty which followed the
death of Conrad IV, of putting himself forward as a candidate for the succession in the Empire. The rank and file
of his subjects opposed the plan quite as vigorously and for
very much the same reasons as their descendants two and
a half centuries later opposed a similar attempt by the first
Hapsburg sovereign of Spain; but while Charles V silenced
complaints by his success, Alfonso only increased them
by his failure. It is happily unnecessary for us to enter
into the details of the Scholar King's efforts to win the
imperial crown; they continued intermittently for a score
of years.[2] He had on the whole the support of France and
of the Ghibelline princes in Italy and Germany, and he was

[1] Colmeiro, *Reyes*, p. 119.   [2] Mondéjar, *Memorias*, pp. 130-200.

lavish in spending money to bribe the electors. On the other hand he had to reckon, save at the very outset,[1] with papal opposition, which became open and pronounced under Pope Gregory X. But the fact that he did not appear personally in the Empire was the fundamental cause of his ill success. Though he held more votes in the electoral college than his nearest competitor, Richard of Cornwall, and was actually proclaimed Emperor, he suffered his rival to come to Aix-la-Chapelle, to be crowned there on May 12, 1257, and to perform various acts of imperial authority, while he himself remained passive in Castile. When Richard died in 1272, Alfonso returned to the charge, only to see the elusive crown once more escape him with the unanimous election of Rudolph of Hapsburg in October, 1273; and a subsequent interview with Gregory X at Beaucaire, in which he protested against the setting aside of his just claims, only served to reveal the full measure of his impotence.[2] He aspired to be emperor, though he was not even able to play the king.[3] He had tried to increase the dignity and preëminence of Castile in Western Europe, but he only succeeded in abasing it, and the chief result of his lamentable failure was to give excuse and opportunity for the great rebellion of his subjects under the leadership of his son which was to bring down his gray hairs with sorrow to the grave.

Alfonso's eldest and favorite son, Ferdinand de la Cerda, who had married the daughter of St. Louis, had died in 1275 during the campaign against the Moors, and had left

---

[1] W. Herrmann, *Alfons X. von Castilien als römischer König* (Berlin, 1897), pp. 37–40; Antonio y Pío Ballesteros, "Alfonso X de Castilla y la Corona de Alemania," in *R. A.*, 3d ser. (1916), xxxiv, pp. 1–23; xxxv, pp. 187–219; xxxvi, pp. 223–242.

[2] Mondéjar, *Memorias*, p. 198; R. St.-H., iv, pp. 190 f., 199 f.

[3] "Como yas solo el rey de Castiella Emperador de Alemaña que foé?" from Alfonso's *Querellas*: cf. Fernández y Gonsales, *Discurso*, p. 43.

two children, Alfonso and Ferdinand, the so-called Infantes
de la Cerda, who, under the law of Las Siete Partidas, were
the legal heirs to their grandfather's throne. But Alfonso's
second son, the Infante Sancho, restless and ambitious,
determined to claim the succession for himself on the ground
of the inexpediency of placing the crown on the head of a
child. Taking advantage of the general disgust caused
by Alfonso's imperial adventure, he gathered round himself a large party of malcontents. His two younger brothers
also sided with him. So powerful was the Infante, that
Alfonso, on his return from his interview with Gregory X
at Beaucaire, weakly yielded to his importunities, reversed
the order of succession established in Las Siete Partidas,
and caused Sancho to be recognized as the heir to the throne.[1]
Furious at Alfonso's failure to support his grandchildren's
claims, the widowed French mother of the Infantes de la
Cerda fled with them to Aragon, where she hoped to
receive aid from Pedro III; but the latter, besides being
anxious to have hostages for the good behavior of France
and Castile during his projected expedition to Sicily, had
already been won over by Sancho, and the final result was
that the Infantes were confined for the next ten years in
the fortress of Jativa.[2] Philip III of France, however,
came forward to support his nephews.[3] At his instance
Alfonso hit upon the fatal idea of dismembering his realm
in order to satisfy both parties; he proposed to erect the
city of Jaen and the neighboring territories into a separate
kingdom for the Infantes, and to leave the rest to Sancho;
but the latter would not accept the compromise, and war

---

[1] Colmeiro, *Reyes*, pp. 124–126.
[2] Cartellieri, *Peter von Aragon und
die sisilianische Vesper*, pp. 43 f., 204–
206; Charles Langlois in Lavisse, *Histoire de France*, iii, 2, p. 112.

[3] On the Cerda claims cf. G. Daumet,
*Mémoire sur les relations de la France et
de la Castille de 1255 à 1320* (Paris,
1914).

ensued between father and son. Castile and Leon supported almost unitedly the cause of Sancho; in 1282, the Cortes were summoned by the latter at Valladolid, and Alfonso was declared deposed. In the following year Alfonso humiliated himself to the extent of begging aid ' from Yusuf the Merinite against his own subjects and children, and even sent him his royal crown as security for a loan of sixty thousand doblas. Such a shameful spectacle provoked the inevitable reaction. Sancho's party was weakened by desertion. The Pope placed him and his adherents under an interdict, and the cause of Alfonso was by no means hopeless, when he fell ill, and died at Seville on April 4, 1284; the device which is still borne on the city's shield commemorates its loyalty to its unfortunate sovereign.[1] Alfonso's last will and testament disinherited Sancho and left the crown of Castile to the Infantes de la Cerda, but it also provided that two separate kingdoms — Seville and Murcia — be carved out of the realm for the benefit of his two younger sons, John and James, with whom he had become reconciled at the last. This arrangement was, of course, in flat contradiction to the fundamental laws of the monarchy, which expressly forbade the dismemberment of the realm; a fact which doubtless made it easier for Sancho to ignore it as well as the provision which disinherited him.[2] At any rate, he succeeded his father on the throne of Castile. The laws and will which the Scholar King had made remained a dead letter for many years to come.

The period of Alfonso X was thus a great turning point in the history of Castile. It saw her launched for the first

---

[1] In this device a curious knot (madeja) appears between the syllables no and do. Read as a rebus, this makes "no madeja do" or "no m' ha dejado"; that is, "she has not forsaken me."

[2] Crónica del Rey Alfonso Decimo, cap. lxxvii, in B. A. E., lxvi, pp. 63–66; Colmeiro, Reyes, pp. 128–134.

time on a number of different lines of development which
were ultimately destined vitally to affect the fortunes of the
Spanish Empire. During the reigns of the nine monarchs
who ruled between the Scholar King and Ferdinand and
Isabella, the nation moved further along these lines, but
undertook little that was new; so that, save for the two great
ventures overseas which are recorded in the next chapter,
the narrative history of Castile in the fourteenth and early
fifteenth centuries may be adequately covered by following
up the results of the policy and impolicy of Alfonso. Of
these, as we have already seen, baronial anarchy and monarchical impotence were at once the most important and the
worst, but further than that it is unnecessary to enlarge upon
them here. The relations of Castile with Aragon, with
Portugal, with Granada and North Africa, with France
and with England, demand more extended treatment, and
we can take up the story in each case at the point where we
left it in the reign of the Scholar King.

It would perhaps be natural, in examining the relations
of Castile and Aragon during the two centuries which
precede the reign of Ferdinand and Isabella, to look for some
evidence of the gradual growth of a policy and sentiment of
union between the two realms, especially on the part of Castile, whose final amalgamation with Leon in the reign of St.
Ferdinand might have been expected to stimulate an ambition to repeat the experiment on a larger scale. Some Spanish historians have thought that they have found such evidence. They harp on the precedents of Sancho the Great
and Alfonso the Warrior. They lay strong emphasis on the
reign of the 'good regent' Ferdinand of Castile in Aragon
from 1412 to 1416, as a foreshadowing of that of Ferdinand
and Isabella, and speak as if the union of the crowns had

been inevitable from the very first.   But an impartial examination of the relations of the two kingdoms during the fourteenth and fifteenth centuries, which does not assume fore-
knowledge of what had not yet occurred, reveals few traces
of anything like a consistent policy of Castile towards her
sister kingdom on the east. If her union with Leon furnished
a precedent for union with Aragon, the powerful current of
Spanish separatism exercised a strong influence in the other
direction.   The elimination of serious danger from the
Moors removed the strongest force which had hitherto
served to draw Christian Spain together.   It is difficult,
in fact, to find *any* thread on which to hang the story of the
dealings of Castile and Aragon during this period, save perhaps the proneness of each to make the most of the internal
dissensions of the other.   Their relations resolved themselves
for the most part into a number of isolated, and on the whole
unedifying, episodes, which doubtless demonstrated the need
of union, but did not betoken the presence of any consistent
effort to attain it.

When Alfonso X died in 1284, his grandchildren, the Infantes de la Cerda, were still retained in honorable captivity
at Jativa by his brother-in-law, Pedro of Aragon; and when
Sancho IV succeeded him, he naturally made every effort
to have them kept there.   Very soon, however, the situation
changed.   France and Aragon were by this time at open
war, and vied with one another for the alliance of Castile;
and Sancho, on the advice of his counsellors, determined
in 1287 that, despite the ties which united him to Aragon,
he could gain the most by taking sides with France.   The
inevitable band of malcontents at once sprang up and took
refuge at the Aragonese court, where the new sovereign,
Alfonso III, promptly adopted the obvious method of defence against his treacherous neighbor by liberating the

Infantes de la Cerda from their captivity, proclaiming the elder of them lawful king of Castile, and finally (in 1289) heading an invasion of that country to vindicate the just rights of his protégé.[1] No serious fighting, however, occurred. There were raids and counter-raids, but neither side was willing to risk a pitched battle. Desultory hostilities, nevertheless, continued into the reign of Ferdinand IV of Castile; both France and Portugal being occasionally involved, first on one side and then on the other.[2] Finally, in 1304, the warring nations agreed to submit their difficulties to three arbitrators, of whom the chief was the king of Portugal. Their verdict was that the Infantes de la Cerda should renounce all claim to the throne of Castile, and receive in return a liberal compensation in money and lands; at the same time the southeastern boundary between Castile and Aragon, which had given so much trouble in the past, was finally fixed on the general line which, though often temporarily changed by subsequent quarrels, it has for the most part followed ever since.[3] The two kingdoms celebrated this reëstablishment of friendship, which is generally known as the peace of Campillo, by a joint attack against the Moors on land and sea; but the results of the campaign, which we shall examine in another place, were hardly commensurate with the expectations that had been entertained of it.

The next period offers little of interest. Peace was preserved till 1327, when Don Juan Manuel, the arch disturber of Castile during the minority of Alfonso XI, allied himself with the kings of Aragon and Granada to raid and harry

[1] R. St.-H., iv, pp. 308, 314.

[2] *Crónica de Don Sancho Cuarto*, caps. v, vi, in B. A. E., lxvi, pp. 78–82; R. St.-H., iv, pp. 322–327.

[3] *Crónica de Fernando Cuarto*, caps.

xi, xii, in B. A. E., lxvi, pp. 129–137; Lafuente, vi, p. 371. The details of the partition are to be found in *Memorias de Fernando IV*, i, pp. 134 f., and in Zurita, i, ff. 420–423.

his native land; but friendship was restored again in the following year by the union of Alfonso IV of Aragon to Eleanor, the Infanta of Castile. When Alfonso of Aragon died in 1336, he was succeeded by his redoubtable son Pedro the Ceremonious, who, being the issue of an earlier marriage, dreaded an effort by his stepmother to disinherit him in favor of her own children, and consequently looked askance at the land from which she came.[1] The need of union between the two realms to oppose the last great effort of the Moors to reconquer the peninsula in 1339–40 prevented any open breach till the accession of Pedro the Cruel of Castile in 1350; but with two such violent kings as he and his namesake of Aragon in power at the same time, it was utterly impossible permanently to preserve peace. In 1356–57, the inevitable war broke out, Pedro of Aragon taking the obvious step of allying himself with his rival's half-brother and enemy, Henry of Trastamara. It continued by land and sea till the latter's accession in 1369, and was followed by a period of bickering which arose out of the unwillingness of the Aragonese king to recognize the validity of the Castilian title to Murcia. Finally, in 1375, terms of peace were arranged, and cemented by the marriage of John, the son and heir of Henry of Trastamara, to Eleanor, the daughter of Pedro of Aragon — a match which deserves notice as the first step towards the ultimate union of the two kingdoms.[2] Another era of good feeling ensued during the succeeding years, largely owing to the fact that the attention of Castile was chiefly turned towards Portugal, while Pedro's successors on the throne of Aragon were lazy and unambitious. On the termination, in 1410, of the old Aragonese royal line, which was descended from the counts

---

[1] R. St.-H., iv, pp. 392–396, 409.
[2] J. Catalina García, *Castilla y León*, ii, pp. 116–120.

of Barcelona, the nine commissioners appointed to decide upon King Martin's successor gave their verdict in favor of Ferdinand of Antequera, uncle and regent of John II of Castile, who accordingly ascended the Aragonese throne in 1412. This judgment, however, does not indicate any settled policy of union on the part of the commissioners, for their decision, as we shall subsequently see in more detail, was rendered on judicial and not on political grounds. Ferdinand was chosen because of his hereditary claims and not for any reasons of expediency. Had another candidate been selected, the great work of the Catholic Kings would in all probability have never been done; but the commissioners were not primarily thinking of plans for the unification of the peninsula when they chose him, and they could not have foreseen the future.[1]

Despite the fact that John II of Castile married the daughter of his uncle, Ferdinand of Aragon, and Alfonso the Magnanimous of Aragon the daughter of Henry III of Castile, trouble broke forth again between the two kingdoms toward the middle of the fifteenth century, owing to the ambition of John II of Aragon to possess himself of the neighboring realm of Navarre. His efforts in this direction were constantly thwarted by the king of Castile, and he naturally revenged himself by interfering in the internal affairs of that kingdom, where his large estates furnished him a pretext for meddling. The marriage of Ferdinand of Aragon to Isabella of Castile in 1469 did not come as the inevitable sequel and logical climax of a long series of antecedents; it is rather as a divergence from the normal trend of the development of both nations that the event which produced united Spain should be regarded.

With Portugal, on the other hand, there is a different

[1] Cf. *infra*, pp. 405 f.

tale to tell. Castile had never forgotten the history of the attainment of independence by the smaller country, and continually longed to reconquer it. From Alfonso X onward there is abundant evidence of a settled policy on her part to reannex the western kingdom, until finally, under Philip II, her efforts were crowned with success. Four times, during the period under review (1250–1450), did Castilian kings [1] marry Portuguese princesses, and three times were Castilian princesses united to Portuguese kings; [2] the corresponding figures for Castile and Aragon are three [3] and two.[4] Castile turned her attention during the fourteenth and fifteenth centuries to the westward rather than to the eastward, and if we look at her problems through the eyes of the statesman of that time, we shall probably agree with him that she was right in so doing. But if her policy in this respect was wise, the ability to carry it out was pitifully lacking. So weak were her kings and so feeble their resources that sometimes it almost seemed as if Portugal would conquer Castile. To this point matters did not actually go, but down to the accession of Ferdinand and Isabella there can be no doubt that Portugal had the best of the exchanges.

We have already seen how Alfonso X's ambitions to possess Algarve were thwarted by his Portuguese contemporaries; we have also seen how the latter even succeeded in making good their hold on rich territories east of the Guadiana. Even after he had received these lands from the Castilian Regent Maria de Molina in 1295 in return for a promise of peace, the king of Portugal joined hands with the king

---

[1] Ferdinand IV, Alfonso XI, John I, and John II.

[2] Affonso III, Affonso IV, Pedro.

[3] Alfonso X, John I, and John II.

[4] Alfonso IV and Alfonso V (the Magnanimous). I do not count Ferdinand I, who wedded Eleanor of Alburquerque when he was Infante of Castile and had no expectation of becoming king of Aragon; nor John II, who only married the daughter of the Admiral of Castile.

of Aragon and invaded Castile in 1297.   He raided the realm
as far as Valladolid, and refused to retire permanently until
a double marriage was arranged to unite the rival dynasties
— Ferdinand IV of Castile to Constance, the daughter of
King Diniz, and Affonso IV of Portugal to Beatrice, the
sister of Ferdinand.[1]   Castile was distinctly on the defensive
during this period.   The alliance of Portugal and Aragon
against her had proved irresistible, and had forced her to
sue for peace at the hands of the state which it was her
ambition to annex.   The policy of fostering union by marriage was continued in the next generation ; in 1327 Alfonso
XI of Castile wedded Maria the Infanta of Portugal.[2]   This
alliance, however, had the opposite effect to that which had
been hoped for ; it actually provoked another war.   For after
Maria of Portugal had borne to her Castilian husband a son,
the redoubtable Pedro the Cruel, Alfonso XI shamefully
neglected her, and devoted himself exclusively to the famous
Eleanor de Guzman, the ancestress of the house of Trastamara.   Naturally the Portuguese could not brook such an
insult to their dynasty.   Allying themselves once more with
Aragon under Pedro IV, and with some of the rebellious
Castilian baronage, they suddenly attacked Badajoz in 1336.
But Alfonso was more ready for them than was the wont
of the Castilian kings.   Not only was the assault on Badajoz
vigorously repulsed, but the Castilian fleet won a useful
victory over its Portuguese adversaries off Cape St. Vincent
in the summer of 1337 — a foretaste of the long maritime and
colonial struggle in which the rivalry of the two realms was
soon to find wider expression.   Two years later, however,
peace was once more restored, owing to the need of union to
repel the great Moorish invasion which ended at Rio Salado ;
and it was in that battle that Affonso of Portugal so dis-

[1] *Ante*, p. 106, note 3; R. St.-H., iv, p. 324.   [2] R. St.-H., iv, p. 409.

tinguished himself by his valor that he won the title of 'the Brave.'[1]

The next stage in the relations of the two realms is exceptionally complicated and difficult. It turns chiefly upon the simultaneous dynastic struggles with which both were convulsed. Portugal naturally sided with Pedro the Cruel, whose mother was a Portuguese princess, in the successional quarrels in Castile, and on Pedro's death in 1369, Ferdinand the Handsome, the last of the ancient line of Portuguese kings, claimed the Castilian throne against Henry of Trastamara. Like his predecessors, he pursued the obvious policy of making common cause with the king of Aragon, who also had his grudges against the Castilian royal house; the sovereigns of Navarre, Granada, and England also took part; there were combats by land and sea.[2] In 1371 the papacy intervened in the hope of restoring peace, and made the Portuguese monarch promise to wed the daughter of his Castilian rival; but Ferdinand, flighty and amorous, refused to abide by his plighted word, and married his mistress, the famous Donna Leonor. To avenge this insult, the army of Castile invaded Portugal and burned part of Lisbon.[3] During the next ten years, the Portuguese king, unable to fight his own battles, endeavored to make the English fight them for him, at least on land. The marriage of John of Gaunt to the daughter of Pedro the Cruel had made the Plantagenets the natural enemies of the Trastamaras. The Earl of Cambridge was sent to Lisbon with a considerable force, but he accomplished little, while the Castilian fleet again defeated that of Portugal.[4] A second Castilian invasion caused Ferdinand to desert his allies, and, after some delay, peace was

---

[1] R. St.-H., iv, p. 419; Fernández Duro, *Marina de Castilla*, pp. 79–81; H. Morse Stephens, *Story of Portugal*, p. 92.

[2] Lafuente, vii, pp. 318–326.
[3] H. Schäfer, *Geschichte von Portugal*, i, pp. 448–465.
[4] Fernández Duro, *op. cit.*, pp. 144 f.

again made between the two realms at Salvatierra on April
2, 1383. The treaty was celebrated by the marriage of
John I of Castile, then a widower, to Beatrice, the daughter
and heiress of Ferdinand of Portugal, with the arrangement
that if Ferdinand should die without male heirs, his
daughter's children should inherit the Portuguese throne.[1]
It was a long step toward Castilian annexation of the western
kingdom — too long by far to suit the Portuguese. On
Ferdinand's death, October 22, 1383, they rose in revolt
under John of Avis, the illegitimate half-brother of the late
king, against the prospective Castilian domination and the
detestable widow regent Donna Leonor, who at that moment
supported it. John of Avis was proclaimed protector of the
realm, and finally, on April 6, 1385, king.[2] He once more sought
the alliance of England and received a force of five hundred
men.[3] Meantime Donna Leonor fled to the court of Castile,
and urged an invasion of Portugal. The king prepared an
army, in which a number of French adventurers were enrolled,
crossed the frontier at Badajoz, and finally, on October 14,
1385, encountered his enemies near the little village of Aljubarrota, some forty miles due north of Lisbon. The Portuguese forces, inferior in numbers, occupied an almost impregnable position on a hill, and successfully repelled two great
assaults which the impetuous king of Castile forced his
army to deliver without adequate preparation and too late
in the day. Froissart has left us a glowing description of the
battle, which, as the evening shades began to fall, was converted into a rout; John of Castile was fortunate to regain
unharmed his own dominions.[4] Aljubarrota was a glorious
confirmation of the independence which Portugal had first

[1] J. Catalina García, *Castilla y León*,
ii, pp. 248–250.

[2] H. Schäfer, *op. cit.*, ii, pp. 109–199.

[3] R. St.-H., v, p. 126.

[4] Froissart's *Chronicles*, tr. Berners
(*Tudor Translation Series*), iv, pp. 197–
202, 273–284; Pedro López de Ayala,
Cronicas, año septimo de Don Juan,

won over three centuries before; it ended for many years to come Castile's hopes of annexing it. During the next few years, in fact, the Portuguese and English armies invaded and ravaged Castile, which was saved rather by the out- break of disease in the ranks of its assailants than by any efforts of its own. The English claims to the throne of the Trastamaras were finally disposed of in 1389, as we shall see more fully in another place; while the Portuguese monarch, convinced at last that he could gain no permanent foothold in Castile, finally consented to a truce, which, though occa- sionally broken, was renewed periodically till 1411, and finally converted into a definitive peace.[1]

During the first half of the fifteenth century, the story of the relations of Portugal and Castile is comparatively un- important. Peace virtually uninterrupted was preserved between the two realms; the marriage in 1450 of John II of Castile to Isabella of Portugal, who became the mother of Isabella the Catholic, is an evidence that they were, osten- sibly at least, on friendly terms. Not that either state had ceased to be jealous of the other — far from it; but both were chiefly occupied with other affairs : Castile with her in- ternal troubles, and Portugal with the fascinating career of maritime exploration and conquest which had been opened for her by the efforts of Prince Henry the Navigator. Yet in this latter fact, namely that Portugal had got a start on Castile in the race for empire, lay the seeds of important developments for the future. The rivalry of the two realms was not dead, but simply temporarily in abeyance; it was soon destined to burst forth again and involve far wider

caps. xiv, xv ; J. Catalina García, *Castilla y León*, ii, pp. 310 ff.; C. Ximenes de Sandoval, *Batalla de Aljubarrota* (Ma- drid, 1872).

[1] Lafuente, vii, pp. 377-386; H. Schäfer, *op. cit.*, ii, pp. 232-259. The treaty of 1411 is given in J. Bernard's *Recueil des Traités* (Amsterdam, 1700), i, pp. 375-383.

areas than ever before. What had been in the past a
purely local matter of Iberian politics, was to develop in
the near future into a competition of world empires.

The story of Castile's relations with Granada and the
Moorish states of North Africa from Alfonso X to Ferdinand and Isabella is also extremely complex, and little of
permanent importance was accomplished by either side.
Christian and Moor were found in alliance, and coreligionists at war, even more frequently than in the preceding age.
Each party strove chiefly to attain its own immediate political ends; in selecting its allies each regarded considerations
of practical utility alone; and since the fortunes of the
struggle changed with incredible rapidity, the combinations
were to the last degree evanescent. The fact that the kings
of Castile, Granada, and Morocco all possessed numerous
rebel vassals, who were ever ready to stretch out the hand
of welcome to hostile invaders, naturally served to make
confusion worse confounded. All these features had, of
course, been present in the struggles of the earlier period,
but never to such a considerable extent. Down to the
middle of the thirteenth century, it had usually been
possible to arouse enough crusading spirit at dangerous
crises to dominate the disruptive tendencies. Now, save
for one great outburst at the middle of the fourteenth
century, religious fervor is almost completely obscured by
other less noble aims, until its final revival by the Catholic
Kings supplied the impetus for the glorious conquest of
Granada.

The three-cornered peace which had been made between
Castile, Granada, and Morocco in the first years of Sancho
IV lasted till 1290. As it had left several towns, hitherto
subject to the king of Granada, in the hands of the Emir of

Morocco, it had never been acceptable to the former, who sought the alliance of the king of Castile against his quondam ally across the Straits, and prepared to wage war on the Merinite. The Moroccan sovereign promptly came over to Spain in quest of revenge; but his operations were hampered by the Castilian fleet, and in 1292 one of his remaining strongholds in the peninsula, the town of Tarifa, fell before the combined assaults of the troops of Granada and Castile. In violation of solemn promises to his ally, King Sancho retained the captured place; but the Granadan Emir consoled himself for its loss by buying back Algeciras from his Moroccan coreligionist, who no longer had any ambition to retain his Iberian possessions.[1]

The next act in the drama brought a complete rearrangement of parties. A new Emir, Mohammed III, had ascended the Granadan throne in 1302. At first he sought aid from Morocco against Castile; but finding that he could gain nothing by this manoeuvre, he made peace with his Christian overlord. Then, seizing the opportunity afforded by the Moroccan ruler's absence on a campaign against Tlemcen, he evened up old scores by possessing himself of Ceuta across the Straits.[2] This town, which had had a most checkered history in the previous century,[3] remained in his hands till 1309, when the aid of the fleet of the king of Aragon enabled the Moroccan Emir to retake it; but the fact that a Spanish ruler, even though he was an infidel, had been able to maintain himself there for seven years was a significant omen for the future.[4] For the present, however, we are more immediately concerned with contemporaneous events in Spain, where Aragon and Castile, temporarily at peace after the settlement of their territorial disputes in

[1] Mercier, ii, pp. 236 f.; Colmeiro, *Reyes*, pp. 147–150.
[2] Mercier, ii, pp. 243 f.
[3] Mas Latrie, pp. 149–151.
[4] Mas Latrie, pp. 299–305.

1304, made a somewhat futile joint attack upon Granada. The king of Aragon failed to capture Almeria; while the king of Castile, though he succeeded in taking Gibraltar by a sudden assault, yet wasted so much time before the walls of the then more important town of Algeciras that his army was decimated by disease, and he finally raised the siege of that town in return for the cession of Bedmar and Quesada. That Granada escaped so cheaply from the combined attack was largely due to the fact that the Emir of Morocco, impressed by the temporary union of the Christian kings of Spain, forgave his coreligionist for the various injuries he had received at his hands and sent him timely reënforcements in his hour of need.[1]

The reign of Alfonso XI began with renewed confusion, but ended with a glorious repulse by the united Christian kingdoms of the last great effort of the Moors to reconquer Spain from North Africa. Hostilities broke out in 1327 between Castile and Granada; and in the midst of them there occurred a Moroccan invasion from across the Strait. The king of Granada was this time equal to the occasion. He utilized the Moors against Castile; then, turning his arms against his allies, he expelled them from the peninsula. The habit of invasion, however, once acquired, was not easily forgotten; and when a few years later the Granadan Emir, again attacked, and this time defeated by Castile, begged aid and succor of the Merinite, the latter returned to the onset, and in 1333 recaptured Gibraltar, which Alfonso was unable to retake.[2] A lull followed during the next six years, but it was emphatically a lull before the storm. The Moroccan Emir yearned to reconquer Spain. The fiery king of Granada lent himself to his plans. Their

[1] A. Giménes Soler, *Sitio de Almería*, pp. 64 f.; *Correspondencia Diplomática entre Granada y Fes: Siglo XIV*, ed. M. G. Remiro (Granada, 1916).
[2] I. López de Ayala, *Historia de Gibraltar*, pp. 137 ff.

alliance presaged the revival of the Holy War as it had been waged in the palmy days of Islam in the peninsula, and evoked a counter-alliance among the Christian kings of Spain. Castile and Aragon forgot their quarrels and made common cause against the invader by land and sea. Though the Castilian admiral sought and found a heroic death in a desperate dash into the centre of the Moorish galleys, he failed to offer any effective resistance to the landing of the Moroccan invader, who promptly joined forces with his Granadan ally and laid siege to Tarifa. The town, however, was able to hold out, largely because of the aid of a fleet of Genoese galleys which Alfonso of Castile had bought for the purpose;[1] and the delay before its walls gave the Christians time to advance against the infidel with an army which is usually estimated at twenty thousand men. The inevitable battle finally took place on the banks of the little stream called the Rio Salado, just north of Tarifa, on Monday, October 30, 1340. Countless acts of heroism were performed by the Christian forces, most of all by the young king of Castile, who was only prevented from plunging single-handed into a group of his foes by a gentle warning from the Primate. A sortie by the garrison of Tarifa against the rear of the Moorish forces finally decided the day.[2] The Christian victory was by all odds the most important that had been won in the peninsula since the days of Las Navas de Tolosa, of which it has been rightly called a fitting pendant. It marked the complete defeat of the last serious effort to invade Spain from North Africa. The Merinite ruler retreated with the remnant of his shattered forces to Morocco, and the vigilance of the Christian fleet which guarded the Strait prevented a repetition of the attempt.

[1] Fernández Duro, op. cit., pp. 77–89.

[2] Crónica de Alfonso XI, caps. cclcclii; Lafuente, vi, pp. 509–516.

Two years later the triumphant Castilian monarch laid siege to Algeciras, which with Gibraltar and Ronda had been left after the battle of Rio Salado in Moroccan hands. So great was the fame of Alfonso's previous exploits that all Western Christendom listened to his appeal for men to come and aid him close the last door open to invasion from the South.   Many valiant sons of France and Italy rallied to his standards : Henry of Lancaster, great-grandson of Henry III, came on from England with the Earl of Salisbury; it will be remembered that Chaucer's "Gentle Knight" was "at the seege of Algezir."[1]   Finally, after a struggle of more than twenty months, the town capitulated on March 26, 1344.   A truce of five years' duration ensued; but in August, 1349, Alfonso was able to continue the task that he had so well begun, by laying siege to Gibraltar.   Had his life been spared he would infallibly have captured it; as it was he fell a victim to the Black Death, before the walls of the great fortress, in March, 1350, cut off in the midst of his labors at the early age of thirty-nine.   The fact that the siege was raised immediately after his death shows what a factor he had been in the victories already won.   Even among his enemies he was held in high esteem.   Yusuf of Granada and all his court wore mourning for him, and many a Moor went unarmed to the Christian camp in order to attend his funeral.   Alfonso was unquestionably the greatest of the Castilian sovereigns between St. Ferdinand and Queen Isabella; he is even worthy, though on a somewhat smaller scale, of comparison with St. Louis.[2]

From 1350 onward the nature of the struggle changes and on the whole degenerates.   The battle on the Salado ended forever all chances of Granada's receiving effectual

[1] I. López de Ayala, op. cit., pp. 161 f.; Prologue to the Canterbury Tales, ll. 56 f.
[2] R. St.-H., iv, pp. 439–441.

aid from the Merinites. In the succeeding years the latter not only lost all their holdings in the peninsula, but even saw their own ports temporarily occupied by Spanish Moors and Spanish Christians. The strife between Castile and Granada is no longer complicated by Moroccan interference as before, and resembles rather the quarrels and bickerings between a suzerain and his rebel vassal on questions of overlordship and tribute than a struggle between Christian and infidel. During the reign of Pedro the Cruel both realms were paralyzed by successional quarrels; but the king of Granada was on the whole loyal to Pedro, and consequently hostile to Henry of Trastamara, from whom, in the first year of his reign, he wrested Algeciras. Rightly believing that he would be unable to maintain himself there against a hostile attack, he determined to destroy the town, and this he so effectively accomplished that it figured no more in the struggles of the time.[1] The remaining thirty years of the fourteenth century saw both Granada and Castile carry their arms across the Strait. The former was in possession of Ceuta during much of the time previous to the Portuguese occupation of it in 1415 ;[2] and in 1399 Henry III of Castile, who had visions of crusades which his untimely death left him small opportunity to realize, sent over a fleet which seized Tetuan and carried off most of its inhabitants to Spain.[3] During the early years of John II, under the regency of his uncle Ferdinand, some progress was made by Castile at the expense of Granada, from which Antequera was taken in 1410 ;[4] but in 1411 Granada recouped

[1] Ibn Khaldûn, *Histoire des Berbères* (trad. de Slane), iv, pp. 380 f.; Mercier, ii, p. 343; I. López de Ayala, *op. cit.*, p. 167.

[2] Mercier, ii, pp. 361 f., 367. On the Portuguese in Ceuta, see E. de Septenville, *Découvertes et conquêtes du Por-ugal*, pp. 12–14.

[3] Mercier, ii, p. 393. Apparently the Spaniards did not keep Tetuan for long; for the place was practically depopulated until the Moors expelled from Granada took refuge there almost a century afterwards.

[4] R. St.-H., v, p. 218.

itself for this loss at the expense of the Merinites by capturing Gibraltar, their last holding in the peninsula.[1] The fortress, however, was not long to remain in the hands of the Spanish Moors. The news of the capture of Constantinople by the Turks in 1453 had filled the Emir of Granada with such reckless enthusiasm that he boastfully hurled defiance at the king of Castile and refused to pay the tribute which was the token of his vassalage, thus giving the latter an excuse for waging war on him; and nine years later an internal revolt in Granada itself furnished the Christian monarch with the desired opportunity. In 1462 Gibraltar was attacked and taken, and has remained ever since in Christian hands.[2] In the following year the town of Archidona to the northward also fell before the Castilian armies, and the payment of the ancient tribute was soon after renewed.[3]

The territorial results of this desultory strife were certainly meagre; and the fact that Granada was able to maintain itself practically undiminished for so long affords the strongest possible proof of the weakness and inefficiency of Castile. The feudal relationship between the two realms, and the tribute, which of course ceased at every declaration of war, only to be renewed again, though in varying amount, at every conclusion of peace, were a perpetual bone of contention; it seems little short of marvellous that the situation should have been tolerated for so many years. One of the most important results of these two centuries of intermittent warfare was that they served to keep the attention of Castile fixed on events across the Strait. The affairs of Granada and Morocco were so closely related that the former served in a sense as a bridge between Chris-

---

[1] I. López de Ayala, *op. cit.*, pp. 170f.   [2] *Ibid.*, pp. 176–189.
[3] Mercier, ii, p. 409.

tian Spain and North Africa. When it fell, it was the logical and inevitable consequence that Ferdinand and Isabella should carry their arms across to the opposite shore, which possessed so much in common with the Iberian Peninsula.

The dealings of Castile with France and England during the fourteenth and fifteenth centuries claim our attention for a few moments; for it is important that we should know something of the early history of her relations with the two great states whose enmity was to be the principal factor in preventing the full realization of Spain's dreams of world dominion in the crucial years of the sixteenth century. In general it may be said that it was the desire of the Castilian kings to live in peace and amity with both these nations. They had plenty to do south of the Pyrenees without interfering to the north of them. Even the versatile Alfonso X, as we have had occasion to observe, sought to cultivate good relations with both England and France by marrying his half-sister to Edward I, and his eldest son to the daughter of St. Louis. But as things fell out, it proved ultimately impossible to maintain an equally close friendship with both powers at the same time. The Hundred Years' War broke out in 1338; both France and England sought the alliance of Castile; and it was ultimately France that won it. For the next hundred years the friendship of France and Castile was virtually uninterrupted. It became a tradition of national policy on both sides; it was renewed at the beginning of each reign; there are in fact few examples in all history of a continuance of friendship between two states more cordial and more prolonged.[1] Yet all this time Castile strove her hardest to avoid being drawn into war with England on account of her

[1] G. Daumet, *Étude sur l'alliance de la France et de la Castille*, p. viii.

friendship with France. She had no real cause of quarrel
with England, and when, in spite of all her efforts, she was
forced to open hostilities against her, she seized the first
honorable opportunity to terminate them. Such are the
main lines of the picture; it now remains to fill in the most
important details.

At the death of Alfonso X, the good relations between
France and Castile were temporarily clouded by the disin-
heriting of the Infantes de la Cerda. The French kings,
however, were so much more interested in ousting the Aragonese from Sicily than in defending the rights of their kinsmen in Castile that no open breach ensued. Even before
the affairs of the Infantes were finally settled by the agreement of 1304, France sought the friendship of Sancho IV
and his successor in order to be able to concentrate her
energies upon Aragon. In 1317 it was arranged that Alfonso XI of Castile should wed Isabella, daughter of Philip
V of France, as soon as she should have attained suitable
age, and that a lasting peace should unite the two nations.
Though the marriage project was subsequently abandoned,
and though there is no further record of any relation between
the two states for a number of years, there is every reason
to think that their friendship was uninterrupted.[1] But
with the opening of the Hundred Years' War matters entered upon a much acuter stage. The contiguity of Castile
to the English lands in the south of France made her friendship of paramount importance to both Edward III and
Philip VI, who promptly engaged in a diplomatic duel to
obtain it. Alfonso XI fully appreciated the strength of
his position, and did his best to keep the two rival monarchs
bidding against one another for his alliance. In 1336 and

---

[1] Daumet, *Mémoire sur les relations de la France et de la Castille*, pp. 86–142;
the same, *Étude*, pp. 1 f.

in 1345 he signed two treaties with France, the second of
which [1] was distinctly anti-English in character; yet in 1346
he strove to secure himself against the hostility of the
Plantagenets by arranging for the marriage of his son,
Pedro, to Jane, the daughter of Edward III. As the
princess, however, died suddenly at Bordeaux on her
way to Spain, the union never took place.[2] It is worth
noting that no treaty of alliance had been spoken of in
connection with it; in fact, at the very moment that
it was being agreed upon, the king of Castile was actually
furnishing ships to France to aid her in liberating Calais
from its English besiegers.[3] In other words, Alfonso was
still endeavoring to preserve good relations with both countries, though events were gradually tending to drive him
more and more into the arms of France.

The beginning of the reign of Pedro the Cruel saw the
Franco-Castilian treaties formally renewed; and on June 3,
1353, the young Castilian monarch married Blanche, the
daughter of Pierre de Bourbon.[4] But this match, instead
of strengthening the ties that united the two realms, almost
resulted in severing them, for Pedro's maltreatment of his
bride was so outrageous that no considerations of political
expediency could prevail upon the French king to ignore it.
At the time of Blanche's arrival in Spain, Pedro had fallen
a victim to the charms of Maria de Padilla. He was only
with difficulty prevailed upon to go through with the ceremony of marriage with Blanche; almost immediately after
it he left her, to return a little later for another visit of two
days, after which he never saw her again.[5] No wonder

---

[1] July 1, 1345: in J. Bernard's
Recueil des Traités, i, pp. 253 ff. See
especially the secret articles, ibid., pp.
256 f.

[2] Daumet, Étude sur l'alliance de la

France et de la Castille, pp. 16 f.

[3] Daumet, Étude, pp. 17 f.

[4] Daumet, op. cit., pp. 22 ff.

[5] Daumet, p. 24; Sitges, Las Mujeres del rey Pedro I, pp. 335–404.

that the Franco-Castilian alliance was shaken by such an
episode as this; and had Pedro succeeded in preserving the
throne of Castile, the whole history of the relations of the
two realms would in all probability have been changed.
But France's need of Castile's friendship was so pressing
that she could afford to neglect no honorable means of retaining it, and when Pedro's wild career of crime and outrage in Spain evoked a counter-claimant to his throne in
the person of Henry of Trastamara, she was quick to seize
her opportunity. She made common cause with the pretender, and sent him a host of marauding mercenaries
under the famous Bertrand du Guesclin, this the more willingly since a temporary peace with England made her anxious
to be rid of these turbulent soldiers of fortune. She enlisted
the support of Pedro, king of Aragon. . Meantime Pedro
of Castile threw himself for protection into the arms of
England, taking refuge at the court of the Black Prince at
Bordeaux, together with his two daughters, one of whom
was later to become the bride of John of Gaunt. The
dramatic story of the successional struggle which followed
in Castile does not directly concern us, save to note that it
was France that had espoused the winning cause. When
Pedro fell a victim to his brother's dagger in 1369, and
Henry of Trastamara mounted the Castilian throne, the
Franco-Castilian alliance which the reign of Pedro had
threatened to break emerged stronger than ever before.
It was by French aid that the pretender had been set on the
Castilian throne; and in the succeeding generations he and
his descendants were to repay the debt with interest by sup-
porting their ally against the common enemy, England.[1]

The naval side of the ensuing struggle was chiefly intrusted
by France to Castile, whose attacks on England in the

[1] Daumet, pp. 26–31; J. Catalina García, *Castilla y León*, vol. i, cap. xxi.

fourteenth century furnished a number of interesting precedents for the days of the Spanish Armada. Certainly
far more damage was done on this occasion than was effected
two centuries later. It seems probable that the French,
knowing that Castile had already made great progress in
maritime affairs, and realizing from the very first their
own inferiority in this respect, approached Henry of Trastamara with a definite request for naval aid in August,
1371.[1]   It was by a Castilian fleet that the Earl of Pembroke
was decisively defeated on June 23, 1372, in the harbor of
La Rochelle, his landing prevented, and his ships destroyed.[2]
In 1373 the English strove energetically but unsuccessfully
to detach Castile from the French alliance : several indecisive actions and a truce of one year's duration ensued ;
but finally the French and Castilian fleets made a joint
demonstration off the southern shore of England in the summer of 1377. The Isle of Wight was overrun and put to
ransom ; Winchelsea was saved by the efforts of the abbot
of Battle ; but Hastings and Rottingdean were sacked, and
the prior of Lewes was carried off. Most of the contemporary English chroniclers represent these raids as a purely
French affair, but there is little doubt that Castilian ships
did the lion's share of the work. The climax was reached
in the spring of 1380 when the Castilian Admiral Fernán
Sanchez de Tovar sailed up the Thames with twenty galleys,
burned Gravesend, and penetrated almost to the city of
London, "whither hostile ships had never attained before."
This raid was obviously regarded as a feat of unparalleled
audacity at the time, and stands out in striking contrast
to the fate of the Spanish Armada.[3]

[1] Daumet, p. 35.
[2] Fernández Duro, *Marina de Castilla*, pp. 130 ff.
[3] *Crónica de Juan I*, año de 1380,
cap. i; *Chronicon Angliae* (ed. Thomp-
son, in *Rolls Series*), pp. 151 f., 166–172;
S. Armitage-Smith, *John of Gaunt*, pp.
230 f.

In return for the naval aid he brought his ally, the king of Castile not unnaturally expected help on land from the French. By this time, too, there was serious need of it, owing to England's support of Portugal in the campaign of Aljubarrota, and to John of Gaunt's subsequent claiming of the throne of Castile by virtue of his marriage with the daughter of Pedro the Cruel. To substantiate this claim, the Duke of Lancaster sailed from England in the ships of the king of Portugal, with more than three thousand soldiers and vast quantities of provisions and stores: for, as Froissart shrewdly remarks, "the English do not willingly go unfurnished with such things." [1]   They finally landed at Corunna on July 25, 1386, but were unable to take the town. Hunting rather than fighting was their chief preoccupation, but they finally succeeded in establishing themselves at Santiago, which surrendered without resistance.[2]   Meantime Charles VI of France had great difficulty in raising troops to succor his ally. Heavy taxes were imposed for the purpose, but men grumbled at being obliged to pay "in order to comfort the king of Castile and expel the English from his dominions." In 1387, however, an advance guard of two thousand men entered the peninsula, and their arrival was enough to cause the army of John of Gaunt to scatter to the four winds of heaven.[3] Clearly the continuance of the semblance of war, at least on land, would be little more than a farce; and the king of Castile, whose only desire was to rid his realm of the presence of his foes, made haste to treat of peace. In return for a liberal money compensation, John of Gaunt agreed to evacuate Galicia and renounce all claims to the throne of Castile;

[1] Cf. Buchon's Froissart, in *Collection de Chroniques Nationales*, xx, p. 141. This significant characterisation is omitted in Lord Berners's translation.

[2] Froissart (tr. Berners), iv, pp. 295–346; Armitage-Smith, *John of Gaunt*, pp. 301–336.

[3] Daumet, pp. 48–50.

it was further arranged that his daughter Catharine should
marry the heir to the Castilian throne, so as to put an end
to the successional struggle between the descendants of
Pedro the Cruel and Henry of Trastamara, as well as to the
quarrel between Castile and England.[1] The treaty was
arranged without consulting the court of France, which
was naturally furious when it heard the news: the Admiral
Jean de Vienne was sent to express to the Castilian monarch
France's opinion of his conduct, and to warn him to do nothing in prejudice of his alliance with France ; and so vigorous
was his language that when the king and his council heard
him they were all "abasshed, and eche of them loked on
other; there was none that gave any answere but satte
styll." [2] The French king, however, had no reason to be
alarmed. The Castilian government had not the slightest
intention of breaking with him, and the alliance of the two
nations was formally renewed, as the custom was, at the
beginning of the next reign.[3]

Henry III, however, was exceedingly careful that alliance
with France should not again bring his country into open
conflict with England. When the French king sent him a
fresh demand for a fleet he was slow to reply, took advantage
of every possible opportunity to delay its preparation and
departure, and when it finally did set sail, gave it instructions which condemned it to ineffectiveness.[4] Under all
the circumstances it is not surprising that the first half of
the fifteenth century saw a considerable loosening of the
bonds of the Franco-Castilian alliance. Formally it was
continued until after the middle of the reign of Henry the
Impotent, despite an attempt of Henry VI of England in

---

[1] Daumet, pp. 50–55.
[2] Froissart (tr. Berners), v, p. 261.
[3] Daumet, pp. 58 f.
[4] Daumet, pp. 67 f., and references

there and in Ballester y Castell, pp.
128 f., to the contemporary chronicle
called the *Victorial*.

1430 to break it, but the Castilian kings were unwilling, and also too weak, to give France any effective help in expelling their foes, and the French kings revenged themselves by refusing to aid their Castilian brethren against their rebel barons and the Aragonese.[1] The palmy days of the alliance were in fact over. Interest and enthusiasm for it had visibly cooled on both sides. Whatever the letter of the treaties might say,[2] the Castilian monarchs were obviously determined to live at peace with England, so that the advantages which France could draw from their friendship were but slight. Finally, in 1467, two years before the marriage of Ferdinand and Isabella, Edward IV of England won away the Castilian alliance from France, and though eleven years later Louis XI succeeded in temporarily regaining it, the old cordiality of feeling was utterly gone, and the way had been already opened for that great regrouping of the powers which bore fruit in the Italian Wars of the sixteenth century.[3] All this, however, may be more profitably considered in connection with the reign of Ferdinand and Isabella. For the present we need only remember that Castile had an unusually long and uninterrupted tradition of amity, during the later Middle Ages, with the nation which was to be her principal foe in the days of the Catholic Kings and of Charles V; while with England, who was to deal the death blow to her imperial ambitions in the reign of Philip II, her relations had on the whole been more friendly than the reverse.

[1] Daumet, pp. 73–77, 82.

[2] Daumet, pp. 69 f. Cf., e.g., the treaty of alliance concluded at Madrid on January 29, 1434, between John II of Castile and Charles VII of France : J. Bernard, *Recueil des Traités*, i, pp. 452–456.

[3] Daumet, pp. 109–111.

BIBLIOGRAPHICAL NOTE

See the bibliographical note at the end of the preceding chapter, and add:

Contemporary Authorities. — *Memorias de Fernando IV de Castilla*, ed. Antonio Benavides for the R. A. H. (Madrid, 1860, 2 vols.); vol. ii (*Colección Diplomática*) contains 586 documents which are indispensable for a study of this reign. *Crónicas de Alfonso X, de Sancho IV, y de Fernando IV* (*Las Tres Corónicas* attributed to Fernán Sanches de Tovar) and *Crónica de Alfonso XI* (attributed to Núñez de Villasán) are also published in *B. A. E.*, vol. lxvi (Madrid, 1875). On the earlier editions of them, see Ballester y Castell, *Fuentes Narrativas*, pp. 115–120. Pedro López de Ayala, *Crónicas de los Reyes de Castilla, Pedro I, Enrique II, Juan I, Enrique III*, ed. E. de Llaguno Amirola in the *Colección de las Crónicas y Memorias de los Reyes de Castilla* (Madrid, 1779–80, 2 vols.); also in *B. A. E.*, vols. lxvi, lxviii (Madrid, 1875–77). On this important writer, whose work marks the transition from the age of the chronicle to that of history in the real sense of the word, see Ballester y Castell, pp. 121–130. *The Chronicles of Froissart*, translated by Lord Berners in the *Tudor Translation Series* (London, 1901–03, 6 vols.), also contain much that is valuable on the history of Castile and of Portugal in this period.

Later Works. — Juan Catalina García, *Castilla y León durante los reinados de Pedro I, Enrique II, Juan I, y Enrique III*, in the *Historia General de España*, edited by the R. A. H. (Madrid, 1891, 2 vols.), is the standard modern authority on the period. Gaspar Ibáñez, Marquis de Mondéjar, *Memorias históricas del rei D. Alonso el Sabio, i observaciones a su Chronica* (Madrid, 1777), contains much that is still valuable on this important reign; the latest monographs on the imperial venture are those of Willy Hermann and of Antonio y Pío Ballesteros, cited *supra*, p. 112, note 1. The best-known of several attempts to vindicate Pedro the Cruel is Prosper Mérimée's *Histoire de Don Pèdre Iᵉʳ, roi de Castille* (new edition, Paris, 1865); J. B. Sitges, *Las Mujeres del rey Don Pedro I de Castilla* (Madrid, 1910), is the latest serious work on the reign, and contains an admirable preliminary essay on the authorities. Heinrich Schäfer's old-fashioned but elaborate *Geschichte von Portugal* (Hamburg and Gotha, 1836–54, 5 vols.) rather inadequately supplies the lack of Herculano in this period; Henry Morse Stephens's *The Story of Portugal* (New York, 1891) is interesting and accurate, though very brief. C. Fernández Duro, *La Marina de Castilla*, in the *Historia General de España* of the R. A. H. (Madrid, 1895), is the standard work on the mediaeval Castilian navy. Georges Daumet, *Mémoire sur les relations de la France et de la Castille de 1255 à 1320* (Paris, 1914) — chiefly devoted to the claims of the Infantes de la Cerda — and his *Étude sur l'alliance de la France et de la Castille au XIV⁰ et XV⁰ siècles* (Paris, 1898), are based on the most thorough research. Andrés Giménez Soler's *El Sitio de Almería en 1309* (Barcelona, 1904) and his *La Corona de Aragón y Granada* (Barcelona, 1908) are typical of the best of modern Spanish scholarship. Ignacio López de Ayala's *Historia de Gibraltar* (Madrid, 1782) is still valuable; several subsequent histories of Gibraltar in English (e.g., that of Captain Frederick Sayer, 2d edition, London, 1865) are largely taken from it.

CHAPTER III

CASTILE IN THE ATLANTIC AND IN THE ORIENT

DESPITE her manifold activities at home and abroad, despite also the limitation of her coast line by Portugal's attainment of independence, Castile did not emerge from the Middle Ages without giving the world a slight foretaste of the tremendous development of her dominions beyond the seas which awaited her under Ferdinand and Isabella and the Hapsburgs. During the reign of King Henry III (1390-1406), whose instincts were far more cosmopolitan than those of most of his predecessors and successors, the conquest and colonization of the Canaries were begun, and a long step incidentally taken on the road to the discovery of America. At the same time the name and fame of Castile were borne eastward to the plains of Central Asia, as far as the court of the redoubtable Tamerlane at Samarcand.

The existence of the Canary Islands was well known to the ancients. Situated in the ocean, which the Homeric poems treated as the barrier between the known world and the Elysian Fields, they were popularly supposed to be the habitation of the blest, hence the classical name of Insulae Fortunatae.[1] Their primitive inhabitants — the so-called Guanches — were almost certainly of Berber stock.[2] All

[1] A map of the Canaries and the adjacent coast will be found in Volume II, p. 171.

[2] F. von Löher in his *Kanarierbuch* (Munich, 1895) maintains that the Canarians are of Vandal origin, but his conclusions have not been generally accepted. Cf. *Historische Zeitschrift*, lxxix, pp. 142 f.

the testimony to be derived from physical aspect, language,[1] religion, and customs, seems to point to that conclusion, and the fact that the islands can be seen from the western extremity of Mauretania (as Strabo[2] was the first to observe) tends to strengthen it still further. Plutarch tells us that Sertorius, in his flight from the ships of Annius, fell in with some Lusitanian sea captains who had visited them, and was almost persuaded by their glowing descriptions to withdraw thither and seek repose from the cares of military life.[3] Fuller and more definite information is to be found in the pages of Pliny, who got hold of a vague itinerary drawn up by a certain Statius Sebosus in B.C. 52 from accounts of navigators of his time; and, still more important, has preserved to us a fragment of a report from King Juba of Mauretania to the Emperor Augustus of an expedition which he had sent out for the express purpose of exploring the archipelago.[4] Finally, the Arab geographer, Edrisi, who finished his famous description of Spain and Africa at the court of King Roger of Sicily in the year 1154, tells at length of a journey of certain Moorish adventurers from Lisbon, to islands whose description tallies closely with what we know of the Canaries. This account has been regarded as apocryphal by the majority of writers, but the naïveté and realism of the story make it seem unlikely that the tale was invented out of whole cloth.[5] In general, however, Europe's knowledge of the Canaries can only be regarded as vague and scanty to the last degree down to the period of the Renaissance.

[1] John Abercromby, "A Study of the Ancient Speech of the Canary Islands," in *Harvard African Studies*, i (1917), pp. 95–129.

[2] Strabo's *Geography*, bk. iii, chap. ii, § 13 (Hamilton and Falconer's translation, i, pp. 225 f.).

[3] Plutarch's *Lives; the Translation called Dryden's*, ed. A. H. Clough, iii, pp. 390 f.

[4] Introduction to the *Canarian* of Bontier and Le Verrier, edited by R. H. Major for the Hakluyt Society, pp. iv–vi; Pliny, *Nat. Hist.*, vi, 37.

[5] Introduction to vol. ii of Eannes de Azurara's *Discovery and Conquest of Guinea*, tr. and ed. C. R. Beazley for the Hakluyt Society, ii, pp. lxxv–lxxvii.

With the fourteenth century, however, we emerge on firmer ground. A passage in Petrarch and several contemporary maps of Genoese, Venetian, and Catalan authorship indicate the presence of Genoese sailors on the island of Lanzarote, the easternmost of the archipelago.[1] Far more important than this was an expedition sent out to explore the Canaries by King Affonso IV of Portugal in 1341, which is interestingly described by Boccaccio. It was composed chiefly of Portuguese and Castilians, but Florentines and Genoese took part in it, and it had a Genoese pilot. The adventurers made no attempt to settle in the islands, but they gained a good deal of knowledge of them and of their inhabitants, and certainly accomplished enough to give Portugal a strong claim to priority of discovery and possession against any other European power.[2] Indeed, the expedition of 1341 furnished the basis of Portugal's later refusal to acknowledge the validity of Castile's occupation of the Canaries; it was the origin of the first of a long series of quarrels between the two nations concerning the limits of their overseas possessions. But the Portuguese were not aroused to the importance of vigorously prosecuting their claims until it was too late. When, in November, 1344, Luis de la Cerda, great-grandson of Alfonso the Learned, was invested by the Avignonese Pope Clement VI with the lordship of the Canaries as a fief of the Holy See, they did indeed object, on the ground of their expedition of three years before, and of the fact that the archipelago lay nearer to Portugal than to Castile. No one, however, seems to have paid much attention to them, and though Luis himself made no serious efforts to realize his sovereignty, "the theory of a Spanish right to the Canaries was established "

[1] Beasley, *Dawn of Modern Geography*, iii, p. 412; Major, introduction to the *Canarian*, pp. xiii ff.

[2] Löher, pp. 34 f.; Beasley, *Dawn of Modern Geography*, iii, pp. 423 ff.

from that moment, " and all that was done in the remaining years of the fourteenth century for the conquest, exploration, and Christianizing of the *Fortunatae* seems to have been the work of Castilians." In fact, Castile "considered that she had earmarked the Canaries through Don Luis "; and when, years later, she prepared to take real possession of the archipelago, Portugal discovered that her opportunity was gone, and that "it was too late to put back the hands of time." [1]

We now come to the famous expedition of the year 1402, which will always be associated with the names of the Norman, Jean de Bethencourt, and of the Poitevin, Gadifer de La Salle. Both were filled to the brim with instincts of maritime adventure and piracy ; both had taken part in a Genoese expedition against Tunis in the year 1390 ; both were keenly desirous to embark in some fresh enterprise, where all the risks and profits should be their own. Joining forces accordingly at La Rochelle, they set sail thence on the first of May, 1402, "for the lands of Canary, to see and explore all the country, with the view of conquering the islands, and bringing the people to the Christian faith." [2] After an adventure at Corunna, indicative of somewhat loose notions of the rights of property, and a brief detention at Cadiz and Seville, from which they were liberated by order of the Royal Council, they continued their voyage; finally, in July, they landed at the island of Lanzarote, and built a fort and called it Rubicon.[3] Most of the inhabitants were

[1] Beasley, *Dawn of Modern Geography*, iii, pp. 426–429.
[2] *The Canarian*, ed. R. H. Major, p. 4. On this work and its various editions, especially the most recent by P. Margry, see bibliographical note at the end of this chapter. When there is any important discrepancy between Major's and Margry's editions, I have followed the latter; but when they agree, I have used the former for quotations, in the interests of convenience.
[3] *Le Canarien*, ed. Margry, pp. 133–138. It is natural to assume, as Beasley (iii, p. 449) evidently does, that the name Rubicon was chosen because of the obvious allusion to the career of Julius Caesar. Millares (iii, p. 27)

very friendly, and listened attentively to the priests' instructions in the elements of the Christian religion, but a few held off in fear and half-hostile suspicion. Soon afterwards Bethencourt and Gadifer passed over with some of their followers to the island of Fuerteventura, where the inhabitants fled before them; but lack of provisions and fears of a mutiny soon obliged them to return without having accomplished anything. At Rubicon, moreover, they found things in evil case. Many of the sailors were discouraged and longed to get away; clearly the conquest of the archipelago was going to prove a far more difficult and serious undertaking than had at first been supposed. The two partners must renounce their original idea of an independent realm. Help from some European sovereign would be indispensable to success, and help would plainly not be given without recognition of overlordship in return. Nothing was to be hoped for from the king of France, for Charles VI, already a victim of insanity, had too many troubles at home to think of such remote possessions; consequently the adventurers were thrown back on the king of Castile, whose government had on the whole treated them generously at Seville earlier in the year. Leaving Gadifer, therefore, in charge of Rubicon, and taking with him such followers as were most anxious to return, Bethencourt set sail in October and landed soon after in Spain. At the Castilian court he was most cordially received, as soon as his errand was known. Henry the Invalid was not likely to neglect such a favorable opportunity to consolidate and reënforce the vague claims to the Canaries which Castile had maintained since the days of Luis de la Cerda. Fair and complimentary words were exchanged between sovereign and adventurer,

however, asserts that it is explained by the reddish color of the soil at the spot selected, which was on the southern shore, opposite Fuerteventura.

with much discussion of the advancement of the Christian faith. Bethencourt begged the king to be permitted to do him homage for the islands. The king congratulated him on his bravery and enterprise, and assured him that 'he showed an admirable disposition in coming to do him homage for a land which as far as he could make out was more than two hundred leagues distant, and of which he had never heard before.'[1] The account really sounds as if the first outpost of Spain's Western Empire was almost forced upon the crown of Castile; certainly her first effective acquisition of the sovereignty of the Canaries cost infinitely less trouble than the retention of it. At any rate King Henry accepted the good fortune which chance had thrown in his way. He received Bethencourt's homage for the archipelago, and granted him the right to appropriate to his own use one fifth of all merchandise brought thence to Spain, the privilege of coining money there, and of preventing any one from landing in the islands without his leave. Finally, Bethencourt made the most of his partner's absence to secure all these important concessions in his own name, and thus to relegate Gadifer to a position of inferiority to himself. In fact, the Norman lord was fully as much occupied in feathering his own nest at the Castilian court as in securing the support and protection of King Henry III. He had promised to return to the archipelago at Christmas, 1402, but he did not actually arrive there till April, 1404, and in the intervening months he had contrived so to arrange matters that the game was left completely in his own hands.[2]

Meantime poor Gadifer in Lanzarote had not only been experiencing grave difficulties with the Guanches, but had also been weakened by the outbreak of rebellion and mutiny

<hr>

[1] *The Canarian*, ed. Major, pp. 44 f.
[2] *Le Canarien*, ed. Margry, pp. 141– 148; Beasley, *Dawn of Modern Geography*, iii, p. 450.

among his own followers. One of the most prominent members of Bethencourt's company, a certain Berthin de Berneval, irritated by the fact that the expedition had not been a more pronounced success, determined to recoup himself for the funds he had invested in it by capturing a number of natives and taking them to Europe to be sold as slaves. Availing himself of a temporary absence of Gadifer, he gathered a small faction of malcontents, pillaged the castle of Rubicon, seized a number of the Guanches, and finally escaped to Spain in a ship that chanced to touch at Lanzarote, together with his confederates, and prisoners to the number of twenty-two; these he handed over to the ship captain and sailors, as the contemporary chronicler says, "after the example of the traitor Judas Iscariot, who betrayed our Saviour Jesus Christ, and delivered Him into the hands of the Jews to crucify Him, and put Him to death." [1] Some of Berthin's accomplices, whom he abandoned at the last moment, were so fearful of the wrath of Gadifer that they attempted to escape to the coast of Africa, where they perished miserably or were enslaved. Meantime Berthin himself was arrested and imprisoned at Cadiz, while the master of the ship in which he had sailed made off to Aragon with his Canarian captives and sold them there. Berthin's misdeeds, however, had an important effect on Gadifer's colony, for they convinced the Canarians that those who had advocated friendship with the Europeans were mistaken, and that a war of extermination must be waged against the invaders. Under the leadership of a certain native by the name of Asche, who aspired to the throne of Lanzarote, a double plan was laid. Asche was to attempt to utilize Gadifer in getting rid of the reigning king, with the intention of turning on his ally and the foreign

[1] *The Canarian*, ed. Major, p. 25.

intruders who had come with him, when the first part of
the programme had been accomplished. But the plot
ultimately recoiled on the head of its originator. With the
aid of Gadifer the king was duly captured, and Asche,
thinking that he had the game in his own hands, rashly
attacked one of the followers of the Frenchman before
putting his prisoner to death; the latter escaped from con-
finement, gathered his friends, seized the treacherous Asche,
and had him stoned and afterwards burned. Gadifer and
his men also took summary vengeance on the party of his
quondam ally, so that many of the Canarians fled to the
caverns in the hills, and more than eighty were terrorized
into being baptized at Pentecost, "with a good hope that
God would confirm them in the faith, and make them a means
of edification to all the country round about." [1] The whole
story would fit well into the history of Cortez in Mexico or
that of Pizarro in Peru.

The next chapter of the story witnesses the culmination
of the inevitable quarrel between Bethencourt and Gadifer.
After the rebellion of Asche had been put down, Gadifer
started on an exploring expedition among the western islands
of the archipelago, accompanied by a number of Castilians
who had just been sent out by Bethencourt. Fuerteventura,
the Grand Canary, Gomera, Ferro, and Palma were visited;
but the explorers apparently did not dare land at Teneriffe,
because of the tales of the strength and ferocity of its inhabitants. On their return to Rubicon in the autumn of 1403,
it was found that the garrison had virtually completed the
conquest of the Guanches of Lanzarote, and in February,
1404, the king of the island and a large majority of his subjects accepted the Christian faith and were baptized. The
'instruction' which was drawn up for their guidance by the

_____
[1] *The Canarian*, ed. Major, p. 59; ed. Margry, pp. 149–182.

priests Bontier and Le Verrier is a marvellously inaccurate
farrago of some of the most famous passages in the Penta-
teuch and the Gospels; whether its divagations were due
to the ignorance of the authors or to their desire to be intelli-
gible and interesting to the natives it is difficult to say.[1]
At this juncture (April 19, 1404) Bethencourt finally arrived
from Spain. He showed no gratitude for what his partner
had accomplished in his absence, and did not hesitate to let
him know that the chief result of his own negotiations at the
Castilian Court had been to deprive Gadifer of all authority
and interest in what had been originally organized as a joint
enterprise. He entirely refused to accede to Gadifer's
very reasonable request that some of the islands be given
to him as a reward for all that he had done, so that the latter,
failing to get immediate satisfaction, threatened to abandon
Bethencourt and return to France. Discussions of the
feasibility of a settlement on the adjacent African coast,
and unsuccessful expeditions and slave hunts in Fuerteventura and the Grand Canary, postponed for a time any open
breach;[2] but the interests of the two adventurers had now
become irreconcilable, and late in the summer of 1404
they went back to Spain to settle their disputes, travelling,
however, by different ships. The result was naturally a complete triumph for Bethencourt, who was already well known
and popular at the court, and was solemnly reinvested with
the islands; Gadifer's just claims were scornfully set aside,
and shortly afterwards he retired to France. The struggle

---

[1] *Le Canarien*, ed. Margry, pp. 192–
233. The Biblical account, moreover,
was often embellished by the inventive-
ness of the narrators, who added a number of items to the regular story. For
example, the Canarians were told that
the Jews, as a penalty for crucifying
Christ, "were destroyed, as everyone
knows, for go where you will, you will
find no Jews who are not in subjection
to others, and who are not day and night
in fear and dread for their lives; this is
how they have become so pale as you
now see them." *The Canarian*, ed.
Major, p. 85.

[2] *Le Canarien*, ed. Margry, pp. 234–
238. The narrative stops abruptly at
this point.

between the two leaders, however, had a far deeper significance than a mere personal quarrel; its most permanent result was to secure the Spanish hold on the archipelago. Throughout the dispute, Bethencourt had been continually reënforced by ships which brought men and provisions from Castile; his own original following of Frenchmen was by this time far outnumbered by the later Spanish arrivals. He had gradually become, in fact, the representative of the king of Castile, while Gadifer, who had not accompanied him on his first expedition to Seville, naturally tended to hark back to the early days of their partnership, and perhaps feebly to cling to the idea of holding the islands as a fief of France. But he had neither the ability nor the resources to carry his plans into effect. Bethencourt remained at the head of affairs, and for the time being reaped all the rewards; and his triumph was the triumph of his patron, King Henry the Invalid of Castile.[1]

In October, 1404, Bethencourt returned again to the archipelago. During the next three months he devoted himself to the subjection of Fuerteventura, an enterprise whose difficulty was enormously enhanced by the not unnatural ill will of the remnant of Gadifer's party, led by the latter's illegitimate son, Hannibal.[2] In January, 1405, Bethencourt went back to France to fetch supplies and colonists, and was highly successful: about one hundred and sixty men accompanied him on his return, of whom twenty-three brought their wives; among them were knights, mechanics, handicraftsmen, and laborers. All of them, however, came on their own initiative. There is no evidence of support by the French government or even of a request for it; Bethencourt obviously was determined to stand loyally by his liege lord,

[1] *The Canarian*, ed. Major, pp. 118–121, 140 f.; Beasley, *Dawn of Modern Geography*, iii, p. 453; Löher, pp. 98–100.

[2] *The Canarian*, ed. Major, pp. 142–164.

Henry of Castile, and to hold the Canaries as his vassal. In May he arrived triumphant at Lanzarote, where he was accorded a reception so enthusiastic that "God's thunder would have been drowned in the noise of the music that they made."[1]   This time Fuerteventura also received him with open arms and gladly acknowledged his supremacy. But when Bethencourt attempted to extend his dominion to the rest of the archipelago, he met with many misfortunes. Expeditions against the Grand Canary and Palma were repulsed by the valor of the natives, after a number of bloody encounters. At Gomera the invaders had a comparatively friendly reception; but at Ferro the clamorings of his followers caused Bethencourt to exchange his schemes of conquest for an attempt to capture slaves. The native king and one hundred and eleven others were decoyed, unarmed, into an ambush and taken prisoners, but almost no progress was made towards the subjugation of the island. Lust for slave hunting was, in fact, one of the most serious difficulties with which the conqueror had to contend. He was by no means entirely superior to it himself, but he was not one to let it interfere with larger aims. With most of his followers, however, it soon took the precedence of everything else. It not only crippled their efficiency in effecting the conquest of the islands; it also constantly diverted their attention to the adjacent African coast, where the opportunities for slave hunting were much more favorable. A great expedition for the purpose was sent over to Cape Bojador in the months immediately succeeding Bethencourt's arrival at Lanzarote. The inhabitants fled at its approach, but a number of them were captured and sold in the slave markets of Spain.[2]

After these various attempts to enlarge his own territories and to satisfy the cupidity of his men, Bethencourt

[1] *The Canarian*, ed. Major, pp. 165–172.   [2] Löher, pp. 120–134.

returned to Fuerteventura, and there established his headquarters.   He next occupied himself with drawing up regulations for the government and administration of the islands
which acknowledged his authority.   The land was divided
up between the loyal natives and the conquerors, the latter
receiving the lion's share and the control of all fortified
places.   Over each of the larger islands two judicial and administrative officers were set, who were to be aided in the
discharge of their duties by an assembly of prominent men ;
"the customs of France and Normandy" were to be observed
as nearly as possible "in the administration of justice and
all other points."   Every one except Bethencourt's Norman
friends, who were exempted from all taxation for nine years,
was to pay annually one fifth of all his income of whatever
sort to support the government : but the most valuable product of the island, the orchil, Bethencourt reserved for himself ; no man might sell any without his express permission.
The interests of the church were to be scrupulously guarded.
Finally, Bethencourt installed his nephew, Maciot, who had
come out with him from Normandy in 1404, as his representative with full powers.   On December 15, 1405, amid protes-
tations of loyalty and gratitude from natives and followers,
he sailed for Spain, partly to get more men and munitions
of war with which to complete the conquest of the archipelago, and partly to secure from the Pope the appointment of
a bishop of the Canaries who would aid him to bring the
inhabitants to the Christian faith.[1]

Bethencourt, however, was not destined to visit the
Canaries again.   He was received with royal pomp at the
Castilian court at Valladolid.   King Henry entered warmly
into his plans for establishing a bishopric in the islands, and

---

[1] *The Canarian*, ed. Major, pp. 185   *Islas Canarias*, iii, pp. 87–92; Löher,
ff.; A. Millares, *Historia General de las*   *Kanarierbuch*, pp. 134–139.

recommended for the purpose a Franciscan, of noble Castilian family, by the name of Albert de Las Casas; for he doubtless fully realized that the appointment of a Spaniard as the chief ecclesiastical authority in the archipelago would incidentally serve to strengthen his own claims to it. To secure the bulls for the new bishop, Bethencourt betook himself to the papal court. The needed formalities were soon completed; and a little later Las Casas was solemnly received in the Canaries, and his see established at Rubicon in Lanzarote.[1] Meantime Bethencourt returned to his Norman home, where he became the victim of successive misfortunes. The last years of his life were embittered by family quarrels and bereavements, the loss of rich cargoes of merchandise from his island realm, and the total failure of his plans for collecting a large military force with which to return and complete the subjugation of the archipelago. One authority says that he maintained close relations with the Castilian court, and actually journeyed there in 1412, to renew his homage for the Canaries to the unfortunate king, John II; but the story lacks confirmation. The year of his death is usually given as 1422, but some authorities put it in 1425, and an inscription,

---

[1] There is a strange tangle of inaccurate statements in connection with the appointment of Las Casas, and it does not seem possible to determine with absolute certainty whether he obtained his bulls from Rome or Avignon. The Bethencourt (1482) manuscript of the *Canarien* tells a long story of how Bethencourt visited Rome and there arranged for the 'provision' of Las Casas; while Abreu de Galindo declares that he settled the matter with Benedict XIII at Avignon. No record of the issuance of bulls to Las Casas has apparently been found in any papal register, and Eubel (*Hierarchia Catholici Medii Aevi*, p. 448) does not place his name in the regular list of the bishops of Rubicon at all, though he mentions him in a reference to Gams (*Series Episcoporum*, p. 474, *q.v.*). The difficulty of the problem is further enhanced by the fact that the allegiance of Castile shifted with such bewildering rapidity at this stage of the Schism (Gams, *Kirchengeschichte Spaniens*, iii, 1, pp. 396 f.) that in default of a precise date of Las Casas's appointment (it probably occurred late in the year 1406), it is impossible to determine precisely where she stood at the crucial moment. N. Valois (*La France et le Grand Schisme d'Occident*, iii, p. 389, n. 6) is unquestionably correct in stating that the *first* bishop of the Canaries received his bulls from Benedict XIII; but the register

placed in 1851 in the church at Grainville where he lies
buried, adopts the later date.[1]

For years after Bethencourt's departure in 1405, the
history of the Canaries is utterly confused and of little
significance. Its salient features are the ebbs and flows
of Castilian control, and the challenging of it by the Portuguese. Bethencourt, as we have seen, had always upheld
the overlordship of Castile, and his brother Reynauld,.
to whom he bequeathed his conquests, did nothing to
alter the situation. But meantime Bethencourt's nephew,
Maciot, whom he had left in the archipelago as his representative, began to plot to emancipate it from Castilian
overlordship and to place it under the protection of the
crown of France. His conduct naturally provoked the
resentment of the Queen Regent Catharine of Castile, who
at once sent out three war caravels under Admiral Pedro
Barba de Campos to force him to return to his allegiance.
Resistance was obviously out of the question; so Maciot,
coolly ignoring the fact that the Canaries were not his to
dispose of, first ceded them to the admiral, and then fled
to Madeira, where he sold them to Prince Henry the Navigator of Portugal.[2] This highly fraudulent proceeding,

which he cites in proof of this assertion
is dated July 7, 1404, and does not
apply to Las Casas at all as he seems
to think, but to a certain Alfonso de
Barrameda, who was appointed bishop
of Rubicon by the Avignonese Pope,
while Bethencourt was still in the Canaries, but who apparently never occupied the see. The fact that this man,
and also Las Casas's successor, a certain Mendo de Viedma, both received
their bulls from Benedict XIII gives
strong ground for supposing that Las
Casas was also appointed from Avignon.
On the other hand, despite all that we
know of the inaccuracy of the 1482
manuscript of the Canarien, it is difficult to brush entirely aside an account

as full and circumstantial as that which
it gives of Bethencourt's journey to
Rome (cf. however, M. Valois's ingenious theory of the probable significance
of the phrase 'voyage de Rome' at this
period). Moreover, it will be observed
that King Henry III had strong reasons
for sending Bethencourt to apply to a
Roman Pope for bulls for a bishop whose
nomination incidentally prejudiced the
French claims to the overlordship of the
lands, and measurably strengthened his
own.

[1] The Canarian, ed. Major, pp. xxvi,
220; Millares, op. cit., iii, pp. 97–99, 101..
[2] The Canarian, ed. Major, pp.
xxxvi–xxxvii; Löher, op. cit., pp. 143–
146.

coupled with the memories of the claims and counter-claims of the fourteenth century, reawakened the long dormant conflict between Castile and Portugal over the possession of the islands. It continued for many years and became inextricably interwoven with other matters which embroiled the two realms. Prince Henry vigorously prosecuted the rights that he had acquired, the more so because the possession of the archipelago would obviously strengthen and facilitate Portuguese progress down the West African coast. Powerful expeditions were sent out in 1424–25 and again in 1445–47; but, owing to the valor of the native resistance and the protests of the king of Castile, they met with no success. The Venetian, Alvisi Cadamosto, also visited the islands in 1455, while in the service of Prince Henry the Navigator, and has left us a most interesting account of them.[1] Meantime on the Spanish side the title which Maciot had turned over to Barba de Campos was passed around with bewildering rapidity among a number of prominent Castilian families — the best possible evidence of the small amount of importance that was attached to it — until finally, in 1443, it fell to Ferdinand, a scion of the ancient house of Peraza.[2] Under this Ferdinand Peraza, and still more under his son-in-law, Diego de Herrera, who inherited his claims, renewed attempts were made to effect the subjugation and conversion of the western islands. But the old lust for slave hunting continued to cripple the efforts of the leaders. Heroic resistance by the natives prevented any effective success in Palma and the Grand Canary; and though the Guanches of Teneriffe showed themselves amenable to gentle treatment at the outset, a subsequent experience of Spanish treachery led to the expulsion of the

[1] *The Canarian*, ed. Major, pp. xxxiii-xxxvi; Eannes de Azurara, *Conquest* of *Guinea*, ed. Beasley, ii, pp. xcvii-xcviii. [2] Löher, *op. cit.*, p. 147.

invaders. Only in Lanzarote and Fuerteventura was Herrera's dominion in any sense fully established.[1]

The solution of all these rival claims was reached in a most unexpected manner. In 1455 King Henry the Impotent of Castile increased complications already great by disregarding Peraza's title, and conferring the islands on the Count of Atouguia, who had brought him his Portuguese bride; the latter sold them to the Marquis of Menisco, who promptly resold them to the Infante Ferdinand of Portugal, younger brother of King Affonso the African.[2] In 1466 an expedition was fitted out under the Portuguese count, Diego da Silva, to substantiate the claims of the Infante; but Diego de Herrera was on hand to oppose him with a force so impressive that da Silva took refuge in negotiations, which were measurably advanced by the fact that he fell promptly in love with Herrera's daughter.[3] The two were shortly afterwards betrothed, and Spaniards and Portuguese jointly attempted once more to carry their conquests to the western islands; but after various failures and repulses, Silva and his Portuguese followers tired of such a strenuous campaign, and longed to return to their native land. Herrera was not sorry to be so cheaply rid of one who, though at present friendly, might easily develop into a dangerous rival. The wedding of his daughter to Silva was celebrated at Lanzarote, and the happy pair departed for Lisbon, whither Herrera soon after followed them for the purpose of extinguishing any surviving Portuguese claims to the archipelago.[4] Meantime, on December 11, 1474, King Henry the Impotent died, and was succeeded by his sister, Isabella, who five years previously had married Ferdinand of Aragon. In addition to effecting

[1] Löher, pp. 164–170.
[2] The Canarian, ed. Major, introduction, p. xxxviii; Fernándes Duro,
Marina de Castilla, p. 253.
[3] Löher, p. 172.
[4] Löher, pp. 173–178.

the union of the crowns and expelling the Moors from
Granada, the royal pair were keenly desirous to carry their
conquests across the straits to Africa; and for this end
they recognized, as the Portuguese had done before them,
the great advantages of a firm foothold in the Canaries.
A series of complaints against the administration of Herrera
arrived most opportunely for their purpose; and the latter,
realizing that the cards were stacked against him, saw the
necessity of coming to an agreement. It was finally arranged that he and his heirs should be secured in the possession of Lanzarote and Fuerteventura, which had been thoroughly conquered, and of Ferro and Gomera, which were
at least partially so; but that they should yield to their
Catholic Majesties, for the sum of 5,000,000 maravedis,
all right to the as yet unsubjugated islands of Grand Canary,
Palma, and Teneriffe. This treaty, which marks the inception of the formal taking over of the archipelago by the
Castilian government, was signed at Seville, October 15,
1477. Herrera consoled himself for his losses by organizing
a series of terrible slave, camel, and cattle hunts on the
adjacent West African coast northward from Cape Bojador.
A fort was erected, attacks by the local Sherif and his followers were repulsed, and raids were organized far into the
interior. It is said that the Berber who served as Herrera's
guide on these expeditions died at Lanzarote in 1591 at
the age of one hundred and forty-six.[1]

Though it seems a far cry from the Canaries to Central
Asia, the spirit of foreign adventure and exploration which
swept over Castile during the reign of Henry III sufficed
to bridge the gap. Hitherto Spain had taken practically

[1] Abreu de Galindo, *Historia de la Conquista*, tr. Glas, p. 59; Viera y Cla-
vijo, *Noticias de la Historia de las Islas de Canaria*, i, pp. 475–486; Millares, *op. cit.*, iii, pp. 235–241.

no part in that extraordinary series of travels and missionary enterprises which immediately followed the age of the Crusades and gave to the states of Western Europe their first knowledge of the Far East. The period of the Polos and of Sir John Mandeville saw her too fully occupied with internal troubles to think of Asiatic exploration. Yet she was to contribute one last stirring scene to the first act of the great drama of the unveiling of the East, before the outbreak of anarchy beyond the Euxine and Caspian and the obstruction of the ancient trade routes by the advance of the Ottoman Turks caused the curtain to fall for another hundred years. The famous mission of Ruy Gonzalez de Clavijo to the court of the great Mongol conqueror Tamerlane deserves an honorable place in the history of Spanish enterprise beyond the seas.

A nation whose life work had been dedicated to the task of driving back the Saracens in the West, could not fail to regard with sympathetic interest the rise of a great empire to the eastward which was hostile to the Ottoman Turk. For nearly half a century the mighty Tamerlane had been building such an empire in the steppes of Asia on the ruins of different kingdoms which had been conquered by his barbarous Tartar hordes, and he was now advancing against the easternmost of the possessions of Bajazet I. Agreement in religion could obviously not long postpone the clash that was necessitated by the rival territorial ambitions of 'the two scourges of God'; and Henry III of Castile determined to inform himself concerning the power and intentions of the great Asiatic potentate whose advent on the confines of the western world promised, temporarily at least, to divert and check the onset of the more immediately terrible Turk. For this purpose he sent two knights, Pelayo de Sotomayor and Hernán Sanchez de Palazuelos, into Asia

Minor, where they witnessed, on July 20, 1402, the famous battle of Angora, in which Tamerlane conquered Bajazet and took him prisoner. After the fight Tamerlane learned of their presence and summóned them before him. Equalling Henry III in his appreciation of the value of a possible ally on the other side of the domains of his principal enemy, the Turk, he surpassed him in his curiosity concerning remote lands and the customs of their inhabitants, and eagerly availed himself of the opportunity to gratify it. The Castilians were most honorably entertained, and dismissed with gifts; and on their departure, they were accompanied by a Tartar ambassador bearing messages of admiration and friendship for Henry III, and by two lovely Christian ladies who had been rescued by Tamerlane from the harem of his Turkish rival.[1]

Henry III promptly responded to these amicable overtures by despatching direct to Tamerlane's court his chamberlain Ruy Gonzalez de Clavijo, a nobleman of Madrid, accompanied by two other persons, and also by the ambassador whom Tamerlane had sent to him. As the latter had retired eastward after his victory at Angora, and was finally found by Clavijo beyond the Oxus at Samarcand, the journey of Henry's representatives turned out to be considerably longer and more arduous than was expected. It has in fact been rightly designated as the "earliest important venture of the Spanish people overland." It started from St. Mary's Port, near Cadiz, on May 22, 1403; it returned to San Lucar on March 1, 1406.[2]

Clavijo kept a careful journal of his experiences, and his descriptions of the places through which he and his com-

[1] *Narrative of Ruy Gonsales de Clavijo*, tr. C. R. Markham for the Hakluyt Society, pp. ii ff.; Beasley, *Dawn of Modern Geography*, iii, pp. 332–335, and footnote on the authorities.

[2] Beasley, *Dawn of Modern Geography*, iii, pp. 335, 356.

panions passed constitute one of the most precious narratives of travel that have come down to us from the Middle Ages. They journeyed by sea as far as Trebizond, touching at Malaga, Naples, Messina, Rhodes, Mitylene, Constantinople, and Sinope by the way. From Trebizond their route lay overland through Erzingan, Tabriz, and Teheran, over the Murgab and the Oxus, which they crossed on a huge bridge of boats constructed by Tamerlane "for the passage of himself and his host." [1] On Monday, September 8, 1404, they reached Samarcand and were summoned into the presence of Tamerlane, whom they found "seated in a portal, in front of the entrance of a beautiful palace. . . . Before him there was a fountain, which threw up the water very high, and in it there were some red apples. . . . He was dressed in a robe of silk, with a high white hat on his head, on the top of which there was a spinal ruby, with pearls and precious stones round it. . . . Three Meerzas, who stood before the lord, and were his most intimate councillors, . . . came and took the ambassadors by the arms, [doubtless as a precaution in case they should prove to be assassins] and led them forward until they stood together before the lord." Tamerlane then asked after the Castilian monarch, saying, "'How is my son the king? is he in good health?' When the ambassadors had answered, Tamerlane turned to the knights who were seated around him, . . . and said, 'Behold! here are the ambassadors sent by my son the king of Spain, who is the greatest king of the Franks, and lives at the end of the world. These Franks are truly a great people, and I will give my benediction to the king of Spain, my son. It would have sufficed if he had sent you to me with the letter, and without the presents, so well satisfied am I to hear of his health and pros-

[1] Clavijo, *Narrative*, tr. Markham, p. 119.

perous state.'[1] . . . The ambassadors were then taken to
a room, on the right hand side of the place where the lord
sat; and the Meerzas, who held them by the arms, made
them sit below an ambassador, whom the emperor Chayscan,
lord of Cathay, had sent to Tamerlane to demand the yearly
tribute which was formerly paid."[2] This tribute, however,
had been suffered to lapse for nearly eight years, and Tamerlane was profoundly irritated that the Cathayan emperor
should have dared to demand its renewal; moreover, he was
quick to seize an opportunity for dramatic effect, and realized
that by publicly setting Clavijo above the representatives
of his Eastern overlord he could pay a most welcome com-
pliment to his 'Western son.' "When the lord saw the
ambassadors seated below the ambassador from the lord of
Cathay, he sent to order that they should sit above him,
and he below them. As soon as they were seated, one of
the Meerzas of the lord came and said to the ambassador of
Cathay, that the lord had ordered that those who were ambassadors from the king of Spain, his son and friend, should
sit above him; and that he who was the ambassador from
a thief and a bad man, his enemy, should sit below them;
and from that time, at the feasts and entertainments given
by the lord, they always sat in that order. The Meerza then
ordered the interpreter to tell the ambassadors what the
lord had done for them."[3]

Many and wonderful are the tales related by Clavijo
concerning his experiences at the court of Samarcand. The
feasts were horrible orgies: "sometimes the company
drank wine and at others they drank cream and sugar."
Caño, the wife of Tamerlane, "called the ambassadors
before her, and gave them to drink with her own hand, and

[1] Clavijo's *Narrative*, tr. Markham,
pp. 132 f.

[2] *Ibid.*, p. 133.
[3] *Ibid.*, pp. 133 f., 172.

she importuned Ruy Gonzalez for a long time, to make him
drink, for she would not believe that he never touched wine.
The drinking was such that some of the men fell down drunk
before her; and this was considered very jovial, for they
think that there can be no pleasure without drunken men." [1]
At one of the festivals, there were several terrible executions;
"the custom is, that when a great man is put to death, he
is hanged; but the meaner sort are beheaded." [2]   Tamerlane
had fourteen elephants, each one "equal in size to four or
five great bulls, and their bodies were quite shapeless, like
a full sack. Their legs were very thick, and the same size
all the way down, and the foot round and without hoofs,
but with five toes, each with a nail, like those of a black
man. . . .   They had much entertainment with these elephants, making them run with horses and with the people,
which was very diverting; and when they all ran together,
it seemed as if the earth trembled." [3]

Clavijo's embassy to the court of Tamerlane is usually
regarded by Spanish historians as an isolated event. It
occurred, as we have already pointed out, at the very end
of that long series of eastern travels initiated by the Polos
almost one hundred and fifty years before, and had no immediately tangible results. Yet on the other hand, if
taken in conjunction with the precisely contemporaneous
expedition of Bethencourt to the Canaries, it certainly indicates that the tide of enthusiasm for foreign discovery and
exploration was running strong in Castile in the opening
years of the fifteenth century. What set the tide in motion,
is difficult to tell; but the example of Portugal and possibly of
Italy, who were already in the field, was doubtless responsible
for much. Why it did not continue is, perhaps, an even

[1] Clavijo's *Narrative*, tr. Markham,
p. 148.
[2] *Ibid.*, p. 150.
[3] *Ibid.*, pp. 156–158.

harder problem; but the internal anarchy and confusion of the reigns of John II and Henry IV furnish the most obvious answer: Spain was too much disrupted at home to think of the prosecution of foreign colonization and conquest till the days of the Catholic Kings. Whatever the final explanation of these different problems, the embassy of Clavijo will always be remembered as an early proof of the Spaniard's passion for adventure in distant lands — of the quality which furnishes the key to his later conquests in the New World. It showed that he had the stuff in him of which empire builders are made. It also afforded an interesting precedent for the attempts which were to be made in the reigns of Charles V and of Philip III to establish relations between the kings of Spain and the shahs of Persia.[1]

[1] On these attempts see F. López de Gómara, *Annals of Charles V*, p. 97, note; P. de Sandoval, *Historia de Carlos V*, lib. xi, xxiv (fol. 593, vol. i of edition of 1614); *Comentarios de García de Silva y Figueroa de la embajada del rey don Felipe III al Rey de Persia*, ed. Sociedad de Bibliófilos Españoles (Madrid, 1903–05, 2 vols.).

BIBLIOGRAPHICAL NOTE

Contemporary Authorities. — The standard account of the first conquest of the Canaries is *Le Canarien*, otherwise called *Le livre de la conqueste et conversion des Canariens*, by two priests, Pierre Bontier (or Boutier) and Jean Le Verrier, who accompanied Bethencourt and Gadifer. All the earlier editions of this work, including that of R. H. Major for the Hakluyt Society in 1872, have been based on a manuscript of about the year 1482, which was revised to suit the views of the family of Bethencourt, and consequently depreciates the importance of his companion. The primitive record, however, was acquired by the British Museum in 1888, and was published at Paris in 1896 by Pierre Margry, in his *La conquête et les conquérants des Iles Canaries*, pp. 129–249; it gives, needless to add, a very different and much more accurate picture of the facts than any of the other editions. It breaks off, unfortunately, in the summer of 1404; so that for the later years of Bethencourt's career we have nothing better than Major's edition and the secondary works based on it. A full account of these and other earlier editions may be found in Margry's book, pp. 1–128, and a briefer one in C. R. Beazley's *Dawn of Modern Geography*, iii, pp. 444 f. Gomes Eannes de Azurara's *Chronica de Guiné*, tr. and ed. C. R. Beazley and Edgar Prestage for the Hakluyt Society (London, 1896–99, 2 vols.), was written in 1452–53; it gives much useful information about the Portuguese in the Canaries.

Ruy Gonzalez de Clavijo, *Historia del Gran Tamorlan, é itinerario y enarracion del Viage, y relacion dela Embajada*, was published in the *Colección de Crónicas de Castilla*, vol. iii (1782), with an introduction by Gonzalo Argote de Molina. It was translated into English and edited for the Hakluyt Society by C. R. Markham (London, 1859); cf. *ante*, p. 160.

Later Works. — Juan de Abreu de Galindo, *Historia de la Conquista de las Islas Canarias*, written in 1632, but first published in an English translation by the Scotchman George Glas at London in 1764, and José de Viera y Clavijo, *Noticias de la Historia General de las Islas de Canaria* (Madrid, 1772–83, 4 vols.), are both valuable. Fuller information about these and other works may be found on pp. 30–65 of Franz von Löher's *Das Kanarierbuch* (Munich, 1895), which is useful for the period of conquest and colonization, but unsound on the ethnological side; cf. *ante*, p. 142, note. The most elaborate modern account of the Canaries is to be found in Agustin Millares, *Historia General de las Islas Canarias* (Las Palmas, 1893–95, 10 vols. in 5). The two portly volumes of Gregorio Chil y Naranjo, *Estudios históricos, climatológicos, y patológicos de las Islas Canarias* (Las Palmas, 1876–80), contain a good deal of miscellaneous information and some excellent maps: historically, however, they are scarcely abreast of modern scholarship. C. R. Beazley's *The Dawn of Modern Geography* (London, 1897-1906, 3 vols.) is the standard account of the early explorations of the surface of the globe, and is invaluable for the two enterprises with which the chapter deals.

CHAPTER IV

THE MEDIAEVAL CASTILIANS

From what has been already said concerning the predominant Spanish tendency towards internal separatism and differentiation, it will be readily inferred that the task of portraying the social, constitutional, and economic condition of the Iberian Peninsula at the close of the Middle Ages is unusually difficult and complex. The only generalization which can be made with absolute accuracy is that generalization is impossible. In every realm of life diversity and variety are the invariably conspicuous facts. There are, in the first place, innumerable lines of cleavage between the two great component parts of Spain — between Castile on the west, and the realms of the Crown of Aragon on the east. In their aims and ideals, in the character and aspirations of their inhabitants, in their social, institutional, and economic life, the two kingdoms were utterly divergent. Then again, within each of the two realms the process of differentiation continues, until the student finds himself confronted with a vast number of apparently unrelated petty units — social, geographical, institutional, and economic. Indeed the process goes so far that the units ultimately become almost indistinguishable from individuals. Another kindred fact which greatly enhances the difficulty of our problem, particularly in Castile, is the wide gulf which separated theory from practice. To read in Las Siete Partidas one might imagine that the mediaeval Castilian government was an effective royal absolutism, tempered perhaps by an unusually large measure of democratic power in municipal affairs, and of popular participation in the Cortes. As a matter of fact, both king and third estate were practically dominated by the rebel aristocracy during most of the two centuries previous to the accession of Ferdinand and Isabella — that is, during the period when the institutional development of the realm made its most rapid strides. In other words, the character of the subject before us does not lend itself to the summarized treatment prescribed for a book which attempts to cover as wide a field as does this. Abridgment, though necessary, is even more than usually likely to give rise to misconceptions.

Let us begin our inquiry by taking up the different ranks and classes of which mediaeval Castilian society was composed, and the conditions under which they occupied the land.

Next below the king, whose positions and powers may best be described in another place, there come, first of all, the nobles. As a class they had inherited high traditions of independence and power from later Visigothic days. Throughout the age of the Reconquest they had improved the various periods of weakness of the monarchy to intrench themselves firmly in the enjoyment of their innumerable privileges and immunities ; and in the period just previous to the accession of the Catholic Kings they reached the summit of their power. Neither sovereign above, nor burgess below could withstand them ; and they made the continuance of peace and efficient government impossible throughout the land.[1] Of these nobles there were, broadly speaking, three different categories: the *ricos hombres*, or, as they came to

[1] Colmeiro, *Curso*, pp. 348–389.

be called in the fourteenth and fifteenth centuries, *grandes* ;
the *infanzones* or *hidalgos* ; and the *caballeros*. Authorities
differ widely as to the precise meaning to be attached to
these different distinctions, but their divergent conclusions
may perhaps be roughly summarized as follows. The title
of *rico hombre* or *grande* at the head of the list, though it
might occasionally be given in recognition of notable services
or as a meed of valor, was primarily indicative of ancient and
noble lineage 'beyond the power of the king to confer.'[1]
That of *hidalgo*, on the other hand, though its very name[2]
connotes distinguished ancestry, came gradually to be
granted as a reward of merit, or of wealth, and was sold so
frequently by the crown as to lose its original significance,
and to become the broad general term most frequently used
to indicate the rank and file of the Castilian aristocracy.[3]
The title of *caballero* also, though it was at first only applied
to men of noble birth, was afterwards conferred on chosen
warriors who went forth to fight equipped with arms and a
horse at their own expense — thus indicating how from an
early date the career of a soldier was held to be a sure road
to social distinction in Castile.[4] Along with these general
categories, the special titles of duke and count make their
appearance in the twelfth century, and that of marquis in

[1] Colmeiro, *Curso*, pp. 393–396 ; *Partida* iv, tit. xxv, ley 10 ; Salazar de Mendoza, *Dignidades Seglares de Castilla*, lib. i, cap. ix ; Salazar y Castro, *Historia de la Casa de Lara*, lib. v, cap. viii ; Moreno de Vargas, *Discursos de la Nobleza* (1659), ff. 17, 51.

[2] Probably from the word 'adalingi,' which meant 'nobles' among the Visigoths and the Lombards, though some derive it from *hijo d'algo*, that is 'son of something,' or 'person of some property'; on the other hand, it may possibly come from *Italicus*, that is, one enjoying the rights of full Roman citizenship or his descendants. Cf. A. Du

Boys, *Histoire du droit criminel en Espagne*, p. 39, note ; Colmeiro, *Curso*, p. 400 ; *Fuero Viejo de Castilla*, lib. i, tit. v, ley 16 ; *Partida* ii, tit. xxi, leyes 2 and 3.

[3] Colmeiro, *Curso*, p. 401 ; Gounon-Loubens, *Essais sur la Castille*, pp. 76–78.

[4] Colmeiro, *Curso*, pp. 399 f. ; *Partida* ii, tit. xxi, ley 14. An *Informe de la Imperial Ciudad de Toledo sobre pesos y medidas*, probably by A. M. Burriel, Madrid, 1780, p. 313, discusses the way in which a *labrador* could make himself a *caballero*.

the fourteenth. The first two were of Visigothic origin and were revived after a period of temporary desuetude by Henry II and Alfonso XI ; that of marquis was granted for the first time by Henry II.[1] Recipients of these dignities, though often deficient in ancientness and nobility of lineage, were for all practical purposes on a par with the *ricos hombres* or *grandes*. The hereditary character of these last three titles was only gradually established ; originally they were held for the lifetime of the recipient, and the remembrance of that fact not infrequently enabled later kings on flimsy pretexts to revoke hastily granted donations and to interrupt lineal successions.[2]

We pass from these different grades to the privileges which they conferred. All the rank and file of the Castilian aristocracy held themselves to be generally exempt from direct taxation ; from imprisonment or seizure of property for debt ; from derogatory punishment such as chastisement with rods or death by the hangman ; and, save in cases of treason and a few other exceptional crimes, from torture.[3] In theory they were preferred over the burgesses in the distribution of offices and other royal favors ; they had a separate place in processions ; and, if arrested, they were confined in a separate prison. They all were entitled to the *riepto* and *desafío*, that is, to the right to avenge an injury or insult and to prove their valor in a formal judicial duel in the presence of the king and twelve of their peers.[4] But the special privileges inherent in the upper ranks of this curiously subdivided baronage go much further still. The *rico hombre*, at the head of the list, could display a standard and a cauldron, as em-

---

[1] Godoy Alcántara, *Ensayo sobre apellidos Castellanos* (Madrid, 1871), pp. 163 f.; Colmeiro, *Curso*, pp. 395 f.

[2] Salazar y Castro, *Historia de la Casa de Lara*, lib. viii, cap. vi; Salazar de Mendoza, *Dignidades Seglares*, lib. iii, caps. xv ff.

[3] Arce y Otalora, *Summa Nobilitatis Hispanicae* (Granada, 1553), p. 344.

[4] Altamira, § 447; Du Boys, *op. cit.*, pp. 113–115.

blems of his cherished right to raise and maintain an army
at his own expense.[1] He had the undoubted prerogative of
renouncing his obedience to his king and sovereign without
further ceremony than sending a follower to make declaration thereof as follows : "Sir, for so and so I kiss your hand,
and from henceforth he is no longer your vassal."[2] He
possessed, theoretically at least, an important place in the
royal councils ; he could remain seated and retain his hat in
the royal presence ; when he entered the royal chamber
the queen rose to receive him. Within his own domains
he often exercised criminal and civil jurisdiction, "saving always the high justice of the king ;" he levied taxes, and even
granted fueros, which were usually confirmed by the crown ;
in some cases the royal officers were forbidden to enter his
lands to collect revenue, punish criminals, or attach their
goods.[3] Next below him, the hidalgo was considerably less
fortunate, especially in the measure of his authority and
jurisdiction within his own estates ; and the caballeros in
turn lacked much which the hidalgos possessed. Still,
taken as a whole, it is impossible to deny that the Castilian
aristocracy was possessed of privileges thoroughly incompatible with orderly or centralized government and inimical
to the best interests of the state. The strange jumble of the
trivial and the important in this long list of baronial prerogatives is particularly significant. It shows that the Castilian nobles could not distinguish the form from the substance of power, and that they knew not how to make a
modest use of their liberties ; it indicates little political sagacity, but unlimited *amour propre*. Yet it would be an
error to regard them as totally deficient in good qualities.

---

[1] Colmeiro, *Curso*, p. 395.
[2] *Fuero Viejo*, lib. i, tit. iii, ley 4 ; cf.,
however, note on the *Fuero Viejo* on p.
288, *infra*.
[3] Colmeiro, *Curso*, pp. 395, 409;
Mariéjol, p. 282.

They certainly formed the backbone of the Castilian armies in the great struggle of the Reconquest, to which the hidalgos proudly boasted that they went of their own free will, at the invitation and not at the orders of the crown.[1] They kept alive more than any one else the military qualities of the Castilian nation, and the high traditions of the profession of arms. If they were a constant menace to their sovereign at home, they were to prove exceedingly valuable in winning new realms for him abroad, in the age of imperial expansion which was so soon to come.

In other countries of mediaeval Europe we are accustomed to attribute the excessive power of the nobles to the opportunities afforded them by the feudal structure of society; it may, therefore, seem difficult to reconcile the extraordinary rights and privileges of the aristocracy of Castile which we have just enumerated with the fact that there was never a fully developed feudal system there.[2] Local conditions — particularly the constantly shifting boundary and the agricultural poverty of the meseta — were distinctly unfavorable to it: "Castile yielded to the current that pushed the world towards feudalism indeed, but did not abandon herself to it." Like Anglo-Saxon England, she possessed "much feudalism but no feudal system." For the act of alienating land by lord to vassal was not *regularly* accompanied in mediaeval Castile by the setting up of the same complicated array of reciprocal rights and obligations by which, under a thoroughly organized feudal system, the two parties to the bargain were almost inextricably bound together. The process here was, in theory at least, much more simple.

[1] Gounon-Loubens, *op. cit.*, p. 78.

[2] Castilian feudalism is still a highly controversial topic. We have no occasion to explore it minutely. The best general account is to be found in Gama Barros, *Historia da Administração Publica em Portugal*, i, pp. 89–206; other standard authorities are given in the succeeding pages and in the bibliographical note at the end of the chapter. Cf. also *Fuero Viejo*, lib. i, tits. iii, iv; *Partida* iv, tit. xxvi.

Ownership as a general rule was granted fully and unreservedly with land, but the crown usually managed to avoid the alienation of political authority with it [1]; so that the vassal was seldom legally entitled to anything like the same measure of jurisdiction over the inhabitants of his domains that he would have had in a thoroughly feudal country like France. To this latter rule there are of course numerous exceptions. The various rights granted to the *ricos hombres*, as described in the preceding paragraph, show that the monarchy occasionally permitted its greatest vassals to exercise powers on their own estates which were wholly incompatible with the maintenance of effective political authority in the hands of the crown. A few instances have even been found in Castile of conditions which possibly justify the statement that the only difference between feudalism there and in other countries is a difference in quantity, not in quality.[2] But it is scarcely fair to argue from special cases such as these. As a general rule the ties that united suzerain and vassal in mediaeval Castile were much too loose and too impermanent to be comparable with those created by a full-fledged feudal system. They could be broken, as we have already seen, at the shortest possible notice.[3] There was no feudal hierarchy. On the basis of the powers which they possessed under the codes, the Castilian aristocracy should have been far less turbulent and troublesome for the central government than the nobles of a country where feudalism was firmly established; it was only the weakness and lack of statesmanship of the majority of the monarchs that permitted the magnates to usurp authority and privileges to which they had no just title, and thus to become a menace to all law and order in the land. Moreover, the

[1] *Fuero Viejo*, lib. i, tit. i, ley 1.
[2] Cf. J. Puyol y Alonso, *El Abadengo de Sahagún: Contribucion al estudio del* *Feudalismo en España*.
[3] *Partida* iv, tit. xxv, ley 10.

evil increased after the middle of the thirteenth century, at the very moment when with the gradual breakup of feudalism in Western Europe it began elsewhere to diminish. There are two chief reasons for this. In the first place the slackening tide of the Reconquest deprived the barons of an outlet for their restless energies in foreign war, and thus increased their proneness to internal revolt. In the second, the power of the aristocracy was enormously enhanced by the institution in the reign of Alfonso X of the *mayorazgos* or great entailed estates.[1] Originally, like their monarchs above them, the nobles had weakened themselves by dividing their domains among their children. Now at last they had perceived their error; and by establishing the principle of primogeniture they handed on their lands undiminished to their heirs, thus perpetuating from generation to generation all the various powers and prerogatives which inevitably went with them.

Next after the nobles come, of course, the clergy, whose valuable services in preaching and supporting the crusade against the Moors as a sacred duty obligatory to all had been rewarded since the earliest days of the Reconquest by numerous grants and privileges. Like the nobles, they were exempt from the payment of regular taxes; in fact, there were certain local levies to which the nobles contributed which the clergy refused to pay. Many of the other privileges of *hidalguía*, such as immunity from certain penalties, or the right to the sum of fifteen hundred sueldos as an indemnity for a blow, were conferred on different groups of clerics at different times by different kings.[2] Often these

---

[1] J. Sempere y Guarinos, *Historia de los Vínculos y Mayorazgos* (2d ed., 1847), especially pp. 85 ff.

[2] J. de Covarrubias, *Máximas sobre recursos* (Madrid, 1829), i, pp. 80 ff.; Colmeiro, *Curso*, pp. 454–457; Altamira, § 429.

privileges were gradually extended so as to be enjoyed not merely by their original recipients, but also by their servants, dependents, and relatives. Meantime the landed possessions and personal property of the clerics increased by leaps and bounds. They were the beneficiaries not only of the royal munificence, but of that of every other estate in the realm as well. Many of the bishops became virtually kings in the territories immediately adjacent to their sees, for the monarchs deliberately divested themselves of their sovereign rights in their favor, and even suffered the episcopal power to extend to the maintenance of special armies to defend the ecclesiastical lands against attacks from neighboring nobles and foreign foes.[1] There can be no doubt that the church rendered numerous services — economic and administrative, as well as military and religious — in return for the privileges which it received from the government. There are constant references in the charters and chronicles of the early periods of the Reconquest to the skill and energy of the clergy in reclaiming the devastated lands, and in tilling the arid soil of the meseta.[2] But the very fact that the interests of the clerics had become so miscellaneous necessarily encroached upon their ecclesiastical activities, and, as time went on, considerably diminished their prestige in the eyes of the mass of the people; certainly their wealth, power, and luxury were a constant source of complaint from the Cortes of the fourteenth and fifteenth centuries.[3] A large portion of the laymen, however, preferred to accept the

[1] Altamira, § 199; Colmeiro, *Curso*, pp. 429–453; A. López Peláez, *El señorío temporal de los obispos de Lugo* (Corunna, 1897).

[2] Cf., e.g., the Valpuesta charter of 804, in *España Sagrada*, xxvi, p. 442. Even if we accept M. Barrau Dihigo's theory that all Leonese and Castilian documents dated before 950 are to be rejected, the evidence on this point is

so abundant that it is impossible to ignore it.

[3] The immorality of the Castilian clerics was of course notorious. The institution of *barraganía*, or licensed clerical concubinage, was universal, open, and avowed. The pomp and adornments of the *barragana* were a thorn in the side of the wives of laymen, and a fruitful cause of angry protest by the na-

situation as it was, and if possible to make capital out of it for themselves. So valuable was the possession of ecclesiastical privilege from a purely mundane point of view, that many essentially nonclerical persons obtained admission to the ranks of the churchmen, and then, having secured to themselves all the rights and immunities inherent in that status, continued to devote themselves to business, law, and even to the occupations of mountebank and buffoon, thus bringing into contempt and disrepute the sacred calling which they had outwardly embraced.[1]

The ecclesiastical hierarchy of archbishops, bishops, and their subordinates was substantially the same in Castile as in other Western European lands. As elsewhere, too, there was a prolonged contest between king and clergy over their respective shares in the important matter of ecclesiastical appointments; and in the early fourteenth century this struggle became three-cornered through the papal claim to the right to 'provide' to certain benefices — a pretension which was resented the more in that it was usually exercised in favor of foreigners, "to the great prejudice of our people and the common weal." The Cortes made vigorous complaints against this practice, which naturally increased apace during the period of the Babylonian Captivity and the Schism, but the monarchs failed effectively to press the national cause at the papal curia. The matter remained in an unsettled and highly unsatis-

tional assembly, but no real improvement was effected till the accession of the Catholic Kings. It is, however, only fair to add that the laymen were equally guilty in this respect: and it is interesting and significant to observe in this connection that there was almost no stigma attaching to illegitimate birth in mediaeval Castile. Indeed, the dignities and emoluments which the natural children of monarchs and of the great magnates often attained were so numerous that one is inevitably reminded of the scathing words of Saint-Simon on the ways of the court of Louis XIV — "The best of all estates was that of bastardy." Cf. Altamira, § 306; Mariéjol, pp. 266, 279; H. C. Lea, *History of Sacerdotal Celibacy*, cap. xix.

[1] *Cortes*, i, pp. 330 f., 403 (Medina del Campo, 1318, pet. 2; Madrid, 1329, pet. 4) · Altamira, § 429.

factory condition down to the accession of the Catholic Kings.[1]

The members of the great orders of military knighthood demanded for themselves the privileges of the clergy and of the aristocracy as well.[2] The ever-present necessity of driving back the Moor rendered the soil of mediaeval Spain particularly favorable to the growth and progress of these institutions : some of which were indigenous, while others, like the Templars and the Knights of St. John of Jerusalem, were merely branches of orders which had been instituted abroad.   Those of purely Castilian origin were three in number.   The oldest was that of Calatrava, founded in 1158 and confirmed by the Pope in 1164, in celebration of the fact that certain soldier monks had successfully defended the town and fortress of that name, which the Templars had been unable to hold against the Almohades.[3]   The beginnings of the order of Santiago are more obscure; despite the fact that it disputed the priority of that of Calatrava, there seems no question that its formal establishment must be placed at least a decade later.   It apparently arrogated to itself the special duty and privilege of protecting the pilgrims who journeyed to the shrine of Compostela.[4]   The order of Alcántara originated in an attempt of Ferdinand II of Leon to introduce that of Calatrava (which was founded in Castile) within his own realm.   The members of the new branch, however, were unable to endure the idea of subjection to a body which originated in another state ; and before

[1] Colmeiro, *Curso*, pp. 457–463, and references to the cuadernos there.

[2] F. Caro de Torres, *Historia de las Ordenes Militares* (Madrid, 1629) ; Colmeiro, *Curso*, pp. 465–471 ; Altamira, § 427. For additional details of. the *Bullaria* of the three orders (Calatrava, edd. I. J. Ortega y Cotes and others, Madrid, 1761 ; Santiago, edd. F. Aguado

de Córdova and others, Madrid, 1719 ; Alcántara, edd. I. J. Ortega y Cotes and others, Madrid, 1759).

[3] Contestación of Manuel Danvila to F. R. de Uhagon in the latter's *Ordenes Militares* (Madrid, 1898 : *Discurso de la R. A. H.*), p. 125.

[4] Colmeiro, *Curso*, p. 466 ; Altamira, § 298.

long they obtained from Lucius III (in 1183) the privilege of complete independence, and adopted the name of the town of Alcántara, which the king of Leon had conferred on them as their headquarters.[1] Down to the middle of the thirteenth century these orders did noble service against the Moors, and were rewarded by a constant stream of privileges and dignities and donations in money and land, by dint of which they were able to constitute themselves veritable *regna in regno*.[2] But the coincidence of this immense accretion of wealth and power with the virtual cessation of the crusading work which they had been called into existence to perform subsequently converted them into a grievous menace to the state. They exchanged the high ideals of their earlier days for the selfish ambitions characteristic of the mass of the Castilian aristocracy; and their power and the extent of their lands made them a rallying point for malcontents. The extinction of the Templars in Castile in 1312 — sequel and counterpart of their abolition four years previously in France — was indubitably a heavy blow to the morale of the other orders, whose internal discipline and condition deteriorated rapidly in the succeeding years. They had in fact outlived their usefulness and were devoting their energies to unworthy ends. The grand master of each one of them was a serious rival to the monarchy; a combination of them all might conceivably overthrow it. One of the very first measures adopted by Ferdinand and Isabella to bring order out of chaos, and to cause a strong central government to prevail in the land, was to terminate the independence of these ancient and powerful institutions.

[1] Caro de Torres, *op. cit.*, ff. 51–53; Colmeiro, *Curso*, p. 467, and references there.

[2] Cf. Fernándes Llamasares, *Historia de las Ordenes Militares* (Madrid, 1862), *passim*; Alvares de Araujo, *Recopilación histórica de las Ordenes Militares* (Madrid, 1866), *passim*; there is a valuable map at the end of this latter volume.

We now turn from the upper ranks of society to the middle
and lower classes. These were subdivided, like every group
of the population of Castile, into a bewildering number of
different categories and varieties, but for our purposes it
will be most convenient to classify and consider them under
two main heads — rural and urban.

The conditions of the rural portion of the third estate were
largely moulded, like those of the clergy and baronage, by the
peculiar circumstances of the war of the Reconquest. The
repeopling of the devastated lands, as the Christians gradually advanced to the southward, constituted a most difficult
problem, and reacted on the whole unfavorably upon the en-
franchisement of the lower classes; for the dangers of living
in a spot exposed to Moorish attack were so obvious and
imminent that few could be induced to settle there without
the promise of protection from nobles or king. Protection
would not be accorded without demanding service in return;
so that the mass of the agricultural population remained in
varying degrees of slavery, semi-slavery, or dependence upon
the magnates as the price of the latter's support. Down to the
end of the twelfth century, at least, they not unnaturally considered their safety first, to the detriment of their aspirations
towards liberty.[1] Gradually there emerged, however, groups
of men who were willing to settle in dangerous territory in
return for a larger measure of autonomy.[2] They were by no
means ready as yet entirely to dispense with royal or baro-

---

[1] Colmeiro, *Curso*, pp. 133 ff.

[2] And also, frequently, for other special rights and immunities, such as a place of asylum for lawbreakers. The monarchy soon discovered that this last privilege was exceedingly effective in attracting restless characters, who, though elsewhere dangerous, were valuable assets on the frontier; and the kings made frequent use of it to that end. A grant of the year 1027 by Alfonso V of Leon and Urraca his wife to the church of Lugo (R. A. H. Mss., Privilegios y Escrituras de las Iglesias de España, vol. iii, pt. ii, fol. 57) throws much light on this. The whole question has been admirably treated in a hitherto unpublished doctoral dissertation by Dr. C. E. McGuire on the *History of the Right of Asylum in Spain*; a typewritten copy may be found in the Harvard College Library.

nial protection, but they demanded at least the privilege of selecting their own lord. Thus originated the *benefactoria* or *behetrías* [1], as they were called, of which there were two kinds — the *behetrías de linaje* or *de entre parientes*, which were obliged to choose their protector from the members of one family, and the *behetrías de mar á mar*, which could select him anywhere within the boundaries of the realm. The latter, if the master that they had chosen failed to give satisfaction, had the right to change him, and even to repeat this process "up to seven times in one day." [2] Below these were the various grades of the *tierras de señorío*. The *cultivadores libres* paid tribute to the king or one of the great feudal lords, in return for the permission to till a portion of their territories and make their living thereon; they might abandon their master if they chose to do so, but lost their lands in consequence. The serfs below them were subdivided into various minor categories.[3] They enjoyed some personal rights and privileges, but, generally speaking, were *adscripti glebae* — that is, inseparable, either by their own volition or the act of their masters, from the land on which they worked. The slave at the bottom of the social structure could hold no property of any kind; but his master, even in the darkest periods, was not entirely absolved from responsibility for the elementary needs of his existence.[4]

Such in brief was the very complicated situation which obtained among the lower and middle classes on the agricultural lands in the period of the height of the Reconquest. In the last two centuries before the accession of Ferdinand

[1] On the etymology of this word cf. *Índice de los documentos de Sahagún en Archivo Historico Nacional* (Madrid, 1874), pp. 272, 594.

[2] *Fuero Viejo*, lib. i, tit. viii; T. Muñoz y Romero, *Estado de Personas en Asturias y León*, pp. 139 ff.; Colmeiro, *Curso*, pp. 608 f.

[3] "Los Solariegos en León y Castilla" by F. Aznar Navarro, in *Cultura Española* (1906), pp. 4–26, 299–326; Muñoz y Romero, *Estado de Personas*, pp. 7–106.

[4] Colmeiro, *Curso*, pp. 597 ff.; Altamira, §§ 195 f.

and Isabella, however, numerous changes and improvements had occurred. In the first place, a general movement of emancipation of the slaves had taken place; the influence of the church, the increasing need of free men to repeople the conquered lands, the efforts of the slaves themselves, and the fact that the cities almost invariably granted aid and protection to fugitives, combined to bring about this happy result. Save for captives taken in the Moorish wars, or in expeditions to unknown lands like the Canaries, there was probably no one left in fifteenth-century Castile who had not succeeded in winning complete *personal* freedom; so that slavery in the full sense of the term had virtually ceased to exist there.[1] Moreover, the lot of the *solariegos* or serfs improved immensely at the same time. Both economically and socially their condition was generally ameliorated by (1) the increasingly strict definition and limitation of the tributes due from them to their masters, (2) the loosening of the ties which bound them to the land on which they worked, and (3) the frequent recognition of their right to marry without their lords' consent.[2] It is, however, even more dangerous than usual to lay down any general rules in this matter; and we must not for one moment imagine that the privileges just mentioned attained anything approaching universal application. In the fourteenth century, when there are numerous evidences of a reactionary movement, it was maintained in certain districts of Castile, notwithstanding all laws to the contrary, that the lord "had the right to take the body of his serf and all that he has in the world."[3] But certainly the status of the servile classes in

[1] Colmeiro, *Curso*, pp. 600–605.

[2] *Partida* iv, tit. xxv, ley 3; Altamira, §§ 276, 431.

[3] *Fuero Viejo*, lib. i, tit. vii, ley 1. The reader should perhaps be warned against taking in too literal fashion such provisions as this and the corresponding law in Aragon, which declares that in case the lord's land is divided up among his children, each of the serfs who lived on it could be "divided in pieces with it." The mediaeval Spanish jurist had

Castile during this period was distinctly preferable to that
of the corresponding portion of the population in Aragon,
as will be more apparent in subsequent pages. The most
salient characteristic of the mediaeval Castilian has often
been described as impatience of restraint and desire to
shake off all authority. As manifested in the upper ranks
of society, this trait was productive of many evils, and rendered order and strong government impossible. It may,
however, be plausibly argued that lower down in the scale
it engendered aspirations towards liberty, which survived
the absolutism of the Hapsburgs and the early Bourbons,
and proved the salvation of the national fortunes in a later
age.

Meantime, while the emancipation of the lower orders
had been progressing, the condition of the inhabitants of the
behetrías tended to deteriorate. No more striking example
could be desired of the wild confusion of titles and jurisdictions which characterized land tenure in mediaeval Castile
than that afforded by the situation in these holdings in the
fourteenth and fifteenth centuries.[1] The unrestricted right
of the *behetrías de mar á mar* to change and choose their protectors at their own discretion gave rise to numerous dissensions and clashes. In the *behetrías de linaje* the rights
and privileges of the overlord were often divided up among
the different members of his family, so that, instead of one
master, the *behetría* not seldom had three or four. When
the king intervened to remedy these difficulties, the usual
result of his efforts was to add himself to the already exces-

---

a mania for drawing absolutely logical
conclusions, no matter how improbable
the result from a practical point of view.
It would be hazardous to infer that such
regulations as the above reflected actual
conditions in the ordinary life of
mediaeval Castile. Cf. F. Kern, "Die
mittelalterliche Anschauung vom
Recht," in *Historische Zeitschrift*, cxv,
pp. 496–515.

[1] Altamira, § 451; Rafael de Floranes, "Apuntamientos sobre behetrías," in *D. I. E.*, xx, pp. 407–475.

sive number of suzerains which he was attempting to diminish. Manifold difficulties also resulted from the fact that many *pueblos de solariego*, or groups of serfs, attempted to convert themselves into *behetrías*, or at least to seek annexation to them, thus rendering confusion worse confounded. The *Becerro de las Behetrías* [1] — a sort of Domesday Book of the time of Pedro the Cruel — describes this curious network of conflicting rights and jurisdictions in great detail. Certainly things had reached such a pass that reform was quite impossible. Nothing short of abolition by royal command, or extinction through internal decadence, could really remedy the situation which had come into being. It was the second of these two possibilities that actually occurred. The prevailing anarchy and confusion of the period immediately preceding the accession of the Catholic Kings made protection more desirable than autonomy, and the nobler aspirations of earlier days sank temporarily into the background. The comparative freedom of the *behetrías* was no longer attractive, and we find constant petitions from their inhabitants to be converted into *pueblos de solariego*. The close of the Middle Ages, then, saw a meeting of the extremes of the long list of categories into which the bulk of the agricultural population had in previous centuries been divided. A general levelling and simplifying process had in fact taken place, from which the large majority of the persons concerned had unquestionably derived advantage. The situation, however, in this as in other matters was far from satisfactory, and was bound to remain so until the overpowerful magnates were curbed and prevented from transgressing the laws of the land.[2]

Far more interesting and important than the development

[1] Printed in 1866; cf. bibliographical note, *infra*, p. 203.

[2] Colmeiro, *Curso*, pp. 609–611; Altamira, § 451.

of the agricultural communities is that of the Castilian cities. We have already seen that the natural conditions of the Iberian Peninsula favored the tendency to concentrate in urban communities. In Roman and in Visigothic days the cities had attained a high degree of importance — the constant state of war contributing still further to foster the natural inclination of the population to seek safety by gathering together behind fortified walls. Whether the constitution of the mediaeval Spanish municipality can be directly traced back to Roman or even to Visigothic days is perhaps the most eagerly debated question in mediaeval Spanish history.[1] Whatever the final verdict on the question of lineal descent may be, we cannot doubt that the high traditions of municipal organization inherited by the mediaeval Castilian from his predecessors favored the evolution of a type of urban constitution which, at its height, gave scope to all that was highest and best in the political life of the time.

Before proceeding further in our consideration of the Castilian municipalities, we must pause to explain some of the principal meanings of a word which one encounters in every phase of mediaeval Spanish history — namely, the term *fuero*. It is descended from the Latin *forum*, one of whose meanings is a tribunal or court, but in Spanish its primary significance is a constitution or code of laws. A fuero, however, was quite as frequently a law of special as of general application; the *Fuero Viejo*, for instance, purported to be a code of privileges of the aristocracy.[2] More often still, a fuero might be granted to the inhabitants of a

[1] The principal modern authorities are the *Discursos* of Seijas Lozano and the Marquis de Pidal before the R. A. H., in 1853 (the gist of these is printed on pp. 300–312 of Pidal's *Lecciones sobre la historia del gobierno y legislación de España*, Madrid, 1880, of which see also pp. 117–158); A. Sacristan y Martinez,

Municipalidades de Castilla y Leon, pp. 27 ff.; E. de Hinojosa, *Historia general del Derecho Español*, i, pp. 238–273, and *Estudios sobre la historia del Derecho Español*, pp. 5–70; Altamira, §§ 58, 59, 134, 202, 289–292, 450.

[2] Cf. *infra*, p. 238, note.

certain locality, and thus become, in effect, a constitution or set of privileges for that particular spot, which the inhabitants invariably defended with the utmost resolution, down to the minutest detail, against encroachment by crown or magnates, in spite of the fact that it was often in manifest contradiction to the provisions of the general law of the land. The number and variety of these local fueros which were given out at different times by different sovereigns, and also, through delegated or usurped authority, by the greater lords and higher clergy, was probably the most fruitful cause of the social and constitutional diversity of mediaeval Castile. 'Though not infrequently granted to rural communities, they were principally employed to encourage the founding of cities, and it is in that connection that we have to consider them here.

The problem of repeopling the conquered lands was in reality far more urban than rural. The boundaries were continually shifting; land which had been captured one day, was likely to be raided and possibly recaptured by the enemy the next. The 'neutral zone' between the rival forces could not possibly be occupied by a scattered and consequently defenceless agricultural population; it was essential for those who ventured to take possession of it to concentrate and intrench themselves in compact groups — in other words, to found cities. Even with this precaution, the sovereigns had to offer strong inducements to persuade their subjects to settle in these outposts of Christendom; and the most obvious of these inducements was to grant to them, as to the agricultural communities which followed on behind, a considerable measure of autonomy in return for the risks which they ran. Consequently, the fueros, constitutions, or charters of the newly founded Castilian cities contained from the very first a greater or lesser number of concessions of the right of self-government. The sovereign voluntarily divested himself in their favor of certain political and judicial powers which normally belonged only to the crown. The measure of their autonomy was obviously, *ceteris paribus*, the degree to which the position which they occupied was exposed; and the terms of their different fueros varied, in general, accordingly. At first the diversity of these fueros was absolutely unchecked; there was a new constitution for each new town; but they all had certain features in common, and as time went on it became the practice to make increasingly frequent use of certain model charters — to grant to a newly founded municipality, for example, the Fuero of Leon or of Sepúlveda — and thus, in some small measure at least, to standardize the methods of local government. Variety rather than homogeneity was doubtless still the rule; but there is at least a sufficient degree of family resemblance between the various municipal constitutions to warrant an attempt to summarize their most striking features.[1]

Almost all the municipal fueros began by granting the inhabitants the right to form a general assembly, *concilium* or *concejo*.[2] It was ordinarily composed of the *vecinos* — heads of families or property owners [3] — and often included

[1] The standard collection of Spanish municipal fueros is that of Muñoz y Romero (Madrid, 1847), of which only one volume was ever published. Many of the fueros of the more important towns have also been separately edited, often with valuable annotations by different scholars: those of Sepúlveda by Feliciano Callejas (1857), of Santiago by Antonio López Ferreiro (1895, 2 vols.), of Zorita de los Canes by R. de Ureña y Smenjaud (1911), and of Cuenca (*Forum Conche*) by G. H. Allen (*Cincinnati University Studies*, 1909–10) may be cited as examples. Others are now being published in the collection known as the *Biblioteca Jurídica Española*, edd. Ureña y Smenjaud and

Bonilla y San Martin. The theory of Adolf Helfferich and G. de Clermont, in their *Fueros francos* (Berlin, 1860), that the French communal organisation seriously influenced the mediaeval municipal government of Spain, was refuted by Tomás Muñoz y Romero in the *Revista general de legislación y jurisprudencia*, xxxi (1867), pp. 28–53, 226–246, 288–313. This refutation, however, applies rather to Castile than to the realms of the Crown of Aragon.

[2] Not to be confused with the word *consejo*, which means a council.

[3] Cf. reference to the fuero of Soria in J. Klein, "The Alcalde Entregador of the Mesta," in *B. H.*, xvii, p. 121, note 3.

many who resided outside of the city walls, for the territory covered by the fuero usually extended some distance into the surrounding country.[1] In this essentially democratic body the chief municipal officers were annually chosen. The methods of their selection varied widely. What we should now call a 'free election' did not invariably prevail even in the most flourishing periods of municipal independence. Ancient local and aristocratic privileges had often to be considered, and a fondness for drawing lots and for a system of rotation in office manifested itself at an early date; still we may fairly say that the municipal magistrates were invested with their several offices under the auspices of the popular assembly, which could thus justly claim for itself the supreme local authority within the town. Of these magistrates the following were the most important. The *regidores*, whose numbers varied from eight to thirty-six, were general administrative officials, whose duty it was to oversee and give advice concerning the management of municipal affairs. They were usually drawn in equal numbers from the ranks of the burgesses and of the caballeros. The municipal *alcaldes* were judges with criminal and civil jurisdiction, and usually fell into two categories — *majores* and *ordinarios*. Some cities had two, others four, six, or even ten. The *alguacil* was a police officer or bailiff; the *alguacil mayor* led the municipal levies in war;[2] the *alférez* carried the standard. The term *fieles* was used to describe minor functionaries with various duties who acted as secretaries of the *concejo*, as inspectors of weights and measures (*fieles almotacenes*), or as superintendents of the public lands and properties of the municipality; sometimes they were employed to prevent merchants from charging excessive prices for the necessaries

[1] Colmeiro, *Curso*, p. 137.
[2] Cf. Carlos Groizard y Coronado, "Las Milicias Locales en la Edad Media," in *Boletín de la R. A. H.*, lv, pp. 353-362.

of life. The *alarifes* took charge of the erection and preservation of the municipal buildings, and of the status of the workmen employed thereon; *andadores* and *mensajeros* carried messages for the *concejo*; and *veladores* kept watch over the city at night. The whole body of these local municipal magistrates, selected in the *concejo* and exercising their functions in its name, was generally known as the *ayuntamiento*.[1]

But the powers of the *concejos* did not cease with the appointment of the principal municipal officers. Regulations for the internal administration of the city, for the raising and collection of its revenue (which was derived from contributions in money and in labor, from fines, and from the income of public lands), for the policing of the streets, for the management of the municipal food supply, and for the punishment of minor delinquents, etc., etc., emanated in the first instance from the general assembly of the citizens. The *concejo*, in other words, both laid down the lines on which the city should be governed, and appointed the magistrates who were charged with the execution of its will.[2] Questions of external, as well as of internal policy were also frequently submitted to it, such as whether or not the city should send its levies on a raid into Moorish territory, or wage war on some overpowerful baron. Some of the Cantabrian cities even went so far as to intervene on their own initiative, without sanction of the central government, in the desultory struggle between France and England during the first half

[1] Colmeiro, *Curso*, pp. 481–486; Sacristan y Martines, *op. cit.*, pp. 103 ff.; Hinojosa, *Estudios sobre la historia del Derecho Español*, cap. i; a series of articles by Fidel Fita on Madrid in the twelfth and thirteenth centuries, in *Boletín de la R. A. H.*, viii, 46–80, 141–160, 399–422, 439–466; ix, pp. 11–157; E. Pérez y Aguado, *Organisación municipal de Madrid en la Edad Media*; and any of the standard municipal histories, such as Diego Colmenares, *Historia de Segovia* (1637), or Manuel Villar y Macias, *Historia de Salamanca* (1887, 3 vols.).

[2] Altamira, § 450; Mariéjol, pp. 294–302.

of the thirteenth century; on one occasion their boldness in seizing English ships evoked a vigorous claim for reparation from King Henry III to St. Ferdinand.[1] Finally, the *concejos* enjoyed, in theory, at least, the right to elect the *procuradores* or municipal representatives to the *brazo popular* or third estate in the Cortes; though we shall later find that here, as in the case of the local magistrates, the methods of choice were too various to permit the full realization of this privilege.[2]

We have here all the appurtenances of a thoroughly democratic régime, and from the middle of the twelfth to the middle of the fourteenth century, when the development just outlined attained its climax, the vigor and liberty of the municipal government of Castile was probably unsurpassed anywhere in Western Europe. Even after the virtual accomplishment of the Reconquest had freed the monarchy from the necessity of seeking the alliance of the cities as outposts in the campaign against the infidel, the value of their friendship in the internal struggle against the turbulent nobles was at once perceived by all the ablest kings. The advice of James the Conqueror to Alfonso the Learned, to court the favor of the municipalities, embodied one of the best recognized principles of strong monarchical government.[3] Fears lest the aspirations of the Castilian cities for democracy and autonomy might some day prove a bar to the progress of the power of the crown, were on the whole far exceeded by the dread of the overweening ambitions of the aristocracy which threatened both. *Parcere subjectis et debellare superbos* was the motto of the monarchy, though it was not always carried out; and the confidence

---

[1] Fernández Duro, *Marina de Castilla*, p. 30; Altamira, § 300.
[2] Colmeiro, *Introd.*, i, pp. 28 ff.
[3] Swift, *James the First of Aragon*, p. 120.

and favor of the crown were often rewarded by the cities'
undertaking on their own initiative to aid it in suppressing
the outbreaks of their common foe. When the days of
monarchical absolutism arrived and the nobles were crushed,
the triumphant kingship avoided the danger of democratic
opposition by a clever utilization of the ever potent forces
of Spanish separatism. But that is another story, which
does not for the moment concern us. During the period at
present under review, royal favor and Spanish impatience
of restraint combined to give the Castilian cities a measure
of independence and self-government which goes far to
justify the claim that Spain was in some respects the most
democratic country in mediaeval Europe. Her democracy
was, of course, rather local than national in its scope. It
manifested itself in characteristically various ways, not only
in the different kingdoms of the peninsula, but also in
the different parts of each of those kingdoms, and could
not make itself fully felt as a national ideal for many
centuries to come. No one, however, can study the history
of the Castilian municipality without recognizing the high
character of the spirit with which it was animated.
On the walls of the great staircase of the town hall at
Toledo, the visitor may still read the lines of a fifteenth-
century Castilian poet, Gomez Manrique, which express
a lofty conception of the duties of a municipal magistrate:

> "Nobles discretos varones
> Que gobernáis á Toledo,
> En aquestos escalones
> Desechad las aficiones,
> Codicias, amor y miedo.
> Por los comunes provechos
> Dejad los particulares;
> Pues os fizo Dios pilares

De tan riquísimos techos,
Estad firmes y derechos." [1]

Modern democracy cannot fail to be stirred by admiration and sympathy for the ideal which these words proclaim.

One of the most significant proofs of the power and prestige of the Castilian municipalities is afforded by the *hermandades* or brotherhoods which they formed for the maintenance of their privileges and the law of the land. Faint traces of such organizations are discernible in the twelfth and early thirteenth centuries,[2] but it is at the end of the reign of Alfonso X that they first emerge as an important factor in the life of the state. In 1282, at the height of the successional struggle between the Scholar King and his rebellious son, an association of the cities of the kingdom of Leon was formed at the instigation of the latter to help him dethrone his father. Two years later, on discovering that the evils of the time had been rather increased than diminished by the change of rulers, the league which Sancho had called into existence reversed its policy, and directed its efforts against him.[3] This *hermandad* of 1282, however, differs from those which followed it in two respects. In the first place, it was formed, not spontaneously, but as a result of a plot of the pretender to the throne of Castile; in the second, it was avowedly anti-royal in its aims. A *hermandad* which was created by the cities of Castile in a meet-

---

[1] This verse has been translated as follows:
"Good gentlemen with high forbears,
Who govern Toledo city,
As you ascend these civic stairs,
Abandon all nepotic cares,
Fear, greed, and undue pity.
Think only of the State's behoof,
Not of the gain that lureth;
Since you're the pillars of the roof
Which God provides, be yours the proof
That honour still endureth."

[2] Montalvo y Jardín, *Discurso sobre las Hermandades de Castilla* (Madrid, 1862), pp. 10 f.; P. Escalona, *Historia de Sahagún*, lib. iii, cap. ii; F. Callejas, *Fuero de Sepúlveda*, p. 87; J. Sanchez Ruano, *Fuero de Salamanca*, p. 77; *Cortes*, i, p. 61.

[3] J. Puyol y Alonso, *Las Hermandades de Castilla y León*, pp. 10-26, and references there.

ing at Burgos in the first year of the reign of Ferdinand IV was, however, much more typical. It was a voluntary association of the representatives of the different municipalities, who, recognizing the dangers of a royal minority, banded themselves together "for the honor and security of the king and his successor and for the honor and safety of the land"; and another *hermandad* of the towns of Leon and Galicia, which was formed simultaneously at Valladolid, proclaimed the same intentions.[1] Both of them pledged themselves to protect the lives and property of their members, to maintain justice, and to prevent illegal taxation. Their constitutions were solemnly confirmed by the king in 1295 and again in 1297.[2] But it is clear that they were not intended to be in any sense permanent. After having tided over the crisis which had evoked them, it was expected that they would cease to exist. Each one had a central deliberative assembly of the representatives of the different cities that composed it, to decide on its method of action. Its expenses were defrayed from a common fund; its letters were despatched under a common seal.[3] Other smaller *hermandades* appeared in the same period in Murcia, Cuenca, and elsewhere,[4] for purposes similar to those of Leon and Castile, and there were also special ones with definite objects of local and particular interest. Among these may be mentioned the famous *Hermandad de las Marismas*, composed of the principal towns on or near the Biscayan coast, which had been given special privileges since the time of Archbishop Diego Gelmirez to stimulate their interest in naval affairs.[5] In this region

[1] *España Sagrada*, xxxvi, pp. clxii–clxx; *Memorias de Fernando IV*, ii, pp. 7 ff.; Puyol y Alonso, *op. cit.*, pp. 27–30.

[2] *Cortes*, i, p. 132; *Memorias de Fernando IV*, ii, p. 133.

[3] Puyol y Alonso, *op. cit.*, pp. 33–40 Cortes, i, pp. 247–272.

[4] Cf. *D.I.E.*, cxii, pp. 1–6, and *Boletin de la R.A.H.*, xxii, pp. 96–99.

[5] Fernández Duro, *Marina de Castilla*, pp. 219–249.

the tradition of autonomy and independence was so strong that the *Hermandad de las Marismas* could not help being affected by it. Its members refused to trade with the interior of Castile, if their local privileges were not observed; it inaugurated what amounted to a separate independent foreign and commercial policy of its own with Portugal, France, and England, and it sent its own representatives to deal with these countries.[1]

We are, however, principally interested in the larger and more general *hermandades* whose primary object was the maintenance of law and order in the realm, and which consequently tended to gravitate towards the monarchy, as the symbol of the governance which Castile so sadly lacked. The long minority of Alfonso XI gave them an admirable opportunity to demonstrate their usefulness. When a new *hermandad*, including "Leon, Castile, Toledo, and Estremadura," was formed in the Cortes of Burgos in 1315, the regent, Maria de Molina, made haste to confirm it, as the best possible means of strengthening the throne. In the century that elapsed between the accession of Pedro the Cruel and the death of John II, the *hermandades* were much less conspicuous. The frequent meetings of the Cortes during this period gave the municipal representatives of the cities a better opportunity than they had pre-

---

[1] It has not seemed worth while to go into the history and constitutions of the three semi-independent provinces of Alava, Viscaya, and Guipúscoa, though they constitute one of the most interesting and permanent proofs of the ineradicability of Spanish separatism. The Basque language and tradition served as a basis of differentiation between them and the other parts of Spain, and for many centuries the three provinces wavered between complete autonomy and partial dependence on Navarre and Castile. Guipúscoa was finally united to Castile in 1200, Alava in 1332, and Viscaya in 1370. But even after their union with the larger kingdom they retained many of the prerogatives of independence. Their juntas or central assemblies coöperated; no evidence of a formal compact between them has been found, but they employed, as a symbol of their unity, a seal with the word "*Iruracbat*," "The Three One," engraved upon it. — Further information may be found in C. de Echegaray, *Las provincias Vascongadas á fines de la Edad Media* (1895).

viously enjoyed of laying their demands before the king; moreover, the sovereigns of the time, though they did not cease to recognize the value of the *hermandades* in cases of special stress and emergency, had also begun to realise that if suffered to establish themselves permanently they might ultimately be converted into a menace to the royal power. The fact that similar associations of nobles and magnates for less patriotic purposes had already begun to make their appearance furnished an additional cause for the misgivings of the crown.[1] During the reign of Henry IV, the *hermandades* again emerged into great prominence, but we can more conveniently consider their development under that monarch in connection with the reign of Ferdinand and Isabella.

The diminished importance of the *hermandades* which is observable after the middle of the fourteenth century is accompanied by the beginnings of decay in the internal government of the cities that composed them.[2] Royal interference and desire to control, which had adversely affected the development of the one, were also the obvious and immediate causes of the contemporaneous decline of the other; but it is a nice question how far the king's meddling in the internal affairs of the municipalities was caused by his dissatisfaction with the rule of the *concejos*, and how far by his fear that unless the crown stepped in to protect and control them the city governments ran grave danger of being subjected to the domination of the rebel baronage. The constant complaints in the proceedings of the Cortes of violent internal upheavals within the city walls seem at first to lend color to the belief that the progress of municipal liberty had outrun administrative order; but

---

[1] Puyol y Alonso, *op. cit.*, pp. 40–47.
[2] Colmeiro, *Curso*, pp. 487–504; Altamira, § 450.

when one comes to look beneath the surface, one finds that most of these broils were rather the result of baronial incursions and ancient family feuds than of any abuse of their privileges by the *concejos*.   The fact that many of the cities petitioned the crown for *cartas* forbidding the nobles to enter their domains is also significant, and indicates that many of the municipal revolts were but a by-product of the excessive powers of the aristocracy.[1]

Whatever the cause of their action, the Castilian sovereigns, from Alfonso XI downward, did their utmost to undermine the independence of the cities of their realms. From open violations of the fueros, the wiser of them shrank. They preferred to work by stealth whenever possible; but their principal methods of operation are reasonably clear. The most important was unquestionably the institution of the *corregidores*, royally appointed officials sent down to the *concejos* to coöperate with, and ultimately to supersede, the locally elected magistrates; as these magistrates, however, were primarily representatives of the central administration, they can most conveniently be considered in connection with it.   But the changes which were effected within the municipalities are almost as notable as the authorities which were superimposed upon them from without.   On all sides we have evidence that the cases of free and open annual election to offices by the *concejo* steadily diminished.   Life tenures, royal appointments, and declarations of the hereditary character of this or that function are encountered with increasing frequency.[2]   When the sovereign found that a city obstinately refused to per-

---

[1] *Cortes*, ii, p. 152 (Burgos, 1367, pet. 14); iii, p. 223 (Madrid, 1435, pet. 28); iii, p. 316 (Madrigal, 1438, pet. 7); iii. p. 515 (Valladolid, 1447, pet. 16); Ortiz y Zúñiga, *Anales eclesiasticos y seculares de Sevilla*, p. 359.

[2] Colmenares, *Historia de Segovia*, cap. xxiv, sec. 18 (año 1345); *Ordenansas para el Gobierno de Leon*, published by that city, 1669, *passim*; Manuel Risco, *Historia de la ciudad y Corte de Leon*, i, pp. 148 ff.

mit the abrogation of the traditional methods of election of
existing magistrates, a host of new positions were often
created, and their holders, invariably royal appointees,
gradually elbowed aside their municipally elected colleagues.
Multiplication of officials and great increase of the funds
that had to be raised to pay their salaries are accompanying
phenomena of this method of procedure.[1] In the reign of
John II occurs the first case of the sale of a municipal post
by the crown as a means of replenishing the royal treasury,
an event the significance of which it is unnecessary to emphasize.[2] And royal interference extended to other things
than the appointment of city magistrates. Sometimes all
the local ordinances of the *concejo* for the government of
the city were so radically reformed by the royal minions as
to retain little or nothing of their original meaning.[3] The
concejos in fact had little left to do. All the real power had
passed from their hands into those of the *ayuntamiento* of
officials, which now no longer represented the voting body
of the inhabitants. Small wonder if the ancient municipal
traditions were forgotten and the spirit of the earlier centuries died away. Doubtless the cities themselves were
much to blame. The early fifteenth century is in every
respect a dark period in the history of Castile, and even if
the crown had left them alone, it is doubtful whether the
municipalities could have preserved their ancient ideals
intact in view of the universal deterioration which was in
progress all around them. But their decadence was certainly accelerated by royal intervention; for though the
king's interference may have been helpful at the outset,

---

[1] *Cortes*, iii, p. 16 (Madrid, 1415, pet. 8); iii, p. 53 (Palenzuela, 1425, pet. 3); iii, p. 119 (Zamora, 1432, pet. 2); G. Gonsales Davila, *Historia de Enrique III* (Madrid, 1638), cap. lxxiii, p. 181.

[2] Colmeiro, *Curso*, p. 502; see also *Cortes*, iii, p. 785 (Ocana, 1469, pet. 7).

[3] *Cortes*, iii, p. 122 (Zamora, 1432, pet. 8); iii, p. 740 (Toledo, 1462, pet. 52).

as a means of protection against baronial control, it ultimately served to undermine the foundations of the finest
and freest life in mediaeval Castile. The complaints of the
Cortes of John II and Henry IV concerning the infringement of the ancient fueros showed that some men realized
the meaning of the change even at that early period; and
a century later its results were evident to all.[1]

It must not be forgotten that the nobles and higher
clergy, who had been granted or else usurped the right to
issue fueros, founded cities on their own domains as well as
the king. These cities never attained at all the same measure of autonomy as did those which received their charters
from the crown, and their decline in the fifteenth century
was considerably more rapid. Hardest of all was the lot
of the town whose lordship was disputed by two hostile
magnates. It was invariably a storm centre of disturbance,
and its streets frequently ran with the blood of opposing
factions.[2]

A few words remain to be said in regard to the status of
the two non-Christian portions of the population of mediaeval Castile — the Jews and the Moors.[3] We have already
seen that the Moors who remained on the territories which
had been won for the Cross were treated, down to the close
of the thirteenth century, with a very remarkable degree
of tolerance and liberality by their Christian conquerors;
and the same may be said of the Castilian Jews. The reign
of Alfonso X marks the culmination of the prosperity of
both races under the sovereignty of the kings of Castile.
The *Partidas* contain numerous laws describing their rights

---

[1] Colmeiro, *Curso*, pp. 487–504.
[2] G. Gonsales Davila, *Historia de
Enrique III*, cap. xxxi (p. 77); Colmeiro, *Curso*, p. 488.

[3] For the standard authorities on
this topic, see the bibliographical note
at the end of the chapter.

and privileges.[1] Both races were segregated in special communities (*aljamas*) surrounded by walls (*barrios*) in the principal cities, and the Moors, or Mudejares, as they were generally called, were sometimes given exclusive possession of smaller towns, which Christians were forbidden to enter. They retained their local officials, their minor courts, and their law codes; and as the Moors came gradually to forget their native language, their law books were translated into Spanish so as to be available for general use. The Christians were strictly forbidden to vex or oppress them, or to force them into acceptance of baptism; no Jew could be summoned to attend court on Saturdays, nor might his religious observances be interfered with in any other way. The value of both races as economic assets was early recognized. In addition to all the regular taxes, they paid a number of special imposts peculiar to themselves; moreover, the management of the capital and commerce of the realm was in large measure intrusted to them; and many of the royal *almojarifes* or taxgatherers were Hebrews.[2] Yet on the other hand, even in the time of the Scholar King, the government made every effort to keep both Jews and Moors from consorting with Christians, and to preserve and accentuate the barriers that kept them apart. In addition to their segregation in separate quarters, they were forbidden under pain of heavy penalties to eat, drink, or bathe with Christians, while sexual intercourse between the different races was punished with terrible barbarity. Finally, regulations insisting that the Jews or Moors wear some distinctive dress or badge, or cut their hair in some peculiar fashion, so as to render them easily recognizable, are found throughout the thirteenth century

---

[1] *Partida* vii, tits. xxiv and xxv.
[2] Lea, *Inquisition of Spain*, i, pp. 64–68, 85–87; Altamira, §§ 432 f.

codes, though the records seem to show that the regulations to this effect were by no means universally observed.[1]

Precisely what factors combined, and in what proportions, to alter these generally satisfactory conditions for the worse in the fourteenth and fifteenth centuries is not entirely clear. That the church pointed the way towards persecution is evident; but it is hard to believe that its attempts in that direction would have met with much success, had they not been supplemented by the great jealousy which the wealth and prosperity of the Moors and Jews aroused throughout the length and breadth of Castile.[2] The association of the Jews with the proverbially unpopular occupation of money-lending rendered them particularly obnoxious, and is probably the chief explanation why they suffered so much more acutely than the Mudejares in the century preceding the accession of the Catholic Kings. Against the Moors, indeed, a number of laws were passed to restrict their acquisition of Christian property, to limit the jurisdiction of their tribunals, and even to increase the facilities for their conversion; but it does not seem to have been possible to enforce these regulations, and it is significant of the continuance of friendly relations between the two faiths, that in 1410 the Mudejares of Cordova and Seville had contributed to the expense of the campaign of the Infante Ferdinand against the Granadan outpost of Antequera.[3] There was, moreover, a notable increase of Mudejarism in the third quarter of the fifteenth century during the reign of Henry the Impotent.[4]

With the unfortunate Israelites, however, the situation was very different. An evil tradition of Hebrew persecu-

[1] Lea, *op. cit.*, i, pp. 68 f., 90; Amador de los Rios, *Historia de los Judíos*, i, pp. 441–498.

[2] Lea, *op. cit.*, i, pp. 68–75, 96 f.

[3] *Crónica de Juan II*, año iv, cap. xxvi (in *B. A. E.*, lxviii, p. 327).

[4] Altamira, § 432.

tion inherited from Visigothic days had not been entirely forgotten,[1] and lay hatred was far easier to stimulate against the Jews than against the Moors. In the Cortes of Burgos in 1315, a number of galling restrictions were imposed upon them. All laws permitting usury were revoked, and many of the provisions by which the Jews had been guaranteed fair treatment in the courts were abrogated.[2] Other privileges were successively removed in the following years, and the fact that the ravages of the Black Death were popularly attributed by superstitious persons to the malign influence of the Hebrews served still further to increase the hardness of their lot.[3] Finally, in the reign of John I, ecclesiastical denunciations and appeals to fanaticism and greed had their inevitable effect. Furious crowds entered and sacked the *aljamas* of the different cities of Castile and massacred hundreds, if not thousands, of the inhabitants; the only sure way to escape death was to submit to compulsory baptism.[4] Thus emerged the class of so-called *Marranos* or *Conversos* — converted Jews, some of whom for a time were not ashamed to lend aid to the Christians against the loyal Hebrews who had refused to abandon the faith of their fathers.[5] By perseverance and efficiency they succeeded in regaining for themselves all the power, wealth, and privileges of which their ancestors had been deprived; but as soon as their position was secured their loyalty to their adopted religion began to waver, so that by the middle of the fifteenth century we find numerous complaints that they were Christians only in name.

How far these complaints were justified by the facts, it is difficult to say. Forced conversions are notoriously in-

---

[1] Lea, *op. cit.*, i, pp. 39–45.

[2] *Cortes*, i, pp. 280–285 (Burgos, 1315, leyes 23–30).

[3] Amador de los Rios. *op. cit.*, ii, 260 ff.

[4] Lea, *op. cit.*, i, p. 107, and references there.

[5] Lea, i, pp. 113 ff.

sincere, and it is altogether probable that a large proportion of the Conversos secretly yearned for the faith of their fathers. On the other hand, it is impossible to deny that by this time "the hatred which of old had been merely a matter of religion had become a matter of race."[1] Detestation of the Jew had been so deeply implanted in the heart of the average Castilian that he was very apt to make groundless accusations of apostasy against the objects of his dislike. Sometimes the kings, fearful of the financial effects of attacking the Conversos, feebly attempted to extend to them their protection; but the mass of the population, and the bulk of the grandees, who dominated the royal policy, were consistently hostile, with the result that there were frequent riots and unpunished murders of the Conversos throughout the reigns of John II and Henry IV.[2] Meantime the professing Jews who had not been killed or exiled, and had not sought refuge in baptism to escape from persecution, lived on, sadly reduced in numbers and wealth, till their expulsion by the Catholic Kings. A schedule, drawn up for purposes of taxation in the year 1474, shows that there were only about twelve thousand families of them left in Castile at that time, and that the large revenues which the Jewish communities or *aljamas* had annually rendered two centuries previously to the Castilian monarchs had by that time dwindled almost to nothing.[3]

The seeds of the evil plant of racial and religious hatred, which was to bear such fearful fruit under Ferdinand and Isabella and the Hapsburgs, had thus been thoroughly sown in the immediately preceding age. Yet the comparatively liberal and enlightened policy which prevailed in the

[1] Lea, i, p. 126.
[2] Diego de Valera, *Memorial de Diversas Hasañas*, cap. lxxxiii (in *B. A. E.*, xx, pp. 77–79).
[3] Amador de los Rios, *op. cit.*, iii, pp. 170 f.; 12,000 'families' are estimated as 60,000 souls.

earlier centuries of the Reconquest should not be forgotten. It shows that the spirit of persecution and intolerance is not a necessary and ineradicable characteristic of the Spaniard, as the modern student is often prone to assume. The fact that the climax of its revival coincided with the age of Spain's unification and expansion was destined, as will subsequently appear, to carry the Spanish reputation for bigotry and fanaticism to the uttermost parts of the earth; but in this, as in the kindred matter of the religious and crusading enthusiasm of her warriors, there is less real than apparent continuity between the periods of Reconquest and of Empire.

BIBLIOGRAPHICAL NOTE

Sources.— Tomás Muñoz y Romero, *Colección de Fueros Municipales y Cartas Pueblas de los Reinos de Castilla, Leon, Corona de Aragon, y Navarra*, vol. i (Madrid, 1847, no more published); invaluable, but should be supplemented by a study of more recent annotated editions of the fueros of individual towns, of which some of the most important are mentioned in the footnote to p. 186, *ante*. *Becerro ; Libro Famoso de las Behetrias de Castilla*, published by Fabian Hernandez (Santander, 1866); drawn up at the command of Pedro the Cruel. Rafael de Floranes, "Apuntamientos curiosos sobre Behetrias," in *D. I. E.*, vol. xx, pp. 407-475.

Later Works.— Eduardo de Hinojosa's *Historia general del Derecho Español* (Madrid, 1887; only one volume published), and his *Estudios sobre la Historia del Derecho Español* (Madrid, 1903), are standard works by one of the greatest living Spanish scholars. Pedro José, Marquis de Pidal's, *Lecciones sobre la historia del Gobierno y Legislacion de España* (Madrid, 1880) deals at once clearly and profoundly with some of the most difficult topics ; Pidal's treatment of the thorny question of the origin of the mediaeval Spanish municipality is particularly good. Henrique da Gama Barros, *Historia da Administraçao Publica em Portugal nos seculos XII a XV* (Lisbon, 1885-96, 2 vols.), contains much that is also applicable to Castile ; the account of feudalism in the Iberian Peninsula is especially valuable. Jules Gounon-Loubens, *Essais sur l'administration de la Castille au XVI⁰ siècle* (Paris, 1860), is comparatively little known, but is a work of sound scholarship. Though it deals specially with a later field, it also throws much light on the mediaeval period.

There are a host of books on the Castilian nobility, most of them written in the sixteenth or seventeenth centuries: three of the best are Juan Arce de Otalora's *De Nobilitatis et Immunitatis Hispaniae Causis Tractatus* (Granada, 1553; in later editions, as, e.g., Salamanca, 1570, the title is *Summa Nobilitatis Hispanicae et Immunitatis Regiorum Tributorum*); Pedro Salazar de Mendoza's *Origen de las Dignidades Seglares de Castilla y de Leon* (Toledo, 1618); and Bernabé Moreno de Vargas's *Discursos de la Nobleza de Espana* (Madrid, 1622, also 1659).

The history of the military orders has also been a favorite subject for Spanish writers. The best of the older books on the subject is Francisco Caro de Torres, *Historia de las Ordenes Militares* (Madrid, 1629); F. R. de Uhagon, *Órdenes Militares* (Madrid, 1898), is the most recent treatment of this topic.

On feudalism, tenures, and the condition of the rural population, beside Gama Barros (cf. *ante*, p. 172, note), the most important works are Tomás Muñoz y Romero, *Del Estado de las Personas en los Reinos de Asturias y León* (2d edition, Madrid, 1883), very valuable; the book is rare, but there is a reprint in the *R. A.*, 2d series, vol. ix (1883), pp. 3-17, 51-60, 86-99, 119-125; Antonio de la Escosura y Hevia, *Juicio crítico del Feudalismo en España* (Madrid, 1856), the first really scientific treatise on the subject, and the basis of subsequent discussions; Francisco de Cárdenas, *Ensayo sobre la historia de la Propriedad Territorial en España* (Madrid, 1873-75, 2 vols.), and Juan Sempere y Guarinos, *Historia de los Vínculos y Mayorazgos* (2d edition, Madrid, 1847), both standard works; Julio Puyol y Alonso, *El Abadengo de Sahagún* (Madrid, 1915), and Francisco Aznar Navarro, " Los Solariegos en León y Castilla," in *Cultura Española* for 1906, pp. 4-26, 299-326, which shed fresh light on feudalism and on serfdom.

On the municipalities Antonio Sacristan y Martinez's *Municipalidades de Castilla y Leon* (Madrid, 1877) is still valuable as a general survey. For special topics, in addition to the study of the different fueros one must depend on the numerous local histories, of which Diego Ortiz de Zúñiga's *Anales eclesiasticos y seculares de la Ciudad de Sevilla* (Madrid, 1677) is an excellent example (—there is a revised and improved edition of this work in five volumes, Madrid, 1795-96, which I have been unable to use); and on a few modern monographs, such as N. Tenorio y Cerero, *El Concejo de Sevilla* (Seville, 1901), and Eduardo Pérez y Aguado, *Organización municipal de Madrid en la Edad Media* (Madrid, 1907). Julio Puyol y Alonso, *Las Hermandades de Castilla y León* (Madrid, 1913), has largely superseded the older works on this topic; the titles of some of these will be found in the footnote to p. 191, *ante*.

On the Jews, José Amador de los Rios, *Historia de los Judíos de España y Portugal* (Madrid, 1876, 3 vols.), is the standard authority; and Joseph Jacobs, *An Inquiry into the Sources of the History of the Jews in Spain* (New York, 1894), will indicate material for further study. On the Moors, Florencio Janer, *Condicion Social de los Moriscos de España* (Madrid, 1857), and Francisco Fernández y González, *Estado Social y Político de los Mudéjares de Castilla* (Madrid, 1866), are both valuable. The first chapters of H. C. Lea's *History of the Inquisition of Spain* (New York, 1906-07, 4 vols.) give the best modern account of the early persecutions.

CHAPTER V

THE INSTITUTIONS OF MEDIAEVAL CASTILE

FROM the different ranks and classes of mediaeval Castilian society we pass to the various organs of the central government, and take up in the first place the king, at the apex of the political structure of the realm.

In the fourteenth and fifteenth centuries and afterwards the kingship of Castile was unquestionably hereditary; but certain explanations and amplifications of this apparently simple statement are essential to a full understanding of it.[1] The Visigothic monarchy, from which the Castilian was descended, was partly hereditary and partly elective. Theoretically, indeed, the elective principle was predominant, for though strong men occasionally seized the throne by deeds of violence, and, having obtained it, sometimes contrived to hand it on to their descendants, such actions were always recognized to be at variance with the laws of the land.[2] The practice of election, moreover, was continued in the earliest days of the Reconquest in the kingdom of Asturias. The legend that Pelayo was descended from the ancient Visigothic monarchs was merely a subsequent invention to strengthen the title which he had derived from the consent of his people on account of his success in war. On the other hand, we may well believe that the

---

[1] Cf. H. Zöpfl, *Sucesión á la Corona de España*, pp. 10 ff.

[2] The old statement that the Visigothic monarchy was first hereditary, down to the extinction of the Balts in 531, and afterwards elective, is far from true; the story is much more complicated. Cf. Colmeiro, *Curso*, pp. 37 ff.

circumstances of the time, especially the pressure of the
Moorish war, tended strongly to promote the counter-
development of the practice, if not the principle, of hereditary succession. The very existence of the little state was
so frequently threatened by external dangers that constitutional purism had to yield to the paramount need of the
moment — the continuity of an efficient executive. Opinions differ widely as to the precise epoch when the practice
of hereditary succession can be regarded as definitely established in the kingdom of Leon; but the preponderance
of authority tends to favor the reign of Ferdinand I (1037–
65), who first united the realms of Leon and Castile.[1] This
new method of determining the succession, however, rested
as yet on no law or ordinance. The Fuero Juzgo, which
remained valid down to the time of Alfonso X, upheld, in
theory at least, the elective principle.[2] It was in Las Siete
Partidas, for the first time, that a definite law of inheritance
of the throne was laid down. This law provided for the
succession of all descendants in the direct line, male and
female, before collaterals;[3] and though it was transgressed
by the succession of Sancho the Bravo in 1284, it was confirmed in the Ordenamiento of Alcalá in 1348, and remained
valid thenceforth till the advent of the Bourbons in the
eighteenth century. From the year 1388, when the future
Henry III of Castile was betrothed to the daughter of
John of Gaunt, the heir of the Castilian throne took the
title of Prince of Asturias.[4]

These different declarations and legalizations of the
hereditary character of the Castilian succession were fortified with elaborate assertions of the divine origin and right

[1] Colmeiro, *Curso*, pp. 166–172.
[2] *Fuero Juzgo*, tit. i, ley 2.
[3] *Partida* ii, tit. xv, ley 2; also
Especulo, lib. ii, tit. xvi, ley 1.
[4] Salasar de Mendoza, *Origen de
las Dignidades Seglares*, ff. 133–137;
Colmeiro, *Curso*, pp. 203 f.

of kingship, and with lengthy disquisitions on the way in
which a monarch should be treated and honored by his
people. They abound in statements of the rights, powers,
and prerogatives inherent in the crown.[1] But enough of
the remembrance of the days of elective kingship was preserved to make it impossible accurately to speak of the
sovereigns of fourteenth- and fifteenth-century Castile as
absolute, even in theory, still less as tyrants.[2] There was
a distinct understanding that the monarch must not abuse
his power; that he must govern according to equity and
righteousness. It was perhaps not enough to warrant the
statement that there was an actual contract between
sovereign and subject, or to justify the deposition of an
unjust king; but it was perfectly adequate as a basis of
a protest against arbitrary uses of royal power. Various
passages in the Partidas show this; particularly noteworthy is the declaration by which the king grants to his
people a certain right of inspection of his political conduct,
and the privilege of guarding him from evil by word and
deed — a privilege which the rebel nobles attempted to
utilize for their own selfish advantage in the fifteenth century, thereby evoking an angry protest from the Cortes
of Olmedo in 1445.[3] The kingship had become hereditary
and the succession fixed before the close of the Middle
Ages; the turbulence of the times demanded this as the
first and most essential condition of necessary centralization.
On the other hand, it was impossible for either subjects or
sovereign to forget the past, or the limitations on monarch-

[1] *Partida* ii, tit. i, ley 8; tit. xiii, leyes 1, 14–26; *Partida* iv, tit. xxv, leyes 1, 2.
[2] Cf. *Partida* ii, tit. i, ley 10, for Alfonso the Learned's definition of this word. Feudalism, moreover, implied certain very important limitations on the power of the crown, and may well have exerted influence in Castile, even though it was not fully established there.
[3] *Partida* i, tit. i, leyes 4, 11; *Partida* ii, tit. i, leyes 2, 8; tit. xiii, ley 25; *Cortes*, iii, pp. 458 ff.

ical absolutism which the days of the elective kingship
implied.

Yet it was not chiefly the theoretical restrictions of the
royal authority that prevented the strong governance which
mediaeval Castile so sadly lacked. The powers with which
the Partidas endow the king, if not enough to create a
tyranny, are at least sufficient to satisfy the demands of a
strong and efficient sovereign. He is there declared to be
the chief lawgiver and judge of the land. He is vested
with supreme administrative and executive authority; he
is the head of the army and the arbiter of the policy of the
realm at home and abroad.[1] In at least one place he is
conceded the right to dispose of or alienate any portion of
his realm at will as if he possessed all its territories in full
ownership; for the distinction between the private domain
of the monarch (*patrimonio privado del rey*) and the revenues
which came to him as head of the state (*patrimonio real*)
was not always sharply drawn in the mediaeval codes, and
their confusion was not seldom utilized by the monarchs
to their own temporary advantage, and the ultimate im-
poverishment of the kingdom.[2] According to the laws of
the land, the royal position was quite strong enough; the
trouble lay not with the codes, but with the impossibility
of enforcing them. Our examination of the narrative
history of fourteenth- and fifteenth-century Castile has
revealed some of the special circumstances which account
for the turbulence of the times: the weak character of
the monarchs, the numerous minorities and regencies, the
prevalence of the trend toward separatism, and above all the
conduct of the rebel nobles. But this description needs
to be supplemented on the constitutional side before the

[1] *Partida* i, tit. i, ley 12; *Partida* ii, tit. i, leyes 5, 6, 8.

[2] *Partida* ii, tit. i, ley 8; cf. also F.

Cos-Gayon, *Historia jurídica del Patri-monio Real* (Madrid, 1881), caps. ii, iv, v.

picture can be regarded as complete. As the king obviously did not exercise in fact the rights with which the law theoretically invested him, it will be necessary for us to take up one by one the organs of the central government and discover what measure of political power (in so far as it was not entirely dissipated by baronial anarchy) was enjoyed by each. In theory they were all created to aid the king in the discharge of his numerous functions, but as time went on, they often used the authority delegated to them not so much to help the sovereign to govern, as to enable themselves to govern in his stead.

Like all the monarchs of mediaeval Europe, the kings of Castile surrounded themselves with a coterie of intimate friends and counsellors, whose titles carry us back to the earlier days when each was assigned some special function in connection with the management of the royal household. Such were the *capellan mayor* or royal chaplain, the *camarero* or chamberlain, the *aposentador* or superintendent of lodgings, the *portero* or door keeper, the *mayor domo* or steward, and a host of others.[1] All of them continued, in theory at least, to discharge the duties indicated by their names; they were also intrusted with minor secretarial and administrative offices in connection with the government of the realm. The *canciller* or chancellor, who was almost invariably a cleric, had charge of the royal correspondence and the promulgation of the royal orders, "so that he represented the living law, and was the faithful guardian of tradition." His signature or seal was generally required to give validity to the king's decrees; he was naturally cognizant of all the different branches of the government's service; a large number of *notarios* and

[1] Altamira, § 443; cf. also the *Libro de la Camara Real del Principe Don Juan*, by Gonsalo Fernández de Oviedo, ed. Sociedad de Bibliófilos Españoles (1870).

escribanos aided him in the discharge of his various duties.[1] The *adelantado del rey* or *sobrejuez* represented the king in his capacity as supreme judge, when the monarch was unable to serve. He also had the duty of supervising, supporting, and, if necessary, of removing the minor judicial officials of the kingdom.[2] The *condestable* and *almirante*, instituted respectively by John I and Ferdinand III, were the heads under the king of the army and navy of Castile; both offices gradually became hereditary, the one in the family of the Velascos, the other in that of Enríquez.[3] The collector of the royal taxes was originally known as the *almojarife mayor*,[4] but the popular wrath at the frequent conferring of this office on a Jew extorted from Alfonso XI a promise that his revenues should in future be gathered by Christians, and that the collectors should no longer be called *almojarifes* but *tesoreros*. Hebrews, nevertheless, were soon appointed to the new office, and it was not long before the *tesorero mayor* was replaced in turn by a *contador de Castilla*; under John II there were two of these, and under Henry IV three.[5] The struggle over the incumbency of this high financial position is very significant. The sovereigns strove their hardest to prevent it from following the lead

---

[1] *Partida* ii, tit. ix, ley 4; Salazar de Mendoza, *Dignidades seglares*, ff. 41–45.

[2] *Partida* ii, tit. ix, ley 19; also *Leyes para los adelantados mayores dados por el Rey Don Alonso el Sabio*, printed in Martínez Alcubilla, *Códigos*, pp. 175 f.; and R. R. Hill, "The Office of Adelantado," in *Political Science Quarterly*, xxviii (1913), pp. 646–648. This office must not be confused with that of the *adelantado de comarca, fronterizo*, or *menor*, which we shall describe in connection with the administration of justice; cf. *infra*, p. 231.

[3] Colmeiro, *Curso*, pp. 544 f.; Fernández Duro, *Marina de Castilla*, pp. 323 ff. Most of the important functions of the *condestable* had been per-

formed, previously to the reign of John I, by the *alférez mayor* or royal standard-bearer; *Partida* ii, tit. ix, ley 16.

[4] *Partida* ii, tit. ix, ley 25; Piernas y Hurtado, *Tratado de Hacienda Pública*, ii, p. 53.

[5] *Colección de las leyes, ordenanzas . . . de la contaduria de cuentas desde Juan II hasta el día*, pp. 1–15; Colmeiro, *Curso*, pp. 546 f.; Piernas y Hurtado, *Tratado de Hacienda Pública*, ii, pp. 53 f.; Conde de Cedillo, *Contribuciones é Impuestos en León y Castilla*, p. 586. The *contador de Castilla* must not be confused with the *contadores reales*, who were subordinate officials.

of those of the constable and admiral and becoming a hereditary possession in some baronial family which would infallibly abuse it; but the tendency of the time was strongly in
the other direction, and the royal revenues suffered wofully
at the hands of those who administered them in the dark
days of the fifteenth century. The kings of Castile were
too weak to control even those officials whose duties brought
them most closely under the shadow of the throne.[1]

The early development of the *Consejo Real* or Royal
Council next claims our attention. The subject is of the
utmost importance, for the Council was to become under
Ferdinand and Isabella the principal organ of the central
government, and the cornerstone of the great administrative system of Spain and the Spanish Empire.

In Visigothic times, and during the earliest days of the
Reconquest, the sovereigns of the different Iberian realms
usually sought the advice of counsellors of proved wisdom
and sagacity whenever any important political or judicial
decision was pending.[2] This was indeed the universal
custom in all the states of Western Europe. But there is
no evidence of the existence of any permanent body of
royal counsellors in that remote period. When the king
felt in need of advice, he asked it of those who seemed to
him best qualified to give it, but any 'meetings of counsellors' which took place were purely accidental in their
nature, and were composed on each occasion as the monarch
should direct.[3] Even the famous *doce sabios* of the reign
of Ferdinand III, in whom Salazar de Mendoza and the
learned Padre Andrés Marcos Burriel thought they discerned the origin of the Consejo Real, have now been shorn

[1] Colmeiro, *E. P.*, i, pp. 484 ff.
[2] Torreánas, *Los Consejos del Rey durante la Edad Media*, i, pp. 50–86.
[3] Torreánas, i, pp. 126 f.

of that distinction.[1] They were apparently rather a body of scholars who occupied themselves principally with discussions of ethical questions, and definitions of "loyalty, covetousness, generosity, piety, and justice," and the office which they held was but temporary. The King's Council had not yet attained definite existence. Its functions were still fulfilled by a vague, accidental, amorphous body of advisers, composed and summoned at the royal will.[2]

The century that followed the reign of St. Ferdinand saw the Consejo emerge on firmer ground. The creation by Alfonso X of a central tribunal, or royal court, relieved it of a large share of its judicial functions, and enabled it to concentrate its attention on political affairs. Legists and *hombres buenos* from the third estate were summoned with increasing frequency in this period to take their places beside the magnates; their 'approximation,' as Torreánaz cautiously terms it, to the Royal Council coincides with their advent to power in the Cortes.[3] The long periods of royal minorities in the fourteenth century were also highly favorable to the increase of the power and permanence of the Consejo, and to the development of the representativeness of its membership. During the minority of Ferdinand IV, his mother, Doña Maria, turned to the cities for help, in order to counteract the influence of the Haros and of the Laras in the government; and accordingly "those of the cities gave her twelve *hombres buenos*"[4] to serve and advise the king and his guardians in matters of justice, finance, and all other affairs of the land. The phrase in the *cuaderno* is far too vague for us to estimate with any certainty the method by which these 'good men' were

---

[1] Torreánas, i, pp. 116–119.
[2] Altamira, §§ 285, 294, 442.
[3] Torreánas, i, pp. 123 f., 126.
[4] ". . . doce omes bonos que me dieron los delas villas del reyno de Castiella": *Cortes*, i, p. 135; Torreánas, i, pp. 128 f.

chosen; but it seems fair to assume that the inhabitants of the municipalities had a considerable share in selecting them. In the early years of the reign of Alfonso XI, moreover, while the king was yet a child, we find the government being carried on with the advice of four prelates and sixteen caballeros and *hombres buenos*, "without whose consent nothing might be done." [1] Apparently these sixteen were chosen on a basis of geographical distribution — four from each of the four quarters of the realm; and a similar method of procedure was adopted by Henry of Trastamara during the stormiest period of his struggle with Don Pedro. When normal times returned, however, the sovereigns continued to choose their advisers, as in earlier days, irregularly, occasionally, and at their own discretion, so that the body of royal counsellors lost much of the stability that it had gained during royal minorities and in the days of civil war. [2]

It was in the reign of John I that the Royal Council became established for the first time on a definite and permanent footing; indeed that sovereign merits the title of the founder of the institution. [3] On his departure in 1385 for the invasion of Portugal, which ended so disastrously at Aljubarrota, he put forth a sort of political testament, in which he stated that "the most necessary of all things is to have a great and good council composed of all sorts of persons, especially of those who bear the burden of the charges and good government of the realm." [4] After his defeat on the field of battle, he returned to Castile and began to give effect to this proposal, by creating in the Cortes of Valladolid (December 1, 1385) a Council composed of twelve persons — four prelates, four nobles, and

[1] Torreánas, i, p. 130.
[2] Torreánas, i, pp. 131–134.
[3] Torreánas, i, p. 145.
[4] *Crónica de Enrique III*, año de 1392, cap. vi (*B. A. E.*, lxviii, p. 188); Torreánas, i, p. 136.

four citizens — all of whom were named in the royal ordinance.[1] All traces of any principles of popular election or representation of geographical divisions now disappear; the crown reserved to itself full power to choose its own advisers, though it actually did select them equally from the three estates of the realm. The functions of the body thus composed were theoretically wellnigh all-inclusive. It was supposed to deal with all the affairs of the realm, save the administration of justice and certain specified matters — chiefly appointments — which the sovereign reserved for himself; and even in these he promised not to act without the Consejo's advice.[2] The organization was further amplified and elaborated in the Cortes of Briviesca in 1387, but the *cuaderno* of the petitions of this body clearly shows that the composition of the Council did not in fact follow the lines laid down for it, and that the representatives of the third estate did not actually take their seats there.[3] At the end of the reign of Henry III, the king provided that the number of councillors should be sixteen "prelados, condes, caballeros . . . y doctores," thus indicating that the place of the *hombres buenos* or *ciudadanos* had now been taken by the *letrados*.[4] Clearly the institution had by this time come to stay. Its composition had not been permanently determined, but it had been invested with powers so extensive that it could never again be crushed out of existence.

During the reign of John II and Henry IV, the Council fell once more on evil days. It was a period of reaction and retrogression in every respect, and the Consejo shared

[1] *Cortes*, ii, p. 332 (Valladolid, 1385, pet. 17).

[2] Torreánas, i, p. 141.

[3] *Cortes*, ii, p. 381 (Briviesca, 1387, pet. 4).

[4] *Crónica de Enrique III*, año de 1406, cap. xx (*B. A. E.*, lxviii, p. 267). This section of the chronicle is often reckoned as belonging to the reign of John II.

the common lot.   The entire reign of John II was dominated by the masterful personality of Álvaro de Luna, the
first of the great *privados* or *validos* of Spanish history;
and it was not that magnate's intention to have his omnipo-
tence limited by any regular body of advisers, who might
conceivably refuse to follow his lead.   In various ways he
contrived to diminish the prestige and importance of the
Council.[1]   Places in it were distributed with reckless prodi-
gality.   In the year 1426 there were no less than seventy-
five councillors, many of whom drew fat salaries without
rendering any corresponding service, and the distinction
which anciently attached to that office was consequently
lost.   Men complained bitterly of the financial burden
which resulted; and finally Álvaro, taking advantage of
the revulsion of public feeling, forced the weak king to
expel from his court all the magnates, "even though they
were of the Consejo," except a small group of his own
immediate adherents; so that thenceforth the Council
became merely a docile instrument of the favorite's ambition.[2]   During the temporary retirement of Álvaro from
1441 to 1445, an attempt was made to reëstablish matters
on the ancient footing, but without permanent success.
After the battle of Olmedo, the *valido* returned to office;
and until his execution eight years later, the composition
and functions of the Consejo were once more completely
dependent on his will, just as they had been on that of the
sovereigns of the early days of the Reconquest.[3]   The next
reign brought no real improvement.   In 1459 an effort was
made to return to the better ways of the previous century
by ordaining that the Council should be composed of
twelve persons — two bishops, two knights, and eight

[1] Torreánas, i, pp. 159 f.   [2] Torreánas, i, p. 166.
[3] Torreánas, i, pp. 175 f.

legists — who were named in the decree;[1] but a glance at
the petitions of the Cortes of the period proves that these
men did not fulfil the hopes that had been reposed in them.
Another attempt at reconstitution in the beginning of 1465
met with no better success — in fact, the king never permitted it to have a fair trial, for fear that it would put too
much power in the hands of the most turbulent of his
vassals, the Marquis of Villena.[2] Before the year was
out, however, the control had been suffered to fall back
into the hands of that unruly magnate, who, with Diego
de Arias and Alfonso Carrillo, archbishop of Toledo, exercised all authority, in the name of a new council of ten
persons which was called into existence chiefly in order to
give a show of legality to his usurpation.[3] Certainly
the Cortes regarded the crown as having capitulated to
the baronage and as having abdicated all pretensions to the
exercise of royal power. "Your Highness has placed in the
Council certain persons, more for the purpose of granting
them favors and honor and of acceding to their requests
than for that of strengthening the government, with the
result that the office of councillor, which used to rank so
high, has now fallen into disrepute. . . . Your commands
which emanate from such Councillors are neither fulfilled
nor obeyed." In these trenchant words the *procuradores*
of the Cortes of Ocaña in 1469[4] told King Henry their opinion
of his government; but the evils of which they complained
were irremediable, until strong monarchs should come to

[1] Marina, *Teoría de las Cortes*, pt. ii,
cap. xxviii. A manuscript of this ordinance may be found in the British Museum, Add. Mss. 9925, ff. 139–153;
there is a copy of it in the Harvard
College Library.

[2] Torreánas, i, pp. 182, 186; *Crónica
de Enrique IV*, cap. lxix (*B. A. E.*, lxx,
p. 141).

[3] Such at least is the inference to be

drawn from an "Arreglo del Consejo
en tiempo de Enrique 4° hacia los años
de 1465," Escurial Mss. Let. Z. plut.
1, n° 8°. A copy of this document is to
be found in the British Museum, Add.
Mss. 9925, ff. 234–240, a transcript of
which is in the Harvard College Library.

[4] *Cortes*, iii, pp. 770, 807 (Ocaña,
1469, pets. 2 and 26).

rescue the royal power from the slough of despond into which it had fallen.

The Consejo had passed through so many vicissitudes that Ferdinand and Isabella could not be at a loss to find precedents for remodelling it along any lines that should seem to them desirable.   Since the middle of the thirteenth century it had at one time been recruited, theoretically at least, according to the principle of popular election; at another the notion of equal geographical distribution of the councillors had prevailed.   After it had become permanently and regularly established under John I, the king reserved to himself the choice of his advisers, but for a time he selected them equally from the three estates of the realm.   Subsequently the *hombres buenos* had given way to the *letrados*, and, last of all, the entire body had been dominated by one or more ambitious nobles.   The functions of the Council had also varied from reign to reign, almost as often as its composition; but it never forgot that, with its various political attributes, it had also inherited from the days of St. Ferdinand and his predecessors a claim to be regarded as the highest court in the land.   During one of its many remodellings in the reign of John II, it was temporarily divided into two *salas* — a *sala de gobierno* and a *sala de justicia*.[1]   The Catholic Kings were in no sense violating tradition when they determined to utilize the Royal Council as a means of concentrating the administration of justice in their own hands.

The Royal Council during the fourteenth and fifteenth centuries had certainly given little promise of the mighty future that awaited it in the sixteenth and seventeenth. We have studied it not so much for what it actually was

[1] Altamira, § 442.

at the close of the Middle Ages, as for what it was subsequently to become. But with the Castilian Cortes, which come next in order, the picture is precisely reversed. The fourteenth and fifteenth centuries see the culmination of their power and prestige; under Ferdinand and Isabella and the Hapsburgs they rapidly decline. Yet even though our examination of the Castilian constitution at the close of the Middle Ages is chiefly important as furnishing a background for what was to follow, it is essential to the truthfulness of the picture that careful attention be given to this very notable national assembly. Its numerous rights and duties afford the best possible evidence of the strong tendency towards democracy characteristic of mediaeval Castile. Its records and petitions furnish an excellent guide to the aims and aspirations of the third estate. Even after it had been deprived of all real power, the history of the realm is in large measure to be read in its proceedings. Like the other organs of the central government, it was first summoned to aid and advise the king in the discharge of his various duties; but, also like them, it gradually developed a measure of independent authority, and ultimately limited in a variety of ways the extent of the royal prerogative.

It is generally agreed among Spanish historians that the origin of the Cortes of Castile and Leon is to be found in the powerful Councils of Toledo, composed of nobles and clergy, which played such an important part in the government of church and state during the last century and a quarter of Visigothic rule in the peninsula, and survived the shock of the Moorish invasion.[1] Soon after their re-

---

[1] Colmeiro, *Introd.*, i, pp. 3 ff., 109 ff. Further references for the following pages may be found in an article by the present author on the "Cortes of the Spanish Kingdoms in the Later Middle Ages," in the *American Historical Review*, xvi (1911), pp. 476-495: some passages in it are reprinted in the text.

appearance in the Christian kingdoms of the north, however, the ecclesiastical functions of these councils began to pass to special assemblies of the clergy alone, so that the attributes of the older body were gradually restricted to temporal affairs.[1] The culmination of this secularization of the functions of the old Visigothic councils is reached in the course of the twelfth and thirteenth centuries, when the kings, discerning in the third estate the strongest possible support against the preponderant power of the nobles, began to summon the representatives of the municipalities to the national assembly — in Leon at least as early as 1188, in Castile probably not till 1250, but in both cases considerably before the corresponding event took place in England.[2] At the same time the name of the institution changed; the older title of *concilio* (and sometimes *curia*) disappeared, and was replaced by that of Cortes, which, though sometimes loosely used to designate assemblies of the earlier sort, is in strict accuracy applied only to those bodies in which the third estate was present.[3] After the final union of Castile and Leon under St. Ferdinand (1230–52) the custom of holding separate Cortes for each of the two kingdoms gradually fell into disuse, and was replaced by the practice of summoning a common assembly composed of the representatives of both.[4] For the purpose of the present inquiry, therefore, it will suffice to describe the united body.

No one had a right to sit or be represented in the Castilian

[1] Colmeiro, *Introd.*, i, p. 10.

[2] Colmeiro, *Introd.*, i, pp. 10–15, 142 ff., 153 ff.; Altamira, "Magna Carta and Spanish Mediaeval Jurisprudence," in *Magna Carta Commemoration Essays*, ed. H. E. Malden (1917), p. 235. The statement in the *Crónica General de España* that *ciudadanos* were present at a so-called Cortes of Burgos in 1169 is not generally accepted today. The assembly at Najera in 1137 was apparently composed of nobles alone.

[3] Danvila, *Poder Civil*, i, p. 160.

[4] Colmeiro, *Introd.*, i, pp. 10–15, 47. The first general Cortes of both realms were held at Seville in 1250; the last separate ones for each kingdom in the first half of the fourteenth century.

Cortes during this period; in this respect the national assembly of the western kingdom forms the sharpest possible contrast to those of the realms of the Crown of Aragon.[1] The Castilian Cortes, being, in theory at least, a council of the king, were composed as the king desired, and varied from session to session accordingly. No two Cortes of this period were composed in exactly the same way. Neither the same prelates nor the same nobles were invariably summoned, nor were the same towns ordered to send procuradores. The clergy were represented by archbishops, bishops, and the grand masters of the military orders selected by the monarch. Custom indeed prescribed the presence of the archbishop of Toledo, and such of the higher churchmen as were resident at court; but even these the king had the unquestioned right to omit to summon if he wished.[2] The representation of the nobles was similarly irregular, and was determined on each occasion by the royal will. All the various ranks of the nobility, down to the *caballeros* and *escuderos*, were apparently eligible for summons to this estate, as were also the great officers of the crown, and, after it had been definitely established in the reign of John I, the members of the Royal Council;[3] but the king selected whomsoever he pleased on each occasion. Subject kings of the crown of Castile were also expected to attend or send representatives, if asked to do so; when the king of Granada acknowledged himself the vassal of Ferdinand III, he promised to come to the Cortes with one of his *ricos hombres*, and the name of 'Don Mahomat Abenazar, rey de Granada, vasallo del Rey,' heads the list of those who confirmed the ordinances of Ferdinand IV in the Cortes of Medina del Campo in 1305. Attendance, when a summons had been

---

[1] Colmeiro, *Introd.*, i, p. 17.
[2] Colmeiro, *Introd.*, i, pp. 16–18.
[3] Colmeiro, *Introd.*, i, pp. 16 f.; *Cortes*, ii, pp. 189, 314; iii, p. 10.

received, was absolutely obligatory in this estate; failure to appear, if not excused, was tantamount to a declaration of revolt.[1]

In theory at least, the representation of the third estate was inseparably attached to the municipalities; as the urban limits, however, did not stop at the city walls, but included neighboring hamlets and isolated houses, the rural communities were not really excluded.[2] During this period, the king selected for summons on each occasion as many towns as he pleased, and whichever he pleased; but the tendency was steadily towards a diminution in the number. In the Cortes of Leon of 1188, of Seville in 1288, and of Alcalá in 1348, there is reason to think that all the towns in the realm were called on to send representatives.[3] In the Cortes of Madrid in 1391, forty-nine municipalities sent procuradores; in the reign of Ferdinand and Isabella the number was finally fixed at eighteen.[4] The causes which combined to bring about this decrease were very numerous, and may be profitably compared to those which effected a similar result in contemporary England. We have not space to examine them here, but we may observe, in passing, that the blame for this unfortunate development is to be laid less at the door of the kings than of the towns themselves, which not only lost their early privileges by failing to insist on their observance, but also actually labored, in a spirit of local antagonism eminently characteristic of Spain, to exclude one another from the right of representation.[5]

[1] Colmeiro, *Introd.*, i, pp. 16 f.; *Cortes*, i, p. 178; *Crónica de Pedro II*, año ii. cap. ii (*B. A. E.*, lxvi, p. 412).

[2] *Cortes*, i, pp. 45, 49; Colmeiro, *Introd.*, i, pp. 18 f.; also Carlos de Lécea y García, *La Comunidad y Tierra de Segovia* (Segovia, 1893), pp. 1, 101 ff.

[3] Colmeiro, *Introd.*, i, pp. 19 f.

[4] *Cortes*, ii, pp. 483–485; iv, p. 111; Colmeiro, *Introd.*, i, pp. 23 ff.

[5] *Cortes*, iii, pp. 782–785; iv, pp. 233, 239; Colmeiro, *Introd.*, i, pp. 27 f.

The number of representatives or procuradores that each town could send varied, until it was fixed at two by a law of John II at the request of the Cortes of Madrid of 1429–30.[1] Another law of the same period specifies that the procuradores must be persons of quality, and not manual laborers.[2] The methods of choice of the procuradores varied according to the fuero or charter of the town that sent them, and were for the most part in general consonance with the methods of selection of the local municipal officers. Usually the matter was determined by lot (*insaculación*); sometimes by election by a more or less restricted number of inhabitants; sometimes by a system under which certain leading citizens served in turn; sometimes by a combination of these methods.[3] Whatever the local practice, it seems clear that down to the second quarter of the fifteenth century the choices were fairly made, without royal interference; but it is equally obvious that from the beginning of the dictatorship of Álvaro de Luna to the accession of Ferdinand and Isabella there were increasingly scandalous corruption and intimidation by the crown and the magnates, until in the reign of Henry the Impotent the king on several occasions actually gave away outright the privilege of representation.[4]

Every city represented in Cortes gave its procuradores credentials and letters of instruction and guidance, or *poderes*, as they were called. These were carefully worded and the procuradores were forbidden to deviate from them in the slightest degree.[5] If some unexpected question arose in the Cortes, the procuradores usually consulted their constituents before giving their votes, and they at-

[1] *Cortes*, i, p. 170; ii, pp. 483–485; iii, p. 85; Colmeiro, *Introd.*, i, pp. 28, 203.
[2] *Cortes*, iii, p. 85.
[3] Colmeiro, *Introd.*, i, pp. 29 f., 33 f.
[4] *Cortes*, ii, pp. 483–485; iii, pp. 85, 101, 135, 270, 407, 569, 715, 782–785; iv, pp. 233, 239; Colmeiro, *Introd.*, i, pp. 28–30, 33 f.
[5] Colmeiro, *Introd.*, i, pp. 37–41; *Cortes*, iii, p. 642.

tempted, though unsuccessfully, to wrest from the king the right of interpretation of the *poderes*, in case there was some doubt as to their meaning.[1] Until the character of these *poderes* was modified in the sixteenth century, their comprehensiveness and definiteness, and the strictness with which they were obeyed, constituted one of the most important safeguards of Castilian parliamentary liberty. The salaries and journey money of the procuradores were paid by the towns that sent them, down to the latter part of the fourteenth century.[2] Under John II the salaries began to be paid by the king, but in the sixteenth century, as we shall later see, it came to be the practice for the Cortes regularly to add a fixed sum for that purpose to the amount which they granted to the crown for the expenses incident to their sessions.[3]

The right to summon the Cortes was inherent in the crown, an inalienable royal prerogative; in case the king was absent, ill, or under age, it was exercised by his representatives in his name and not of their own right.[4] Time and place of meeting were left absolutely to the royal discretion; there was no rule as to the frequency of sessions, or the size, locality, or importance of the place where they occurred; on one occasion the Castilian Cortes met at Bubierca in Aragon.[5] At the opening session, which was attended by the king and all three estates, the first business was the presentation of the *poderes* by the procuradores. Then followed the speech from the throne, in which the purposes of the meeting were set forth, and formal replies were made by each estate: the head of the house of Lara

---

[1] *Cortes*, iii, pp. 407 f.; *Crónica de Juan II*, año de 1430, cap. iii (*B. A. E.*, lxviii, p. 479).

[2] *Cortes*, ii, p. 140.

[3] Colmeiro, *Introd.*, i, pp. 37–41; *Crónica de Juan II*, año 1422, cap. xx;

año de 1430, cap. iii (*B. A. E.*, lxviii, pp. 421, 478 f.).

[4] Colmeiro, *Introd.*, i, pp. 45–48.

[5] *Crónica de Pedro I*, año xiv, cap. iii (*B. A. E.*, lxvi, p. 525).

answering first, for the nobles; the archbishop of Toledo
next, for the clergy; and finally the city of Burgos for the
third estate.[1] These formal proceedings over, the estates
usually separated for deliberation, but communicated with
one another by messengers. Of the nature of the debates
it is almost impossible to learn anything, but it seems probable that they were very quiet and generally ineffective
and disorganized. The session lasted till the business was
done, but there is no record during this period of prolonged
meetings such as took place in the time of Philip II. Lastly
occurred the presentation of petitions by the estates to the
crown. There was apparently no final meeting of the
king and the three estates for formal ratification of what
had been done. The estates usually separated without
any guarantees that their wishes would be respected, though
it was the usual custom for the government to send back
to the cities, and sometimes to the bishops and nobles,
full copies of the *cuadernos*, or lists of petitions, with the
royal answers.[2]

Parliamentary privilege in the Castilian Cortes stood
very high. In 1302 and 1305 complete security and freedom from arrest and seizure of property were promised the
procuradores during sessions of the Cortes and while they
came and went; and in 1351 this promise was confirmed,
save in a few exceptional cases, though subsequent petitions would seem to indicate that the rule was not always
enforced.[3] By an ordinance of 1379, the procuradores were
granted the same entertainment which Las Siete Partidas
accorded the king and his immediate followers — a privilege which, again, was by no means invariably realized in

[1] Colmeiro. *Introd.*, i, pp. 52–
55.
[2] *Cortes*, i, p. 476; Colmeiro, *Introd.*, i, p. 91; J. Gounon-Loubens,
*Essais sur l'administration de la Cas-
tille*, pp. 108 f.
[3] *Cortes*, i, pp. 163, 180; ii, pp. 20,
62, 541.

fact.[1] There was apparently no restriction whatever on freedom of speech during sessions in the period which at present concerns us. The sole recorded instance in which the king attempted in any way to rebuke or punish a procurador for his conduct was that of Mosen Diego de Valera, who wrote a most insolent letter to John II, "on account of which he was in great peril, and it was ordered that nothing which was due him from the king should be paid him, not even his wages;" but this was for an act done outside the Cortes, not a part of his official functions.[2]

The powers of the Castilian Cortes in this period may be classified under three heads — financial, legislative, and miscellaneous.

From at least as early as the middle of the thirteenth century, it was a recognized custom that when the king desired an extra grant, or *servicio*, over and above what came to him regularly of his own right, he must ask it of the national assembly. In 1307 this custom passed into written law and was confirmed as such in 1329, 1391, 1393, 1420, and afterwards.[3] At the close of the fourteenth century, when the Cortes were at the height of their power, this important privilege was fortified by several temporarily successful demands for an audit, and occasional insistence on a reduction of the sums the king required. Three times the Cortes even secured a partial right of appropriation of the sums they voted, and once they forced the king to deposit their grant with two persons, with the stipulation that nothing should be taken from them save for the Moorish war, for which it had been given.[4] This seemingly

---

[1] *Partida* ii, tit. ix, ley 15; *Cortes*, ii, p. 287; iv, p. 425; Colmeiro, *Introd.*, i, p. 90.

[2] *Crónica de Juan II*, año 1448, cap. iv (*B. A. E.*, lxviii, pp. 658–660); Colmeiro, *Introd.*, i, pp. 90–96.

[3] *Cortes*, i, pp. 187, 428; ii, pp. 489, 527; iii, pp. 23–25, 29; iv, p. 378; Colmeiro, *Introd.*, i, p. 72.

[4] *Cortes*, ii, p. 408; iii, pp. 6, 7; *Crónica de Juan II*, año 1406, caps. xi, xii; año 1411, cap. vi; año 1418, cap

impregnable financial position was, however, seriously weakened in two different ways. First, the fact that the nobles and clergy were generally exempt from taxation (despite several attempts to subject them to it) left the procuradores to bear alone the brunt of every financial struggle against the crown, so that they usually submitted tamely to the royal demands, as the records plainly show.[1] Secondly, by utilization of loans, invention of new imposts, and above all by perpetually postponing the definite settlement of the difficult question as to whether or not certain taxes (especially the blighting *alcabala*) could be levied without the consent of the national assembly, the crown was able to gain alternative means of supply, and thus to circumvent the opposition which it might occasionally be unable to overthrow.[2] Their failure to make the most of their financial rights naturally undermined the position of the Castilian Cortes in other respects.

The share of the Castilian national assembly in legislation rested on a somewhat different basis. The power to make laws, as we have already seen, resided exclusively in the crown. According to an ordinance of 1387, on the other hand, the consent of the Cortes was necessary for the revocation of a valid law, though it is by no means clear that this enactment was rigidly enforced during this period; certainly it was not in the sixteenth century.[3] The most important part of the Cortes' share in legislation, however, lay not here, but in their right to draw up a set of petitions to the crown, which if accepted became the law of the land.

viii; año 1425, cap. x (*B. A. E.*, lxviii, pp. 281 f., 336, 376, 433).

[1] *Cortes*, ii, pp. 402, 408; Colmeiro, *Introd.*, i, pp. 79 f., 84 f.

[2] *Cortes*, ii, pp. 257, 489, 527; iii, p. 97; *Crónica de Juan I*, año x, cap. iii (*B. A. E.*, lxviii, p. 121).

[3] *Cortes*, ii, pp. 371 f.; iii, pp. 406 f.; cf. also an article by the present author on "Control by National Assemblies of the Repeal of Legislation" in *Mélanges d'histoire offerts a M. Charles Bémont* (Paris, 1913), pp. 437-458.

This practice, begun in 1293, became fixed in 1317, and was utilized sometimes by the nobles and clergy, though most frequently, of course, by the third estate.[1] The petitions range over the very widest diversity of topics — administration of justice, measures of police and public safety, dealings with Moors and Jews, granting of letters of naturalization, standards of weights and measures, *barragania*, or licensed concubinage of the clergy, etc.; some were of general, some of local, import.[2] Though the Cortes had no means of enforcing compliance with these requests, they were often accepted and acted upon. That the Castilian assembly was unable to turn this right of petition into a right of legislation (as did the English Parliament in this period) was due to its ineffective procedure, to its failure to make redress precede supply,[3] and to the general lack of coöperation and of political opportunism which characterized its members.

Though based on royal promises and valid ordinances, most of the powers of the Castilian Cortes not included under legislation or finance were really only exercised according to the discretion of the crown. Such was the case in respect to their control of the foreign policy, and the provision that they must be consulted in matters of importance to the wellbeing of the realm.[4] Their share in the recognition of a new sovereign, however, demands more careful definition. The theory of the older historians, that the validity of a king's accession depended on his recognition by the Cortes and on his oath in their presence to observe the established laws, can certainly no longer be maintained.

[1] *Cortes*, i, pp. 106 ff., 299 ff. Hence the various *ordenamientos de prelados* and *hidalgos*, e.g., in 1295, 1315, 1351, 1390, etc.

[2] *Cortes*, i, pp. 145, 179; ii, pp. 14, 249, 303; iii, pp. 389 f., 496.

[3] *Cortes*, iii, p. 496, and the unfulfilled law, *Nueva Recopilación*, lib. vi, tit. vii, ley 8.

[4] *Cortes*, i, p. 40; iii, pp. 21, 809 f.; Colmeiro, *Introd.*, i, pp. 57 ff.

It was customary, indeed, for the national assembly to meet
when a king died, to swear to the heir and receive his oath,
but this was by no means indispensable to the making of a
new monarch.   In the case of the accession of a king under
age the powers of the Cortes were somewhat more extensive,
and included considerable influence in the nomination of
regents and their exercise of power; and they usually recognized the heir to the throne during the lifetime of his predecessor, and were empowered to accept royal abdications.[1]

Allowing for all limitations, the composition and powers
of the Castilian Cortes in the fourteenth and fifteenth centuries indicate, in theory at least, a very high degree of
parliamentary development for that period.   Whether
their authority would have been greater or less, had the
realm been in order and the aristocracy controlled, is a
question which it is easier to ask than to answer.   Certainly
they were to furnish priceless aid to Ferdinand and Isabella
in deposing the rebel nobles from the high place they had
usurped; but after the common enemy had been subdued,
they were to show themselves pitiably unable to reap any
of the rewards of the victory they had helped to win.

The contrast between theory and practice, which we have
already encountered in so many different branches of the
government of mediaeval Castile, is particularly evident
in the administration of justice.   All the various codes,
from the Fuero Juzgo down, declare the king to be the highest judge in the land; they provide for a complete hierarchy
of courts, all of them directly or indirectly dependent on

---

[1] *Partida* ii, tit. xiii, leyes 19 ff.
Cortes, i, p. 132; iii, p. 1; Marina,
Teoría de las Cortes, ii, pp. 24 ff., 47 ff.
There are several instances of royal
accessions without any meeting of the
Cortes till long afterwards. On the
other hand, when Charles V abdicated
without consulting the national assembly, he frankly recognised that he was
violating precedent.

the royal authority; they proclaim all the principles of a perfectly centralized judicial system.[1] But as a matter of fact, the condition of mediaeval Castile in this respect was utterly chaotic. More perhaps than in any other branch of the government service was the weakness of the monarchy reflected in the shortcomings of the law courts.

Let us begin at the top of the ladder with the highest judicial bodies. Down to the middle of the thirteenth century, it is impossible to discern any trustworthy evidence of the existence of a regularly organized royal court. When the king meted out justice, he surrounded himself with a number of magnates whose advice he valued, and the tribunal thus constituted soon came to be known as the *Curia* or *Cort*; but it was not always composed of the same persons; its authority was purely consultative; and no clear line of demarcation was as yet drawn between it and the equally irregular and amorphous Royal Council.[2] Under Alfonso X, however, whose zeal for the creation of the forms of strong monarchical government was only exceeded by his inability to invest them with any real vitality or power, the first steps were taken toward the definite, permanent, separate organization of a central royal court. By an ordinance of the Cortes of Zamora in 1274 he created a supreme tribunal, composed of twenty-three *alcaldes de corte* — nine of them from Castile, eight from Leon, and six from Estremadura — some of whom were to be always present in the royal household to administer justice continually. In addition to these twenty-three alcaldes, the Ordinance of 1274 also provided that there should be three special judges, "good men who knew and understood the fueros of the land, to hear appeals"; it also laid down rules

---

[1] *Fuero Juzgo*, lib. ii. tit. i, ley 13; *Partida* iii. tit. iv, leyes 1, 2; *Fuero Real*, lib. i, tit. vii, ley 2. [2] Altamira, § 294.

for the exercise of appellate jurisdiction, and enumerated
the cases of which the king claimed cognizance in the first
instance.[1] At the outset Alfonso promised to sit in person
three days a week for the administration of justice; but as
time went on, the pressure of other business limited the royal
presence to Friday, which became and remained from thenceforth the special day for the sovereign to exercise his function as the highest judge in the land.   When the king was
absent, the alcaldes sat in judgment under the leadership
of the *adelantado del rey* or *sobrejuez*; in other words, the
central court, whose function had hitherto been solely advisory, was gradually beginning to acquire a jurisdiction and
authority of its own.[2]

From the death of Alfonso the Learned to the accession
of the house of Trastamara, the royal tribunal fell on evil
days. During the reign of Sancho the Bravo, who owed his
throne to the support of the aristocracy, it practically ceased
to exist. Under Henry II and his son John I, however, it
was reconstituted on a more permanent basis and came to be
known as the *Audiencia* or *Chancillerta*.[3] At first it held its
sessions at the court of the king; in 1387 it was ordered to
divide its time equally between Medina del Campo, Olmedo,
Alcalá de Henares, and Madrid; in 1390 it was set up at
Segovia; in 1405, at Valladolid; but the constant complaints of the Cortes show that when separated from the
monarch it was not seldom terrorized by the aristocracy
into neglecting its duties. During this period and subsequently its composition varied again and again. Its judges
were of course exclusively recruited from the ranks of the
clergy and of the *letrados*; and efforts were made to appor-

[1] *Cortes*, i, pp. 89–92 (Zamora, 1274, leyes 17–35); Colmeiro, *Curso*, pp. 560 ff.

[2] Altamira, § 444.

[3] On the different shades of meaning of these two names, see F. Mendizábal, in *R. A.*, 3d ser., xxx (1914), pp. 62–65.

tion them fairly among the different quarters of the realm. By 1433 the Audiencia was divided into two main *salas* for civil and criminal suits; the judges in the former were generally known as *oidores*; those in the latter as *alcaldes*. There was also a special *sala de los hijos-dalgo* for the adjudication of baronial suits, and a *procurador fiscal*, or special prosecutor on behalf of the crown. From the verdicts of the Audiencia there was, generally speaking, no appeal; but the records show that the king not seldom inhibited it from proceeding with the more important cases that came before it, in order that he might deal with them himself.[1] The complaints of the procuradores, as well as the frequency with which changes occurred in the composition and powers of the tribunal, furnish ample proof that the institution was not working satisfactorily in the period immediately preceding the accession of the Catholic Kings.[2]

Below the Audiencia was a whole hierarchy of minor local courts, presided over for the most part by *adelantados menores* (*de comarca* or *fronterizos*) and *merinos*. These functionaries were originally crown appointees, but from the thirteenth century onward their offices, particularly that of the *adelantados*, tended to become hereditary in certain prominent families, greatly to the prejudice of the effective administration of justice in the districts committed to their charge.[3] They possessed executive and military as well as judicial powers; one authority describes the *adelantados* as "captains rather than magistrates," and

[1] The Royal Council, presided over by the monarch, was still, of course, the supreme tribunal of the nation.

[2] On this paragraph cf. Colmeiro, *Curso*, pp. 563-569; F. Mendizábal, "Origen, historia, y organización de la Real Chancillería de Valladolid," in *R. A.*, 3d ser., xxx (1914), pp. 61-72, 243-253. Both these authorities give ample references to the sources.

[3] *Espéculo*, lib. ii, tit. xiii, ley 3; *Partida* ii, tit. ix, leyes 22, 23; R. R. Hill, "The Office of Adelantado," in *Political Science Quarterly*, xxviii (1913), pp. 648-652; and note to p. 210, *ante.* There were *merinos menores* as well as *merinos mayores*; the former were appointed by the latter or by the *adelantados.*

the *merinos* as " magistrates rather than captains." [1]   They often lost touch, however, with the central power they were sent out to represent, and their tribunals were frequently overawed by the aristocracy.   At the bottom of the ladder came the municipal alcaldes, whose selection had usually been delegated by the sovereign to the Concejo in the local charter or fuero ; there were, moreover, a certain number of minor judges whose appointment had been usurped by the great lords in defiance of the rights of the crown.   Numerous conflicts of jurisdiction were the natural result.   In certain exceptional cases the lesser authorities claimed the power of overriding the decisions of the central government ; but, generally speaking, the theory was that appeal lay from the locally appointed magistrate to the lowest crown judge, and from him through the successive grades of *merinos* and *adelantados* to the Audiencia and the king.

This apparently adequate system of local judicial officers, however, broke down in practice even more completely than the central court, or Audiencia, above it.   Very significant in this connection are the numerous efforts of the kings of the fourteenth and fifteenth centuries to strengthen and protect their minor judges in the faithful performance of their duties.   Royal inspectors, called *pesquisidores*, were frequently sent out to inquire about them, and to report on their work at headquarters.   The name of these officials recalls the fact that there was inaugurated, in this period, a new form of judicial procedure called the *pesquisa*, by which the king or his judges were empowered to bring action, *motu proprio*, against any notorious delinquent, without waiting for specific accusation by a regular plaintiff.   Henceforth this new method gradually began

---

[1] Colmeiro, *Curso*, pp. 548–550. With the *adelantado fronterizo*, on whom rested the duty of defending the realm against foreign invasion, the military side took the precedence of everything else.

to supersede the older forms of public and oral trial, which
had often resulted in the past in the escape of powerful
hidalgos whom lesser men dared not openly accuse.[1] More
important still was the sending out of the first *corregidores*
in the reign of Alfonso XI. These were royally appointed
magistrates imposed upon the municipalities for the purpose of aiding and ultimately of superseding those who had
been locally elected. They may be regarded as the successors of the so-called *jueces de salario*, whom we find
mentioned in the Cortes of 1293, and were intended, like
them, to carry the king's authority and jurisdiction into
every corner of the realm.[2] The corregidores, however,
soon attained a measure of authority which their predecessors had never known. In addition to their judicial
functions, they rapidly developed wide powers in administration and in finance.[3] They were not merely judges;
they soon converted themselves into the 'state's men of
all work.' For the present the possibilities of their office
were not evident to the world at large, because of the abasement of the central power which they represented. But
when the monarchy had emerged triumphant over the
factions, and the crowns of Castile and Aragon had been
united, the corregidores were to become the cornerstone
of the administrative edifice of Spain and of the Spanish
Empire.

It must not be imagined that the municipalities endured
these invasions of their liberties and privileges without a
protest. The procuradores in the Cortes steadily main-

---

[1] *Partida* iii, tit. xvii; Altamira,
§ 446. An interesting English parallel
to this is the form of procedure temporarily legalized by the Statute 11
Henry VII, c. 3 (1495). Cf. Busch,
England under the Tudors (tr. Todd), p.
274.

[2] Colmeiro, *Curso*. p. 531; *Cortes*, i,
p. 120 (Valladolid, 1293, pet. 4). Castillo de Bovadilla, *Política para Corregidores* (Barcelona, 1616), i, pp. 17 ff.,
traces the origin of the office back to
God and the days of the Creation.

[3] Mariéjol, p. 172.

tained that no corregidor could be imposed on any town
without a definite request from the inhabitants, on the
ground that such action was a breach of the fueros. The
constant recurrence of petitions to this effect is doubtless an
indication that the principle was not always fully observed,[1]
but there were certainly many cities which succeeded in
preserving their immunity. The *cuadernos* are filled with
requests that the corregidores be not permitted to hold
office for more than one year, that they be selected, not
among the minions of the king, but from the inhabitants
of the region over which they are set, and that they be men
of character and ability suitable to their exalted functions.
In the weak reigns of John II and Henry IV we find many
complaints that they abused their authority, increased the
evils that they were sent out to suppress, and, above all,
that they were scandalously corrupt, and cared only for the
money that they could make out of their position.[2] And
finally, as a means of controlling the acts of wicked appointees, the procuradores demanded of the crown, at least
as early as the year 1419, that corregidores, at the expiration of their term, be obliged to remain for at least fifty
days in the region where they had held office, so that any one
who believed himself to have been wronged by their verdicts might state his case and have justice.[3] This seems
to be the first intimation in Castile of the institution of
the *residencia*, which was to be developed so much further
under the Catholic Kings. All these items show that the
corregidores were far from popular among the mass of the

[1] *Cortes*, ii, pp. 187, 207, 301 (Medina del Campo, 1370, pet. 12; Toro, 1371, pet. 8; Soria, 1380, pet. 1); iii, pp. 37, 205 f. (Ocaña, 1422, pet. 2; Madrid, 1435, pet. 17).

[2] Colmeiro, *Curso*, pp. 535 ff.; *Cortes*, ii, pp. 152, 297 (Burgos, 1367, pet. 14; Burgos, 1379, pet. 30); iii, pp. 677 f., 704 f. (Cordoba, 1455, pet. 3; Toledo, 1462, pet. 2).

[3] *Cortes*, iii, pp. 15, 206 f., 272 f., 327 f. (Madrid, 1419, pet. 6; Madrid, 1435, pet. 18; Toledo, 1436, pet. 15; Madrigal, 1438, pet. 19).

people; but the fact that most of the complaints occur during the reigns of the weaker kings is an indication that the protests were evoked quite as much by the unworthy character of the officials themselves and of the monarchs they served, as by the principle of centralization which they represented. Certainly local conditions were bad enough to demand a remedy, provided one could be discovered that was not worse than the disease.

It will be evident that the different institutions described in the preceding paragraphs represent rather the longings and aspirations of the Castilian kingship for a more efficient central government than any accomplished result. Nothing permanent could be effected until order had been reestablished by the strong hand of the Catholic Kings; and the chief significance of the constitutional experiments of their predecessors lies far less in what they achieved at the time, than in the fact that they afforded Ferdinand and Isabella precious material to work with, when at last the opportunity came. Confusion remained the salient feature of the Castilian judicial régime throughout the period at present under review; and if we are to appreciate the full extent of it we must supplement our examination of the hierarchy of courts and judges with a brief account of the various legal codes which they were supposed to administer. Of all the nations of Western Europe, Spain traces her legal system back to that of Rome in most direct descent; but the struggle between the Roman and Visigothic elements was long and bitter, and was immensely complicated by the incorrigible particularism which caused each class and each locality to lay claim to a special law of its own. In the twelfth century, at the time of the great revival of Roman law in Western Europe, Castilian students visited the famous schools of northern Italy and southern France, and brought back the knowledge they had gained there to their native land.[1] This furnished a foundation for Alfonso the Learned to build on, so that he was enabled to infuse the Roman principles into the greatest and most notable of his law books, and to evoke some measure of order from the wild confusion which had reigned in earlier years. But precedents in the legal history of his native land were as essential to the great legislative work of the Scholar King as were the teachings of the glossarists of Bologna; and in order to discover what these precedents were, we must briefly trace the development of legislation in Leon and in Castile from the time of the barbarian invasions.

When the Visigoths arrived in Spain, in the early fifth century, they brought with them all their barbarian customs, which were subsequently written down by King Euric. The native Hispano-Romans, however — numerically by far the largest portion of the population — were suffered to retain their own laws, which were, of course, almost exclusively Roman in origin. Nay more, Alaric II in the year 506, before his departure for the battle of Vouillé, took pains to codify and arrange these Roman laws for the use of the conquered population in the famous Breviary of Alaric or *Lex Romana Visigothorum*, based chiefly on the Theodosian Code, the Institutes of Gaius, and the *Sententiae* of Paulus. But the Visigoths did not long remain content with this double system of law, which divided them from the subject population. Of all the barbarian nations they were the most inclined to imitate the ways of imperial

[1] A college for Spanish students was founded at Bologna by the will of the famous Cardinal Albornoz, who died in 1367; it still exists, "under the control of the Spanish government, which sends to it candidates for the diplomatic service [and other persons] who have previously taken the B.A. degree in a Spanish University." Cf. Rashdall, *Universities of Europe in the Middle Ages*, i, pp. 200–204. There is a fuller account of this interesting foundation at the end of J. G. Sepúlveda's life of Cardinal Albornoz, which may be found in his *Opera* (Madrid, 1780, 4 vols.), iv, pp. 77–85.

Rome, whose superiority they clearly discerned. As long
as the barrier of religion separated them from the native
Spaniards a complete fusion of the two legal systems was
out of the question; but with the conversion of Reccared
in 587, the way was opened for a new code, which should be
valid for both portions of the community. Such a code
was put forth in the seventh century, chiefly through the
instrumentality of Kings Chindaswinth and Recceswinth;
and it is commonly known as the *Fuero Juzgo*. Dispute
rages hotly over the relative strength of the Visigothic and
Roman elements in it, but the weight of opinion seems to
favor the view that the latter was distinctly predominant.
Whatever the facts may be in this particular, it is certain
that the Fuero Juzgo remained the law of most of Christian
Spain down to the middle of the thirteenth century, except in so far as it was contradicted or superseded by local
fueros.[1]

The importance of this last exception, however, is almost
certain to be underestimated by any one who has not studied
in detail the history of mediaeval Spain. In addition to
the struggle for mastery between the Visigothic and Roman
systems, the traditions of Spanish separatism rendered impossible, for centuries to come, the observance of any
universally binding central code. In the first place, each
locality had its own fuero, or custom, which was not seldom
invoked to the prejudice of the law of the land. In the
second, each class of society had its own special privileges
and immunities. Those of the nobles were naturally of
first importance; they were apparently written down and
codified at the so-called Cortes of Najera in 1137. Exactly
to what extent and for how long they were valid are dis-

[1] Antequera, *Historia de la Legisla-
ción Española*, caps. v, vi; Ladreda, *Estudios históricos sobre los Códigos de
Castilla*, caps. ii, iii.

puted questions; but they were certainly regarded as a
basis for the definition of the rights of the aristocracy in
later codes of undoubted authenticity.[1]   Those of the clergy
and of the monasteries, and of special corporations like the
Mesta, were scarcely less extensive.   Many communities
recognized no law whatsoever, and were governed merely
according to local custom and tradition, and the judgments
of arbiters selected among the inhabitants, "por fazañas,
albedríos, y costumbres" as the phrase ran.[2]   All these
incongruities were considerably less abhorrent to the
mediaeval jurist than they would be to his successor of
today; but even contemporaries realized the crying need
of unification and reform.

St. Ferdinand cherished plans of far-reaching improvements, but death cut him off in the midst of his labors, and
he bequeathed the unfinished task to his learned son.   No
better illustration could be desired of the many contrasts
and contradictions in the character and career of Alfonso
X than is afforded by the history of his various legislative
enterprises.   Whatever their faults and the inability of the
monarch to enforce them, they entitle Alfonso to a fame as
a lawgiver which will long outlive his reputation as a king.
In general, the codes which he put forth fall into two fairly
distinct groups.   The first includes those in which the

[1] Cf. *Ordenamiento de Alcalá*, prólogo
to tit. xxxii.   The so-called *Fuero Viejo*
or *Fuero de los Fijos-dalgo* states in its
prologue that it was drawn up in its
final form by Pedro the Cruel in 1356,
on the basis of earlier compilations of
the privileges of the aristocracy, whose
validity previous monarchs had constantly striven to impugn; cf. Antequera, *Legislación*, pp. 167 ff.; Ladreda,
Códigos, pp. 76–78.   The inaccuracies in
this prologue, however, are so numerous, that it seems more than doubtful
whether any of its statements can be
accepted; and a strong case has recently
been put forward for the theory that
the *Fuero Viejo* was merely a private
compilation of the fifteenth century,
which never attained legal validity.
Altamira, § 456.   But whatever the
facts about the *Fuero Viejo*, the other
codes contain plenty of evidence of the
enormous extent of the privileges of the
aristocracy.

[2] M. and M., ii, pp. 220 ff.; cf. also
J. Costa, *Derecho Consuetudinario y
Economía Popular de España*, *passim*;
Antequera, *op. cit.*, pp. 160 f.

national Visigothic features predominate; the second comprises those in which the influence of Roman law is supreme. To the first belong the *Fuero Real* and its various special supplements and the mass of municipal charters; to the second, the *Especulo* and *Las Siete Partidas*.[1]

The *Fuero Real* or *Fuero de las Leyes* was promulgated in 1254–55, and is in effect a summary, codification, and reconciliation of all existing fueros, whether of local or national scope, from the Fuero Juzgo down[2] — an attempt to substitute one law book for the many partially conflicting ones previously in force. In the Prólogo we find the statement that the king, having taken counsel with his advisers and those learned in the law, had determined to give the people this fuero to be judged by at their own request.[3] Pursuant to this intention, the Fuero Real was adopted as law by the royal courts; it was granted as a local municipal fuero to a number of important towns; for seventeen years it apparently even superseded the aristocratic privileges promulgated at Najera, until their reëstablishment in the Cortes of Burgos in 1271.[4] In general, it may be said that the Fuero Real remained the principal law book of the realm for nearly a century after its promulgation, and was actually observed whenever it did not conflict with the established custom of this or that locality or place. This is perhaps an unsatisfactory definition of the state of affairs; but in view of the facts as they have come down to us, it is impossible to be more specific. The

---

[1] We know too little of the compilation called the *Setenario*, begun by St. Ferdinand and apparently finished by Alfonso X, to enable us to place it definitely in either of those categories. Cf. Altamira, § 455; Ladreda, *op. cit.*, pp. 87 f.

[2] There are also, however, certain traces of the influence of Roman law discernible in it, as, for instance, in its provisions concerning intestacy. Cf. Altamira, *Cuestiones de Historia del Derecho*, p. 128.

[3] In Martínez Alcubilla, *Códigos*, p. 105.

[4] Antequera, *op. cit.*, pp. 254 ff.; Colmeiro, *Introd.*, i, p. 162.

national tendency towards diversity and variety — more noticeable perhaps in the domain of law than anywhere else — was destined to withstand for many generations to come all the strivings of the monarchy for unification.

The minor codes supplementary to the Fuero Real are chiefly important as indicating the immense range of Alfonso's knowledge and interest in matters of legislation; they also show the difficulties which the central government experienced in obtaining any general observance of the Fuero Real. The Leyes Nuevas deal with questions of usury and debt, inheritance, and the relations of Christians and Moors; in their Prólogo they frankly state that the judges cannot determine how these matters are to be treated under the Fuero Real, and that additional regulations are necessary to enlighten them.[1] The Leyes del Estilo are rather a statement and explanation of the law by eminent jurists than a code in the proper sense of the word. They comprise two hundred and fifty-two capitulos and attempt to reconcile the differences between the Fuero Real and the many local laws with which it came into conflict.[2] The Leyes de los Adelantados consist of a set of five ordinances concerning the rights and duties of these magistrates.[3] Of another character was the Ordenamiento de las Tafurerías, or ordinance concerning gaming houses, which paid the state a tax in return for the permission to remain in existence, and which had not been adequately regulated in the earlier codes.[4]

The other side of Alfonso's legislative work — including the Especulo and the Partidas — shows foreign Roman influence as plainly as the Fuero Real shows the national,

---

[1] Martínez Alcubilla, Códigos, pp. 176 f.

[2] Ibid., pp. 149–173.

[3] Ibid., pp. 175 f.; ante, p. 210, note 2.

[4] Martínez Alcubilla, op. cit., pp. 184–188; Antequera, Historia de la Legislación, pp. 259 f.

and represents far more accurately the real leanings and theories of the Scholar King. The *Especulo* or *Espejo de todos los derechos*, which is generally regarded as the first legislative work of Alfonso in point of time, has been only partially preserved. Its preface states that it comprises a choice of all the best fueros of the land, made with the advice and consent of the ecclesiastical authorities, *ricos hombres*, and jurisconsults, and given to the people to be ruled by; but there is no evidence that the latter part of this programme was ever actually carried out. The *Especulo* was in fact only the first attempt of Alfonso radically to alter legislation in Castile by the introduction of Roman principles; it served as "a preliminary sketch of the *Partidas*" and was "intended to pave the way for the greater code, to which, as Alfonso plainly foresaw, there was bound to be strenuous opposition." [1] It never was recognized as the law of the land, but was doubtless utilized by the jurists of the period as a book of reference and consultation. [2]

We are thus brought to the last and greatest of the legislative works of the Scholar King, the *Libro de las Leyes*, or *Las Siete Partidas*, as it is usually called on account of the seven great sections into which it is divided. It seems probable that it was begun in 1256 and finished in 1265 by a number of jurists whose names have not come down to us, under the supervision and direction of the king himself. [3] Its sources were: (1) the fueros and good customs of Castile and Leon, such as the Fuero Juzgo and Fuero Real, and the principal municipal charters; (2) the canon law as set forth in the Decretals; and (3) the Pandects of Justinian and the commentaries of the most famous Italian jurists thereon. [4]

[1] Colmeiro, *Reyes*, p. 327.
[2] Antequera, *Historia de la Legislación*, pp. 248 ff.; Martínez Alcubilla, *Códigos*, p. 190. The text of the *Especulo* is given on pp. 7–206 of vol. vi of *Los códigos Españoles*, ed. Rivadeneyra.
[3] Antequera, *op. cit.*, cap. xiv.
[4] Altamira, § 455.

THE INSTITUTIONS OF MEDIAEVAL CASTILE

Of these three elements the last two were unquestionably predominant, so that the Partidas may justly be described as an attempt to unify the laws on a Roman basis; but the principles of the older Castilian legislation were by no means entirely forgotten. Alfonso knew that his people could never be induced to abandon their ancient laws and customs at once; and every now and then one encounters passages in the Partidas which betray a defiantly Germanic origin utterly at variance with the Romanist ideals of the Scholar King. One illustration will suffice: "If a father is so closely besieged in a castle which he holds for his lord, as to be utterly deprived of all food, he may kill and eat his son without prejudice to his honor, rather than surrender the castle without his lord's command."[1]

But the Partidas are much more than a mere compilation of laws. They contain a number of moral and philosophical reflections of a legal nature, a quantity of political maxims, and many disquisitions on the qualities and characteristics which ideally perfect rulers and institutions should display. A few titles may be cited by way of illustration. "How a king should be moderate in eating and in drinking";[2] "How the children of a king should be trained to be well dressed and cleanly";[3] "How doctors and surgeons who represent themselves as learned and are not so, deserve to be punished if any one dies through their fault";[4] "That no monk should be permitted to study physic or laws."[5] And this curious medley of apparently incongruous elements naturally leads us to inquire what was the real purpose of Alfonso in preparing this great code. Was it

[1] *Partida* iv, tit. xvii, ley 8. For further light on the subject of the Germanic element in Spanish law, and particularly in the local fueros, cf. E. de Hinojosa, "Das germanische Element im spanischen Rechte," in the *Zeitschrift für Rechtsgeschichte*, germ. Abth. xxxi, pp. 282–359.
[2] *Partida* ii, tit. v, ley 2.
[3] *Partida* ii, tit. vii, ley 5.
[4] *Partida* vii, tit. viii, ley 6.
[5] *Partida* i, tit. vii, ley 28.

intended to be a great legal encyclopaedia, a guide to the
basic principles of legislation, for use by the king and great
jurists of the realm? Or, did the Scholar King intend to
put it at once into practice as the common law of the land
to the prejudice of the Fuero Juzgo, the Fuero Real, and the
different lôcal charters? The Chronicle of Alfonso X states
that the king commanded all his subjects to accept the
Partidas as their law and fuero, and ordered his judges to
decide cases accordingly,[1] and there are passages in the code
itself which support this assertion;[2] yet on the other hand,
the prologue to the Partidas describes them as a 'book for
the instruction of kings,'[3] while a royal order to the alcaldes
of Valladolid, of August, 1258, specifically prohibits the
use of Roman law in Castile.[4] Besides, if the Partidas
were intended to be observed as the law of the land,
why, in addition to promulgating the Fuero Real, did
Alfonso continue to confirm ancient local charters and
also to issue new ones almost down to the day of his
death? Was it understood that these local charters should
be valid save when they conflicted with the law of the land?
These questions are scarcely susceptible of definite answers;
they will probably long remain among the unsolved problems in which the career of this strange sovereign abounds.
A possible explanation may be offered by the theory that
though the king himself preferred the absolutist principles
of the Roman law, he realized the intensity of his people's
attachment to the national codes, and catered to their
prejudices by compiling, simplifying, and confirming these
at the same time that he drew up another law book inspired
by the ideas in which he believed.

Whatever the final verdict on these matters, the fact

---

[1] *Crónica*, cap. ix (*B. A. E.*, lxvi, p. 8).

[2] Ladreda, *op. cit.*, p. 112.

[3] Martínez Alcubilla, *Códigos*, p. 196.

[4] Altamira, § 455.

remains that Las Siete Partidas were never formally declared
to be the law of the land during the lifetime of the Scholar
King; not until the famous enactment known as the *Ordenamiento de Alcalá* in 1348 did they attain even theoretical validity.   During the eighty-three years which elapsed
between their completion and their definite acceptance, the
Fuero Real and the municipal charters remained in force.[1]
On the other hand, it would be a great mistake to suppose
that Las Siete Partidas exerted no influence during this
period.   Though technically invalid, they were being constantly consulted by lawyers, legal professors, and students
at the universities.   They turned a generation of jurists
to the study of the Roman law — the predecessors of the
letrados who were to render such invaluable service to the
monarchy in the days of the Catholic Kings.   Some of their
principles were undoubtedly introduced into the actual
practice of the courts; the Ordenamiento de Alcalá itself
speaks of the conflicts of jurisdiction which arose as a result
of this.[2]   We may well believe that Alfonso XI, who was as
ardent a believer in royal absolutism as his namesake had
been before him, and far more capable of carrying his ideas
into practice, was not slow to seize an opportunity to strike a
blow for the code which formed the basis for his own theories
of government.   If, without formal promulgation, Las Siete
Partidas could vindicate themselves to the extent that they
had already done, might they not hope to take precedence
of all other codes and charters, when supported by a solemn
declaration of their validity by the king?   At any rate, Alfonso XI thought it worth while to give the plan a trial;
and in the year 1348 he accordingly established Las Siete
Partidas as the law of the land, save where they were con-

[1] Antequera, *Historia de la Legislación*, cap. xv.

[2] Altamira, *Cuestiones de Historia
del Derecho*, pp. 132–134.

tradicted by the Fuero Real, the municipal charters, and the privileges of the aristocracy; the great code was thus formally declared for the first time to be in force in Castile, though it was relegated to a subordinate position.[1] Several important modifications in the Partidas were introduced at the same time — most of them in the direction of concessions to the national fueros — which served to increase their popularity. The legislative activity of the kings and Cortes of the period further strengthened the forces of unification and centralization; while the increasingly absolutist sentiment of the age all over Western Europe furnished an invaluable support for the tendencies which Alfonso desired to promote. To imagine that variety, diversity, and confusion ceased to be the distinguishing features of Castilian law after the Ordenamiento de Alcalá, would be a grievous misconception; but the period which elapsed between Alfonso XI and Ferdinand and Isabella saw them sensibly diminish and the Partidas emerge "from the position of a subordinate and supplementary law to that of the principal law of the land."[2] During that long interval there was in theory no alteration in the relative position of the different codes established in the Ordenamiento de Alcalá, but as a matter of fact the Partidas steadily increased in prestige and popularity, and the national fueros correspondingly declined. The extreme turbulence of the times prevented the meaning of this change from being entirely apparent to contemporaries, but it is doubtful whether Ferdinand and Isabella could have found an adequate legal basis for their absolutism, had it not been for the various legislative reforms of their predecessors.

A number of changes in judicial procedure and penalties were also effected during the two centuries between

---

[1] *Ordenamiento de Alcalá*, tit. xxviii.   [2] Altamira, § 456.

Alfonso X and the Catholic Kings. In addition to the use of the *pesquisa*, which we have already noticed, and the corresponding decline in the practice of oral accusation, all the so-called *pruebas vulgares*, such as judicial combat and the ordeal, were definitely abolished after the early fourteenth century, excepting the *rieptos* or duels of the aristocracy, which Alfonso X and his successors wisely judged it to be impossible to do away with, and therefore attempted to regulate. The legislation on this subject in the various codes is extremely interesting, and gives a vivid picture of the spirit of the Castilian aristocracy.[1] The cruel and ferocious punishments of earlier days were little abated, if at all. One section in the Partidas forbids branding in the face, cutting the nostrils, exoculation, lapidation, crucifixion, and throwing over a precipice;[2] but these regulations were not observed, and some of them were specifically contradicted in another part of the same code.[3] The use of torture continued, but was strictly limited to certain types of criminals, and was only permitted in the presence of witnesses. Cognizance of the crime of heresy, which was regarded as a heinous form of treason, was vested by the Partidas in the bishops; if found guilty, the culprit was handed over, as in other lands, to the secular arm for punishment. Death by the fire was the penalty prescribed in the Alfonsine codes; and at an earlier date St. Ferdinand caused several heretics to be boiled alive.[4]

Still another illustration of the wide gulf that separated theory from practice in the institutional life of mediaeval Castile is presented by the state of the national finances

---

[1] *Partida* vii, tits. iii and iv; *Ordenamiento de Alcalá*, tit. vi, leyes 7-11; tit. xxxii, ley 4; Altamira, §§ 446 f.

[2] *Partida* vii, tit. xxxi, ley 6.

[3] *Partida* vii, tit. xxxviii, ley 4.

[4] *Partida* vii, tit. xxvi, ley 2; Altamira, § 446.

at the close of the period under review. The number and variety of the revenues to which the king was in one way or another legally entitled were enormous; elaborate machinery had been devised, and numerous officials appointed for their collection, and yet the poverty of the Castilian monarchs was a jest in the mouths of their subjects. Undoubtedly a similar condition obtained in the treasuries of all the sovereigns of Western Europe during the period of baronial anarchy immediately preceding the establishment of absolute monarchy. The emptiness of the royal coffers was everywhere the measure of the impotence of the central government. The situation in Castile, however, was probably much worse than the average, just as the abasement of the royal power was more complete; and it presents a number of features of special interest.[1]

In the early days of the Reconquest, the royal revenues were largely derived from contributions of a preëminently feudal nature. These did not vary essentially in number or variety from those prevalent in mediaeval times in other lands. The *petitum* or *moneda*, a special contribution levied by the crown on occasions of special importance, such as the marriage of a member of the royal family; the *conducho* or *yantares*, that is, the royal right of purveyance and entertainment or its pecuniary equivalent; the *fonsadera*, or indemnity for exemption from military service; and the *calonna*, or fine incident on a locality for permitting a crime to go unpunished within its limits, may be cited as typical examples.[2] But as time went on, and the framework of a regular central government gradually

---

[1] For the standard authorities on this topic, cf. bibliographical note at the end of this chapter, p. 270, and Boissonnade's bibliographical studies in the *Revue de synthèse historique*, described on p. 42, *ante*.

[2] Conde de Cedillo, *Contribuciones é Impuestos en León y Castilla*, pp. 126–149, 186 ff.; Colmeiro, *E. P.*, i, pp. 464 ff.

made its appearance, these feudal dues began to fall into
the background and to be supplanted by a more modern
set of revenues. In other words, a system of national taxation began to emerge. Sometimes the feudal due was itself
converted into a national tax, as, for instance, the *moneda*,
which was at first levied on special occasions, but after the
thirteenth century apparently became a regular annual contribution, until it was abolished in the reign of Henry III.[1]
The *moneda forera* also, which was originally a lump sum ·
paid by the municipalities for exemption from all feudal
dues, except from the *fonsadera* and the *yantares*, appears
in the sixteenth century as a septennial levy incident on all
men in recognition of the sovereignty of the crown.[2] Often
the feudal due was gradually suffered to fall into abeyance
and the newer types of taxation permitted to replace it.
Of these the most important were as follows.

1. The *capitación* incident on Moors and Jews who were
permitted to remain in Christian territory. A petition of
the Cortes of Valladolid in 1312 indicates that the standard
rate was six thousand maravedis per day from each *aljama*
or community in the realm; but there were numerous local
variations, and even complete exemptions, which were the
cause of constant complaint. In Segovia it appears that
the Jews paid annually thirty dineros apiece as a perpetual
reminder of the sum for which Christ was betrayed, but
as this impost was collected by the bishop, it seems
probable that it was a special local levy in excess of the regular capitation.[3]

2. The *servicio*, or special tax, which could be voted

---

[1] At least in time of peace: the frequent abuses of it in the preceding
period were believed by a contemporary
to have been the cause of the depopu-
lation of Castile; cf. Conde de Cedillo,
op. cit., pp. 515 f.

[2] Colmeiro, *E. P.*, i, p. 469.

[3] *Cortes*, i, p. 220 (Valladolid, 1312,
pet. 102); Colmenares, *Historia de Segovia*, cap. xxiii, § 14; Colmeiro, *E. P.*,
i, p. 471.

only by the Cortes, and has already been considered under
that head. The procuradores made strenuous, though not
always successful, efforts to subject forced loans or *emprés-
titos* to the same condition.[1]

3. The *sisa*, or tax on food stuffs, first established by
Sancho IV, but withdrawn, owing to its intense unpopu-
larity, by his widow Doña Maria during the minority of
Ferdinand IV. It was, however, to reappear.[2]

4. Revenues from mines and salt pits. Laws of Alfonso
X and Alfonso XI declared these to be a part of the royal
domain and their products the property of the crown. In
the case of the mines, the demands of the monarchy were
apparently often satisfied by an arrangement that a fraction
of their output should be handed to it; with the salt pits
the royal monopoly, theoretically at least, was maintained
in full.[3]

5. The so-called *tercias reales*, or royal thirds of the tithe
that was due to the church, which the kings retained on the
pretext that the clergy ought to contribute directly to the
crusade against the Moors. This right, which was only
provisionally recognized by the ecclesiastical authorities
in the Middle Ages, became regular and permanent in the
days of Ferdinand and Isabella. As the government usually
handed back one third of the third received, for the benefit
of the buildings of the parish churches, its share was ultimately reduced to two ninths.[4]

[1] On this question of *emprés titos*, see *Cortes*, ii, pp. 257, 408, 489, 527 (Bur-
gos, 1373, pet. 1; Palencia, 1388, pet. 1; Madrid, 1391, orden. 8; Madrid, 1393, pet. 3); Colmeiro, *Introd.*, i, pp. 79 f.; the same, *E. P.*, i, pp. 497 ff.
[2] Conde de Cedillo, *op. cit.*, pp. 384 f. The *sisa* apparently originated in Ara-
gon; cf. Canga Argüelles, ii, p. 578, and Berganza, *Antiguedades de España*, ii, p. 183.

[3] *Partida* iii, tit. xxviii, ley 11; *Orde-
namiento de Alcalá*, tit. xxxii, leyes 47 f.; *Cortes*, ii, p. 397 (Briviesca, 1387, pet. 49); Gallardo, *Rentas Reales*, vi, pp. 1–19; Colmeiro, *E. P.*, i, p. 470.
[4] *Nov. Recop.*, lib. i, tit. vii, ley 1; Canga Argüelles, *Diccionario de Ha-
cienda*, ii, p. 592; Colmeiro, *E. P.*, i, p. 470; Conde de Cedillo, *op. cit.*, pp. 299–301.

6. National customs duties, or *derechos de aduana*. From the thirteenth century onward, all commodities were subject to the payment of a duty on entering and leaving the realm. The rate was ordinarily one tenth the value of the commodity in question, which doubtless accounts for the fact that the word *diezmo* was often used to denote it as well as the ecclesiastical tithe.[1] This duty was levied in return for the protection given to the traveller or merchant and his goods; and it is worth noting that the treatment which strangers were accorded at the frontiers of mediaeval Castile contrasts favorably with that meted out in many European and American custom houses today. The personal effects of the average traveller were exempt from payment; the oath or declaration of the merchant was accepted in regard to the content of the cases he brought with him, which he was not obliged to unpack; but if an intent to defraud was discovered, the penalty was death and the confiscation of the goods.[2] Some commodities could not, in theory, be exported at all, especially silver and gold; and there were an infinite number of local exceptions and exemptions. Theories of protection of national industries, however, were not yet fully developed, and the revenues from the *aduanas*, though considerable, were not comparable to the income derived from this source by Ferdinand and Isabella and their successors.[3]

7. Local customs duties. The traditions of Castilian separatism favored the maintenance of internal tolls. The

[1] Colmeiro, *E. P.*, i, p. 471. The commercial *diezmo* was usually called the *diezmo de mar*, or *diezmo de puertos secos*, as the case might be, to distinguish it from the ecclesiastical *diezmo*, or the *medio diezmo* of the military orders. Further references and much further information on this complicated subject may be found in Dr. J. Klein's as yet unpublished doctoral dissertation on the Mesta (especially chapters iii and xi) in the Harvard College Library

[2] *Partida* v, tit. vii, leyes 5, 8; Colmeiro, *E. P.*, cap. xxxvii.

[3] *Cortes*, ii, pp. 57, 59, 70 (Valladolid, 1351, pets. 17, 20, 70); *Leyes del Estilo*, ley 201; *Memorial Histórico Español*, ii, p. 29; Canga Argüelles, *op. cit.* (under "Rentas Reales"), ii, pp. 491 ff.; Colmeiro, *E. P.*, i, pp. 335 ff.

foreigner who had passed the frontier found other barriers
awaiting him within the realm, and those Castilians whose
business took them from one end of the country to another
were obliged to pay dearly for that privilege. The terms
portazgo, *pontazgo*, and *montazgo* indicate the sums levied
for the right to pass with one's belongings through the gates
of a town, over a bridge, or across a wooded pasture (*monte*).
Their meanings varied, however, as time went on, and *portazgo*, and still more *montazgo* came to be used almost exclusively of the heavy imposts levied on the great flocks
of sheep which annually migrated from the rainy pastures
of Galicia to the sunny plains of Andalusia and back again.[1]

8. The *alcabala*, or tax on commercial transactions, the
most lucrative of all, but also the most disastrous in its
ultimate effects on the economic welfare of Spain. This
source of revenue, which is generally believed to have been
borrowed from the finances of the Moors, was first regularly established in the reign of Alfonso XI, though there
are occasional and local traces of its existence at an earlier
date.[2] It was apparently imposed in 1342 to provide for
the special needs of the campaign against Algeciras, with the
distinct understanding that it should cease when peace was
made.[3] The rate was one twentieth the value of the trans-
action, and there is no evidence that the Cortes formally
sanctioned it.[4] But instead· of ceasing when the war was
over, it continued, and the rate was increased in 1366 to

[1] *Partida* v, tit. vii, leyes 5-9; *Partida* vi, tit. 1, ley 2; *Ordenamiento de
Alcalá*, tit. xxvi; Canga Argüelles, *op.
cit.*, ii, p. 418; Colmeiro, *E. P.*, i, p. 470.
[2] Its name probably comes from the
Arabic *kabala*; despite Spanish philolo-
gists to the contrary it does not seem
likely that it is in any way connected
with the French word *gabelle*. (Cf.
Littré, *Dictionnaire de la Langue fran-
çaise*, under this word; also Dozy and

Engelmann, *Glossaire des mots espagnols
dérivés de l'arabe*, second edition, 1869,
pp. 74 f.) — On irregular and exceptional
alcabalas before Alfonso XI, cf. Ortiz y
Zúñiga, *Annales de Sevilla*, pp. 179, 189,
and Llorente, *Noticias históricas de las
provincias Vascongadas*, ii, p. 138.
[3] Canga Argüelles, *Diccionario*, i, pp.
24 ff.
[4] *Crónica de Alfonso XI*, caps. cclxiii-
cclxv (*B. A. E.*, lxvi, pp. 329-331).

one tenth.[1] The Cortes apparently had not yet entirely
relinquished all claim to control it; in 1388 they granted
it for special purposes for a period of two years, and again,
three years later, for one. In 1393 they granted a *servicio*
on the express understanding that the *alcabala* should not
be levied again without the consent of the three estates
of the realm;[2] but the lack of any adequate machinery for
enforcing the bargain rendered their action nugatory.
Meantime, the kings continued to treat the new impost
according to their own desires. During the minority of
Henry III, the rate was once more dropped to one twentieth;
but when the young monarch took the reins of government
into his own hands, it was restored to one tenth and there
remained.[3] This tax, which had originated in such irregular fashion, was to become a cornerstone of the royal finances
in the succeeding centuries, and was bound to operate unfavorably to the general economic welfare of a nation which had
little natural aptitude for trade. Exactly how blighting
its effects were, cannot be accurately determined, till far
more minute and painstaking research has been accomplished
in the still almost totally unexplored field of Spanish economic history.

In the course of the fourteenth and fifteenth centuries a
royal treasury (*hacienda*) was gradually organized for the
collection and administration of these revenues. At the
head of it was the *almojarife* or *tesorero mayor*; under him
were a number of subordinates — *diezmeros, cojedores*, etc.
— each of whom was charged with the collection of the revenue of the source or locality committed to his care, and its

---

[1] *Crónica de Pedro I, año de 1366,*
cap. xix (*B. A. E.*, lxvi, p. 547).
[2] *Cortes*, ii, pp. 410, 511, 527 (Palencia, 1388, orden. 4; Madrid, 1391,
"respuesta de Fernandes de Villegas";
Madrid, 1393, "tercera cosa"). It is
worth noting that the second of these
grants (1391) put the rate at three
meajas per *maravedí* or 50 per cent.
[3] Conde de Cedillo, *op. cit.*, pp.
452 ff.; Gounon-Loubens, *Essais*, pp.
281 f.

deposit in the royal coffers. In the reign of Pedro the Cruel *contadores reales* were appointed to keep track of these officials and to check up their results.[1] Nevertheless, there were constant complaints by the Cortes of the period concerning the harshness and corruption of the royal tax-gatherers. The procuradores doubtless exaggerated the extent of the evil, but their grievances were certainly not imaginary, particularly under the weaker kings. Curiously enough, the turbulent reign of John II witnessed several efforts to estimate the yield of the different sources of revenue. Schedules of rates for the various customs houses were prepared in 1431 and 1446; and in 1429 a sort of budget was drawn up, in which the total annual income of the Royal Treasury was estimated at 60,812,930 maravedis. Payments were ordinarily made in money during this period, though contributions in kind were not wholly unknown.[2]

Theoretically, then, the revenues to which the sovereigns of Castile were legally entitled were amply sufficient to provide for the needs of their government. Of all the sources of income which we have described, only one, the *servicio*, was entirely within the control of the Cortes; the status of the *empréstito* and *alcabala* was possibly doubtful; but the levy and rate of the others remained entirely in the hands of the crown. The almost proverbial emptiness of the Castilian treasury thus demands some explanation; and the causes which combined to account for it may be briefly summarized as follows.

1. Exemptions. The payment of taxes was essentially an affair of the third estate — so much so, in fact, that the

[1] Cf. note 5 to p. 210, *ante*.
[2] Cf. "Ordenansas del rey Juan II en 2 de Noviembre de 1437 y en 30 de Setiembre de 1442" in *Colección de leyes* *de la contaduria de cuentas*, pp. 1–15; Altamira, §§ 448, 449; Colmeiro, *E. P.*, i, pp. 481 ff.; Conde de Cedillo, *op. cit.*, pp. 567 ff.

word *pechero*, or taxpayer, connoted an absence of social distinction.[1] The exemption of the nobles and clergy was not in any sense complete; they were subject to many of the indirect taxes, notably (despite violent protests) to the *alcabala*, and to certain minor contributions for the upkeep of roads and bridges, and for the destruction of grasshoppers.[2] Alfonso X, moreover, protested against the canons of the Lateran Council declaring all payments of imposts by the clergy to be of a voluntary or exceptional nature; and strenuous efforts were made by various Castilian sovereigns to prevent lay property from passing into clerical hands, and, in case it did so, to provide that it should continue to be taxable as before;[3] still there is no denying that the wealthier portions of the community got off much more cheaply than they deserved. Local as well as class exemptions were not infrequent. Cities whose position exposed them to Moorish attacks were often granted immunity from certain imposts. Sometimes the crown handed over directly to the municipal treasury the product of some of the national taxes levied in that locality.[4] And there were also countless special cases and individual immunities which defy classification. Certainly the incidence of national taxation was far from general or uniform.

2. The lavishness of the crown in grants and donations, of which we have had constant examples from the earliest days of the Reconquest. Since these grants were originally a product of the circumstances of the Moorish war, they might have been expected to cease when the enemy was limited to the little kingdom of Granada. Unfortunately the Castilian monarchs found the nobles at home even

[1] *Fuero Viejo*, lib. i, tit. i, ley 3; Altamira, § 448.
[2] Gounon-Loubens, *op. cit.*, p. 282; Mariéjol, p. 279.
[3] Colmeiro, *E. P.*, i, pp. 474 f.; Altamira, §§ 429, 448.
[4] Altamira, § 448.

more difficult to cope with than the infidel abroad; and it was by the continuance and increase of ill-considered munificence that most of them purchased immunity from baronial revolt. Alfonso X started the ball rolling in the wrong direction, and Henry of Trastamara made matters much worse. In the reigns of John II and Henry IV the central power was so deeply abased that the barons scarcely waited for the crown to give, but seized what they desired for themselves. Moreover the confusion which had been suffered to grow up between the private personal patrimony of the king, and the national property of which he was the trustee, extended the scope of these royal donations. The monarchs disposed of both with equal freedom in this period, to the ruin of the national fortunes.[1]

3. Last, but not least, the general state of anarchy, which marked the end of the Middle Ages in Castile, was incompatible with the prosperity of the national finances. It was literally impossible, under the conditions which actually prevailed, to collect the sums due to the crown. The restoration of the national resources in the reign of Ferdinand and Isabella was not brought about by the invention of new imposts. It was not primarily due to the great Act of Resumption or to the annexation of the grand masterships. The fundamental explanation of it was the reëstablishment of peace and strong government, which enabled the central power to make itself felt in every quarter of the realm, and made possible an approximation between the amount theoretically due to the crown and the sums which it was able to gather in.

Warfare was one of the principal occupations of mediaeval Castile, and the special function of the aristocracy; the

___
[1] Cos-Gayon, *Historia jurídica del Patrimonio Real*, caps. ii, iv.

caballero who was unable to provide himself with arms
and a horse soon fell back into the social limitations of the
'pecheros.'[1] The first duty of all the nobles was to follow
the king's banner when called upon, with whatever forces
they could muster; the privileges of the *ricos hombres*
might entitle them to an invitation rather than a summons
from the king to go to war, but they were supposed invariably to accept it. The higher clergy too were expected
to accompany the monarch in his campaigns against the
Moors, or if not, to send some one in their place; a kind of
scutage was apparently paid by those who were unable to
join the royal forces.[2] The obligations of the municipalities
were far less clear. Their fueros often entitled them to
exemptions of one sort or another; but since every city
was intensely proud of its standard — the emblem of its
fitness to engage in the noble profession of arms — and
profoundly anxious not to be outdone by its neighbors
in this respect, the municipal levies not seldom attained
considerable proportions.[3] But if the numbers of the host
were not inadequate, its lack of unity and discipline was
deplorable. In the first place, there was every probability
that many contingents would desert at the outset, if the
campaign did not meet with their approval, or if the prospect of booty was small; indeed, the monarch would have
reason to think himself fortunate if none of his forces were
ultimately found in the ranks of the foe. Even in the
rare cases when all the army was loyal to its sovereign, the
number and inequality of its different units, the immense
variety in their methods of waging war, and the lack of
any regulated scale of authority among its leaders were
fatal barriers to any real efficiency. The only reason that

[1] Mariéjol, p. 196.
[2] *Partida* i, tit. vi, ley 52; Danvila,
Poder Civil, i, pp. 167 f., and references

there; Colmeiro, *Curso*, p. 573.
[3] Colmeiro, *Curso*, pp. 570 f.

it won its fair share of victories was the fact that its foes were usually in a similar plight.[1] In the fourteenth and fifteenth centuries, indeed, some efforts were made to introduce order and discipline. The crown succeeded in superimposing on the feudal levies a number of trained commanders (*adalides*); and in the reigns of Alfonso XI, John I and II, and of Henry IV, a permanent, regularly paid royal guard occasionally made its appearance — the nucleus for a standing army.[2] The creation, in the reign of John I, of the office of *Condestable de Castilla* marks another step along the road to a more efficient military organization. Still, down to the days of Gonsalvo de Cordova, the rate of progress towards the desired goal was very slow. The best asset of the mèdiaeval Castilian forces was the valor of the individual soldiers — a quality in which the Spaniard has never been deficient, but one which, if unsupported by discipline and effective leadership, was bound to be decreasingly important in proportion to the progress of military science.

The armament and fighting methods of the mediaeval Castilian soldier offer certain peculiarities, which are to be attributed to the fact that he had been chiefly occupied in fighting the Moors, and that he had seen almost no service north of the Pyrenees. He was trained and equipped to wage the sort of warfare that the nature of the Reconquest imposed — that is, a war of rapid raids and counter-raids in a mountainous and difficult land.[3] For this purpose cavalry was of the first importance, and we consequently find that the Castilian armies were largely composed of horsemen. But most of these horsemen were not heavily armed like those of France and England. The nobles and

[1] Altamira, §§ 297, 299.
[2] Altamira, § 457; Colmeiro, *Curso*, pp. 575–577.
[3] Oman, *Art of War in the Middle Ages*, pp. 673 ff.

the military orders furnished a nucleus of mailed knights
of the standard mediaeval pattern (though their steeds
were unprotected by armor), but the greater part of the
Castilian cavalry consisted of *genetes*, so-called from the
jennets or light coursers which they rode. They were
equipped with a steel cap, shield, and quilted jacket for
defence, and a couple of darts or javelins which they hurled
at their foes. Their favorite manoeuvre was to hover
around and harass their opponents, in the hope of breaking
their formation and gaining an opportunity for a swift
charge.[1] Against the Moors, who were similarly armed,
these troops were fairly successful; but against a combination of knights and bowmen, such as had been evolved
in the first half of the fourteenth century in England, they
were almost powerless, as the battle of Navarrete (1367)
was to prove.[2] Unfortunately the Castilians did not
profit at once by the lessons of that fatal campaign. Heavier
armor was only gradually and irregularly adopted by them
in the succeeding century, and missile weapons did not
make any notable progress till the days of Gonsalvo de
Cordova; but on the other hand, the tradition of speed
and mobility, inherited from the earliest times, was not
forgotten, and was to be cleverly utilized by the Great
Captain when he re-created the military forces of the
Catholic Kings. The date of the introduction of gun-
powder and cannon in Spain is a much disputed point, but
it is safe to say that neither attained any great importance
until the final siege of Granada.[3] For the capture of walled
towns, huge catapults, movable wooden towers, and
battering rams were usually employed. Tactics and
strategy were practically nonexistent; only in the peren-

[1] Clonard, *Historia de las armas Españolas,* i, pp. 381 ff.; Altamira, § 457.

[2] Oman, *op. cit.,* pp. 644–647.
[3] Altamira, §§ 370, 457.

nial occupation of devastating the enemy's lands and terrorizing their defenceless population was there any sort of system.[1] Yet even for these rudimentary stages of the development of the military art, a number of rules and regulations were evolved. The second of the Siete Partidas and the earlier *Fuero Viejo de las Cabalgadas* lay down laws for the conduct of campaigns, and describe the military methods of the day.[2]

The mediaeval Castilian navy was by no means equal to that of the realms of the Crown of Aragon; the fact that Castile had been deprived of the best part of her seaboard by the declaration of Portuguese independence is probably the best explanation of her backwardness in this respect. From the middle of the ninth to the middle of the eleventh century, the Galician, Cantabrian, and Asturian coasts were frequently raided by Scandinavian and occasionally by Moorish pirates. In 970 the former penetrated inland and sacked Santiago de Compostela; and, by a bit of poetic justice, it was one of the most famous archbishops of that ancient see — the restless Diego Gelmirez — who afterwards took the lead in providing his native land with a navy adequate for her defence. As there was no one in Spain at that time who understood the art of naval instruction and navigation, he applied to the maritime republics of Italy for aid; and about the year 1120 he induced a Genoese master shipwright named Ogerio to come and visit Galicia. A dockyard was prepared at Iria; shipbuilding began; and before the end of the twelfth century a Christian fleet had fought the Moors on the sea. We must not suppose, however, that anything like a regularly organized Castilian navy existed at this early period.

---

[1] Clonard, *Historia de las armas Españolas*, i, pp. 447 ff.

[2] Altamira, § 457. See J. Almirante's elaborate *Bibliografía Militar de España* for fuller information in regard to the literature of this subject.

The ships were owned by private persons or by the municipalities; if the sovereigns needed them for national purposes,
they simply summoned them to their aid like the feudal array.[1]

The chief centre of Castilian maritime affairs remained
in the Biscayan ports down to the middle of the thirteenth
century, when the scene of interest shifts to Seville.   When
St. Ferdinand captured that town with the aid of Ramón
Bonifacio of Burgos, he rewarded the followers of his victorious admiral by granting them a special quarter of the
conquered city, with special privileges and a special jurisdiction; and a number of naval men from the northwest
migrated thither in the succeeding years.[2]   The office of
almirante, as we have already seen, was created by Ferdinand III.   From that time onward, Seville and the Guadalquivir became the naval centre of Castile.   Alfonso X,
whose zeal for maritime affairs fully equalled that of his
father, established a shipyard and arsenal there, and took
the first steps towards the creation of a permanent royal
navy for purposes of war.   The capture of Cadiz from the
Moors (September 14, 1262), which greatly enhanced the
security and importance of Seville, may be regarded as
the first signal triumph of the king's ships.[3]   Meantime
Alfonso also strove to keep alive the naval interest in the
Biscayan towns.   Whether new shipyards were constructed
there is not certain; but a sort of subsidiary admiralty was
created at Burgos to stimulate and direct the shipping of
the northwestern ports, and the Castilian contingents which
coöperated with the French against the English in the
naval struggles of the Hundred Years' War were chiefly

[1] Fernández Duro, Marina de Castilla, pp. 9–23; Murguía, Diego Gelmires, pp. 186 ff.; A. Navarrete, Historia Marítima Militar de España, i, pp.
117–130.

[2] Fernández Duro, op. cit., p. 29;
F. J. de Salas, Marina Española de la
Edad Media, cap. ii.
[3] Fernández Duro, op. cit., p. 42.

recruited in that region.[1] Altogether, the prestige of the
Castilian navy, both in the Mediterranean and the Atlantic,
was distinctly high during the two centuries following the
death of St. Ferdinand. Even England was not ashamed
to take hints from it in the construction of ships, and in
battle she treated it with marked respect.[2] The naval
foundations for Castile's future career of imperial expansion
to the westward were firmly laid before the close of the
Middle Ages. One of the most essential links of the chain
that bound the Reconquest to the conquest had been forged
previous to the accession of the Catholic Kings.

The ships were of various sorts and sizes, and depended
for the most part on both oars and sails for their propulsion. The two principal types were the lighter vessels
called *cocas*, which were introduced by the Cantabrians but
chiefly used in the Mediterranean, and the heavier galleys
or *navas gruesas* such as were employed in the Hundred
Years' War; the largest of these had complements of over
two hundred men. There was no very notable variation
in the general lines of construction during the fourteenth
and fifteenth centuries, though there were a number of
minor improvements, and the size tended steadily to increase.[3] Fighting was almost exclusively done in close
contact by ramming and boarding; there is some reason
to believe that Alfonso XI began to use artillery in his ships
in his wars with the English navy, but it is by no means
certain. The Partidas devote an entire chapter to "La
Guerra que se faze por mar," explaining in detail its rules
and conditions, the number and quality of the men and the
armament, and the ranks and duties of the different officers.[4]

[1] Altamira, § 457.
[2] Fernández Duro, *op. cit.*, pp.
159 f.
[3] Fernández Duro, *op. cit.*, pp. 55,
158 ff., speaks of *naves gruesas* carrying
500–900 combatants or 1000 passengers.
[4] *Partida* ii, tit. xxiv; Fernández
Duro, *op. cit.*, pp. 72 f.

During the first five centuries of the Reconquest the conditions of existence rendered wellnigh impossible any considerable development of agriculture, pasturage, industry, or commerce; but when the Moors were at last driven back to the confines of Granada the earlier difficulties were largely removed, and serious efforts were made to develop the resources of the land. The agricultural problem was, of course, by far the most discouraging. Some progress was made, but not sufficient to enable the fields to support the population or to render their tillage generally profitable or successful. The lists of foodstuffs imported into the realm during this period plainly indicate its agricultural shortcomings; the natural infertility of the bulk of the land, coupled with the devastations of the war of the Reconquest, were a constant discouragement to activity in this direction, and stamped on the average Castilian an aversion to labor in the fields which has clung to him ever since, and was to affect most adversely his imperial ambitions at a later day.[1] Pasturage, on the other hand, had flourished in the peninsula from the time of the Romans, and during the later Middle Ages made rapid strides. The rainy valleys of the northwest furnished admirable facilities for grazing sheep in the summers, as did the warmer plains of the south in the winters; during the intermediate seasons vast flocks were driven back and forth across the intervening lands along certain well established routes called *cañadas*. Since the passage of the sheep could not fail to injure the agricultural interests of the localities which they traversed, there was a constant series of quarrels between farmers and graziers. The latter, in order to protect themselves against the complaints of their enemies, obtained permission, at least as early as the

[1] Colmeiro, E. P., cap. xxxi.

reign of Alfonso the Learned, to form themselves into an association or gild, called the 'Mesta,' which secured from the crown, particularly under Alfonso XI, a number of important privileges, jurisdictions, and immunities, and a regular code of laws defining them. The policy of favoring pasturage at the expense of agriculture, which was to be continued and carried much further under the Catholic Kings, was another contributory cause of Castile's poor showing in the latter field.[1]

The industrial and commercial organization of mediaeval Castile was naturally of a preëminently local type — far more so in fact than that of the other Western European states of the period, for the separatistic character of the country revealed itself in economic as well as in political affairs.[2] The products of the different towns of the realm varied widely, as did the organization of the various gilds which controlled their output, and the lines of local custom houses discouraged communication between the different parts of the realm.[3] The crown favored the establishment of annual or biennial fairs of two to four weeks' duration in the principal cities, in order to facilitate the exchange of commodities. Those of Seville, Medina del Campo, and Murcia were perhaps the most important, but they did not suffice to break down or even seriously to lower the economic barriers by which the land was internally divided.[4] Endless confusion in money, weights, and measures was an accompanying phenomenon of the times. Several

[1] Colmeiro, E. P., cap. xxxiv. The first (and only) volume of L. Redonet y López-Dóriga's *Historia del Cultivo y de la Industria Ganadera en España* (Madrid, 1911) does not reach the period of Alfonso X. Much fuller and more accurate information on this topic may be found in a doctoral dissertation in the Harvard College Library by J. Klein; a portion of it, on the "Alcalde Entregador of the Mesta," was printed in B. H. (see p. 270, *infra*), and it is expected that the whole will soon be published in book form.

[2] Altamira, §§ 510 f.

[3] Colmeiro, E. P., caps. xxxvii, xxxviii.

[4] *Partida* v, tit. vii, ley 3; C. Espejo and J. Paz, *Las antiguas ferias de Medina del Campo.*

different types of currency were in circulation, and also much debased coin;[1] it will be remembered that the Scholar King himself set his subjects an evil example in this respect. The foreign commerce of the realm was in somewhat better case. The Castilian merchant marine developed rapidly during the fourteenth and fifteenth centuries, hand in hand with the Castilian navy, and Castilian traders were to be found in all the great markets of Western Europe.[2] There was a gild of Biscayan pilots, established at Cadiz soon after the capture of the town from the Moors, and consuls were appointed every year to settle all questions which came up in connection with navigation and commerce.[3] The idea of helping the nascent industries of the realm by the imposition of protective tariffs appears plainly in different places in the Alfonsine codes,[4] and various *aranceles* or schedules of the period bear witness to the crown's desire to regulate the commercial activities of the realm in accordance with universally applicable standards. The royal interference in this matter, however, was nothing in comparison with what it was to become in the days of Ferdinand and Isabella and the Hapsburgs. Fishing, also, received the royal attention and encouragement from an even earlier date, and was expected to yield a portion of its profits to the crown; in a fuero which he granted to the little Biscayan town of Zarauz in the year 1237, St. Ferdinand provided that whenever the inhabitants succeeded in capturing a whale, they should give him a strip of its flesh the length of the body.[5]

---

[1] Despite the fact that *Partida* vii, tit. vii, ley 9 decrees the penalty of death for the crime of false money. For further information about the literature of Castilian coinage, cf. Juan de Dios de la Rada y Delgado, *Bibliografía Numismática Española* (Madrid, 1886).

[2] Colmeiro, *E. P.*, caps. xli, xlii; cf. also Eloy García de Quevedo y Concellón, *Ordenanzas del consulado de Burgos*, pp. 9–46.

[3] Fernández Duro, *op. cit.*, pp. 157–161.

[4] As, e.g., *Partida* ii, tit. xi, ley 1.

[5] Fernández Duro, *op. cit.*, p. 162.

The intellectual life of Castile during the later Middle Ages was naturally somewhat stunted by the turbulence of the times. At the time of the accession of Alfonso the Learned, there was only one university in the realm — that of Salamanca — which had been projected in 1230 by Alfonso IX of Leon and was really founded twelve years later by St. Ferdinand.[1] The Scholar King's zeal for learning led him to draw up extensive regulations for it, and to confer upon it numerous privileges; and a long section in the Siete Partidas dealing with the organization of study in the realm bears further witness to Alfonso's interest in education and to his determination to keep it under royal control.[2] Without doubt he expected that other universities would soon spring up, and in 1293 his successor Sancho IV took the first measures to found a *studium generale* at Alcalá, which was to become under Ferdinand and Isabella the foremost centre of learning in Spain.[3] But from Sancho's reign to that of the Catholic Kings not a single new university was established in Leon or Castile, a fact which is the more remarkable when we consider that no less than six similar institutions were set up within the same period in the much smaller realms of the Crown of Aragon.[4] Lack of governance was, as usual, the underlying cause. The kings, some of whom were

[1] A number of Masters of Theology, Law, Logic, and Grammar had taught at Palencia since 1212–14, and St. Ferdinand took steps towards giving them corporate existence, but the institution, such as it was, had virtually disappeared in 1263, and scarcely deserves the name of a University. A so-called *Studium Generale*, which was set up at Valladolid about the middle of the thirteenth century, and attained considerable distinction, may perhaps be regarded as the successor of Palencia. Cf. H. Rashdall, *The Universities of Europe in the Middle Ages*, ii, 1, pp. 66–85, and

G. Reynier, *La vie universitaire dans l'ancienne Espagne*.
[2] *Partida* ii, tit. xxxi.
[3] Rashdall, *op. cit.*, ii, 1, p. 99.
[4] Rashdall, *op. cit.*, ii, 1, pp. 86–96, 99 f.; V. de la Fuente, *Historia de las Universidades en España*, i, caps. xiv, xvii, xxvi, xxvii, xxix; P. Melon, *L'Enseignement supérieur en Espagne* (Paris, 1898). The Aragonese universities, with the dates of their foundation, were Lerida, 1300; Perpignan, 1349; Huesca, 1359; Valencia, 1411 (Rashdall does not reckon this as a university till 1500); Barcelona, 1450; Saragossa, 1474.

really interested in education, and whose authority and control were, in theory at least, more dominant in university affairs than was the case in any other country in Europe, were too completely in the hands of the rebel baronage to be able to carry their plans into effect.

Yet it would be a mistake to suppose that Castile was so completely wrapped up in its own internal troubles during the fourteenth and fifteenth centuries as to be incapable of literary, artistic, or scientific productivity, or deaf to the intellectual influences of other lands. In art, architecture, and literature one can easily find traces, all the way from Alfonso X to Ferdinand and Isabella, of the fashions of the other states of Western Europe, especially of Italy, with which Castile had numerous opportunities to become intimate owing to the Aragonese expansion in the Mediterranean.[1] In painting, the style of Giotto was carried over to Castile by the Florentine artist Gherardo Starnina during the years 1380–87; a sort of 'Giotto School' was subsequently set up at Seville, but the attempts of the native Castilian painters to imitate the foreign models which had been set before them were not remarkably successful. In the reign of John II, a certain Nicolao Florentino, who was almost certainly none other than Dello Delli, visited Spain; the mural paintings in the apse of the old cathedral of Salamanca furnish perhaps the best existing examples of the work that he did there.[2] Flemish influences are also traceable in Castilian painting of the fifteenth century. The famous journey of Jan Van Eyck to the peninsula in 1428–29 was probably the origin of them, though their

[1] A significant evidence of the Italian influence on Spain in the domain of education and of law is afforded by the college of Spain at Bologna, to which reference has been made on p. 236, note 1, supra.

[2] A. Michel, Histoire de l'art, iii, 2, pp. 752 ff., and bibliography at the end of the chapter for further references.

results were not evident in the work of the native artists till some thirty years afterwards.[1]

In sculpture and architecture Gothic models began to be introduced from France in the course of the twelfth century, and gradually took their place beside the native styles; the cathedrals of Burgos, Toledo, and Leon (all begun in the thirteenth century) exhibit them at the climax of their power, and the wonderful towers of the first named, which is usually considered the most beautiful church in Spain, were apparently the work of a fifteenth-century German, Meister Hans of Cologne.[2] In architecture, however, the national and Moorish fashions were by no means forgotten. 'Mudejar' buildings of various sorts were constantly being erected in Castile till well into the sixteenth century. Indeed, traces of Arab influence keep continually cropping out even in edifices built by architects who had been imported from north of the Pyrenees. There was certainly no 'pure' style of any kind in the Castile of the later Middle Ages.

In the domain of literature Italian influence again comes to the fore. From the end of the fourteenth century onward, we find numerous writings which evince a keen appreciation and understanding of Dante, and a lively interest in Boccaccio; at times it almost seems that the popularity of the older literary works of the distinctively national type, like the *Poema del Cid*, was quite overshadowed by that of the new importations. Francisco Imperial, the son of a Genoese jeweler established at Seville, is generally regarded as the first of these Italianate Castilians; the famous Marquis of Santillana, Enrique de Villena, and Juan de Mena,

[1] Michel, *op. cit.*, iii, 2, pp. 783 ff.
[2] Usually known in Spain as Juan de Colonia; cf. V. Lampéres, *Historia de la Arquitectura Cristiana Española*, ii, pp. 127, 220. There is a monograph by the same author on Juan de Colonia, published at Valladolid in 1904.

carried the new fashion considerably further a half century afterwards.[1] English literature also had some few followers in Castile during this period. Robert Gower's *Confessio Amantis* was translated into Spanish by a certain Juan de Cuenca in the reign of John II, whose chief title to fame was his passion for learning and letters.[2]

Altogether it is evident that in her intellectual as well as in her political life, Castile was no longer cut off from the rest of Western Europe, as she had been before the virtual accomplishment of the Reconquest by St. Ferdinand. The great national task on which the full force of her energies had been concentrated for five centuries was practically finished; she was beginning to reach out into new fields. Internal chaos prevented her from accomplishing anything very great in these new spheres of activity until the advent of strong government under the Catholic Kings, but at all events she had succeeded in immensely broadening her horizon. In every phase of the national life, the two centuries which followed the accession of Alfonso the Learned are a period of necessary transition between isolation and empire.

---

[1] J. Fitzmaurice Kelly, *A History of Spanish Literature*, pp. 97–102; cf. also C. B. Bourland, "Boccaccio and the Decameron in Castilian and Catalan Literature," in *R. H.*, xii, pp. 1–232.

[2] Fitzmaurice Kelly, *op. cit.*, p. 98; Puymaigre, *La cour littéraire de Juan II, roi de Castille, passim*; *D. I. E.*, xix, pp. 435–454.

BIBLIOGRAPHICAL NOTE

See bibliographical note at the end of the preceding chapter, and add:

Sources. — By far the most important of these are of course the *Partidas* and the other codes, and the *cuadernos* of the Cortes of Castile: these have been described among the general authorities, in the note at the end of the Introduction. A *Colección de las leyes, ordenanzas, y reglamentos expedidos para gobierno del tribunal y contaduría mayor de cuentas desde el Reinado del Señor Don Juan II hasta el día*, published by the Imprenta Real at Madrid, 1829, gives the text of two important financial ordinances of John II, though the bulk of the work covers the later period.

Later Works. — General. Francisco de Berganza, *Antiguedades de España* (Madrid, 1719–21, 2 vols.), is a mine of miscellaneous information, and is based partially on manuscript sources; it needs, however, to be controlled by the studies of more recent authors. On the monarchy, Heinrich Zoepfl, *Bosquejo histórico sobre la sucesión á la corona de España*, translated from the German by Santiago de Tejada (Paris, 1899), and Fernando Cos-Gayon, *Historia Jurídica del Patrimonio Real* (Madrid, 1881), are both useful. Gonzalo Fernández de Oviedo's *Libro de la Camara Real del Principe Don Juan*, written in 1546–47 and published by the Sociedad de Bibliófilos Españoles (Madrid, 1870), throws much light on the royal household in the later mediaeval period. The standard work on the Council, and one of the most admirable products of recent Spanish scholarship, is the Conde de Torreánaz's *Los Consejos del Rey durante la Edad Media* (Madrid, 1884–90, 2 vols.). On the national assembly, F. M. Marina, *Teoría de las Cortes* (Madrid, 1813, 3 vols.), contains much that is still valuable, though the reader must never forget that it was written chiefly to prove the case of the Spanish liberals a century ago, and is therefore strongly biassed. Juan Sempere y Guarinos, *Histoire des Cortes d'Espagne* (Bordeaux, 1815), is a good antidote. Francisco Mendizábal has thrown much new light on the central courts by his articles on the "Origen, historia, y organización de la Real Chancillería de Valladolid," in the *R. A.*, 3d series, vol. xxx, pp. 61–72, 243–264, 437–452, and vol. xxxi, pp. 95–112, 459–467. J. M. Antequera's *Historia de la Legislación Española* (4th edition, Madrid, 1895) is a standard work, but needs to be supplemented by more recent investigations, such as J. Costa's *Derecho consuetudinario y Economía Popular de España* (Barcelona, 1902, 2 vols.) and Rafael Altamira y Crevea's *Cuestiones de Historia del Derecho y de Legislación Comparada* (Madrid, 1914); M. F. Ladreda's *Estudios históricos sobre los Códigos de Castilla* (Corunna, 1896) is also a most convenient little book. Geronimo Castillo de Bovadilla's *Politica para Corregidores y Señores de Vassallos* (Madrid, 1597; Medina del Campo, 1608; Barcelona, 1616; and Antwerp, 1750, 2 vols.) is a mine of information, by a most learned lawyer, on the whole question of local administration in Spain. My references are to the edition of 1616.

On financial and economic matters Manuel Colmeiro's standard *Historia de la Economía Política en España* (cf. *ante*, p. 47) should be supplemented by Francisco Gallardo Fernández, *Origen, Progresos, y Estado de las Rentas de la Corona de España* (Madrid, 1805–06, 7 vols.), with the supplementary volume *Prontuario de las Facultades y Obligaciones de los Intendentes*; José Canga Argüelles, *Diccionario de Hacienda* (Madrid, 1833–34, 2 vols.); Jerónimo López de Ayala y Álvares de Toledo, Conde de Cedillo, *Contribuciones é Impuestos en León y Castilla durante la Edad Media* (Madrid, 1896); and J. M. Piernas y Hurtado, *Tratado de Hacienda pública y Examen de la Española* (5th edition, Madrid, 1900–01, 2 vols.). There are also a large number of excellent modern monographs on special economic subjects: Cristóbal Espejo and Julián Pas, *Las antiguas Ferias de Medina del Campo* (Valladolid, 1908), and Julius Klein, "The Alcalde Entregador of the Mesta," in the *B. H.*, vol. xvii, pp. 85–154, may be cited as examples.

The Conde de Clonard's *Historia orgánica de las armas de infantería y caballería Españolas* (Madrid, 1851–59, 16 vols.) is an elaborate work, but devotes little space to the mediaeval period. Francisco Javier de Salas, *Discurso [sobre la Historia Marítima de Castilla y Aragón] leido ante la R. A. H.* (Madrid, 1868), and Adolfo Navarrete, *Historia Marítima Militar de España* (one volume published, Madrid, 1901), may be used to good advantage to supplement C. Fernández Duro's book, already cited, on the Castilian navy.

Vicente de la Fuente, *Historia de las Universidades, Colegios, y demás Establecimientos de Enseñanza en España* (Madrid, 1884–89, 4 vols.), and Vicente Lampérez y Romea, *Historia de la Arquitectura Cristiana Española en la Edad Media* (Madrid, 1908–09, 2 vols.), are the principal books on these subjects. James Fitzmaurice Kelly's admirable *History of Spanish Literature* (latest edition, New York, 1917) may be supplemented for the important period of John II by the Comte de Puymaigre's *La cour littéraire de Don Juan II, roi de Castille* (Paris, 1873, 2 vols.).

BOOK II

THE REALMS OF THE CROWN OF ARAGON

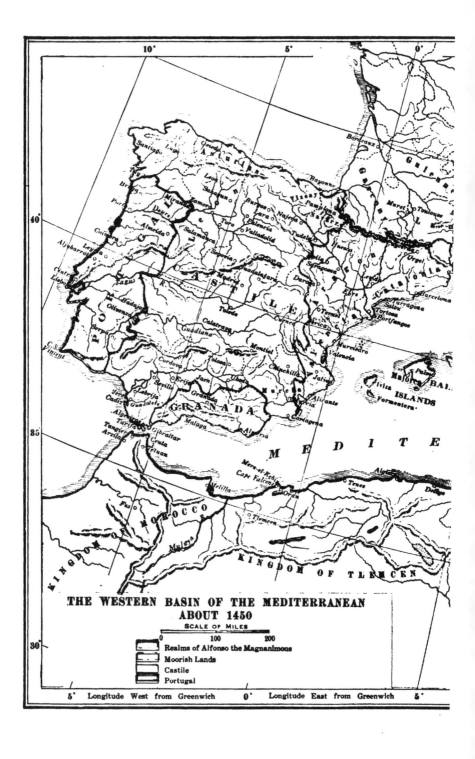

THE WESTERN BASIN OF THE MEDITERRANEAN
ABOUT 1450

SCALE OF MILES

0   100   200

Realms of Alfonso the Magnanimous
Moorish Lands
Castile
Portugal

5°   Longitude West from Greenwich   0°   Longitude East from Greenwich   5°

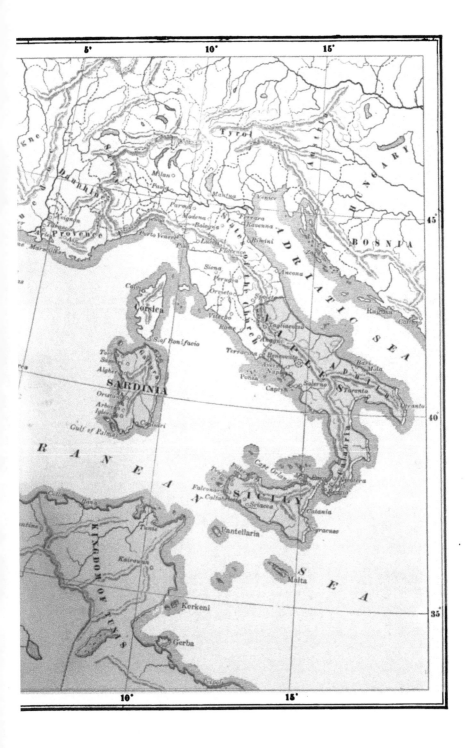

CHAPTER VI

ARAGON AND CATALONIA IN FRANCE, SPAIN, AND NORTH AFRICA

THE interest of the mediaeval history of the realms of the Crown of Aragon lies quite as emphatically on the side of external expansion, as does that of the contemporaneous development of Castile in internal affairs and the war of the Reconquest. The Spanish Empire was even more preponderantly Aragonese [1] in the Middle Ages, than Castilian in the sixteenth and seventeenth centuries. We must therefore deal with the growth of the eastern realms in the Iberian Peninsula and the adjacent lands as rapidly as possible, in order to have more space to devote to their conquests overseas.

The origins of the little kingdom of Aragon are even more obscure than those of Asturias. It appears in the first place as a countship, rather than as an independent realm, and its original territories lay along the banks of the river Arago, from which it took its name. In the ninth century its capital was at Jaca; and it subsequently extended its dominions at the expense of the Moors in the regions of Sobrarbe and Ribagorza. [2] In these early years of its existence, however, the question of its independence or subjec-

[1] It has proved impossible to avoid using the words 'Aragon' and 'Aragonese' as denoting both the kingdom of that name in the more restricted sense, and also the combination of the three eastern realms and their dependencies; but, with this preliminary caution, it is hoped that the reader will find no difficulty in making for himself the necessary distinction in each case.

[2] F. Codera, *Estudios críticos de historia Árabe Española*, 1st series, pp. 95–111, 135–140, 169–201; T. Ximenes de Embun, *Orígenes de Aragón y Navarra*, pp. 174 ff.

tion to foreign overlordship was far more important than
the speed of its progress against the infidel. At first it
seems to have been often under the suzerainty of the Frankish monarchs; at times, in all probability, it was virtually
autonomous; but as the years went by it gradually fell
more and more completely under the control of Navarre.[1]
This kingdom, by the middle of the ninth century, had successfully vindicated its independence of the domination of
Charlemagne's successors, thus greatly enhancing its own
prestige, and incidentally weakening the Frankish hold
over Aragon. The latter, on the other hand, was still too
small and weak to be able permanently to dispense with
outside protection and support; so that the Navarrese
monarchs naturally fell heirs to all the authority over its
rulers which they had forced the Carolingians to relinquish.
For a time it was overlordship: later, owing to deaths,
marriages, and unwise divisions of inheritances, it became
considerably more. By the end of the tenth century Aragon
had lost all claims to existence as a separate state; she had
been practically absorbed by the kingdom of Navarre.[2]

The next period saw Navarre take the lead of all the
Iberian states, and for one brief moment unite them under
her sceptre. The hero of this most glorious epoch of his
country's history was King Sancho the Great, who ruled
from 970 to 1035. Already master of his own realm and
of Aragon, he skillfully alternated and combined the time-
honored methods of matrimony, intrigue, and war, to win for
himself the succession in Castile, and the effective occupation
of most of Leon. At the close of his life he ruled over
an uninterrupted expanse of territory which stretched from
the mountains of Galicia to the confines of the county of

[1] J. de Jaurgain, La Vasconie, ii, pp.
334 ff.; also L. Barrau-Dihigo, "Les
Origines du royaume de Navarre," in
R. H., vii, pp. 141–222, 505 f.
[2] T. Ximenes de Embun, op. cit., pp.
187 ff.

Barcelona. But it was not possible for such an extended realm to remain long united in mediaeval Spain. The reign of Sancho was a final and most brilliant outburst of the flame of Navarrese power south of the Pyrenees; but the succeeding period witnessed its virtual extinction. At his death in 1035 the great king divided his realms. To his eldest son, García, he gave Navarre. To his second, Ferdinand, he left Castile and his claims to Leon, which the latter subsequently prosecuted with such vigor that the two kingdoms were united under his rule in 1037. To the third, Gonzalo, he gave Sobrarbe and Ribagorza, and to the fourth, Ramiro, the original territory of Aragon; as Gonzalo, however, soon after died and left no heirs, Ramiro was able to gather in his inheritance. The latter also increased his dominions by conquests to the south, and on his death in 1063 was able to leave to his son an Aragon territorially more extensive than ever before, and, for the first time, completely independent of foreign sovereignty.[1]

From 1063 to 1134, the history of Aragon offers the usual spectacle of internal confusion, intrigues with the neighboring realms, and sporadic progress against the Moor. In 1076 the murder of the Navarrese king gave it an opportunity to turn the tables on the realm which had previously absorbed it; for fifty-eight years after that date Navarre was annexed to Aragon. The most famous monarch of this stormy period was Alfonso the Warrior (1104–34), whom we have already encountered as the second husband of Urraca of Leon and Castile, and a notable disturber of the peace of those kingdoms. His victories over the Moors have entitled him to a fairer fame. Under his leadership the Christian arms were carried across the Ebro. In 1118 Saragossa was taken — an event which, for Aragon, is

[1] Lafuente, iv, pp. 139–152, passim; Zurita, i, ff. 17–18; also pp. 72 f., supra.

comparable to the capture in 1085 of Toledo for Castile; the surrender of many minor places to the south of it followed shortly afterwards, and raids were made into Valencia, Murcia, and Andalusia, as far as the shores of the Mediterranean.[1] Unfortunately Alfonso had no surviving children to whom he could leave these conquests; he therefore provided in his will that his dominions should be parcelled out between the Templars and the Knights Hospitallers. As this arrangement, however, was highly distasteful to his subjects both in Aragon and in Navarre, they coolly ignored it, and both states chose new rulers to suit themselves. The Navarrese, who were above all anxious to regain their autonomy, elected as their sovereign a grandnephew of their king who had been murdered in 1076; from the descendants of this monarch the realm finally passed, in 1234, into French hands for more than two centuries, so that we lose sight of it henceforth for a long time to come.[2]

[1] Ximenes de Embun, *op. cit.*, pp. 202–229; Domingo y Gines, *Estudio crítico sobre la conquista de Zaragoza por Alfonso I* (Saragossa, 1888).

[2] The relationships of the kings of Aragon and of Navarre in this early period are shown by the following table.

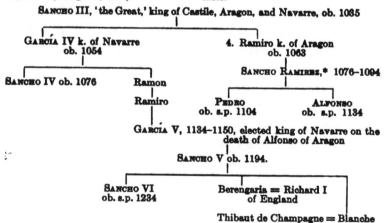

SANCHO III, 'the Great,' king of Castile, Aragon, and Navarre, ob. 1035

GARCÍA IV k. of Navarre ob. 1054

4. Ramiro k. of Aragon ob. 1063

SANCHO IV ob. 1076   Ramon

SANCHO RAMIREZ,* 1076–1094

Ramiro

PEDRO ob. s.p. 1104

ALFONSO ob. s.p. 1134

GARCÍA V, 1134–1150, elected king of Navarre on the death of Alfonso of Aragon

SANCHO V ob. 1194.

SANCHO VI ob. s.p. 1234

Berengaria = Richard I of England

Thibaut de Champagne = Blanche

* This man is sometimes reckoned as Sancho V of Navarre, the Sancho who died in 1194 becoming Sancho VI, and the one who died in 1234, Sancho VII.

The Aragonese, in the meantime, dragged from a monastery in Narbonne a brother of their late king, named Ramiro, and set him on their throne. Nay more, in order to make the succession safe, they persuaded this Ramiro to procure a papal dispensation from his vows of celibacy, and to marry a sister of the duke of Aquitaine. But Ramiro had no desire or talent for reigning. The nobles were restless at home. The Moors harried his frontiers. Navarre and Castile on the north and west clamored for revenge for the insults and humiliations to which they had been subjected by the late king. Alfonso the Emperor actually invaded the realm, and temporarily incorporated Saragossa and other towns in the domains of the crown of Castile; only by recognizing his feudal overlordship was it possible to check his advance. Ramiro was only too glad to acknowledge himself incompetent to cope with all these dangers, and when, in 1135, his Aquitanian wife presented him with a daughter, Petronilla, he saw a way out of his difficulties. The little princess was betrothed [1] while still in the cradle to Ramon Berenguer IV, the reigning count of Catalonia, with a provision for the latter's succession to the Aragonese throne in case Petronilla should die without issue. The important support of the powerful eastern countship was thus secured against the manifold dangers which threatened Aragon at home and abroad, and the continuance of that support was guaranteed in the future by the assured prospect of the union of the crowns. Ramiro, on his own confession incapable of reigning, had probably done more for his native land than a powerful monarch could have accomplished. In 1137 he retired into a monastery, leaving his infant daughter under the

---

[1] Zurita, i, fols. 56 ff.; M. and M., iv, p. 496. The marriage was actually celebrated in 1151.

guardianship of her future husband. He had certainly
earned his rest.[1]

The separation of Aragon from Navarre, and its union
with the county of Catalonia, are epoch-making events
in the history of Spain and also of the Spanish Empire.
Ramiro could not possibly have foreseen the consequences
of his work. He had sought union with the eastern state
as a means of protecting Aragon against foreign and internal
dangers. What he had really accomplished was far more
than that; he had changed the whole current of his country's development, and laid the basis for her imperial domain.
Hitherto her history had been, like that of Leon, Castile,
and Navarre, an alternation of internal feuds and Moorish
raids. Her attention had never been directed to events
beyond the limits of the peninsula. She was narrow, self-
absorbed, and totally without cosmopolitanism or ambitions for empire. Now, all at once, her destinies were
permanently linked with a state of Frankish origin, whose
boundaries crossed the Pyrenees, which was possessed of a
long seacoast and splendid harbors, and whose fleets had
already begun to cruise in the Mediterranean Sea. An
entirely new and dazzling prospect was suddenly opened
before her. Naturally she could not abandon and forget
all her ancient traditions in a moment. On the contrary,
she clung to them tenaciously, and the fact that she maintained her separate institutions (despite the union of the
crowns) gave her an opportunity to assert herself which
she did not neglect. Still, the operation of Catalonian influence, however strongly resisted, was bound ultimately to
make itself felt; and though the name of the kingdom
prevailed generally over that of the county in designating

[1] *Gesta Comitum Barcinonensium,
scripta a monacho Rivipullensi,* cap. xxi
(in *Marca Hispanica,* coll. 549 f.); Zurita, i, ff. 51–58: Ximenes de Embun,
pp. 230–239.

the united realms, the triumph of the maritime, commercial, and imperial influence of the latter is evident in the diminishing effectiveness of the Aragonese opposition to the great ventures of the fourteenth and fifteenth centuries which emanated from Catalonia. The coincidence that Castile was partially shut off from access to the sea by the declaration of the independence of Portugal, at almost precisely the same moment that Aragon acquired it by union with Catalonia, produced results of lasting importance. It explains why Spain's first imperial ventures were made to the eastward, in the Mediterranean Sea, rather than to the westward in the Atlantic. Had the positions been reversed, the history of the two chief states of the peninsula in the next three centuries would in all probability have been utterly different, and the policies of the empire which arose from their united resources more different still.

In an earlier chapter we have had occasion to speak briefly of the Frankish origin of the county of Catalonia, of its attainment of independence of French control in the end of the ninth century, of its subsequent turning on the land that gave it birth and annexing, at its expense, important territories north of the Pyrenees.[1] At the time of its union with Aragon in 1137, these territories included Cerdagne and the greater part of Provence, Millau, and Gévaudan — the lion's share of the country of the Langue d'Oc — a generous portion of the south of France. In the next two generations these Catalonian holdings were further augmented by the addition of Roussillon (1172), and, under foreign suzerainty, of Montpellier (1204), by the acquisition of the overlordship of Foix, of Nîmes, and of Béziers (between 1162 and 1196), and by temporary extension of

[1] Cf. ante, pp. 31–33; also P. Tomic, Historias y Conquistas dels Reys de Arago (Barcelona, 1886), caps. xxiii– xxxvi. On this work, cf. J. Massó Torrents in R. H., xv, pp. 595–603.

direct authority over the county of Urgel.[1]   But the counts
of Catalonia were also interested in expansion in other
directions than across the Pyrenees in France.   They bore
their share in expeditions to the southward against the
Moors.   Though their gains in that direction were not very
permanent, they had raided the lands of the infidel as far
as Murcia before the end of the eleventh century.[2]   Last but
not least, they had already evinced a lively interest in maritime affairs.   In 1114–15, in alliance with the Pisans, they
had made an expedition against Majorca and Iviza.   Its
success in its main objective was but evanescent, as the
Moors soon retook the islands, but it led indirectly to the
permanent occupation of Tarragona and the neighboring
coast, which had not hitherto been safe from Moorish
attack.[3]   Maritime commerce also began to flourish.   Barcelona was already known as a seaport of real importance.
Clearly, then, at the time of its union with Aragon, the
Catalonian state was confronted with a large variety of
opportunities for growth and expansion in at least three
different directions — northward in France, southward
in Spain, eastward in the Mediterranean Sea.   Vital, ambitious, and cosmopolitan, reënforced and encouraged by the
acquisition of Aragon, the descendants of Ramon and
Petronilla began to push their fortunes with equal vigor in
all these fields at once, but with very different success.
In France, after heroic efforts, the tide turned against them
and they had to acknowledge defeat.   In the south, against
the Moors, under the leadership of Aragon, they succeeded
in annexing those portions of the peninsula in which they
had not been forestalled by their neighbors on the west.

[1] Devic and Vaissete, *Histoire générale
de Languedoc*, vi, pp. 50 f., 88–92, 213 f.;
Baudon de Mony, *Relations politiques
des comtes de Foix avec la Catalogne*, i, pp.
38–48; Lecoy, i, pp. 141 ff.; Swift,
James the First of Aragon, p. 266.
[2] Bofarull, ii, pp. 327 ff.
[3] Bofarull, ii, pp. 398 ff.

The capture of Valencia was the crown and fine flower of the Reconquest on the eastward, but, as we have already seen, the glory of driving the Moors out of Spain is preëminently the glory of Castile. It was to the eastward, in the Mediterranean, that the destiny of the Aragonese-Catalonian state really lay; and even before the possibilities of expansion by land had been entirely exhausted, on the north by failure, and on the south through accomplished success and the fact that there was no more territory to regain, Catalonia had perceived that the future of the eastern kingdoms was on the sea. From that moment onward she proudly led the way, with Aragon rather reluctantly tagging at her heels.[1]

Everything which it is essential for us to know in the narrative and external history of the realms of the Crown of Aragon down to the middle of the fifteenth century may, in fact, be most conveniently summarized under these three heads: the loss of the French lands; the completion of the Aragonese reconquest in Spain and the ensuing relations with the Moslem powers of Granada and North Africa; and the acquisition of an empire in the western basin of the Mediterranean. The first two were virtually accomplished before the end of the reign of James the Conqueror in 1276, and may, therefore, be dismissed in short space in the present chapter. The history of the third, on the other hand, is exceedingly complicated and difficult, and prolongs itself not only to the close of the mediaeval period but beyond. The study of it will, therefore, necessarily demand more space, and will involve some investigation of the principal events of the different reigns in chronological order; for, with a single possible exception, every one of the Ara-

---

[1] On this paragraph cf. Denk, *Die Grafen von Barcelona von Wilfred I bis Ramon Berenguer IV* (Munich, 1888).

gonese kings from James the Conqueror downward was more
or less intimately concerned with the development and
increase of the Aragonese possessions beyond the seas. But
though, for the sake of convenience, we shall take up these
different lines of development one by one, it would be the
greatest possible mistake to conceive of them as unconnected
with one another or as succeeding each other in any strict
chronological order. In the critical period of the thirteenth
century, they were all closely interdependent and synchro-
nous. The loss of the French lands, though chiefly caused
by the events of the reign of Pedro II (1196–1213), was not
formally legalized till the treaty of Corbeil in 1258, twenty
years after the conquest of Valencia had virtually completed
the reconquest of the eastern part of the peninsula. The
conquest of Valencia was undertaken largely in deference
to the demands of the kingdom of Aragon, which had been
somewhat offended by the fact that King James had given
precedence to the maritime ambitions of his favorite Catalonians, and had sent out the first expedition against the
Balearics nine years before. It was only after the Conqueror's death that the Mediterranean programme of the
East Spanish realms began to eclipse their activities in
other directions.

The story of the gain and loss of the lands north of the
Pyrenees was largely determined by the fact that the
Aragonese-Catalonian sovereigns, like their Castilian contemporaries to the westward, were often unable to resist
the temptation to divide their inheritance by will between their different children. Though well planned marriages, assertions of feudal suzerainty, and fortunate ex-
tinctions of collateral lines not seldom served to draw
the errant portions of their extended domains together,

the Aragonese sovereigns were so addicted to the practice
of division that any hopes of permanently welding all
their lands into a single homogeneous realm were necessarily foredoomed to failure. Ramon Berenguer III (1096–
1131), who, as we have already seen, was one of the founders
of the territorial greatness of Catalonia north of the Pyrenees,
was also one of the most flagrant offenders in this regard.
To his eldest son, Ramon Berenguer IV, the husband of
Petronilla of Aragon, he left only the lands south of the
mountains; the French territories, which he had labored
so hard to augment, passed to a younger son, Berenguer
Ramon.[1] Fortunately, instead of flying at one another's
throats in fratricidal strife according to the Castilian fashion,
the two sons of Ramon Berenguer III maintained most
cordial relations with one another. Nay more, when the
younger was threatened in the possession of his domains
in France, the elder, in alliance with the Emperor Frederick
Barbarossa, successfully maintained him and his heirs in
the possession of their lawful inheritance.[2] A happy result
of this act of fraternal loyalty was the temporary reunion
of all the territories north and south of the Pyrenees under
Alfonso II, the son and heir of Ramon Berenguer IV, who
possessed himself of Provence on the death without male
heirs of his cousin, the son of Berenguer Ramon, and subsequently defended himself there against the attacks of the
count of Toulouse.[3] But unfortunately the old mistake was
once more repeated in the next generation, and in a manner
which prepared the way for the final loss of the French holdings in the thirteenth century. Alfonso II (1162–96), who
had inherited all the lands on both sides of the mountains,
was also successful in increasing them. We have already

---

[1] Bofarull, ii, p. 426.
[2] Zurita, i, f. 69.

[3] Devic and Vaissete, op. cit., vi, pp. 24 ff.; Bofarull, iii, pp. 67 ff.

seen that Roussillon and the feudal suzerainty of Nîmes and
the adjacent lands were acquired under his rule.[1] To the
south, also, he made notable advances against the Moors,
taking from them the territories about Caspe and Albarracin,
and founding the city of Teruel. In 1177, moreover, he
captured Cuenca for his ally, the king of Castile, who, in
gratitude for this notable service, withdrew the claim of
feudal overlordship over Aragon which Castile had maintained, in theory at least, since the days of Alfonso the
Emperor.[2] But it was probably this very preoccupation
about Spanish affairs that led Alfonso of Aragon to turn over
the administration of Provence to his brothers Ramon Berenguer and Sancho, and finally, in 1193, to his second son,
who bore his father's name. On the elder Alfonso's death
in 1196, this second son inherited Provence and some of the
smaller territories adjacent to it, under the feudal suzerainty
of his elder brother Pedro; while the latter succeeded his
father as ruler of all the Spanish lands south of the Pyrenees,
together with Roussillon, and later acquired Urgel and the
fief of Montpellier. But Provence had once more passed
out of the direct possession of the kings of Aragon, and this
time it never really returned.[3]

The confusion and disunion which reigned in these Aragonese-Catalonian holdings north of the Pyrenees were
greatly increased, at the close of the twelfth century, by the
progress of the heresy of the Albigenses. Alfonso of Provence strove hard, and for a long time successfully, to prevent
his lands from being involved, but numerous converts were
made within the French territories of his brother and feudal
suzerain Pedro of Aragon; while Raymond, count of Toulouse, who had married Pedro's sister Eleanor, was the

[1] *Ante*, p. 279.
Zurita, i, ff. 77–82.

[2] Devic and Vaissete, *op. cit.*, vi, pp.
175 ff.; Lecoy, i, pp. 141 ff.

staunch friend of the heretics from the beginning, and did
his utmost to enlist the sympathies of the Aragonese monarch
in their behalf.[1] But King Pedro was still a most devoted
son of the church.   In November, 1204, he actually went
to Rome to receive the crown of Aragon at the hands of
Innocent III, declaring himself at the same time the faithful
vassal of the Holy See, and even promising the payment
of an annual tribute.[2] Eight years later he played a prominent and heroic part in the battle of Las Navas de Tolosa
against the Moors, and Innocent III doubtless felt that when
the affair of the Albigenses should finally come to a head
he could count on the active support of the king of Aragon.
During the early years of the thirteenth century the crisis
gradually approached.   Despite the thunderings of St.
Dominic, the heresy increased so fast as to constitute a
real menace to the Church; and at last the murder of
Pierre de Castelnau, the papal legate, on January 15, 1208,
gave the signal for an army of crusaders to collect under
the banner of Simon de Montfort, and carry flame and sword
throughout the Albigensian lands.[3] For four years more,
until after the campaign of Las Navas had been concluded,
Pedro abstained from taking arms, and did his best to mediate between the belligerents.   But in the year 1213 his
hesitations came to an end.   The Moorish danger was past.
The Pope had refused his offers of mediation.   His subjects,

[1] Devic and Vaissete, op. cit., vi, pp.
216 ff.; Bofarull, iii, pp. 129 ff.

[2] The underlying reasons for this
novel departure have never been satisfactorily cleared up. Need for papal
consent to a divorce from his wife,
Maria of Montpellier, and desire to enlist papal and Italian support for a projected expedition against the Balearics,
were doubtless important factors in
Pedro's decision; and there were apparently some precedents for his action
in the history of Aragon in the eleventh

century. It is, however, clear that the
whole proceeding roused deep indignation among the Aragonese, who did not
relish seeing the realm which they had
won from the infidel by their blood thus
lightly handed over by their monarch
in vassalage to Rome. Cf. Zurita, i,
ff. 22, 27, 90; Bofarull, iii, pp. 108 ff.;
R. St.-H., iv, pp. 45–48; Colmeiro,
Reyes, pp. 199 f.; Altamira, § 250.

[3] A. Luchaire in Lavisse, Histoire de
France, iii, 1, pp. 266 f.

who had suffered cruelly from de Montfort's armies, begged
him to intervene. His brother-in-law, the count of Toulouse, came and threw himself on his protection. Honor,
and loyalty to his relations and vassals, forbade him any
longer to withhold his hand. First he made sure that the
king of France would hold aloof. Then, after signing an
offensive alliance with the counts of Foix and Toulouse,[1]
he gathered his armies and declared war on Simon de Montfort. Finally, on September 12, 1213, the rival forces met
on the plain beneath the ramparts of Muret. The battle
there was brief and decisive. The generalship of de Montfort and the exhortations of St. Dominic rendered the charge
of the crusaders irresistible. Their victory was speedy and
complete, and the body of King Pedro was found among
the slain.[2]

The results of the Albigensian crusade presaged the ruin
of the power of Aragon in the south of France. The war
kept on during the minority of Pedro's son James, Simon
de Montfort continuing to advance until his own death in
1218. His son Amaury inherited his claims, but, being
unable to substantiate them unaided, finally made them
over to Louis VIII, king of France, who captured in rapid
succession Avignon, Nîmes, and Carcassonne (1226), and all
the country up to the walls of Toulouse.[3] By the peace of
Paris in 1229, Nîmes, Béziers, and Carcassonne were ceded
to the French crown, without regard to the Aragonese
claims of feudal suzerainty; and in the succeeding years
the count of Toulouse further complicated matters by turning around on the ancient allies of his house, attacking

[1] Baudon de Mony, *Relations de
Foix avec la Catalogne*, i, pp. 136–
145.
[2] Zurita, i, ff. 99–101; Devic and
Vaissete, *op. cit.*, vi, pp. 421–429. For
further authorities on the battle of
Muret cf. A. Molinier, *Sources de l'histoire de France*, iii, p. 68.
[3] Devic and Vaissete, *op. cit.*, vi, pp.
604–616.

the count of Provence, cousin and feudal vassal of the king of Aragon, and even attempting to oust the latter from the tenure of Montpellier.[1]

By this time James the Conqueror, the son and successor of Pedro the Catholic, had reached man's estate and was firmly seated on his throne. In 1226 also St. Louis had become king of France; so that the claims of the two states were worthily represented wherever they came in conflict. Of the two monarchs James was decidedly in the less advantageous position, and his only hope of complete success lay in uniting the rival counts of Provence and Toulouse in amity with one another and in joint allegiance to himself. To this truly Herculean task he bent his efforts during the crucial year 1241, but without success.[2] Divorce and remarriage were to be the means to the end. The count of Toulouse was to be separated from his wife in order that he might be wedded to Sancia, the third daughter of the count of Provence; it was doubtless James's ultimate intention that the issue of this union should some day marry one of his own descendants, and thus pave the way for the reunion of all the Aragonese holdings south and north of the Pyrenees. The divorce was duly secured; but the long interval which elapsed between the death of Pope Gregory IX and the election of his successor caused fatal delays in securing the dispensation for the count's second marriage, and in the meantime the lady who had been selected for him became the bride of Richard of Cornwall. With Sancia thus disposed of, the Conqueror centred his attentions on her younger sister Beatrice. It seems probable that he favored a scheme of substituting her for her sister as the bride of the count of Toulouse in the early part

[1] Devic and Vaissete, *op. cit.*, vi, pp. 632 ff.   [2] Devic and Vaissete, *op. cit.*, vi, pp. 725–734.

of 1245: but when her father died on August 19 of that
year, he suddenly changed his tactics, and advanced to Aix
in the hope of seizing her for himself; had he been successful in so doing, there is little doubt that he would have
found means of making her his wife.   But he had not a
sufficient number of troops to enable him to carry out the
attempt, and on January 31, 1246, he was once more forestalled by the celebration of the marriage of Beatrice to the
redoubtable Charles of Anjou.[1]   With this, all hope of Aragon's retaining Provence vanished forever. All that the Conqueror could hope for hereafter was to retain the scattering
bits of French territory which he continued to claim or hold
farther westward, some as feudal suzerain, some as vassal,
and others in full ownership.

Of these the most important and also by far the most
troublesome was the county of Montpellier, which had been
acquired in 1204 by the marriage of its heiress, the granddaughter of the Eastern Emperor Manuel Comnenus, to
James's father, Pedro the Catholic.   Its suzerainty, however, had been retained by the bishops of Maguelonne,
who were almost never on good terms with the kings of
Aragon and tended to support against them the counter
claims of the kings of France.[2]   On the other hand, the
ancient pretensions of the French monarchs south of the
mountains, in the county of Barcelona or Spanish Mark,
had never been entirely forgotten; and they had been
recently revived, doubtless in retaliation for James's intrigues with the counts of Provence and Toulouse.   There
were, moreover, an enormous number of conflicting claims
of a minor nature, provocative of ill will and of occasional
acts of violence.   Obviously, from every point of view, the

[1] Devic and Vaissete, op. cit., vi, pp.
775–777; Swift, op. cit., pp. 74–76, 82, 83.

[2] Lecoy, i, pp. 139 ff.; Swift, op. cit.,
pp. 12 f., 72, 94.

time was ripe for a definite and permanent settlement of all these outstanding questions. At last, on March 14, 1258, at Tortosa, the king of Aragon appointed three commissioners to take up the whole series of problems with France, and also to arrange, if possible, a marriage between his daughter Isabella and Philip, the second son of Louis IX. These representatives finally found the French court at Corbeil, near Paris; and there, on May 12, signed a treaty in which the king of France renounced all claim to Barcelona, Urgel, Besalú, Ampurias, Gerona, and Osona, south of the Pyrenees, and to Roussillon, Cerdagne, and the subsidiary territories of Conflans and Valespir, to the north of them; while the commissioners for the king of Aragon gave up his rights in Carcassonne, Agde, Foix, Béziers, Nîmes, Albi, Redes, Narbonne, Toulouse, Millau, and Gévaudan, and all other territories north of the mountains over which he pretended to authority or jurisdiction, save Montpellier, which he retained under the suzerainty of the king of France. The marriage contract of Philip and Isabella was drawn up at the same time, and both treaties were confirmed on July 16, 1258, by James the Conqueror at Barcelona; and on the following day the king of Aragon solemnly divested himself of any last shadow of a title to the possession of the suzerainty of Provence, by making over all his claims to that territory to Margaret, the eldest daughter of the late count, who had married Louis IX.[1]

[1] Devic and Vaissete, op. cit., vi, pp. 858 ff.; Swift, op. cit., pp. 94 f. The delicate question of Montpellier was not actually settled at Corbeil; and it gave rise to some difficulties in the succeeding years. The claims to suzerainty of the bishops of Maguelonne disappear at this stage, and in 1293 a small portion of the town of Montpellier, known as Montpellieret, was ceded in full ownership to the crown of France. We shall revert to this matter in another place in connection with the history of the kingdom of Majorca. Cf. C. V. Langlois in Lavisse, Histoire de France, iii, 2, p. 95, note 2; iv, 1, p. 84; Lecoy, i, pp. 139–148, 311–337. One other minor exception to the renunciations of James north of the Pyrenees may also be noted, namely, the little viscounty of Carlat, between Quercy and Gévaudan, whose suzerainty he retained, to-

In general the king of Aragon was undeniably the loser
in this treaty. The rights to the lands south of the Pyrenees
which Louis IX renounced may have been historically and
theoretically valid in the eyes of a feudal lawyer, but they
were for all practical purposes obsolete; while the Aragonese
claims to Provence and most of the other French possessions
which James the Conqueror gave up rested on far more
recent and solid foundations. Geographically, however, the
facts were on the whole against him, as was also his constant
preoccupation with outside matters; though we may incidentally observe that his sporadic though unsuccessful efforts to acquire Navarre [1] may be regarded as an attempt to
indemnify himself for his losses at Corbeil. On the other
hand, we must remember that the Conqueror's territorial
losses in France, though heavy, were as yet by no means
absolutely complete. Cerdagne and Roussillon and Montpellier (the latter under French suzerainty) still remained,
and, in pursuance of the ineradicable Spanish practice of
dividing royal inheritances, were erected, together with
the Balearic Islands, into a separate realm with the title of
the kingdom of Majorca; this kingdom was conferred at the
Conqueror's death on his younger son James, under the
suzerainty of the latter's elder brother, the heir of Aragon.
The relations of the subsidiary dynasty thus set up with
the sovereigns of the older line were distinctly the reverse
of cordial, and finally, in the reign of Pedro IV, gave
way to open war, with the ultimate result that Cerdagne,
Roussillon, and the Balearics were reunited to the Crown of
Aragon, and Montpellier was sold by its despairing sovereign

gether with Montpellier. Practically,
however, the matter made little difference, for the territory was too small and
too remote for the kings of Aragon to
enforce their rights. Lecoy, i, pp. 146

f., 326; ii, pp. 45, 55, 67 f., 123, 139,
161, 167–172, 303 f., 313, 329.
  [1] Swift, op. cit., pp. 91–94, 98, 116,
118, 121, 131–133.

to the king of France. The lopping off of that rich fief, however, put a term to the losses of the Crown of Aragon north of the Pyrenees for over three centuries to come. Cerdagne and Roussillon, save for a temporary cession to France in the end of the fifteenth century, continued to remain in Spanish hands until the Peace of the Pyrenees in 1659.[1]

From the story of the loss of the Aragonese lands in France, we pass to that of the completion of the Aragonese reconquest in Spain and its results, and therewith return once more to the reign of James the Conqueror. His grandfather and father before him had set him a glorious example by their victories against the Moors; the battle of Las Navas de Tolosa had been fought when the Conqueror was four years old, and the story of it may well have been the delight of his childhood hours. But the memory of that great campaign served not only to recall past triumphs to the mind of the youthful king; it also spurred him on to seek new ones. Though it had been won by the united armies of Christian Spain, its fruits had been reaped almost exclusively by Castile. The eastern realms had gained much glory but little land; and James was determined to right the balance, and increase the extent of his peninsular dominions.

It was some time, however, before the young king could give his attention to foreign conquest. He had not completed his sixth year, when his father's death before the walls of Muret left him heir to a realm with sadly diminished prestige; indeed, he remained a prisoner for several months in the hands of Simon de Montfort, before a stern mandate

[1] The southern part of Cerdagne is still Spanish; only the portions north of the mountains were ceded to France in 1659.

from Pope Innocent III procured his release. Suppression
of internal rebellion occupied all his energies during the
next fourteen years. Every one seized the opportunity
afforded by the weakness of the monarchy to compass his
own advantage; not until the year 1228 could the young
king call his throne his own.[1] By this time his character
had fully developed. Warmth and intensity of passion,
both good and bad, formed its basis; restraint and self-
control had no part in it at all. Waves of ferocious anger
and tender pity succeeded one another like the showers
and sunshine of an April day. In the heat of a terrible
campaign against the Valencian Moors, when it was essential for him to be everywhere at once, he found that a swallow had made her nest by the roundel of his tent, and "so
I ordered the men not to take it down till the swallow had
taken flight with her young ones, as she had come trusting
in my protection."[2] None could punish or avenge more
cruelly; none, on the other hand, could be more generous
or loyal to his friends. His valor in war was famous throughout Western Europe; yet he could not bear to sign a death
warrant, "and when it was necessary to let justice take its
course, he bewailed the heavy responsibility of being forced
to cause a man to die." He was a scandal to Christendom
for his licentiousness; "but the fault seemed the less, when
allowance was made for his unrivalled beauty and his noble
and gentle mien, which caused all women to cast longing
eyes upon him, so that his only problem was to choose between them."[3] His genius was preëminently military. He
inherited notable ability in this respect from his maternal

---

[1] Swift, op. cit., pp. 11–33. The
royal victory was largely due to the
support of the church and of the cities,
and James never forgot it. His advice
to Alfonso the Learned 'to keep the
church and the people in his grace' was
the fruit of his experience in these early
years.

[2] The Chronicle of James I, King of
Aragon, tr. by John Forster, i, p. 322.

[3] These two quotations are taken
from the very rare fifteenth-century

great-grandfather, the Emperor Manuel Comnenus, and it
is as a warrior and conqueror that he won his most enduring
fame; but as a statesman, administrator, and lawgiver he
stood very high, while his various literary productions, as
well as those of his descendants, have earned for the sovereigns of the house of Barcelona an honorable place in the
history of mediaeval poetry and prose.[1] With such energy
and versatility, it was obvious, now that the factions had
been dominated at home, that the new king would not long
rest content without embarking on conquests abroad. The
rich kingdom of Valencia still remained in Moorish hands,
and offered a tempting prey. The heart of the kingdom
of Aragon was set on acquiring it, and, after the conclusion of the Balearic campaign in 1229–30, James determined
to concentrate his efforts on the attainment of that end.

Some preliminary measures had, in fact, already been
taken. As early as 1225, three years before the flames of
civil war had been entirely extinguished within the realm,
a strong force had been launched against the fortress of
Peñiscola, a miniature Gibraltar, some forty miles south of
Tortosa. The campaign was unsuccessful; but when
word came of renewed preparations in the following year,
Abu Zeid, the Moorish king of Valencia, took alarm and
offered to pay tribute to the extent of one fifth of his revenues
as the price of peace. James gladly accepted these terms,
the more so as the success of his projected campaign was,
for the time being, more than dubious;[2] but three years
later, on the very eve of his departure for the conquest of
Majorca, the whole affair was reopened by the dethrone-

Corónica de los Reyes de Aragon by
Gauberte Fabricio de Vagad (pp. 74 f.),
as cited by R. St.-H., iv, pp. 184 f.
On Vagad and his work, which was published in Saragossa in 1499, cf. Gallardo,

Ensayo de una Biblioteca, iv, coll. 850 f.;
Fueter, *Histoire de l'historiographie
moderne*, p. 290.
[1] Swift, *op. cit.*, pp. 143 ff., 255 ff.
[2] Swift, pp. 26 f.

ment of Abu Zeid, who fled to the court of Aragon to demand the Conqueror's aid in the recovery of his realm. All that James could do for the moment was to conclude a most advantageous treaty with the Moorish sovereign, in which he promised the latter the military aid he desired in exchange for an extensive territorial compensation.[1] Abu Zeid, however, was unable to regain his kingdom, so that in 1232, on his return from his third visit to the Balearics, the Conqueror prepared to take up the question of the Valencian campaign and press it vigorously himself. Adequate pretexts for war were not lacking. The new Valencian ruler who had displaced Abu Zeid was contemptuous and belligerent; he refused to pay all the tribute due to Aragon since James's treaty with his predecessor, and even raided the Christian lands.[2] Funds were granted by the Cortes of Aragon and Catalonia. Abu Zeid, going beyond the terms of the treaty of 1229, now transferred to the Conqueror all his claims to his former kingdom. A bull of Pope Gregory IX, declaring the forthcoming campaign to be a crusade, was published with due solemnity at Monzon. In January, 1233, the campaign began, interest centring in the siege of the little town of Burriana on the seacoast north of Valencia. The forces engaged on both sides were apparently very small, despite the exaggerated estimates of earlier writers, but the resistance was heroic, and the place did not fall till midsummer. In the succeeding months, most of the towns northward from Burriana to the Catalonian border, including Peñiscola, surrendered to the forces of the king of Aragon.[3]

The years 1234 and 1235 saw a lull in the Valencian campaigns, the Conqueror's attention being chiefly occupied with his marriage with Violante of Hungary, and with dis-

<hr/>

[1] Swift, p. 37.   [2] *Chronicle*, i, pp. 389 f.; Swift, pp. 55 f.   [3] Swift, pp. 56–58.

putes with the sovereigns of France, Castile, and Navarre. In 1236, however, he returned to the attack and possessed himself, after considerable resistance, of the fortress of Puig de Cibolla, twelve miles north of Valencia, and two miles from the coast, valuable as a base of operations against the Moorish capital. During the next year and a half, the king's attention was again distracted by other problems in the northern part of his dominions. The unpatriotic conduct of the Aragonese nobles, who placed the maintenance of their privileges before the welfare of the realm, gave him constant cause for alarm. In the summer of 1237, the Moorish sovereign of Valencia attacked Puig with a large force, and was only with great difficulty beaten off. Finally, however, in January, 1238, all other difficulties were cleared away, and the Conqueror led his armies to the southward, swearing a solemn oath not to return to Catalonia or to Aragon until Valencia was in his hands.[1] A proposal of the Moorish sovereign to hand over a number of strongholds and to pay an annual tribute of 10,000 byzants in return for peace, elicited from James the ominous reply that 'he intended to have both the hen and the chickens'; and so deeply were the Moors impressed by the vigor of his preparations, that before the end of April the most of the country north of the Guadalaviar surrendered itself at discretion. The siege of the city of Valencia now began. At first James's army did not exceed 1500 men, but subsequent reënforcements, some of them from foreign lands, brought it up to several times that number. At one time, a fleet of twelve galleys arrived from Tunis to succor the beleaguered town, but it sailed away without accomplishing anything. The details of the siege are of the characteristic mediaeval sort. They exhibit the Conqueror's military skill, and occa-

[1] Swift, pp. 62–64.

sionally the ferocity of his vengeance against those who resisted him. When the defenders of one of the city's towers refused to yield, the tower was set on fire and its inmates burned alive, despite subsequent offers of surrender. In September it became obvious that the town could hold out no longer, and generous terms of capitulation were finally granted by James, who permitted the inhabitants to depart with their goods, and promised them an escort as far as Cullera, some twenty-five miles to the southward. The bishops and nobles, when they learned of this arrangement, "lost color, as if some one had stabbed them to the heart,"[1] so disappointed were they at being deprived of an opportunity to enrich themselves; but the king was undeterred by their grumblings, and actually executed some of his own soldiers who dared to offer violence to the departing Moors.[2] The surrender of Valencia virtually placed in James's hands all the towns north of the Jucar, except Denia and Cullera, which remained temporarily in Moorish control; and five years later an infidel raid into the conquered land gave him a pretext for attacking the strip of territory which lay between the Jucar and the confines of Murcia. Jativa and Biar alone offered effective resistance, but the first surrendered in June, 1244, and the second in February, 1245; and with the expulsion of the Moorish king from Cullera and his voluntary surrender of Denia

---

[1] *Chronicle*, ii, p. 396.

[2] The treatment of the Moors who remained in Valencia was also very generous, and far more consonant to the usual practice of the Aragonese monarchs than the harsher fate that was meted out to many of the inhabitants of the Balearics. They were suffered to retain their native customs, and no attempt was made to induce them to abandon their religion. It is true that a revolt which occurred in the winter of 1247–48 elicited from the Conqueror an edict for the expulsion of the entire Moslem population of the kingdom; but the desperate resistance he encountered when he attempted to carry the edict into effect resulted in a notable relaxation of its enforcement. Most of the Christian landholders, also, apparently recognised the vast superiority of the Moorish knowledge of agriculture, and protested violently at the royal projects of expulsion. Cf. "Repartimiento de Valencia," in vol. xi of *D. I. A.*, pp. 143–656; Swift, pp. 85–87, 253.

the triumph of the Conqueror was complete.[1] His difficulties had not been lessened during the campaign by the fact that representatives of his future son-in-law, Alfonso the Infante of Castile, constantly hovered around with the obvious intention of picking up whatever territories they could for their master — a performance which the entirely indefinite state of the boundaries rendered less difficult than might have been supposed. Though furious at this invasion of his rights, the Conqueror saw that he could not afford, at that moment, to quarrel with Alfonso; and in March, 1244, a temporary arrangement for the division of the disputed territories was made between the two realms. The line then adopted, however, was soon destined to be rectified to the advantage of the king of Aragon, as the sequel will show.[2]

During the next eighteen years James was so busy with other cares that he did not push his conquests against the Moors any further in the Iberian Peninsula. In 1263, however, a fresh opportunity came, when the Moorish ruler of the province of Murcia, who had been suffered by his Castilian conquerors to remain and to retain some measure of autonomy, was incited by the Emir of Granada to break out in revolt. Alfonso X had, as usual, far too many irons in the fire himself to undertake the task of quelling the insurrection; he therefore sent his wife to beg aid of his father-in-law, who with wise generosity determined, against the advice of his counsellors, not to refuse it; for "if the king of Castile happen to lose his land," he shrewdly remarked, "I shall hardly be safe in mine."[3] An exhortation from Pope Clement IV contributed to whet his crusading

[1] Swift, pp. 64–70, where full references to the older authorities will be found; V. Boix, *Historia de la Ciudad y Reino de Valencia*, i, p. 121.

[2] Swift, pp. 78–81.
[3] *Chronicle*, ii, pp. 495–503; Swift, pp. 107 f.

ardor; and in 1265 the Conqueror invaded Murcia. Until
he sat down before the capital of the realm in 1266, his advance was little more than a triumphal procession. Most
of the towns gave up without striking a blow, though the
surrender of Elche had to be accelerated by a brief interview
with one of its notables, during which James seized the opportunity to drop "into the sleeve of his gown 300 byzants,"
at which "he was delighted, and promised on his Law that
he would do all he could for my advantage." [1]   A month's
siege was necessary before the city of Murcia would consent
to treat, but in February, 1266, it bowed to the inevitable,
and with its fall the resistance of the surrounding country
was at an end. When James returned to Valencia in the
following April, he left 10,000 men behind him to prevent a
recurrence of the revolt. A number of Catalans, moreover,
were subsequently transplanted to Murcia and settled there,
and lands were freely distributed to some of the Aragonese
nobles who had aided in the conquest.[2] The possession of
the entire territory, however, was definitely given over by
the Conqueror to Castile, in loyal fulfilment of his plighted
word; and Alfonso the Learned lost no time in formally
incorporating it in his own dominions. The boundary between it and the Aragonese kingdom of Valencia remained
in doubt until the year 1304, when it was finally drawn
under Portuguese arbitration, as we have already seen,
considerably to the south of the line fixed by James and
Alfonso in 1244.[3] The resulting enlargement of the lands
of the king of Aragon may be fairly regarded as a recognition of the fact that James had done the lion's share of the
work of subjugating the Murcian realm, and deserved some
territorial reward.

The final conquest of Murcia for Castile in 1266 marks

[1] *Chronicle*, ii, p. 540.   [2] Swift, p. 116; Altamira, § 254.   [3] Cf. *ante*, p. 117.

an important turning point in the history of the realms
of the Crown of Aragon. From henceforth they were no
longer contiguous at any point to land held by the infidel ;
and this fact exercised an important influence on the development of their national ambitions and ideals. On the
one hand, it naturally caused them to lose interest in the
great task of expelling the Moors from the peninsula, because they could no longer hope to reap any territorial
reward from its accomplishment. When Granada should
fall, Castile, which completely encircled it on the land side,
would obviously be the sole beneficiary ; the western kingdom, therefore, now became more than ever the land of the
Reconquest *par excellence*. But there were other sides to
the picture as well. If Granada was 'a hope for Castile,'
whose capture would bring a great reward, it was also, until
that capture should be effected, very much of a thorn in
her side.[1] Aragon had no such thorn, and could, therefore, concentrate freely on other things—especially on her
career of maritime expansion to the eastward — in a way
that was impossible for her western neighbor. Moreover,
in that career of expansion and in other matters, she needed
no longer to feel herself burdened, as Castile, in theory if
not in practice, still was, by the weight of mediaeval crusading traditions. She was comparatively free to deal with
the Moorish states of Granada and North Africa on the
same basis as she would with any foreign land—to make
commercial treaties and traffic with them, to forget that
they were the 'hereditary foe.'[2] What she lost in possi-

[1] A. Giménes Soler, *El Sitio de Almería*, p. 9. It may also be observed
that the fact that Aragon was prevented
from gaining further lands in Spain by
the Castilian acquisition of Murcia,
is one reason why the western kingdom
was so long in conquering Granada;
she lacked the incentive of a competitor
in the race for territorial expansion in
the peninsula. Cf. A. Giménes Soler,
La Corona de Aragón y Granada, p. 9.
[2] L. Klüpfel, *Die äussere Politik Alfonso's III. von Aragonien*, pp. 103 f.

bilities of territorial aggrandizement within the peninsula, Aragon more than regained by increased freedom of action outside of it. All these different considerations go far towards explaining the wide divergence between the paths travelled by the eastern and western portions of Spain during the period previous to their union.

The points that have been made in the preceding paragraph are well illustrated by the story of the relations of Aragon to Granada and the Moorish states of North Africa during the fourteenth and fifteenth centuries. Towards Granada her attitude was primarily determined by the ebbs and flows of her policy in regard to Castile and Morocco. It was during the reign of James II (1291-1327), who made more treaties with Moorish rulers and enjoyed greater prestige in the Moslem world than any other sovereign of his house, that the two realms came into closest contact. James had inherited from his two predecessors a tradition of friendship rather than of hostility to the Moorish realm; and he continued it by signing, on May 16, 1296, a treaty with the Granadan sovereign which may be regarded as the norm for subsequent agreements between the two states. It provided for the protection in each of the subjects of the other, and declared that each would remain neutral in case the other were attacked by a third party.[1] Obviously the king of Aragon desired to guard against the hostility of Granada in case his smouldering disputes with the king of Castile should burst into flame; and the state of his relations with the king of Morocco also dictated the advisability of preserving friendship with the latter's coreligionist across the Strait. But a few years later all was changed. A new king, Mohammed III, ascended the throne of Granada in 1302, and, reversing

[1] A. Giménes Soler, *Aragón y Granada*, pp. 25, 41, 45 ff.

the policy of his predecessor, crossed over and seized Ceuta from the Merinites; while, two years later, the settlement of the Murcian boundary removed all cause of hostility between Aragon and Castile. The natural result of these developments was that the king of Aragon made common cause with the king of Morocco against Granada, and sent him a fleet, with the aid of which he was able to expel the latter from Ceuta; then, joining forces with the king of Castile, the Aragonese monarch attacked the Emir of Granada in his own dominions. But the results of the campaign were disappointing. The capture of the town of Almeria had been assigned as his share to James of Aragon, but though he remained four months and three days before the town, and won a notable battle outside its walls, he was unable to take it. The siege was raised on January 26, 1310, and though peace was not finally made between the two states until thirteen years later, James's failure before Almeria may justly be said to mark the last appearance of Aragon as a 'reconquering power.'[1] Thenceforth her relations to Granada were determined solely by the political exigencies of the moment. They varied almost from year to year, but it is not worth while to follow them in detail. That they were preponderantly friendly was due chiefly to the fact that Aragon was so often in difficulties with Castile that she could not afford to neglect any obvious opportunity to make trouble for her; and the desire of Aragon to maintain mercantile relations with Morocco also doubtless contributed to the same result. The only notable deviation from this policy occurred in 1340, when Aragon made common cause with Castile to repel the last great Moorish invasion from across the Strait, which was supported by

[1] A. Gimónes Soler, *Sitio de Almería*, pp. 59 f.; idem, *Aragón y Granada*, pp. 171, 218.

the Granadan king. The fate of that expedition has already
been recounted. It only remains to observe that the king
of Aragon hastened to make peace with both Morocco and
Granada at the earliest opportunity, in 1345, leaving Alfonso XI of Castile to conduct alone his final campaign
against the infidel.[1]

If Aragon, in this period, was far less deeply involved
with Granada than was Castile, she was much more intimately concerned than was her western neighbor with the
Moorish states of North Africa. Castile, as we have already seen, was frequently brought into contact with the
Merinite rulers of Morocco through her bickerings with
the Emirs of Granada; and the North African lands to the
west of the Muluya River were specifically assigned to her
as a field for conquest under an arrangement between
Sancho IV and James II of Aragon in 1291.[2] But at the
same time that she obtained recognition of the priority of
her own rights in the territories to the west of the Muluya,
Castile conceded to Aragon the same privileges in those to
the east of it; and the majority of the Aragonese sovereigns strove their hardest to make the most of them.
They aspired to commercial predominance in all the North
African ports; and, except in Morocco, where Castile had
forestalled them, they also cherished the ambition to demonstrate their military and political superiority over the
different Moorish rulers, and whenever possible to collect
tributes in token of it. Their political dealings with Tlemcen, Tunis, and the occasionally independent state of Bugia
form a significant if subsidiary chapter in the history of
their foreign policy; while their commercial activities in
these states, and also in Morocco, give us an admirable

[1] Mas Latrie, p. 326.
[2] *Memorial Histórico Español*, iii, p.
456; A. Giménez Soler, "Episodios de
las relaciones entre la Corona de Aragón
y Túnez," in *Anuari de l'Institut d'Estudis Catalans*, 1907, p. 197.

illustration of their keen interest in economic advancement.[1]

Before entering upon the story of Aragon's relations with each one of these different realms, it is worth noting, as a striking evidence of the complete extinction of the ancient religious animosities between them, that large numbers of Aragonese and Catalonian mercenaries were enrolled during this period in the armies of the various emirs. The king of Morocco had at one time as many as ten to twelve thousand Christian soldiers in his service, while the rulers of Tunis and Tlemcen each maintained a force of two to three thousand. And it must not be supposed that the men who composed these levies were all, or even chiefly, renegades. Their recruitment and employment by their Moorish masters were specifically approved by various Christian kings, and even by the Popes. Pedro III of Aragon set the example by a treaty with the king of Tunis on June 12, 1285. The practice spread rapidly to Italy, France, Germany, and even England. Castilians also occasionally enrolled themselves among these foreign mercenaries, but the majority of them invariably came from the East Spanish realms. They almost always retained their own banners while on service in the North African forces; they were also usually subject to recall at the will of their lawful sovereigns; but they were highly esteemed and eagerly sought for by the Moorish rulers, who generally used them as a sort of rampart to give solidity to their more lightly armed and mobile native troops. There were also considerable numbers of Berber soldiers serving at various periods, and on a more informal basis, in the armies of the Christian kings of Spain; they were, for the

[1] Cf., on these matters, Claudio Miralles de Imperial, *Relaciones diplomáticas de Mallorca y Aragón con el* *África Septentrional* (Barcelona, 1904), p. 35; also Mercier, vol. ii, *passim*.

most part, cavalry, and were used for scouting duty and for sudden raids.[1]

Coming now to the relations of Aragon with the individual North African states, we find that in Morocco, where the interests of Castile were recognized as paramount, the story is principally economic. In the early years of the thirteenth century Catalan merchants were established at the town of Ceuta,[2] and in 1227 James the Conqueror, jealous of the competition of the Genoese, put forth an ordinance providing that no merchandise of Aragonese origin should be borne to that port in foreign vessels as long as national ones were available for the purpose.[3] In 1274 the Merinite sovereign successfully appealed to the king of Aragon for military aid in suppressing a revolt of the inhabitants of the town; and in 1309 another Aragonese army earned his gratitude by expelling from Ceuta the troops of the king of Granada, who had seized it seven years before.[4] During the next three decades there was a violent reaction, owing to the fears awakened by the sudden increase of the power of the Merinites, which gave them temporary preponderance over the other North African states, and finally led to the last great Moorish invasion of Spain in 1340.[5] But as soon as that danger was past, the kings of Aragon made haste to return to the policy of their predecessors. In 1345 Pedro the Ceremonious formally renewed friendly relations with the Moroccan ruler, and twelve years later concluded with him a most complete and inclusive treaty, political and commercial, against

[1] Mas Latrie, pp. 266–276; J. Alemany, "Milicias Cristianas al servicio de los sultanes Musulmanes del Almagreb," in *Homenaje á F. Codera* (Saragossa, 1904), pp. 133–169; A. Giménez Soler, "Caballeros Españoles en África y Africanos en España," in *R. H.*, xii, pp. 299–372.

[2] A. de Capmany, *Memorias históricas de Barcelona*, i, 2, p. 80.

[3] Mas Latrie, p. 140.

[4] Mas Latrie, pp. 255 f., 303 f.

[5] Cf. *ante*, p. 128, and Mercier, ii, pp. 281 ff.

their common enemy, Pedro of Castile.[1] In this case there is no evidence of any effort to assert any kind of political superiority. Peace, in order to facilitate commerce, was the main object on both sides, and was thenceforth for the most part preserved.

With regard to the kingdoms of Tlemcen and Bugia, on the other hand, there is a different tale to tell. Lying east of the River Muluya, they fell within the Aragonese sphere of influence; smaller and weaker than their neighbors, and perpetually at odds with one another, they offered a much more favorable opportunity for the exercise of some measure of political domination. During the reign of James II (1291–1327), who took the liveliest interest in North African affairs, vigorous efforts were made to obtain specific acknowledgement of overlordship from the kings of both these realms; and if no formal or explicit recognition of vassalage was ever received, a certain amount of tribute of an irregular sort was unquestionably collected. James utilized every chance to play off Bugia against Tlemcen, and vice versa; his warships were constantly present in the ports of both nations, and exercised no inconsiderable influence on the ebbs and flows of their rival powers. All these efforts to attain political dominance could not fail to react unfavorably on the commercial activities of Aragon in this part of North Africa. The economic side falls distinctly into the background here; though this is partly explained by the fact that the trade of Tlemcen and of Bugia was less valuable than that of their neighbors.[2]

In Tunis, as in Tlemcen and in Bugia, we find a conflict between the political and the commercial objects of the

[1] Mas Latrie, pp. 326, 392–394.
[2] Mas Latrie, pp. 320–325; A. Giménez Soler, in *Anuari de l'Institut d'Estudis Catalans*, 1907, pp. 195–224;

Miralles de Imperial, *Relaciones diplomáticas*, pp. 63 ff.; Klüpfel, *Aussere Politik Alfonso's III.*, pp. 103–115.

Aragonese monarchs, in which the former, at least during the thirteenth and fourteenth centuries, remain distinctly to the fore. As that side of the story, however, is much more intimately bound up with the Aragonese power in Sicily than in Spain, it may be most conveniently reserved for consideration in that connection. But the economic relations of the two states were also of considerable importance. Tunis was unquestionably the chief centre of European trade in North Africa, and regular Aragonese factories and consulates were set up there during the reign of James the Conqueror.[1] Vigorous competition not unnaturally ensued with the Genoese, Florentines, Venetians, and other Italian powers who were already on the ground; but the Aragonese were generally able to hold their own.[2] During its brief period of separate existence, moreover, the kingdom of Majorca possessed its own factories and officials in Tunis, and also in Tripoli and Alexandria. It signed commercial treaties with the Moorish kings, and threatened to enter upon a really serious rivalry with its parent realm.[3] There was an elaborate set of duties and tariffs on this thriving trade; but in return the European merchants were most effectively protected against fraud or maltreatment in the North African ports. Most of the custom houses there employed a Christian scribe, selected by the European residents; moreover, the chief Moorish officials, who were invariably men of rank and importance, often performed the functions of consuls, and acted as guardians and protectors of resident and transient Christians in all their dealings with the native inhabitants.[4]

[1] Swift, op. cit., pp. 226 f.
[2] Mas Latrie, pp. 233–236; Miralles de Imperial, Relaciones diplomáticas, pp. 63 ff.
[3] Mas Latrie, pp. 316–320; Miralles de Imperial, op. cit., pp. 55–62.

[4] Mas Latrie, pp. 336 ff., 373, 404–407. There was apparently some traffic in slaves with these North African ports, but there is no reason to think that it attained any very considerable proportions. Swift, p. 190, note.

Much of this admirable organization was directly traceable
to the needs and demands of the merchants of the Aragonese
realms, whose preëminence among the various foreign traders
in the North African ports was unquestioned for a brief
period during the first half of the fifteenth century.[1]

In dealing with the various North African activities of
Aragon, we have used that name in its larger sense, as the
sole convenient means of designating all the three realms
which were ruled by the Aragonese kings; strictly, it
would have been much more accurate if we had spoken instead of Catalonia. For Aragon, in the more limited meaning of the word, had little or no interest in such distant
things. It was at Barcelona that all the foreign and naval
activity of the realm, both political and commercial, was
centred; it was the Catalans who built the ships and
manned them; it was the Catalans who cherished visions
of expansion and a maritime career. When, therefore, just
after the middle of the fifteenth century, the county was
paralyzed by internal revolt and civil war, their effects were
promptly felt in North Africa. After a period of unex-
ampled strength and prosperity, the commercial relations
of the East Spanish kingdoms with the Moorish states began rapidly to dwindle and decay; and before any real
recovery could take place, the marriage of Ferdinand and
Isabella united the crowns of Aragon and Castile, and altered the whole course of the development of the Iberian
realms. North African projects were by no means abandoned in the succeeding age, but they were pursued under
different auspices, with changing methods and divided
aims, and they were subordinated, even more completely

[1] Cf. *infra*, pp. 493 ff., 503 ff. The 'golden age' of Aragonese commerce in Tunis falls between the second expedition of Alfonso the Magnanimous against Gerba in 1432, and the beginning of the decline of Barcelona in the reign of John II.

than before, to the prosecution of other schemes. One of the most logical and hopeful paths of Iberian development was gradually suffered to fall into desuetude, owing chiefly to the multitude of new interests which presented themselves in the age of Ferdinand and Isabella and the Hapsburgs.[1]

[1] Cf. J. Arias y Miranda, *Examen del influjo que tuso en el comercio, indus-* *tria, y poblacion de España su dominacion en América* (Madrid, 1854), pp. 39 ff.

BIBLIOGRAPHICAL NOTE

See notes at the end of the Introduction and of Chapters I and II, and add:

Sources and Contemporary Chronicles. — The *Colección de Documentos inéditos del Archivo General de la Corona de Aragon*, ed. Próspero Bofarull y Mascaro and others (Barcelona, 1847–76, 1910, 41 vols.), is the most important collection of sources for the realms of the Crown of Aragon. "Episodios de la Historia de las Relaciones entre la Corona de Aragón y Túnez," and "Documents de Túnez del Archivo de la Corona de Aragón," ed. Andrés Giménez Soler, in the *Anuari* of the Institut d'Estudis Catalans for 1907, pp. 195–224, and for 1909–10, pp. 210–259, furnish valuable source material, preceded by excellent introductions, on the relations of Aragon to the North African states. Antonio de Capmany y de Montpalau, *Memorias Históricas sobre la Marina, Comercio, y Artes de la antigua ciudad de Barcelona* (Madrid, 1779–92, 4 vols.), is a mine of information on the subjects with which it deals. As two of the four volumes are exclusively composed of documents, it seems best to class it as a source, and to regard the other two as introductions. For further information see Prescott, i, pp. 91 f. Capmany published also the *Llibre del Consolat* or maritime code of Barcelona (Madrid, 1791); this is often, though incorrectly, listed as volume v of the *Memorias*. James the Conqueror, *The Chronicle of James I, King of Aragon*: English translation by John Forster (London, 1883, 2 vols.). On the authenticity, value, and different editions of this important authority, see Auguste Molinier, *Les sources de l'histoire de France*, iii, p. 163; Ballester y Castell, *Fuentes Narrativas*, pp. 132–140; and José Massó Torrents in the *R.H.*, xv, pp. 503–523. The *Gestas del Rey Don Jayme de Aragon*, first published in 1909 by Raymond Foulché-Delbosc for the Sociedad de Bibliófilos Madrileños, is a translation and rearrangement of the Chronicle, which was appended to *La Grant Crónica de los Conquiridores*, compiled at the command of Johan Ferrándes de Heredia, grand master of the order of St. John of Jerusalem, in the latter part of the fourteenth century. Cf. Ballester y Castell, pp. 153 ff., and K. Herquet, *Juan Ferrandez de Heredia* (Mülhausen, 1878), pp. 89 f.

Later Works. — Jerónimo Zurita, *Anales de la Corona de Aragon* (2d edition, Saragossa, 1610, 6 vols. — the last two volumes of this edition have the subsidiary title of *Historia del Rey Hernando el Católico*), was written in the middle of the sixteenth century; the first edition was published from 1562 to 1580. It is largely based on the sources, particularly the latter part, and marks a great advance over any historical work previously produced in Aragon; it is a standard authority, which becomes increasingly valuable as it approaches the period in which the author lived. For further information see F. López de Gómara, *Annals of Charles V*, p. 137, and references there, and E. Fueter, *Historiographie*, pp. 290–292.

Antonio de Bofarull y Brocá, *Historia Crítica de Cataluña* (Barcelona, 1876–78, 9 vols.), is the most elaborate general work on that subject, and naturally throws much light on the history of Aragon and of Valencia; its value, however, is much impaired by a lack of footnotes and references. On the gain and loss of the French lands, Claude Devic and Joseph Vaissete's *Histoire générale de Languedoc* (revised edition, Toulouse, 1872–93, 18 vols.) is much more valuable; written in the eighteenth century, it has been brought thoroughly up to date, and contains a wealth of documents. It furnishes the groundwork for numerous recent monographs, such as Charles Baudon de Mony's excellent *Relations politiques des comtes de Foix avec la Catalogne* (Paris, 1896, 2 vols.).

For the beginnings of Aragon, Tomás Ximenes de Embun, *Ensayo histórico acerca de los Orígenes de Aragón y Navarra* (Saragossa, 1878); Jean de Jaurgain, *La Vasconie* (Pau, 1898–1902, 2 vols.); and Louis Barrau-Dihigo, "Les Origines du royaume de Navarre," in *R. H.*, vii, pp. 141–222, 505 f., all are important. Charles de Tourtoulon's *Jacme 1ᵉʳ le Conquérant* (Montpellier, 1863–67, 2 vols.) has been in large measure superseded by F. D. Swift's *James the First, the Conqueror, King of Aragon* (Oxford, 1894); the footnotes in this last work are a boon to all serious students of the reign.

Vicente Boix, *Historia de la Ciudad y Reino de Valencia* (Valencia, 1845–47, 3 vols.), is the best book on the subject; it practically supersedes Gaspar Escolano (d. 1619), *Decadas de la historia de la Ciudad y Reino de Valencia*, although the latter was reëdited and continued by J. B. Perales in three volumes in 1878–80; pages 579–583 of volume iii of Boix's work contain a brief bibliography. Claudio Miralles de Imperial, *Relaciones Diplomáticas de Mallorca y Aragón con el África Septentrional durante la Edad Media* (Barcelona, 1904), supplements Mas Latrie's *Relations et Commerce*; cf. *ante*, p. 93.

CHAPTER VII

THE FIRST CONQUESTS OVERSEAS

FROM the subsidiary phases of the external history of the realms of the Crown of Aragon during the later Middle Ages, we turn for the next three chapters to the study of their conquests in the Mediterranean. This remarkable story of territorial expansion deserves the most prominent place in the mediaeval portion of any history of the Spanish Empire. It laid the foundations for Spain's preëminence in Europe during the sixteenth century. It directed her imperial aspirations to the eastward before the discovery of America diverted them to the west. It made the conquest of the Canaries by Castile seem almost insignificant. Nor must we forget that the glory of taking the lead in this great outburst of maritime and territorial expansion in the Mediterranean — even more than in the contemporaneous activities of the realms of the Crown of Aragon in North Africa — is essentially the glory of Catalonia. Not only was it through Catalan energy and valor that the necessary expeditions were made possible and the majority of land and naval battles fought; it was in deference to Catalan tradition that the movement was first begun. In the early twelfth century, as we have already seen, the Catalans had made joint attacks with the Pisans on the Moors of Majorca and Iviza; and from that time onward they never ceased to cherish the ambition to repeat the experiment on a larger scale. The Balearics had formed a part of Spain under

the Carthaginians, the Romans, and possibly under the
Visigoths : their reconquest for Christendom was, therefore, quite as obvious a duty as that of Valencia ; for the
Catalans, indeed, there was no question that it should have
precedence.[1] James the Conqueror shared their feelings,
and his determination was further strengthened by the
fact that his Catalan subjects had given him far less trouble
than the Aragonese during the stormy years of his minority.
To reward them, he initiated his reign with the expedition
in which they were preëminently interested : if the Aragonese
supported the Balearic campaign at all, they did so as the
king's feudatories and not by national sanction.[2]

The Almohades had taken the Balearics from the Almoravides in the year 1203 ;[3] and though they had been unable
after Las Navas to retain complete control of them, they
maintained in the islands a pirates' nest which menaced
the commerce of the entire western Mediterranean. The
seizure of two ships of Barcelona had evoked from James
the Conqueror a demand for reparation, and when the
ruler scoffingly inquired, "Who is the king who makes this
request?" he promptly received the minatory reply, "The
son of that king of Aragon who won the battle of Las
Navas."[4] When the subject of an attack on the Balearics
was broached at a meeting of the Catalan Cortes in December, 1228, the three estates responded with enthusiasm;
and though the Aragonese held back, and urged the superior
advisability of an expedition against Valencia, King James
pushed forward his preparations vigorously in the early

[1] Cf. ante, pp. 25–27 and p. 293.
[2] Swift, James the First of Aragon, p. 36.
[3] Lecoy, i, p. 13, and Mas Latrie, p. 100, put the Almohade conquest in 1187; but cf. also Mercier, ii, p. 128.
[4] Crónica de Fray Pedro Marsili, ed. Quadrado, p. 257; Lecoy, i, p. 23; Swift, op. cit., p. 35. Desclot (Cronica del Rey En Pere, cap. xiv) asserts that James declared in full Cortes, "Let me no longer bear the name of king if I go not and take him [the king of Majorca] by the beard."

months of 1229.[1] Realizing the importance of clothing the
enterprise of which he was to reap the benefit in the panoply
of a crusade, the king received the Cross with his followers
at the hands of the papal legate; and on September 5,
1229, they set sail from the harbor of Salou with 155 ships,
including those contributed by Genoa, Provence, Marseilles,
and Narbonne, carrying probably some 15,000 foot and
1500 horse.[2]

The expedition arrived in the nick of time, for the Moorish
king, Abu Yahya, had not yet received the reënforcements
which he had solicited from North Africa, and he was also
threatened by rebellion at home. Nevertheless, the Balearic
sovereign was able to prevent the Christians from landing
at Palomera near the western extremity of Majorca, where
they first cast anchor. A hot race for the harbor of Santa
Ponza then ensued; but King James, with a detachment
of his swiftest ships, outstripped the Moors on shore who
attempted to head him off, so that he was able to land his
men in spite of some resistance from the advance guard of
the Saracens. The young king slew four or five of his
enemies with his own hand, and was gently rebuked by his
followers for his rashness. On Wednesday, September 12,
a pitched battle was fought, in which the Moors were
finally forced to abandon a strong position on an eminence
above Santa Ponza. The victory, however, was dearly
bought by the death of James's trusted friends and counsellors, Ramon and Guillen Moncada, whose loss drew from
the Conqueror a flood of tears. Meantime the other ships
had brought up the rest of the troops, and the reunited
Christian forces advanced to the attack of the city of
Palma.[3] For three and a half months the siege continued.

[1] L. Dollfus, *Études sur le moyen âge
espagnol*, pp. 168 ff.
[2] Swift, *op. cit.*, pp. 38 f.

[3] Usually known, at that period, as
the city of Majorca.

.

All the regular mediaeval engines for attack and defence
were employed — mines and countermines, windlasses and
catapults, mantlets and trebuchets. At one time a Moorish
detachment on the hillside above the Christian camp cut
off the stream that supplied it; but the hostile party was
eventually dislodged and captured, and the head of its
leader was slung over the walls of the town. On a later
occasion fortune unexpectedly came to the rescue of the
Christians, when a disloyal Moorish chieftain brought
them an "angel's present" of supplies.[1] Twice did the
besieged attempt to buy off the besiegers, but in vain; a
savage lust for slaughter animated the army of the Conqueror, who finally, on December 31, marshalled all his
forces for a grand assault. After a violent struggle the
Moors gave way. Their king was found hiding in a house
and was made prisoner. A ruthless butchery of the inhabitants ensued; though it would be foolish to accept
literally the figures of the contemporary chroniclers, there
can be no doubt that the horrors of the surrender were unusual even for that barbaric age.[2] Indiscriminate looting
followed; and afterwards there was an auction of the
prisoners and booty taken, at which every one bought but
refused to pay for his purchases. Discontent and quarrelling were the natural result, until James interfered: "I will
first hang so many of you in the streets," he threatened the
rioters, "that the town will stink of them."[3] A systematic
pursuit of the Moors in the mountain country now began.
The enemy took refuge in huts and caves hewn out of the
face of a high cliff; from these they were finally expelled
by a Christian soldier who was lowered on a rope over the
face of the rock, with fire brands which he hurled among

---

[1] *Chronicle of James I*, i, p. 148.   [2] Cf. Swift, p. 48; Lecoy, i, p. 66.
[3] *Chronicle*, i, p. 179.

the foe; "and I was very glad," as the Conqueror naïvely records, "to see the fire as I was eating."[1]

The Moors now began to surrender in large numbers. The conquered land was divided into allotments between the king and his nobles;[2] and after the arrival of reënforcements sufficient to remove all chance of any hostile outbreak, the Conqueror returned to Spain in the end of October, 1230, after an absence of nearly fourteen months. A rumor that the Hafside king of Tunis was preparing a fleet for the recovery of Majorca caused him to revisit the island in 1231. The alarm proved false, but James persisted with his expedition, and gained the submission of a number of the mountain Moors. In the following year the Conqueror returned to the island for the third time to receive the surrender of the last bands of his enemies; by the use of an ingenious stratagem he also secured the recognition of his overlordship by the king of Minorca on this occasion. More than three hundred bonfires were lighted at Cape Pera on the Majorcan shore, and the Minorcan ruler was thus led to believe that a mighty host was preparing to attack him, whereas in reality, as James assures us, "I had with me only six knights, four horses, one shield, five esquires to attend on my person, ten servants and some scouts."[3] In 1235 the Sacristan of Gerona, who was primate elect, aided by the Infante of Portugal[4] and other knights, took possession of Iviza and Formentera (the latter of which was uninhabited), and the reconquest of the islands was therewith complete.[5]

---

[1] *Chronicle*, ii, p. 192.

[2] "Repartimientos de Mallorca" in D. I. A., xi, pp. 1–141; Swift, pp. 48–54. The method here described bears some analogy to that employed in the conquest and colonisation of the Indies; cf. *infra*, Vol. II, p. 232, note 3.

[3] *Chronicle*, i, p. 214.

[4] On this man see Swift, pp. 38, 52, 61, 78, 81, and elsewhere.

[5] The *Historia General del Reino de Mallorca* by J. Dameto, V. Mut, and G. Alemany, i, pp. 250–452, may also be consulted on this and the two preceding paragraphs.

Most of the Moors who had offered to surrender in Majorca were made slaves, and distributed among the various estates into which the island had been divided. Colonists from the seaboard cities of Catalonia and also from Marseilles were imported in great numbers, and freedom from customs duties was granted alike to all classes of the inhabitants, so that the population of Palma became "the most honorable and cultured in the world", and "its liberties and franchises superior to those of any other city."[1]   In Minorca, on the other hand, where there had been no conquest but merely a recognition of over-lordship, the Moorish inhabitants were left practically un-disturbed in the enjoyment of autonomy and independence, save for the payment of an annual tribute to the king as feudal suzerain, and the cession of the town of Ciudadela and all the forts of the island.   The results of this liberal treat-ment were, however, apparently unfortunate; for Minorca revolted against the Aragonese domination in the succeeding reign, and had to be reconquered afresh by Alfonso III.[2]

Though virtually completed so early in his career, the capture of the Balearics was the last great venture over-seas which was undertaken by James the Conqueror.   Dur-ing the remaining forty years of his life, his attention was constantly distracted from the work of maritime expansion, which was nearest his heart, by the pressure of other and less welcome cares.   Still, it is as a conqueror and a cru-sader that the great king deserves chiefly to be remem-bered, for to the day of his death his mind was filled with schemes for different expeditions beyond the boundaries of his realm.[3]   A project for the recovery of the Holy

[1] Muntaner, *Chronique* (ed. Buchon), cap. viii (i, p. 25); Lecoy, i, pp. 69 ff.

[2] Lecoy, i, pp. 73–76; Parpal y Marqués, *Conquista de Menorca por Alfonso III*, pp. 11 ff.

[3] P. Tomic, *Historias e Conquestas*, cap. xxxix.

Sepulchre was entertained in 1260, and the king actually
set sail, only to be driven back by a storm. Again, in 1268–
69, invitations from the Khan of Tartary and from the
Emperor Michael Palaeologus urged him for a last time to
the East: again he embarked, and again a gale forced him
back into the port of Aigues Mortes, so that he finally
returned to Aragon. "It seems to me," so he said to his
knights, "that it is not our Lord's will that we should go
beyond sea, as once before when we had prepared." [1]
Events which paved the way for the Aragonese acquisition
of Sicily and southern Italy in the succeeding reigns took
place during his lifetime, but the Conqueror did not live
to see the results of them. In 1276 he died at Valencia,
worn out by his ceaseless activities, in the sixty-ninth year
of his life and the sixty-fourth of his reign — a great hero
of the Reconquest, and one of the principal founders of the
Spanish Empire.[2] But so deeply was this mighty monarch
imbued with the separatistic traditions of his native land,
that he endangered the fabric that he had reared with so
much difficulty by dividing his realms at his death. By
his first wife Eleanor, daughter of Alfonso VIII of Castile,
he had a son, Alfonso; by his second, Violante of Hungary,
four sons and six daughters; he also had several bastards
by various mistresses. Beginning in the year 1229, he had
made a number of different wills disposing of his inheritance,
dividing it and subdividing it as the number of his children
increased. By his testament of 1250, his dominions were
actually parcelled out among all five of his legitimate male
heirs.[3] Of these five, however, Ferdinand, a younger son
of Violante, died in 1251, and Alfonso, the son of Eleanor,

[1] *Chronicle*, ii, pp. 603 f. R. Röh-
richt, "Der Kreuzzug des Königs Jacob
I von Aragonien (1269)", in *Mittheilungen des Instituts für oesterreichische*
Geschichtsforschung, xi, pp. 372–395.
[2] Swift, pp. 140–147.
[3] Swift, p. 88; Zurita, i, ff. 160 f.

in 1260; while another, Sancho, who had entered the
church, became archbishop of Toledo in 1268. With the
number of his male heirs reduced to two, James, in 1270,
made his last will and testament, by which Pedro, the
eldest son of Violante, was declared his successor in Aragon,
Catalonia, and Valencia; while James, his younger brother,
was assigned the Balearics and the lands north of the
Pyrenees which had remained to the Conqueror after the
treaty of Corbeil.[1] The unhappy result of this unwise
division of the Aragonese inheritance was corrected in the
succeeding century, when the Majorcan realm was rein-
corporated with the rest of the kingdom; but the bad example was followed by James's successors in the disposition
of the later Italian conquests, to the grave prejudice of
the unity of the Aragonese empire.

The importance of the long reign of James the Conqueror,
both in the internal and the foreign history of his native land,
is equalled if not exceeded by that of the brief rule of
his elder son and successor, Pedro, who amply deserves the
appellation of 'the Great.' At home, the constitutional
struggle which accompanied and profoundly influenced the
course of external affairs reached its climax; while abroad,
the mounting energies of Pedro's subjects were given a new
direction by the acquisition of Sicily. To the origin and
early phases of this great drama of foreign conquest we
now turn. It irrevocably committed the realms of the
Crown of Aragon to the career of territorial expansion
in the Mediterranean on which they had been already
launched. It ultimately paved the way for that long
struggle between the royal houses of France and Spain,
around which the whole development of the Spanish Empire

[1] Swift, pp. 89, 102, 117, 121; Lecoy, i, pp. 101–110, 119–121.

revolved from the time of Ferdinand and Isabella to that
of Philip II.

The source of the Aragonese claims to Sicily and southern
Italy lies in Pedro's marriage on June 13, 1262, to Constance, daughter of the Hohenstaufen Manfred, and granddaughter of the Emperor Frederick II.[1] On the Hohenstaufen
side the match was arranged primarily as a means of support against the hostility of the Holy See, possibly also
against the imperial ambitions of Alfonso the Learned of
Castile. For Aragon, it offered far reaching visions of
external conquest, the more welcome because of the recent
defeat at Corbeil of James the Conqueror's plans of expansion in southern France. Against the allies was arrayed
the might of the papacy and Charles of Anjou, who came
and slew Manfred at Benevento in 1266, and received the
kingdom of Sicily[2] as a fief of the Holy See. Two years
later, Manfred's nephew Conradin, last scion of the Hohenstaufen dynasty, was defeated by the terrible Angevin at
Tagliacozzo, and soon after suffered a traitor's death, with
heroic fortitude, on a scaffold overlooking the bay of Naples.
Tradition tells us that, before he bowed his head to the ex-
ecutioner's axe, the youthful victim took off his glove and
tossed it down to the crowd below, where it was picked up
and carried overseas by an Aragonese knight and delivered
to Conradin's cousin, the Lady Constance.[3] It was a royal
gage that cried for vengeance, but James's hands were tied
by the recent treaties with Louis of France, and by his
fears of the hostility of Castile and of internal rebellion.
Not until the Conqueror had been six years in his grave
was Conradin's death avenged.

Meantime the kingdom of Sicily groaned under the cruel

[1] Cartellieri, *Peter von Aragon und die sicilianische Vesper*, p. 6.
[2] That is, Naples and the island of Sicily.
[3] M. Amari, *The War of the Sicilian Vespers*, tr. Ellesmere, i, pp. 69 f.

and oppressive rule of its new sovereign.[1]   The rights and
privileges of the inhabitants were consistently ignored.
Frenchmen were preferred for almost every office.   Complaints were answered by barbarous executions.   Charles
cared little or nothing for the wishes of the people over
whom he ruled.   His entire attention was centred on
conquests in the eastern Mediterranean, and he regarded
his Sicilian realm chiefly as a means to provide funds for
that end.   Only from Aragon could the oppressed inhabitants have any hope of redress.   While James the Conqueror
was still alive, John of Procida, the friend and counsellor
of the last of the Hohenstaufens, arrived at the Aragonese
court, and begged for aid; together with Roger de Lauria,
foster brother of the Princess Constance, he besought the
heir to the throne to devote himself to the recovery of his
wife's inheritance.[2]   The result of these efforts was plainly
evident when Pedro succeeded his father in July, 1276.
The young sovereign burned to distinguish himself in the
field of foreign conquest.   For a long time he had been
obliged to restrain his martial ardor in deference to the
cautious policy of the Conqueror's later years; now, at
last, his chance had come.   But first it was essential to
make sure of the attitude of Castile and of France.   In the
former kingdom the struggle between Alfonso the Learned
and Sancho the Bravo was reaching its height, and in January, 1278, Pedro took the decisive step of seizing and im-
prisoning the Infantes de la Cerda, thus putting himself
in possession of hostages for the friendship of both factions
in the western realm and also for that of Philip of France.[3]
Protracted negotiations with all three parties followed:

[1] See Amari, *op. cit.*, i, caps. iv–viii,
and iii, pp. 300–347, for a good account
of the older authorities; Cartellieri, *op.
cit.*, cap. v.

[2] Cartellieri, *op. cit.*, pp. 23 f.
[3] Cartellieri, pp. 43 ff., 204–206; and
ante, p. 113.

the Aragonese king utilizing his advantage to the utmost, alternately betraying Alfonso and Sancho into advantageous territorial concessions, and hoodwinking Philip III. Treaties were made with the king of Portugal and with Edward I of England, whose daughter Eleanor was subsequently betrothed to Pedro's son and heir, Alfonso. An alliance was also concluded, through the instrumentality of John of Procida, with the Eastern Emperor Michael Palaeologus, who was threatened by the projects of Charles of Anjou.[1] Meantime Pedro used all possible efforts to provide himself with an adequate fleet, men, and armaments. He was resolved no longer to be dependent on aid from Genoa and Pisa, as his predecessors had been whenever they undertook a naval campaign in the Mediterranean. At all the ports in his realm there was feverish activity and excitement. At Collioure the blacksmiths forged nothing but anchors; ships were constructed in all the coast towns as far south as Valencia. Even the inland cities occupied themselves with the manufacture of arms and munitions of war; provisions were plentifully supplied by the country districts; all parts of the king's dominions seemed anxious to do their share.[2]

Pedro's subjects, however, were not enlightened as to the true object of all these preparations; for the king had spread it abroad that he intended to use them for a campaign against the Moors. It is not difficult to discern the policy that lay behind this announcement. War against the infidel was sanctioned by the most ancient of national traditions. Enthusiasm for fighting on purely religious grounds was doubtless practically dead, but interest in possibilities of territorial and commercial conquest at the

<hr>

[1] Cartellieri, pp. 63-66, 77 f., 87-89, 189 f.

[2] Muntaner, *Chronique*, ed. Buchon, i, pp. 125, 128 f.; Cartellieri, p. 94.

expense of the Moslem ran higher than ever, and would unquestionably evoke far more unanimous support from Pedro's subjects than an expedition against a protégé of the church. Moreover, the particularistic Aragonese, cut off from the sea and intensely jealous of the Catalans, might very likely have opposed a plan for the conquest of Sicily, which, if successful at all, would inevitably redound chiefly to the advantage of their maritime neighbors; of a crusade, however, even though they might not be precisely informed of its destination, they would find it almost impossible to complain. Most important of all would be the effect of King Pedro's announcement upon Pope Martin IV, a Frenchman through and through, and the servile instrument of his terrible Sicilian vassal. However great his hostility to the king of Aragon, the head of the church could scarcely refuse to approve of his plan for attacking the infidel. He doubtless guessed what Pedro's real objective was, and it is significant that he forbade him to appropriate the tithes of the province of Tarragona for the purposes of the holy war. Nevertheless, the king of Aragon had publicly proclaimed his zeal for the welfare of the Church of Christ in a way that could not easily be forgotten, and would stand him in good stead when the moment for his attack on the kingdom of Sicily should finally arrive.[1]

It will readily be conceived that Pedro of Aragon was not the man to announce his intention of going on a crusade without being able to carry out the pretence in deeds as well. Fortunately for his purposes, the situation in one of the Moorish kingdoms of North Africa was such as afforded him an admirable opportunity to do this, and at the same time to realize his original plan for the conquest of Sicily.[2] From at least as early as the year 1180, the

[1] Cartellieri, pp. 79–87.   [2] Cartellieri, p. 82.

Moslem rulers of Tunis had maintained good relations with the Norman and Hohenstaufen sovereigns of the court of Palermo, and had paid them, with some measure of regularity, a small annual tribute, as a guarantee of immunity from attacks by Sicilian pirates and of access to Sicilian ports for the purpose of buying grain.[1] But when Charles of Anjou was invested with the Sicilian crown in 1266, the Hafside sultan across the sea refused to recognize him as the rightful heir of his Hohenstaufen predecessors. The tribute ceased, and hostilities threatened to break forth. Tunis became a place of refuge for the Angevin's enemies, and it was largely Charles's cries for revenge that led his brother, Louis IX, to divert the crusade which he was preparing for the Holy Land into an expedition against the North African port.[2] But the followers of the French king found the Saracen ruler admirably prepared for resistance and ably supported by the Christian enemies of Charles of Anjou; a pestilence decimated their ranks and finally carried off their royal leader. They therefore determined to treat for peace, and secured it on terms notable for the advantages which they granted to the king of Sicily, whose enemies were ordered out of Tunis, while the arrears of the tribute, which had not been paid since 1265, were fully made up, and the amount of it doubled for the future.[3] The whole course of events, however, had been carefully noted by Pedro of Aragon and its lesson taken to heart. Long before the death of his father, he had cherished plans for the conquest of Sicily; and in Tunis he saw numerous possibilities for a vantage ground from which to launch an attack whenever the time should be ripe.[4] His father had carefully cultivated friendly re-

[1] Mas Latrie, pp. 95–97, 223.   [3] Mas Latrie, pp. 248–252.
[2] Mas Latrie, pp. 244, 247 f.   [4] Cartellieri, p. 80, note.

THE FIRST CONQUESTS OVERSEAS

lations with the Hafside sultans;[1] from the time of his
accession he himself had interfered, whenever possible,
in Tunisian affairs; in fact he received a considerable
annual pension from the Tunisian ruler as a reward for his
surveillance of the latter's rebel brother, who had taken
refuge at his court. After the death of El Mostancer
(1277), Pedro reversed his policy, and supported the brother
against the legitimate heir, who had refused to continue
the pension which had been paid by his father; and later
still (1281), when the brother made a similar error, the king
of Aragon took sides against him with Abu Bekr, the governor of Constantine, who desired to win independence of
Tunisian control. Various advantageous concessions were
gained by Pedro in return for this alliance. He was thus
enabled to get his fleet and his army into convenient proximity to his real objective, Sicily; and, at the same time,
to appear to redeem his pledge to undertake a crusade. In
fact it may well have been the situation in Tunis that suggested the announcement which so well suited his plans
in other ways.[2]

A diligent German scholar has conclusively shown that
the old idea that Pedro of Aragon bore a part in the con-
spiracy leading up to the famous massacre of the Sicilian
Vespers, which began in Palermo on March 30, 1282, is no
longer tenable. News of the massacre reached him in
Valencia probably about April 20, and was almost certainly unwelcome, because the rebels at the outset put
themselves under the protection of the Holy See, thus
threatening to render doubly difficult a conquest by the
king of Aragon.[3] Pedro had, however, by this time gone

[1] *Memorial Histórico Español*, i, pp. 158 f.; Swift, p. 227.
[2] Mas Latrie, pp. 259 f.; Cartellieri, pp. 80 ff.; Mercier, ii, pp. 217–219;
L. C. Féraud, "Expédition du Roi Pierre III à Collo," in *Revue Africaine*, xvi (1872), pp. 241–258.
[3] Cartellieri, pp. 98, note, 185.

too far to draw back; and he fully realized the advantages of a foothold in Tunis for the purpose of negotiating with the insurgents. In early June of 1282, therefore, he set sail with a considerable force, which was apparently in ignorance of its destination, and landed on the twenty-eighth of the month at Collo on the North African coast. On his arrival he found that his protégé, Abu Bekr, the governor of Constantine, had already been defeated.[1] A few encounters with the Saracens sufficed to save his reputation as a crusader and to keep his army in fighting trim;[2] but his attention was chiefly directed towards Sicily and her affairs. Negotiations with the rebels there began at once; the conditions under which the Aragonese monarch should govern the realm were discussed at length; in early August, at Palermo, the Sicilians definitely decided to summon Pedro to be their king.[3] Four knights and four burgesses were sent across to the Aragonese ruler, to tell of the woes they had suffered under Angevin rule and to beg him to hasten to their rescue. The envoys, clad in deep mourning, were conveyed in ships with black banners and black sails.[4] After hearing their story, Pedro hesitated no longer. He utilized the Pope's refusal of help for his crusade to persuade some of the more reluctant of his followers that he was justified in accepting the proffered throne. In late August he left the North African coast. On the thirty-first he arrived at Trapani. On September 4 he was welcomed at Palermo by the enthusiastic plaudits of the rejoicing populace, assumed the crown of Sicily in the cathedral

[1] Cartellieri, pp. 192 (and note), 193.
[2] Cartellieri, p. 194; Muntaner, Chronique, i, pp. 138-154. Contemporaries lay great stress on the fierceness of the fighting and on the number of the slaughtered Moors; but there can be little doubt that they exaggerate.

Pedro had little crusading ardor, and wanted to stand well with the North African powers for commercial reasons.
[3] Cartellieri, pp. 195-197.
[4] Muntaner, i, p. 147; Cartellieri, p. 198.

there, and sent a formal defiance to Charles of Anjou, who was already besieging Messina.[1] An insolent reply caused Pedro to make ready for battle, and the Sicilians, seeing his preparations, asked what he intended to do. "I go," said the Aragonese monarch, "to attack King Charles." "In the name of God," replied the Sicilians, "take us with you and do not leave us behind."[2]

A detachment of 2000 light-armed troops was sent on in advance to prevent the fall of Messina before the king's arrival. They slipped through the besieging forces of Charles of Anjou by night, and subsequently made a sortie which wrought havoc among their foes, so that the Messinians, who had been at first unfavorably impressed by their beggarly equipment, took courage and prepared to resist to the last.[3] The time of their deliverance, however, was now at hand. The king of Aragon came on from Palermo with all his available troops. Every male Sicilian between the ages of fifteen and sixty had been summoned to join him; while the Aragonese fleet advanced along the coast, ably led by the gallant Roger de Lauria, "the most illustrious of those great seamen whom Pedro had attracted to his service by permitting them to enjoy at once the authority of an admiral, and the liberty of a corsair."[4] Their united forces were plainly irresistible, and Charles of Anjou did not await their onslaught, but transferred himself with as many of his followers as possible to Reggio on the mainland. Those that were left behind, together with an enormous quantity of provisions and booty, fell into the hands of Pedro's army; and "so great," says Muntaner, "was the loot, that Messina became rich for evermore, and florins were as plentiful as coppers."[5] The

[1] Cartellieri, pp. 200 f.
[2] Muntaner, i, p. 161.
[3] Muntaner, i, pp. 162, 164.
[4] R. St.-H., iv, p. 272.
[5] Muntaner, i, p. 166.

Aragonese fleet was meantime sent in chase of the Angevin ships in the strait; they were but twenty-two against one hundred and fifty, if the figures of the contemporary chroniclers are to be believed, but they won a glorious victory and captured forty-five of the foe. Apparently the Messinians could not believe their eyes when they saw the returning vessels, and thought, at first, that Charles was coming back with reënforcements to take a terrible revenge. But for the moment at least the Angevin was reduced to impotence. From the shores of Calabria he had witnessed his rival's triumph without being able to lift a finger to prevent it; in fact some of Pedro's forces even succeeded in crossing the strait and sacking Nicotera, almost under his very eyes.[1] Charles, however, was by no means at the end of his expedients. Defeated in open war, he determined to try his fortune in other fields, and as a preliminary sent a challenge to his rival to meet him, each with a hundred knights, in a battle à outrance, in closed lists at Bordeaux on English ground, June 1, 1283 — the issue of the combat to determine the fate of Sicily. Pedro, though by no means blind to the advantageous position he had already won, was chivalrous enough to accept; and the two rivals, leaving their sons to represent them in Sicily and Italy during their absence, departed for their respective countries to prepare for the coming encounter.[2]

It is more than doubtful whether either of them had ever taken it seriously, or thought that there was any likelihood of its actually occurring. For Charles of Anjou it was probably but a pretext to enable him to gain papal aid, and possibly to obtain possession of the person of his rival; and it was not long before Pedro was informed of the Angevin's

---

[1] Muntaner, i, pp. 167-177, who calls the place 'Nicotena' by mistake.

[2] Amari (tr. Ellesmere), ii, pp. 15 ff.; Muntaner, i, pp. 187-195.

plots. On his way back to France, Charles passed through Rome and obtained the support of Pope Martin IV, whom he persuaded to forbid the combat at Bordeaux, to declare that Pedro had forfeited his dominions as penalty for his interference in Sicily, to preach a crusade against him as the enemy of the church, and to place his realms under an interdict. It was, in a sense, the age-long struggle between the empire and the papacy that threatened to break forth afresh. The mantle of the Hohenstaufen had fallen on the shoulders of the king of Aragon, whose offence was doubtless aggravated by the memory of the way in which his grandfather — another Pedro — had championed the cause of heresy against the church. Clearly, Rome could not rest quiet till the dynasty was brought to its knees. Charles of Anjou was to be used as the chief instrument for the attainment of that end, and could rely at the outset on the support of Philip of France, who longed to carry further the work that his father had begun at the treaty of Corbeil, and make new conquests to the south of the Pyrenees. Altogether, the king of Aragon was confronted by a most formidable array of foes; but he never faltered. Returned to Spain, he set about the selection of the hundred knights who were to accompany him to Bordeaux; but on learning, in the midst of his preparations, that the king of England would not undertake to guarantee him a fair combat in closed lists, and that if he appeared with his followers he ran grave danger of capture and death, he changed his plans. Disguised as the servant of a horse dealer, he crossed the mountains, and three days later arrived at Bordeaux. He made known his identity to the English seneschal, formally demanded that the combat which had been arranged should take place, circled the lists on horseback, with his lance in rest, and finally, after re-

pairing to a church, solemnly and publicly to thank God
for His support and protection, regained his own dominions
in safety, having loyally fulfilled his plighted word as a
gentleman and a king.[1]

When this romantic but inconclusive farce had been
terminated, the forces of the rival monarchs began to
struggle with one another again.   Roger de Lauria defeated
the French fleet off Malta, which he finally captured in
June, 1284,[2] and subsequently won another victory in the
Bay of Naples.   On this occasion the young Prince of
Salerno, son of Charles of Anjou, was taken prisoner and
condemned to death, as retribution for the execution of
the youthful Conradin in 1268 ; but the Infante of Aragon
relented at the last moment and preserved his life.[3]   On
the sea there could be no question which of the two rivals
was superior.   The Aragonese fleet was already triumphantly asserting its control of the entire western Mediterranean — a long step towards the upbuilding of the
Aragonese empire.   Charles of Anjou led an army into
southern Italy, in the hope of retrieving his fortunes by
land, but death overtook him before he could accomplish
his purpose (January 7, 1285).   Meantime, however, in
France and Spain there was another tale to tell.   The
papal sentence hung like a dark cloud over the Aragonese
realms.   The king of France had collected a formidable
army to give effect to it.   Worst of all, a terrible rebellion
against King Pedro had broken out in the kingdom of
Aragon.   We shall have occasion to follow the course of

[1] Muntaner, i, pp. 196 ff. ; Desclot,
Cronica del Rey En Pere (ed. Buchon),
pp. 642 f., 648–654 ; Zurita, i, ff. 251,
254, 257–259.

[2] Muntaner, i, p. 231.   Malta thereafter followed the fortunes of Sicily,
under the subsidiary and direct lines of
the kings of Aragon, until it was finally
granted to the Knights of St. John of
Jerusalem by Charles V in 1530.   Cf.
Miège, Histoire de Malte, ii, pp. 97–125.

[3] Amari (tr. Ellesmere), ii, pp. 90
ff. ; R. St.-H., iv, p. 280.

this great revolt in another place; for the present we need only observe that one of its chief causes was the resentment of the Aragonese at Pedro's absorption in enterprises overseas, for which they had no interest or enthusiasm, and that its principal result was temporarily to paralyze the efficiency of the resistance to the French invasion. And to cap the climax of the king's misfortunes, his younger brother, James of Majorca, who had been left by his father in possession of Cerdagne, Roussillon, Montpellier, and the Balearics, turned traitor and joined forces with Philip of France. On January 20, 1279, Pedro had forced him formally to acknowledge himself his feudal vassal; and James, who had never forgiven his brother for refusing to recognize his independence, seized this opportunity to take his revenge.[1]

But Pedro was one of those from whom the most desperate crises evoke the most splendid efforts. A dash at Perpignan failed to capture the wretched James, who fled away under cover of night; but when the invading French army reached the mountains, they were exposed to all the hazards of a guerilla warfare with which they knew not how to cope. Night attacks decimated their forces. Stones were hurled down on them from the cliffs above. Singly or in small companies they were lured away into devious paths and cut off. Finally, after having crossed the range, they made the grievous error of waiting to lay siege to the comparatively unimportant fortress of Gerona, instead of pushing straight on and striking at the Catalonian capital. Meantime the courage of Pedro and his adherents was roused by the news of a fresh naval victory near Rosas, won by the few ships which he had kept in Catalonian waters over the much larger fleet that had been sent to coöperate with the army

[1] R. St.-H., iv, pp. 281-293; Lecoy, i, pp. 151-206.

of the king of France. Even the rebel Aragonese, who had hitherto stood aloof from the contest, came forward, in July, 1285, with offers of aid, when they saw the heroic fight which their king was making against tremendous odds. Finally, after a magnificent resistance of two months and a half, Gerona fell; but the long delay before its walls had given Pedro time to organize the defence of the country to the south of it, so that the French could advance no farther; and in the meantime the arrival of Roger de Lauria from Sicilian waters served to complete the destruction of the French fleet, and necessitated the retreat of the invading army which it supplied. The retirement of the French forces was to the last degree disorderly. Pedro's troops hung mercilessly on their rear, and pillaged their baggage train; not until they had reached the shelter of Perpignan and the protection of the forces of the king of Majorca could they feel that they had escaped from the 'gates of hell.' For King Philip the issue of the conflict brought complete though tragic disillusionment. During the long and weary retreat, the conviction forced itself upon him that he had been throughout merely a tool in the hands of Rome. More and more harshly did he reproach the papal envoy who accompanied him for all the disasters that he had suffered; more and more bitterly did he bewail the loss of the "noblest army that had ever followed the Oriflamme." Under the circumstances his death at Perpignan, on the fifth of October, 1285, doubtless came to him as a deliverance: he had no ambition to outlive his defeat.[1]

The same year, 1285, saw, in fact, a clean sweep of all the protagonists in the great drama which had arisen out

[1] The best modern account of this campaign is to be found in Lecoy, i, pp. 207-279. Interesting details are given in Muntaner, i, pp. 357-427, and in Zurita, i, ff. 281-297.

of the Aragonese conquest of Sicily. Besides Charles of
Anjou and Philip of France, Pope Martin IV had died on
March 29, and on November 11 Pedro of Aragon, the best
and greatest of them all, followed his rivals to the grave.[1]
The moment that the French army had been driven from
his realms, he had planned to punish his traitor brother,
the king of Majorca, who had given Philip free passage
through Cerdagne and Roussillon, and had otherwise
aided and abetted him. He had determined to strike his
first blow in the Balearics: he had already gathered together a fleet and an army for the purpose, when he was
seized with a chill and fever, to which he soon succumbed.
His son Alfonso, who was to have accompanied him, hastened to his bedside, only to be sent off to carry through
the Balearic campaign alone. "Who told thee to come
hither, Infante?" queried his dying father; "Art thou a
doctor that canst cure me? Thy presence here can do no
good. Depart at once for Majorca; for God wills that I
should die, and neither thou nor any one else can prevent
it." Reverently and obediently the Infante kissed his
parent on the hands and feet, and Pedro kissed him on the
mouth and gave him his blessing; "and the Infante went
forth with the grace of God."[2] Anxious to see his realms
reconciled with the Holy See, the king, in his last moments,
persuaded the archbishop of Tarragona to raise the interdict which Pope Martin had placed upon his dominions,
in return for an admission by Pedro of his fault, and for his
promise to do all in his powel to have Sicily restored to
Rome. This was obviously, however, merely a case of
deathbed repentance, whose sincerity was more than
doubtful; moreover it was in flat contradiction to the will
which Pedro had previously made, and which was accepted

[1] Muntaner, i, p. 440.   [2] Muntaner, i, pp. 434 f.; Lecoy, i, pp. 284 f.

as valid by his successors.[1] By that will the king bequeathed to his eldest son, Alfonso, Aragon, Catalonia, and Valencia, with the suzerainty of the Balearics and the French lands pertaining to them; and to his second, James, the kingdom of Sicily and all his conquests in Naples. Two younger sons were left, for the time being, without inheritance; but the death of Alfonso without male heirs, and the subsequent succession of James to the Spanish realms, was ultimately to bring the elder of them, Frederic, to the Sicilian throne.[2] The fatal tendency to division had not, in this case, been permitted to go to its customary extremes, though the cutting off of the newly won realm of Sicily, under a separate king, indicated that it was by no means extinct. The history of Sicily during the succeeding century, however, makes it very doubtful whether any other arrangement would have been practicable under the existing circumstances.

Pedro was one of the greatest of mediaeval kings. Many of his predecessors, both in Aragon and Castile, had been either heroes or saints; but Pedro was almost, if not quite, the first in whom the virtues of valor and discretion were so mingled as to entitle him to be regarded as a statesman. Dante's verdict upon him goes, as usual, straight to the heart of the whole matter:

" D'ogni valor portò cinta la corda."[3]

When we come to the examination of the internal history of his reign, we shall perhaps conclude that he died at the most fortunate moment for his reputation. Be that as it may, there can be no question of the importance of what

[1] This final scene in Pedro's life is described in detail in Desclot, *Cronica del Rey En Pere*, pp. 733 f.; Muntaner makes no mention at all of the matter. Cf. also L. Klüpfel, *Die äussere Politik*

Alfonso's III., pp. 19 f.
[2] Muntaner, i, pp. 436–438; R. St.-H., iv, p. 306.
[3] *Purgatorio*, vii, 114.

he accomplished in the brief nine years of rule that were allotted to him. Pedro was the first mediaeval Spanish sovereign to make his influence deeply felt in the settlement of problems of Pan-European importance. Hitherto the Iberian realms, chiefly occupied by the Reconquest, had been largely ignored in the regulation of international affairs; but henceforth Aragon at least would have to be reckoned with as an important power. The conquest of Sicily had opened for her a splendid imperial vision, whose realization was to be the glory of the succeeding age. Lastly, it is important to remember that this first important entrance of the East Spanish kingdoms into the international arena brought them at once into the sharpest conflict with Rome. Like his grandfather and namesake before him, Pedro did not shrink from battle with the Holy See when the interests of his people demanded it. Together with the crown of Sicily, he gladly assumed the arduous task of carrying on the great struggle against papal supremacy from the point where his Hohenstaufen predecessors had laid it down; in the long list of champions of the temporal power against the spiritual he deserves an honorable place. His reign forms the indispensable link between those of the Emperor Frederick II and of King Philip the Fair. It was a step on the road to Anagni. That a French monarch ultimately reaped the rewards of his efforts in this direction, and perhaps abused his triumph, is one of the ironies of history, but it must not be suffered to dim the glory of King Pedro. Whatever the Spanish Empire of the sixteenth and seventeenth centuries became, its Aragonese progenitor was certainly not conceived in subservience to Rome.

The history of the Aragonese realms, both internal and foreign, continues to unfold itself in dramatic fashion during the brief six-year reign of Pedro's son and successor, Alfonso III. The new king was by no means the equal of his father. All the contemporary accounts unite in praising his personal bravery and energy in war, but he lacked the statesman's power of determining in advance the main aims and methods of his policy, and of resolutely adhering to them. He never seemed quite to know his own mind, and was consequently too much swayed by the advice of others.[1] At home his rule witnessed a further humiliation of the monarchy by the rebel baronage; while abroad, though the story of territorial expansion and political development becomes steadily more intricate and confused, the power of Aragon makes little permanent progress.

The principal achievement that stands to Alfonso's credit is the completion, in 1287, of the conquest of Minorca, which had never been captured from the Saracens except in name. Its subjugation was the logical sequel to the expedition against Majorca, on which he had gone forth, obedient to the wishes of his dying father, in the autumn of 1285. Contemporaries would have us believe that he experienced little difficulty in winning away the larger island from his treacherous uncle, James: the latter had never been popular in the Balearics, and was frequently absent in Montpellier and Roussillon. It seems, however, that considerable resistance was encountered and overcome before Alfonso, who was powerfully seconded by the fleet of Roger de Lauria, could enter Palma on December 19, and receive the oath of allegiance from its citizens.[2] Had he not been recalled to Aragon by the news of his father's death, he would probably have attacked Minorca then and there. Certainly he had ample justification for so doing,

---

[1] L. Klüpfel, *Die äussere Politik Alfonso's III.*, p. 9, note.

[2] Lecoy, i, pp. 286 f.; L. Klüpfel, *op. cit.*, p. 17.

because the *arraez* or local Moorish ruler, who had been permitted to remain there, virtually supreme under the suzerainty of Aragon, had lent treacherous aid to the North African enemies of Pedro III at the time of his expedition to Tunis, and still remained unpunished.[1] But for the time being Alfonso was obliged to content himself with a smaller expedition to make sure of the loyalty of Iviza; the more arduous Minorcan campaign was postponed for a more favorable opportunity. This came at last in the autumn of 1286, on the conclusion of a temporary truce with France which afforded a brief respite from the never ending cares and worries of the Sicilian problem; and Alfonso made the most of it. He sought and obtained a special grant of funds from his Catalan subjects. He collected a large fleet of his own, and again received aid from the ubiquitous Roger de Lauria. On November 22, 1286, he left Salou.[2] Two days later he arrived at Majorca, where he levied a tribute in money and kind on the inhabitants and sent a declaration of war to the Minorcan ruler. Tempests and cold of unusual severity delayed him and scattered his fleet. When he finally arrived at Port Mahon, on January 5, 1287, he had only twenty ships with him; but after eight days' fruitless waiting for the rest to arrive, he determined to risk a battle against superior numbers, and marshalled his forces for the attack. The Minorcans had meantime received considerable reënforcements from North Africa, and apparently made a desperate resistance; but when a decisive battle ensued on January 17, they were unable to withstand the onslaught of the Catalans and Aragonese, and retreated to the shelter of the castle of Port Mahon.[3] On January 21, the capitulation was

[1] Parpal y Marqués, *Conquista de Menorca*, p. 13; Klüpfel, *op. cit.*, pp. 31 f. and note; Lecoy, i, p. 289.

[2] Parpal y Marqués, *op. cit.*, p. 22.
[3] Muntaner, ii, pp. 50–55; Klüpfel, pp. 31 f.; Lecoy, i, pp. 294 f.

signed. Minorca was handed over to Alfonso. The arraez and his immediate following were given free transportation to the Barbary coast, while the rest of the Moorish inhabitants were declared slaves of the crown, and sold as such in Catalonia and Sicily.[1] Catalan colonists were soon established in the island, and concentrated in the neighborhood of Port Mahon, which increased rapidly in prestige and importance, and soon became an invaluable half way station for the ships which plied between Spain and Sicily. All the Balearics remained in the possession of the Crown of Aragon till after Alfonso's death, though his uncle, James of Majorca, succeeded in maintaining himself in Montpellier, Cerdagne, and Roussillon. It was not till 1298 that the latter was at last restored, under Aragonese suzerainty, to his island realm, where he and his successors continued to hold sway until the separate existence of the whole Majorcan kingdom was finally terminated in the middle of the following century.[2]

But the affairs of the Balearics were by this time scarcely more than a side issue. The crux of the situation lay in Sicily. Alfonso's younger brother, James, had been crowned there, at Palermo, on February 2, 1286, in accordance with the wishes of his father; but from the first moment of his reign he was threatened by internal rebellion, foreign attack, and above all by the bitter hostility of the new Pope, Honorius IV, who promptly excommunicated him and ordered him out of his dominions.[3] Everything depended on the attitude of the new king of Aragon. Would he take advantage of his father's dying promise to do his best to

[1] Save for those who were able to purchase liberty at the price of six and one half doblas apiece. Cf. Parpal y Marqués, pp. 40 f.; Klüpfel, p. 32; Lecoy, i, p. 295, who gives the date of the capitulation as January 1; there seems better authority, however, for January 21.

[2] Klüpfel, p. 32; Lecoy, i, pp. 296, 338–364; Bofarull, iii, p. 561.

[3] Klüpfel, pp. 20 ff.

restore Sicily to the papacy as an excuse for abandoning
his brother? Or would he choose the harder part, follow
his father's political testament and the career of empire
and expansion to which his country had so recently been
committed, and support James against every foe in his own
dominions?   It was a momentous question, and it is greatly
to the credit of Alfonso that he chose the latter alternative.
There were strong inducements for him to decide the other
way; for though the papal legate in France had published
his excommunication, and preached the holy war against
Aragon, Honorius used every pretext to postpone any definite action against him.[1] The Pope obviously drew a sharp
distinction between the positions of the two sovereigns.
With James there could be no possible reconciliation, but
for Alfonso, if he would abandon his brother and acknowledge his fault, the road to forgiveness was still open; it
was the papal policy to separate and, if possible, to embroil
the two kings.   But Alfonso, for the time being, was staunch.
What his father had won at so much labor and cost, he could
not bear to let go.   With the fleet of Roger de Lauria he
held unquestioned command of the western Mediterranean,
and could therefore easily communicate with his brother
in Sicily.   An alliance for mutual defence in their respective
possessions was made between them on Christmas day,
1285, and confirmed on February 12, 1286. They were
also both encouraged by the increasingly obvious fact
that Philip the Fair, the new king of France, was far less
enthusiastic than his predecessor for the prosecution of the
papal and Angevin claims, and if anything desirous of an
excuse to withdraw from the conflict.[2] But even without
him the array of foes with which the two brothers were
confronted was extremely formidable. The bitterness of

[1] Klüpfel, pp. 24 f.   [2] Klüpfel, pp. 17, 20, 22.

the papal hostility was increased rather than diminished
when Nicholas IV succeeded Honorius in February, 1288.
The Angevins in Naples were still exceedingly powerful.
James of Majorca was hand in glove with any combination
which promised to injure his Aragonese kinsman; while Castile, under Sancho the Bravo, was eager to deprive Alfonso
of those invaluable political pawns, the Infantes de la Cerda,
and lent a willing ear to the summons of his foes. It is
needless to add that both sides sought aid from the Moorish
states in North Africa. At one stage in the proceedings,
James and Alfonso made an alliance with the Soldan Kela-
wun of Egypt against their Christian foes.[1]

We need not follow the story of the desultory fighting
by land and sea which continued intermittently during the
rest of the reign. No military or naval action of decisive
importance occurred, and hostilities were constantly interrupted by negotiations, truces, and temporary peaces,[2]
arranged through the mediatorial offices of Edward I of
England but never loyally observed. On at least two occasions, Alfonso could have had satisfactory terms as far as
Aragon and his own reconciliation with the papacy were
concerned; but the question of Sicily, "which no one seemed
willing to renounce," remained apparently insoluble. Finally,
in November, 1288, the Prince of Salerno, son and heir
of Charles of Anjou, who had remained in the hands of the
king of Aragon since 1284, was set at liberty, on the understanding that he should bring about a three years' peace
within two months, or else return to captivity.[3] In March,
1289, he departed for Rome on this errand, together with
certain Aragonese ambassadors, but he did not fulfil his
promise. Whether he had ever intended to do so is more

---

[1] Klüpfel, pp. 44, 71, 88 ff.
[2] Notably at Bordeaux and Oléron
in 1287, and at Campfranch in 1288.
Klüpfel, pp. 29–58.
[3] Klüpfel, pp. 51 f.

than doubtful; in any case it is certain that he was but wax in the hands of Nicholas IV, who soon converted him into a servile instrument of papal policy, and finally crowned him king of Sicily on May 29, 1289.[1] The crusade was thereupon preached against his rival James from one end of Italy to the other. Alfonso's excommunication was proclaimed afresh. All the treaties previously concluded with him were declared null and void; and Philip the Fair was granted the ecclesiastical tithes within his realms to finance an invasion of Aragon. Of the two brothers, James was unquestionably threatened the more seriously; but he put a bold face upon the situation, and proceeded to besiege Gaeta so vigorously that his rather inefficient adversary soon agreed to a two years' truce.[2] Alfonso, on the other hand, was by this time heartily tired of fighting over the interminable question of Sicily. The internal situation in Aragon and the necessity of dealing with Sancho of Castile imperatively demanded his attention. Everything dictated the wisdom of seeking reconciliation with Rome. Yet on the other hand he did not intend absolutely to abandon his brother if he could possibly help it; most anxiously did he seek for some middle way, which should offer to all parties concerned an honorable escape from an intolerable situation. Throughout the latter part of 1289 and most of 1290, matters trembled in the balance. Alfonso kept sending messengers to Rome to induce the Pope, if possible, to consent to a discussion of terms, while James in Sicily bravely attempted to make his policy keep time with the ebbs and flows of that of Aragon. A touch of comedy was supplied by Charles of Salerno, who, on the expiration of the time within which he had promised to secure peace, presented himself for reincarceration in fulfilment

[1] Klüpfel, p. 57.   [2] Klüpfel, pp. 60 ff.

of his plighted word; but took great care to come so well
guarded by Majorcan troops, and to select so discreetly
the time and place of his appearance, that no jailer was
on hand to receive him.[1]   Finally, with the aid of the pacifi-
catory efforts of Edward I, the Pope was induced to send
two cardinals to France to discuss a peace; after protracted
negotiation, a treaty was signed at Tarascon, in February,
1291, between all the parties concerned in the Sicilian quarrel,
except James, on terms which most historians have agreed
in regarding as humiliating to the dignity of Aragon.   The
provisions which affect the king of France do not concern
us here; the Aragonese-Castilian quarrel was suffered to run
its course; the main lines of the settlement of the affairs
of Aragon and Sicily were as follows.

In return for a formal acknowledgment of his faults and
a request for forgiveness, to be subsequently repeated in a
personal interview between Alfonso and Nicholas, the
former's excommunication and the various papal edicts
against his realm were to be revoked, and he was to be
recognized as lawful sovereign in his dominions, including
the Balearics.   The king, furthermore, promised to take
the Cross at the Pope's behest, with 5000 foot and 200
horse, for the recovery of the Holy Sepulchre, in formal
ratification of their reconciliation.   Thus far the text of
the treaty, which contains no word of any promise to pay
tribute to Rome, nor any mention of Sicily;[2] to judge by
it alone, James was simply left to his fate, while the Aragonese difficulty was solved on terms generally favorable
to the king.   But in all the histories, from the usually trustworthy Zurita[3] down, we find it recorded that the king

[1] Klüpfel, pp. 67 f.
[2] Save that Alfonso promised to give
no further aid to his brother there, and
to withdraw all Aragonese troops from
the island. The text of the treaty is
printed in Rymer's *Foedera* (second edition, ed. Holmes), vol. ii, pp. 501–504.
[3] Zurita, i, f. 345.

bound himself to pay to Rome an annual revenue of thirty ounces of gold, in token of the vassalage of his realm, as in the days of Pedro II; and also, if necessary, to lend armed support for the expulsion of his brother from Sicily and the restoration of the Angevins there. Obviously the final verdict on Alfonso's reign must depend on whether or not the statements of these historians are true. On the one hand, it does not seem likely that so many writers would have asserted that such humiliating conditions were imposed on the Aragonese king without some basis in fact; on the other, all that we know of the earlier history of Alfonso's reign is in flat contradiction to such an unworthy abandonment of his brother and the Sicilian inheritance, as are also the provisions of his will. The difficulty of the problem is, of course, greatly enhanced by the fact that Alfonso outlived the treaty of Tarascon but four months; had he been granted a longer life his subsequent actions would have spoken for themselves. His most recent historian strongly inclines to the opinion that, whatever concessions he may have made at Tarascon, it was Alfonso's ultimate intention to arrange an acceptable peace for his brother in Sicily; certainly he wrote to James and also to the king of Granada to that effect. Possibly he may have had some plan of directing the crusade, which he had bound himself to undertake, against Sicily rather than the Holy Land; such things had often been done before, and at times when crusading enthusiasm was at a far higher pitch than at the end of the thirteenth century.[1] Clearly matters were still far from their final solution, when everything was upset and all the work of the reign thrown into the melting-pot again by the sudden death of the king, at the early age of thirty-seven, on June 18, 1291.[2] Un-

[1] Klüpfel, pp. 80–87.
[2] Not March 18, as H. Rohde, *Der Kampf um Sicilien*, p. 6, has it.

married and childless, he left his throne and that of Majorca
to his brother James, with instructions that the latter should
hand over Sicily to his younger brother, Frederic. If James
should die childless, Frederic was to succeed him in Aragon
and in Majorca, and Sicily was to go to Pedro, the youngest
brother of all. Under no circumstances were Aragon and
Sicily to be united under a single monarch.[1]

The new king, however, was energetic and ambitious,
and at first saw no reason why he should renounce Sicily
as the price of his succession in Aragon. In sharp contrast
to his father and brother, who had appreciated the difficulties in the way of uniting the two realms under the same
ruler, he fully believed that he could retain them both.
When the news of Alfonso's death called him across to Aragon
to receive the homage of his subjects there, he summoned
the Sicilian estates to Messina, and as a pledge of his future
intentions presented to them his younger brother Frederic,
not as their king but merely as his own lieutenant and representative.[2] This policy, however, did not have the effect
that was expected of it. The hearts' desire of the Sicilians
was national autonomy and independence. They had no
mind to remain subjects of a sovereign whose principal
possessions lay in another part of Europe. They had aided
the Aragonese to expel the Angevins, because they had been
encouraged to believe that they would ultimately be permitted to have a king of their own; and the events of the
reign of Alfonso III had naturally served to strengthen this
expectation. But now that it was apparent that James of
Aragon intended to retain Sicily in his own hands, to convert
the island into a portion of the Aragonese empire, and to
stifle all aspirations for independent national existence,
the enthusiasm of the Sicilians for their Aragonese 'libera-

[1] Zurita, i, f. 347.   [2] H. Rohde, *Der Kampf um Sicilien*, p. 8.

tors' was exchanged for enmity and distrust. A patriotic party, recruited largely among the more highly educated citizens, began to take shape; and it gained added strength day by day from the fact that the young Frederic steadily gravitated towards it.[1] The latter had lived long enough in Sicily to have become imbued with all the native aspirations for autonomy. He naturally was ill pleased with the way in which he had been deprived of the kingship of the island in defiance of the will of Alfonso. He was not, indeed, openly at odds with the king of Aragon; ostensibly they maintained friendly relations, and James repeatedly professed himself to be most solicitous to safeguard his brother's interests. But, on the other hand, it must have been increasingly plain, as time went on, that the permanent retention of both realms under a single sovereign was impracticable, as long as the enemies of the house of Aragon remained so numerous and powerful.

It was, indeed, the attitude of the outside powers that ultimately proved to be the determining factor in the situation, and finally convinced James that his original plan could not possibly be carried out. His attempts to retain Sicily and incorporate it into the Aragonese empire had nullified all the efforts of his predecessors to secure a durable peace. The treaty of Tarascon was a scrap of paper; and the enemies of the king of Aragon began to arm themselves for a fresh trial of strength. But no military events of decisive importance occurred either on land or sea. 'Glorious victories' were constantly reported by both sides, but in reality there was little fighting; the solution, if it came at all, was obviously going to be reached by diplomacy and not by war.[2] For four long years, by constantly

[1] Rohde, op. cit., pp. 80, 86.
[2] Rohde, chaps. ii–viii passim; Amari (tr. Ellesmere), chap. xiv. Roger de

Lauria, at this period, though primarily fighting for his own advantage, stood closer to Frederic than to James, and

shifting his methods of defence, James managed to hold his various enemies at bay. He succeeded for a brief moment in relieving himself of the hostility of Sancho of Castile by abandoning the cause of the Infantes de la Cerda.[1] He was fortunate, also, in having a temporary respite on the side of the papacy, his bitterest foe; for Nicholas IV died in April, 1292, and the cardinals were unable to elect a successor till July, 1294. The absence of leadership in Rome was significantly reflected in the evanescence of the political combinations of the period, and James took advantage of it to stave off his inevitable defeat as long as possible. His period of grace was prolonged for five months beyond the end of the interregnum at Rome by the pitiful pontificate of Celestine V,

"Che fece per viltate il gran rifiuto";[2]

but finally the foes of the king of Aragon got the leader for whom they had looked so long by the election, on Christmas Eve, 1294, of the redoubtable Boniface VIII, masterful and dominant, raised to the papacy by the votes of the French cardinals and the support of the son of Charles of Anjou — a truly strange introduction for the pontiff who was to be smitten by Sciarra Colonna at Anagni.[3] But if nine short years sufficed to send France all the way from the extreme of intimate alliance with the Holy See to that of open defiance of it, an even briefer space was enough to swing Aragon an equal distance in the opposite direction. ‹ Ever since the reign of Pedro II, and more especially since that of his grandson, she had struck out a line of policy notable for its attitude of independence and even hostility toward Rome. She had picked up the torch of

thereby increased the confidence of the Sicilians. Rohde, pp. 77 f.

[1] Daumet, *Mémoire sur les relations de la France et de la Castille de 1255 à 1320*, pp. 111 ff.

[2] Dante, *Inferno*, iii, 60.

[3] Rohde, chaps. ii–viii *passim*, especially pp. 33, 102, 123.

Ghibellinism where the Hohenstaufens had set it down, and had borne it bravely forward; but now her turn to relinquish it had come. For in Boniface James of Aragon recognized a power with whom he could not hope to contend — another Hildebrand or Innocent III — no servile tool of princes and potentates, but an arbiter of the destinies of monarchs and of realms. The new Pope had obviously resolved to restore peace in Christendom on his own terms. At the very beginning of his pontificate he had taken the decisive step of opening negotiations with Frederic, offering him a marriage with Catharine of Courtenay, daughter of the titular Emperor of Constantinople and niece of Charles of Anjou, together with her claims to the succession of the Empire of the East, in return for his abandonment of Sicily. Frederic did not accept this proposal. His increasing love and respect for his Sicilian subjects, as well as a natural scepticism concerning the Pope's ability to perform his promises, held him back; but he at least consented to negotiate, and thus gave Boniface a chance to make overtures to Aragon, France, and Anjou.[1] It is probable that James, before this time, had been convinced that his original plan of retaining Sicily could not be carried out; and provided territorial compensation was elsewhere forthcoming, he did not propose to stand by Frederic. He had, moreover, for some time past been secretly negotiating with France, with a view to indemnifying himself for a loss which he foresaw was inevitable. He had even gone so far as to offer to marry the daughter of Charles II of Anjou on condition that the Pope should grant him Sardinia; and he had also spoken of a match between himself and that Catharine of Courtenay whom Boniface had offered to his brother, in the hope of gaining the succession to the Latin Empire of the East.[2]

[1] Rohde, p. 144.   [2] Rohde, pp. 118–120.

All this made it comparatively easy for Boniface to carry out his plans for the settlement of the Sicilian question. The representatives of Aragon, France, and Anjou were accordingly summoned by him to Anagni in June, 1295, and they there evolved a most comprehensive treaty, of which the following stipulations concern us here.

James renounced all his rights and titles to Sicily, which was to be restored to the Holy See for the house of Anjou. The king of Aragon agreed to marry the daughter of his Angevin rival as sign and seal of their reconciliation, and there was to be a mutual surrender of captives and hostages. The excommunication and interdict against James and Frederic and their dominions were to be raised, and the king of France renounced all right and pretension to the realms of the Crown of Aragon. At the same time, a papal bull commanded in categorical terms that the Balearics be restored to James of Majorca, under the suzerainty of the Aragonese king — a sentence which, however, was not fully executed till three years afterward.[1] Lastly, we may be reasonably sure that the cession to the Aragonese king of Corsica and Sardinia, as indemnification for his renunciation of Sicily, was at least fully discussed at Anagni. James had had his eye on these islands for some time past, and was exceedingly anxious to annex them to his dominions. They were held at the time by the Pisans and Genoese, but the church had claimed the overlordship of them since the end of the eleventh century, and Boniface, who bore no love to their actual occupants, was not averse to handing them over to James, to conquer if he could on his own resources, and to hold at an annual tribute of two thousand silver marks under the suzerainty of Rome. The matter

[1] R. Starrabba, "Documenti riguardanti l' abdicazione di Giacomo II al trono di Sicilia" in *Archivio storico Siciliano*, n. s., vii, pp. 275–293; Rohde, *op. cit.*, pp. 146–152; Lecoy, i, pp. 346, 353 ff.

was not settled till January, 1296; the formal ceremony of investiture was deferred till April 3, 1297; and it was many years later before the king of Aragon was able to enter into possession of his new dominions. The first military expedition against them was not launched till 1323, and must be reserved for examination in another place; but there seems every reason to think that their cession was virtually arranged in 1295.[1]

Altogether, the peace of Anagni was only a partial triumph for Boniface VIII.[2] He had succeeded, it is true, in wresting Sicily from the possession of James and in settling for the time being the quarrels of Aragon with France and Majorca. But he had by no means put an end to the war to which the Sicilian question had given rise; he had rather altered and perhaps enlarged its scope, and changed the personalities of the combatants. For the Sicilians found in Frederic a worthy champion of their independence, so that the struggle in that quarter continued with unabated violence; while the contest for Corsica and Sardinia and the campaigns of the Catalan Grand Company in the eastern Mediterranean simply served to transport the war to other lands. The current of Aragonese imperial ambition had begun to run so strongly that even Boniface VIII was powerless to stop it. Checked in one direction, it promptly burst forth in others, constantly gathering headway, and seeking for new worlds to conquer.

From 1295 to 1327, that is, during the remainder of the reign of James II, the history of the expansion of Aragon in the Mediterranean Sea falls into three separate divisions,

[1] On this complicated matter cf. 33, 42; Rohde, p. 132; R. St.-H., iv, Amari (tr. Ellesmere), iii, p. 64; E. p. 358, speaks of a secret article in the Besta, La Sardegna medioevale, i, pp. 78 treaty, relative to Corsica and Sardinia. ff., 261; Finke, Acta Aragonensia, i, pp. [2] Rohde, pp. 149 f.

which correspond to the three principal ramifications already noted of the war over the question of the Sicilian inheritance. The first is the struggle of Sicily under Frederic to maintain itself against the assaults of Pope and Angevin. The second is the beginning of the conquest of Sardinia. The third is the origin and early progress of the Aragonese domination in Greece. The affairs of Sicily and of Sardinia, down to the end of the reign, can conveniently be recounted in the immediately succeeding pages, while the rise and fall of the Catalan duchy of Athens forms an episode so remote from the rest of the Aragonese Empire in the western basin of the Mediterranean that it will be easier to describe it in a separate chapter.

In Sicily there was consternation when the news of the peace of Anagni was known. Ambassadors were sent to the king of Aragon to beg him to reconsider his decision. On their arrival at Barcelona, they found preparations being made for the marriage of James to the Angevin princess, 'the Queen of the Holy Peace,' which they regarded as the sign and seal of his dishonor;[1] when they learned that the king of Aragon had already abandoned all his rights in Sicily to Charles of Naples, "they grieved like men who have received sentence of death," and caused the sails of the ships that bore them home to be painted black.[2] But the valor of the Sicilians was proof against the desperate circumstances in which they were placed. Their desertion by the king of Aragon was perhaps a calamity; but it also could be converted into a great blessing, if only they could maintain themselves against the papacy without his aid; for in case of triumph their reward would be the greater — namely, the national autonomy of which they had so

---

[1] Amari (tr. Ellesmere), iii, pp. 27–29.   [2] R. St.-H., iv, p. 360.

long dreamed, instead of continued subjection to a foreign prince. Young Frederic, brave, handsome, and beloved, was by this time completely won over to the cause of Sicilian independence. On December 11, 1295, the Sicilian parliament conferred on him supreme power, with the title of 'Lord of the Island,' and received in return his pledge to defend his subjects with his life and his substance. On May 25, 1296, followed the more solemn act of his coronation and anointing as king of Sicily, in the cathedral church of Palermo; and this was accompanied by an extensive remodelling of the Sicilian constitution, which remedied sundry abuses, strengthened and confirmed individual liberties and franchises, and increased the power of the national estates.[1]

Having thus made doubly sure of the enthusiastic loyalty of his Sicilian subjects, Frederic persuaded a large proportion of the Aragonese troops in the island to enroll themselves in his service, and to ignore the missives which James sent forth to summon them home. He then turned his thoughts to war. Comprehending the immense advantage of seizing the initiative, he promptly crossed the strait of Messina with a considerable force, and began to ravage Calabria and Apulia. The feeble Angevin levies of the indolent Charles of Naples were quite unable to stem the onrushing tide; and Boniface saw that immediate measures would be necessary to save his protégé. The most obvious plan was to draw closer to James of Aragon, who would be more than ever anxious to please the Pope in order to insure the satisfaction of his ambition to annex Corsica and Sardinia; to call on him as a loyal son of the church to aid in effecting the subjugation of Sicily, and even to take arms if necessary against his own brother. Negotiations

[1] Amari (tr. Ellesmere), iii, pp. 30-48.

for this purpose were prolonged throughout the latter part of 1296 and 1297. James, who, not unnaturally, was reluctant to comply with the papal mandates, used every effort to persuade Frederic to come to terms. The latter, however, proved obdurate, and as Boniface possessed a strong hold over the king of Aragon through his control over the as yet unsettled question of Corsica and Sardinia, James finally came to Rome early in 1297, prepared to enlist in the papal service. The next weeks were occupied in winning away the all-powerful admiral, Roger de Lauria, from the service of Frederic, who had been unable to avoid disagreements with this haughty and independent spirit; and when Lauria finally passed to the papal side, the naval preponderance passed with him. In the summer of 1298 there assembled under his leadership, in the harbor of Naples, one of the most formidable fleets that had ever sailed the seas — upwards of 100 galleys — to which most of the Western Mediterranean states had furnished their contingents. The undaunted Frederic did not hesitate to appear at the mouth of the harbor with an inferior force, but soon after deemed it prudent to retire to Sicily without a battle; according to a contemporary historian, his withdrawal was caused by the receipt of a secret warning from his brother, who had not really desired to fight him, and hoped to fulfil his obligation to Boniface without a serious conflict.[1] A series of inconclusive operations followed; but finally, on July 4, 1299, the king of Aragon and the admiral won a bloody victory off Cape Orlando, which ended the resistance of the Sicilians on the sea. Frederic, however, managed to effect his escape with nineteen galleys. Far from discouraged at his defeat, he and his followers gloried in the fact that

[1] N. Specialis, *Historia Sicula*, lib. iv, caps. 3 and 4 (in Gregorio, *Biblioteca*, i, pp. 387–388). On this point, however, see also Amari (tr. Ellesmere), iii, pp. 101 f.

they had so long held at bay the fleets of the principal maritime state of the time, and they were more than confident that they could retrieve their fortunes by land at the expense of the armies of the prince of Naples. Their hopes were justified by the event. At Falconaria, on December 1, 1300, Frederic's infantry, by an impetuous charge, drove the horsemen of their foes in headlong flight, and vindicated the honor of a noble cause.[1]

The effect of the desperate resistance of the Sicilians was enhanced by the fact that after the naval battle off Cape Orlando, James of Aragon had departed for Spain. He had accomplished the task which had been assigned to him, and though still in much terror of Boniface, he felt bitterly ashamed of the part he had been made to play.[2] The Pope was hard put to it to find a champion for his cause. Charles of Naples had already proved a broken reed, and the Count of Valois, to whom Boniface next applied, lost the bulk of his forces through a pestilence before Sciacca. No one else seemed to be immediately available, and the final result was the signature of a peace at Caltabelotta in August, 1302, which finally terminated a struggle of twenty years' duration, and rewarded Frederic for his splendid fight against overwhelming odds.[3] He was recognized as king of the island of Sicily during his lifetime,[4] in absolute sovereignty, independent alike of Naples and of the Pope, and all previous papal sentences against him and his subjects were revoked. His Angevin rival retained the whole of Naples on the mainland, including Calabria, and there

---

[1] Amari (tr. Ellesmere), iii, pp. 48–137, gives an excellent account of these events, based chiefly on N. Specialis. See also Zurita, i, ff. 370–393.

[2] Finke, *Acta Aragonensia*, i, pp. 65 ff. Much useful information in regard to the relations of Rome and Aragon in this period may be found in Paul Diepgen's *Arnald von Villanova* (Berlin, 1909).

[3] Amari (tr. Ellesmere), iii, pp. 256 ff.

[4] The precise title which he assumed was 'king of Trinacria': on the reasons for this cf. Mas Latrie, pp. 281 ff.

was a mutual restoration of conquered places on both sides of the strait of Messina, so that the historic kingdom of Sicily was henceforth divided. Frederic further agreed to marry Eleanor of Anjou, the daughter of his foe, in token of the reconciliation of the rival houses; and there was further inserted, to save the papal dignity, a clause which, as every one must have realized, stood little or no chance of fulfilment, to the effect that after Frederic's death Sicily should revert to the Angevins, in return for an indemnity to his children of 100,000 ounces of gold. Even with these concessions, however, the peace of Caltabelotta proved too bitter a humiliation for Boniface to accept. Before he would consent to ratify it, he obliged Frederic to exchange the full and complete sovereignty over Sicily, which had been conferred upon him by the original treaty, for an arrangement by which he should consent to acknowledge the feudal supremacy of Rome and pay 3000 ounces of gold in recognition of it. "The terms honorably obtained by the sword," says Amari, "were thus defaced by negotiation."[1]

Despite all these modifications and reservations, it is undeniable that at Caltabelotta the papacy suffered an important loss of prestige. Seven years before, at Anagni, James of Aragon had forsaken the ways of his fathers and bowed the knee of submission to Rome; but Frederic had proved more obstinate, and was finally rewarded with the recognition of the virtual independence of his kingdom. More than a century later the separate line of Sicilian sovereigns which had been founded by Frederic died out, and the island was finally and formally incorporated in the Aragonese Empire; but nothing in the checkered course of Sicily's later history should cause us to forget that its first acquisi-

[1] Amari (tr. Ellesmere), iii, p. 272.

tion by a Spanish monarch was effected through open defiance of the Holy See.   In the conquest of Sardinia, however, which next claims our attention, we shall find Aragon
and the papacy in alliance.

We have already seen that in 1296–97 Pope Boniface
had granted to King James of Aragon, as a part of the price
of his abandonment of his brother Frederic, the right to
conquer and hold the islands of Corsica and Sardinia, under
the suzerainty of the see of Rome.   This apparently magnificent papal donation, however, was emphatically of the
sort that it is more blessed to give than to receive.   Bitterly
as he detested the rival republics of Genoa and Pisa, which
were actually in occupation of the two islands, Boniface
realized that he did not possess the military power to expel
them; he was, therefore, only too happy to find a sovereign
amenable to his authority who would engage, on his own
resources, to do so for him.   It is also quite clear that the
king of Aragon fully realized the difficulty of the task he
had undertaken.   He postponed action again and again,
until the pressure of other more immediate problems had
abated, and thus gave Boniface and his successors an
opportunity to prepare the way for the final military campaign by ecclesiastical admonition and diplomatic intrigue.
The existing conditions in both islands, more particularly
in Sardinia, furnished an admirable opportunity for the
exercise of the papal talents in this direction.   Not only
were Pisa and Genoa at odds with one another over the possession of them; but both, in different ways and degrees,
were exceedingly unpopular with the natives.   They had
been called over from Italy in the eleventh century to expel
the Saracens from the islands; having successfully accomplished that task, they felt that they were entitled to remain,

and this the inhabitants not unnaturally resented. In Sardinia, the latter had been governed since very ancient times by four *giudices* or judges, each of whom was virtually a king in the district committed to his charge; at the period with which we are dealing the most powerful of them was unquestionably the Judge of Arborea, whose domains occupied the southwestern quarter of the island. The Pisans, who were dominant in that region, had irritated these magistrates by sundry exactions and demands. They were generally unpopular also because of their intense Ghibellinism, and since their power in both Corsica and Sardinia was distinctly on the wane (the Genoese held practically all of one and the bulk of the other) the Pope and the king of Aragon determined to concentrate their efforts against them. At first they strove to widen the breach between the Pisans and the Judges of Arborea, and with excellent results. Secret negotiations were opened between Hugo, Judge of Arborea, and the king of Aragon in 1321; they terminated in an arrangement by which the former was given assurance that he would be maintained in all his dignities and titles, in return for his support against the common foe. Next King James approached the Genoese in Sardinia, and made sure that they would not actively support the Pisans. The powerful families of the Dorias and the Malespini, the greatest feudatories in the island, were even won over to the cause of Aragon; while in the commune of Sassari, where the Genoese showed some signs of taking the other side, the inhabitants rose and expelled them. Only in Iglesias and Cagliari did the Pisans keep the upper hand, and even there signs of the presence of an Aragonese party kept constantly cropping out; one man was beheaded for having been heard to exclaim, "Please the devil that those Catalans come!" Meantime the papacy, transferred to

Avignon in 1309, continued to do everything in its power
to emphasize its ancient claims to the overlordship of both
Corsica and Sardinia, and its consequent right to dispose
of them; it also interfered on all possible occasions in the
affairs of the Sardinian clergy, in order to assure itself of
their loyalty and support. In Italy, too, matters shaped
themselves in a way favorable to the Aragonese invasion.
Pisa was weak, distracted by internal broils, and discouraged
by the death, in 1313, of the Emperor Henry VII; on the
other hand, all the Guelf powers in the peninsula supported
the Pope and the king of Aragon. The king of Naples
formally approved of the enterprise, while Frederic of Sicily,
unable to prevent it, vainly attempted to mediate between
his brother and the Pisans.[1]

By the time, then, that King James was ready to begin
military operations, the diplomatic foundations for them had
been pretty thoroughly laid. Meantime, no precautions
had been neglected in Aragon and Catalonia that would
serve to insure success. The Infante Alfonso [2] was placed
in command of the expedition, and was furnished with a
fleet so great, says Muntaner, "that the whole world trembled every time that the eagle of Aragon made ready to fly."
The names of those who rallied to Alfonso's standard included
all the best and bravest in the realm, and such was the enthusiasm for the enterprise that no less than 20,000, according to the contemporary chronicler, were forced to remain
behind. At the very last moment the Avignonese Pope,
John XXII, grew fainthearted and attempted to draw
back, reminding King James "that there were already wars

[1] On this paragraph cf. Zurita, ii, ff.
45–51; Besta, La Sardegna medioevale,
i, caps. vi–xiii, especially pp. 275–279,
and also his preface for bibliography.
The most important documents on the
history of mediaeval Sardinia are to be
found in Historiae Patriae Monumenta,
edita jussu Regis Caroli Alberti, vols.
x–xii (Turin, 1861–68).

[2] His elder brother James had renounced his right to the succession. Cf.
Zurita, ii, ff. 33–36.

and tribulations enough in Christendom"; but the latter
was not thus to be diverted from his purpose.[1] On May
31, 1323, the Aragonese fleet left Portfangos under the
orders of the valiant admiral Francisco Carroz, with upwards
of 10,000 soldiers under the Infante. A small detachment
furnished by the kingdom of Majorca joined them at Port
Mahon. On June 12 they anchored in the Gulf of Palmas,
as had previously been arranged with Hugo of Arborea.[2]
After the latter had met them and solemnly recognized the
overlordship of Aragon, preparations were made to attack
the two chief Pisan strongholds, Iglesias and Cagliari.
The first-named was considerably the less formidable, but
it required a four months' siege by the bulk of the invading
forces before it yielded, on February 7, 1324, to starvation
and thirst. After its surrender the Infante was able to concentrate his army and navy before Cagliari, where Admiral
Carroz had already preceded him.[3] As an earnest of his
determination to capture it at any price, he proceeded to
construct directly in front of it a fortified town and castle,
which he called Bonayre, so placed that it enabled him immediately to detect any attempt at a sortie of the garrison
or at relief from without, and there awaited developments.
A Pisan squadron, reënforced by a detachment of Germans,
which attempted to break through the blockade, was beaten
off with great slaughter, and the expected sortie of the garrison of Cagliari met with a similar fate; the invaders were,
moreover, still further strengthened by the arrival of a fresh
fleet from Aragon.[4] On the other hand, the forces of the
Infante had been decimated by the ravages of the terrible
'intemperia' or Sardinian fever, which had made the
climate of that island the synonym for death since Roman

[1] Muntaner, ii, pp. 354–356; Zurita,
ii, ff. 45–47.
[2] Besta, op. cit., i, pp. 279 f.
[3] Besta, i, pp. 280–282.
[4] Muntaner, ii, pp. 357–372; Besta,
i, pp. 283–286.

times.[1] Bonayre, as its name implies, was far less destructive than the region of Iglesias in this respect, but Alfonso's losses were quite sufficient to make him think twice before refusing terms somewhat less favorable than he had originally hoped to obtain. Through the mediation of Bernabe Doria and Hugo of Arborea, a treaty was finally arranged on June 19, 1324, by virtue of which the Pisans surrendered to the Infante all their possessions in Sardinia, except Cagliari, and promised to hold that as 'a fief of the Crown of Aragon, at an annual tribute of 3000 lire.[2]

This somewhat lame and halting peace served rather to postpone the end of the struggle than to terminate it. Cagliari became a center of Pisan intrigue; the Genoese, reversing their policy, now joined forces with their quondam foes. It was not until Admiral Carroz, a year and a half later, won a decisive victory over their combined fleets in Sardinian waters that the town was finally delivered up, and the king of Aragon could boast that he was really master of the whole island.[3] According to Muntaner, the treaty of 1324 led the inhabitants of Corsica, which was practically entirely under the control of Genoa, to follow the example of their brethren in Sardinia and acknowledge the suzerainty of King James; but Zurita offers a number of excellent reasons for doubting this statement, the chief of which is the fact that King Pedro IV of Aragon, who afterwards did much fighting in Sardinia, makes no mention of the matter in his chronicle.[4] Certain projects which were broached, though not accomplished at the time, for the invasion and conquest of Corsica seem to afford additional evidence that the claims of the Aragonese monarch to the overlordship

[1] Zurita, ii, ff. 52-54; and also Muntaner's curious 'sermon en vers,' ii, pp. 346-353.

[2] Besta, i. p. 286.

[3] Muntaner, i, pp. 385-406; Zurita, ii, ff. 69-73.

[4] Muntaner, ii, pp. 372-374; Zurita, ii, ff. 61 f.

of that island can in no sense be regarded as established, despite the fact that he undoubtedly continued to style himself the king of it in virtue of the papal donation of 1297.

A few other scattering events of this important reign remain to be mentioned, all of them indicative of the spirit of foreign enterprise and expansion that animated alike the sovereigns and subjects of the realms of the crowns of Aragon and Sicily; in some respects it never rose so high again. The most significant of these was the struggle over the possession of the little island of Gerba, just west of Tripoli, and close to the North African coast. Captured from the Moors, first by the Normans and later, in the end of the thirteenth century, by the Admiral Roger de Lauria, it was defended with difficulty by the heirs of the latter against repeated infidel assaults. Outside aid was indispensable to its permanent retention in Christian hands, and in 1310 Frederic of Sicily sent the chronicler, Ramón Muntaner, who had abundance of military experience, to organize and maintain its defence. The latter accomplished his mission so effectively that he was rewarded by his grateful master with a three years' grant of the lordship of Gerba and also of Kerkeni, to the northwest of it, under the suzerainty of the Sicilian crown. At the expiration of his term he went back to Spain, leaving the island in the possession of Frederic; for the farce of continuing to recognize the rights of the heirs of Roger de Lauria had by this time been given up, so completely incapable were they of enforcing them. A score of years later, in 1335, the Saracens won Gerba back, and the subsequent attempts of Genoa and Sicily to recapture it for Christendom were not attended with permanent success.[1] The little island of Pantellaria, however, was

<hr />

[1] Muntaner, ii, pp. 281–295, 326–328; Mas Latrie, pp. 282–293, 415 f., 417; Bofarull, iv, pp. 155 ff.

reconquered in this period from the Saracens, and subjected to the payment of a tribute by King Frederic. After numerous vicissitudes it passed to the Crown of Aragon in the early fifteenth century, and in 1492 it was conferred on the great family of Requesens, which continued to administer it as a hereditary possession for three hundred years.[1]

The struggle over Gerba brings us back to the question of the status of the tribute to Aragon from the king of Tunis, of which mention has already been made.[2] Certain sums had been irregularly paid by the Hafside sultans to the Aragonese kings during the previous century, in return for the Christian soldiers whom the latter had permitted to serve in the Moorish armies. In 1285, moreover, Pedro III had established a claim for himself and his successors to a more permanent contribution from the same source, when the Tunisian sovereigns recognized him as lawful king of Sicily, and as heir to the annual tribute which the rulers of Tunis had anciently paid to the Sicilian crown. But when on Pedro's death Sicily was separated from Aragon under an independent line of kings, this Tunisian tribute naturally became an object of competition between the two rulers. The Angevins in Naples also refused to abandon their claim to it; and the triple controversy thus aroused finally resulted in a complete cessation of the disputed revenue, pending its settlement. In 1309, after King James of Aragon had abandoned all rights to Sicily, he was selected as arbiter between the two remaining claimants, and finally gave his verdict in favor of the king of Naples, on the ground

---

[1] R. Gregorio, *Opere Rare riguardanti la Sicilia* (2d edition, 1873), p. 669. The island had been taken from the Saracens by Roger II of Sicily, and in the reign of the Emperor Frederick II it was under Christian jurisdiction; but the infidel inhabitants had regained control of it during the period of the Angevin wars. I can find no authority for the statement in the *Encyclopaedia Britannica* that "a Spanish fleet, under the command of Requesens, won a considerable victory here in 1311."

[2] *Ante*, p. 324.

that the exact. title of his brother Frederic was only king
of Trinacria. As the Angevin, however, was totally unable
to enforce his claim, the sentence remained practically inoperative, and the king of Aragon subsequently acknowledged the right of Frederic of Sicily to collect a fresh tribute
from the king of Tunis, if he could do so, by force. The
fact that the Christians were established in Gerba, where
they could menace the Tunisian coast, apparently enabled
Frederic to accomplish this, down to the recapture of the
island by the Saracens in 1335; it seems that the king of
Aragon was also in receipt of an annual contribution of 5000
doblas from the Hafside ruler during this period, on the old
ground that the latter had Christian soldiers in his service.[1]

Other evidences of the interest and enthusiasm of King
James for the extension of the power and prestige of Aragon
in distant lands are his second marriage in 1314 with Mary,
the sister of Henry of Lusignan, king of Cyprus, and his
sending of an embassy, apparently with the most successful
results, to the Soldan of Cairo, to ransom all the Aragonese
and Catalan crusaders and merchants who were prisoners
within his domains.[2] His reign marks an important epoch
in the development of the Aragonese Empire. James was
neither great, save possibly as a legist, nor beloved, and
it is hard to forgive his treatment of the Sicilian question
and his abandonment of his brother Frederic; but he prof-
ited by his early errors and did not repeat them, and as
time went on, he gave evidence that he possessed caution
and determination, quickness to seize his opportunities,
and many of the other qualities of statesmanship.

[1] Zurita, ii, f. 19; Mas Latrie, pp. 279–281, 290 ff.; A. Giménes Soler, "Episodios de la historia de las Relaciones entre la Corona de Aragón y Túnes" and "Documentos de Túnes," in *Anuari de l'Institut d'Estudis Catalans*, 1907, pp. 195–224; *ibid.*, 1909–10, pp. 210–259.

[2] Zurita, ii, ff. 23–24. The practice of sending embassies to Cairo was continued under Pedro IV. Zurita, ii, ff. 344–345.

BIBLIOGRAPHICAL NOTE

See bibliographical note at the end of the preceding chapter, and add:
Contemporary Authorities. — Heinrich Finke, ed., *Acta Aragonensia* (Berlin, 1908, 2 vols.), is an invaluable collection of documents on the reign of James II of Aragon, with an excellent introduction and notes. Bernat Desclot, *Cronica del Rey En Pere* (Pedro III), ed. J. A. C. Buchon in *Chroniques étrangères relatives aux expéditions françaises pendant le XIII* *siècle* (Paris, 1840), and Ramón Muntaner, *Crónica del Rey Don Jaime I y de muchos de sus descendientes*, French translation, ed. Buchon (Paris, 1827, 2 vols.), are the two most important contemporary chronicles; on the various editions of them, cf. J. Massó Torrents in *R. H.*, vol. xv, pp. 523–543. Pere Marsili, *Crónica*, Catalan text and Spanish translation, ed. and tr. J. M. Quadrado in *Historia de la Conquista de Mallorca* (Palma, 1850), gives a good account of the conquest of the Balearics. Nicolaus Specialis, *Historia Sicula* (ed. Rosario Gregorio in *Biblioteca Scriptorum qui Res in Sicilia gestas sub Aragonum Imperio retulere*, Palermo, 1791–92, vol. i, pp. 283–508), covers the period 1282 to 1337. Bartholomaeus de Neocastro, Saba Malaspina, and the other contemporary writers on Sicily will also be found in Gregorio's collection. For further information about them, see Auguste Molinier, *Les sources de l'histoire de France*, vol. iii, pp. 168–171.

Later Works. — Otto Cartellieri, *Peter von Aragon und die sizilianische Vesper* (Heidelberg, 1904), is the best and latest treatise on the subject. Ludwig Klüpfel, *Die äussere Politik Alfonso's III. von Aragonien, 1285–1291* (Berlin, 1911–12), and H. E. Rohde, *Der Kampf um Sizilien, 1291–1302* (Berlin, 1913), are two admirable monographs which evidently owe much to the inspiration and guidance of Finke. The *Historia General del Reino de Mallorca*, by Juan Dameto, Vicente Mut, and Gerónimo Alemany (2d edition, by Miguel Moragues and J. M. Bover, Palma, 1840–41, 3 vols.), has been largely superseded, at least for the purposes of the present work, by Albert Lecoy de la Marche, *Les relations politiques de la France avec le royaume de Majorque* (Paris, 1892, 2 vols.), which is indispensable. Cosme Parpal y Marqués, *La Conquista de Menorca en 1287 por Alfonso III de Aragon* (Barcelona, 1901), is a solid study, based on the sources, to which full references are given. The standard history of the Sicilian wars down to the peace of Caltabelotta is Michele Amari, *La Guerra del Vespro Siciliano*. My references are to the Earl of Ellesmere's translation, *History of the War of the Sicilian Vespers* (London, 1850, 3 vols.). Enrico Besta, *La Sardegna Medioevale* (Palermo, 1908–1909, 2 vols.), marks an epoch in the study of Sardinian history; unfortunately it stops with the Aragonese conquest in 1324.

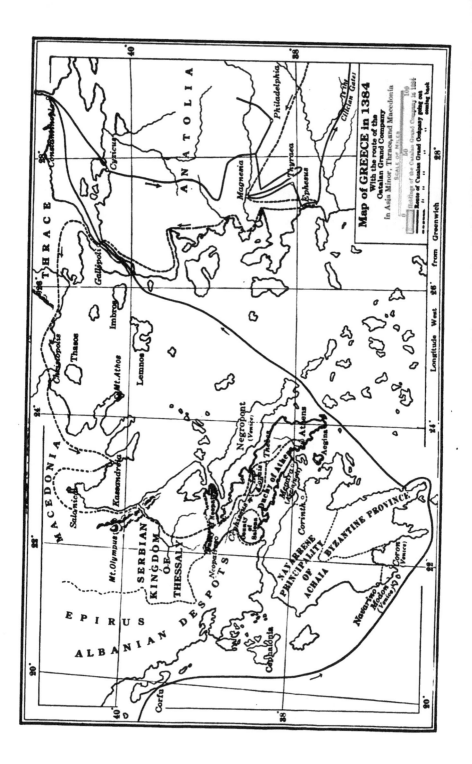

Map of GREECE in 1384
With the route of the
Catalan Grand Company
in Asia Minor, Thrace, and Macedonia

SCALE OF MILES

Holdings of the Catalan Grand Company in 1384
Route of Catalan Grand Company going out
" " " " " coming back

Longitude West   from Greenwich

THRACE

Constantinople

Gallipoli

Chersonesos
Thasos
Mt.Athos
Lemnos
Imbros

MACEDONIA

Salonica
Kassandrea

Mt.Olympus

SERBIAN
KINGDOM
OF
THESSALY

EPIRUS

ALBANIAN DESPOTS

Corfu

Cephalonia

Neopatras
County
of
Salona
County of
Neopatras
Zeitouni
Thebes
Duchy of Athens
Megara
Aegina
Athens
Corinth
Negropont (Venice)

NAVARRESE
PRINCIPALITY
OF
ACHAIA

BYZANTINE PROVINCE

Navarino
Modon (Venice)
Coron (Venice)

ANATOLIA

Philadelphia

Magnesia
Thyraea
Ephesus
Cyzicus

Cilician Gates
The
Cilician Gates

CHAPTER VIII

THE CATALAN GRAND COMPANY

BEFORE proceeding further with our study of the development of the Aragonese empire in the western basin of the Mediterranean, we must devote one short chapter to the story of a much remoter outpost of it, which was won and lost during the fourteenth century in the Levant. The history of the Catalan Grand Company and of the duchy of Athens under its dominion is one of the dramatic episodes of the Middle Ages, and has been described from many different points of view; but as the whole affair exercised no lasting influence on the fortunes of the Spanish Empire, it need only be dealt with briefly here. We shall also find it convenient to carry the story through to its conclusion in the present chapter, even though by so doing we shall ｜ be taken somewhat beyond the point which we have reached in the development of the more permanent portions of the Aragonese Empire farther westward. The matter is episodic rather than fundamental for our main purpose, and may therefore best be considered by itself.

The terrible confusion into which Greece had been thrown by the Fourth Crusade had been in no wise diminished by the reconquest of Constantinople by the Emperor Michael Palaeologus in 1261. The domains of the reëstablished Empire of the East were small and scattered, "a feeble, crippled body, which could ill support its enormous head." The bulk of the Grecian peninsula remained more or less completely independent of it, split up into a number of

minor principalities, most of which acknowledged the sway
of Western rulers. Even the parts which remained nominally under Byzantine control were in reality managed
by rival Genoese and Venetian mercenaries and colonists,
who were practically masters of the situation. The way in
which Charles of Anjou contrived to extend the dominion
of his house into this sadly disrupted land need only be
briefly touched on here; we have already seen that the possession of an empire in the East had been the goal of his
ambition from the very first, and, indeed, that he regarded
the conquest of Sicily chiefly as a stepping-stone to that
end.[1] He began in 1267 by seizing the island of Corfu, which
had belonged to his rival, Manfred of Sicily. In the same
year a treaty with Baldwin II, the deposed Latin Emperor
of Romania, gave him the suzerainty over the great principality of Achaia, which was held by William of Villehar-
douin and comprised the bulk of the Peloponnesus; and
soon afterwards a marriage between his second son and
William's daughter converted the Angevin suzerainty into
virtual possession. The rich duchy of Athens also, com-
prising ancient Attica and Boeotia, and ruled over from
1205 to 1308 by the French house of de la Roche, specifically
acknowledged the authority of Anjou; even in Cephalonia
and Epirus Charles considered himself to be overlord.
"In almost every part of the Greek world the restless
Angevin had a base for his long projected attack on Constantinople"; and the Emperor Michael Palaeologus and
his son, Andronicus II, had fully as much cause to dread
the assaults of the fierce Frenchman on the west as those
of the infidel Turk on the east.[2]

---

[1] *Ante*, p. 320. The same idea appears at the time of the raid of Charles
VIII, who, as Bacon (*Henry VII*, ed.
Lumby, p. 82) put it, hoped "to make
the reconquest of Naples, but as a bridge
to transport his forces into Graecia."

[2] Good accounts (with maps and
bibliographies) of the topics treated in

It was entirely natural that in seeking aid to ward off the threatened danger, the Byzantine emperors should look to the house of Aragon. That dynasty was already at swords' points with the Angevins in the western Mediterranean, and it had also been in close touch with Oriental affairs ever since the marriage of Pedro II to the granddaughter of the Emperor Manuel Comnenus in 1204. During the reign of James the Conqueror, Aragonese traders had frequently made their appearance in the Levant; and just before the Sicilian Vespers the rulers of Aragon and Constantinople had been drawn nearer than ever together in common enmity to Charles of Anjou, through the instrumentality of John of Procida.[1] On the other hand, the famous ravaging expedition of Roger de Lauria into Grecian waters in the year 1292 must have made the Byzantine emperors think twice before employing the warriors of the West. Plunder, ransom "enough to satisfy five armies," and indiscriminate slaughter, sufficient, according to Muntaner, to explain the lack of good men to defend the Morea at a later day, were the sole objects of Lauria's men; and apparently the territories of the Byzantine emperor suffered quite as severely as those of his Angevin foe, for the admiral justified himself in attacking the former on the ground that Andronicus had failed to pay the king of Aragon a subsidy promised to the father of Pedro the Great.[3] The expedition, however, certainly served the purpose of reminding these western marauders of the glories of the East, whatever it may have caused the East to think of them. It had indicated to them an unrivalled opportunity for booty and spoil, and

this paragraph may be found in W. Miller, *The Latins in the Levant*, chapters i–v, and in R. Rodd, *The Princes of Achaia*, chapters iii–ix. Cf. also "Notes on Athens under the Franks," by W. Miller, in *English Historical Review*, xxii (1907), pp. 518–522.

[1] *Ante*, pp. 320 f., and Cartellieri, *Peter von Aragon*, pp. 76 f.

[3] Muntaner, *Chronique* (ed. Buchon), ii, pp. 27 ff. (cap. clix); W. Miller, *Latins in the Levant*, pp. 184–186.

when the chance came they would not fail to take advantage of it.

Under the circumstances, then, we need not wonder that when the peace of Caltabelotta closed the war in Sicily, the soldiers in Frederic's armies cast longing eyes to the eastward, in the hope of finding fresh employment there. Clearly Frederic wanted to get rid of them, so much so, in fact, that he recked little where and how they found service; for despite the traditional friendship of his house with the Palaeologi, he apparently began by offering them to Charles of Valois, husband of that Catharine of Courtenay to whom Boniface VIII had once planned to marry him, to be used against Andronicus II. This project, for a number of reasons, fell through, but Roger de Flor,[1] the most redoubtable of Frederic's generals, who had set his heart on getting to the Levant, did not propose to be balked by the ebbs and flows of diplomatic negotiation; and it occurred to him that the easiest way to effect his purpose was to offer his services to the very emperor whom he had previously expected to attack. Andronicus, hard pressed by the Turks, accepted his proposal, even though he must have been fully aware of the exceedingly unstable character of his new allies. Roger was given the title of 'Grand Duke,' the hand of the Emperor's niece, and a promise of double pay for his men — four months of it in advance. On these terms he sailed for Constantinople in the summer of 1303,[2] with 36 ships and

[1] On this man cf. G. Schlumberger, *Expédition des 'Almugavares' en Orient*, pp. 5–17.

[2] I have followed Muntaner's *Chronicle* (caps. cxcix–cci) and Moncada's *Espedicion de los Catalanes* in dating the departure of the Company from Sicily in 1303; Schlumberger (p. 32) and (by implication) Rodd (ii, p. 71) place it one year earlier. Nobody, so far as I know, has attempted to ex-plain this discrepancy. All agree that the Company reached the Gallipoli peninsula in the autumn of 1304, and Schlumberger (pp. 37, 51, 69) and Rodd (ii, pp. 73–75) fill up the intervening period by extending to nearly two years the length of its sojourn in Asia Minor. The chief reason for adopting the later date is that the former does not allow adequate time for the negotiations of Roger with Andronicus after the peace

THE ENTERPRISE OF ROGER DE FLOR

about 6500 men, most of them light-armed infantry skirmishers, or Almogavares,[1] as they were called; a number of
whom brought with them their wives, mistresses, and children. The expedition at its inception cannot be regarded
as indicating any real intention on the part of the Aragonese
rulers, either in Spain or in Sicily, to extend their empires
into the Levant, or to continue in that region their struggle
with the Angevins, which had been interrupted in the
West by the peace of Caltabelotta. Roger de Flor's enterprise originated as an accidental and independent venture,
and might just as well have been undertaken in opposition
to the ancient Byzantine friends of Aragon as in alliance with
them. On the other hand, as we shall later see, the home
government was not unwilling to turn the issue of the expedition to its own profit and advantage, when the course
of events had sufficiently demonstrated the power of the
Almogavares.[2]

The latter did not wait till they got to Constantinople to
show the stuff they were made of : they incidentally ravaged
the Angevin island of Corfu as they passed.[3] At Constantinople there were great rejoicings over their arrival. Roger
was solemnly invested with the promised title of Grand
Duke, and married, with ceremonies of the utmost magnificence, to the Emperor's niece. But in the midst of the
festivities a violent quarrel broke out between Roger's
troops and the Genoese, who had dominated Constantinople
for some years past, and hated the sight of the Emperor's
allies. Furious fighting ensued, and Muntaner tells us that
over 3000 Italians were found dead in the city streets.

of Caltabelotta, which are described in
chapter cxcix of Muntaner.
    [1] On the meaning and derivation of
this term see Miller, *op. cit.*, p. 214, and
G. Schlumberger, *Expédition des 'Almu-*

gavares' en Orient, pp. 38 f.
    [2] Miller, *op. cit.*, pp. 213 f.; Schlum-
berger, *op. cit.*, p. 33.
    [3] Schlumberger, p. 36.

Andronicus, angered beyond expression by the 'insolent
Latin vagabonds' whom he had enthusiastically welcomed
so shortly before, was now all on fire to get rid of them, and
the threatening approach of the Turks on the other side
of the Bosphorus gave him the desired excuse.[1]   In January, 1304, Roger and his warriors were induced to cross over
into Asia Minor, nominally for the purpose of fighting
the battles of Andronicus against the infidel, practically as
an independent and wellnigh irresistible band of marauders,
whose savage bearing had already cowed their titular
master into sullen submission.   After a bloody encounter
with the Turks, from which they emerged victorious, the
Almogavares settled down to pass the remainder of the
winter at Cyzicus, where they gave themselves up to every
sort of orgy and outrage.   With the coming of spring they
were once more on the march.[2]   Southward across the
great plain of Anatolia they took their way, forcing the
Turks to raise the siege of the ancient city of Philadelphia,
but subsequently levying a war contribution of such immense proportions on the inhabitants that the latter's
joy at their deliverance was speedily exchanged for mourning.   It was much the same story in the succeeding weeks
at Magnesia, Thyraea, and Ephesus.   Meantime the
company kept receiving numerous reënforcements from
Constantinople and from the West; for the fame of its exploits had spread far and near, and all the adventurers of
Europe longed for a place in its ranks and a share in its spoils.
In midsummer, with strengthened forces, the Almogavares
penetrated south and east to the famous Cilician Gates,
which connect the mediaeval Armenia and Anatolia, and
there, on St. Mary's day, under the scorching rays of an

[1] Schlumberger, pp. 38–51.
[2] Schlumberger, pp. 59–69;   Rodd, ii, pp. 73 ff.

August sun, drove a huge army of hostile Turks in headlong flight.[1] Only the prudence of Roger de Flor prevented the band from pushing on to the valleys of the Tigris and Euphrates. As it was, they returned by slow stages, impeded by their enormous booty, to Magnesia, where Roger had left the spoils which had been captured in the previous spring. But the town was now in full revolt against him. The Emperor Andronicus, who had by this time, begun to hate the Catalans " even worse than the double procession of the Holy Ghost," had doubtless inspired the uprising, as a means of putting a spoke in the wheel of his too powerful allies; and when the Almogavares sat down to a siege, he at once intervened and recalled them to Constantinople, on the pretext that he needed them to defend it against a threatened attack by the Bulgars; permission to remain longer in Asia Minor could not fail to render them absolute masters there. With no very good grace, Roger decided to obey, the more readily because of the stout resistance of the Magnesians. It doubtless cost him many a pang to abandon his dream of an independent realm, which had come so near to being realized, but some of his men were getting out of hand, and the risks of staying where he was were very great.[2] In the autumn of 1304, accordingly, the whole Company crossed the straits, and went into winter quarters on the Gallipoli peninsula, which Muntaner describes as "the most delightful cape in the world, with good bread, good wine, and all the fruits in great abundance."[3]

It will readily be believed that the winter of 1304–05 was largely occupied with wrangles between the Emperor and the Catalan leader over the question of pay; Roger kept going back and forth between Constantinople and the

[1] Muntaner, *Chronique* (ed. Buchon), ii, pp. 150–158 (caps. ccv–ccvii); Moncada (ed. Champfeu), pp. 69–98 (lib. i, caps. xli–xvi).

[2] Schlumberger, pp. 106–118.

[3] Muntaner, ii, p. 160 (cap. ccix).

Gallipoli peninsula to settle them. Meantime, matters were greatly complicated by the arrival of a fresh detachment of Catalans, under the famous Berenguer de Entença of ancient Spanish lineage, "in every way Roger's equal as a warrior and plunderer, and his superior in insolence and pride." Very reluctantly, Roger was obliged to recognize the new arrival; he finally passed over to him his title of Grand Duke, though not until he himself had been given permission to assume the still more resounding one of Caesar. But Roger's days were numbered. His negotiations with the Emperor concluded, on terms generally satisfactory to himself, he prepared, in April, 1305, to cross over once more to Asia Minor. Before his departure, however, he visited Constantinople to bid farewell to Michael, the son and colleague of Andronicus, who was vastly less yielding than his father, and was angered beyond measure at the concessions that the Catalan leader had already obtained. The only way to rid himself of the man whom he detested and feared was by murder, but Michael did not shrink from it. A great feast was tendered to Roger at the palace; at the conclusion of it a band of soldiers rushed into the hall, and cut down the guest of honor and his companions.[1]

Furious at the murder of their chief, the Almogavares, under the leadership of Entença, intrenched themselves at Gallipoli and sent a formal defiance to Michael; but the latter put the envoys to death, and ordered the massacre of all the Catalans that could be found in Constantinople. The ranks of the Company were further depleted by numerous desertions, but several thousand still remained; and as the old lust for conquest and rapine burned stronger than ever within their breasts, they improvised a fleet, and

[1] Muntaner, ii, pp. 161–173 (caps.   ii, caps. i–ix); Schlumberger, pp. 119–
ccx–ccxv); Moncada, pp. 109–163 (lib.   157.

began a wild career of piracy in the adjacent waters. They were no less efficient on sea than on land. A number of victories were won against superior forces, till finally Entença and his followers were induced to board a Genoese galley under a safe conduct, which was promptly violated. The Catalan fleet was dispersed, and Entença was held by his captors for an enormous ransom, first at Trebizond, and finally at Genoa. But even now the courage of the Almogavares never flagged. Berenguer de Rocafort, a soldier of humble origin, was chosen captain of the band in solemn council. With his election all traces of aristocratic influence in the Company's organization disappeared. An ultra-democratic form of government was gradually installed, in which military efficiency was the only road to authority, the supreme power being vested in a council of twelve captains. In vain did the Greeks besiege the Gallipoli peninsula. A handful of men sufficed to hold at bay the entire Empire of the East. Catalan ravaging expeditions into Thrace and Macedonia invariably returned laden with booty and captives, which were sold at enormous profit. From 1305 to 1307 Gallipoli became in fact the great slave market of the East, and a source of supply for the harems of the emirs of Asia Minor. In the midst of all these activities, Entença returned, liberated at last from his Genoese prison through the efforts of James of Aragon, to whom the Company had thrice applied for the purpose; as he could not possibly get on with the plain, blunt Rocafort, the Company soon split into two independent bands. The inevitable quarrel between them broke out in the end of the year 1307, and resulted in the death of Entença, Rocafort being left for the time the dominant personality in the situation. At about the same time the Company, having exhausted the possibilities of Gallipoli, moved across to the mainland of Thrace and Macedonia, where its previous devastations had convinced the inhabitants of the futility of resistance.[1]

And now new factors came into play, which were destined to terminate the wanderings of this strange marauding band. Even in its palmiest days, it had never abandoned the pretence of being in the service of King Frederic of· Sicily. Officially all its acts were accomplished in his name, and it carried the banners of Sicily and of Aragon with it into battle.[2] All this made it natural that the Sicilian monarch should attempt to recover effective control of it and of the territories which it had conquered; and as a preliminary step toward this end, he sent out his cousin [3] Ferdinand, a younger son of King James I of Majorca, to take command of it. But Rocafort, who had tasted the sweets of independent power and had no mind to surrender his leadership to this scion of Aragonese royalty, plotted against him from the moment of his arrival, and forced him to return with his mission unaccomplished;[4] then, realizing that his action amounted to a declaration of revolt against his sovereign, he anxiously cast about him for means of support in case his authority should be challenged again. In so doing he naturally turned his attention first of all toward the potentates of the Grecian peninsula, to whose domains he was being brought nearer and nearer every day, as the Catalans pursued their spoliations in

[1] Moncada, pp. 164–332 (lib. ii, caps. x–xxviii; lib. iii, caps. i–vi); Schlumberger, pp. 158–292.

[2] Miller, p. 215.

[3] Not 'nephew,' as Schlumberger (p. 271) has it.

[4] On the subsequent career of Ferdinand, who was accompanied by the chronicler Muntaner on his return, cf. Muntaner, ii, pp. 214–230 (caps.

ccxxx–ccxxxiii); *Historia General del Reino de Mallorca*, by J. Dameto and others (second edition by Moragues and Bover), iii, pp. 8 ff., 25 ff.; Schlumberger, pp. 297–311 and 324 ff.; Miller, pp. 215–217, 253 ff. Rubió y Lluch has published a study of him in vol. viii of *Estudis Universitaris Catalans*, which I have not been able to see.

Macedonia and Thrace;[1] and he finally opened negotiations
with the last of the de la Roche dukes of Athens, who had
been established there as a result of the Fourth Crusade.
There were plans of a marriage between the Catalan leader
and a kinswoman of the duke, and of joint action against
their various foes; but before matters could come to any
definite conclusion a strong faction in the ranks of the
Company itself, irritated at Rocafort's dealings with outside powers, and suspicious of his personal ambitions, rose
in revolt, and finally handed him over to the custody of a
French noble, Thibaut de Chepoy; the latter surrendered
him to the tender mercies of the Angevin king of Naples,
and he died shortly afterwards of starvation in the dungeons
of Aversa. But the elimination of Rocafort did not terminate the dealings of the Company with the Athenian authorities. The Catalans were by this time ravaging Thessaly
with a vengeance; but that warlike country yielded them
more hard knocks than booty, and the fierce inhabitants
pointedly assured their unwelcome guests that better opportunities for plunder awaited them in Boeotia and Attica.
Obviously the Company was destined to appear in the neighborhood of Athens before many months elapsed; obviously,
also, it would depend on the attitude of the authorities there
whether it came as friend or foe. Meanwhile the last of
the de la Roche dukes died (October 5, 1308) and was succeeded by his cousin, Walter de Brienne; and the latter,
who had taken the measure of the Catalans and did not
relish the prospect of having them any nearer to himself
than was absolutely necessary, offered them a substantial
reward to remain in Thessaly and complete the conquest
of it in his name. This programme was successfully carried

[1] Until the spring of 1309, however, their headquarters were at Kassandreia — the ancient Potidaea — at the neck of the westernmost of the three peninsulas to the southeast of Salonica. Miller, pp. 216, 221 f.

out in the summer of 1310; but its accomplishment was followed by a violent quarrel between the Athenian duke and the Company, because of the latter's unwillingness to vacate the territories it had won.   On the insolent refusal of the Catalans to depart, Walter contemptuously announced that he would expel them, and summoned all the great princes of the Morea to rally to his standard.   The friendly Angevins in Achaia, for whose cause he had fought in Sicily, gladly sent him a large contingent; the Venetians in Negropont supported him: whether we accept Muntaner's estimate — 24,700 [1] — or that of the Chronicle of the Morea — 6000 [2] — as the size of his army, we may rest assured that it was the mightiest host that had ever assembled under the banner of a duke of Athens, brimful of confidence, and eager for victory.   But the savage Catalans were more than equal to the occasion.   Issuing out into the great Boeotian plain, they took up their position in some marshy ground, which they further extended by diverting the waters of an adjacent stream, hard by the spot where Philip of Macedon, more than sixteen centuries before, had won "that dishonest victory of Chaeronea, fatal to liberty"; and there they awaited the onslaught of the chivalry of Frankish Greece.   On March 15, 1311, the battle of the Cephissus took place.   Walter's horsemen plunged all unsuspecting into the treacherous morass; stuck fast in the clinging mud, they were ingloriously shot down or stabbed by their crafty foes; Walter and the great majority of his knights were numbered among the slain. Like the battle of Courtrai, nine years before, it was one of the earliest and most striking demonstrations of the superiority of infantry, properly handled, over cavalry; of

[1] Muntaner, ii, pp. 251 f. (cap. ccxl).   Latin, p. 120.   The French translation
[2] *Chronique de Morée*, ed. by A.   overlooks the word "dos" before "mil"
Morel-Fatio for the Société de l'Orient   on the opposite page, line 8.

a democratic over an aristocratic fighting machine. Thus at last, after a life of a hundred and six years, the French duchy of Athens came to a sudden and tragic end.[1]

By this time the Catalans were ready to abandon their roving life, and they accordingly determined to settle down and establish themselves permanently in the territories they had won. With the adoption of a sedentary existence, however, they began to feel the need of outside recognition and support. They were surrounded on every side by foes whom they could not, unaided, hope permanently to withstand; they consequently reversed the policy of Rocafort, and applied to Frederic of Sicily to send them one of his children, to be their leader in peace and war. Frederic was only too glad to avail himself of this opportunity to extend his dominion over the conquests of the Almogavares. As his oldest available son, Manfred, was still too young to assume the Company's leadership, he sent out Berenguer Estañol, a knight of Ampurias, to govern for the time being as Manfred's representative. From the date of Berenguer's arrival, we may justly regard the duchy of Athens as formally connected with the kingdom of Sicily, and therefore as a semi-independent eastern outpost of the Aragonese Empire.[2] On Estañol's death in 1316, King Frederic appointed his illegitimate son, Alfonso Fadrique, in his stead; since Manfred, whose representative the latter theoretically was, died in November, 1317, Alfonso Fadrique governed Athens in the name of Frederic's third legitimate son, William, who was likewise a minor, until his retirement in 1330.[3] In the following period the duchy continued to be ruled by a series of governors in the name of the suc-

[1] The best modern account of these events is given in Miller, op. cit., pp. 216–229; there is a valuable note on the battle of the Cephissus on p. 229.

[2] Miller, pp. 235 f.

[3] Miller, pp. 242 f.; S. V. Bosso, Note storiche Siciliane del Secolo XIV, pp. 456 f.

cessive descendants of King Frederic, who one after another inherited the title of duke of Athens, though they never visited Greece. In 1355 the Catalan conquests in the East were bound for the first time in personal union to Sicily, through the deaths of all Frederic's legitimate offspring except one grandson, who bore his name, and fell heir to all his dominions.[1] At the death, twenty-two years later, of this Frederic — whose feeble rule in Sicily was painfully reflected in the incompetent government of his representatives in Athens — he left all his domains to his daughter Maria.[2] The Sicilians accepted her, but the Catalans in the East refused. Knowing that they stood in need of more vigorous outside aid against their many foes than Maria would be able to accord, they offered their sovereignty to Pedro IV, the mighty king of Aragon, who promptly accepted it, and promised to send out a governor to represent him on the ground.[3] Thus at last was the duchy regularly incorporated in the empire of Aragon itself, the ancient Sicilian connection which it had maintained for so long being definitely and permanently broken. Many years earlier than this, moreover, the papacy, which had originally visited the Catalans with excommunication, decided that it would be wise to absolve them, and permit them to be reconciled with Mother Church. They might be 'sons of perdition,' but they were also a bulwark against the Turks. Now that they had won for themselves a permanent habitation, it was possible to give them official recognition as respectable members of society.[4]

At the same time that their status was being secured with the outside world, the Catalans proceeded to remodel the internal government of the duchy of Athens. Beginning

---

[1] Miller, p. 278; also Stokvis, *Manuel d'histoire*, ii, p. 467.
[2] Miller, p. 305.
[3] Miller, pp. 305 f.
[4] Miller, pp. 276–278.

under the rule of Estañol, they gradually evolved a constitution, closely resembling that of Catalonia, for their new domain, of which Thebes, not Athens, was the capital. There were a vicar-general and a marshal, appointed by the king's representative, and holding under him the chief political and military powers in the state; there was an elaborate system of local government under *veguers*, *castellanos*, and *capitans*; there was a large measure of popular liberty, and a sort of parliament, or meeting of the *sindici*, representing the principal towns and villages. No offices were to be granted to any outsiders, not even to Sicilians or Aragonese; Attica was to be for the Catalans who had taken it and their descendants — the 'Conquistadores,' as they called themselves, like the later Castilian empire builders in America. 'The Usages of Barcelona' supplanted the 'Assizes of Romania,' and Catalan became the official as well as the ordinary language. The conquered Greeks were treated as a subject race; they were excluded as a rule from the enjoyment of civic rights, and the Greek church was relegated to a position of inferiority to that of the West.[1] During the early part of their rule, moreover, the Catalans continued to extend their conquests. After successfully repelling an attempt of the heirs of Walter de Brienne to recover the duchy,[2] they attacked the Venetians in Negropont, and would probably have conquered the island had they not been ordered by Frederic of Sicily to desist.[3] In 1318, on the extinction of the reigning dynasty in Thessaly, they promptly occupied the southern part of that

[1] Miller, pp. 235–239; A. Rubió y Lluch, *La Expedición y Dominación de los Catalanes en Oriente* (Barcelona, 1883); also three monographs by the latter on "Atenès en Temps dels Catalans," "Els Castells Catalans de la Grecia continental," and "Els governs de Matheu de Moncada y Roger de Lluria en la Grecia Catalana," in *Anuari de l'Institut d'Estudis Catalans*, 1907, pp. 225–254; 1908, pp. 364–425; 1911–12, pp. 3–58.
[2] Rodd, ii, pp. 171–174.
[3] Miller, pp. 243 f.

country and erected it into the Catalan duchy of Neopatras, whose title was proudly borne, together with that of Athens, by Sicilian kings and Aragonese sovereigns long after the effective domination of the Catalans in the Near East had passed away.[1]   But it is interesting to observe that the subsequent years of the Catalans' dominion in Athens saw no further extension of these easy conquests.   The period of the rule of Alfonso Fadrique (1316–30) witnessed the zenith of their power; from that time onward they began to lose those magnificent fighting qualities which had won them their place in the world.   Despite occasional raids into hostile territory to kindle enthusiasm for war, the life of Thebes and Athens bore little resemblance to that of the Anatolian plains and the peninsula of Gallipoli. Discipline could no longer be maintained; luxury and corruption crept in; the drunken descendants of the hardy victors of the Cephissus surrendered themselves to a life of sloth and debauchery on their great estates.   By the time that the Catalan duchy had transferred itself (1377) from Sicilian to Aragonese obedience, its occupants were no longer invincible.   Their dominion was approaching its end.[2]

The power that was ultimately destined to oust the Catalans from their possessions in Attica and Thessaly was an upstart family of Florentine 'steel kings' and bankers, called the Acciajuoli, who had long been attached to the Angevins in Naples, and, while furthering their patrons' ventures in the Morea, financially and otherwise, had incidentally managed to acquire territory there for themselves.   In 1358 they got Corinth, and in 1373 Megara — this last on the ground of the refusal of the Catalans to hand over to them certain fugitive vassals — and thus possessed themselves of the

---

[1] Miller, pp. 246–248.   [2] Miller, pp. 277 ff.

high road into the Athenian duchy from the south.[1] Further than this they did not venture for the present to advance, for the Catalans were still regarded as formidable
foes — more formidable by far than they actually were —
and the Acciajuoli did not dare to attack them until the
assaults of other enemies had weakened them still more.
This necessary preliminary, however, was speedily accomplished by the famous Navarrese Company, composed,
like its Catalan predecessor, of a host of professional soldiers, whom the peace of Bretigny had permitted their
original employer, the notorious Charles the Bad, to dis-
miss from his service, but whom Jacques de Baux, a claim-
ant of the duchy of Achaia and also one of the numberless
titular Emperors of Constantinople, had determined to
utilize for purposes of his own.[2] As a preliminary to the
conquest of Achaia, de Baux launched these Navarrese
mercenaries against the Catalan Grand Company from the
northward; in 1380 they advanced triumphantly across
Boeotia, but were finally stopped by the defences of the
Acropolis.[3] The delay before the walls of the Athenian
citadel gave the Catalans time to meet and memorialize
their absent sovereign, Pedro IV of Aragon.   In a petition
which clearly indicates how completely their pristine vigor
had been sapped, they begged him to send them a vicar-
general who would protect them from the invaders.   After
some delay, the king complied, and finally despatched to
Athens Philip Dalemar, Viscount of Rocaberti; the latter
arrived in the autumn of 1381, and, turning on the Navarrese Company, speedily drove it out of the duchy into the
Peloponnesus, where it subsequently established itself in
Achaia.[4] But the expulsion of the Navarrese was only a

---

[1] Miller, pp. 270–272, 285 f., 304.
[2] Cf. Rubió y Lluch, *Los Navarros en Grecia* (Barcelona, 1886).
[3] Miller, pp. 310–312.
[4] Zurita, ii, ff. 377–378; Miller, pp. 312–316.

preliminary to a fresh invasion of the Acciajuoli.   The latter
had keenly watched from their outposts at Corinth and
Megara the gradual disintegration of the Catalan state,
and realized how completely the expulsion of the Navarrese
had exhausted it.   When at last Rocaberti fell into dis-
favor with King Pedro and was recalled, they saw that
their chance had come.   The scornful rejection by the chief
heiress of Catalan Athens of an offer of marriage from the
leader of the Acciajuoli served as the pretext for launching the long postponed attack.   The details of the invasion
are almost unknown to us.   It probably began in 1385,
but the conquest was not finally accomplished till May,
1388, owing to the resistance for sixteen long months,
after the rest of Athens had surrendered, of a handful of men
in the Acropolis.[1]   Frequent embassies were despatched
to the home government to beg for relief; but Pedro,
though his enthusiasm for the architectural glories of ancient
Greece was outspoken and unbounded,[2] was unable to render any practical aid in the defence of his distant dominions.
With the fall of the Acropolis in 1388, the Catalans disappeared from the soil of Attica like clouds in the rays of
a summer sun.   Whither they all went, and how they were
so rapidly dispersed, it is impossible fully to explain.   Many
took ship and sailed westward to Sicily or Barcelona;
others lingered on in the East, but there was no element of
permanence in their conquests.   Few, if any, traces of their
presence can be detected in Athens today; and the fact
that the word 'Catalan' was long used there as a term of
opprobrium and reproach sufficiently indicates the general

---

[1] Miller, pp. 322–326.

[2] Miller, p. 315: cf. Pedro's order
to send twelve men-at-arms to guard
the Acropolis (Sept. 11, 1380): "major-
ment con lo dit castell sia la pus richa
joya qui al mont sia e tal que entre tots
los Reys de cristians envides lo porien
fer semblant." Rubió y Lluch, Los
Navarros en Grecia, p. 233.

impression they left on the native Greeks. The sister duchy
of Neopatras fell to the Acciajuoli with that of Athens, but
the Catalans managed to maintain themselves in the adjacent county of Salona till 1394, and their pretensions to the
island of Aegina were not entirely abandoned until 1451.[1]

It is not easy to pass judgment on this curious episode
in the development of the Aragonese Empire. However
remiss they may have been in failing to take practical measures to prevent the loss of their possessions in Greece, it
is certain that the Aragonese and Sicilian sovereigns, their
successors, and their subjects were intensely proud of their
brief connection with the home of classical civilization.[2]
The humanist Alfonso the Magnanimous actually made an
abortive attempt to recover the lost duchies, and the titles
to them continued to figure among the dignities of the
Spanish crown down to the end of the seventeenth century.[3]
But whether or not it would have been 'practical politics'
for Pedro IV to have attempted to retain them, in the
circumstances that obtained in the end of the fourteenth
century, is quite another question. They were, after all,
remote, and isolated amidst hostile states; moreover,
since they had been acquired as it were accidentally, rather
than by a regularly organized national effort with the support of the home government, there was comparatively little

[1] Miller, pp. 325–330, 347. On the
subsequent history of the Navarrese
Company in Achaia see Rubió y Lluch,
Los Navarros en Grecia, pp. 160–204.
Its career was much briefer and more
checkered than that of the Catalans;
but it maintained a high reputation for
military efficiency during the closing
years of the fourteenth century. Its
name is perpetuated today in the famous
town and harbor of Navarino (Rubió y
Lluch, op. cit., p. 168), which it had
captured in 1382. In 1430 its dominions
were acquired by Thomas Palaeologus,
who thirty years later retired to Rome,
after having been deprived of his possessions by the Turks, and died a pen-
sioner of Pope Pius II. His son Andrew
made over his claims to Achaia first to
Charles VIII of France in 1494, and
then, ten years later, to Ferdinand the
Catholic of Spain, after the latter had
completed the conquest of Naples.
Hence the title of 'Prince of the Morea'
which was borne by the Spanish monarchs for two centuries to come.
[2] Miller, p. 325.
[3] Miller, pp. 411, 416, 429–431; F.
Cerone, in Archivio storico per le Province Napoletane, xxvii (1902), pp. 427 ff.

loss of prestige in letting them go. Certainly the Aragonese monarchs had on their hands a host of other problems, of greater importance and far nearer home, and could ill afford to dissipate their energies. When one remembers how the Spanish Empire suffered in later days from the wide dispersion of the territories that composed it, one is inclined to applaud the restraint of the monarch who declined to exhaust his resources in the endeavor to preserve a dominion so remote.

BIBLIOGRAPHICAL NOTE

See note to the preceding chapter, and add:

Contemporary Authorities. — *Libro de los Fechos et Conquistas del Principado de la Morea*, compiled at the order of Johan Ferrándes de Heredia, grand master of the Order of St. John of Jerusalem: Spanish text and French translation (*Chronique de Morée*), ed. Alfred Morel-Fatio (Geneva, 1885). On this interesting chronicle, which was finished in 1393, see the preface to the above edition, and also Ballester y Castell, *Fuentes Narrativas*, pp. 153 ff.

Later Works. — Francisco de Moncada's *Espedicion de los Catalanes y Aragoneses contra Turcos y Griegos* (Barcelona, 1623; also Madrid, 1858, in vol. i of *Historiadores de Sucesos Particulares*, in *B.A.E.*; excellent French translation, with a good introduction, by the Comte de Champfeu (Paris, 1828); my references are to this) is the work of a noted scholar and statesman, viceroy of the Spanish Netherlands, and ambassador at the Imperial Court, who lived from 1586 to 1645. Gustave Schlumberger's *Expédition des 'Almugavares,' ou routiers catalans, en Orient* (Paris, 1902) is a brilliant study, which unfortunately stops in 1311. William Miller, *The Latins in the Levant* (New York, 1908), is indispensable, and Sir Rennell Rodd, *The Princes of Achaia* (London, 1907, 2 vols.), and S. V. Bozzo, *Note storiche Siciliane del Secolo XIV* (Palermo, 1882), are very useful. Antonio Rubió y Lluch, in his *La Expedición y Dominación de los Catalanes en Oriente* (Barcelona, 1883), and in his *Los Navarros en Grecia y el Ducado Catalán de Atenas* (Barcelona, 1886), has made the most thorough study of the latter years of the existence of the Catalan duchy; and Francesco Cerone, in "La Politica Orientale de Alfonso di Aragona" in *Archivio storico per le province Napoletane*, anno xxvii (1902), pp. 3–93, 380–456, 555–634, 774–852, and anno xxviii, pp. 154–212, tells of the efforts made to revive the power of Aragon in Greece during the fifteenth century.

CHAPTER IX

A MEDITERRANEAN EMPIRE

We now return to the realms of the Crown of Aragon and their dependencies in the western basin of the Mediterranean, which we left at the death of James II in 1327. The brief and generally unimportant reign of the latter's son and heir, Alfonso IV, is little more than a transition period. As far as the history of Aragonese expansion in the Mediterranean is concerned, it is absolutely without significance, save for a serious revolt in the newly conquered island of Sardinia. In this the lead was taken by the Genoese, who had now turned their arms against their quondam allies from Aragon, and attempted to expel them from the island. The rebellion began at the instigation of the Dorias, who had come into conflict with the Aragonese officials in the commune of Sassari. As the viceroy who represented Alfonso in the island was unable to maintain himself alone, it became necessary to send him reënforcements; and in order to obtain these in sufficient numbers the king was obliged to desist from a campaign which he had begun against the Moors of Granada. Meantime the Genoese redoubled their efforts. A furious struggle blazed up all over Sardinia and in the adjacent seas as far as the coasts of Italy and Catalonia. On land, the Genoese had emphatically the better of the argument. In a few years they mastered all the island except Sassari, Cagliari, and Iglesias; and these might well have fallen also, had not Alfonso opened negotiations for a treaty, which was not concluded till after his death, and was in general so lame and ambiguous as to make it little more than the prelude to another war. On the sea the contest was somewhat more even, and the fighting violent in the extreme; so much so, in fact, as to suggest that there was more at stake between the rival powers than the possession of an unprofitable and unhealthy island. As a matter of fact, the conflicting economic interests of the two powers were the underlying cause of their hostility. Both aspired to the commercial hegemony of the western Mediterranean, and were determined to go to any length to attain it. They had already encountered one another in North Africa and in the Levant, and now the Sardinian question had brought them more openly into collision than ever before; but the title to the island was, after all, rather a pretext than a cause of their strife. The struggle between them went on intermittently throughout the remainder of the fourteenth century and beyond, until the decline of Genoa made it impossible for her to continue it; and it was in Sardinia that she contrived with the aid of the native population to maintain the fight the longest. The island was not wholly conquered by the Aragonese, as we shall later see, till 1421.[1]

Alfonso IV was twice married, first to Teresa de Entença, a noble dame of Aragonese birth, and second to Eleanor, sister of Alfonso XI of Castile. Each wife bore him two sons: those of the first were called Pedro and James, and those of the second Ferdinand and John; and the last years of Alfonso's life were clouded by a bitter feud between Queen Eleanor on the one side and the Infante Pedro on

[1] Zurita, ii, ff. 95–98, 100 f.; Bofarull, iv, pp. 260 ff.; R. St.-H., iv, pp. 391 f.; G. Manno, *Storia di Sardegna*, ii, pp. 23–30.

the other. For us the main interest of the conflict, in which
at one time it seemed probable that Eleanor would win
for her children the crown that was unquestionably Pedro's
by hereditary right, lies in the fact that it served to develop
at a very early age the character and ability of the Infante.[1]
When in his twentieth year he finally succeeded to the throne
of his father — Eleanor and her children having fled to
Castile at the last moment — he had already reached ma-
turity. Within a frail and sickly body he concealed a
bold, crafty, rancorous, and defiant heart. To reign in
fact as well as in name was his life's ¦study and object, re-
lentlessly pursued through all the vicissitudes of fortune.
Neither family ties nor friendships held him back. The
attainment of the end justified in his eyes the use of any
and every means. He was most dangerous when seemingly
impotent, and a past master of sheltering himself in his
most atrocious acts behind the technicalities of the law.
He has often been compared to Louis XI of France; but
he differed sharply from that monarch in his fondness for
pomp and outward magnificence, and in his implicit belief
in their value as a means to impress the multitude. He is
known in the long history of the Aragonese kings as the
'Ceremonious'; he was the author of a special treatise on
the duties and privileges of the officials of his court; and
like King Frederick I of Prussia, and in defiance of ancient
precedent, he insisted on crowning himself at his accession,
"to show that he held the throne of God alone and of no
earthly power."[2]

The main interest of his reign lies in domestic affairs, in
his successful efforts to raise the monarchy from the depths
of degradation to which baronial revolt and constitutional

[1] Bofarull, iv, pp. 262-278.
[2] *Crónica de Pedro* (ed. Bofarull), pp.
80 f.; R. St.-H., v, pp. 1 f., 13 f., 53;

Lafuente, vii, pp. 143-145; K. Schwarz,
Aragonische Hofordnungen, pp. 41-
121.

limitations had consigned it; and all this we shall examine
in another place. Abroad, however, he was by no means
inactive, and in the fifty-one years during which he occupied the throne he succeeded in strengthening in three
different directions the position which Aragon had already
won beyond the seas. He put an end to the separate existence of the kingdom of Majorca, and incorporated the
greater part of it in his own domains. He kept alive the
power of Aragon in Sardinia through a difficult and turbulent
period. He prepared the way for the reunion with Aragon
of Sicily. We will take up these different phases of Pedro's
activities in the order named.

At the time of Pedro's accession in 1336, the throne of
the Majorcan realm had been occupied for twelve years
by the third of the separate line of kings — James, the
grandson of that James of Majorca who had been expelled
from the Balearics by Alfonso III, but had been subsequently restored to them under Aragonese suzerainty in
1298, as a sequel of the treaty of Anagni. In addition to
Majorca, Minorca, and Iviza, it will be remembered that
his realms also included Cerdagne, Roussillon, and Montpellier on the mainland; but over the last of these three
territories the suzerainty of the king of France had been
recognized since the middle of the thirteenth century, while
a small part of the town of Montpellier, commonly called
Montpellieret, had been ceded, in 1293, in full ownership
to the French monarch, and formed an integral part of the
royal domain.[1] It will readily be understood that the
relationship between the sovereigns of France and Majorca
which this complicated situation in Montpellier created
was delicate in the extreme. The Majorcan rulers often
entirely disregarded the rights of the French kings in

[1] Cf. ante, p. 289, note 1; Lecoy,'l, pp. 139, 148, 311-337.

the districts in question and insisted on exercising all the
jurisdiction and privileges of full ownership; the French
kings equally resolutely refused to be elbowed aside. So
irksome, indeed, was the position during part of the reign
of the comparatively pacific Sancho (1311–24), the second
king of the separate Majorcan line, that the latter forgot his grudges against his cousin, the king of Aragon,
who was his feudal suzerain in the rest of his dominions,
and sought to make common cause with him against the
king of France.[1] It was, in fact, by a skilful process of
playing off their two overlords, the French and Aragonese
monarchs, against one another, that Sancho and his father
had managed to preserve the separate existence of their
scattered domains;[2] but when in 1324 the second King
James, nephew of Sancho, ascended the Majorcan throne,
a bolder but ultimately fatal policy was inaugurated.
James of Majorca was the equal of his cousin and brother-
in-law,[3] King Pedro of Aragon, in violence if not in craft.
Nothing short of absolute autonomy in his domains would
satisfy him, and he rashly defied both his suzerains at once.
He openly flouted the representatives of Philip of Valois
in Montpellier, and eagerly availed himself of every possible
opportunity to pour contempt upon his overlordship. At
the same time he scornfully ignored the repeated summons
of Pedro of Aragon to come and do him homage for the
Balearics, and intrigued with the latter's worst enemies in
Castile, in Naples, and in Morocco.[4] In the year 1339,
indeed, he had a change of heart. Yielding to papal entreaties, he crossed to Barcelona to acknowledge formally
the suzerainty of his brother-in-law; but the ensuing
ceremony was such as served to increase rather than to

[1] Lecoy, i, pp. 379 ff.
[2] Lecoy, i, pp. 394 f.
[3] He had married Constance, the
daughter of Alfonso IV. Lecoy, ii,
p. 13.
[4] Lecoy, ii, pp. 31–36, 40–54.

diminish the friction between the two monarchs. The Aragonese king apparently took a malicious pleasure in causing James to remain standing for a quarter of an hour, while he solemnly discussed with his counsellors whether or not it would be advisable to provide him with a cushion to sit on; and when the question was finally decided in the affirmative, it was observed that the cushion which was brought was conspicuously lower than that of Pedro. A subsequent clash between the attendants of the two sovereigns angered the king of Aragon so terribly that he was only prevented from killing James on the spot by the fact that the sword of state which he was wearing and attempted to draw could not be extracted from the scabbard. Memories of the past faithlessness of Majorcan monarchs surged up in the mind of the rancorous king of Aragon, and he resolved, then and there, to seize the first possible chance to correct the error of his ancestor James the Conqueror in dividing his inheritance, and definitely and finally to incorporate the Balearic realm and its continental dependencies into his own dominions.[1]

The opportunity which he sought was not long in presenting itself; and it was the direct result of James's reckless dealings with King Philip of France. In the year 1341 their quarrel in Montpellier came to a head. The Majorcan king had recently strengthened himself by a treaty with Edward III of England, whose armies had already made their appearance in Normandy. More confident than ever in the support of this new ally, he gloried in publicly defying the behests of his French overlord.[2] The culmination of his rebellious deeds was reached in the month of March, when, after publicly protesting that he no longer recognized the suzerainty of France, he presumed to organize and

[1] Lecoy, ii, pp. 60 f.; Zurita, ii, f. 138.   [2] Lecoy, ii, pp. 30 ff.

celebrate a tournament at Montpellier, in direct violation of Philip's commands, and further, on the attempt of the royal representatives to interfere, caused the king's scutcheons in the city to be torn down and the king's officers and notaries to be expelled.[1] Open hostilities were sooner or later inevitable, and James, foreseeing them, approached the king of Aragon; for so completely had his last quarrel with the king of France obliterated the remembrance of his earlier broils with Pedro, that he now hoped to convert the latter into an ally.[2] But Pedro had a longer memory than his rash brother-in-law, and a statesman's ability to discern that the moment for which he had waited so long had at last arrived. To James's petitions for aid he replied with deceitful counsels to avoid hostilities, and thus furnished the French king an opportunity to occupy Montpellier. Having thus increased rather than diminished his brother-in-law's perplexities in one quarter, he subjected him to fresh humiliation in another by convoking the Catalan Cortes at Barcelona and summoning James to appear at once, under threat of a declaration of feudal felony and forfeiture if he refused.[3] Against methods like these the king of Majorca was powerless; on his failure to arrive at the appointed time, King Pedro, in February, 1343, declared that his domains were reunited to the Crown of Aragon. When, too late, James finally did appear, Pedro falsely accused him of plotting against his life, and thus provoked him into a defiance which gave an excuse for carrying the sentence into effect.[4] Needless to add, every preparation had been already made. Tithes which had been wrung from the clergy to be used in a crusade against the Moors in North Africa were diverted to furnish

[1] Lecoy, ii, pp. 36–38.
[2] Lecoy, ii, p. 43.
[3] Lecoy, ii, pp. 58 ff.
[4] *Proceso contra el Rey Jaime III* in *D. I. A.*, vols. xxix–xxxi; *Crónica de Pedro IV*, pp. 122–130.

a fleet to attack the Balearics; the king himself was in command of it, while his brother led a simultaneous expedition against Cerdagne and Roussillon. The Balearic campaign lasted only one month. The population was probably less hostile to James than is usually represented, and many isolated deeds of valor were performed in his cause; but the Majorcans stood no chance against the disciplined soldiers of the king of Aragon, and after a feeble attempt to dispute his advance on the heights above Santa Ponza, resistance was virtually at an end. Minorca and Iviza promptly followed. The Pope, who dreaded the increased power of the king of Aragon, attempted to effect a compromise, but only postponed the inevitable. The incorporation of the islands into the realms of the Crown of Aragon was virtually complete by the end of June, and James of Majorca confessed it by fleeing overseas to Cerdagne and Roussillon, whither he was immediately followed by his implacable brother-in-law.[1]

The struggle over the continental portions of the Majorcan realm was much more prolonged. A campaign of devastation, vigorously pursued, finally resulted in the submission of all Cerdagne and Roussillon, except the fortress of Perpignan, which defied every assault of Pedro's Almogavares; but when his military forces were inadequate, the king of Aragon was more than able to supply their deficiencies by masterful diplomacy and intrigue. On July 15, 1344, he held an interview with his brother-in-law under the walls of Perpignan, which Pedro describes in his chronicle in terms of haughty satisfaction.[2] It resulted in an arrangement by which James gave up Perpignan and all the other strong places in the counties to Pedro, in return

[1] On this and the preceding paragraph see *Historia General del Reino de Mallorca* by J. Dameto and others, iii. pp. 143–215.
[2] *Crónica de Pedro IV*, pp. 215 f.

for the latter's pledge "to treat him with pity and grace"
— a phrase which was certainly susceptible of many inter-
pretations, but which James, in view of certain preliminary
negotiations, was fully justified in regarding as a promise of
pardon, peace, and recognition of his royal title. Needless to add, Pedro had no intention of redeeming his pledge
in any such way as this; but for the present his treachery
had served its purpose. The keys of Perpignan were
handed over to him; the garrison welcomed him within its
walls. After an entry characterized by all the pomp and
magnificence which were so dear to his heart, he proceeded
to the church of St. John, and there, on the twenty-second
of July, solemnly proclaimed and confirmed the annexation
of Cerdagne and Roussillon to the rest of his hereditary
domains. The struggle was not, as a matter of fact, quite
over, either here or in the Balearics, but the invader had
gained a hold on his prey, and was not destined to relinquish
it.[1]

It did not take James of Majorca long to discover that
the hopes which he had built on Pedro's promises were the
merest castles in the air. His first disillusionment came
in the shape of a contemptuous offer from his brother-in-
law of a miserable pension of 10,000 livres, in return for his
renunciation of all title to Cerdagne and Roussillon and the
Balearics, coupled with a scornful promise to recognize his
rights in Montpellier, which Pedro, on account of its re-
moteness and predominantly French sympathies, had wisely
determined to leave alone. Stung to madness by this
insulting proposal, so different from what he had anticipated, James gathered a few faithful followers around him
and fled to France. On the way he passed through a corner
of Cerdagne, where the inhabitants, who still cherished some

[1] Lecoy, ii, pp. 109-135.

devotion to him, offered their support in an attempt to regain his lands; but the affair was so badly managed and Pedro so keenly on the watch, that after a few encounters, in which James had all the worst of it, the royal fugitive was driven to seek safety in Montpellier.[1] There the representatives of Philip VI received him cordially. The king of France bore no lasting grudge against him for his former conduct, and dreaded the progress of the armies of the king of Aragon north of the Pyrenees. Had it not been for the fact that the war against England, which was going badly, occupied all his attention in the North, it is more than probable that Philip would have actually supported James against Pedro. But as things were, it would have been madness for him to offend the powerful king of Aragon, who, though he was too prudent to attempt to win Montpellier for himself, had determined that the French monarch should not give shelter to his enemy, and loudly complained of an attempted expedition for the recovery of the Balearics, on which James, with French support, embarked in 1347.[2] Finally in the spring of 1349, as the easiest way out of an intolerable situation, Philip purchased all the rights of the king of Majorca in Montpellier for 120,000 écus d'or, thus terminating the separate existence of the only portion of the Majorcan realm which had escaped the clutches of Pedro by annexing it to the lands of the crown of France.[3] The unfortunate James utilized the funds which he had received from this sale to fit out a final expedition for the recovery of the Balearics. He managed to effect a landing at Majorca, but was completely defeated there on October 25, 1349, in a pitched battle between Palma and Luchmayor, by Pedro's Almogavares. The latter had been instructed beforehand to secure at all costs,

[1] Lecoy, ii, pp. 136–145. [2] Lecoy, ii, pp. 146–154. [3] Lecoy, ii, pp. 154–163.

either dead or alive, the body of the Majorcan king; and when one of them, cutting his way through the densest of the mêlée, attained his object and held up James's severed head to the gaze of the combatants, the battle ceased as if by magic. It was a fitting end for a prince whose dauntless courage redeemed a multitude of faults.[1]

Pedro's new possessions caused him considerable difficulty during the remaining years of his reign. The old desire for independence in the different portions of the Balearic realm was by no means extinguished, and when the son and namesake of James of Majorca, who had been taken prisoner by Pedro's Almogavares in the battle of 1349, escaped, thirteen years later, from his jailers, and married, as her third husband, the notorious Joanna of Naples, he managed to breed constant trouble for the king of Aragon until his death in 1375.[2] He played a considerable rôle in the war with Castile, was the ally of Pedro the Cruel and Edward the Black Prince, and a prisoner of Henry of Trastamara; in the last year of his life he vainly attempted a descent on Catalonia through Cerdagne and Roussillon on the north. His claims passed at his death to his sister Isabella, and from her to Duke Louis of Anjou, who made some show at an attempt to enforce them, but failed to accomplish anything. Finally, in 1390, a marriage treaty was arranged between the latter's son Louis and Pedro's granddaughter Violante, in which the latter received a large dowry in return for a complete renunciation for herself, her husband, and her successors of all right and title to the Majorcan realm.[3]

Such were the last phases and aftermath of a conquest which had been initiated more than a century and a half before. That the end was delayed so long is simply another

[1] Zurita, ii, ff. 234-235; *Historia General del Reino de Mallorca* by J. Dameto and others, iii, pp. 267-271.

[2] Lecoy, ii, pp. 179 ff., 201.
[3] Lecoy, ii, pp. 267-276.

testimony to the intensity of the passion for autonomy
which characterized the inhabitants of the territories concerned. Most of the historians of Majorca exhaust themselves in invectives against the outrageous means by which
James's spoliation was effected, and emphasize the happi-
ness of the Balearic kingdom under its separate line of
sovereigns; but however dastardly his methods, it is impossible to doubt that Pedro's resolve to terminate the separate existence of the subsidiary realm was justified by
every consideration of statesmanship. James the Conqueror
had made a grievous error in severing it from Aragon, with
which it had been traditionally united since ancient times;
and since Aragon after his death had blossomed out into a
great Mediterranean power, the wisdom of reannexation was
more obvious than ever. During the period of its autonomy it had really been a hindrance to the growth of the
Aragonese empire, whereas it ought to have served as an
invaluable stepping-stone to the remoter possessions to the
eastward; nor was its case for one moment comparable
to that of Sicily, for whose independence there were a host
of reasons, both geographical and historical, that did not
apply in the Balearics. And we must not omit to pay
tribute to the practical good sense of Pedro IV in refraining
from any serious effort to take Montpellier. Save for
Cerdagne and Roussillon, the ancient holdings of Catalonia
north of the Pyrenees were gone forever, and it would have
been the height of folly to have attempted to maintain an
isolated outpost which was so completely at the mercy of
the king of France. The solution of the whole matter was
probably, in fact, by far the best that could have been devised; and as we shall later see, those portions of the
Majorcan realm that were reannexed to the domains of
the Crown of Aragon were to some extent consoled for

their loss of a separate line of kings by being permitted to retain a very considerable measure of institutional autonomy. Spanish particularism was indeed proof against such trifles as the extinction of a local dynasty.

The Majorcan affair, the pressure of his relations with Castile, and above all his bitter internal struggle with the forces of the Union, which we shall consider elsewhere, prevented King Pedro from seriously attacking the difficult problem of Sardinia during the first fifteen years of his reign. The Aragonese garrisons in the island were only partially and tardily reënforced, while the Genoese, spasmodically aided by the Pisans, utilized every opportunity to solidify and increase the gains they had made in the period of Alfonso IV. They had all the best of sundry desultory military and naval operations in 1347–48, so that by the middle of the fourteenth century the Aragonese power in the island was perilously near extinction. Corsica, despite the papal donation, had never been conquered by Aragon except on paper.[1] Altogether it was only too obvious that Pedro would have to bestir himself vigorously, if he wished to reap the fruits of the labors of his predecessors in these islands.

For this purpose the king of Aragon sought and obtained in 1351 an alliance with the powerful maritime republic of Venice, which shared his hostility to the Genoese. The united fleets pursued their foes to the eastern waters of the Mediterranean, finally overtaking them in the Bosphorus, where on February 13, 1352, there took place one of the fiercest conflicts of the age.[2] At the last moment the Aragonese and Venetians received a reënforcement of nine galleys

[1] R. St.-H., v, pp. 40 ff.
[2] Zurita, ii, ff. 243–246; A. Navar-rete, Historia Marítima Militar de España, i, pp. 274 f.

from the Emperor at Constantinople, and with their aid barely managed to defeat the Genoese; but the losses which the latter inflicted on them were so terrible, both in ships and in men, that they also claimed the victory. No prisoners were spared on either side — all captives being either drowned or starved to death. The battle was, however, totally without effect on Sardinian affairs. The Genoese refused to surrender a single one of their possessions there, and were even encouraged to further resistance by the fact that Mariano, son and successor of that Hugo of Arborea who had been one of the staunchest adherents of the Aragonese cause during the reign of James II, abandoned the ways of his father, and rose in rebellion against the authority of Pedro. For two years matters hung in the balance, a continuation of Pedro's naval victories being more than equalized by Genoa's diplomatic success in stirring up Mariano of Arborea to make trouble for their common foe by proclaiming Sardinia independent. Finally, in the summer of 1354, the king of Aragon, at the head of one of the most formidable fleets that his country had ever sent forth, crossed over to Sardinian waters and laid siege to the town of Alghero in the northwestern corner of the island. Despite the assistance of Venice, however, he was unable to take it; disease decimated his forces, and negotiations followed, in which the new Judge of Arborea steadily strengthened his own position and the cause of Sardinian independence by playing off Aragon and Genoa against one another. On November 9, 1355, an arrangement was concluded by which the Genoese were permitted peacefully to evacuate Alghero, and Pedro to enter into possession of it; and from that time onward the power and interest of the former in the island steadily waned.[1] They continued

[1] Zurita, ii, ff. 251-258, 260-262.

to interfere there sporadically, it is true, for many years, but rather with the idea of making trouble for the Aragonese than of gaining control for themselves.

Henceforth the possession of Sardinia lay between the rival forces of the king of Aragon and the natives under the Judges of Arborea. Clear through to the very end of the reign and beyond they continued their inconclusive strife. In the sixties the Aragonese cause was seriously weakened by the hostility of the Avignonese Pope, Urban V, who was angered at Pedro's appropriation of the clerical possessions in Aragon to furnish funds for his Castilian wars, and attempted to punish him by depriving him of the title to Sardinia; this naturally encouraged the natives to renewed efforts. During the last years of the reign there was a particularly violent outburst of hostilities between Pedro and Eleanor, daughter of Mariano of Arborea, who had strengthened herself against him by a marriage alliance with the famous Genoese knight, Brancaleone Doria; this quarrel was terminated by a treaty, in August, 1386, in which the king of Aragon had distinctly the worst of the bargain.[1] One cannot help feeling a curious lack of enthusiasm on the part of Pedro in reading the weary story of his Sardinian campaigns. He certainly did not exhibit in them anything like the same sustained and relentless energy which characterized his operations elsewhere. Whether it was a haunting memory of the somewhat ignoble origin of the Aragonese claim to the island, or the unexpected tenacity of the natives, or, as seems most probable, the horrible ravages of the detestable climate — a foe more potent than the mightiest army — it is impossible to say; but whatever the cause, it is a noteworthy fact that the king of Aragon consistently postponed the vigorous prosecution of Sardinian affairs in

[1] Lafuente, vii, pp. 126–132.

favor of every other problem, internal or foreign, that presented itself for solution. Certainly the completion of the Aragonese conquest of the island cannot be regarded as any nearer at the end of his reign than at the beginning; and under a less energetic king it might well have been abandoned. The reign had seen Genoa eliminated as a serious competitor for the prize; but on the other hand, it had also witnessed the conversion of the natives from alliance and benevolent neutrality to active and effective opposition. From Pedro's point of view, the change was not altogether favorable; and the most that can be claimed for the Sardinian policy of the 'Ceremonious' monarch is that it tided over a danger point in the history of the Aragonese occupation of the island.

The history of Pedro's policy in Sicily occupies a distinctly minor place in the history of the reign, at least until the very close. Its principal object was to pave the way for the ultimate incorporation of the island in the Aragonese dominions, as soon as the opportunity should present itself through the extinction of the line of monarchs established there by Frederic III. One obvious way to accomplish this was to secure the good will of the Sicilian kings and their subjects by lending them military aid in the interminable struggle with the Neapolitan Angevins which chiefly occupied their reigns; another was to strengthen the ties that united the two dynasties by a series of marriages. Such assistance as Pedro gave his cousins in their difficulties with the sovereigns of Naples cannot be described as generous. Several times Sicilian petitions for help went absolutely unheeded. In 1360 a fleet of galleys was sent to escort his daughter Constance on her way to marry Frederic IV of Sicily (1355–77), and aided in inflicting a timely defeat on the forces of Joanna of Naples; but further

than this little or nothing was done.[1] On the other hand
the policy of matrimonial alliance between the two realms
was vigorously pursued. In addition to the above mentioned marriage of Constance and Frederic, Pedro himself
wedded, as his third wife, Frederic's sister Eleanor, thus
becoming the uncle as well as the grandfather of Frederic's
only legitimate child, Maria.[2] The relationship between
the two dynasties was now so close, that when, in 1377,
Frederic died without male heirs, Pedro came boldly forward and claimed the Sicilian throne for himself, in virtue
of a provision in the will of Frederic III which excluded
females from the succession. Papal opposition, the threat
of an interdict, and the fact that the liberty-loving Sicilians
were as yet in no mood to tolerate annexation to Aragon
prevented Pedro, however, from pressing the claim on his
own behalf. He prepared a huge fleet, and kept the whole
western Mediterranean in suspense for at least two years
by threatening a raid on the Sicilian coasts; but his counsellors were almost unanimous in opposition, and the king
himself was far too practical a statesman to strike when
there was so little hope of success.[3] Yet though he recognized that the moment was scarcely ripe for the actual
reunion of the two realms, Pedro was determined to do
his best to prepare the way for it. In the year 1380, accordingly, he made over his rights to the kingdom of Sicily
to Martin, his second son by Eleanor, the sister of Frederic
IV, granting him, in effect, full authority over the island,
with the title of vicar general, and merely reserving to
himself, during his lifetime, the title of king.[4] The result
of this donation was, of course, to establish another col-

[1] Zurita, ii, f. 304. 'Frederic IV' is of course 'Frederic II' of the Aragonese line of Sicilian kings. See Genealogical Table, p. 311.

[2] Zurita, ii, ff. 236–238; I. La Lumia, Storie Siciliane, ii, p. 231.
[3] La Lumia, op. cit., ii, pp. 250 ff.
[4] Zurita, ii, f. 374.

lateral line of Aragonese sovereigns in the Sicilian realm, since Martin's elder brother John was the heir of his father in all his other dominions; it had thus the advantage of placating the Sicilians by securing them a continuance of their separate line of kings, yet on the other hand it brought the two dynasties closer together than they had been for three generations, and consequently facilitated reunion whenever issue should fail in either one. As the Sicilians were at that time divided into various factions, each of whose leaders, as Zurita says, "desired to seise" the Infanta Maria, and by marrying her, to acquire the realm," [1] Pedro deemed it essential to the success of his plan to possess himself of her person and thus forestall all opposition; and in the year 1382 this end was accomplished for him by the Viscount of Rocaberti, of Athenian fame, who, on his way back from the Catalan duchy in Greece, kidnapped the Infanta and had her brought by way of Sardinia to Barcelona.[2] We shall soon see how an unexpected series of deaths without issue among the descendants of Pedro IV effected the incorporation of Sicily in the realms of the crown of Aragon, far earlier than the 'Ceremonious' monarch could reasonably have ventured to hope.[3]

The relentless energy and perseverance which formed the basis of the character of Pedro IV were conspicuously absent in that of his son and successor John, who, after issuing triumphant from the throes of the inevitable successional quarrel with his step-mother, Sibylla of Forcia,

---

[1] Zurita, ii, f. 374.
[2] Zurita, ii, f. 378.
[3] I have not attempted to deal with the complicated story of the internal history of Sicily during this period, since it is not an essential part of the main narrative. Those who are interested will find an admirable account of it in La Lumia, *Storie Siciliane*, ii, pp. 221-335.

abandoned himself to the pleasures of music and the chase.
The most notable singers of the day flocked to his court.
He possessed the finest collection of falcons in Europe.
The grave Aragonese disapproved of these pastimes; the
Cortes spoke their mind about them with characteristic
frankness, and talked of cutting off the royal revenues if
the king did not mend his ways. Their protests, however,
were of little affect, for John remained to the end of his
days a 'carefree hunter,'[1] who consistently neglected the
direction of the affairs of state. The natural result was
that the foreign policy of Aragon, which under Pedro had
been so vigorous and well defined, was suffered for a time
to drift aimlessly whithersoever the more dominant forces of
other powers combined to impel it.

Curiously enough, however, the outside influence to
which Aragon first succumbed was exerted in such a way
as to lead her into active continuance of the Sicilian policy
of the late king. The Babylonian Captivity of the papacy
had by this time given place to the Great Schism of the
West; and the Avignonese Pope, Clement VII, conceived
that the best possible way to breed trouble for his Roman
rival would be to unite those ancient foes, the houses of
Anjou and of Aragon, in a common hostility against him.
In 1390, accordingly, he arranged a marriage between
John's daughter Violante and Louis of Anjou and Provence,
who had claims on the kingdom of Naples against Ladislaus
of Durazzo, the actual occupant of the throne. He also
made a match between Maria, the captive heiress of Sicily,
and Martin, nephew of King John, and son of that Martin
to whom Pedro IV had granted his rights to the island;
he thus brought sensibly nearer the ultimate annexation

[1] Zurita, ii, f. 394; R. St.-H., v, pp. 162–167. John is known in Aragon as 'El Casador,' and in Catalonia as 'Lo Descurat.'

of Sicily to Aragon, which had been the aim of the late
king's policy from the very first.[1] In March, 1392, the
two Martins, father and son, passed over to Sicily, which
had been rent by internal anarchy and rebellion ever since
the departure of Maria, to try to make good their pretensions
to the realm. It was a difficult task. The Roman Pope,
Boniface IX, was violently in opposition, and did not scruple
to bring the papal weapons of interdict and excommunication to bear. Ladislaus of Durazzo in Naples, jealous of
the claims of the younger branch of his family, which was
now united to the Aragonese by the marriage of Louis of
Anjou and Violante, showed himself consistently hostile.
The Sicilians themselves plainly foresaw that the acceptance
of Martin as their king would ultimately mean the end of
their independence, which they were determined at any cost
to defend; and when they succeeded in blocking up the
chiefs of the Aragonese expedition in the castle of Catania,
King John was so slow in sending reënforcements to deliver
them as to lend color to the belief that his jealousy of his
brother took precedence of his solicitude for his success.
Had it not been for the energy of the Aragonese admiral,
Bernaldo de Cabrera, the real hero of the enterprise, the
whole affair might well have ended in disaster.[2] As it
was, the struggle continued without any decisive results
until the death of John of Aragon, on a hunting party, in
May, 1395. As the king left no male heirs, the crown of
Aragon devolved on his younger brother Martin, who,
after a year's delay in Sicily, returned to claim it, leaving
his son Martin, with his bride Maria, to continue as best he
could the struggle for recognition as king of that turbulent
island. The fact that the Aragonese Cortes recognized
the younger Martin as heir to the Aragonese throne at the

---

[1] Zurita, ii, ff. 398 f.   [2] Zurita, ii, ff. 402–408.

same time that they swore allegiance to his father as their sovereign, shows that the fears of the Sicilians for the loss of their independence were by no means groundless.[1] The end of it, however, was to come in a way which none of them could have anticipated.

King Martin of Aragon was a kindly soul, but scarcely more efficient as a monarch than his predecessor. He succeeded in rendering valuable aid to his son in reducing Sicily to obedience, both by the support he gave him before his departure, and still more by despatching a fresh expedition from Barcelona to bear a hand in quelling the last revolt in 1397; but save for this he soon subsided into comparative insignificance.[2] The younger Martin of Sicily, however, was a man of different stamp. With the same restless activity that had characterized his grandfather, he coupled a knightly bearing, and a personal solicitude for the welfare of his subjects, which speedily won for him their devoted affection.[3] As soon as he had secured himself in Sicily against the attacks of internal rebels and foreign foes, he launched boldly forth on a vigorous campaign in North Africa, which resulted in a temporary reconquest of the island of Gerba, and the reopening of the interminable question of the political, financial, and commercial relations of Aragon and Sicily with Tunis.[4] Nay more, as an evidence of his keen interest and solicitude for the welfare of the Aragonese Empire as a whole, the heroic young prince undertook to deal with another problem which properly belonged to his father, but was obviously far beyond the latter's capabilities — namely, the suppression of a revolt

[1] Zurita, ii, ff. 414, 425–427.
[2] Zurita, ii, ff. 427–429, 433–435.
[3] R. Starrabba, "Documenti riguardanti la Sicilia sotto Re Martino I," in Archivio storico Siciliano, 1st ser., iii (1876), pp. 137–176; G. Beccaria, "Note critiche sul Parlamento di Catania del 1397," in Archivio storico Siciliano, nuova serie, xiii (1888), pp. 345–368.
[4] Mas Latrie, pp. 432–434.

in Sardinia which had been suffered to go on unchecked since the reign of King John. In 1408 the opportunity for this was exceedingly favorable, for the last of the rebel Judges of Arborea, Mariano V, had died in the previous year, and William of Narbonne, whom the natives chose as his successor, was clearly unequal to the task. Martin of Aragon sent reënforcements to his son; the Genoese, as was their custom, supported the Sards; a furious battle between them finally took place near Cagliari on June 26, 1409, from which the Sicilian king, though greatly outnumbered, issued victorious. During the next few weeks the young conqueror passed from one town to another as if on a triumphal march. Resistance seemed at an end, and the Aragonese possession of Sardinia no longer a dream but a fact, when suddenly, on July 24, 1409, the hero of the hour fell ill and expired, in all probability a victim to the Sardinian fever.[1] His death was the signal for new things. His first wife Maria and her son Pedro had predeceased him; his second, Blanche of Navarre, had no children who survived; so that the crown of Sicily passed on his death to his father, and all the scattered dominions of the Aragonese Empire were at last reunited in one hand. But old Martin of Aragon himself was now childless and a widower, so that the future was doubtful and dark. Unwilling to neglect any opportunity to secure the succession, he married again, in September, 1409; but his hopes were disappointed, and in the following May he also passed to the grave [2] — the last of the old line of the counts of Barcelona, which was assuredly one of the most remarkable dynasties in the history of mediaeval Europe. Its most illustrious names challenge comparison with the best

[1] Zurita, ii, ff. 450–454; G. Manno, *Storia di Sardegna* (3d ed., Milan, 1835),   ii, pp. 84–87.
     [2] Zurita, ii, ff. 454–458.

and greatest monarchs of any nation. Its average level
was exceedingly high ; and if the reigns of its last two representatives in Spain were an anti-climax, all its pristine
splendors were gloriously revived in the heroic young
Martin of Sicily, flaming up in added brilliancy for one
fleeting moment, like the light of a lamp before it expires.

A stormy interregnum of two years' duration followed,
and was finally terminated on Tuesday, June 28, 1412, by
the selection of Ferdinand of Antequera, brother of Henry
III of Castile, as the successor of King Martin in all his
dominions.[1] The story of these events is complicated and
very interesting, but as it belongs rather to the history of
Aragon than to that of the Aragonese Empire we cannot
linger over it for long. It is, however, important to observe
that the nine magnates who met at the little town of Caspe
on the lower Ebro to settle the question of the succession
were not 'electors' in the true sense of the word, but rather
judges; and their function was not to choose one of the
rival candidates on the basis of his merits and deserts, but
to determine which of them had the best legal claims,
according to the Aragonese law of hereditary succession.
The question which lay before them was, in other words,
not political but judicial: strictly speaking, Ferdinand of
Antequera was selected not because of the admirable
qualities which he had displayed as regent for his nephew,
John II of Castile, but because, through the fact that his
mother was the sister of the last two kings of Aragon and the
daughter of Pedro IV, he was lineally nearer the throne than
any of the other competitors. The violent invectives that
the older Aragonese and Catalonian historians have hurled

---

[1] Zurita, iii, f. 71, who however gives the date incorrectly as July 28, which fell
on a Thursday in this year.

against the magnates of Caspe, on the ground that their
decision was a shameful signing away of the independence
of the realm and a bringing in of Castilian bondage, are
thus totally without foundation. This important step
toward the union of the crowns of Aragon and Castile under
Ferdinand and Isabella was based on strictly legal grounds;
indeed, it is more than doubtful whether a verdict so contrary to the ineradicable tendencies of Spanish separatism
could otherwise have survived. But the 'Nine of Caspe,'
conscious of the justice of their case, were strong enough
to ignore the menaces and cajoleries of the political factions
that stormed around their quiet retreat. It would be idle
to deny that their position was immensely strengthened by
the spotlessness of Ferdinand's record, and by the violence
of his chief rival, the count of Urgel;[1] but it needed all
the majesty of the law and the claims of hereditary right,
in a land where respect for the law was ever a dominant
characteristic, to bring a scion of the house of Trastamara
to the throne of James the Conqueror and Pedro the Great.[2]
Zurita has left us a memorable description of the ceremony
of the publication of the verdict. From a lofty dais outside the church of Caspe a sermon was preached and the
sentence of the 'Nine' read to the vast concourse of people
by St. Vincent Ferrer. The royal standard was displayed
before the altar in Ferdinand's name; and the multitude,
in the fulness of their gratitude at the termination of their
long suspense, burst forth into a splendid hymn of praise
and thankfulness to God.[3]

From the moment of his accession the new king was

[1] Lorenzo Valla (*De Rebus a Ferdinando Aragoniae Rege gestis Libri Tres*:
in Schott, i, p. 759) asserts that the count
threatened to replace the mitre of the
archbishop of Saragossa with a red-
hot helmet, and to shave the head of
the Pope, "non aqua, sicut fieri solet,
ante perfusum."
[2] Cf. F. Janer, *El Compromiso de
Caspe* (Madrid, 1855); Cayetano Soler,
El Fallo de Caspe (Barcelona, 1899).
[3] Zurita, iii, ff. 71–72.

naturally confronted with great difficulties in each of his new dominions. His four years' reign was so brief that he could not possibly deal with them all; the only wonder is that he managed to accomplish what he did. In his Spanish lands he found difficulty in accommodating himself to the various limitations of monarchical power which the Aragonese constitutions imposed: brought up in a land where kingship was, in theory at least, omnipotent, and himself endowed with the highest possible conception of the duties and privileges of the royal prerogative, he could not restrain his impatience at the checks he received from the national and municipal assemblies and the law courts.[1] The hostility of his unsuccessful rival James of Urgel demanded serious measures; it was not till the latter part of 1413 that the pretender was willing to admit defeat and humbly to accept the royal offer of perpetual imprisonment in lieu of execution.[2] The king was also much preoccupied with the termination of the Triple Schism which had resulted from the Council of Pisa. Gregory XII and John XXIII had been disposed of at Constance; but the Avignonese pontiff, Benedict XIII, a scion of the ancient Aragonese house of Luna, had refused, with truly Spanish obstinacy, either to abdicate or even to recognize his deposition. Since 1403, when he broke with the king of France, he had been established in Catalonia, where he had exerted his influence in favor of the choice of Ferdinand at Caspe; he now expected a return, with interest, of this act of amity, and demanded that the king of Aragon should support him and his claims to the papacy against the steadily increasing opposition of the bulk of the rest of Western Christendom. For a long time Ferdinand stood loyally by Benedict; but finally, foreseeing that complete isolation

[1] R. St.-H., v, p. 208.   [2] Zurita, iii, ff. 97–99.

from the rest of Europe would be the inevitable result of persistence in this attitude, he consented to meet the ubiquitous Emperor Sigismund and the refractory pontiff at Perpignan, in the autumn of 1415, in the hope of arranging a compromise. Benedict, however, was so utterly unreasonable in his demands that Ferdinand bowed to the inevitable and finally withdrew his allegiance, and the haughty prelate, gathering around him such adherents as he could muster, retired to the lonely fortress of Peñiscola, a possession of his family overlooking the Mediterranean, and there continued to defy authority, both temporal and spiritual, till his death at the age of ninety, in 1424.[1] The whole episode, so thoroughly characteristic of the persons concerned in it, forms a curious chapter in the ever changing history of the relations of the Aragonese kings and the Popes.

In the Mediterranean, the immediate attention of Ferdinand was naturally centred on Sardinia and Sicily, both of which had seized the opportunity afforded by the confusion of the interregnum to rise in revolt. In Sardinia it was the viscount of Narbonne, heir to the Judges of Arborea, that sought to overthrow the authority of the Aragonese representatives in the island; he was supported, as usual, by the Genoese, and was in close touch with James of Urgel in Aragon. But after Ferdinand's accession the latter was defeated, and the former made a five years' truce with the king; so that in 1414 the viscount of Narbonne, recognizing the futility of further resistance, offered to sell to Ferdinand all his holdings in Sardinia for 153,000 florins of gold. The price was so high that Ferdinand, who realized that he had the game in his own hands, refused to

---

[1] Zurita, iii, ff. 115–122; Creighton, *History of the Papacy* (edition of 1905), ii, pp. 59–63, 82, 89 f., 154.

pay it, and negotiations dragged on between the two parties until the following reign; but the final consummation of the Aragonese conquest of the island, which was reserved for Alfonso the Magnanimous, was inevitable from the time of Ferdinand, if not from that of the expedition of Martin the younger in 1409.[1]

Sicily, too, "ever longing to possess a king who would find her crown so fair that he would not desire any other," made one last bid for independence in 1410. Against Blanche, the widowed queen of the younger Martin, who had been left in the island as the representative of the Crown of Aragon, two hostile parties arose. The one was led by the Admiral Bernaldo de Cabrera, who had hitherto been the most ardent and efficient champion of the Aragonese cause, but now, according to Lorenzo Valla, aspired to the Sicilian throne and the hand of the regent;[2] the other was composed for the most part of Sicilian barons, who desired to place the crown on the head of Martin's illegitimate son Fadrique. In the three-cornered struggle that ensued the admiral had the best of it, until at last, in 1412, an accident delivered him into the regent's hands, and he was thrown into prison; in the following year he was released by the orders of Ferdinand, on acknowledgment of his offence, payment of an enormous fine, and a promise to leave Sicily forever.[3] With Cabrera eliminated, the warring elements subsided. The party of Fadrique saw the uselessness of continued resistance, and somewhat sullenly accepted defeat. Ferdinand, moreover, had the wisdom to use his victory with moderation, and flattered Sicilian pride by ordering that one half the members of the council which aided the

[1] Zurita, iii, ff. 46, 104.
[2] L. Valla, *De Rebus a Ferdinando Aragoniae gestis Libri Tres*, in Schott, i, pp. 766 f.
[3] Zurita, iii, ff. 7, 58 f., 76, 88; R. Gregorio, *Opere rare*, pp. 426-434; R. St.-H., v, pp. 202-204.

Regent Blanche should be natives. The Sicilians now directed all their efforts towards persuading Ferdinand to let them have his second son John as their king, probably in the hope of making ultimately possible the reëstablishment of an independent line of sovereigns; and finally, . in 1415, Ferdinand yielded to their entreaties to the extent of sending him over to them as his lieutenant. His real reason for taking this step, however, was probably his hope that by so doing he might pave the way for the annexation of the Angevin kingdom of Naples to the Aragonese domains — an end which had not been lost sight of since Pope Clement VII, in 1390, arranged the marriage of King. John's daughter Violante and Louis of Anjou. In January, 1415, before John set sail for Sicily, he was betrothed, at the age of eighteen, to Queen Joanna II of Naples, forty-five years old, sister and successor of Ladislaus of Durazzo, who had died a few months before. According to the accompanying agreement, the Aragonese Infante was to share the throne of his bride, and retain it alone if he survived her. But the fickle Joanna changed her mind while her youthful lover was crossing the seas, and upset everything by marrying instead the Count de la Marche, who was ardently supported by France, Genoa, and the other foes of the house of Aragon, though bitterly unpopular with . the queen's own subjects. Clearly the time was not yet ripe for the Aragonese to win Naples by gentle means, and John was not ready or able to assert his claims by force. He therefore wisely devoted himself to solidifying his power in Sicily and putting out the last embers of revolt, until, a year later, he was recalled to Spain. But Aragon had by this time gone too far with her Neapolitan plans to desist from them. Alfonso the Magnanimous and Ferdinand the Catholic were to carry on and finish the work which had already been begun, and were thereby to give an entirely new complexion to the foreign and imperial policy of the realm.[1]

Ferdinand died on April 2, 1416, at the age of forty-three, and in his final will and testament left all his realms to his eldest son, Alfonso, thus ending John's hopes of the succession in Sicily, and those of the Sicilians for an independent line of kings.[2] The new monarch was active and energetic, a diplomat of high merit, and a passionate lover of the art and learning of the Renaissance. He lacked his father's high sense of royal duty, and vastly exceeded him in his detestation of Aragonese constitutionalism. From the moment of his accession he longed to exchange the stern landscapes of his native Spain for the fertile fields and sunny skies of Italy; and the fact that his father had forsaken the testamentary example of his predecessors, and left him to rule over all of his dominions, ultimately gave him the opportunity to gratify his heart's desire. Nearly all the early acts of his reign may be regarded as paving the way for this change of abode. He at once recalled his brother John from Sicily, and in 1419 married him to the widowed Blanche of Navarre, who had preceded him as regent there; he thus rid himself of all possible rivals for the Sicilian crown, and diverted the ambition of the turbulent Infante in the direction of the little Pyrenean kingdom.[3] One of the last acts of the previous reign had been the arrangement of Alfonso's marriage to his cousin, Maria of Castile; and in 1418 the new king strengthened the tie by making a match between his sister Maria and his wife's brother John, which he vainly hoped would forestall the

---

[1] Zurita, iii, ff. 109 f., 113 f., 126 f.; G. Desdevises du Desert, *Don Carlos d'Aragon*, pp. 93-95.
[2] Zurita, iii, ff. 123-124.
[3] Zurita, iii, ff. 126-127, 135-136; Desdevises du Desert, *Don Carlos d'Aragon*, p. 95.

possibility of trouble with the western realm and leave him free to pursue his Italian policy undisturbed.[1] Clearly the young monarch, the first to have a really fair chance to try the difficult experiment of ruling all the scattered territories of Aragon from a single throne, was contemplating a departure which would necessarily give a totally new direction to the activities of that mighty empire: he would make Italy rather than Spain the head and centre of his dominions.

But before he could hope to set foot in the land of his aspirations, it was essential that he should make certain of the Mediterranean possessions which he already had. Sicily, exhausted by ceaseless anarchy and civil war, had no longer either the power or the wish to oppose him; but in Sardinia the fact that the late king had not been able to come to terms with the viscount of Narbonne gave rise to a most difficult situation. Neither side trusted the other; the forces of rebellion had been checked but not crushed; the presence of the young king at the head of a powerful army was clearly essential to the establishment of a durable peace.[2] On May 13, 1420, accordingly, Alfonso set sail with a large fleet of galleys and transports, which was strengthened by an additional detachment from Majorca on the way. On his arrival all signs of resistance vanished, and Sassari, where he had anticipated violent opposition, opened its gates to him on August 11. The rights of the viscount of Narbonne were finally bought off for 100,000 florins — a sum less than two thirds the size of that which he had offered to sell them for in the previous reign — and were soon after granted out to the family of Cubello, which was remotely connected with the old line of the Judges of Arborea. These

[1] Zurita, iii, ff. 112, 134.
[2] J. Ametller y Vinyas, *Alfonso V de Aragón en Italia*, i, pp. 46–50.

Cubellos remained in possession of the Arborean territories till 1478, with the title of Marquises of Oristano; and as they were from first to last loyal supporters of the authority of the kings of Aragon, no further trouble was experienced from that quarter. The summoning to Cagliari, in 1421, of the representatives of the three estates (*stamenti*) of the realm, to form a national assembly on the model of the Catalan Cortes, may be regarded as the culmination of Alfonso's success. From that time onward, the Aragonese mastery of the island was assured.[1]

It was but natural that Alfonso should think of following up his triumphs in Sardinia by an attempt to realize the Aragonese claims to Corsica. These dated, it will be remembered, from the donation of Boniface VIII in 1297; but they had been so utterly neglected that, according to at least one account, the papacy had actually regranted the island to the Genoese. In any case the latter had been in full possession there since the middle of the fourteenth century; but their rule had so alienated many of the principal inhabitants that Alfonso, from his coign of vantage in Sardinia, had little difficulty in persuading one faction among them to deliver up to him the important town of Calvi. Thence he proceeded in October, 1420, to lay siege to the fortress of Bonifacio, which commanded the strait between Corsica and Sardinia. The place was too strong to be taken by assault, but a strict blockade by land and sea had almost effected its surrender when a rescuing squadron, sent by Genoa, broke through to the inner harbor and delivered it. After this mishap Alfonso apparently lost heart, and abandoned the Corsican campaign, so that the island re-

---

[1] Zurita, iii, ff. 139 f.; Ametller, *op. cit.*, i, pp. 54–56; Manno, *Storia di Sardegna*, ii, pp. 97 ff.; Stokvis, *Manuel*, iii, p. 744. There is an article by L. Aresio in vol. iii of the *Archivio storico Sardo* (1907) on Alfonso V and Sardinia from 1435 to 1444, which I have not been able to see.

mained thenceforth in the hands of the Genoese.[1] Whether he had ever been really in earnest about it may well be doubted. Certainly he cared far less for it than for the prospect of gaining a foothold in Italy; and it was probably the arrival of an urgent message from Queen Joanna of Naples which really accounts for his sudden raising of the siege of Bonifacio in the winter of 1420–21.

Alfonso had kept a sharp watch on Neapolitan affairs from the moment of his accession. The unspeakable Joanna, who had so unexpectedly thrown over the marriage which had been arranged for her with his brother John, had already cast off and ultimately exiled James, Count de la Marche, the husband of her choice; she was now giving free rein to the adulterous instincts which formed the basis of her character. The condottiere Muzio Attendolo Sforza and the seneschal Giovanni Caracciolo were the principal rivals for her favors and the political power that would naturally go with them; and when the influence and prestige of the former began to wane, he sought to recover them by making common cause with Louis III of Anjou, the son of Violante of Aragon, whom he proposed that Joanna should make her heir. Joanna, under the influence of Caracciolo, refused to entertain this proposal; and both parties, foreseeing the need of further support for their respective causes, simultaneously applied for it to Alfonso of Aragon in 1420, at just the moment when he had completed the conquest of Sardinia.[2] That monarch, who discerned in the situation an admirable opportunity to advance his own designs, made haste to adopt the cause of Joanna; for the succession of Louis of Anjou, though he was descended on his mother's side from the old line of Aragonese kings, would in no way further the actual interests of Aragon in

[1] Zurita, iii, f. 144; Ametller, i, pp. 75–82.   [2] Ametller, i, pp. 57–65.

Naples but rather defeat them, while support of Joanna might ultimately be rewarded by the Neapolitan throne. Moreover Alfonso wisely decided that it would be well to back up his promises with a show of military force. Before his departure for Corsica he detached a portion of his fleet for service in Neapolitan waters; in early September the Aragonese ships appeared off Capri.[1] Sforza and the Angevins mustered their forces to oppose them; and the Aragonese leaders, perceiving that decisive action was inevitable, landed and requested an interview with Joanna in order to make certain of her adherence. The ensuing conference terminated in an arrangement by which the Neapolitan queen agreed to adopt Alfonso as her son and heir, "seeing that the Kings of the House of Aragon had ever been renowned for their justice and clemency, and were known as most Christian and glorious sovereigns"; she furthermore invested him with the duchy of Calabria. In return for these favors it was understood that the king of Aragon should come and deliver the licentious queen from the factions who were striving to control her.[2] The moment that Alfonso learned of her decision, he broke camp before Bonifacio, and at once betook himself to Sicily with all the forces at his disposal. Thence in the spring of 1421 he crossed to the mainland and engaged the power of his Angevin rival by land and sea. Fortune seemed to smile on him at every turn. His adversaries, Sforza and Louis of Anjou, retreated before him. Joanna welcomed him at Naples, perhaps rather in fear than in love; but she at least delivered up to him the castles that dominated the city and the bay. Meantime the Aragonese fleet defeated the Genoese, who had come to the rescue of the Angevins. Pope Martin V, alarmed at the rapidity of Alfonso's progress, was induced

[1] Ametller, i, pp. 64 f.   [2] Zurita, iii, f. 142; Ametller, i, p. 85.

to confirm his adoption and conquest by a threat of the king
of Aragon to support Benedict XIII, who was still alive
at Peñiscola. At the end of the year 1422 Alfonso was to
all intents and purposes in full control of the lovely kingdom
which he longed to possess.[1]

But the victories which the Aragonese monarch had won
on the field of battle were lost in the heart of the queen. A
coolness sprung up between them when Joanna discovered
that her adopted son was to be no mere puppet in her hands,
and it soon developed into a bitter hate. Joanna longed
for the return of Sforza; she loudly proclaimed that Alfonso
was practically holding her in captivity; and the fact that
each lived in a separate and strongly fortified castle, whence
they issued only on rare occasions, and under strong guards,
to pay one another formal visits, lent color to the pretence.
Finally, in 1423, a battle was fought outside of Naples
between the Angevin and Aragonese forces, in which the
latter were defeated; and soon afterward Sforza succeeded
in carrying off Joanna to Aversa.[2] Liberated from the tutelage of Alfonso, there was little doubt what the fickle queen
would do. She revoked her adoption of the Aragonese
monarch, and announced her intention of taking his rival,
Louis of Anjou, as her son and heir in his stead. Without
an overwhelming military and naval preponderance, the
king of Aragon was powerless against such treachery as
this; and though the issue of such combats as occurred
between the rival forces was on the whole favorable to his
cause, he determined to retire for the time being to Spain
and watch events. Leaving his brother Pedro with a small
army to defend as best he could the places which he still
retained, he set sail in October, 1423, for Barcelona, taking

[1] Zurita, iii, ff. 150–151; Ametller, i, pp. 103–144.
[2] Zurita, iii, ff. 151–155.

a mild revenge on his enemies by plundering the Angevin town of Marseilles on the way.

It was nine long years before Alfonso got an opportunity to return to the land of his choice. During that interval his brother was gradually driven from one fortress to another, and finally obliged to take refuge in the Castello dell' Ovo in Naples, the only place which remained to him. In the diplomatic field, however, fortune veered around in favor of the king of Aragon the moment that he had departed from Italy. Pope Martin, like all the pontiffs of the period, had no desire to see the existing powers in Naples too strong, and had tended in the days of Alfonso's prosperity to support Anjou and Sforza; but now that the circumstances had changed, he was easily induced to assume an attitude of benevolent neutrality. In Henry VI of England, too, Alfonso found a useful ally. He also made successful overtures to the duke of Milan. Even in Naples sentiment began to declare in his favor. The duke of Anjou, relegated to the duchy of Calabria, enjoyed no real authority. The seneschal Caracciolo was the true sovereign of the realm under the queen, and consequently incurred the jealousy and hatred of the Neapolitan baronage. He knew that his power could not possibly be perpetuated beyond the term of his mistress's life, if indeed as long, unless he obtained outside support. Consequently in the year 1431 he began to make secret overtures to the king of Aragon.[1]

Encouraged by these fresh developments, Alfonso began to prepare a new fleet and army for a fresh campaign against Naples. Since he was somewhat uncertain, however, as to the exact position of the different parties there, he took a leaf out of the book of his illustrious predecessor, Pedro

[1] Ametller, i, pp. 145–305, passim; Zurita, iii, ff. 208 ff.

the Great, and gave out that he was embarking on an expedition against Tunis. As usual, pretexts were not lacking: the most obvious being the interminable quarrel over the islands of Gerba and Kerkeni, which, despite an Aragonese ravaging expedition from Sicily in 1424, had fallen back once more into the hands of the Hafside sultans. In August, 1432, Alfonso landed with a considerable force at Gerba, and defeated the forces of the Tunisian sovereign in a battle, which Zurita describes in glowing terms, and in which many splendid trophies were doubtless won. Of permanent political results, however, this victory was absolutely barren. The Moors entirely refused to give up the island, and Alfonso, convinced of the futility of attempting to capture and hold it, soon abandoned all thought of fighting the North African powers. This expedition was in fact the last military enterprise of Spain against Tunis till the time of Charles V. It marks, in other words, the abandonment for one century of the schemes of political domination of the Hafside realm which had occupied earlier kings of Aragon, and the beginning of a period in which commercial relations take precedence of everything else.[1]

But it was Naples, not Tunis, that really interested Alfonso; so that he desisted with but little regret from the North African campaign. In September, 1432, the king of Aragon crossed over to Sicily, where he learned of the sudden fall and death of the favorite Caracciolo; Queen Joanna had cast him off and he was soon after assassinated. As no one paid much attention to Louis of Anjou, the elimina-

[1] Zurita, iii, ff. 210–211; Mas Latrie, pp. 476 ff.; A. Flandina, "La Spedisione di Alfonso nell' Isola della Gerbe," in Archivio storico Siciliano, nuova serie, i (1876), pp. 422–453; Ametller, op. cit., i, pp. 347–352; F. Cerone, "A proposito di alcuni documenti sulla seconda spedi-

sione di Alfonso V contra l'isola Gerba," in Anuari del Institut d'Estudis Catalans, 1909–10, pp. 51–89. It seems that a futile attack was launched against Tripoli in 1433 (Zurita, iv, f. 220), but nobody took it seriously.

tion of the grand seneschal paved the way for negotiations between Joanna and Alfonso; and, thanks to the skill with which the Aragonese agents manipulated the Neapolitan baronage, an arrangement was made in December, 1433, by which Joanna's adoption of Louis of Anjou was annulled, and Alfonso reinstated in the position which he had occupied twelve years before. But, as on former occasions, the moment of Alfonso's apparent triumph was the moment of his greatest danger. Pope Eugenius IV refused to ratify his recent treaty with Joanna, and soon after formed a league with the Emperor and the North Italian states to put him out of the peninsula. Before the year was over, Alfonso saw himself again obliged to retire to Sicily. In 1434 Louis of Anjou died, and his decease was followed, in February, 1435, by that of Queen Joanna herself; treacherous to the very end, she again disinherited Alfonso in her final will and testament, and left her throne to René, the younger brother of Louis of Anjou, who was at that time a prisoner in the hands of the duke of Burgundy. With the chief counter-claimant temporarily powerless, Alfonso promptly put forward a bold assertion of his rights to the kingdom of Naples, basing them on his adoption by Queen Joanna and on his descent from Constance, the wife of Pedro the Great. The immediate effect of this declaration, however, was to draw down upon the king of Aragon the heavy displeasure of the Pope. Eugenius demanded Naples as a fief of the Holy See, and, supported by the Genoese and the Visconti, made every preparation to fight for it. Alfonso opened the inevitable contest by besieging the town of Gaeta; the inhabitants were about to surrender when a Genoese fleet appeared to relieve it. As the king of Aragon had an enormous numerical superiority in galleys, he offered battle with absolute confidence, despite a considerable inferiority in lighter vessels; but in the ensuing action, August 5, 1435, which is usually known as the battle of Ponza, the Genoese fought with unusual skill and a truly desperate fury, and were completely victorious. The king and the majority of his forces were captured, his brother Pedro being the only one of prominence who escaped. Most of his ships were taken and burned before his eyes. It was a terrible setback for the power which had been generally and justly regarded as supreme in the western Mediterranean for more than one hundred years.[1]

Again, however, the spectacle of the humiliation of one side brought the inevitable revulsion of feeling in its favor, and desertion from the ranks of the other. Fifteenth-century Italy, as has been often observed, was a microcosm of Europe in the succeeding age; the principle of the balance of power had begun, almost without men's realizing it, to make itself felt, and this time it was the king of Aragon who was to profit by it. Moreover Alfonso's charming manners and personality stood him in good stead at this crisis. The Genoese admiral who had captured him entertained him as a guest of honor at Porto Venere, thus sparing him the humiliation of a sojourn among the rancorous Genoese. When he was handed over to Filippo Maria Visconti, who had been the leader of the coalition against him, the Milanese nobility came to the city gates to welcome him. The duchess of Milan received him on bended knees, and her husband, though at first he deemed it wise to avoid a personal meeting with his royal captive, sent word to assure him that, far from regarding him as his prisoner, he was proud to be able to place himself and his dominions at his disposal.[2] It was a fitting return for countless examples

[1] B. Facius (Fazio), *De Rebus gestis ab Alphonso Primo Libri Decem*, pp. 86–90; Zurita, iii, ff. 216–218, 227, 229– 231; Ametller, i, pp. 353–488, *passim*.
[2] Zurita, iii, ff. 231–232.

of loyalty to friends in distress and of chivalry towards
vanquished foes which Alfonso had given in the past, and
which had won him his title of the 'Magnanimous.' The
crafty Filippo Maria was shrewd enough to discern which
way the wind was blowing, and quickly saw that it would
be the height of folly for him to deprive Alfonso of his liberty. Since he could not possibly hope to conquer Naples
himself, he preferred to see it in the hands of Spaniards
rather than of Angevins; for the latter would be constantly passing through his own dominions on their way to
and from it, while the former could reach it by sea. It was
a line of reasoning which frequently suggested itself to his
Sforza successors in the course of the next hundred years,
and explains many a subsequent French defeat in the
peninsula. On this occasion it received additional emphasis
from the popular enthusiasm for Elizabeth, the wife of the
captive René of Anjou, whom that unfortunate prince had
sent to represent him in Naples. She was warmly received
by the inhabitants, and her husband was forthwith proclaimed king of the realm. The Aragonese surrendered
one castle after another to her advancing armies, and were
finally reduced to the fortress of Scylla on the strait of Messina. Obviously, if Filippo Maria did not promptly liber-
ate Alfonso, the cause of Anjou would triumph. In the early
spring of 1436, accordingly, the duke set his royal prisoner
free, despite the protests of the unforgiving Genoese, who
vented their anger by a revolt against their Milanese overlord. Meantime Alfonso, joining forces with his brother
Pedro, prepared once more to invade Naples.[1] Gaeta and
Terracina were taken in rapid succession; but much hard
work remained to be done before the king of Aragon's
triumph was complete. The proximity of his forces to the

[1] Zurita, iii, ff. 233-235; Ametller, ii, pp. 14 ff.

Patrimonium Petri again aroused the resentment of Eugenius IV, who strove to enlist the support of Genoa, Florence, and Venice against him, and sent a fresh army of invaders into Naples under his legate apostolic, Giovanni Vitelleschi, patriarch of Alexandria. Not until Alfonso began to negotiate with the refractory Council of Basel and the anti-pope elected by it, was Eugenius brought to terms. Angevin opposition, also, became increasingly vigorous at the same time. In 1438 Alfonso's rival René was released from captivity, returned to Naples, and received a royal welcome. The first attempt of the king of Aragon to besiege him there ended in a disastrous failure and the death of his brother Pedro; but finally, in June, 1442, Alfonso's army found a way into Naples by a subterranean aqueduct, which a tradition, accepted by Zurita, asserts was the same that was used for a similar purpose by Justinian's famous general Belisarius, nine centuries before. The capture of the town followed at once. Alfonso won golden opinions by forbidding wanton pillage and protecting the Neapolitan women from outrage by the licentious soldiery, while René of Anjou, defeated beyond the possibility of recovery, escaped on a Genoese galley from the realm over which he had aspired to rule. After making certain of the allegiance of the outlying portions of the kingdom, and as far as possible of the friendship of the papacy, the king of Aragon, on February 26, 1443, celebrated his triumph by a state entry of unparalleled magnificence into the conquered capital. Thus at last, after a struggle of twenty-two years' duration, the chief goal of his ambition had been attained, and a new realm added to the Aragonese Empire.[1]

[1] B. Facius (Fazio), De Rebus gestis ab Alfonso Primo Libri Decem, pp. 147 ff.; G. Pellegrini, Historia de Actibus Regis Alfonsi, published by Lecoy de

Alfonso the Magnanimous did not return again to Spain, but spent the rest of his days in Italy, and for the most part in Naples. He was one of the foremost figures in the wars and diplomacy of the peninsula until the day of his death. He took an active interest in the affairs of the Near East. He rivalled the Medici in his enthusiasm for humanism, and in the generosity of his patronage of the scholars and artists of the Renaissance. The most noteworthy feature of his political career in Italy was his relations with the Visconti and Sforza dukes of Milan. His consistent refusal to fight with the treacherous Filippo Maria prevailed over the latter's efforts to breed trouble for him; finally, on his death in 1447, the Milanese duke actually bequeathed to him the bulk of his lands, to the prejudice of his son-in-law, Francesco Sforza.[1] But Alfonso, who perceived that the Milanese would not willingly tolerate the rule of Aragon, nor the rest of Italy such an upsetting of the balance of power, wisely refrained from prosecuting his rights. On March 25, 1450, Francesco Sforza entered Milan and was solemnly proclaimed and recognized as duke.[2] The Aragonese claims, however, were not by any means forgotten. Alfonso's nephew Ferdinand subsequently attempted to revive them, and under Charles V the duchy was finally incorporated in the Spanish Empire. In the last few years of his life Alfonso had the satisfaction of humbling his ancient rivals, the Genoese, with a fleet which he had collected at the instance of Pope Calixtus III to fight the advancing Turks, and had paid for with the tithes of the church. Genoa itself was

---

la Marche in *Le Roi René*, ii, pp. 401–428; anonymous *Cronica del regno di Napoli*, also published by Lecoy de la Marche in *Le Roi René*, ii, pp. 428–435; Ametller, ii, pp. 31–457, *passim*; Lecoy de la Marche, *Le Roi René*, i, cap. iii; N. F. Faraglia, *Storia della lotta fra*

Alfonso V d' Aragona e Renato d' Angiò (1908). On the entry by the aqueduct cf. Procopius, *De Bello Gothico*, i, 9, 12 ff., and Zurita, iii, f. 273.

[1] Zurita, iii, ff. 306–308.
[2] Ametller, ii, pp. 680 ff.

blockaded, and was only delivered at the last moment by
the withdrawal of the hostile ships on the news of the death
of the king; but the days of its greatness were gone forever,
and it was henceforth relegated to the position of a satellite
of France or of Milan.[1] Outside the peninsula, also, the
Aragonese king's political and diplomatic activity was
incessant. He sent aid to Scanderbeg against the Turks
in Albania. He might possibly have prevented the fall of
Constantinople in 1453, if the other Italian states had supported him. He did his best to revive the Aragonese claims
to the duchies of Athens and Neopatras.[2] At his death, on
June 27, 1458,[3] he followed the precedent set by the majority
of his predecessors, and divided his inheritance. Having
no legitimate children, he bequeathed Naples to his bastard son Ferrante, while the rest of his realms, including
Sicily, passed to his brother John.[4] It was doubtless the
only practical settlement under the circumstances. Aragon would not have tolerated Ferrante, and Alfonso would
never have been content to leave Naples to any one else.
That he did not attempt to bequeath more than the realm
he loved best to the child of his love is a tribute to his
political sagacity and restraint.

Altogether the reign of this brilliant monarch was fraught
with tremendous possibilities for the future. It had given
a new and fateful turn to the destinies of the Aragonese
Empire. Alfonso had continued and carried further all the
imperial, land-conquering projects of his predecessors, and
he had added a host of military, diplomatic, and political
responsibilities besides. Most significant of all, he had

---

[1] Ametller, ii, pp. 826 ff.

[2] Ametller, ii, pp. 665 ff., 744 ff.;
ante, p. 381.

[3] *Itinerario de Alfonso V*, ed. A.
Giménes Soler (Saragossa, 1909), p. 306.

[4] Ametller, ii, p. 850. Ferrante was
born in 1423. There has been much
discussion concerning his parentage. Cf.
A. A. Messer, *Le codice Aragonese*, p.
xxviii, note 2.

shifted the centre of gravity of the Aragonese Empire from Spain to Naples. He had refused to dwell in his native land; he either ignored it completely or else attempted to make use of it to pay the bills of his political and diplomatic ventures outside, or of his sumptuous Neapolitan court. All this was gall and wormwood to the sober Aragonese, and even the more enterprising Catalans became increasingly restless. As soon as the Aragonese Empire ceased to be directed from the realms of the Crown of Aragon their enthusiasm for it began to wane. In their eyes the fresh glories which Alfonso's reign had brought with it were no compensation for the reckless infringement of their constitutional liberties. The language used by a deputation of the Cortes of Aragon sent over to the king in 1452 is very noteworthy: "Sire, the war which has continued for seven years without ceasing has depopulated your frontiers to such a degree that men have ceased to till the soil there; Aragon, during these seven years, has expended four hundred thousand florins in the ransom of prisoners alone; all industry, all commerce is at a standstill. . . . For such manifold evils, the country can find but one remedy — and that is the presence of its king." [1] No words could have been more prophetic. They sum up the grievances of sixteenth-century Spain against the Emperor Charles V. They foreshadow a Spanish Empire ruled in non-Spanish interests and in non-Spanish ways. The Magnanimous King had sown the seeds of future conflict between national and dynastic interests. He had bequeathed to his successors an enlarged empire, but dissatisfied subjects. What was the solution to be? The future alone could tell, and the future was on the knees of the gods.

[1] Cited in R. St.-H., v, p. 278. The war referred to is the desultory struggle with Castile, which took its rise in the territorial ambitions of Alfonso's younger brother, the future John II, who represented him in Aragon during his absence.

BIBLIOGRAPHICAL NOTE

See bibliographical notes to the three preceding chapters, and add:
Contemporary Authorities. — *Crónica del Rey Pedro IV.* Spanish translation, ed. A. de Bofarull (Barcelona, 1850). Much has been recently written concerning this interesting work and its authorship, which is almost certainly to be attributed to Pedro's secretary, Bernardo Descoll; there can be little question, however, that he worked under the king's guidance and supervision. Cf. Ballester y Castell, *Fuentes Narrativas*, p. 146, note. Lorenzo Valla's *Historiarum Ferdinandi Regis Aragoniae Libri III* is rather the work of a most intelligent humanist and man of letters than of an historian. It was finished in 1445, and first published in Paris in 1521. I have used the edition in Schott, i, pp. 727–785. The most important contemporary writer on Alfonso the Magnanimous is Bartholomaeus Facius (Fazio), *De Rebus Gestis ab Alphonso Primo Neapolitanorum Rege Commentariorum Libri Decem* (Naples, 1769). On this man and the various editions of his work, see Fueter, *Historiographie moderne*, p. 46, and Bartolommeo Capasso, *Le Fonti della Storia delle Provincie Napolitane* (Naples, 1902), pp. 169 f. Capasso is apparently unaware that extracts from G. Pellegrini's manuscript *Historia de Actibus Regis Alfonsi* (Bibl. Naz. di Napoli, Ms. ix, c. 22) have been printed by Lecoy de la Marche, in *Le Roi René*, ii, pp. 401–428; nor does he mention an anonymous manuscript *Cronica del Regno di Napoli* (Bibl. Brancacciana di Napoli, Ms. 2 G 11), a part of which was also printed by Lecoy de la Marche, *Le Roi René*, ii, pp. 428–435.

Later Works. — The standard history of Sardinia by Giuseppe Manno, *Storia di Sardegna* (3d edition, Milan, 1835, 2 vols.), leaves much to be desired. Rosario Gregorio's *Opere Rare riguardanti la Sicilia* (2d edition, Palermo, 1873) is still useful; Isidoro La Lumia's *Storie Siciliane* (Palermo, 1881–83, 4 vols.), and his *Studi di Storia Siciliana* (Palermo, 1870, 2 vols.), are indispensable. J. Ametller y Vinyas, *Alfonso V de Aragón en Italia* (Gerona, 1903, 2 vols.), is a most exhaustive work, which is comparatively little known; its usefulness, however, is much impaired by lack of references. Albert Lecoy de la Marche, *Le Roi René* (Paris, 1875, 2 vols.), is excellent, and contains a number of well chosen documents. Georges Desdevises du Dezert, *Don Carlos d'Aragon* (Paris, 1889), is the standard biography of that prince, and also gives much valuable information about Navarrese institutions. Useful monographs on special subjects are Karl Schwarz, *Aragonische Hofordnungen im 13. und 14. Jahrhundert* (Berlin, 1914); Florencio Janer, *Examen de los Sucesos y Circunstancias que*

motivaron el Compromiso de Caspe (Madrid, 1855); Cayetano Soler,
El Fallo de Caspe (Barcelona, 1899); Antonino Flandina, "La Spedizione
di Alfonso nell' Isola della Gerbe," in *Archivio storico Siciliano*, nuova
serie, i (1876), pp. 422–453; and N. F. Faraglia, *Storia della Lotta fra
Alfonso V d' Aragona e Renato d' Angiò* (Lanciano, 1908).

CHAPTER X

THE LIBERTIES OF ARAGON

THE history of the institutional development of the realms of the Crown of Aragon differs widely, as might be expected, from that of Castile. In the first place, we have here to do with a number of different states, each governed under a constitution of its own. When the Crowns of Aragon and Catalonia were joined by the marriage of Ramon and Petronilla in the twelfth century, each land retained its separate institutions, as did Valencia and the Balearics after they had been conquered. The sole tie between these realms was the fact that they possessed the same king and occasionally sent their representatives to meet in a joint Cortes; even the kingship of the Balearics, as we have already seen, was most of the time separated from that of Aragon until their final annexation in 1349. In the matter of language, moreover, there was the sharpest sort of division. The Catalan tongue is very similar to the Provençal, but quite different from the Aragonese, which is a dialect of Spanish. In Valencia a modified form of Catalan prevailed, but in a few regions which were permanently settled by Aragonese nobles, the Aragonese language maintained itself and is spoken today. The sovereigns of the house of Barcelona spoke Catalan, and were therefore linguistically at variance with their Aragonese subjects; those of the house of Trastamara, which succeeded them in 1412, spoke Castilian and Aragonese, and were therefore unintelligible to the Catalans. In addition to all this internal differentiation, the overseas possessions, Sardinia, Sicily, and Naples — the *tierras de allá mar* — continued to maintain their own methods and framework of government after their conquest by Aragon; during much of the time, also, the last two were ruled by collateral lines of kings. Thus the development of Spanish separatism more than kept pace with the growth of the Spanish Empire to the eastward. There was to be no merging in the parent state; the new possessions, as they were acquired, retained their constitutional autonomy.

Each one of these different states possessed certain distinguishing characteristics which reflected themselves in its institutions and political life. In Catalonia, originally an aristocratic and agricultural country, which afterwards became commercial and democratic, we have at first the nearest approach to a full-fledged feudal system which any of the Iberian lands offers; this subsequently gave way to a most remarkable urban development — both political and economic — of which Barcelona was the centre. The Aragonese respect for law is shown by the growth and power of the Justicia — an officer of a sort which no other European state can boast. The preponderance of the city of Valencia is perhaps the outstanding fact in the government of the Valencian kingdom. The Italian and Mediterranean lands also all had their peculiarities. But, though each one of these different realms is sharply differentiated from all the rest, there is noticeable everywhere — or at least within all of the Spanish realms of the Crown of Aragon — a certain unity of purpose on the part of all classes and of the different individuals within each class which stands out in sharp contrast to the conditions prevalent in Castile, and gives to the constitutional history of these eastern realms a meaning and sequence which are conspicuous by their absence in the west. This spirit of co-öperation, this sinking of individual differences for the common good, so utterly at variance with all that we have hitherto encountered in the history of Castile, makes itself principally evident in the crises of the great struggle against monarchical absolutism which raged intermittently from the reign of James the Conqueror to that of Pedro IV. The kingdom of Aragon proper was the centre of it. Catalonia and Valencia, too royalist perhaps to initiate such a revolution themselves, were yet powerfully affected by its ebbs and flows, and not ashamed to share in the spoils after the victory was won. A brief glance at the narrative history of this mighty conflict, in which the Aragonese aristocracy constituted itself the protector of the realm against all the encroachments of the royal prerogative, will serve as the best possible background for a study of the institutions of the eastern kingdoms. It will make clear the nature of the spirit that animated them, and will illustrate, as nothing else can do, the many contrasts between the Castilians and the Aragonese. It goes to show that old Lord Brougham was not far wrong in asserting that "we meet with more strict limitations of the prerogative of the Crown in the former constitutions of some of the Peninsular Kingdoms than are anywhere to be found among the old governments of the European Continent, except perhaps in Hungary." [1]

The struggle begins to take definite shape in the reign of James the Conqueror. At the time of his accession he was less than six years old, and virtually a prisoner in the hands of Simon de Montfort. His father, "the most bounteous king that ever was in Spain," had reduced the realm to bankruptcy. The land was torn by factions, in which the

[1] Brougham, *Political Philosophy*, chapter xix, par. 1.

king's uncles and the most powerful nobles disputed the precedence. The situation was in fact closely analogous to that which was constantly occurring in Castile, but the outcome was utterly different. Instead of seizing the opportunity for further abasement of the royal power, the warring barons at once recognized that the king's immediate liberation and restoration were of paramount necessity to the safety of the state, and accomplished them within eight months of his father's death. When the young monarch had been restored to his own dominions, the magnates indeed resumed their quarrels, but the aged Ximeno Cornel, "the wisest man in Aragon and the best adviser," who "grieved for the evils that he saw so great" in the realm, devoted himself to the maintenance of the central power; the church and the cities rallied loyally to its support, and James himself, as time went on, became increasingly expert in the difficult art of reigning. After thirteen years of turbulent minority (1214–27) he emerged triumphant, largely, no doubt, through his own efforts and those of his advisers, but also because of the fact that the mass of his people were thoroughly tired of factional strife and recognized its futility. Even the baronage had apparently realized that excessive restrictions of monarchical power were bound to work out badly in the end.[1]

Half a century later the king and the aristocracy encountered one another again, but with a very different distribution of forces. James had meantime enlarged his dominions by the acquisition of Valencia and the Balearics. Internal strife was for the moment in abeyance. The king had carried the power of the Aragonese monarchy to a far higher point than it had ever attained before. With

[1] Swift, *James the First of Aragon*, pp. 15–33; S. Sanpere y Miquel, *Minoria de Jaime I*.

the aid of the civilians and canonists he had modified the laws of the land by the Fueros of Huesca of 1247 in a sense hostile to feudal privilege. He was recognized as one of the foremost sovereigns of the day. In the hour of his strength his hapless son-in-law, Alfonso X of Castile, appealed to him for aid against the Moors of North Africa, and James deemed it expedient to grant it, even though extra funds were imperatively necessary in order to enable him to fit out a fleet. Maritime Catalonia came forward with a conditional grant of bovage; but when the king attempted to extort a similar tax from the Cortes of Aragon at Saragossa he was met with a stern refusal: "We do not know in Aragon what bovage is," retorted one of the members.[1] Despite all his power and prestige, the fact that James had dared to propose an unconstitutional levy had put all the Aragonese baronage up in arms; not only was bovage denied him but every other sort of impost as well. Encouraged by this initial success, the Cortes passed from their refusal of funds to an enumeration of their grievances. A Union or league of the nation — forerunner of a mightier Union soon to follow — was formed, and twelve articles were drawn up, in which various infractions of the power of the aristocracy by the triumphant monarchy were alleged. In reply the king tried to justify himself, promised respect for the fueros, and grumblingly compared his treatment by the Aragonese nobles to the persecution of Christ by the Jews.[2] Some further concessions were granted at a Cortes at Exea in 1265, where feudal privilege "attained the highest point it was destined to reach in the Conqueror's reign"; but others were refused, and "the result of the struggle was a compromise, by which the nobility secured

---

[1] Swift, pp. 108–110. Bovage was a tax on each yoke of oxen. Cf. Zurita, i, ff. 106–107; *Chronicle of James I*, ii, pp. 507–520.

[2] *Chronicle of James I*, ii, p. 520.

indeed the confirmation of the privileges of their order, but otherwise failed to trammel the King's liberty of action in any vital respect."[1]   In the fact that complete abasement of the monarchy did not follow the restriction of royal encroachments lies one of the chief differences between mediaeval Aragon and Castile.

In the next two reigns the struggle reached its culmination.   Under Pedro III the expedition to Sicily and its consequences served once more to light the fires of Aragonese discontent.   To all the old grievances was added anger at the cost of a distant enterprise of which the Aragonese did not see the value, and from which they were sure that Catalonia would derive the real profit.[2]   There was also deep dread of the hostility of France, and of the papal interdict which had followed in its train.   Altogether, the Aragonese felt that they had not been taken into the king's confidence, and that the project on which he had embarked without consulting them had ended disastrously.   All these grievances burst forth at the Cortes of Tarazona, in September, 1283, after the king's return from the Sicilian expedition.   So deep was the national resentment that the cities supported the nobles, and when Pedro answered their petitions for the observance of their fueros and liberties with a haughty speech, they proceeded to form a new Union for the defence of them.   The members of this formidable confederation solemnly promised one another mutual support for the redress of their grievances, saving their due allegiance to the crown.   They agreed to proceed by force against any who should play them false, and to defend one another's persons and goods against any royal processes initiated without the consent of the Justicia of

[1] Swift, pp. 111-113.
[2] Klüpfel, *Die äussere Politik Alfonso's III.*, pp. 4-8.

Aragon — holding that in such cases they were absolved
from their oath of fidelity to their sovereign. They even
went so far as to declare that under such circumstances
they regarded themselves as free to make common cause
with the Infante Alfonso, the heir to the throne, and to
expel King Pedro from the realm. "They were all of them,"
says Zurita, "so unanimous on this point, that the Ricos
Hombres and the Knights labored no more strenuously for
the maintenance of their privileges and liberties than did
the commons and the lower classes; for they all were of
the opinion that Aragon existed, not by virtue of the forces
of the kingdom, but of liberty, and it was the will of them
all that when liberty should perish, the realm also should
perish with it."[1] The king was naturally alarmed at the
seriousness of the opposition he had encountered, and
prorogued the Cortes to Saragossa, promising at the same
time to examine the complaints alleged. In the interim
fresh demands were added to the old. The nation was
obviously in deadly earnest, and in view of the threatening
aspect of foreign affairs Pedro was obliged to yield. The
instrument in which the royal concessions were made is
known to history as the General Privilege, and it has sometimes been compared to Magna Carta. Both are singular
mixtures of feudal and national claims. Both aim at putting
a term to monarchical usurpations without prejudice to
the position of a king who keeps within the law. Both
strenuously assert that they are not innovations but a
return to ancient liberties which had been infringed by
the crown. But there is, of course, the widest possible
divergence between the circumstances of their origin and
the character of the kings from whom they were extorted.
The members of the Union continued even in the moment

[1] Zurita, i, f. 265.

of their triumph to preserve a respect for Pedro III which the barons at Runnymede never accorded to John Lackland. Their great seal represents the sovereign seated on his throne and the members of the Union on their knees before him, in the attitude of suppliants, as a sign of their loyalty. On the other hand, a long line of spears in the background of the picture indicates that the confederates had the means at their disposal to enforce their demands, in case the king should refuse to listen to them.[1]

The chief provisions of this memorable act[2] are as follows. The king swore to observe all the ancient fueros and privileges of the realm, and promised that in future no Aragonese subject should be tried or convicted without due process of law; all lands and goods confiscated during the reigns of Pedro and of his father were to be returned; all donations and grants from the royal domain to the *ricos hombres* were to be validated and confirmed; no fief was to be forfeited without the consent of the Justicia and of the royal council. All nobles were to have the unquestioned right to leave the service of the king and to seek another lord outside the realm for any cause whatsoever; and to recommend to the king's favor and protection on their departure their wives and children, vassals and goods. No *rico hombre* was to be obliged to render military service beyond the boundaries of the realm or overseas, on the ground of any fief or honor held of the king. Representatives of all ranks and classes of society were to have a place in the royal council, and to be consulted in regard to peace and war and the general welfare of the realm. Only natives of the kingdom were to be permitted to sit as judges. No

[1] Hallam, *View of the State of Europe during the Middle Ages* (Boston, 1861), ii, pp. 48-50.

[2] The text is to be found in vol. i, ff. 6-8 of the official edition of the *Fueros y Observancias del Reyno de Aragon* (Saragossa, 1667, 2 vols.).

new impost or tax was to be established; the salt tax and the *quinta* were to be abolished. Finally, annual Cortes were to be held at Saragossa, and the members of the Union were to have the right to present fresh demands from time to time.

The concessions of King Pedro to his Aragonese subjects were reëchoed in Valencia and Catalonia. As the operation of the fueros in Aragon had been specifically extended to the former kingdom in the reign of James the Conqueror, the Valencians were permitted to appropriate to themselves all the rights granted in the General Privilege as a matter of course; moreover the fact that Valencia and Valencian affairs are constantly mentioned in the text of the instrument indicates that this had been intended from the first.[1] A series of parallel privileges was also granted to the Catalonians — the more willingly because they had greatly aided Pedro in the conquest of Sicily, and were about to bear the brunt of an invasion from France. But it was one thing to accede to the demands of his subjects in theory and another to observe them in practice. The Valencians were bullied into a repudiation of the 'Fuero of Aragon' within a short time after they had been granted it; while the Aragonese, who discerned unmistakable signs that Pedro intended ultimately to evade his promises to them, strengthened the bonds of their Union, began to raise troops, and opened negotiations, as a sovereign power, with the king's enemies in Navarre.[2] Whether or not they would have dared to do so much if Pedro had not been laboring under the terrible incubus of papal censure may well be doubted; but as it was, despite the royal entreaties, and the pressure of the danger of invasion from France, they continued in their revolt, and threatened to paralyze the military efficiency of

[1] Zurita, i, f. 265.   [2] Zurita, i, f. 266.

the realm. The fact, however, that zeal for the assertion of class privilege was now beginning to take the precedence of patriotism in the ranks of the rebels was speedily perceived by King Pedro, who cleverly utilized the fact for his own advantage. He wisely ignored the demands of the members of the Union, in the hope that the untimeliness of their complaints would deprive them of popular sympathy, and that their rebellious ardor would cool for lack of an object to vent itself upon. In July, 1285, his foresight was justified by the event. The insurgents decided to postpone the redress of their grievances and aid the king against the French. Pedro, however, was not destined to reap the reward of his statesmanship; for at Perpignan, on St. Martin's Day, he died.[1]

The absence of Alfonso III on the Majorcan expedition at the moment of his father's death afforded the members of the Union an opportunity to organize a fresh resistance; while the fact that the danger from France was temporarily set aside gave them an excuse for returning to their grievances. Beginning with the complaint, unjustifiable under the circumstances, that Alfonso had dared to assume the title of king of Aragon without waiting to swear to the maintenance of their fueros, they went on to demand the reformation of the royal household, and the banishment of all the royal counsellors of whom they did not approve. The monarch was rudely summoned to Saragossa to discuss the affairs of the nation with the Cortes, and to revoke all grants of fiefs made since the death of Pedro. The malcontents threatened to refuse all payment of taxes in case he failed to comply, and to unite to resist him by force.[2]

[1] Zurita, i, ff. 280, 289, 297–299. A number of curious details of this struggle are given by the fifteenth-century Catalan chronicler, P. M. Carbonell, in his *Chroniques de Espanya* (Barcelona, 1547), ff. lxx–lxxx.

[2] Zurita, ii, f. 302.

The king appeared, but showed unexpected firmness in refusing the Union's demands, with the result that the more fainthearted of the confederates deserted the cause. The rest Alfonso tried to win over by concessions, and was making good progress towards the desired end when he was called away on the expedition against Minorca. Then, when his back was turned, all the elements of revolt broke forth afresh. The malcontents ravaged Valencia. They sent messengers to France, to Castile, and to Granada begging for alliances. They almost went so far as to recognize the right of the papal protégé, the French king's son, to the throne of Aragon.[1] There could no longer be the slightest question that they had gone far beyond the widest possible interpretation of the fueros and privileges of the realm. Constitutional and feudal progress by this time had outrun administrative order with a vengeance, but the king was at present too weak to defend his just rights. All attempts at compromise failed; the Union had the power in its hands and proposed to use it. On Christmas day, 1287, Alfonso made a solemn entry into Saragossa, and there signed two documents known to history by the significant name of the 'Privileges of Union,' and described, with only slight exaggeration, as "the most tremendous power ever conceded by a king to his subjects."[2] By them he promised not to proceed against any of the members of the Union save by sentence of the Justicia and with the consent of the Cortes, which were to be convoked annually at Saragossa; and the national assembly was given the right to elect and assign to the king certain persons who were to have seats in his royal council. Sixteen castles were handed over by the monarch as security for the ob-

[1] Zurita, ii, ff. 303–305, 307–308, 311–315, 316–318.   [2] Zurita, ii, ff. 321–323; Burke, History of Spain, i, p. 375.

servance of his promises; and finally, in case he should evade them, he formally recognized the right of the Union to depose him and to choose another king in his stead.[1] In the following year, the members of the Union further declared that the 'Fuero of Aragon' and all the liberties and privileges which went with it were extended to the kingdom of Valencia.[2]

Most of the provisions of the Privileges of Union, even more than those of the General Privilege which preceded them, remained unfulfilled in fact. The castles were not all handed over; the decrees and decisions of the Justicia were not executed; though the counsellors whom the Privilege of Union imposed upon the king were chosen, their advice was often ignored; and the Cortes did not meet annually. The organization of the Union, however, remained unshaken throughout the rest of the reign of Alfonso III and the first ten years of that of James II. The latter's caution and known respect for the law, and also possibly the emigration of a number of the nobles to Italy, which he secretly encouraged, prevented any open breach for a time; but finally, in 1301, the news that an outbreak similar to that of 1287 was imminent forced the king to take vigorous measures for the defence of his authority. On this occasion, however, the royal cause was completely victorious. That the Cortes and the Justicia promptly rallied to its support may be taken as a significant proof that Aragon realized that the Union had gone too far for the good of the realm. Certainly their alliance facilitated the king's triumph. James was able to pose as defender of parliamentary privilege and of the authority of the courts against the assaults of a dis-

---

[1] The text of the two privileges may be found in M. and M., v, pp. 34–40; in V. de la Fuente, *Estudios críticos sobre la historia y el derecho de Aragón*, iii, pp. 119–131, 186 f.; and in Danvila y Collado, *Las libertades de Aragon*, pp. 234–245.

[2] Zurita, i, ff. 332–333.

loyal and selfish baronage. After a brief struggle the
Justicia pronounced the annulment of the Union as an illegal institution; he revoked all its acts, and delivered
over all its members and their goods to the royal mercy.[1]
James had the wisdom to use his victory with moderation,
and this, coupled with the fortunate circumstances under
which he had won it, prevented a recrudescence of trouble
for many years to come. Indeed, it is not too much to say
that the most notable triumphs of the reign of this king
were gained in his dealings with his rebel subjects at home.
In a work on the development of the Spanish Empire they
must necessarily be relegated to an inconspicuous place, but
they are quite worthy of a separate volume in themselves.
James's patience, perseverance, and, above all, his skilful
utilization of the legists that flocked to his court, are the
chief elements which combined to give him the victory;
and his success in converting the Justicia into an ally of
the monarchy was the outward and visible sign of his
triumph. His deathbed boast was fully justified: "I
have passed many a sleepless night," he protested, "in
planning how to cause my subjects to enjoy the blessings of
justice and peace."[2]

The final stage of the struggle of king and barons was
postponed till the reign of Pedro IV. For though the
Union of James II's day had been dispersed, the Privileges
of Union were still extant; and as long as the Privileges
remained, a new Union might at any time be created. A
quarrel in the royal family over the succession to the throne
gave the signal for a fresh outbreak in 1346–47. Pedro's
first wife, Mary of Navarre, had borne him no male children who survived. As the law of Aragon excluded women

[1] Zurita, i, ff. 401–403.   385–387; V. de la Fuente, *Estudios*
[2] Zurita, ii, f. 81; R. St.-H., iv, pp.   *críticos*, iii, pp. 145–173.

from the throne, the heir presumptive was Pedro's younger brother, James. Pedro, however, had many reasons to dislike and mistrust this man — particularly because of his friendship with King James of Majorca — and determined, in defiance of the custom of the land, to leave the throne to his daughter, Constance, in default of male heirs in the direct line. This decision was much resented by the mass of his subjects, not only as a violation of the fundamental laws, but also because the proud spirit of the Aragonese bridled at the thought of being ruled by a woman. The cause of James found adherents on every hand. The discontent, moreover, spread rapidly to Valencia, always closely in touch with Aragon, and especially so on this occasion since it was the regular residence of the Infante. Feeling that he could not be safe as long as his brother remained in the southern kingdom, Pedro summoned him to leave it, and conferred its governorship in his absence on one of his own adherents. But if James's departure from Valencia promised to give Pedro quiet in that quarter, his presence in Saragossa, whither he at once repaired, served to redouble the discontent there. Skilful utilization of the magic words 'liberties' and 'fueros' produced the inevitable effect. The Union, abolished in the reign of James, reconstituted itself with spontaneous and unbounded enthusiasm. The fact that the cities, with but few exceptions, unhesitatingly threw in their lot with the nobles was of evil augury for the monarchy, which was thereby deprived of its strongest support; while their accession to the ranks of the Union relieved the latter of the charge of being devoted merely to feudal and aristocratic ends. The reservation that it pursued its aims "saving its due allegiance to the crown" was also most useful as a rallying cry in a land where respect for the law has ever been very great, and at

the same time it was not sufficiently specific to hamper
freedom of action.   And the example of Saragossa was soon
followed by Valencia.   Despite all that Pedro's representative there could do, another Union, modelled on that of
Aragon, was promptly formed in the southern kingdom;
moreover the two bodies soon came to an agreement that
they should fight in unison for their common ends, and
that neither should treat with the king without the consent
of the other.   In Catalonia alone did Pedro find support.
There the principles of the Union had not penetrated; and
the long established partiality of the Aragonese monarchs
for the inhabitants of this maritime and commercial province was richly rewarded in their hour of danger and
distress.[1]

Despite the support of the Catalonians, Pedro was as
yet in no condition to defeat his enemies by force; but it
was in just such crises as this that he invariably displayed
his highest talents as a diplomat and intriguer.   After demanding a safe conduct, to the great indignation of his subjects, who could not bear the thought that their honor or
loyalty was doubted, he acquiesced in the rebels' petitions
that he should come to Saragossa and summon the national
Cortes.   Having satisfied himself on his arrival that his
foes had the military power to enable them to enforce whatever demands they elected to make, he acceded to most
of their demands.   Annual Cortes, expulsion of unpopular
(Catalonian) counsellors, and acceptance of new ones selected by the Union, together with the confirmation of
other concessions embodied in the second of the two Privileges of 1287, were granted one after the other.   Hostages
were given, and sixteen castles delivered up as security for
the performance of the royal promises; Pedro himself was

[1] Zurita, ii, ff. 187–190, 191–194, 195–198.

virtually a prisoner of the Union in his palace at Saragossa, while at the same time his presence there served to give a show of legality to the rebels' cause.[1] But just at the moment that the king of Aragon seemed about to drain the cup of humiliation to the dregs, his fortunes began to revive. Despite all the hostages demanded of him, he had managed to retain about his person his mayor domo, Bernaldo de Cabrera, a violent royalist,[2] whose powers of diplomacy and intrigue were not exceeded by his own. The latter began by detaching from the Union Lope de Luna, the richest noble of the three realms, whom he won over by promising him the much desired post of governor-general of Aragon; he also opened communications with the remnant of the royalist party in Valencia. Encouraged by these signs of returning fortune, Pedro ventured roundly to accuse his brother James of treason and felony in a solemn session of the Cortes, and to challenge him to mortal combat. The duel was declined, but a scene of extraordinary violence ensued; the crowd broke into the church where the session was being held, but the king and his adherents escaped unharmed. Not even yet, however, did Pedro feel strong enough to appeal to arms. In late October, 1347, he left Saragossa for the friendlier soil of Catalonia, after confirming all his concessions to his foes, and annulling all oaths of allegiance to his daughter Constance. But though he outwardly preserved a calm demeanor, and apparently yielded every point that his enemies demanded, the fires of fury were raging within him at the check he had received. Though seemingly powerless, he was in reality plotting busily to regain all and more than he had lost, as his enemies were soon to discover to their undoing.[3]

[1] Zurita, ii, ff. 199–200, 200–204.
[2] Grandfather of the admiral of the same name, who distinguished himself in Sicily in the early years of the next century.
[3] Zurita, ii, ff. 206–207; Crónica de

The next event was the death of the Infante, on November 19, 1347, at Barcelona, whither he had gone for a meeting of the Catalonian Cortes. So convenient was his demise for the purposes of the king, that Pedro was universally believed to have brought it to pass. Of course James's death was the signal for the outburst of war both in Valencia and in Aragon; but it was in Valencia, where the Infante was deeply beloved, that the struggle was by far the most serious. The royal representative there, Pedro de Exerica, was totally unable to make head against the rebellion. The king, who rushed to his rescue with a small force of loyal Catalonians, was promptly shut up in Murviedro and forced to confirm the Valencian Union, grant the Valencians a Justicia, and exclude Cabrera and other confirmed royalists from his council. A subsequent attempt of Pedro to escape to Teruel was discovered and forestalled. Amid the threatenings of a furious crowd, the king and queen were handed over to the heads of the Valencian Union and escorted to the capital, where the populace welcomed them with jeers. A series of fresh humiliations, vividly described in the king's chronicle,[1] followed; but even at the lowest ebb of his fortunes Pedro continued to intrigue and plot, while the indefatigable Cabrera labored night and day in Barcelona to fan the fires of Catalonian loyalty. Finally the outbreak of the pestilence gave Pedro an excuse for demanding license to depart from Valencia, where he had been kept virtually a prisoner for two months. After extorting from him a renewal of past concessions, the authorities finally suffered him to escape (June, 1348). It was a grave error, for with the king at liberty all the forces of royalism raised their head. The scene of interest shifted

Pedro IV, ed. Bofarull, pp. 267–270. The king's truly dithyrambic utterances after his safe arrival on Catalonian soil afford dramatic evidence of his predilection for his Catalan subjects.

[1] *Crónica de Pedro IV*, pp. 274 f.

in the next few weeks to Aragon. Lope de Luna, the chief of the royalist forces there, prepared for a trial of strength on the field of battle; while the king, by intrigue and bribery, ably seconded his efforts, and actually succeeded in detaching hostile Castile from the ranks of his enemies, and in gaining from Alfonso XI a force of six hundred horsemen. The final encounter occurred at Epila, on the self-same spot where, seven months before, the forces of the Valencian Union had won a temporary victory over Exerica. Despite a considerable inferiority in numbers, the royalists charged with such vigor that the troops of the Union gave way all along the line. Most of the rebel chiefs remained dead on the field, though their principal leader, the Infante Ferdinand, who was wounded and taken prisoner by the king's Castilian auxiliaries, was ultimately suffered to escape to the western kingdom. On every hand the king's victory was complete (July 21, 1348).[1]

The battle of Epila was the death knell of the Union in Aragon. Saragossa submitted at once to the royalist forces, and purchased an ignoble immunity from punishment by delivering over those leaders of the insurrection (thirteen in number) who had not taken refuge in flight. They were straightway hung at the gates of the town; and similar executions occurred in other cities of the realm. All the royal concessions of the previous months were, of course, revoked; all the acts and treaties of the Union were solemnly annulled as illegal; its seal was broken and its name formally abolished. The Privileges of Union of 1287, "the root and cause of all the evil," were destroyed in most dramatic fashion. The original parchment was produced, and in the presence of his subjects the king furiously cut and hacked it into a hundred pieces with his dagger, wound-

[1] Zurita, ii, ff. 209-226.

ing himself slightly in the process, so careless had he become in his blind rage.[1] "From that time forth," says Zurita, "the name of the Union was permanently abolished, and also that license and lawlessness which men called liberty, but which, born as it was of a popular uprising and seeking to maintain itself by force of arms, perished justly by them, as is usually the case, and succumbed to the might of the power of the Crown."[2]

From Aragon Pedro turned on Valencia, where the insurrection had continued at full blast, undismayed by the fate of the Union in the sister kingdom. Though Pedro had a powerful fleet and an army at his disposal, though Aragon as well as Catalonia was now supporting him, and though Castile remained strictly neutral, the Valencians refused to surrender without a struggle. They withdrew within the walls of their capital, making occasional sorties to harass the royal troops, and meantime strove desperately, though ineffectually, to secure relief from without. But when they saw their fair country ruthlessly devastated by the king's forces, and the lines of the besieging army drawn so tightly round their city as to preclude the possibility of their escape, they were convinced that "the anger of God had fallen upon them to punish them for their sins," and prepared to treat for peace. So angry was Pedro at the resistance of the Valencians that he was with difficulty dissuaded by his counsellors from razing their city to the ground. After much argument he reluctantly agreed to accept its complete submission and an acknowledgment of

---

[1] *Crónica de Pedro IV*, pp. 281-283; Zurita, ii, f. 229. It seems that Pedro exhibited his wound to the populace, with the remark that privileges which it had cost so much blood to win could not be suppressed without the shedding of more. The scene evidently made a tremendous impression on those who witnessed it, and thereafter 'Pedro el Ceremonioso' was usually spoken of as 'Pedro del Punyalet,' or 'Pedro of the Dagger.'

[2] Zurita, ii, f. 229.

his unquestioned right to dispose of all its liberties and immunities according to his own discretion.   Finally he granted
the inhabitants a pardon, from which all active participants
in the preceding revolt were specifically excluded.   Needless to add, the Valencian Union was utterly shattered by
this defeat.   "From that day onward," as Pedro significantly puts it in his chronicle, "Valencia remained in our
grace and love."[1]   But the punishment of the guilty rebels
which paved the way for this happy consummation was far
more frightful than that which had fallen on their Aragonese
comrades a few months before.   It reminds us of the horrors enacted in Valencia two and a half centuries before in
the days of the Cid; clearly the king had much faith in
the power of terrorism.   One example will suffice : the metal
of the bell which had summoned the leaders of the Union
to council meetings was poured, red hot, down the throats
of the condemned.[2]

Thus ended after a struggle of more than a century this
singular contest between sovereign and subject, around
which the whole internal history of Aragon during the
period in question revolves, in which Valencia actively
participated, and to which Catalonia was not entirely a
stranger.   It is still too early to attempt to pronounce definite judgment upon it ; much new material remains to be
discovered ; many doubtful points need to be cleared up.
There are two fundamental questions on which the final
verdict will inevitably depend.   First : Can the aims of
the rebels be said to have been in any sense really national
in their scope, or was their uprising in effect solely a revolt
of a powerful and united feudal aristocracy, bent on the
assertion of its special privileges, but clever enough to associate with itself at certain stages representatives of the

[1] *Crónica de Pedro IV*, p. 289.   [2] Zurita, ii. ff. 230–234.

third estate in order to disguise the true nature of its aims, and to gain for itself the appearance of popular sanction? Second: Even granting that the Union was in some degree national in its character and aspirations, was it safe for any nation, at the stage of development which Aragon had then attained, so considerably to limit the power of its king? Would not anarchy have been the sole real result of a premature attempt to anticipate modern constitutionalism? Was not absolutism, at that period, the only sure road to peace and order, as England, France, and Castile were to learn in the next century, to their cost? Certainly the writings of patriots like Zurita and Blancas are distinctly favorable to the royal cause, and strongly assert that the defeat of the Union was for the best interest of the realm.[1] Moreover, it is worth noting that though Pedro punished ferociously at the moment, he used his victory in later years with remarkable moderation. Against the higher nobility he remained indeed inexorable; their power was broken beyond the possibility of repair; but he extended the rights of the lesser baronage, and restored and amplified the charters of the cities that had risen in arms against him. Most important of all, as we shall see in detail in another place, he confirmed and strengthened the authority of the Justicia, who, though his appointment was now unreservedly in the royal hands, continued in the next period to perform the work which the warmest apologists of the Union had declared to be the true function of his office — the defence of the subject against breach of privilege and sentence contrary to the law. Pedro's successors, moreover, at least down to Alfonso the Magnanimous, followed on the whole the same wise course, with the gratifying

[1] Blancas, *Comentarios*, tr. Hernandes, pp. 181 f. Of the modern writers, Danvila y Collado (*Libertades de Aragon*, pp. 405 ff.) takes the same view, while V. de la Fuente (*Estudios críticos*, iii, pp. 100–204) is more progressive.

result that the history of Aragon, during most of the century previous to the accession of the Catholic Kings, presents an agreeable contrast to contemporary Castile in the general stability of its institutions, and in the absence of baronial rebellion.   Yet, on the other hand, even the bitterest critic of the aims of the Union and the most ardent advocate of royal absolutism will not be prepared to deny that the cause for which the Aragonese rebels lived and died was far more deserving of our sympathy than the savage, wanton, disorganized outbursts of the self-seeking nobility of Castile. They certainly fought for an ideal; it may have been a wrong one, but it was unquestionably higher than individual aggrandizement.   The whole tone of the contest in Aragon connotes a more advanced stage of political development than the western kingdom had yet reached.   It has justly been compared to the struggle for the charters in thirteenth-century England; it has a meaning and sequence; it appeals to the sympathy and intelligence of the modern student, who often finds himself at a loss to account for the strivings of the aristocracy in Castile.   And lastly, though the aims of the Union were not attained, the attitude of the Aragonese sovereigns after the battle of Epila plainly shows that they realized that their subjects would never let them push their victories too far, or tolerate lawless despotism.   Though the Union had doubtless attempted to impose excessive limitations upon the king, it had so strengthened the spirit of resistance to unjustifiable monarchical encroachments that things could never go to the opposite extreme.   Though the mediaeval Castilian barons subjected their weak sovereigns to humiliations far more degrading than any which their Aragonese contemporaries suffered, they were unable to oppose any barrier to the well organized despotism of Ferdinand and Isabella.   In Aragon, on the other hand, the defences against royal absolutism remained so strong that the Catholic Kings wisely refrained from any attempt to overthrow them by force, and instead followed the policy of leaving the eastern realms alone, in the hope that their passion for liberty would die down from lack of fuel to feed the flames.

BIBLIOGRAPHICAL NOTE

See bibliographical notes to the four preceding chapters, and add:

Sources. — *Fueros y Observancias del Reyno de Aragon*. Edited by order of the Diputacion Permanente del Reyno (Saragossa, 1667, 2 vols.). Indispensable for the study of the constitutional history of the realm.

Later Works. — Pere Miguel Carbonell, *Chroniques de Espanya* (Barcelona, 1547). Carbonell was born in Barcelona in 1434 and died there in 1517; he was archivist of the Crown of Aragon from 1476 to his death. His chronicle deals only with Aragon down to the year 1488. For further information about him and his work see *Enciclopedia Universal Ilustrada*, vol. xi, p. 753. Jerónimo de Blancas, *Commentarii Rerum Aragonensium* (Saragossa, 1588); Spanish translation by Manuel Hernandez (Saragossa, 1878); my references are to the latter. On Blancas, who was chronicler of the realm under Philip II, see Prescott, vol. i, p. 91. Vicente de la Fuente, *Estudios críticos sobre la Historia y el Derecho de Aragón* (Madrid, 1884–86, 3 vols., or series), is invaluable; vols. ii and iii contain several excellent essays on the different phases of the constitutional struggle. Manuel Danvila y Collado's *Las Libertades de Aragon* (Madrid, 1881) is the only monograph on the struggle as a whole, but its statements and conclusions should be accepted with caution. Salvador Sanpere y Miquel's *Minoria de Jaime I* (Barcelona, 1910) is a useful essay. The war has unfortunately made it impossible for me to obtain H. E. Rohde's edition of Klüpfel's posthumous work on the *Verwaltungsgeschichte des Königreichs Aragon zu Ende des 13. Jahrhunderts* (Stuttgart, 1915).

CHAPTER XI

THE INSTITUTIONS OF THE EASTERN KINGDOMS AND OF THEIR DEPENDENCIES

THE great internal struggle which has been described in the preceding chapter affords the principal explanation of the fact, already frequently noticed, that Aragon and Valencia held themselves largely aloof from the ambitious plans and enterprises of their sovereigns in Italy and in the Mediterranean Sea. Their attention was turned inward, not outward; they were, in fact, rather negatively than positively important in the upbuilding of the Aragonese Empire. Consequently we are justified in restricting our examination of their institutions to the smallest possible space, in emphasizing only those features which are unique and distinctive, particularly those which served to limit the royal power; for it is really almost as a hindrance to imperial development that we are concerned with them. The constitution and internal conditions of maritime and commercial Catalonia, on the other hand, will have to be more fully discussed : for it was from Catalonia that all the great adventures overseas were launched; she was the true centre of the Aragonese Empire. A few words must also be added concerning the methods of governing the Mediterranean possessions as they were successively acquired. Of course the real life of the system we are about to describe was destined to be but short. After the union of the crowns under Ferdinand and Isabella, Castile so completely took the precedence of the eastern kingdoms that she swallowed up many of their institutional peculiarities, in fact at least, if not in name. Though the ancient framework of the mediaeval constitutions of the Aragonese realms and their dependencies was permitted to subsist as a matter of form, Castilian methods and principles practically prevailed after the beginning of the sixteenth century throughout every portion of the Spanish Empire. On the other hand, it would be impossible to give any adequate idea of the real nature of that extraordinary agglomeration without some account of the infinite variety of its component parts. It is therefore essential for us to familiarize ourselves with the more salient characteristics of its eastern and ultimately less important portions.

ARAGON

The predominance and power of the aristocracy of Aragon is the outstanding characteristic of the social structure of that kingdom. In its long struggle with the monarchy it had won for itself a position so high, that, though defeated at Epila, it never ceased to boast that it was the truest guardian of the national liberties. Other forces, moreover, had been at work from earliest times to assure its preëminence. Aragon had played so small a part in the work of the Reconquest that the need to concentrate in walled towns was not felt there to the same degree that it was in Castile. A more sedentary and rural existence was therefore possible, and a system of large landed holdings — the first essential for a flourishing nobility — grew up and was perpetuated. There was, moreover, something more nearly resembling a regular feudal system in Aragon than in Castile; and it was considerably accentuated by the union with Catalonia — a still more feudal state — in 1137. By the second half of the thirteenth century, at the time of the

Cortes of Exea, a very real feudalism may be said to have been in existence in Aragon, where, curiously enough, it began to flourish at the very moment that elsewhere it showed signs of decadence.[1]

Perhaps the most obvious outward sign of the power and importance of the Aragonese aristocracy lies in the fact that it comprised two great categories — an upper and a lower nobility, each with a separate representation in the Cortes — so that there were, with the clergy and burgesses, not three but four estates of the realm. The upper nobility, who claimed descent from the first conquerors of the land, were known as barons or *ricos hombres*; of these there were but nine in the reign of James the Conqueror. They held of the king fiefs and 'honors,' consisting of the revenues of different towns, and were obliged in return to render him military service from one to three months each year at the rate of one knight for every five hundred Jaccic sols (about $175) of rent. They were exempt from corporal punishment, from the jurisdiction of the ordinary tribunals of the realm, save that of the Justicia, and from the payment of regular taxes; they also possessed the unquestioned right of renunciation of allegiance to their sovereign. They could be deprived of their lands only for certain specified crimes, one of which was falsely ascribing, under oath, the attributes and privileges of noble birth to any one who did not actually possess them.[2]

The lower nobility were divided into three classes, *mesnaderos*, *caballeros*, and *infanzones*. The first originated in the reign of James the Conqueror, and, as their name (from *mesnada* or royal household) indicates, were specially

[1] Vicente de la Fuente, "Los señorios en Aragón," in vol. ii of his *Estudios críticos*, pp. 165–240; Swift, *James the First of Aragon*, chap. xix.

[2] M. and M., vi, pp. 6–25; Altamira, §§ 310, 466, 471; Swift, *op. cit.*, pp. 187 f.

attached to the royal person; they were supposed to be descendants in the male line of *ricos hombres*, and were only slightly inferior to them. They were vassals of the king alone, but could live without dishonor at the expense of a *rico hombre* — though only as a friend and not as a vassal.[1] *Caballeros*, or knights, enjoyed exemption from taxation and certain other privileges of nobility, such as that no one should lay hands on the bridles of their horses to detain them. The title, however, connoted rather an acquired dignity than a status by birth, and it could, apparently, be conferred by prelates and *ricos hombres* as well as by the crown. The *infanzones*, at the bottom of the ladder, were sons of knights, and were naturally very numerous; but the possession of a number of more or less important privileges marked them off sharply from the burgesses.[2] In general, one gains the impression that the kings deliberately increased the number and prerogatives of these lesser nobles as a counterweight to the excessive powers of the *ricos hombres*; but they certainly did not succeed in breeding any permanent dissension in the ranks of the baronage. The Aragonese aristocracy stood united, on the whole, in a way which furnishes a most impressive contrast with their self-seeking Castilian contemporaries; and they were not only zealous for the welfare of their order as a whole, but also for that of the entire body politic. Their division into two estates served to strengthen, not to weaken them; they thus constituted themselves one half of the national assembly,[3] and vindicated their title to the high position to which they laid claim.

The clergy and the municipalities were far less impor-

---

[1] Blancas, *Comentarios*, pp. 278–317; M. and M., vi, pp. 25–27.

[2] "Los infansones nacian, los caballeros se hacian": *Fueros y Observancias del Reyno de Aragon*, ii, fols. 22 ff.; M. and M., vi, p. 29.

[3] Cf. *infra*, p. 460.

tant in mediaeval Aragon than in Castile,[1] as was natural in view of the comparatively modest part borne by the Aragonese in the war of the Reconquest. Down to the battle of Epila, the churchmen and most of the larger cities tended in general to throw in their lot with the baronage against the monarchy, and sought to win for themselves privileges like those of the aristocracy;[2] after the close of the internal struggle, both these orders made some independent gains at the expense of the defeated nobles. The fueros granted to the different cities do not offer the same variety and divergence as do those of Castile; but the capital city of Saragossa claimed and attained a practical predominance over all the other towns of the realm, to which we have no parallel in the western kingdom. It is indicated by the fact that Saragossa invariably demanded the right to represent one half the *brazo real* or fourth estate whenever a committee was appointed to do business in its name, and also by the so-called *Privilegio de los Veinte*, a sort of special constitution granted to the city by Alfonso I in 1119, which vested extraordinary powers in a body of twenty of the principal inhabitants, and conferred exceptional rights and prerogatives upon the municipality as a whole.[3]

The mass of the rural population led a hard existence; and the lot of the Aragonese serf was even worse than that

[1] Despite the statements to the contrary of Prescott, i, p. 65, who probably based his conclusions on the erroneous theory that the cities sent representatives to the Cortes of Aragon in 1133: cf. on this V. de la Fuente, *Estudios críticos*, ii, pp. 14 ff.

[2] Save in the South, where there are evidences of a more democratic attitude; cf. Altamira, § 466.

[3] M. and M., vi, pp. 217–220; Sans y Ramón, *Privilegio de los Veinte*. There were also in Aragon three so-called *comunidades* — Daroca, Calatayud, and Teruel. These were groups of villages and hamlets, whose constitution and government present a number of curious anomalies. The fuero of Teruel, which is closely akin to those of Cuenca and of Sepúlveda in Castile, has been published with an excellent introduction by F. Aznar y Navarro, in vol. ii of the *Colección de Documentos para el Estudio de la Historia de Aragón* (Saragossa, 1905).

of the Castilian *solariego*. There were but few free landed proprietors, except among the ranks of the nobles; the peasants were all of them more or less at the mercy of their masters, who could "treat them well or badly, according to their own desires, and take away their goods without appeal, without the king's having any right to interfere." [1] So completely were some of them bound to the soil, that, in case the land on which they lived was partitioned among the sons of the lord, each of the serfs who dwelt thereon could, according to the strict letter of the law, "be divided in pieces with it." [2]

The condition of the Aragonese Jews in the later Middle Ages is not strikingly different from that of their coreligionists in Castile. Like them, they were very numerous, and enjoyed in the thirteenth century wider freedom and privileges than were accorded to them in the other nations of Western Europe. They were segregated in special localities, or *aljamas*, in the most important towns of the realm, and their rights and prerogatives were strictly defined. James the Conqueror was particularly active in protecting them; he recognized their high economic value, and frequently employed them in the financial business of the crown. At the same time, however, the ecclesiastical authorities were mustering their forces for the campaign of proselytism and persecution which began in earnest in the fourteenth century. The Castilian massacres of 1391 had their counterparts in all the realms of the Crown of Aragon, though certainly to a much less extent in Aragon proper than in Catalonia and Valencia. Large numbers of Hebrews were slain outright; most of the rest accepted baptism — some,

[1] *Fueros y Observancias*, ii, f. 38, ley xix. In 1381 the nobles successfully protested against an attempt by Pedro IV to prevent one of their number from maltreating his serfs. Zurita, ii, f. 375.

[2] R. St.-H., v, p. 71; and *ante*, p. 181, note.

no doubt, because of the preachings of men like St. Vincent
Ferrer and Gerónimo de Santa Fé, others in order to escape
from further outrages.[1] In one respect it seems that the lot
of the *conversos*, if they showed any signs of relapsing, must
have been worse in Aragon than in Castile; for the papal
Inquisition, though it had not been extended to the western
kingdom, had been established in the eastern realms since
the time of its foundation in the thirteenth century, and
furnished the machinery, ready to hand, for the detection
and punishment of religious backsliders. But as a matter
of fact the Inquisition "had sunk into a condition almost
dormant in the spiritual lethargy of the century preceding
the Reformation," while on the other hand the Aragonese
as a whole, and especially their rulers, were considerably
more alive than the Castilians to the financial and economic
value of the Jewish portions of the population, and consequently more reluctant to persecute them. We therefore
find the *conversos* occupying the highest offices in the government, in the army, and at the court, and marrying their
children into the foremost families of the land; while the
first part of the fifteenth century witnessed a distinct revulsion of feeling in favor of the professed Jews who had
remained loyal to the faith of their fathers. Many of the
legal restrictions under which they lived were not rigorously
enforced; by the time of the accession of the Catholic Kings
they had regained, in practice, a large part of the privileges
which in theory they had previously lost.[2]

The Moors in the kingdom of Aragon were even better
off, and were also more fortunate than their brethren in
Castile. The intimate commercial and political relations

[1] Amador de los Rios, *Historia de los Judíos en España*, i, caps. vi, ix; ii, caps. i, iii, v, vii, viii, x; F. Baer, *Studien zur Geschichte der Juden in Aragonien, passim*.

[2] Lea, *Inquisition of Spain*, i, caps. iii, v, *passim*.

which most of the Aragonese sovereigns maintained with the North African states had their natural counterpart in the very notable degree of liberality in their treatment of the Moorish inhabitants of their own dominions. A large measure of religious and political freedom was permitted them in return for the payment of certain special and extra imposts, and for their subjection to a number of economic limitations of which the Christian population reaped the benefit. There was virtually no attempt at proselytism or conversion; they had escaped the odium which proverbial Hebrew avarice had fastened on the Jews; there are many evidences that they were generally regarded as valuable members of society. The practice of selling into slavery Moorish prisoners captured in war practically ceased in the fourteenth and fifteenth centuries with the completion of the Reconquest and the capture of the Balearics.[1]

We pass from the different ranks and classes of society to the various organs of the central government. The Aragonese kingship was hereditary, like that of Castile,[2] but the royal powers and prerogatives, in theory at least, were much less extensive. The king's oath before the Justicia and the representatives of the four estates of the realm to observe all the laws and privileges of the land was indispensable to the validity of his accession; and the formula of allegiance, which, according to contemporary authorities, was still in use in the sixteenth century, clearly indicates that the sovereign was regarded rather as the servant than as the master of his people. "We who are as good as you," so it ran, "swear to you who are no better than we, to accept you as our king and sovereign lord, provided you

---

[1] Altamira, § 467.

[2] Save that it excluded females from the succession. Zurita, i, f. 66; M.

and M., iv, p. 498; Danvila, *Poder Civil en España*, i, p. 321.

observe all our liberties and laws; but if not, not." [1] Here
there is certainly no trace of absolutism on the one hand or of
servility on the other; a contract is made between sovereign
and subjects, in which deposition is openly recognized as
the proper penalty for a king who seeks to override the laws.
And the constitution erected a host of other barriers against
the despotism of the crown. Most of them will be taken
up incidentally to our study of the position and power of
the other portions of the body politic. For the present we
need only observe that the Aragonese monarchs were far
more limited than their Castilian contemporaries by the
extensive powers of the Cortes in legislation, taxation,
finance, and even in the management of foreign affairs, and
by the authority of the Justicia in matters of justice.[2] Even
in the appointment of their intimate advisers and counsellors, and of the officers of their royal household, they had
by no means a perfectly free hand. During the period of
the Privileges of Union, the Cortes exercised extensive powers
in the selection of them; and even after the Privileges were
abolished in 1348 there are a number of cases in which they
continued to interfere.[3] Particularly strict were the regulations to prevent the king from introducing foreigners —
especially Catalonians — into the royal council in Aragon;
chiefly, no doubt, for fear lest their presence should further
stimulate the king's interest and ambition for foreign enterprise and expansion, which were always regarded with ill
concealed hostility by the law-loving, self-righteous, and
rather uncosmopolitan Aragonese.[4]

[1] *Fueros y Observancias*, i, ff. 14–15;
Antequera, *Historia de la Legislación*,
pp. 311–313; Lea, *Inquisition of Spain*,
i, p. 229, note; also R. St.-H., iv, p.
340.
[2] M. and M., vi, pp. 188 f., 195; V.
Balaguer, *Obras*, vii (Discursos académicos), pp. 113–127.

[3] Finke, *Acta Aragonensia*, i, preface, pp. xxx ff.; K. Schwarz, *Aragonische Hofordnungen*; M. and M., v,
p. 38; vi, p. 194; Zurita, ii, ff. 380–
381, 394–395. On the Royal Council
in Aragon, see Torreánas, *Consejos del
Rey*, i, pp. 249 ff.
[4] *Fueros y Observancias*, i, ff. 37–38.

The Aragonese Cortes differed considerably from those of Castile in respect to their composition and procedure, and enjoyed much more extensive powers. The division of the nobility into two classes raised the number of the estates from three to four.[1] The right to attend was not, as in Castile, primarily dependent on the receipt of a royal summons. Proof of rank and lineage entitled to representation in the two *brazos* of the aristocracy, while in the *brazo de las universidades*, or *brazo real*, such cities and towns as could show that they had sent representatives in the past continued to enjoy that privilege. Membership in the clerical estate was also fairly definitely fixed, so that the complexion of the whole assembly could not be changed, as in Castile, at the behest of the crown. The presence of the Justicia as 'juez de las Cortes' was absolutely necessary, and constitutes another anomaly of Aragonese parliamentary practice.[2] The clauses in the General Privilege and the Privileges of Union demanding annual Cortes were superseded by a law of 1307 providing for biennial ones: the records show, however, that neither of these requirements was actually observed.[3] In the matter of procedure, extremely minute and careful regulation of the smallest and most unimportant details is the outstanding feature. There was a complicated arrangement for three prorogations of four days each in order to give tardy members a chance to arrive; the process of *habilitación*, or formal proving by each member of his right to sit, was exceedingly strict and almost interminable. In theory absolute unanimity of the members of each *brazo* was required on every measure, a fact which has caused some writers to exclaim that the

---

[1] Blancas, *Modo de proceder en Cortes de Aragon*, cap. vi.

[2] J. de Martel, *Forma de celebrar Cortes en Aragon* (Saragossa, 1641),

caps. x, xvi, xviii–xxi, xxxvii; M. and M., vi, pp. 170–178.

[3] *Fueros y Observancias*, i, f. 6; M. and M., vi, p. 203.

passage of any law was a miracle in Aragon.[1] The *solio* or
final formal meeting of the king and estates — in which all
the measures of the session were solemnly proclaimed and
sworn to — served to prevent the sovereign from ignoring
those doings of the assembly which were not to his liking;
and as a further method to secure this end, a committee of
the estates, or *Diputación del Reyno*, usually composed of
two members of each *brazo*, was chosen to remain in session
during intervals between sessions, to watch over the observance of the laws, and report to the Cortes any infraction of
them.   A full account of the duties and powers of this body
will be found in the fueros. They may perhaps be summarized under three heads: (1) to oversee the administration of the public revenue (not the *patrimonio real*); (2)
to deal with all infractions of the fueros by public officials
or private persons; (3) to keep the peace, in company with
the Justicia of Aragon.[2] Finally, we may note that the
consent of the Aragonese Cortes was always necessary to
the passing of all laws; the king, unlike the Castilian monarch, could not legislate without them. By them alone
could an extra grant, over and above what came to the king
in his own right, be made; without their consent no new
tribute or duty could be imposed, nor the rate of an old
one diminished or increased. The Cortes received the
oath of a new king to observe the laws, and recognized him
as monarch; they alone could grant letters of naturalization; truces, peaces, and declarations of war were usually

[1] Practically, however, it would seem
that a great many pieces of business
were decided by majority vote, and
moreover the custom of electing a committee of four or more members for
each *braso*, with full powers, often rendered nugatory the provision demanding
unanimity. In such cases the deputies
of Saragossa demanded the right to
constitute themselves one half the *braso
real*. Cf. *ante*, p. 445. M. and M.,
vi, pp. 217–220; Martel, *Forma de celebrar Cortes en Aragon*, caps. xxx, xxxiii,
xxxiv, xlii, xliii, xlv–l.
[2] M. and M., vi, p. 222; *Fueros y
Observancias*, i, ff. 26, 46, 66, 72, 75, 107,
213–215, 221, 223–225, 236, 242, 244,
265, 266, 268–270.

ratified by them; occasionally they confirmed and even nominated ambassadors.[1] Their claim to a voice in the appointment of the principal officers of state has already been described; and we shall later see that they exercised a large measure of control over the Justicia. Lastly, they had a most extensive power of investigating, in conjunction with the Justicia, *greujes*, or wrongs done by the king, his officers, or the estates, to one another, to individuals, or groups of individuals of whatever rank, or vice versa, in defiance of the laws, and of demanding that justice be done.[2] The procedure and other powers of the Cortes were such as insured attention to these demands.

There is no need for prolonged consideration of Aragonese finance,[3] local government, or military affairs, interesting and important though they are; for none of them vitally affects the development of the Spanish Empire. The attempts of the Aragonese to restrict arbitrary taxation were numerous and not entirely unavailing: the General Privilege limited to eight the number of imposts to which *villeros* could be subjected, and the Cortes constantly protested against the introduction of new burdens from Catalonia. Comment on the Aragonese army may most conveniently be made in connection with Catalonia, where it was principally recruited. The efforts of the Aragonese were chiefly directed to limiting it to the smallest possible dimensions.[4] In the domain of legislation and justice, a struggle similar to that in Castile took place between the

[1] Blancas, *Modo de proceder*, caps. xviii–xix; Martel, *Forma de celebrar*, caps. lxxi–lxxv; M. and M., vi, pp. 186–189, 195.

[2] Blancas, *Modo de proceder*, cap. xiv; Martel, *Forma de celebrar*, caps. liv–lix. Fuller references to the authorities on this paragraph may be found in the footnotes to my article on "The Cortes of the Spanish Kingdoms in the Later Middle Ages," in the *American Historical Review*, vol. xvi (1911), pp. 477 f., 486–490.

[3] Cf. L. Klüpfel, "Die Beamten der aragonischen Hof- und Zentralfinanzverwaltung," in *Vierteljahrschrift für Sozial und Wirthschaftsgeschichte*, xi, pp. 1–44.

[4] Altamira, § 471.

native and Roman codes and methods; and the victory of
the latter was considerably earlier and more pronounced.
The famous Fueros of Huesca, compiled in 1247 by the great
jurist bishop, Vidal de Canellas, correspond to Las Siete
Partidas and the Ordenamiento de Alcalá, and mark the
turning point in the conflict; after that time the national
laws and customs, from the more or less mythical Fuero of
Sobrarbe downward, fall steadily into the background.[1]
The hierarchy of royal and local courts was not widely
different from that which we have found in Castile, though
there are a number of peculiarities of nomenclature — e.g.,
the *zalmedina* or petty judge, "without jurisdiction of
limbs or blood." The *sobrejuntero* was a knight in command
of a *junta* or federation of towns for police purposes — something resembling the Castilian *hermandad* on a minor scale
— though indeed the small size and comparative orderliness
of Aragon rendered organizations of that kind for the most
part superfluous.[2]

It remains for us to study the office of the Justicia —
unquestionably the most original and interesting of Aragonese institutions, and the one which was destined in the
sixteenth century to offer the sturdiest resistance to mo-
narchic encroachments from Castile. We are fortunately not
obliged to enter here into the thorny question of its origins.
Certainly it did not go back to the days of the Fuero of
Sobrarbe, as one of its earliest incumbents asserted; and an
ingenious theory that it was borrowed from the Arabs in
1118 does not seem to have received general acceptance.[3]

[1] V. de la Fuente, *Estudios críticos*,
ii, pp. 77–145; R. de Ureña y Smenjaud, *Las Ediciones de los Fueros y
Observancias del Reino de Aragón an-
teriores á la Compilación de 1547*
(Madrid, 1900); Swift, *op. cit.*, pp.
205–208.

[2] *Fueros y Observancias*, i, ff. 7, 33–
35; Swift, pp. 171–173.

[3] J. Ribera, *Orígenes del Justicia de
Aragón*; A. Giménez Soler in *R. A.*
3d ser., v, pp. 201–206, 454–465, 625–
632; also i, pp. 337–348; iii, pp. 385–
391; x, pp. 119–126.

Our knowledge of the office during the entire twelfth century is in fact both vague and scanty. Even in the early part of the rule of James the Conqueror it is clear that it was in no sense fully developed. Zurita, it is true, inserts an enthusiastic description of the duties and powers of the Justicia at the close of his account of the rule of Pedro II (1196–1213), referring to him as "a rampart against all oppression and a personification of the Justice from which he took his name";[1] but Vidal de Canellas, writing a half century later, makes it clear that at that period he enjoyed almost no independent power and was little more than the spokesman of the king, whom he obeyed, and of the magnates, whom he was obliged to consult.[2] However, the Justicia clearly enjoyed sufficient prestige in the reign of James the Conqueror to make his alliance, or the power to control him, distinctly worth fighting for; and from that time onward to the middle of the fourteenth century there ensued a violent struggle between king and nobles to secure this valuable prize.

From the very beginning of the conflict the king enjoyed and retained the immense advantage of the right of appointment;[3] but even before the death of the Conqueror the barons managed, in some measure at least, to weaken the royal control over the Justicia by investing him with the right to sit in judgment in suits between the king and themselves. They also successfully insisted, at the Cortes of Exea in 1265, that the Justicia should always be chosen among the knights, and not among the *ricos hombres*, who were exempt from corporal punishment.[4] In the stormy days of the struggle over the General Privilege and the Privileges of Union, the attempts of the nobles to withdraw

[1] Zurita, i, ff. 101–103.
[2] Cited in Blancas, *Comentarios*, pp. 271 f.
[3] Altamira, § 312, 468.
[4] *Fueros y Observancias*, i, ff. 21–23.

the Justicia from crown influence, and to subject him as far as possible to their own, made further progress.[1] For a time baronial support enabled the Justicia virtually to usurp the king's position as principal judge of the realm, and even to seek, in derogation of the Roman legislation introduced by the Crown, to lead the nation back to the observance of the ancient laws and fueros; in the Privileges of Union of 1287, Alfonso III went so far as to promise not to proceed against any adherent of the Union without the mediation of the Justicia and the consent of the Cortes.[2] But the excesses of the baronial triumph brought the inevitable reaction, and the law-loving James II cleverly took advantage of it both to enhance the authority of the Justicia and to regain his alliance for the monarchy. On every possible occasion he exalted and magnified the powers and prerogatives of the office by appointing notable men to fill it, and above all by declaring that no appeal could be lodged against its decisions; so that the authority of the Justicia, which, as Blancas says, "had hitherto slumbered like a sword in its scabbard, was drawn forth for the first time in this reign and never sheathed again."[3] The successive Justicias, on their part, were not slow to recognize in the king the true cause of their mounting prestige, and steadily gravitated towards the monarchy; and finally, when in 1348 Pedro the Ceremonious issued victorious from his struggle with the forces of the Union, the results of the developments of the previous half century were for the first time fully revealed. The office enjoyed its greatest power and prestige in the period succeeding the battle of Epila. The nobles, who had hitherto aspired to control it, were broken, while the triumphant monarchy had wisely re-

[1] M. and M., vi, pp. 265-295.　　　　[2] Altamira, § 468.
[3] Cited in R. St.-H., v, p. 81.

solved to respect and defend the independence of the Justicia, as a proof of its own determination to uphold the laws. In the ensuing period the Justicia was recognized as 'juez superior y medio' — a superior and intermediate judge, with special powers, whom all other judicial authorities of the realm were obliged to consult in the interpretation of the laws. He was declared to be the sole judge of delinquent officials, and in such cases the royal prerogative of pardon was specifically stated to be inoperative. He was given a permanent seat at Saragossa, the capital of the realm, and two lieutenants were appointed to aid him in determining the law and in rendering his decisions. It is true that the king at the same time sought to augment his own judicial power by the organization of a special tribunal which followed him whithersoever he went; he also strengthened his control over the minor courts of the realm. It could scarcely have been otherwise in the height of the monarchical reaction that followed the battle of Epila. There was, however, plenty of room for his own jurisdiction and for that of the Justicia also; and for many years afterwards the two did not collide.[1]

The Justicia, as we have already seen, was always appointed by the crown. During the period of the struggle over the General Privilege and the Privileges of Union the kings had occasionally undertaken to remove refractory incumbents;[2] but this practice was deeply resented by the Cortes, and after 1348 the national assembly strove to give the occupants of the office a life tenure, in order to render them perfectly independent of crown control. During the latter part of the fourteenth century the efforts of

[1] Danvila, *Poder Civil*, i, pp. 337–343. See also list of Justicias in Blancas, *Comentarios*, pp. 390–470; and V. de la Fuente, *Estudios críticos*, iii, pp. 405–434.

[2] As, e.g., in the case of Pedro Martínez Artasona: cf. Blancas, *Comentarios*, p. 412.

the Cortes in this direction were entirely unavailing; and in the early years of the fifteenth, when legislation on the subject seemed imminent, the kings attempted to forestall the effects of it by obliging each Justicia at the time of his appointment to sign a letter of resignation, which could be subsequently produced by the monarch in case he should prove himself to be obnoxious. The famous Juan Jiménez Cerdán (1389–1420) was eliminated in this way, and one of his successors, Martin Díaz de Aux (1433–40), who refused to abide by his resignation, was subsequently murdered in prison at the behest of Alfonso V. In the year 1441, a law was finally passed rendering the Justicia irremovable by the king without the consent of the national assembly; but the victory which the popular party had won came so late that it was robbed of any real significance. The office of the Justicia had by this time passed its zenith, and henceforth became practically hereditary in the powerful and generally royalist family of Lanuza; the monarchs were generally satisfied with the attitude and conduct of the successive incumbents, and made no attempt to remove any of them for many years to come.[1]

The efforts of the Cortes to control the Justicia's tenure of office having thus proved abortive, they centred their energies on a series of attempts to limit the scope of his authority, and to render him responsible to the nation rather than to the king. In 1461 they arranged to have the Justicia's two lieutenants drawn by lot, instead of appointed, as previously, by the Justicia himself; and in 1467 the tenure of these magistrates was reduced to one year, so that they should not get out of touch with the national will. In cases of exceptional importance, the lieutenants were

---

[1] Zurita, iii, ff. 139, 255, 271–272; Blancas, *Comentarios*, pp. 443 ff.; Altamira, § 468.

empowered to call together all the legal lights of the realm in solemn conclave; and the dicta of this *consilium extraordinarium*, by which the independent authority of the Justicia was naturally much restricted, were preserved and respected to almost the same degree as the regular laws of the land. And as a final means to prevent the Justicia from becoming the tool of the triumphant monarchy, the Cortes began to appoint, from as far back as the year 1390, a commission of four members, representing the four *brazos*, to receive complaints against the conduct of the Justicia and his lieutenants and to report accordingly.[1] In 1467, by the so-called *Forus Inquisitionis Officii Justitiae Aragonum*, this commission attained considerably fuller development.[2] The number of its members was raised to seventeen, and the method of their selection changed to an elaborate system of *insaculación*, in which all the four *brazos* were to be represented. The Aragonese were apparently well aware of the danger of equity being lost sight of amid the technicalities of the law; and great care was taken to prevent this important committee from being exclusively composed of legists. Elaborate regulations were also made to secure speedy and effective procedure.[3] The net result of all these·developments was naturally to diminish the Justicia's authority and independence; his office was not nearly so important at the accession of Ferdinand and Isabella as it had been a century before. The mounting prestige of the monarchy limited it on the one side; the demands of the Cortes and of the nation, though they doubtless originated in a laudable determination to emancipate the Justicia from royal control, served rather to hamper it on the other. A decline in its power and prerogatives had in fact

---

[1] Blancas, *Comentarios*, pp. 333–343; Mariéjol, pp. 190–192.

[2] *Fueros y Observancias*, i, ff. 76–85.

[3] Blancas, *Comentarios*, pp. 359–368.

already set in, and was to continue and increase until the final catastrophe in the reign of Philip II.

A few words remain to be added in regard to the scope of the Justicia's powers. The office was certainly unique in the countries of Western Europe. Other lands possessed magistrates with attributes which remind one of it — as, for instance, the chancellor in England — but there is really nothing to which it can be fairly or profitably compared.[1] Its chief function was to watch over infringements of the law of the land, to protect subjects from verdicts contrary to that law, "to guarantee the rights of each against the tyranny of all, the liberties of the nation against the encroachments of the central power, the fortunes of the subject against the exactions of the tax collector, the freedom of the individual against the abuses of royal, seigniorial, or ecclesiastical jurisdiction."[2] These functions were chiefly exercised in two ways, namely, by the utilization of the kindred rights of *manifestación* and *firma*, which Blancas justly describes as "two shields to defend all our laws and liberties."[3] The first was designed to protect prisoners, particularly prisoners awaiting judgment, from violence or maltreatment by jailers or judges. Whenever any one dreaded such maltreatment he applied to the Justicia, who sent for him and removed him to a special prison — the so-called *carcel de los manifestados* — to which the ordinary authorities were refused access; in case of resistance to such removal, the Justicia was expected to use force. This intervention created no presumption against the validity of the action under which the criminal was accused; and if it was found that it had been demanded without adequate cause, it was

[1] It is difficult to see why Hallam likens it to the office of Chief Justice of the King's Bench: *View of the State of Europe in the Middle Ages* (Boston, 1861, 3 vols.), ii, p. 51.

[2] Mariéjol, p. 189; cf. also Ribera, *Orígenes del Justicia*, pp. 135 f.

[3] Blancas, *Comentarios*, pp. 325 f.

promptly revoked. For the purpose for which it was intended, however, it served as a most precious guarantee, which, according to the old Aragonese proverb, it was not too late for the accused to demand, even "after the hangman's cord had been actually passed about his neck."[1] *Firmas*, on the other hand, were special guarantees which were granted by the Justicia to those who demanded them, and which protected their lives and their property from judgments contrary to the laws. Such a *firma* suspended the trial if it had been begun, or the execution of the sentence if it had been already rendered, until the Justicia should have had time to investigate the case and determine whether or not it had been conducted in conformity to the fueros; and during the period of the suspension, the person of the defendant was especially protected against ill usage of any kind.[2] The Justicia, moreover, according to Blancas, had not only the right but the positive duty of interfering to prevent (1) the torture of any free man in Aragon save for the crime of false money, (2) the imposition of any tax without the consent of the Cortes, (3) the citation, trial, or condemnation of any Aragonese by a foreign judge or beyond the boundaries of the realm, (4) any compulsion to hospitality or entertainment, (5) alterations of the value of the coinage without constitutional sanction, (6) the intrusting to a foreigner of any castle or fortress within the realm, and (7) secret trials or imprisonments.[3] He also was the king's most eminent counsellor, and, as we have already seen, 'juez superior de las Cortes.' Finally, on the occasion of a royal accession it was the Justicia's prerogative to administer the coronation oath, which he received, seated and covered, from the kneeling and bareheaded monarch:

---

[1] A. Du Boys, *Droit criminel de l'Espagne*, p. 527.

[2] Du Boys, pp. 530 ff.

[3] Blancas, *Comentarios*, pp. 324 f.

a ceremony, as Prescott rightly says, "eminently symbol-
ical of that superiority of law over prerogative which was so
constantly asserted in Aragon."[1] In the discharge of these
exalted functions the Justicia occasionally found himself
in the position of umpire or mediator between the king and
the nobles;[2] but this was rather an accidental and exceptional result of his more distinctive duties than a regular
attribute of his office, as some authors have attempted to
represent it. The conjunction of powers which he did
possess, however, was certainly most impressive, and we
cannot wonder that the Justicia Cerdán at the close of
the fourteenth century was led to declare that his was "the
greatest lay office that existed anywhere in the world."[3]

VALENCIA

The internal conditions and institutions of the kingdom
of Valencia need not long detain us. Though somewhat
more sympathetic (largely on account of its maritime location) than was Aragon with the territorial ambitions of its
sovereigns beyond the seas, its small size and the violent
conflicts that raged within its boundaries prevented it from
rendering any very effective aid in the prosecution of foreign
conquest until the early part of the fifteenth century. From
the very beginning it was a strange compound of Aragonese
and Catalonian influences. Conquered chiefly through
the support of the Aragonese aristocracy, it had been largely
colonized by burgesses from Catalonia; moreover, the
policy of James I and of his successors tended generally to
exalt the latter element at the expense of the former, to
place the government as far as possible in its hands, and to
favor the Catalan language to the prejudice of the Aragonese.

[1] Prescott, i, p. 75.
[2] As, e.g., is described in Zurita, i, ff. 280-281.
[3] Cited in Danvila, Poder Civil, i, p. 342.

On the other hand, the Aragonese nobles were naturally quite unwilling to see themselves thus elbowed aside, and protested vigorously. They regarded Valencia as their own special perquisite, and in 1285 openly demanded that the new realm be governed by the fueros of Aragon. Around the conflict thus initiated the whole internal history of Valencia centred until the abolition of the Privileges of Union in the middle of the fourteenth century. In the domain of legislation the effects of the struggle are chiefly visible in the sharp contrasts between the two chief codes in use in the two different portions of the Valencian realm. Most of it was governed under the so-called Valencian 'Furs' drawn up by James the Conqueror in 1250, and revised and enlarged in 1271.[1] This code was "saturated with Roman principles, especially on the civil side", but it also contained many concessions to native and Gothic jurisprudence. It was published in Provençal; it forbade any Roman jurist or advocate to plead in a Valencian court, and prescribed that all disputed legal points should be settled "according to the discretion of the justiciar and good men of Valencia and the kingdom to the exclusion of canon and civil law." It sanctioned private vengeance and even private war, composition for minor offences, a liberal use of torture for non-privileged persons, and regular penalties of extreme severity and barbarity.[2] But there were a number of regions, especially those which belonged to the aristocracy, which were excluded from the operation of this famous code, and were subject to the fueros of Aragon.[3] Most of them lay just north of the capital of the kingdom, and opposed an insurmountable barrier to the unchallenged predominance

[1] P. H. Taragona, *Instituciones dels Furs de Valencia, passim*; Swift, *op. cit.*, pp. 209–214.
[2] M. and M., viii, pp. 3 ff.
[3] M. and M., viii, p. 19. The most important were Arenoso, Almasora, Benaguacil, Jerica, and Manises.

of the Furs throughout the realm. Indeed, at certain stages of the struggle over the maintenance of the Privileges of Union, it looked as if the fueros of Aragon were going to prevail over the Furs. Even the city of Valencia itself became, as we have already seen, a most vigorous centre of opposition to the royal cause. But when the monarchy finally emerged victorious, the power of the Aragonese aristocratic party in Valencia began to decay. The urban, Catalan portion of the population, supported by the crown, prevailed in the field of legislation as well as in other respects; so that the lovely realm which Aragon had striven at the outset to mould according to its own laws and traditions, ultimately followed rather the lead of Catalonia, and began to play an active if subordinate part in the process of expansion in Italy and in the Mediterranean.[1]

A few specialties of Valencian institutional history may be briefly noticed. The predominance of the capital was even more marked than that of Saragossa in Aragon. It held no less than five votes in the *brazo real* of the Valencian Cortes; and it invariably demanded that its representatives should constitute one half of the membership of that chamber, no matter how many other cities sent delegates; this exaggerated pretension, however, was not made good.[2] The estates enjoyed the unusual privilege of meeting separately without the royal summons after the Cortes had been dissolved by the king, to deal with such matters as concerned each one, and to present petitions to the crown; and on these occasions the deputies of the capital were apparently the sole representatives of the *brazo real*, since the other towns were not permitted to send delegations without the king's command. When the estates met in

[1] Altamira, § 491.
[2] Boix, *Historia de la Ciudad y Reino de Valencia*, i, pp. 193 f.; M. and M., vii, p. 456; Danvila, *Estudios acerca de la Legislación de Valencia*, pp. 284 f.

this way, they took the name of *estamentos*.[1] Several attempts were made to introduce into Valencia a Justicia similar to that of Aragon, but they were never permanently successful.[2] The Moorish and Jewish portions of the population were very large. The former were chiefly concentrated in the rural districts, especially in the Aragonese *señorios*, where they rendered invaluable service in tilling the soil. The latter, on the contrary, were for the most part found in the capital itself. As in Aragon, the tolerant and liberal policy towards the Jews which had prevailed in earlier days was suddenly exchanged, in the latter part of the fourteenth century, for one of violent persecution; and the massacres, forced conversions, and wanton destruction of Hebrew property which ensued in the city of Valencia were in some respects more horrible and ruthless than anywhere else in the peninsula.[3]

The climax of Valencia's power and prosperity was reached in the period of Alfonso the Magnanimous. The sunny kingdom was far more congenial to that splendor-loving monarch than the barren plains of Aragon or the busy streets of Barcelona. It reminded him of his beloved Italy, and he took pleasure in favoring and beautifying it in every way.[4] Its commercial prestige in this period mounted so high as to arouse the jealousy of the Catalans, who strove to limit its merchant marine by navigation ordinances. It was by Valencian sailors under a Valencian admiral, Juan de Corbera, that Alfonso was enabled to force the harbor of Marseilles and sack the town in the year 1423.[5] We have also many interesting evidences of the closeness

---

[1] M. and M., vii, pp. 456 f.; Danvila, *Estudios*, p. 285.
[2] Zurita, i, ff. 332–333.
[3] Altamira, § 490; Amador de los Rios, *Historia de los Judios*, ii, pp. 363 ff.

St. Vincent Ferrer was a native of Valencia.
[4] Boix, *Historia*, i, pp. 318 ff.
[5] Zurita, iii, ff. 156–157.

of Valencia's connection with Italy throughout the reign of the Magnanimous King. The Borgias, who were destined to become so famous in the succeeding years, originated in the Valencian town of Jativa; they were introduced into Italy through Alfonso, and one of them was elected to the papacy, with his full approval, in April, 1455, under the name of Calixtus III.[1] It was largely through Valencia, moreover, that the realms of the Crown of Aragon became acquainted with the art and literature of the Italian Renaissance. Ausías March, the greatest master of the Valencian tongue, "a philosopher who happened to write in verse," was a devoted admirer and imitator of Petrarch; the "Ladies' Book" of Jaume Roig owes much to the Decameron of Boccaccio.[2] In all these respects the fame of Valencia spread far and wide in the middle of the fifteenth century, and though its political prestige waned rapidly under the efficient absolutism of the Catholic Kings, it maintained its place as a literary, artistic, and commercial centre until a much later day.

CATALONIA

We now come to the county of Catalonia, the real source and mainspring of the Spanish Empire in the Mediterranean, and consequently, for our purposes, the most important portion of the realms of the Crown of Aragon. We have hitherto had occasion to emphasize the urban, commercial, and democratic features of it, and from the fourteenth century onward these tendencies were unquestionably predominant; on the other hand, it must never be forgotten

[1] Ametller, *Alfonso V de Aragón*, ii, pp. 806 f.

[2] Cf. Roque Chabás's edition of Roig's *Spill o Libre de les Dones* (Barcelona, 1905), pp. xiii–xiv; M. Menéndez y Pelayo, *Historia de las ideas estéticas en España*, i, 2, pp. 209–222. A critical edition in two volumes of the works of Ausías March was published in 1912–14 by Amédée Pagès for the Institut d' Estudis Catalans.

that Catalonia possessed an early mediaeval, aristocratic, and feudal background, which had no parallel elsewhere in the Iberian Peninsula. Its origin was French, not Spanish; from the time of Charlemagne and Louis the Pious it had taken its customs, institutions, tradition, and language from north of the Pyrenees. On the expulsion of the Moors its territories had been parcelled out among a number of nobles from the South of France, who for a long time vied with one another for preponderance in characteristically feudal fashion. By the end of the ninth century the counts of Barcelona were doubtless *primi inter pares*; but the forces of centralization operated slowly, and until the union with Aragon in 1137 their triumph cannot be regarded as assured. After that date the political power of the other Catalonian nobles was gradually broken, and the history of the county began to revolve around the struggles of the crown and the commercial plutocracy of Barcelona; but the fact that the upper orders succeeded in keeping the third estate from being represented in the Cortes until the year 1283 warns us that the change was not rapidly completed.[1] Even in the fourteenth and fifteenth centuries the student is being constantly reminded of the intensely feudal and aristocratic nature of the country's origin. In the domain of legislation this feature is particularly prominent. The *Usatges*, put forth by Ramon Berenguer I in 1064–69, are the earliest known feudal code; and they survived all the efforts of James the Conqueror to supplant them, though they were indeed considerably modified in the next two centuries by different monarchs, and supplemented by the introduction of Roman jurisprudence.[2] Economically, and

[1] M. and M., vi, pp. 399 ff.; vii, pp. 311 ff.

[2] The text of the *Usatges* is published in Charles Giraud, *Essai sur l'histoire du droit français*, ii, pp. 465–509, and more recently in the *Cortes de Cataluña* (ed. R. A. H.), i, pp. 10–46. The date usually given for their promulgation —

territorially also, the power of the old Catalonian nobility is attested by a schedule of the year 1359 which estimates the number of houses on seigniorial land as more than double that of those situated on the royal domain; while a seventeenth-century author asserts that only twenty-five per cent of the towns and cities of the county were held directly by the crown. This last statement is chiefly explained by the great number of alienations to the nobles which the crown made in the sixteenth and seventeenth centuries with the idea of filling the royal treasury; but the fact that such a large proportion of the soil remained in the hands of the baronage must never be forgotten, however absorbing the interest in the political and commercial development of the Catalan cities.[1]

Perhaps the most lamentable result of the survival of the feudal and baronial control of the rural portions of the county was the wretched condition of the Catalonian serfs. Of course their treatment varied with the different localities; but, generally speaking, they were unquestionably far worse off than the Castilian *solariegos*. As elsewhere, they were for the most part bound to the soil (*adscripti glebae*), unable to leave or dispose of the farms they held without the lord's consent; their rights over their personal property, and their privileges of marriage and inheritance, were seriously limited by seigniorial interference; and they staggered under a heavy burden of dues of various sorts, which were payable in money, labor, and kind, and were imposed in most vexatious ways.[2] But what made the

---

1068 — is not entirely accurate; cf. Fidel Fita, "Cortes y Usajes de Barcelona en 1064," in *Boletín de la R. A. H.*, xvii, pp. 385–428, and J. Ficker, "Ueber die Usatici Barchinonae," in *Mittheilungen des Instituts für Oesterreichische Geschichtsforschung*, Ergänzungsband ii, pp. 236–275; the latter shows that some of the laws in this code should be assigned to later years. The study by J. Coroleu, entitled "Código de los Usajes de Barcelona, Estudio Crítico," in *Boletín de la R. A. H.*, iv, pp. 85–104, is still valuable, and gives a list of the earlier authorities.

[1] Altamira, § 474.

[2] Hinojosa, *Cuestión Agraria en Cataluña*, pp. 137 ff., 169 ff.

lot of the Catalan peasant peculiarly hard was the special set of exactions commonly known as the *seis malos usos* — the six evil customs. The first of these, and in a sense the foundation for all the rest, was the so-called *remensa personal* — that is, the obligation of the serf to purchase personal redemption from his status as such, at a price satisfactory to his lord, before he could be permitted to leave his land. From this the Catalan peasants took their name of *homines de redemptione* or *payeses de remensa*.[1] The second was the *intestia* or the right of the lord to a share — one third or even one half — of the goods of a peasant who died intestate. The third, the *exorquia*, gave the lord the privilege of appropriating a portion of the property of a serf who died without issue.[2] The fourth, the *cugucia*, adjudged to him the whole or part of the property of any peasant's wife who was guilty of adultery. The fifth, the *arsina*, compelled the peasant to pay the lord an indemnity if the whole or part of his farm should be burned.[3] Lastly, the *firma de spoli* permitted the lord to exact a contribution from a serf who desired to pledge the proceeds of his farm to the woman he proposed to wed, pending the payment of her dowry and the performance of the marriage ceremony.[4] Over and above these *seis malos usos* there were in some localities other occasional and exceptional exactions of an even more outrageous nature. Such was the right of the lord to compel his serf's wife to leave her own child without sustenance, in order to be able to suckle his own;[5] and his pretension to the infamous *derecho de pernada* or *jus primae noctis*, with his serf's bride.[6]

Now most of these barbarous customs were familiar

---

[1] Hinojosa, *op. cit.*, pp. 212 f.
[2] Hinojosa, pp. 233–236.
[3] Hinojosa, pp. 237–241.
[4] Hinojosa, pp. 241–244; J. A. Bru-tails gives a somewhat different explanation of this term, in *B. H.*, v, pp. 78 f.
[5] Hinojosa, p. 367.
[6] Hinojosa, p. 307 and note.

enough in all feudal countries; but in Spain, where, with
the exception of Catalonia, feudalism had never been thoroughly and firmly established, they were distinctly unusual
and provoked much complaint. In the course of the
fourteenth and fifteenth centuries, moreover, a number of
different forces were at work which paved the way for emancipation. The steady improvement in the lot of the Castilian *solariego* doubtless had its effect in Catalonia, especially after the house of Trastamara supplanted the old
royal line of the counts of Barcelona in 1412. The decline
of the political power of the nobles and the growth of that
of the king and cities operated in the same direction; and
the humanitarian precepts of the church doubtless counted
for something. Under James the Conqueror there began
a process of granting to certain localities exemptions, more
or less complete, from the *malos usos* and other kindred
exactions, and it was continued and increased in the succeeding reigns. When a territory was thus exempted the
serfs on the adjacent lands naturally strove with might and
main to migrate thither; and by the end of the fourteenth
century the great majority of the Catalan peasants had managed in one way or another wholly or partially to emancipate themselves. In 1395 there were probably not more
than fifteen to twenty thousand families subject to the
malos usos; and these were, for the most part, localized
in the neighborhood of Gerona, Vallés, and Vich, and were
situated, curiously enough, chiefly on ecclesiastical lands.
In the next half century Maria de Luna, the wife of King
Martin I, and the illustrious jurist Tomas Mieres of Gerona
labored actively to promote the cause of freedom. Finally,
on July 1, 1448, King Alfonso the Magnanimous, in Naples,
put forth a 'constitution' granting to the serfs the right to
meet and discuss the abolition of the *malos usos*; and later,

in 1455, he actually proclaimed their temporary suspension. There was a brief reaction under John II, when the question of the liberation of the serfs became for a time fused with other issues of foreign and internal policy, but the process of emancipation had already reached a point from which it was impossible permanently to turn back. The glory of promulgating the instrument which completed the liberation of the Catalan peasant was reserved, as we shall later see, to Ferdinand the Catholic, in 1486; but it is only fair to his predecessors to.point out that the famous 'Sentencia Arbitral de Guadalupe' did little more than crown and consummate a work of which the greater part had already been accomplished.[1]

Before passing on to the remarkable political and economic development of Barcelona, which is undeniably the salient feature of the domestic history of Catalonia in the later Middle Ages, a few social and constitutional peculiarities remain to be mentioned. There were probably more slaves in Catalonia in proportion to the population than anywhere else in Spain, because of the activity of its foreign and commercial relations. They were acquired either by purchase or as prisoners of war, and during the period of the Catalan Grand Company there were a number of Greek slaves in Barcelona.[2] The story of the gradual superseding of the Usatges by the Roman law does not differ widely from that of the corresponding process in the other Iberian realms. In 1409 King Martin, with the consent of the Catalan Cortes, established a 'hierarchy of Codes' similar to that set up by the Ordenamiento de Alcalá of 1348 in Castile; in this the 'common' (i.e., the Roman) law was formally recognized as 'supplementary' to the Usatges,

[1] Hinojosa, op. cit., pp. 283–305.
[2] M. and M., vii, p. 331; Altamira, § 479.

constitutions, and acts of the king and Cortes, and to the customs and privileges of the realm.[1] There were a large number of different kinds of taxes and tributes, some of which came to the crown of its own right, while others could be imposed only with the consent of the Cortes; of the latter one of the most important was the bovage, or tax on each yoke of oxen, first granted in 1217.[2] The crown's facilities for collecting these imposts, however, were lamentably deficient, and a large share of the financial work of the county consequently devolved upon the *Diputación General de Cataluña*, or standing committee of the Cortes, which maintained a special treasury and set of revenues of its own, deposited the funds received in the great bank or Taula of Barcelona, and subsequently superintended their distribution and employment.[3]

Consideration of Catalan finances naturally leads on to that of the Catalan Cortes, to which representatives from the Balearics also came; for the Majorcan realm never enjoyed the privilege of having a national assembly of its own, even during the period when it was ruled by a separate line of kings.[4] There were but three *brazos* in the Catalonian Cortes; several attempts were indeed made in the late fourteenth and early fifteenth centuries to create a *braç dels cavallers generosos é homens de paratge*, on the model of the *brazo de caballeros* of the Cortes of Aragon,

[1] Altamira, §481. The famous *Libre de las Costums de Tortosa* (1279), a sort of pact between the lord and the inhabitants of that city, is one of the most complete of the mediaeval municipal codes; it has been made the subject of an exhaustive study by B. Oliver under the somewhat misleading title of *Historia del Derecho en Cataluña, Mallorca, y Valencia* (Madrid, 1876–1881, 4 vols.).

[2] Zurita, i, ff. 106–107; and *ante*, p. 432.

[3] Bové, *Institucions de Catalunya*, pp. 94 ff.; J. Coroleu and J. Pella y Forgas, *Fueros de Cataluña*, pp. 576–586; Altamira, §483.

[4] *Cortes de Cataluña*, ed. R. A. H., i, pp. x–xi. The *Historia General del Reino de Mallorca*, by J. Dameto and others (iii, pp. 313–318), is quite wrong in implying that the representation of the Balearics in the Catalonian Cortes only began in 1343.

but they never met with any permanent success.[1] About a dozen towns and cities were usually represented in the third estate; most of them sent one *procurador* or *síndico*, several sent two, but Barcelona sent five and sometimes more. Apparently each town had but one vote, irrespective of the number of its representatives, but Barcelona's predominance was perfectly obvious and deeply resented.[2] The method of selection of the municipal representatives varied in this period according to local custom — not until the reign of Ferdinand and Isabella did *insaculación* become the regular practice.[3] Full and definite instructions were given to the *síndicos* by the concejo of the municipality they represented. In Barcelona this function was performed by the *Vintiquatrena de Cort* — a most interesting body — a sort of permanent commission of the Concejo, consisting of twenty-four persons selected for the special purpose of supervising and counselling the *síndicos*, even down to the minutest details of their private life. Neglect of these instructions might subject the delinquents to the censures of the church or even to a revocation of their powers.[4] The process of *habilitación* was formal, rigid, and very complicated. No less than thirty-six rules were laid down concerning the qualifications of members.[5] Unanimity of votes, theoretically obligatory in all four estates in Aragon, was here restricted to the nobles.[6] There was, of course, no Justicia. At the concluding session or *solio*, which resembled that of Aragon, the sovereign was obliged to swear to the measures which the Cortes had passed, before he was granted the *donativo*.[7] But the surest guarantee

---

[1] *Cortes de Cataluña*, vii, pp. 46 ff.; Coroleu and Pella, *Las Cortes Catalanas*, pp. 58 f.

[2] *Cortes de Cataluña*, vii, pp. 46 ff., and *passim*; Coroleu and Pella, *Cortes*, p. 61; Altamira, § 324.

[3] Coroleu and Pella, *Cortes*, pp. 69-83.

[4] *Ibid.*, pp. 84-94.

[5] M. and M., vii, pp. 206-209.

[6] Coroleu and Pella, *Cortes*, pp. 116-131.

[7] *Ibid.*, pp. 131-133.

against any infringement of the rights and privileges of the Catalonian Cortes was the above-mentioned *Diputación General*. It originated in the end of the fourteenth century, and was composed of six persons, one from each estate and three *oidores de cuentas*; it held office for a term of three years, and its members had special privileges, special titles, and a special costume. In addition to its financial powers already described, it had the duties (1) of publishing and explaining the acts of the Cortes as well as the Usatges and other codes and of seeing to their observance; (2) of furnishing arms and munitions to the military forces of the county if they were called upon to resist an invasion or to deal with an infraction of the fueros; (3) of sitting in judgment in cases of dispute between the inhabitants and authorities of the land, and of arresting criminals denounced by the public prosecutor; and (4) of providing adequate naval defence for the Catalonian coasts, harbors, and shipping. It performed, in fact, all the functions of the *Diputación del Reyno* of Aragon, and many of these of the Aragonese Justicia besides, and insured to the Catalonian Cortes, whose servant it was, a measure of efficiency which probably exceeded that of any other similar body in the peninsula.[1]

Besides the separate national assemblies of the three different realms of the Crown of Aragon, there were also the so-called General Cortes of the eastern kingdoms. These were composed of representatives of Aragon, Catalonia, and Valencia, and also of the Balearics, and met ordinarily at Monzon or Lerida, which lay in debatable ground between Aragon and Catalonia. They were summoned only to deal with matters of general concern to all the Spanish dominions of the Aragonese kings, and were in

[1] Coroleu and Pella, *Fueros de Cataluña*, pp. 557–586; Calmette, *Louis XI et la révolution catalane*, pp. 33–38; Bové, *Institucions de Catalunya*, pp. 47–108.

effect little more than a juxtaposition of the separate assemblies already described. By an arrangement made in the year 1383, the king made his opening address, stating the purpose of the meeting, in Catalan, and the Infante answered him in the name of the Cortes in Aragonese.[1]

The organization of the army and navy of Catalonia deserves some notice, since it was largely by Catalan soldiers and sailors that the Italian and Mediterranean conquests of the fourteenth and fifteenth centuries were made. Feudal methods of recruitment continued throughout the fourteenth and fifteenth centuries, though most of the work of the Italian and Mediterranean campaigns was done by mercenaries — especially by the light-armed 'Almogavares' or skirmishers, who formed the greater part of the Catalan Grand Company.[2] But the real nucleus of the military forces of Catalonia was the armed contingents of the municipalities, who were called out by the process commonly known as the *somatent*.[3] This could be used in case either of national peril or of merely local disturbance, to punish a murderer, put down a revolt, or prevent the infliction of unjust penalties by rebel barons in contravention of the law of the land. The *veguer*, or chief royal official of the town, mounted the balcony of the Casa Consistorial, called out the words "*Via fora, Somatent,*" ordered the bells to be rung, and then raised a banner in the public square, around which the gathering inhabitants could rally. Competent leaders were on hand to marshal and direct the troops thus raised; if the cause of their summons was merely local, they dealt with it alone; in

---

[1] *Cortes de Cataluña*, i, pp. xii–xiv; Coroleu and Pella, *Fueros de Cataluña*, pp. 500 ff.; Altamira, § 314, 480.

[2] Cf. *ante*, p. 367.

[3] Pella, *Llibertats y Antich Govern de Catalunya*, pp. 267–286; Coroleu and Pella, *Fueros de Cataluña*, pp. 108–111. The etymology of the name is very doubtful; cf. Pella, *op. cit.*, p. 277; Calmette, *Louis XI et la révolution catalane*, p. 36, note.

case of invasion or national danger, they joined forces with the *somatents* of the adjacent cities, and, with them, formed the backbone of the country's defence. There was also a less formal and authorized type of *somatent* known as a *sacramental*, composed of a voluntary association of the inhabitants of a certain neighborhood, to expel criminals and malefactors; but these *sacramentals* proved highly dangerous to the public peace, on account of the bitterness of feeling which reigned between the upper and lower rural classes, and Ferdinand of Antequera was obliged to adopt strenuous measures to regulate and control them.[1] There are many obvious parallels between these *sacramentals* and the *hermandades* of Castile previous to the reforms of Ferdinand and Isabella; but the regular *somatents* differed sharply from both in the fact that they were not spontaneous growths, but were regularly authorized and controlled by the crown. Indeed, it is not improbable that the reform of the Castilian *hermandad* accomplished by the Catholic Kings was suggested by their knowledge of the Catalan *somatent*. These municipal levies served rarely, if ever, beyond the borders of the county. They were primarily intended to preserve order at home and prevent invasion from abroad. That of Barcelona was naturally by far the most important. It was composed of thirty-four companies, organized by the different commercial corporations and gilds, commanded by captains selected therein, all under the leadership of the *conceller en cap* of the municipality.[2]

The history of the development of the Catalonian navy is also intimately bound up with that of Barcelona, and the commercial side of it will be briefly treated in that connection. But the maritime trend and tradition of the

[1] Coroleu and Pella, *Fueros de Cataluña*, p. 110.   [2] Altamira, § 484.

county extended far beyond the limits of its capital, and antedated the period of the latter's preëminence; they reached back to the ninth century and the early days of the Spanish Mark, when Armengol, count of Ampurias, won a notable victory over a Saracen fleet in the neighborhood of the Balearics.[1] Subsequent rulers did much to increase the national interest in naval affairs, and the Catalans themselves proved the aptest of pupils in all matters pertaining to the sea; so that when James the Conqueror and Pedro III launched their realms on a career of expansion in the Mediterranean, there was no lack of ships to enable them to carry out their programme. On the other hand, there was crying need of centralization and system in the entire naval organization. Many of the great lay and ecclesiastical lords of the country possessed small fleets, which they not only often refused to allow to be employed in the royal service but sometimes actually utilized for piratical purposes of their own; even the ships of the capital were by no means always available for the purposes of the crown.[2] By a series of royal privileges and ordinances of the thirteenth, fourteenth, and fifteenth centuries, however, the naval forces of the country were organized in more permanent fashion. Ships of war were thenceforth furnished in four different ways. There were, first, the royal galleys, either constructed, equipped, and maintained at the king's expense, or else hired, often with their crews, from other lands; these formed the nucleus of most of the conquering expeditions sent forth into the Mediterranean. Next came the ships of the *Lonja de Contratación*, or Board of Trade, which were also usually hired, and were dedicated especially to the task of protecting the Catalonian com-

[1] F. de Bofarull y Sans, *Antigua Marina Catalana* (Barcelona, 1898), p. 1. The date of this event is usually given as 813.

[2] Altamira, § 484.

mercial fleets. Thirdly, there were the naval forces maintained and paid by the *Diputación General*, which were
principally employed in defending the coast against the
attacks of pirates. Lastly, there were the special ships
which Barcelona was permitted to arm and maintain as
guardians of the port.[1] The admiral, appointed by the
crown as the head of this imposing armament, was, generally
speaking, the most important man in Catalonia after the
monarch. Sometimes, indeed, his power was so great as
occasionally to threaten that of his sovereign, as, for example, was the case with Roger de Lauria, and, a century
later, with the second Bernaldo de Cabrera.[2] There were
an enormous number of different kinds of ships, of which
the most common were the galleys (*galeras*) both heavy
(*gruesas*) and light (*sutiles*), and also a special type called
uxers, which were distinguished by heavy castellated struc-
tures or turrets on the bow and the stern. There were also
smaller auxiliary ships called *galeotes* and *corces*, besides
transports and little boats of various sorts (*taridas, cocas,*
and *falucas*). The principal method of propulsion was by
oars; sails were distinctly secondary and supplementary.[3]
The famous *Ordenanzas Navales* of 1354, drawn up at the
behest of Pedro IV by his admiral, the first Bernaldo de
Cabrera, grandfather of the one above mentioned, contains
a number of interesting details concerning naval preparations and tactics, sailors' pay, and sailing directions for the
various fleets. Particularly noteworthy were the means
employed to guard the coasts against the raids of pirates.
An elaborate system of watch towers and lighthouses, with
bells, horns, and messengers on foot and on horseback,

[1] Capmany, "Antigua Marina de Barcelona," libro ii, in *Memorias his-tóricas de Barcelona*, i, pp. 57–70, 105–123.
[2] Cf. *ante*, pp. 351, 409.
[3] F. de Bofarull y Sans, *Antigua Marina Catalana*, pp. 8–16.

revealed the peril before it was too late, and notified the adjacent inhabitants to stand to their arms.[1]

All the internal history of Catalonia in this period, political, constitutional, military, and economic, really converges and is focussed at Barcelona, whose astonishing growth and prosperity in the thirteenth, fourteenth, and fifteenth centuries overshadow all other features of the evolution of the Catalonian state, and afford the best possible explanation of its change from a predominantly feudal and aristocratic, to an essentially urban and commercial existence. The foundations of this remarkable development were laid in the famous charter which was granted to the city by James the Conqueror in the year 1257, and which superseded the primitive constitution inherited from the days of the Spanish Mark. Under this new charter, the *veguer* and *bayle*, royal appointees and representatives, were henceforth to be aided in governing the city by a small council of eight burgesses, who met every week and really dominated the entire municipal administration; and also by a larger one of two hundred persons which was occasionally called into consultation.[2] The main features of this charter were preserved throughout the fourteenth and fifteenth centuries, though the size and method of recruitment of both the bodies it had created underwent a number of important variations. The membership of the smaller (the *Concell*) was reduced to six and later to four, and finally, in 1265, fixed at five. That of the larger sank to one hundred, where it remained during the fourteenth century, thus causing it to acquire the name of the *Concell de Cent*; in 1387 it was raised to 120, in 1455 to 128, and

[1] *Ordenansas Navales de 1354*, ed. Capmany, *passim*.
[2] Printed in Capmany, *Memorias*, ii, pp. 464 f. The primitive charter was really first displaced by one granted in 1249, which, however, soon gave way to that of 1257. Cf. Swift, *James the First of Aragon*, p. 167.

finally, in 1493, to 144, where it remained till its extinction in 1714. The original members of the smaller Concell were appointed by the crown and elected their own successors; but after 1274 they were chosen by a body of twelve electors selected by the Concell de Cent, whose members were in turn elected by the smaller Concell.[1] The members of both bodies held office for terms of one year only, and their gradual democratization is very noteworthy. At first they were almost exclusively recruited from the ranks of the richer and privileged citizens, but by the middle of the fifteenth century we find only two of the smaller Concell chosen from the municipal aristocracy; the others had to be taken, one from the merchants, another from the artisans, and the last from the laboring men.[2] In the larger body, also, the popular classes apparently began to predominate at an even earlier date. As time went on the functions of the two councils gradually became defined. The smaller was essentially an executive and administrative body. It saw to the maintenance of public order, to the distribution and spending of the municipal revenues, and the preservation from infringement of all the fueros and privileges of Barcelona. It was perfectly ready, if the circumstances demanded it, to assert its rights against nobles, ecclesiastics, royal officers, or even against the crown itself. It appointed the minor officials of the municipality to carry out its decrees. It had the privilege of petitioning the monarch at any time. Its members bore the proud title of 'magnificos.' They could sit covered in the royal presence; they were preceded by mace bearers on their journeys; and their representatives at the royal

[1] D. I. A., viii, pp. 120–122, 137–139, 143–146, 233–237, 282–288; Capmany, Memorias, ii, appendix, pp. 67–72; Bové, Instituciones, pp. 109 ff.

[2] Cf. Manual de Novells Ardits, edd. Schwartz y Luna and Carreras y Candi, passim.

court were afforded all the privileges of foreign ambassadors.[1] The functions of the larger Concell de Cent were, on the other hand, rather legislative and advisory; its approval was necessary for the passing of new ordinances and for the imposition of municipal taxation. Jointly with the *veguer* and *bayle* the two bodies possessed many of the prerogatives of absolute sovereignty, particularly in economic matters, as will hereafter more fully appear. They had the right to make independent commercial treaties with foreign powers, and to exercise an extensive mercantile jurisdiction, which they intrusted to two *consols de mar.*[2] Whether or not, as has been suggested, the development of this interesting system of municipal government was largely directed or influenced by that of the Italian cities of the same period, with which the Catalans became familiar in their commercial and military enterprises to the eastward, it is impossible definitely to say; but it is certain that the resemblances were numerous and very close.

The power of Barcelona did not stop with the city walls. In common with the other chief Catalan municipalities, she managed to extend her jurisdiction over the adjacent villages and territories by granting them what were called *derechos de vecindad* or *carreratge*. The places to which this right of *carreratge* had been given were thenceforth regarded by a legal fiction as streets[3] of the capital itself, endowed with all its privileges and immunities, in fact virtually annexed, so that Barcelona became to all intents and purposes a little *regnum in regno*. This process of municipal aggregation was generally favored by the Catalan rulers, first as a means of curbing the power of the baronage, and second because it served to replenish the treasury; for

---

[1] Capmany, *Memorias*, ii, appendix, pp. 108 ff.

[2] Bové, *Institucions de Catalunya*, pp.

109-146; M. and M., vii, pp. 378-393.

[3] Hence the name, *carreratge*, from *carrera* or street.

almost every extension of the municipal boundary by the
method just indicated was purchased by a substantial
contribution to the royal coffers. The nobles naturally
opposed it, and in the cases of the smaller towns not seldom
succeeded in forcing the king to revoke the donations made
(though never to return the funds received for them).
But the preëminence of Barcelona, fortified by its advantageous maritime location and immense political and commercial reputation abroad, made the right of association
with it so valuable that nothing could permanently arrest
its extension and development. The name of Catalonia
was often quite unfamiliar in foreign lands at the close of
the fifteenth century; but every one spoke of the glories
of its capital. Barcelona *was* the whole county, in the eyes
of most of Western Europe, and even in the Catalan legal
and judicial treatises of that period one constantly finds
the name of the city loosely applied to the entire principality.[1]
The mounting prestige of the capital and the pride and
prosperity of its citizens revealed themselves in various
quarrels with the Catalan nobles on the subjects of rival
jurisdictions and precedence, and in numerous conflicts of
authority with the Diputación General. Some of these
were serious, and affected the whole political life of the
county; others were absurdly trifling, as when in 1444
the Concellers objected to the placing of a standard on the
grave of one of the most noted statesmen and jurists of the
day, on the ground that such an honor would show a dangerous favoritism to a counsellor of the king. But the best
of all proofs of the high position which Barcelona had won
for herself was the dignities and privileges attached to

[1] Pella y Forgas, *Llibertats y antich
govern de Catalunya*, pp. 241 ff.; Calmette, *Louis XI et la révolution catalane*,
pp. 38 f. and notes. A full though unsystematic bibliography of Barcelona
may be found in vol. vii, pp. 759–761,
of the new *Enciclopedia Universal Ilustrada Europeo-Americana*.

membership in the ranks of her 'honored citizens' (*ciudadanos honrados*). These were the richer and more powerful burgesses, who had raised themselves, principally by their success in business, above the regular level of the mass of the urban population, and were socially regarded as being on the same plane with the lower nobles — the so-called *generosos* or *hombres de paratge*. Their numbers were limited, but on the other hand any man who possessed the necessary qualifications might gain admission to their ranks by vote of the representatives of the municipal government, who met annually on the first of May to consider possible candidates. The political privileges of the *ciudadanos honrados* were equivalent to those of the knights of the military orders; they were entitled to the *desafio* and *riepto*; they were exempt from all imposts save the municipal taxes of Barcelona. Altogether the *ciudadania honrada* was unquestionably the highest privilege of urban life which the Iberian Peninsula afforded; and men of today, had they lived at that time, would doubtless have valued it even above admission to any of the ranks of the aristocracy. Yet Barcelona was fully alive to the danger of permitting these privileged persons to monopolize the city government and guarded against it, as is indicated by the changes already described in the composition of the two Concells during the fourteenth and fifteenth centuries.[1]

But, after all, the fundamental cause of Barcelona's greatness was her commerce. It made her richer than all the realms of the Crown of Aragon put together; "it paved her streets with gold;" it was the ultimate source of her political preëminence. The notion, which one continually encounters in the history of Castile, that trade and manual labor were dishonorable and degrading, never ob-

[1] Altamira, § 478; Coroleu and Pella, *Fueros de Cataluña*, pp. 48 f.

tained in Catalonia; in fact, commercial success, as we
have already seen, was the high road to social recognition.[1]
The history of the various gilds and industrial organizations in Barcelona is vastly interesting and important,[2]
but as the emphasis in this book is necessarily laid rather
on external than on domestic affairs, it seems wiser to
forego any attempt to describe them, in order to have
more space for the history of Barcelona's foreign trade.
From ancient times the city had been an important commercial centre, and though its prosperity was interrupted
during the period of the Goths and Moors, it revived in
the early days of the Reconquest. In the second half of
the eleventh century Ramon Berenguer II granted his special encouragement and protection to its shipping.[3] Documents of the next two hundred years reveal active trade
relations between Barcelona and Genoa and Pisa, whose
merchants thronged the Levant; before the accession of
James I the way had been prepared for the expansion of
Catalonian commerce to all parts of the Mediterranean.
We have already seen that great emphasis was laid in the
succeeding period on the maintenance of trade with the
more westerly states of North Africa, complicated though
the situation there was by ambitions for political control.
Farther eastward this latter difficulty did not obtain, and
we find, throughout the fourteenth and fifteenth centuries,
constant evidences of the efforts of Catalan merchants to
establish themselves in Tripoli and in Egypt. The occasional embassies despatched by the Aragonese sovereigns
to the 'Soldans of Babylonia' were primarily due to commercial considerations; and in 1437 Barcelona showed that

[1] Capmany, *Memorias de Barcelona*,
i, 3, p. 40.
[2] Capmany, *Memorias*, i, 3; Bové,
Institucions, pp. 147–252; M. Gonsáles

y Sugrañes, *Contribució a la Historia dels
antichs Gremis de Barcelona* (Barcelona,
1915; one volume so far published).
[3] Capmany, *Memorias*, i, 1, p. 10.

she realized the value of the Egyptian trade by petitioning
Alfonso the Magnanimous to make peace with the Soldan
in order that it might be reëstablished in its pristine vigor.
But the commercial ambitions of Catalonia were by no
means limited to the Mediterranean. In the fourteenth
century her ships began to make their appearance in the
ports of England and Flanders; in 1389 a Catalan 'factory'
was set up at Bruges, and Catalan goods thence distributed
to the merchants of Germany and the Baltic lands.[1]

The commodities exported included salt, wine, iron, steel,
arms, coral, honey, saffron, and fruit; but unquestionably
the most important products which Barcelona sent abroad
were raw wool and manufactured cloths. So deafening,
in fact, was the noise coming from the cloth factories in
Barcelona, that in 1255, on petition of the citizens, they
were segregated in especially secluded quarters.[2] Among
the principal imports may be mentioned silk, oil, dyestuffs,
paper, drugs, and glassware. In the reign of James the
Conqueror a number of edicts were put forth to protect
Catalonia from the competition of foreign Italian merchants; in 1273 a citizen of Barcelona was authorized to
seize the goods of some Genoese who had robbed him, while
eight years earlier an order was issued for the wholesale
expulsion of all Lombards, Florentines, Sienese, and Luccans
trading there.[3] But with the accession of Pedro III a more
reasonable spirit began to prevail, and in the next two
centuries Catalonia settled down to a policy of permitting

[1] Swift, *James the First of Aragon*, pp.
225–229; Capmany, *Memorias*, i, 2, pp.
138–146; ii, pp. 233–235; W. Heyd,
Histoire du commerce du Levant (enlarged French edition of the original
German, Leipsic, 1885–86, 2 vols.), i,
pp. 421 ff.; A. Schaube, *Handels-
geschichte der romanischen Völker des
Mittelmeergebiets bis zum Ende der
Kreuzzüge* (Munich and Berlin, 1906),

pp. 539–615. (This last for the earlier
period.) 'Soldan of Babylonia' means,
of course, Soldan of Cairo or Egypt.
Cf. Stanley Lane-Poole, *History of
Egypt in the Middle Ages* (New York,
1901), p. 3, note 3.
[2] Capmany, *Memorias*, i, 2, pp. 239–
260; ii, pp. 22 f.
[3] Swift, *James the First of Aragon*, p.
228.

the importation at merely nominal duties (usually less than one per cent) of commodities not produced in the principality;[1] at the same time, however, she generally prohibited completely the entrance of such goods as were manufactured at home, and thus protected her own industries. It is also worth noting that, in view of her lack of agricultural advantages, and of the possibilities of famine, she often flatly forbade, or else imposed heavy duties upon, the exportation of grains.[2] The maintenance of her merchant marine and the retention of her carrying trade were objects of most anxious solicitude. In 1227 a royal order was issued to the effect that all traffic with the ports of Egypt and North Africa must be borne by ships of Barcelona alone, to the exclusion of foreign vessels. The application of this edict was extended in the succeeding reigns, until finally in 1454 Alfonso the Magnanimous ordained that no foreign ship whatever could be loaded in the ports of his dominions.[3] The Catalan merchant marine responded bravely to the efforts that were made in its behalf. The *ataranzas* or dockyards of Barcelona, which had to be frequently rebuilt and enlarged in the fourteenth and fifteenth centuries, were the most famous in the Mediterranean, and far surpassed those of Seville. Foreign visitors repeatedly asserted that the Barcelonese equalled the Venetians, and excelled all others, in the number and variety of their ships.[4]

The organization of the thriving foreign trade of the Catalan capital was both liberal and efficient. In 1279 Pedro III issued an important charter of privileges to the town of Barcelona, in which he authorized its merchants to elect two special officers to sit in judgment on commercial

[1] Capmany, *Memorias*, i, 2, p. 232.
[2] Altamira, §515.
[3] Capmany, i, 2, pp. 221, 234.
[4] Capmany, *Memorias*, i, 1, pp. 26–32; Calmette, *Louis XI et la révolution catalane*, p. 37.

cases.[1] In the beginning of the fourteenth century they took the name of *consols de mar* ; in 1347 their power and jurisdiction were more strictly defined, and the right to elect them was transferred to the city magistrates.   They presided over the Lonja de Contratación or Board of Trade, composed of the leading merchants of Barcelona, membership in which was highly prized but very difficult to obtain.[2] The protection of Catalan merchants in foreign lands received the attention of the government at an even earlier date. A privilege of the reign of James the Conqueror authorized the Concell de Cent of Barcelona to appoint consuls to reside in all the foreign lands with which Barcelona traded, and these consuls were given full authority and jurisdiction to govern, punish, and judge not only all the Catalonians, but also all other subjects of the Crown of Aragon, resident in the place to which they were sent.[3] But what unquestionably served to extend the naval and commercial power and prestige of Barcelona more than anything else was the famous *Llibre del Consolat,* one of the earliest codes of maritime and commercial law, compiled by a group of celebrated sailors and merchants of the Catalonian capital, probably in the reign of James the Conqueror. In the fourteenth century it was enforced throughout the Levant, translated into almost all the different languages spoken there, and universally recognized as the basis for the regulation of the intercourse of the Mediterranean peoples in the matters with which it dealt. It is thoroughly international in form and substance; no mention is made in it of the place of its compilation or of the king of Aragon who sanctioned it; the sums of money set down in it are reckoned in byzants and not in sols of

[1] Capmany, *Memorias,* i, 2, p. 153.   [2] Capmany, *Memorias,* i, 2, pp. 183–
[3] Bové, *Institucions de Catalunya,*   204.
pp. 253–284.

Barcelona. It was a notable contribution to world civilization, unfettered by any national limitations or restrictions;
and its speedy and wellnigh universal adoption bears elo-
quent testimony to the high prestige of the country of its
birth.[1]

Cosmopolitanism, enterprise, and greed of gain abroad,
restless energy, patriotism, and love of liberty at home were
the qualities which these different developments fostered
in the Catalonians. They were also naturally led on to
celebrate their glorious deeds in stately prose and joyous
verse in their native Catalan tongue. The chronicles of
the kings of the house of Barcelona rank among the best historical narratives of the later Middle Ages. Troubadours
from Provence found the warmest of welcomes in the
Catalonian cities, especially at Barcelona and Tortosa;
and for a long time the author of the finest poem of the
year was rewarded with a magnificent prize, "thus mani-
festing to the world the superiority which God and nature
have assigned to genius over dulness." [2] And the versatility, progressiveness, and daring of the Catalonians are
the more remarkable when contrasted with the sombre
conservatism and stiff-necked obstinacy of the Aragonese.
Seldom has history furnished a more striking contrast
than that afforded by the union of these two realms under
a single line of rulers. They had literally nothing in common save their passion for freedom; and even that they
evinced in totally different ways. In language, in outlook,
in interests, and in ideals they remained absolutely divergent — another of the innumerable examples of the ineradicability of Spanish separatism. The effect of this

[1] Capmany, *Memorias*, i, 2, pp. 170–
183; ii, appendix, pp. 79–88; and Capmany's edition of the "Llibre del Consolat," cf. *ante*, p. 309; Bové, *Institucions*, pp. 285–314.
[2] G. Mayans y Siscar, *Orígenes de
la Lengua Española* (new edition, 1873),
p. 273.

characteristic upon the development of the empire which had begun to be built up beyond the seas was already very marked; and the union with Castile, through the marriage of Ferdinand and Isabella, was destined to extend that effect to wider fields. When the discovery of America furnished a western outlet to imperial energies hitherto almost exclusively occupied to the eastward, the hardest of all the problems which confronted the Catholic Kings and their successors was that of endowing the gigantic agglomeration with the unity which was essential to its permanence.

THE BALEARICS

We now pass to a brief examination of the constitution and internal conditions of the Aragonese dependencies in the Mediterranean and in Italy, and begin with a few words concerning the kingdom of Majorca. As first constituted under the separate line of sovereigns which began with the death of James the Conqueror, the realm included the islands of Majorca, Minorca,[1] and Iviza, the counties of Cerdagne and Roussillon and the adjacent lands, and those parts of Montpellier which recognized the sovereignty of the king of Aragon. But with the extinction of the separate line of kings in 1349, the county of Montpellier, as we have already seen, fell out of the combination and was sold to the king of France, so that the history of its internal development, though both interesting and important, particularly on the urban and economic side, ceases to affect Spanish affairs, and consequently need not be considered here.[2]

---

[1] Of course Minorca, strictly speaking, did not come into the kingdom of Majorca till its final conquest by Alfonso III in 1287; during the previous half century it was governed by a Moorish ruler under the suzerainty of the king of Aragon. Cf. ante, p. 336,

and Vaquette d'Hermilly, Histoire du royaume de Majorque, pp. 78–80, 115–118.

[2] References to it may be found in Swift, James the First of Aragon, pp. 169, 177, 215, 230, 234; in Heyd, Commerce du Levant, ii, pp. 13 ff., 23 f., 421

The counties of Cerdagne and Roussillon, on the other hand, never enjoyed quite the same measure of autonomy as the Balearics. They had insisted, for instance, at the time of the separate constitution of the Majorcan realm, that the Usatges of Catalonia should continue to be in force within their boundaries,[1] while the islands refused to observe them; moreover the fact that Cerdagne and Roussillon were actually adjacent to Catalonia made it inevitable that the measure of their independence should be somewhat diminished in consequence. Theoretically, of course, they remained part of the Majorcan realm even after the termination of the separate line of kings; practically, however, their autonomy counted for so little that we are justified in restricting our attention to the islands.

Under the arrangement by which the distinct Majorcan monarchy was finally constituted in the reign of Pedro III, the Balearics were granted a distinct code of laws and independent judicial and financial systems.[2] Moreover, as we shall later see, the municipal assemblies of the towns of Palma and Ciudadela were permitted gradually to extend their authority over the islands of Majorca and Minorca respectively in such a way as to make them virtually national in their scope. All this certainly savored of complete autonomy. But at the same time the kings of Aragon insisted that the Majorcan sovereigns should render them feudal homage in token of their vassalage, that they should be summoned to the Catalan Cortes with the other great feudatories, that they should never be permitted to hold Cortes of their own, and that they

ff., 707–717, *passim*; in A. Schaube, *op. cit.*, pp. 539–615; and in A. Germain, *Histoire de la commune de Montpellier* (1851).
[1] Zurita, i, f. 233; Altamira, § 495;

J. de Gazanyola, *Histoire de Roussillon* (Perpignan, 1857), p. 233.
[2] Vaquette d'Hermilly, *Histoire de Majorque*, pp. 95 f.; Altamira, § 495; Lecoy, i, chap. iv.

should promise to aid the kings of Aragon against all their foes.[1] Even with these limitations, however, the sovereigns of the separate line labored strenuously and continuously to consolidate and increase their own monarchical power; and though they were unable to shake off the galling suzerainty of the kings of Aragon above, they certainly contrived to assert their authority over their subjects below, more completely perhaps than any of the contemporary kings of the different Iberian realms. The absence of baronial traditions was of course a distinct advantage for them; and they followed with considerable success the policy of impressing their subjects by a show of outward magnificence and ostentation. Naturally the annexation of Majorca to the other realms of the Crown of Aragon in 1349 militated somewhat against these developments, since the executive power was thenceforth represented by a viceroy sent out by the Aragonese sovereign; on the other hand it is important to observe that the termination of the separate line of Majorcan kings did not affect the constitutional autonomy of the Balearics, which, in accordance with the immemorial principles of Spanish particularism, was left entirely untouched. We have therefore to sketch the main features of the independent internal organization and local government of the islands, which survived long after the extinction of the separate dynasty of Majorcan kings.[2]

In Majorca itself the whole story revolves around the efforts of the capital, Palma, to extend its jurisdiction over the entire island, and there is a parallel development of the town of Ciudadela in Minorca. As the Balearics were conquered from Catalonia, the bulk of the expeditionary

---

[1] *Cortes de Cataluña*, i, p. x.
[2] Altamira, § 495; *Historia General del Reino de Mallorca*, by J. Dameto and others, iii, pp. 302–306.

force and also of the colonists who followed it were of an essentially urban type. The wealth and energy of the Balearics thus became early concentrated in the cities, and the rapid development of Majorcan commerce strengthened the tendency of the more valuable portions of the community to desert the countryside. The numbers and activity of the Majorcan Jews also, to whom the kings extended their special protection, were an added source of prosperity and attractiveness for the municipalities, particularly the capital,[1] so that during most of the fourteenth century the town of Palma monopolized the life of Majorca more completely even than did Barcelona that of Catalonia; all the wealth and talent of the island were concentrated there. The history of its government and administration during the fourteenth and fifteenth centuries furnishes a significant commentary on this development, and on the fruitless efforts of the rural communities to arrest it.

At first Palma was ruled by a royal *bayle* and *veguer* and a general assembly of the citizens; but about the middle of the thirteenth century this general assembly began to be gradually elbowed aside by a small, self-perpetuating body of six annually elected *jurados*, who managed to concentrate in their own hands the chief power, not only over the munic- ipality, but also over the rural districts which it had al- ready begun to dominate and control.[2] In the course of the fourteenth century, however, the situation changed again. The annexation to Aragon, as we shall subsequently see, ruined Majorcan commerce, and caused the inhabit- ants of the capital to turn back to the country districts with the idea of exploiting them; and this naturally caused the *forenses* or rural population, who had never had any

[1] Cf. Morel-Fatio in *Révue des études Juives*, iv (1882), pp. 31–56.
[2] Lecoy, i, pp. 82 ff.

voice in the government of the island, to clamor more loudly than ever for representation. The most obvious way of meeting this demand, and at the same time of keeping all real authority in the hands of the municipal government, was to revamp the larger and more general assembly (usually called the Consell) of the citizens, and to give the *forenses* seats in it. By a number of successive reforms, of which the most important were made in 1398 and 1448, this end was gradually accomplished. The Consell recovered its earlier predominance and the *jurados* were subjected to it; the rural population was given representation there, though its delegates never formed more than a minority.[1] The *forenses*, however, were not satisfied with this. As long as the Consell of Palma dominated the entire island, their hands were really tied. They therefore now strove to secure some measure of autonomy for themselves, particularly in financial affairs, and were so far successful as to obtain an arrangement by which a portion of the taxes should be set apart to be used by them for their own special purposes.[2] But even these reforms did not go to the root of the matter. The differences between the *forenses* and the *ciudadanos* lay far too deep to be remedied by regulations and institutions. The inhabitants of Palma looked on the rural population with disdain and contempt. The ruin of their commerce by the annexation had led them to gamble and speculate on their country domains, and to overtax and oppress those who labored on them, but they had no real sympathy or interest in agricultural development; indeed, like some of the early conquistadores in America, they regarded their association with it as a disagreeable and degrading necessity. The quarrels and corruption

---

[1] J. M. Quadrado, *Forenses y Ciuda-danos*, pp. 61–81; J. M. Bover, *Noticias de Mallorca*, pp. 197–201.

[2] Quadrado, *Forenses y Ciudadanos*, pp. 83–93.

which disgraced the government of Palma were not calculated, on the other hand, to increase the respect of the
forenses for the *ciudadanos*; and the final result was that
in the year 1450 a peasant insurrection burst forth in the
island of Majorca which literally deluged it with blood.
A royal amnesty caused a temporary cessation of the strife
without any definite decision in the year 1454; but under
John II it broke out again and ultimately became involved
with the contemporaneous revolt which was in progress
against that monarch in Catalonia. At the close of the
reign a statement of grievances by both sides was presented
to the sovereign, but the latter died before he was able to
provide any real remedies. Meantime the insurrection
had so reduced the population that the economic life of the
island had virtually come to a standstill; in addition to
the number who had perished in the risings, there was a
considerable exodus of *forenses* to Corsica.[1]

But the indubitably miserable and disrupted state of the
Majorcan realm at the accession of Ferdinand and Isabella
must not blind us to its immense prosperity and wealth
in the earlier and happier stages of its development. The
soil was rich and fertile, and the Moors had done much to
improve it; despite its tragic neglect, due to the urban trend
already described, the agricultural output of Majorca was
very large, and formed a considerable portion of the wealth
of the community. The truest source of Majorca's greatness, however, was its commerce. Palma was an almost
obligatory stopping place for ships plying between Spain
and the Levant and North Africa. Its inhabitants were
inevitably caught up and carried along on the commercial

[1] *Historia General del Reino de Mallorca*, by J. Dameto and others (2d ed.,
edd. Moragues and Bover), iii, pp. 405
ff.; Quadrado, *Forenses y Ciudadanos*, caps. vii–xx; and also *Privilegios y Franquicias de Mallorca*, ed. Quadrado
(Palma, 1894), vol. i (no more published); Altamira, §§ 496 f.

currents which flowed past them. It was a microcosm
of Barcelona in this respect, with consuls and factories
established for the benefit of its merchants in most of the
lands with which it dealt, with a commercial fleet of at
least three hundred and sixty larger vessels, and with more
than thirty thousand foreign sailors and traders dwelling
within its walls. It was especially noted as a centre for the
exchange and barter of slaves. The extinction of the separate line of Majorcan kings was of course a severe blow to
Palma's commercial prestige. Barcelona did not propose
to be hampered any longer by its competition, and soon
succeeded in restricting it. Moreover the capture of Constantinople by the Turks a century later further limited
the eastern trade of the Majorcan capital, though even at
the time of the Catholic Kings it had not fallen so low that
it would have been impossible to resuscitate it. But during
the thirteenth and early fourteenth centuries it is not too
much to say that Palma was a sort of Mecca for millionnaires.
All contemporaries bear witness to the luxury and elegance
of its houses and of the villas of the neighboring countryside. The children of the greater commercial families
were described by a writer of fifty years afterwards as
"richer than the merchants of his own day." [1] And this
great efflorescence of Majorcan commerce was accompanied
by notable progress in letters and in science. The sailors
of the Balearics knew and used the magnetic needle. as
early as 1272.[2] The Majorcan school of cartography was
famous throughout Western Europe, where its maps were
almost universally employed for purposes of navigation.
Ramon Lull, "knight errant of philosophy, ascetic and
troubadour, novelist and missionary," who travelled through

[1] Altamira, § 517; Mas Latrie, pp. 316-320.

[2] Fernández Duro in *Boletín de la R. A. H.*, xix, pp. 366-377.

Europe and Palestine and was finally stoned to death outside the walls of Bugia by the Mohammedans whom he was striving to convert, was born in Palma in the year 1235.[1]

SARDINIA

Though Sardinia had been granted by the Pope to the kings of Aragon in 1297, it will be remembered that no serious attempt had been made to take actual possession of it till 1323; and that for more than a century after that date the island was in confusion and turmoil, owing to the interminable conflicts of the Pisans, Genoese, and Judges of Arborea with the Aragonese invaders. Even after the judgeship was suppressed in 1409 and the feudal marquisate of Oristano substituted for it, there were constant revolts and insurrections; so that the constitutional machinery of the new Aragonese government never fairly got into working order during the period with which we are now dealing.[2] We cannot, therefore, at present do more than indicate the foundations upon which the Spanish administration of Sardinia in the sixteenth and seventeenth centuries was ultimately to be built up.

The chief administrative problem with which the Aragonese were confronted in Sardinia was that of centralizing and unifying the government of the island and of effacing the lines of its ancient division into four separate and independent judgeships.[3] As an obvious method of accomplishing this purpose, the kings of Aragon began in 1323 to

[1] Menéndez y Pelayo, *Historia de las ideas estéticas en España*, i, 2, pp. 163–190; *Histoire Littéraire de la France*, ouvrage commencé par des Réligieux Bénédictins et continué par des membres de l'Institut, xxix, pp. 1–386 (Paris, 1885); also *Historia General del Reino de Mallorca*, by J. Dameto and others (2d ed. by Moragues and Bover), iii, pp. 37–103.

[2] G. Manno, *Storia di Sardegna*, ii, lib. ix, *passim*.

[3] On Sardinia's constitutional history in the preceding periods cf. E. Besta, *La Sardegna medioevale*, *passim*.

appoint viceroys to represent their sovereign authority there. Down to the middle of the fifteenth century, or as long as the rebellions and internal wars continued, these viceroys were chiefly occupied with military affairs, and were therefore able to accomplish relatively little in the line of constitutional reform. Moreover, they were not always implicitly trusted by the monarchs who sent them out. The kings of Aragon were alive to the danger that ambitious viceroys might strive to make themselves too independent in their remote domain and strike out a line of policy inimical to their own; and they attempted to guard against this peril by appointing them for very short terms. All the Sardinian historians speak of a stringent regulation which limited the viceregal tenure of office to three years.[1] The records show that this was by no means invariably observed; but it is fair to add that the terms which fell below the statutory limit were more numerous than those which exceeded it.[2] Save, however, for this restriction of the period of their rule, the Sardinian viceroys during the fourteenth and fifteenth centuries were virtually absolute under the crown. Down to the time of Ferdinand and Isabella there was practically no council or advisory body to aid or control them in the discharge of their duties. Nearly all the minor officials of the island were appointed by them, or on their recommendation, and obediently carried out their instructions.[3] To this general rule, however, there was one noteworthy exception. The Aragonese sovereigns were determined that the administration of the royal revenues in Sardinia should be kept out of the hands of the viceroys, who might otherwise be tempted to use their authority to enrich themselves at the expense of the crown.

[1] Manno, op. cit., ii, pp. 187–193.   Manuel, iii, p. 745.
[2] Cf. list of viceroys in Stokvis,   [3] Manno, ii, pp. 188, 194.

In 1341 a *procurador real* was nominated to take charge of the king's finances in the island, and the viceroy was strictly enjoined not to meddle with his affairs.[1] This separation of the management of the *patrimonio real* from that of the other branches of the government of the overseas dependencies grew to be one of the characteristic features of Spanish imperial administration, as will hereinafter more fully appear.

The appointment of viceroys, however, was not the only way of breaking up the old quadripartite division of the island, and of making its inhabitants conscious of the unity of the new administration. Another equally effective means to the same end, and one fully in keeping with the best traditions of the government of all the Spanish kingdoms, was the inauguration of a national assembly. In the reign of King Martin, the Sardinian cities of Cagliari and Alghero were granted the right of representation in the Cortes of Catalonia, but the records do not show that this privilege was ever exercised; the prevailing policy from the outset was to treat Sardinia like Sicily and Naples, as a *reino de allá mar* — a separate kingdom with a system of administration entirely distinct from that of the realms of Aragon — and therefore to endow it with a parliament of its own. Zurita tells us that in the year 1355 Pedro the Ceremonious summoned the three estates of the Sardinian Cortes to meet at Cagliari, and that they were composed of Aragonese and Catalonians as well as of the inhabitants of the island; but he is exceedingly indefinite as to what was accomplished there, and the Sardinian historian, Dexart, emphatically denies that this body should be given the name of a parliament, "quia nullas leges tulit nec

[1] Manno, ii, pp. 188, 212, note. The *procurador real* must not be confused with the *abogado del fisco*, first appointed under Ferdinand the Catholic to conduct financial suits on behalf of the crown; cf. *infra*, Vol. II, p. 165.

capitula."[1]   No such doubt, however, can exist about the assembly held by Alfonso V in 1421 ; it marks the real beginning of the Sardinian representative system, and entitles the Magnanimous King to the credit of its foundation.[2]   It was modelled in general on the Cortes of Catalonia, in three estates, and had similar regulations for elections, summonses, and meetings.   There were six *habilitadores* to determine the qualifications of members to sit; sixteen *tratadores* to carry on negotiations between the different *brazos* and particularly to settle the difficult question of the proportional incidence of taxation; and also eighteen *provisores* whose duty it was to listen to complaints of the arbitrary conduct of royal officials.   It was also customary for the different estates to meet separately as *estamentos* without special summons and to deliberate, each one upon its special affairs.[3]   Efforts were made to introduce the Catalonian custom of holding triennial parliaments, but they never attained permanent success; the intervals between sessions were subsequently limited to ten years, but even this rule was not invariably observed.[4]   The principal function of the parliament of Sardinia, at least from the royal point of view, was the granting of subsidies or *donativos*; and the obvious correlative of this was the right to petition the crown for the redress of grievances, and to present requests, which, if accepted by the monarch or his representatives, acquired the force of laws.   The generosity of the Sardinian estates in voting funds for the prosecution of Alfonso V's Italian campaigns was such as to elicit from

[1] J. Dexart, *Capitula regni Sardiniae sub Aragonum Imperio* (Cagliari, 1645), § 16 of proem; Zurita, ii, ff. 262–263.

[2] Manno, ii, pp. 98 ff.

[3] The practice of holding separate meetings was particularly common with the *brazo militar* or house of barons in Sardinia. It was doubtless taken from

the kingdom of Valencia (cf. *ante*, p. 473), with which, as we have already seen, Alfonso was far more intimate than with any other of his Spanish realms.

[4] Manno, ii, pp. 98 ff., 107, 143, 214; Dexart, lib. i, tit. i,[1] cap. ii; lib. i, tit. ii, cap. ii.

that monarch, in a burst of gratitude, a favorable response to a request for the election of a special tribunal (over and above the *provisores*) to sit in judgment on the viceroy and other royal officials, in case of alleged violation of the laws of the land. This institution never came into actual existence, for, as Manno shrewdly observes, "those things that are born of an excessive effervescence of enthusiasm cannot survive";[1] nevertheless the fact that it was even contemplated indicates that the king and the Sardinians were by no means out of sympathy with one another, and that the island parliament faithfully discharged its function of informing its sovereign of his subjects' desires.

There is little more that needs to be said concerning the Aragonese administration of Sardinia previous to the accession of the Catholic Kings. Some effort was made to settle the interminable conflicts of lay and ecclesiastical jurisdiction in the island — a heritage of the papal claims to sovereignty there — by the election of a special tribunal of appeals in the reign of John II;[2] and in 1460, at the General Cortes of Fraga and Lerida, that monarch solemnly reconfirmed "the perpetual union and incorporation" of both Sardinia and Sicily "in the kingdom of Aragon and the royal Crown thereof."[3] The institutional autonomy of the island, however, was not disturbed, and we hear little or nothing of the problems of its administration in the works of contemporary historians. On the whole, one gains the impression that the Sardinians, though constantly complaining of the corruption, greed, and arbitrary conduct of the officials of the island, were by no means dissatisfied with the fate that had united them with the realms of the Crown of Aragon. The very fact that they grumbled about the conduct

---

[1] Manno, ii, p. 106.   [2] Manno, ii, p. 111.
[3] Zurita, iv, f. 75; Cipolla, *Signorie Italiane*, i, p. 314.

of the local administration indicates that they believed that their new sovereigns intended to treat them well. And it is noteworthy that almost all the Sardinian historians speak enthusiastically of the numerous benefits conferred on their native land by the rule of the kings of Aragon, particularly of their measures to eliminate the abuses of antiquated feudal jurisdiction, of their gradual abolition of slavery, of their solicitude for the military defence of the island, and most of all of the favor they showed to the Sardinian municipalities, to which they granted privileges and immunities comparable to those of the cities of Catalonia.[1] Agriculture received far more attention from the government here than in most of the other lands over which the Spanish monarchs held sway; the commerce of the island, though it was of course not comparable to that of Majorca or Catalonia, unquestionably improved after the Aragonese occupation; while the diminution of the population in this period, of which all contemporaries complained, is probably in great measure to be ascribed to the number of deaths on the field of battle.[2] Most of the benefits of the Aragonese rule in Sardinia were not fully realized till the time of Ferdinand the Catholic, who consolidated and enhanced them, but there can be no question that the first two centuries of Spanish administration in the island, though far from ideal when judged by modern standards, showed a considerable improvement over the form of government which it supplanted.

SICILY

The Aragonese administration of the island of Sicily was powerfully affected from the beginning by two special considerations. The first of these was the undying love of

---

[1] Manno, ii, pp. 193-197, 220-226.
[2] Manno, ii, pp. 226-234; D. A.
Asuni, *Histoire de la Sardaigne* (Paris, 1802, 2 vols.), i, pp. 116-121.

independence and liberty, which was the dominant characteristic of the Sicilians, and which revealed itself in their
repeated demands for a separate line of kings. The second
was the high tradition of free institutions and self-government which the island had inherited from the times of the
Norman and Hohenstaufen, and which the Aragonese, as
heirs of these dynasties, felt themselves in some measure
bound to maintain.

We have already encountered numerous evidences of the
Sicilian passion for autonomy, and of the readiness of the
earlier Aragonese kings to respect it. It is natural to ascribe the establishment of a separate Sicilian dynasty by
the will of Pedro the Great to the irresistible influence of
Spanish separatism, and to attribute James II's abandonment of his original resolve to rule in Sicily as well as in
Aragon to that monarch's reluctance to fight with the papacy; but it is impossible to avoid the conclusion that Sicily's
unwillingness to recognize any sovereign whose attention
was distracted by the government of other realms was a
most important element in causing both these decisions.
And it will be remembered that for over one hundred years
— from the treaty of Anagni in 1295 to the death of the
younger Martin in 1409 — the Sicilians were successful
in maintaining a separate dynasty, and therefore in preventing themselves from being brought under the sceptre
of the kings of Aragon. Of the independent Sicilian sovereigns of this period, Frederic, the son of Pedro III and the
brother of James II of Aragon, whose reign lasted from 1296
to 1337, was unquestionably the greatest. He had come
to the island so young that he felt himself almost a native.
As he had defended his realm, not only against the Pope
and the Angevins, but also against his brother the king of
Aragon, who had deserted him at the treaty of Anagni,

he won for himself and for his dynasty the affection and
good will of the Sicilians. Instead of serving to make Sicily
Aragonese, his reign committed his successors to the cause
of Sicilian independence.[1] And in addition to defending
his new kingdom against foreign foes, the reign of Frederic
did much to improve its internal administration, which
had suffered grievously from the cruelties and oppressions
of the Angevins. All the free institutions inherited from
Norman and Hohenstaufen times were strengthened and
renewed. Particularly important was Frederic's revival
of the powers of the Sicilian Parliament, which had been
virtually in abeyance under the house of Anjou. In all
the greatest affairs of the realm, in peace, in war, in treaties,
and in finance, the Sicilian national assembly attained in
this period an authority so extensive that the history of
its manifold activities is virtually the history of the island.[2]
It is true that Frederic's three rather unworthy successors,
Pedro II, Louis, and Frederic IV, were for the most part
puppets in the hands of the rebellious baronage, and lost
much of the ground that Frederic had gained. The national
assembly was rarely convoked under them, and when it
did meet was little more than a battleground of factions.[3]
Nevertheless the parliamentary tradition was not suffered
to die out, and under the younger Martin, who saw the
necessity of courting popularity in order to gain recognition,
it was once more revived in full force. At a Parliament
held in Syracuse a number of 'good laws' and regulations
were passed to bring back the ancient liberties of the realm;
and as a means of diminishing the excesses of baronial power,

---

[1] A good account of the narrative
history of the reign of Frederic after the
peace of Caltabelotta may be found in
S. V. Bozzo, Note storiche Siciliane del
secolo XIV (Palermo, 1882).

[2] C. Calisse, Storia del Parlamento in
Sicilia (Turin, 1887), pp. 46 f.; R. Gregorio, Considerazioni sopra la storia di
Sicilia (Palermo, 1831–39, 4 vols.), ii,
pp. 473–477.

[3] Calisse, op. cit., p. 66.

a royal council of twelve members was created, of which one half was elected by the commons and one half appointed by the crown. Order and free government were on the high road to restoration, when the death of young Martin in 1409 and of his father in the succeeding year threw everything again into confusion, and left Sicily as well as Aragon without a king.[1]

During the interregnum and the first three years of the reign of Ferdinand of Antequera, Blanche of Navarre, the widow of the younger Martin, managed to maintain herself in Sicily as the representative of the Crown of Aragon against the local factions which were attempting, in one way or another, to set up a new line of independent sovereigns. In 1415 Ferdinand sent his younger son, John, to replace Blanche as viceroy; but the Sicilians, foreseeing that the rest of the Aragonese dominions would ultimately fall to John's elder brother, Alfonso, straightway attempted to revive their autonomy by securing for John the title of independent king of the island. This naturally resulted in the recall of John to Aragon at the moment of Alfonso's accession; for the latter did not propose to tolerate any division of the Aragonese inheritance.[2] On the other hand, the Sicilians had no wish to accept Alfonso as their sovereign; in fact, the Magnanimous King, not daring to run the risk of a point blank refusal by the Sicilian Parliament, secured recognition from separate assemblies of barons and the representatives of the third estate, summoned successively to the Castello Ursino in Catania. Moreover, as Alfonso rarely paid his Sicilian subjects the honor of visiting them, they continued their efforts, down to the very close of the reign, to establish a dynasty of their own. When,

---

[1] Gregorio, *Considerazioni*, iii, pp. 166–188; Calisse, *op. cit.*, pp. 69–74. Some authors maintain that this parliament was held at Catania.

[2] La Lumia, *Studi di storia Siciliana*, ii, pp. 59 f.

in 1458, Alfonso died, and John succeeded him as king in Aragon and in Sicily, the islanders attempted to induce the latter to fix his residence among them; failing in this, they sought to persuade him to set up his son, Charles of Viana, as his representative there, with the thinly disguised intention of making him an independent sovereign. Naturally John II did not accede to these desires; but the fact that he found it advisable solemnly to confirm the annexation and incorporation of Sicily with the realms of the Crown of Aragon in the Cortes of Fraga and Lerida in 1460 [1] may be taken to indicate that the ambitions of his Sicilian subjects for autonomy caused him a good deal of anxiety. Even as late as 1477, when the heiress of the richest fief in the island announced her intention of wedding a prince of the Neapolitan royal house, the king of Aragon was so much worried lest the match result in the setting up of a separate line of Sicilian kings, that he actually attempted, though unsuccessfully, to prevent it, by offering himself, despite his eighty years and his blindness, as a rival candidate for the lady's hand.[2]

But though the Sicilians failed in their efforts to maintain a dynasty of their own, they strove the harder for that very reason to preserve all the other emblems and organs of their national and institutional freedom. The intensely separatistic character of the Spanish methods of government doubtless facilitated their efforts in this direction, but it is impossible to withhold a tribute of admiration to the Sicilians themselves for their heroic though not always judicious determination to maintain their liberties. A brief examination of the chief component parts of the Sicilian constitution in the middle of the fifteenth century will serve to make clear the measure of success which these efforts attained.

[1] Zurita, iv, ff. 75-76.   [2] La Lumia, Studi, ii, pp. 60 f.

The representative of the Aragonese king in the island was a viceroy, but the office, in the fifteenth century, was not seldom in commission — conferred, that is, on two or even three persons at the same time. Its duration was exceedingly variable. At a later date the normal term came to be regarded as three years, but it was often less and not seldom more. The viceroys, through the powers delegated to them, could summon, prorogue, and dissolve the Parliament; exercise all the rights of a legate of the Holy See (claimed by the Sicilian sovereigns since the days of Pope Urban II); appoint all subordinate officers, save a few who were nominated directly by the crown; pardon criminals; grant feudal fiefs; put forth proclamations which did not infringe the laws and liberties of the realm; deal directly with the see of Rome in matters ecclesiastical; oversee the publication and execution of papal bulls in Sicily; and represent the island in its dealings with foreign states. They were selected, during the fifteenth century, quite as often from among the prominent families of the island as from those of Aragon. They were paid a large salary; they dwelt in the royal palace at Palermo; and they were invested with all the pomp and prerogatives of kings.[1] Of the great officers of the crown, who had been so prominent in Angevin times, when Sicily and Naples were under a single rule, only the chief Justiciar of the royal court, the Constable, and the Admiral remained in the island; and their functions were rather advisory than authoritative.[2] Over and above the *donativo*, which, as we shall subsequently see, could be granted only by the Parliament, there was a long category of revenues which came to the viceroy as a matter of course; among these customs duties, profits of jurisdiction, feudal

[1] La Lumia, *Studi*, ii, p. 68; and list in Stokvis, *Manuel*, iii, pp. 708 f.
[2] La Lumia, *Studi*, ii, pp. 68 f.

dues, revenues of vacant benefices, and the sale of bulls of crusade were the most important. Taxation was not, however, anywhere nearly so oppressive in this period as it subsequently became; and though it was not absolutely impossible even at this early date for small sums occasionally to find their way across the sea to Spain, the revenues were largely used for Sicilian purposes.[1] The administration of justice was also completely dominated by the viceroy: he had a seat and a vote in both the chief courts of the realm, the *Magna Curia* for civil and criminal affairs, and the *Real Patrimonio* for financial ones; they followed him about wherever he went, and were guided by his wishes in rendering their decisions.[2] There was also a so-called *Sacro Consiglio*, composed of the members of both these courts, and of as many other officials as the viceroy was pleased to summon, by whose advice he was supposed to be guided in judicial questions of supreme importance and other 'grave affairs.'[3] In spite of vigorous protests from the Sicilians, the practice of sending certain cases across to Spain for final settlement gradually began to establish itself in this period.[4]

The authority of the viceroy, though in general strongly supported by that of the subordinate officers and of the courts, was also seriously limited, throughout the fifteenth century, by the powers of the island Parliament. This body had behind it a strong local tradition; on its maintenance and development the Sicilians concentrated their strongest efforts; and the unquestioned importance of the Cortes of the realms of the Crown of Aragon doubtless operated indirectly in its favor. It was composed of three estates or

---

[1] La Lumia, *Studi*, ii, pp. 78 f.
[2] La Lumia, *Studi*, ii, pp. 75 f. The feudal barons maintained, however, almost complete judicial independence in their great fiefs.
[3] R. Gregorio, *Opere rare* (Palermo, 1873), p. 465.
[4] La Lumia, *op. cit.*, ii, pp. 75 f.

bracci — barons, clergy, and representatives of the cities; and there were numerous and elaborate regulations concerning parliamentary procedure and privilege. The place and time of convocation were determined by the viceroy. The ancient Hohenstaufen maxim of annual Parliaments had now fallen into desuetude, so that during most of the fourteenth and fifteenth centuries the assembly was summoned whenever convenient; but in 1488 it became triennial, owing to the establishment of a rule that the sums which it was invariably requested to grant should be paid up within three years. Its chief functions were to receive the oath of each new sovereign to preserve the laws and privileges of the realm, and to watch over the subsequent performance of it; to propose *capitoli*, which if accepted by the kings acquired the force of laws; and to vote taxes, to which, as in Aragon, the significant title of *donativos* was always given. The fact that the royal treasurer, in his capacity of custodian of the revenues of vacant sees and confiscated fiefs, was given access to both the upper houses, and was generally recognized as the principal representative of the viceroy in the Parliament, indicates that the financial functions of that body were regarded by the government as of primary importance. Various documents in this period bear witness to a constant attempt to make the grant of funds by the Parliament dependent on the acceptance of the *capitoli* by the viceroy; but it may well be doubted whether this principle was ever rigorously observed in practice.[1]

In one respect the advent of the Spanish domination in Sicily actually strengthened the local Parliament, and that was in the establishment of a *Diputazione del Regno*, on the

[1] A. Mongitore, *Parlamenti generali del Regno di Sicilia dall'anno 1446 sino al 1748* (Palermo, 1749, 2 vols.), i, pp. 49– 104, *passim*; Calisse, *op. cit.*, pp. 65–188, *passim*, especially 111, 165 ff., 182 ff.; La Lumia, *Studi*, ii, pp. 69–73.

model with which we have become familiar in the realms of the Crown of Aragon. This originated during the reign of Alfonso the Magnanimous, in a demand that representatives of the realm should oversee the raising, collection, and spending of the *donativo* in the manner and for the purpose voted. In 1475, under John II, its functions were extended to include the right to defend the nation against all infractions of its privileges and laws. It would seem that the only way it had of actually exercising this right was to complain to the viceroy or to the king himself; but the records show that this prerogative was frequently and effectively used. The members of the Diputazione were at first nine, then fifteen, and finally twelve in number; each *braccio* elected one third of them; and they were paid moderate salaries.[1]

Other indications of the determination of the Sicilians to preserve the largest possible measure of independence might be multiplied without number. They invariably held that they had been united to the realms of the Crown of Aragon by their own free will and not by conquest; and that therefore they were entitled to resist any encroachment on their liberties and privileges, in a way that Naples and Sardinia were not. In spite of their annexation to Aragon, they maintained their own system of currency, their own flag, their own consuls abroad, and their own representatives at the church councils of Constance and Basel. When envoys from the Sicilian Parliament came to Barcelona they were received with all the pomp and circumstance of ambassadors of a foreign state. Indeed, in a list of precedence of European lands, published by Julius II in 1504, Sicily was placed fifth in the order, after the Empire, France, Spain, and England; and before Scotland,

---

[1] Mongitore, i, pp. 81–88; Gregorio, *Considerazioni*, iv, pp. 260–235; Calisse, pp. 189–209, *passim*.

Hungary, Bohemia, Portugal, and Venice.[1] Theoretically without doubt it was well that the preservation of all these ancient liberties and franchises should compensate for the evils of an absent sovereign; but practically this resulted in the maintenance of feudal anarchy, confusion, and lawlessness — the more pitiful because brought into strong relief by contrast with the orderly if absolute monarchies that were consolidating themselves in other European states. Unquestionably the island lacked governance. Economically it was in a wretched condition. The population was probably little more than half a million souls; the fields were cultivated only when in close proximity to the towns; there were vast waste spaces with few paths and no roads. Commerce was in abeyance owing to the Turkish raids; and the discovery of America and of the new trade routes was soon to bring it almost to a standstill.[2] Nearly all the wealth in the island was in the hands of the Jews, who enjoyed under Alfonso V and John II a very unusual number of privileges, and a large measure of local autonomy under their own elected officers or *proti*. They were generally well liked, and constituted, in fact, a veritable *regnum in regno* until the reign of Ferdinand the Catholic, who expelled them.[3] Intellectually the state of Sicily was chaotic. Though printing was introduced at Palermo before 1473, the vast mass of the people was densely ignorant. On the other hand, the founding of the University of Catania by Alfonso the Magnanimous in 1445 relieved law students from the necessity of going to Bologna, while names like those of Antonio Beccadelli (Panormita) and Lucio Marineo Siculo

[1] La Lumia, *Studi*, ii, p. 74.
[2] La Lumia, *Studi*, ii, pp. 63 f., 79 f.
[3] La Lumia, *Studi*, ii, pp. 1–55. King Martin diminished the importance of the *proti* by appointing a sort of judge-in-chief of all the Israelites in Sicily, called the *Dienchelele*; but the Jews, by dint of a generous bribe, soon persuaded Alfonso the Magnanimous to abolish this office.

show that the island produced notable scholars, though they unquestionably found more congenial fields for their activities in other countries. In all walks of life we encounter "the same singular contrast of civilization and barbarism, of light and darkness, of apparently heterogeneous and discordant facts, which is the chief characteristic of Sicily in this period." [1]

NAPLES

"When the Kingdom of Naples was transferred from the Family of Anjou to Alphonsus King of Aragon, although it came under the Dominion of a most powerful King, possessed of so many hereditary Kingdoms, such as Aragon, Valencia, Catalonia, Majorca, Corsica, Sardinia, Sicily, Roussilion, and many other flourishing Dominions; and new Families, new Customs, and Fashions were brought to it from Spain, yet it luckily happened that this magnanimous King did not treat it as a foreign Kingdom; nor did he look upon it as a Province of the Kingdom of Aragon, but had as great a Regard for it as if it had been his antient and native Kingdom. . . . Whether it was upon account of the Sweetness of its Climate, or its Grandeur, and the vast Number of its illustrious Barons and Nobility; or whether it was his Love for his dear Lucretia Alagna, it is evident that he preferred this Kingdom to all his other Dominions, and it never was in so flourishing a Condition, as in his Reign. He fixed his Royal Residence in Naples, where he resolved to pass the Remainder of his Life; and, as if he had forgot his paternal Dominions, all his Care, and all his Thoughts were employed about this Kingdom." [2]

In these striking words, a famous eighteenth-century historian sums up the essential features of Alfonso's rule

[1] La Lumia, *Studi*, ii, pp. 80 f.
[2] Giannone, *History of Naples*, tr. Ogilvie, ii, p. 337.

in Naples: he treated it not as a dependency of the realms of the Crown of Aragon, but rather as the head and centre of all his dominions.   It was of course inevitable that Alfonso should import many "new Families, new Customs and Fashions" into Naples, not only from the realms of the Crown of Aragon but also from Castile, his native land, where he had passed his early years.   His edict that all poor and indigent people should have a public audience every Friday and that an advocate should be appointed for them — with a yearly salary from the royal treasury — has a distinctly Castilian flavor.[1]   Moreover, he spoke Spanish to the day of his death, in contrast to his illegitimate son and successor, Ferrante, the first 'Re di Napoli,' who was Italian in speech, in character, and in education.[2]   But there can be no doubt that Neapolitan interests generally prevailed over those of the Spanish realms during the reign of the Magnanimous King.   It was not till the early years of the sixteenth century, when, under the lead of Ferdinand the Catholic, the last French attempt to recapture Naples was defeated, that the realm became thoroughly Hispanicized and the inherited local and Angevin traditions and institutions completely superseded by those of its new masters.[3]

The type of administration which Alfonso inherited from his Angevin predecessors in Naples was much more feudal than national; and as it was his aim rather to make himself popular in his new realm than to assimilate it to his other possessions, he continued and maintained the system which he found there.   He upheld and increased all the ancient rights and privileges of the Neapolitan baronage, and doubled their numbers.   He endowed the petty lords as well as the

[1] Giannone, tr. Ogilvie, ii, pp. 338 f.; also pp. 230 ff., *supra*, and Vol. II, pp. 123 f.

[2] Cipolla, *Signorie Italiane*, i, pp.

486–488; Messer, *Codice Aragonese*, pp. xxix–xxxiv.

[3] Giannone, tr. Ogilvie, ii, p. 475.

greater with *merum et mixtum imperium*, to the detriment of his own royal rights. More than six-sevenths of the lands of the realm were in the hands of the feudal nobles at the time of Alfonso's accession; under him and his immediate successors the proportion was further increased, so that the Spanish kings of the sixteenth century were unable with all their efforts to set the current flowing in the opposite direction.[1] All the great crown officers of Angevin times, the Constable, Chancellor, Prothonotary, Lord High Chamberlain, and Steward, were maintained by Alfonso; not until the reign of Ferdinand the Catholic was there any serious attempt to diminish their importance.[2] The Neapolitan national assembly, on the other hand, which inherited high traditions from Hohenstaufen times, was now only a shadow of its former self. The clergy had practically ceased to send representatives; the barons showed their indifference by frequently permitting substitutes to take their places; and these substitutes, as well as many of the municipal delegates, were usually legists, who obediently carried out the wishes of the monarchs, and made no difficulty about voting taxes.[3] In order to make certain that funds should not be wanting for the prosecution of his wars and for the maintenance of his luxurious court, Alfonso reorganized the financial system of his kingdom. All the ancient imposts and exactions — feudal rather than national in their character — were preserved and increased, and certain new ones were added to them; moreover, their collection and administration were completely reformed on a new and

[1] Giannone, ii, p. 367; Bianchini, *Storia delle Finanse di Napoli*, pp. 123–136. According to Bianchini, there were 1619 'terre' in Naples in the year 1579, of which only 53 belonged to the royal domain, while the rest were in feudal hands.

[2] Giannone, ii, pp. 481–487; L.

Cadier, *Administration du royaume de Sicile*, pp. 168–275, gives a full account of these officers as they were in Angevin times.

[3] Reumont, *The Carafas of Maddaloni*, tr. Bohn, p. 76; Amétller, *Alfonso V de Aragón*, ii, pp. 458–461.

more efficient basis by the fusion into a single body — henceforth known as *Camera della Sommaria* — of the ancient tribunals of the Mint and of the Royal Chamber. It was supereminent above all the other councils of the realm, with but one exception, of which anon; and a new division of the kingdom into twelve provinces facilitated its proceedings. It was given charge of everything that concerned the royal revenues and patrimony, in order that the king's ministers "might be more careful and diligent in providing him with Money."[1]

Despite the recklessness of his grants to the Neapolitan baronage, Alfonso made one heroic effort to centralize the administration of justice by the erection of the *Sacro Regio Consiglio di Santa Chiara*, so called from the great monastery in which, down to the middle of the sixteenth century, it held the majority of its sittings.[2] It was modelled partly on the type of royal council whose acquaintance we have made in the Spanish realms, and partly on the Roman Rota, with whose forms and procedure Alfonso had become familiar through his friend Alfonso Borgia, bishop of Valencia and afterwards Pope Calixtus III. It was composed, under the king, of a president, who was usually the king's eldest son or else one of the greatest prelates of the realm, two 'military' assistant counsellors to represent the baronage, a vice-prothonotary, and a number of learned doctors of the law — at first nine, later six and seven, and afterwards ten and twelve. It was a general court of appeal from all the minor tribunals of the realm and also from the

---

[1] Giannone, ii, p. 356–360; Bianchini, *op. cit.*, pp. 137–160 (especially pp. 148 f.).

[2] "It got the name of Sacred," says Giannone, ii, pp. 348 f., "on account of the sacred Person of the King, who declared himself Head of it, and because it was his own particular Council, wherein he sat in Person . . . whence the Nobility are not allowed to enter this sacred Tribunal with their Swords or other Arms, nor even those, who can wear their Swords in the King's Closet."

Camera della Sommaria; and Giannone goes further and
maintains that cases were brought up to it from the courts
of Sicily, and even from those of the other Aragonese lands
as well, "whence we are convinced," he further adds, "of
the Vanity of the Opinion, that [Naples] from the beginning
of Alphonsus's Reign became dependent upon the Crown of
Aragon."[1] The list of authorities cited by Giannone in
support of these assertions is certainly impressive;[2] their
statements, however, are not always specific, and a large
allowance must necessarily be made for the patriotic bias
of Giannone himself. It was natural that much of the business of his other realms should be referred to Alfonso, and
it is highly probable that he frequently discussed it with
the members of the Santa Chiara; but it would certainly
be difficult to prove that that tribunal possessed any constitutional authority of its own outside the kingdom of
Naples. It was unquestionably the most important body
in the realm in which Alfonso fixed his residence, and could
therefore scarcely fail to be informally consulted in regard to
the affairs of the rest of his dominions; but there is no reason to ascribe anything more to it than this.

As the Aragonese had originally come into Sicily and
Naples as heirs of the imperial house of Hohenstaufen,
they inherited friction with the papacy, which had claimed
suzerainty over Naples as well as Sicily since 1059, and had
in general supported the Angevins there. This friction
was considerably more serious in the kingdom of Naples
than in the island, partly because the Aragonese authority
there had been so much more recently established, and partly
because of greater geographical proximity.[3] Even after

---

[1] Giannone, ii, p. 349.
[2] The most important of them are
Tapia's *Jus Regni Neapolitani* and N.
Toppi's *De Origine Tribunalium*, neither

of which I have been able to see, save
in so far as they are quoted in Giannone.
[3] Giannone, ii, pp. 489 f.

his recognition and investiture by Eugenius IV in 1443, there were interminable quarrels over boundaries, and countless conflicts of jurisdiction between Alfonso and his successors and the contemporary Popes, particularly about the question of the revenues of vacant benefices. Even the Borgia Calixtus III refused to recognize Alfonso's illegitimate son, Ferrante, as king of Naples, on the former's death in 1458; and a similar attitude on the part of subsequent pontiffs encouraged John, the son of René of Anjou, to make another effort to expel the Aragonese in 1462-64.[1] Giannone complains that Alfonso and the kings that came after him failed to apply against the papal encroachments "those strong and effectual Remedies which were begun to be made use of in France", but rather attempted "to cure the wounds with Ointments and Plasters." In political and institutional ways the accusation is perhaps well merited, but on the other hand we must not forget that it was under the patronage of the Magnanimous King that Lorenzo Valla shattered the foundations of the papal claims to temporal sovereignty by his investigations into the historical validity of the so-called Donation of Constantine.[2] The mention of the name of Valla tempts one to go further and study the development of the Renaissance at Alfonso's luxurious court, but this fascinating topic lies so far from the field to which this volume is devoted that it must of necessity be left aside.[3]

Nor can we dwell on the internal side of the reigns of Alfonso's illegitimate son and successor in Naples, Ferrante

---

[1] Lecoy de la Marche, *Le Roi René*, i, pp. 288, 335–342.

[2] Cf. M. von Wolff, *Lorenzo Valla* (Leipsic, 1893), pp. 60 f. and chapter iv.

[3] References on this topic may be found in the footnotes to pp. xlviii–xlix of A. Messer's *Codice Aragonese*.

To the list there given should be added V. Balaguer, "Alfonso V de Aragón y su Corte Literaria" in his *Discursos Académicos* (*Obras*, vol. vii, pp. 241–278), and B. Croce, *La Spagna nella vita Italiana durante la Rinascensa* (Bari, 1917).

I (1458–94), nor on the briefer rule of his different descendants during the next ten years. Naples ceases to form a part of the Aragonese Empire in this period, and though an intimate political alliance was maintained between Ferrante and his uncle John, the history of the kingdom has little to do with that of Spain until the opening of the Italian wars. Certainly Ferrante had absorbed all his father's passion for the Italy of the Renaissance. There was little or nothing Spanish about him; he possessed the characteristic virtues and vices of the typical fifteenth-century Maecenas and petty despot, and belongs wholly to the annals of the peninsula where his life was lived. The Neapolitans themselves regarded him with enthusiasm; "they preferred a native bastard to a foreign pretender",[1] whatever his lineage and descent. In other words, Naples was as yet in no sense truly Aragonese; indeed the fifteen years (1443–58) during which the two realms had been united under a single sceptre had served rather to make the Aragonese king Neapolitan.

Yet in spite of all its weaknesses and limitations, we cannot contemplate the position of the great Mediterranean empire which James the Conqueror and his successors had built up without being profoundly impressed by its grandeur. It had been won from infidel and Christian alike, often against heavy odds and by means and for ideals of which there was much reason to be proud and little to be ashamed. It had secured for the East Spanish realms a position of unquestioned predominance in the western basin of the Mediterranean Sea. It went far to counterbalance the

---

[1] Messer, *Codice Aragonese*, p. xxxi; Burckhardt, *Civilisation of the Renaissance in Italy*, tr. Middleman, p. 21, has an interesting paragraph on the absence of prejudice aginst illegitimacy in the Italy of the Quattrocento. Was this attitude possibly traceable to Spanish influence? Cf. p. 175, note 3, supra.

isolation from the affairs of Western Europe which characterized fifteenth-century Castile, and to preserve for the Iberian kingdoms as a whole their place in the family of European states. When united with the other dominions which the events of the next century were to bring to Spain, it was destined to contribute its share towards giving her preëminence among the nations of the earth.

BIBLIOGRAPHICAL NOTE

See bibliographical notes at the end of the preceding chapters, and add :
Contemporary Authorities. — The *Colección de documentos para el estudio de la Historia de Aragón* (9 vols. so far published, Saragossa, 1904–1913) is an invaluable repertory of miscellaneous fueros, donations, ordinances, and other documents (mostly of the mediaeval period), edited by some of the foremost scholars in Spain. To the Aragonese *Fueros y Observancias*, cited in the note to the previous chapter, correspond the *Constitutions y altres· Drets de Cathalunya* (Barcelona, 1588, 3 vols.) and the various editions of the 'Furs' of Valencia, on which see J. P. Fuster, *Biblioteca Valenciana*, i, pp. 83–85. The proceedings of the Concell of Barcelona (*Dietari del Antich Consell Barceloní*) from 1390 to 1649 have been published in 14 volumes (Barcelona, 1892–1913) by Frederich Schwartz y Luna and Francesch Carreras y Candi, under the title of *Manual de Novells Ardits*. On the naval history of Catalonia, the *Ordenanzas de las Armadas Navales de la Corona de Aragon, aprobadas por el Rey Pedro IV, año de MCCCLIV*, ed. Antonio de Capmany y de Montpalau (Madrid, 1787), are useful; as are the *Privilegios y Franquicias de Mallorca* (ed. J. M. Quadrado, 1894) for the study of the constitutional history of the Balearics. A number of valuable documents in the Neapolitan archives and in the Bibliothèque Nationale have been published by Francesco Trinchera and A. A. Messer respectively, under the title *Codice Aragonese* (Naples, 1866–74, 3 vols., and Paris, 1912). Both these collections deal with the period of Ferrante I and his successors, but they incidentally throw light on the reign of Alfonso the Magnanimous.

Later Works. — For Aragon, Jerónimo de Blancas, *Modo de proceder en Cortes de Aragon*, and Jerónimo de Martel, *Forma de celebrar Cortes en Aragon*, published together at Saragossa in 1641, give a good picture of the national assembly; on these authors see Prescott, i, p. 91. Albert Du Boys, *Histoire du droit criminel en Espagne* (Paris, 1870), is valuable, and Julián Ribera y Tarragó, *Orígenes del Justicia de Aragón* (Saragossa, 1897), ingenious and original; this last work, however, should be controlled by the articles of Andrés Giménez Soler in the *R. A.*, cited in note to p. 463, *ante*. Francisco Sanz y Ramón, *El Privilegio de los Veinte* (Saragossa, 1891), and Fritz Baer, *Studien zur Geschichte der Juden im Königreich Aragonien* (Berlin, 1913), are both good monographs.

For Valencia, Pere Hierony Taraçona, *Institucions dels Furs y Privilegis de Valencia* (Valencia, 1580), is a most learned work, with ample citations of the original authorities. Manuel Danvila y Collado, *Estudios críticos acerca de los Orígenes y Vicisitudes de la Legislación escrita del Reino de Valencia* (Madrid, 1905), is a convenient but not an invariably safe guide; it has the secondary title of *Estudios e Investigaciones acerca de las Cortes y Parlamentos de Valencia.*

For Catalonia, Eduardo de Hinojosa, *El Régimen Señorial y la Cuestión Agraria en Cataluña durante la Edad Media* (Madrid, 1905), is a masterpiece of sound scholarship and of lucid presentation. José Coroleu and José Pella y Forgas, *Los Fueros de Cataluña* (Barcelona, 1878), is prolix and unscientific, but contains much useful information; *Las Cortes Catalanas* (Barcelona, 1876), by the same authors, is better. Salvador Bové, *Institucions de Catalunya* (Barcelona, 1894); Francisco de Bofarull y Sans, *Antigua Marina Catalana* (Barcelona, 1898); and José Pella y Forgas, *Llibertats y Antich Govern de Catalunya* (Barcelona, 1905), are all valuable.

On the Balearics, Vaquette d'Hermilly, *Histoire du Royaume du Majorque* (Maestricht, 1777), may still be consulted with profit, and J. M. Quadrado's *Forenses y Ciudadanos* (Palma, 1895) is excellent.

On Sardinia, J. Dexart, *Capitula sive Acta Curiarum Regni Sardiniae* (Cagliari, 1645), is important, though somewhat rare.

For Sicily, Antonio Mongitore's *Parlamenti generali del Regno di Sicilia dall' anno 1446 sino al 1748* (Palermo, 1749, 2 vols.) has not been entirely superseded by Carlo Calisse's excellent *Storia del Parlamento in Sicilia* (Turin, 1887). Rosario Gregorio's *Considerazioni sopra la Storia di Sicilia* (Palermo, 1831–39, 4 vols.) is still valuable also.

For Naples Pietro Giannone's *Istoria civile del Regno di Napoli* (first edition, Naples, 1723, 4 vols.) is still essential on the institutional side, particularly when Carlo de Tapia's *Jus Regni Neapolitani* (Naples, 1605–43, 7 vols.) and Nicoló Toppi's *De Origine Tribunalium* (2d ed., Naples, 1666, 3 vols.) are not available. My references are to James Ogilvie's excellent translation (*The Civil History of the Kingdom of Naples*, London, 1729–31, 3 vols.). On Giannone's work and place among the historians see Fueter, *Historiographie moderne*, pp. 342–345. Carlo Cipolla's *Storia delle Signorie Italiane dal 1313 al 1530* (Milan, 1882, 2 vols.) contains a number of useful references, though it deals chiefly with narrative history. Alfred von Reumont's *The Carafas of Maddaloni* (English translation, London, 1854) gives a few items of interest in regard to the government of Naples; and Lodovico Bianchini, *Storia delle Finanze del Regno di Napoli* (3d ed., Naples, 1859), is the standard authority on revenue and taxation. So little serious work, however, has been done on the constitutional history of Naples under the Aragonese, that one is fain to glean what one can from works on adjacent fields and periods; e.g., Léon Cadier's admirable *Essai sur l'Administration du royaume de Sicile sous Charles Ier et Charles II d'Anjou* (Paris, 1891), which furnishes an excellent point of departure for the study of the age of Alfonso the Magnanimous.